... to see things as they are, to find out true facts, and store them up for the use of posterity.

George Orwell, "Why I Write" (1947)

THE
LOSING BATTLE
WITH ISLAM

DAVID SELBOURNE

 Prometheus Books

59 John Glenn Drive
Amherst, New York 14228-2197

Published 2005 by Prometheus Books

Inquiries should be addressed to
Prometheus Books
59 John Glenn Drive
Amherst, New York 14228–2197
VOICE: 716–691–0133, ext. 207
FAX: 716–564–2711
WWW.PROMETHEUSBOOKS.COM

09 08 07 06 05   5 4 3 2 1

Library of Congress Cataloging-in-Publication Data

Selbourne, David, 1937–.
    The losing battle with Islam / David Selbourne.
        p. cm.
    Includes index.
    ISBN 1–59102–362–9 (hardcover : alk. paper)
    1. Islam—20th century. I. Title.

DS35.6.S45 2005
320.5'57—dc22

                                                                            2005018397

Printed in the United States of America on acid-free paper

THE LOSING BATTLE WITH ISLAM

ALSO BY DAVID SELBOURNE

Against Socialist Illusion

The City of Light (Jacob d'Ancona)

Death of the Dark Hero: Eastern Europe 1987–90

A Doctor's Life

An Eye to China

An Eye to India

In Theory and in Practice

Left Behind: Journeys into British Politics

The Making of a Midsummer Night's Dream

Moral Evasion

Not an Englishman: Conversations with Lord Goodman

The Principle of Duty: An Essay on the Foundations of the Civic Order

The Spirit of the Age

Through the Indian Looking Glass

Contents

Preface   9

1. The Misnaming   11

2. A Bad Press   47

3. The Hostile Round   89

4. Beyond Reason   127

5. Israel and Jews   171

6. Into the Moral Labyrinth   225

7. Taking Liberties   273

8. Thinking within Limits   337

9. The Force of Faith   387

10. Against Illusion   437

Index   489

Preface

Work on what was to become this book began in the 1980s, with the gradual building up of an archive of materials on the Islamic world, and of the non-Muslim world's responses to events taking place in it. All these materials were in the public domain. The public domain—that of press agency reports, the findings of governments, information on the World Wide Web, public statements and so on—has remained my principal source. This was supplemented by observations and findings of my own, published earlier in my journalistic work, in Afghanistan, India, Pakistan and Kosovo as well as on domestic fronts where Muslims issues were to the fore: as in controversies over the Rushdie case, local conflicts about education and other contentious social issues in which Muslims and non-Muslims were involved.

This is a book written neither from the 'left' nor from the 'right'. In any case the terms are now out of date, not least in relation to debates about Islam. It is intended to be balanced, fair-minded and objective, insofar as this is possible, and to serve the truth—that truth of which George Orwell spoke in the epigraph chosen for this work. It is based, as the reader will see, on a labour of accumulation not of prejudices but of recorded facts, and of reports of events. I am neither an 'Islamophobe'—a disorder of the mind, like any prejudice of similar kind—nor an 'Islamophile', which is a prejudice too.

One of the governing assumptions of the work is that the responses of non-Muslims to the challenges posed by the Islamic revival and advance have been as significant as the revival and advance themselves. I therefore pay close attention throughout the book to these non-Muslim responses, not least because many of them have served Islamism's cause. By 'Islamism' I mean Islam in its form as a radical political movement, whether pitted against Muslim and Arab regimes of which it disapproves, or against the 'infidel' non-Muslim world, whose actions it opposes.

Another of the assumptions which govern this book is that the Western media, especially network television, have served us ill in understanding the matters discussed and analysed here. The 'anchor', the commentator and even the news-gatherer too often stand between us and the dispassionate information we require. They cast their shadows across events, rather than shedding light upon them.

There are, of course, distinguished exceptions to this. Above all, the international press agencies—most notably the Associated Press and Reuters—have set high standards in the scope of their coverage of events in the Muslim and Arab worlds. Even the best of the 'quality' newspapers, on both sides of the Atlantic, contain reports of only a small proportion of what we need to know; most television channels and programmes contain even less. I do not claim that this book makes up for such lack. It had its origin in a personal attempt by the author to grasp what was afoot. The result of this effort follows.

CHAPTER ONE
The Misnaming

It has been said that Arabs and Muslims have a sense of loss at the decline of their power and influence in the world; that they have fallen from past political and cultural heights; that they have failed to meet the 'challenges' of 'modernisation'. If so, the seeking of compensation, much of it by violence, for this supposed 'sense of loss', defeat or humiliation—or a correction of the imbalance between themselves and 'the other'—has been under way for decades in the 'reawakening' of the Arabic and wider Islamic worlds.

This 'reawakening', resurgence or insurgency of Muslims has expressed itself in different ways since the end of the Second World War, aided by the processes of decolonisation. In the hope of attaining 'Arab unity', it has taken political form in 'Arab nationalism', of the kind expressed by the politics of the Egyptian leader Gamal Abdul Nasser; economic form, as in the seizure of the Suez Canal by Nasser in 1956 or in the use from October 1973 to March 1974 of the 'oil weapon' against the West, when OPEC imposed an embargo on petroleum exports to the United States; and religious form, as in the holy fervour aroused by the revolution in Iran in 1989 and the hostilities inspired by it.

These forms cannot be schematically distinguished from, or opposed to, one another. It was the same stirring-to-life in the Muslim world which gave to 'nationalism', 'pan-Arabism' and 'fundamentalism' their impulse and force. The Ba'ath ('Resurrection') parties in Syria and Iraq espoused a secular national-socialism, in part derived from Nazi and Italian fascist models, and

11

black-robed Khomeinism was the Party of God. Yet the stimulus for each was furnished by the renewal of a just sense of entitlement in Muslims—both the secularised and the religiose—to an unshadowed place in the political sun, free of subordination to Soviet and Western tutelage alike.

The relation between the 'nationalist' and 'fundamentalist' forms of Muslim upheaval is clear enough, and has become clearer with the passage of time. It is a relation not made less clear where the nationalist impulse has been instrumentally harnessed by 'fundamentalists', as in Chechnya, or where Islam was instrumentalised by a Ba'athist regime more Satanic than Koranic. The 'secularist' Ba'athist Saddam Hussein long invoked Allah's aid in his enterprises—including when attacking other Muslims—and called for a 'holy war' in October 1990 against Western forces in the Gulf. During the 1991 Gulf War, he was accurately described to me by a devout worshipper at London's Regent's Park Mosque as a 'child of Arab nationalism'; but after he had fired missiles at Israel, fellow-Muslims denoted him a 'great Muslim leader, standing up for what he believes in, against the might of the world'.

In January 1991, to shouts of 'You are the new Saladin!' and addressing an Islamic conference in Baghdad, the nominally secularist Saddam went further in blurring the distinction made by Western 'experts' between Arab nationalism and the Islamic revival. The coming battle would be a 'struggle' not for the aggrandising Iraqi conquest of Kuwait and hopefully of Saudi Arabia, but 'between believers and infidels'; he would 'clear the infidels out of Saudi Arabia and Palestine'; and after his defeat in the Gulf War he added the words '*Allahu Akhbar!*'—'Allah is Mighty!'—to the Iraqi national flag.

Despite his regime's killing (by the tens of thousands) of the Muslim faithful, clerics included, Saddam called in his 'Christmas letter' of December 2000 for a jihad by Christians and Muslims against Israel. Likewise, he expressed his objections to the Chechen seizure of hundreds of hostages in Moscow, in October 2002, on the grounds that the act would 'undermine Islam and Muslims'. In February and March 2003, on the eve of the Iraq War, he again adopted Islamic imprecations against those preparing an attack upon Iraq, calling the US-led invasion an 'aggression on the fortress of faith'; and in April 2003, after the fall of Baghdad and citing a Koranic text, described the Iraqis as having both 'Arabism and Islam' in their 'hearts and minds'. This was an appeal to nationalism and to faith conjoined. The 'awakening' of the Bosnians, Chechens, Kosovars and Palestinians and of the Muslims of Kashmir, Sudan and Thailand has similarly been both nationalist and Islamic.

The declaration of 'war' by the US against an abstraction called 'global terror' has masked the true lineament of things. Dictated by prudence and *realpolitik* as this terminology was, there was no war to declare. There has been 'a war on' for decades. It has included hostilities among Muslims of different persuasions, as in Algeria, Egypt, Iran, Jordan, Pakistan and Syria; between Islamists—a term increasingly used, including by Muslims, for those who seek to make Islam into a politics and a political movement—and the West; and between the West and the world of Islam. Russia, China and many other countries have been caught up in this 'reawakening' and in the belligerencies it has spawned.

Indeed, there have been few boundaries, whether of territory or moral principle, of method of combat or falsification of word, that have not been transgressed on this battlefield. Yet taboo, a false 'tact', short-term memory loss and wishful thinking have between them served—with other factors to be discussed—to cloud our knowledge of what has been at issue, and what is afoot.

There have been many wars since 1945, especially in Africa, which have nothing to do with Islam, and many (including in Africa) in which Islam stands at the heart of the conflict. Moreover, from the late 1940s and early 1950s, and especially once the fall of Communism in 1989–91 had freed the Muslim states in the Soviet bloc—including in the Middle East—from their strait-jackets, both a revived Arab nationalism and a renewal of ardour for Islam in politicised form have come to make the anti-Western running in many parts of the globe. This revivalism has brandished guns in one hand and sacred texts in the other. Demonising America, 'Zionism' and often Christianity also, it has been demonised in turn.

Anti-Arab feeling and a wider 'Islamophobia' have exacted their own toll. They have included attacks on Muslims settled in non-Islamic states, the targeted assassinations carried out by the Israelis, the savaging of Chechnya by the Russians, the hangings of Islamists in Xinjiang by the Chinese, the coalition 'turkey-shoot' of the defeated Iraqi army after its predations in the Gulf War upon a Muslim neighbour, the shooting-down by the US of an Iranian passenger airliner in July 1998, the near-genocide of Muslims in Bosnia, the killing of Muslim Albanians in Kosovo, and so on.

There are few areas in the world from the Caucasus to Kashmir, from the Moluccas to Manhattan, from Tunisia to Tanzania (and even to Trinidad and Grenada) which have not suffered from the Islamic convulsion. It has often been of large scale. It is a convulsion that has been carried to the heart—bleeding in more than one sense—of the West. But Western 'mind-sets' are easily bamboozled, as the teaching of history fades in schools and universities, and the media fails genuinely to inform. Most are not really in a position to understand what is occurring. A faith of global reach, hostile to the *zulm* or 'tyranny' of the West, demands a dominant role in the world order and intends to get it by hook or by crook. Moreover, with the weapons now available to them, Muslim absolutists and despots, whether secular or religious, are of ever greater potential danger. And who can perceive—or, if perceiving it, say— that a bin Laden may with some justice be held to be a good Muslim, not a bad, and that the use of any means against the 'infidel' can be justified by Holy Writ; or fully grasp that a call for the destruction of 'the United States and the Jewish people' can be regarded as a badge of virtue and not as the voice of psychosis?

At the same time, Islamists who profess to loathe the United States not only seek their education and fortunes in America but look to it—have even pleaded with it, in the Palestinian case—to intervene in their problems, both political and economic. The skills and devices Islamists have employed in their cause have been many-sided. They have combined a mixture of justified objection to Western policy, throat-cutting crudity and technological skill in acts of violence, moral evasion of responsibility for them, and subtlety in playing on the West's weaknesses, including those weaknesses which derive from dependency on the Muslim world's natural resources and from wishful thinking. It was wishful thinking which at the time led to the boast that Israel had been able to see off its foes in 'six days', that the 1991 Gulf War 'lasted only six weeks', the 2003 Iraq War 'three weeks', and the 'liberation of Afghanistan from the Taliban' a 'mere six weeks'.

Resort to suicide-bombing, a lethal weapon, has gone hand-in-hand with, say, the Muslim exploitation of Christian sensibilities, as during the Israeli siege in 2000 of the Church of the Nativity in Bethlehem. Elsewhere in the Muslim world—the West Bank and Gaza included—Christians have been mistreated in conflicts which derive from the primary cause of the Islamic revival. Similarly, public lynchings of Palestinian collaborators with Israel have been combined with well-judged appeals to anti-Semitism, that great deformity of mind. The latter is particularly absurd when most Arabs are Semites themselves.

In previous historic upsurges, as in the seventh century and onwards, Islam gained an empire from the trans-Himalayas to the trans-Pyrenees. It created the aesthetic glories (and sufferings) of Islamic Spain, and in another resurgence brought the Turks and their Ottoman Empire to Byzantium and the gates of Vienna. The former Yugoslavia was largely under Muslim control until 1913.

Black-masked, fist-brandishing, chest-beating and flag-burning Islamist militants, or Islamist students of the arts of hijacking and self-destruction, are hard to connect with their predecessors who created the Alhambra in Granada, or Seville's Alcazar. Suicide-pilots would seem to have little in common with the great Islamic poets, philosophers and doctors of the Middle Ages, the friends and intellectual peers of Christian and Jewish sages of those times. But the fount of Islamic energy, of its destructiveness and high aspiration, is the same as it has always been: the desire to protect the purity of the Islamic faith, and to vindicate its claim to be the final revealed religion on earth.

This present war, a Third World War, has already taken a bewildering variety of forms and struck in many places: in St. Peter's Square, at the Munich Olympics, in the skies over Scotland, in downtown New York, in the London Underground, in a theatre in Moscow. On its battlefields Islamists have been fighting for their own states—and others, including fellow-Muslims, have been fighting to stop them—in the southern Philippines, in Kashmir, in the Levant, in the Maghreb, in southern Russia, in the Balkans. On top of it all, there has been an endless round of cease-fires, peace talks, peace brokerage, accords made and accords broken, while the wider war has continued.

It is a war of great complexity which has taken millions of lives in open and bloody conflicts, as in Afghanistan, Algeria, Bangladesh, Biafra, Bosnia, Chechnya, Iran, Iraq, Lebanon, Nigeria, Somalia, Sudan, Tajikistan, Xinjiang and so on. The Algerian civil war from 1992 has cost between 150,000 and 200,000 dead. The Pakistan-Bangladesh war in 1971 is said by some to have taken the lives of two million; some estimates suggest that as many as a million—Iraqis and non-Iraqis alike—were killed by Saddam Hussein during his twenty-five-year rule. The 1991 Gulf War took many tens of thousands of lives; more thousands died in the wake of the occupation of Iraq from March 2003 and the insurgency which followed. Since 1983, civil wars, famine (as in 1998) and displacement in Sudan, Africa's largest country, have led to more than 2 million deaths. In western Sudan's Darfur region, the civil war which broke out in February 2003 between non-Arabs and the Islamist Arab government in Khartoum was taking a toll of some 10,000 to 15,000 deaths a month from violence, disease and malnutrition between October 2003 and March 2005; as many as 300,000 may have died in all.

The Biafran civil war in 1967, triggered by riots in northern Nigeria between the dominant Muslim majority and Christian Ibo immigrants, which this time led to an attempted Christian secession, killed some one million people, many 'slaughtered like cattle'. The civil war in Lebanon from 1975 to 1990 left 150,000 dead and reduced much of Beirut to a heap of rubble. Even the largely unheard-of 1992–97 Tajikistan civil war in Central Asia, provoked by Islamist secessionists, claimed tens of thousands of lives and created half a million refugees. There have also been tens of thousands of dead in the Islamic and separatist insurgency since 1989 against Indian rule in Kashmir, and over 100,000 dead in the two wars between Chechen separatists and Russia from 1994 to 1996, and from 1999; there were tens of thousands of dead in the Soviet Union's 1979–89 war in Afghanistan, and tens of thousands of dead in 1991 and 1992 in the civil war between Armenians and predominantly Muslim Azeris in Nagorno-Karabakh.

There have been, in total, tens of thousands more dead in the Muslim separatist rebellions in Indonesia and the Philippines, in the Ba'athist massacres of Islamists in Syria in 1982, in the Palestinian *intifadas* and in the struggles against Islamists in Afghanistan and Muslim separatists in southern Thailand. Many others have been done to death in plane-hijackings, suicide-bombings, kidnappings, embassy attacks and the rest.

Millions over the years fled the Soviet bloc, millions have fled Africa's and other lesser wars, millions the poverty and instability of the Third World in search of better lives. In addition have come the refugees, the migrants and the asylum-seekers driven from their homes by the turmoil in the Islamic world. More than 600,000 Palestinians fled the Arab-Israeli war of 1948–49 into camps in Jordan, Lebanon and Syria, or went elsewhere, and half a million left Lebanon in the 1975–1990 civil war. Assault on Muslims and inter-ethnic hatreds brought some 100,000 Bosnians and 25,000 Kosovars to Austria and 350,000 Bosnians and 160,000 Kosovars to Germany alone, in the latter case to join some two million Turks. Between one and two million Afghans sought refuge in Iran and Pakistan—many later returning home—and some 20,000 Afghans came to New York. In fact, some three-quarters of the world's migrants in the last years are said to have been Muslims.

Two million Somalis are said to have been driven from their homes in the chaos and civil war which followed the overthrow of the regime of Mohamed Siad Barre in 1991; over one million Azeris were displaced in their civil war with Armenians; up to ten million East Pakistanis, Muslims and Hindus alike, fled into India in 1971; up to four million Iraqis are said to have gone into exile during Saddam Hussein's rule; four million Sudanese, according to the United Nations, have been displaced by civil wars, with hundreds of thousands taking refuge in Chad, Ethiopia and other countries; and since the 1990s half a million Uighurs have fled Chinese efforts to stifle the Muslim separatist movement in Xinjiang, taking their refuge in Pakistan and neighbouring Central Asian nations, themselves in the grip of varieties of turmoil.

From the theatres of Islamic upheaval there have come into the United States and Western Europe Afghans, Albanians, Algerians, Bosnians, Chechens, Egyptians, Iranians, Iraqis, Kashmiris, Kosovars, Kurds of Iraq and Turkey, Lebanese, Macedonians, Nigerians, Pakistanis, Palestinians, Somalis and Sudanese, among others. They have been variously escaping Muslim Sharia law, inter-Muslim conflict, economic hardship, Muslim-Christian violence and anti-Muslim aggression. The latter has included aggression by nations—the United States, Britain, Russia and China, among others—which had nonetheless helped build, and continue to help build, the Islamic world's war potential. Escapees, victims, scapegoats, malefactors and 'sleepers' awaiting their moment, they signify that an aroused and angered Islam is 'on the move' in every sense.

For politicians to diagnose these phenomena as the consequences of 'terror', and then to declare war upon such 'terror', may itself appear politic, but is foolish. It has led, among other things, to the inordinate focus upon al-Qaeda—meaning 'the base', 'the model' or 'the principle'—as the embodiment of such 'terror'. Yet the false (and crude) naming of 'the West's foe' as 'terror' is also self-revealing. There is fear in it; in part self-terrorisation and in part a justified fear, as in all wars.

In 1956, in Oxford, I stood among a crowd of students at the Martyrs' Memorial—retrospect invests the very word 'martyr' with irony, the irony of the significance it was later to gain in Islamist war-talk—protesting at the Anglo-French invasion of Nasserite Egypt. Forty-five years later I was outside Boston as the World Trade Center was brought down. The Third World War has been fought, according to its own distinct rhythms, during most of my lifetime. The effects of the twentieth-century awakening of the world of Islam have spread ever wider in a dialectic of violent action and reaction. In another of its theatres, India, I saw it expressed in Hindu-Muslim 'communalism' and in intermittent reciprocal attack; in Serbia and Kosovo, as hatred and preparation for civil war.

Indeed, this Third World War could be argued to have broken out almost immediately after the end of the Second; one of the reasons, perhaps, why the world would rather not think it. To some extent masked and contained by the Cold War and the Soviet imperium—which made many leading Arab and Muslim nations (among others) its satrapies and instruments—much of the open conflict which has broken out since the Soviet Union's fall was earlier held in check. When the Soviet imperium fell, Arab nationalism and Islam were among the first of the suppressed forces to emerge from Leninism's shadows.

Volatile, expansionist and often appearing irrational, with its complex and shifting enmities and alliances, its sudden upsurges and quiescences of militancy like the flaring and dying-down of sunspots, Islam's present awakening looks, and is, hard to understand in all its aspects. This is not least because some Islamist actions in this war have been suicidal, both knowingly and unknowingly, and some fratricidal. The Third World War of the mid-twentieth to perhaps the mid-twenty-first centuries—or another mediaeval Hundred Years' War—has also unfolded in its own way. It had no starting-pistol shot as at Sarajevo in the First, nor an equivalent to Hitler's invasion of Poland in 1939. However, if you wish, you can pick 29 November 1947 as one possible beginning, when the UN called for the establishment of two states in Palestine, which the Jews accepted and the Arabs—who wanted no Israeli state at all—refused. Here, war after war—in merely one of the theatres of the Third World War—has followed: in 1948–49, when Israel was attacked within hours of the declaration of the new state, in 1967, and in 1973 when Egypt was defeated.

Other marker-events and dates in this particular arena have been 1976, when Syria sent its army into Lebanon during the latter's fifteen-year civil war; the 'normalisation' of relations between Israel and Egypt in 1979—after the Camp David 'peace accord' of the previous year; 1981, when Israel pre-emptively bombed the Iraqi nuclear reactor under construction at Osirak, and annexed the Golan Heights from Syria. In 1982, the Syrian regime crushed in bloodshed an internal five-year rebellion by the Muslim Brotherhood, the Israelis invaded Lebanon—occupying its southern border areas until May 2000—and Hezbollah (the 'Party of God') was established in Lebanon by Iran and Syria. The first Palestinian uprising took place from 1987 to 1993; relations were restored between Israel and Jordan in 1994, and a temporary peace was secured between Israel and the PLO in 1993–94 under the 'Oslo accords'.

The second Palestinian uprising from September 2000 to February 2005 brought further thousands of Palestinian and Israeli deaths. According to the Institute for Strategic Studies in London, in the Muslim nations surrounding a nuclear-armed Israel there were by 1999 some two million men under arms, with some 15,000 tanks and 2,200 combat aircraft between them. These totals excluded the forces and war *matériel* possessed by Saudi Arabia, Sudan and Turkey, and also excluded the means available to the 'radical', 'militant' or 'terrorist' forces—the adjective a matter of choice and contention—which were operating in the region.

Or begin elsewhere. A military coup in July 1952 swept away a newly-independent Egypt's nascent democracy, and was to bring Nasser to power. Pakistan, created in 1947, took the decision in 1953 to call itself an 'Islamic

Republic'. Algeria gained independence from 130 years of rule by France in a
ferocious war from 1954 to 1962, which slew one-tenth of its population of
ten million. In 1956, the same year in which Sudan gained independence from
Britain, Nasser's Egypt was invaded by the British and French, with covert
Israeli support. Other coups brought the Ba'athists to power in Syria in 1963
and in Iraq in 1968, while Tripoli fell to Gaddafi in 1969, Khartoum was seized
by Siad Barre in the same year and Hafez Assad took over in 1970 in Damascus. In December 1968, an early hijack—of an El Al aircraft—was carried
out in Athens by the People's Front for the Liberation of Palestine.

In 1971, with Muslim butchering Muslim—and with Hindus slain *en masse*
as India intervened—East Pakistan broke free from rule by Karachi under its
military dictator, Yahya Khan. By the 1970s, Gaddafi was beginning to have
nuclear ambitions; in 1974, Turkey invaded Cyprus; Saudi Arabia's King Faisal
was assassinated by an Islamist militant in 1975; also in 1975, Morocco seized
territory claimed by Algeria in the western Sahara, with war breaking out
between Morocco and Polisario guerrillas for its control. Libyan weapons and
explosives are said to have reached the IRA in Belfast by 1977.

Khomeini came to power in Iran in 1979, seized the US embassy in
Teheran and held fifty-seven American hostages captive for 444 days until
1981, ruling for a decade of intensifying ferment in the Muslim world;
Saddam Hussein took over in Baghdad in 1979 also. By the early to mid-1970s,
Muslim separatists had already begun their long struggles in Indonesia and the
southern Philippines, while the goal of creating an Islamic state in Muslim-
dominated areas of south-east Asia, including Malaysia and southern Thailand, began to take root; and Mohammed Zia ul-Haq seized power in Pakistan
in 1977, seeking to advance further the Islamisation of the country until he
was killed in a plane crash in 1988.

In 1980, Iran and Iraq went to war over a border dispute and fought each
other to a standstill until 1988; in 1980 also, the US recalled its ambassador
from Libya after a mob sacked its embassy in Tripoli. In 1981, Egypt introduced emergency laws to help combat the Egyptian Islamist movement, a
movement which it sought to crush with violence, but whose embers smoulder
still; also in 1981 more than two decades of war began in Afghanistan. In 1982,
a military coup brought General Hossain Mohammad Ershad to power in
Dacca; in 1983, as its Islamist regime sought to impose Sharia law in the
country, Sudan's civil war began between radical Muslim government forces in
the north and Christian and animist secessionists in the south.

It was in 1983 also that an attack on a US Marines' barracks in Beirut
killed 241 American servicemen; and in 1986 US planes bombed Tripoli and

Benghazi in retaliation for an earlier attack on American servicemen in Berlin. The United States also imposed sanctions on the Gaddafi regime, at the same time as Pakistan was assisting Tripoli in its weapons ambitions.

Or look to the late 1980s and early 1990s. In 1987, Zine el-Abidine ben Ali seized power in a palace coup in Tunisia and began to pursue an aggressive policy against the country's Islamist movement. In March 1988, Saddam Hussein carried out a poison-gas attack on Iraqi Kurds in Halabja, and massacred some 80,000 Kurds in Anfal. Hamas, inspired by Khomeinism, was also formed in 1988 at the height of the first intifada; the militant Islamic Salvation Front was born in Algeria; al-Qaeda is said to have been created at the end of the Soviet occupation of Afghanistan; and Pan Am Flight 103 was brought down over Scotland in December of the same year. Also in 1988, war broke out between predominantly Christian Armenia and predominantly Shi'a Muslim Azerbaijan.

In February 1989, as Teheran's incipient nuclear ambitions were being assisted by Pakistan, the Iranian *fatwa* against Salman Rushdie was pronounced by Khomeini and repeatedly endorsed thereafter. Kashmiri Islamists began their bloody struggle with India in 1989 for an independent Muslim state. Also in 1989 the new Islamist leader of Sudan, Omar Hassan Ahmed al-Bashir, described his regime's continuing battle with its 'southern rebels' as a jihad. In 1990, the then Soviet Union was struggling with Islamist insurgents in Tajikistan in Central Asia, while successor Russian forces were engaged in fierce fighting around the capital, Dushanbe, in December 1992. In 1990, again, the Chinese were deploying tens of thousands of troops in order to crush a Muslim separatist (or 'counter-revolutionary') movement in the Xinjiang region, where about half the population is Muslim; there had been earlier violent uprisings in 1981, 1988 and 1989.

In July 1990, there was even an attempted coup in Trinidad—where some 6 per cent of the population is Muslim—by a Black Muslim group, Jamaat al-Muslimeen. Led by Yasin Abu Bakr, a local Muslim leader with ties to Libya—which had provided some training to the insurgents—the group also had a 'loose relationship' with Louis Farrakhan's 'Nation of Islam' movement in the US. The Trinidadian prime minister, Arthur Robinson, and his cabinet were taken hostage by seventy gunmen. Electrically-wired explosive devices were (characteristically) placed in a car outside one of the buildings in which the hostages were held; the television station and many other buildings in Port of Spain were set on fire, with gangs of looters roaming the streets. After some thirty deaths in the fighting which ensued, the hostage-takers were tricked, the hostages released and 114 insurgents charged with kidnapping, murder and treason.

On a much larger scale, but in the same year and in the same war of 'reawakening', Saddam Hussein invaded Kuwait. In November 1991, the Soviet Union was finally defeated in Afghanistan by Islamist forces. Also in that year, and until 1997, there was not only civil war in Tajikistan, but Muslim separatists first declared independence in Chechnya—they did so again in 1996—and declared a jihad against Moscow. In 1991–92, civil war broke out in Somalia, almost the whole of whose population is Muslim, and which was to become one of al-Qaeda's bases of operations. In 1991, too, Muslims and Christians were fighting in the Indonesian Moluccas.

Algeria's civil war—Muslim against Muslim—broke out in 1992 after the Islamist movement seemed headed for electoral victory, was denied its spoils and also proclaimed a jihad. A military government, declaring a state of emergency, took power to crush it. In Tanzania, the government was driven to ban the Islamist Balukta Party in 1993, while the Kenyan government acted likewise after violent clashes with Islamists in Mombasa in the same year. From 1992 to 1995 there was civil war in Bosnia, as Bosnian Muslims fought for an independent state; some quarter of a million Serbs, Croats and Muslims are said to have died. In 1994, war was launched against the Chechens by Moscow; and after an intermission of three years was relaunched in late 1999, when 80,000 Russian troops were sent in to deny Chechnya's self-proclaimed independence as a Muslim state. Also in 1994 a US-led effort to end Somalia's civil war ended in debacle, and perhaps from the mid-nineties Pakistan's nuclear scientist, Abdul Qadeer Khan, began providing further help to Iran's nuclear programme. From 1997 to 1999 there was a Muslim separatist uprising in Kosovo.

The complexities of these world-wide upheavals generated by the Islamic *risorgimento* have been great. They have included crises, lulls, truces and resumptions of conflict, as in Algeria, Chechnya, Kashmir, the Palestinian territories, Sudan or Thailand; bloody rivalries (as in Darfur in western Sudan, and in Iraq) between Islamist factions in battle for control of a nation; struggles for control of oil resources; ethnic conflicts, as between Arabs and Africans, including where the latter are also Muslim; and familial, clan and tribal struggles, as in the Palestinian territories, Afghanistan, Iraq, Somalia and Sudan, which are interwoven with wider political ends. Other battles between Muslim and Muslim have cut across Islamism's larger purposes in its advance against the world of 'unbelief'.

In this global conflict, the inter-relations of the combatants—to which I will return in later chapters—have also been bewildering. The murder in early September 2001 of the leading Afghan opponent of the Taliban, Ahmed Shah Massoud, was carried out by Algerians with Belgian passports and with visas to enter Pakistan issued in London. Along the fifty-year-old road that postwar and postcolonial Islamism has taken, links have been established and armouries amassed by many Islamic states, often with the aid of the historically-unseeing West; before 1990, the US even facilitated the acquisition by Iraq of the means to produce chemical and biological weapons. Above all, no individual event in this war—and certainly not the 2001 attack on New York's World Trade Center—can properly be described as a 'bolt from the blue'.

It is the complexity of these events and relationships that has helped confuse analysis and kept understanding at bay. So, too, has lack in the West of historical knowledge of Islam, recent historical knowledge included. It is a lack fully matching and even exceeding the ignorance among Muslims of Western history. It is easier by far, and tempting, to wish a plague on all their houses and to retreat. But the West especially cannot afford it, no more than it can afford to think that a resurgent Islam can be 'defeated' by smart bombs, invasion, 'sanctions', 'democratisation' or mere contempt, or that the non-Muslim world is facing mere 'terror'.

Many of the connections and affiliations in the present war, unlike in the First and Second World Wars, have been covert, suppressed, denied. In its opening decades, this war has been not only a battlefield of visible combat but a war of shifting position, changing alliances and hit-and-run methods. It is also a war both of the long haul and of the short-term; a war of large goals and small men also, as in most wars. On its front-lines there has been no latter-day Saladin, nor a Churchill, Saddam Hussein's violent posturings (until cut down to size) and Osama bin Laden's 'aura' notwithstanding. Much has been sordid on all sides, merely blood-letting or murder, attacks on civilian targets, rhetoric and waste of money, men and arms.

The links and changing loyalties between the nations and movements of the Arab and wider Islamic arousal have been among the most intricate, but also most important, features of this renaissance. Egypt ruled with an iron rod over Gaza before 1967. Iran helped fund and otherwise supported the Algerian, Egyptian and Iraqi Islamist insurgencies; was a key ally of the Sudanese Islamist regime; supplied arms to the Bosnian Muslims; inspired and aided the formation of Lebanese Hezbollah; armed Hamas; and worked hard to develop its nuclear programme. It was also active in the insurgencies in Tajikistan, Turkmenistan and other Central Asian Muslim countries and regions. It aided the Kosovars; funded mosque-building in Kuwait, Abu Dhabi and other places; bankrolled the effort in 1991–92 to set up a British Muslim 'Parliament' and masterminded the bombing of a Jewish community centre in Buenos Aires in July 1994.

Iraq supported the Egyptian Islamist insurgency which began in 1993, and helped fund the PLO and the Palestinian Authority. In 1991, it was alleged to have given technical help with Algeria's attempt to produce a nuclear bomb, and in 1998 with Libya's biological warfare programme. Iraq even provided £2 million to build Birmingham's Saddam Hussein mosque, symbol of the conflation of secular nationalism with Islamism. In the late summer of 1991 Libya in its turn supported the attempted coup against Gorbachev as the Soviet Union collapsed, helped the IRA, and was involved in support for the anti-white Mugabe regime in Zimbabwe. Jordan supported the PLO when it was based in its country, before turning on it with massacre and expulsion in 1970. And despite the appearance of standing aside from the war between Islam and the non-Islamic world, Jordan permitted the port of Aqaba to be used to rearm Iraq before the Iraq War of 2003 and to break the UN embargoes against it.

Since its Islamist takeover in 1983, Sudan has also been a place of energy and violence. It has supported fellow-Islamists in their insurgencies in Algeria, Egypt and Tunisia, aided—while denying it—Islamists in Somalia, and sided with Saddam Hussein in the Gulf War, as did Yasser Arafat. Syria, on the other hand, was Iran's only Arab ally in the bloody Iran-Iraq war, murdered its own Islamists by the thousands in 1982, overran Christian Lebanon, has been a patron and protector of Hezbollah, and has sheltered and funded Hamas and Islamic Jihad. It gave refuge to leading figures in the fallen regime of Saddam Hussein, and ordered and supervised numerous hijackings, hostage-takings and suicide-bombings.

For his part, Yasser Arafat had his principal base successively in Jordan— whose government he nevertheless attempted to overthrow—in Lebanon and in Tunisia, despite the ostensible political differences between the PLO and their regimes, and notwithstanding the ill-concealed hostility of most Arab and Muslim nations towards him. Pakistan, a country that has alternated between semblances of democracy and military dictatorships, has provided arms and training to many insurgent Islamist groups, including the Chechens and the Afghan Taliban movement. In defeat, or seeming defeat, the Taliban found shelter in Pakistan, while North Korea, Iran and Libya were provided with advanced weapons technologies, to the knowledge both of the senior Pakistani military and its secret services.

Pakistan was also said to have been involved in Islamist bombings in Bombay and Calcutta at the end of 1992 and in early 1993—with large loss of life—in reprisal for the Hindu destruction in December 1992 of the Babri Masjid mosque in Ayodhya, originally built on a site sacred to Hindus. It was also implicated in the attack on the Indian parliament in New Delhi in December 2001, and in arming and funding Muslim separatists who continued to fight India in Kashmir, despite intermittent efforts to find a peaceful solution to the conflict.

Regimes threatened by Islamist insurgency have themselves backed, and continue to back, insurgencies elsewhere. Among other recipients of its largesse, violent Islamist groups in Algeria and Chechnya were funded from Saudi Arabia. It gave aid to other militant Islamic movements beyond its borders which might otherwise be a danger to itself, or in order to outgun those which were. It has been, and continues to be, involved in most aspects of the always-widening Islamic revival, despite its seeming support for the West.

What is clear, too, is that many non-Muslim nations, both in the West and beyond it, have been engaged in these often covert connections. Russia was alleged in 1997 to have helped Syria to produce nerve gas, as well as supplying the Hafez Assad regime with arms as the predecessor Soviet Union had done. It helped build Iran's nuclear reactor at Bushehr; had close relations, military and commercial, with Saddam's Iraq; and remained one of Teheran's principal supporters. Yet at the same time as aiding Iran and Iraq it was fighting a fierce war against the Muslim Chechens—in turn aided by the Iranians—which left much of their country in ruins. Belarus, Ukraine and Romania also helped Iraq with weapons supplies after the latter's defeat in the 1991 Gulf War.

Similarly China, despite its own troubles with Iranian-backed insurgencies in its Muslim-populated regions, has aided Iran with its nuclear missile and arms programmes since the early 1990s. Indeed, China is said at different times to have provided nuclear and other advanced weapons know-how to Algeria, Iran, Iraq, Pakistan and Syria. As for the nuclear-armed 'rogue' state of North Korea, it is reported to have supplied Iran, Iraq, Pakistan and Syria with missiles and missile technologies.

The Western world has no genuine right to complain about any of this. France, under Mitterrand, and Britain helped make Pakistan a nuclear power. Germany assisted Iraq's missile programme before the 1991 Gulf War. Western arms suppliers, secretly or with the knowledge and assistance of their governments, have armed many of the Islamic nations to the teeth, as the US and other countries have helped arm Israel. Israel has in turn helped arm others—such as India and Turkey—who are actual or potential combatants in this global conflict between the Islamic and non-Islamic worlds.

Nor can Saudi Arabia or China be blamed for policies of uniquely low cunning. In this game of strategically-shifting alliances, the US (with Britain) backed and armed Iraq in the Iran-Iraq war of 1980–88. It also helped fund and arm the Afghan Muslim insurgency when Afghanistan was still under Soviet occupation. But the US, like other non-Muslim countries, was insufficiently aware at the time that the Iraq and Afghanistan which it was supporting were already among the theatres in a global war whose principal target was to be the US itself.

The 1990s were also a decade when Jemaah al Islamiyah (or 'Islamic Community') began creating operational units in Singapore, Malaysia, the Philippines and Australia; when the Muslim separatist movement in Chinese Xinjiang (or East Turkestan to the Muslims of the region) gained strength; when the Algerian and Egyptian Islamist insurgencies and the struggles against them steadily grew more brutal; when civil wars were being fought in Afghanistan, Iraqi Kurdistan, Somalia and Sudan; when inter-ethnic violence devastated the Balkans, and the Indonesian army's military offensive against Islamist rebels continued.

It was the Gulf War which was to be something of a catalyst, and in which the scales at last began to fall from some Western eyes. A vicious inter-Muslim conflict, Iraq's predatory attempt to annex the American neo-colony of Kuwait in August 1990 was met not only by Australia, Britain, France and the US (among others) but by military contingents of one kind and another from Bangladesh, Egypt, Morocco, Pakistan, Qatar and Syria (among others). Some were motivated by traditional enmities, others by calculation of interest; some by Islamic fraternity, others again by the settling of scores.

Saddam Hussein, savaged on the battlefield, proclaimed a glorious triumph and indeed lived to fight another day, putting down a Shi'a rebellion in Iraq in 1991 with barbarous methods. More significant, in the context of renascent Islam's much wider war, was the support shown to Saddam Hussein by militant Islamists in Afghanistan, Egypt, Jordan, Malaysia, Pakistan, Syria, Tunisia and even South Africa, as well as by many Muslims in Europe, Britain included. Hundreds of thousands of Muslims—50,000 alone in one Pakistani city, Lahore—protested against the participation of troops from their countries in the fight to 'liberate Kuwait'. Protests in Bangladesh brought down the Ershad goverment, deposed in December 1990, and pro-Iraqi demonstrations were held from one end of the Muslim world to the other, including the Muslim world in Europe, exactly as they were to protest again against the 2003 Iraq War. In 1991, Yasser Arafat proclaimed that 'Iraq and Palestine' would 'pray together in Jerusalem after the great battle, God willing'. God was not willing, and they did not.

However, it is not the conscripted troops of Muslim and Arab national armies who should, for the time being, be looked to as the non-Islamic nations' most redoubtable adversaries in this Third World War. Instead, it is its irregulars, its martyr-warriors, its *mujahideen*, its 'extremists', its 'terrorists', its suicide-bombers, its hijackers, and its hostage-takers who have rediscovered a redoubtable mission. In its name they have done battle—a just battle in their own terms—with the 'infidel' world.

In Bosnia, in 1993, as Muslims were put to the Serbian sword, there were to be found such irregulars, or *mujahideen*: Afghans, Iranians, Jordanians, Pakistanis, Turks, Yemenis and even British Muslims from Yorkshire fought for Islam on the soil of the former Yugoslavia. The arms they carried came from Iran, Pakistan and Turkey, and political support was given by Malaysia, the United Arab Emirates and Saudi Arabia, among others. Irregulars from Pakistani and Afghan terrorist training camps were found alongside Chinese Muslims in Xinjiang in 1990 and in the Tajikistan civil war in 1992; Egyptian Islamists were fighting in the Somali civil war in 1992, carrying Iranian-supplied arms; Egyptians, Iranians, Jordanians, Saudis, Syrians, Yemenis and others besides, including Muslim 'Britons', joined the fight-back against the 'coalition' occupation of Iraq from March 2003.

Veterans of the Islamist victory over the Soviet Union in Afghanistan reappeared in the planning and execution of the attack on the World Trade Center, in the Chechen war against the Russians and in the Muslim insurgencies in the Philippines and Indonesia. Chechen Islamists in turn offered in October 2000 to send 150 fighters to help Hamas in its struggle with Israel; arms used by *mujahideen* in Kosovo were passed on, after their 'victory', to 'ethnic Albanians' during the attempted uprising in Macedonia in 2001; and a new 'foreign legion'—with many Arabs among them—of former trainees and combatants in all these and other Islamist theatres of battle are among the cadres of al-Qaeda, who have been found in its associated groups and cells from Buffalo to Bali, and as co-participants in Islamist actions in many parts of the world.

A bomb, a local attack or an insurgency, even an open confrontation with Western forces in an Afghanistan or an Iraq—and whether they be 'successes' or 'failures'—are no more than incidents in what Islamists and most 'ordinary' Muslims alike see as a wider struggle and a settling of accounts. It is a struggle larger than any that Muslims may have with one another. In other respects, too, this is no 'ordinary' war. Rather, it is a war to end all wars, a last war—even if, after the passage of several decades, it is still in its early stages—to restore Islamic pride, and even to remake the world in its image.

But to the non-Islamic nations it remains 'global terror'. Indeed, in the case of the West, such misnaming compounds the delusions and illusions, the confusions and unrealities which govern the West's own relations with itself and its grapplings with its internal social and ethical disorders, as well as those which govern its relations with the non-Western world. Western politicians and intellectuals have thus given barely any acknowledgment to the Islamic resurgence despite the fact that Muslims themselves refer to it often, and are emboldened by their recovered self-belief to act decisively upon its promptings. Thus, it was in keeping with Western evasions that Bernard Lewis's conception in 1990 that there was a 'clash of civilisations' between the Islamic and non-Islamic worlds—a notion later 'borrowed' from him by Samuel Huntington—should have been nervously shied away from. Yet both Muslim clerics and Western Muslim intellectuals proclaim that such a 'clash' is in progress.

In 1991, the exiled Iraqi writer Falih' Abd al-Jabbar declared that 'Islamic fundamentalism'—or 'neo-Islamism', as he also called it—had 'gradually come to dominate [sc. Islamic] social and political thinking for the past twenty years and more'. To him, such 'neo-Islamism' expressed the 'decay' of Arab nationalism as represented by Nasserism. The rise to power of the Ba'ath movement in Syria and Iraq appeared to al-Jabbar in 1991 to be 'almost aberrations'. The failure of 'nationalist modernisation' in the Islamic world and the 'disintegration of the left'—the Soviet empire had by then vanished—had left an 'ideological and political vacuum', he declared. The door was 'wide open to neo-Islamism' which, al-Jabbar asserted, had 'managed to integrate' nationalism and Islam.

Although a strong sense of the 'Islamic wave' was already part of Muslim self-consciousness by the 1970s, the mere word 'Islamism' was still being placed in quotation marks in Britain in the mid-1990s. This was despite the passage of a convulsive decade of Khomeinite fundamentalism from 1979 to 1989, and five years and more after the ayatollah's death. In December 1993, no fewer than five hundred Islamic radicals—whose names, obviously, were not disclosed to inquiring Western journalists—met in Khartoum to discuss what they chose to call 'their future strategy towards conflicts involving Muslims'; which was to say Islam's challenge to the West.

Organised by Sudan's National Islamic Front, delegates were present from throughout the Middle East, as well as from what were called 'the growing Islamic movements in the United States and Europe'. There were delegates from Bosnia and Somalia; from South Africa; from Washington; and 'a large delegation from Britain', among many others. One month earlier, Sudan had been put on the US State Department's list of countries suspected of 'sponsoring terrorism', and was also being accused of harbouring and training prominent Islamists from Lebanon and Palestine.

This event merits being singled out from a host of other conclaves, both
clandestine and open, for the illustration it offers of the continuous (and still
continuing) unwillingness in the West to recognise the fact of the Islamic
'reawakening', and to call its battles by their right names. In 1997, Dr. Hassan
Turabi, who was then the leading figure behind the Islamist Sudanese regime,
spoke correctly not only of a 'resurgent Islam' but disparagingly of Europe's
'post-Christian civilisation'. A lawyer, a London University graduate and a
self-professed 'admirer of Arnold Toynbee', Turabi was nevertheless reductively presented in Western commentary as no more than a Grand Guignol
'terror mastermind'.

Even minor spokesmen of the Islamic cause in Britain during the 1991
conflict over the Iranian *fatwa* against Salman Rushdie could be heard arguing,
justly, that 'the passionate and firm response to Rushdie's provocation' had
become 'possible only with the rise of militant Islam. If the Rushdie episode
had transpired before the mid-1970s', a chronology which coincided with that
given by the above-quoted Falih' Abd al-Jabbar, 'the Muslims' reaction would
have been negligible', it was declared.

The dominant sense in the world of Islam has rightly been one of pride
in its own resurgence. This was so, despite minoritarian confessions by Muslims of their 'backwardness' in the face of the West, or the assertions—as by
Fareed Zakaria, a *Newsweek* editor, in September 2002—that 'radical political
Islam is past the peak of its power'. For its part, the West has preferred, or
needed, to see in the Islamist movement only 'barbarism' and 'terror'. To one
British editorialist, the 'defeat' of the Taliban was thus a 'triumph of civilisation over the self-destructive forces of barbarism'. To a second, it was 'difficult
for the civilised man or woman to admit that barbarism can take possession of
a soul, or a society. But unless we do, we cannot stop its advance'. To a third,
more obtuse, 'We are at war with the world's losers.... We're rolling'. A true
sense of the Islamic 'reawakening' has barely figured at all in the Western
mind. The 'foe', therefore, is being both misjudged and underestimated.

Western responses to the Islamic revival, being anxious responses, are off-
balance. As we shall see, untruths have been rife on both sides of the conflict.
Hence, the Western public has had no clear sense of what has been occurring.
In such vacuum of understanding the portmanteau terms 'terrorism', 'international terrorism', 'terror networks', 'terror suspects' and so forth have had
their uses. They have covered (and concealed) a multitude of unanalysed and
evaded historical, political, cultural and ethical issues in this accelerating
phase of the Islamic upsurge. When a British foreign secretary could declare
that Osama bin Laden's 'theology' was 'terror', that his 'religion' was 'terrorism'

and that it was 'the religion of terrorism with which we are in conflict', it was plain that comprehension had ended.

Simple confusion plays a large part in such Western visionlessness and reductiveness. This is explicable on several grounds. First, there is the intricacy of the events themselves, as I have already indicated. To take one brief phase of this world war at random: at exactly the same time, but in different theatres of the war, the Israelis were besieging (and effectively destroying) Yasser Arafat's headquarters on the West Bank, Egypt was arresting its own Islamic militants, the shelling in Kashmir was continuing, Muslims were setting upon Hindus (and vice versa) in India, Christians were being killed by Muslims in Indonesia, Donald Rumsfeld was visiting US troops in Central Asia, Chechen and Russian violence was continuing in southern Russia, al-Qaeda struck in Tunisia and European Muslims were taking part in demonstrations in Europe in common cause with 'anti-globalisers', anti-Americans and anti-fascists.

The second cause of Western confusion is that our historic memory grows shorter. As Bernard Lewis has pointed out, 'in current American usage the phrase "that's history" is commonly used to dismiss something as unimportant'; I was myself told by a senior editor at the *New York Times*, less than a fortnight after the attack on the World Trade Center, that an early version of part of this chapter was 'very interesting, but we don't do history'. Conversely, as Lewis has also argued, Islamist pronouncements—such as those made by bin Laden—often contain historical references and allusions to the longevity of Islam's perceived humiliation at the West's hands or to the evocation of past Islamic glories.

Such references rightly seek to link present acts to a chain of historic causation. But who in the West, and especially in a mass media most at home with the instantaneous and the immediately dramatic—or, better, the catastrophic—wants a collation of events and dates which discloses how we got here? Look at some of them again: Suez in 1956; the PLO created in 1964, and the hijackings and hostage-takings that followed year after year; the India-Pakistan war over Kashmir in 1965–66; the 'Six Day War' in 1967; the assassination of Senator Robert Kennedy by a Palestinian, Sirhan Sirhan, in 1968; the slaughter of Palestinian guerrillas in Jordan in 1970; the Syrian-Egyptian attack on Israel in 1973; in 1974 the use of the 'oil weapon'; the Islamic revolution in Iran in 1979; the years of the Iran-Iraq war from 1980—each has brought us to where we are now.

So, too, with the assassination in 1981 of Egyptian president Sadat after making peace with Israel; or the Muslim uprisings in western China from

1981; or the acquiring of nuclear weapons by Pakistan in the 1980s; or the Israeli invasion of Lebanon in 1984; or Lockerbie in 1988; or the *fatwa* against Salman Rushdie in 1989—on and on, the momentum of things has continued, yet with each event or development generally perceived in the West discretely, often as a sensation, and shorn of context.

It is uninteresting to our ahistoric times to trace links between, and understand historically, the fact that Muslim Chechnya first declared itself independent in 1991; that the Soviet Union was defeated in Afghanistan in the same year; that the World Trade Center was first attacked in 1993; that Hamas was offered full support by Iran in 1994; that the first Russian-Chechen war also began in 1994; that there was a wave of unrest even in the sheikhdom of Bahrain also in 1994, when the Shi'ite majority demanded political reforms; that bomb attacks were carried out against Americans in Saudi Arabia in 1995 and 1996, allegedly with Iraqi help; that the victorious Taliban, largely funded by Saudi Arabia, entered Kabul in September 1996; that the so-called International Islamic Front for Jihad Against Jews and Crusaders, which included al-Qaeda among other militant groups, is said to have been founded by bin Laden in February 1998 in a training-camp in eastern Afghanistan; and that the US embassies in Kenya and Tanzania were brought down in the same year.

It was also 1998 in which Cruise-missile attacks were launched in reprisal, but randomly, by the US on an Afghan training-camp and a factory in the Sudan; in which Pakistan first tested a nuclear weapon; and in which the dictatorial Suharto, who had been backed by the United States, was overthrown in Indonesia. Yet without such chronological sense, the sense of the unfolding of things, there can be no true vision of what has brought the Islamic, non-Islamic and anti-Islamic worlds to their present pass. Thus, General Musharraf came to power in Pakistan in a bloodless coup in 1999; thousands of Nigerians died in Muslim-Christian violence from 1999 as Sharia law was introduced in twelve of Nigeria's thirty-six states; clashes took place between Albanian Muslim insurrectionists and the Macedonian security forces in 2001; there was an attempted military coup in the Ivory Coast in 2002 in which Islamists were involved; and martial law was declared in the Muslim provinces of southern Thailand in 2003, while attempts were being made, in 2003 and 2004, to settle the twenty-year civil war in Sudan.

The ahistoricity of Western mentalities is today increasingly shaped by media-governed attention-spans. But our failure to grasp truly what is happening is also owed to the intellectual confusion sown in the world of 'progressivism'—and therefore in the mental worlds of many Western opinion-formers—by the socialist debacle in the late 1980s and early 1990s. The limits upon what may now be 'correctly' thought and said about the world is most restrictive when those who are perceived to be victims of the West's economic and political power are the issue. Here, a sense of the victimhood of the Islamic world—a sense which most Muslims themselves share—is a self-sufficient pose for much of what remains of the Western 'left'. But a grasp of the nature and meaning of the Islamic revival requires more than sympathy for the underdog, even if such sympathy is just.

This step most of the Western 'left', embattled by intellectual and political defeat and socialism's passing, are not disposed—and generally no longer able—to take. Moreover, telling the truth about the strengths of the Islamic revival is also inhibited by the secular 'left's' unease in treating of, or its entire recoil from, all matters to do with religious faith. Or, as Western Muslim intellectuals have themselves seen, the 'problem for the left' is that 'there is no place in it for understanding that religion can be the core of someone's identity'.

In this third main cause of inadequate and confused Western responses to the Islamic revival, the Muslim-as-victim joins the Muslim-as-'terrorist' in a cartoon reductiveness as great as that which once made of Hitler a maniac, and Mussolini a buffoon. Today, 'progressives' in the West understand least about Islam and Islamism, but believe they understand most; and certainly believe that they understand more than 'the cowboy' whose first instinct is to shoot at Muslims from the hip. Nevertheless, the 'left's' moral and political confusion about how to respond to Islam's challenge to the West is plain.

In 1990 and 1991, fellow-'left' intellectuals in Britain admitted to me in conversation that 'socialists' had 'lost their confidence and sense of direction' in knowing how to respond 'correctly' to the Gulf War. As between Saddam Hussein and the coalition forces, I was told, 'you can't place your sympathies unequivocally in any one place'; or, again, Saddam was 'a horror' but the war against him was 'essentially an American operation' and thus, by implication, impossible to support. In 2003, before, during and after the outbreak of the Iraq War, the latter position was a general one; and hundreds of thousands joined hands with Muslims in the non-Muslim world in order to protest against the assault upon Saddam Hussein's dictatorial regime. Similarly, Muslims and non-Muslims alike found explanations, and even justifications, for the London suicide-bombings of July 2005 in British support for US policy in Iraq, while simultaneously expressing revulsion at the attacks.

Such ambivalence seems unlikely to diminish; on the contrary. 'Anti-Americanism' has increasingly become a *leitmotif* as the Islamic 'reawakening' has advanced, and as muddled Western responses to Islam and Islamism have intensified. In addition, the print and televisual media have contributed greatly to bring us to our present confusion. 'Catastrophism' and instantaneous

responses to each new stimulus of our appetite for event have contributed to
the daily Babel. So, too, has a mire of mis- and dis-information, the blurring
of the distinction between objective fact and subjective opinion, and the mere
need to fill space and time, to say nothing of the distortion and paranoia
expressed in the striking of seemingly 'progressive' poses.

Overheated obsessions with the Jews and the making of Israel into the
root-of-all-evil have also clouded judgment, as have equally aberrant forms of
hero-worship of the malefactor. Moreover, the 'intoxicating allure in some
sections of the Islamic world of the power of terrorism', as it has been called,
has also exerted its influence in the non-Islamic world. This the shrewdest of
Muslims themselves know. As Shabbir Akhtar, of Bradford's Council for
Mosques, sardonically put it in January 1991, in reference to Islamist violence,
there are many in the West who 'merely pretend to despise it while secretly
admiring it'. Such insights are the further fruits of the Islamic 'reawakening':
to be several steps ahead of where the non-Islamic world thinks the 'backward' Muslim is.

There has also been a sharpening deterioration, during the last decade, in
the quality of public 'debate' about what it is that Western and other nations
with a 'terrorist' problem are facing. Of the deterioration none can be in
doubt. Even the *New York Times* could give space in September 2002 to the
crude view that 'Osama bin Laden didn't care twopence for the Palestinians.
He was—let's hope the past tense is correct—a bloodthirsty religious maniac,
and his followers were deluded fanatics for whom murder was some obscure
compensation for failure'.

Unhappily for the non-Islamic world, low-level response of this kind has
coincided with the steady political and cultural progress of the Islamist cause.
It is a deterioration which may be measured by comparing the relatively high
intellectual level of exchanges and moral engagement from 1989 to the mid-
1990s over the Rushdie affair. It was demonstrated by Western press commentators, academics and others, as well as by Muslims in favour of, and (although
widely ignored) opposed to, the *fatwa*.

Public argument then had its great crudities also—there is little as crude
as burning a book of which one disapproves. But the standard of debate on
the subject among the contending parties, whose terms I will look at later, was
worthy of the ethical and other complexities of the issue. In general, it is not
the case now. Moreover, many of yesterday's libertarian anti-Islamists have in
effect 'changed sides' in the intervening period; where they once unequivocally opposed the threats being made against Rushdie for his *Satanic Verses,* they
now perceive the conflict between Islam and the West with different eyes.

Arguably, many such have more intellectual sympathy for Islamist opponents of Western liberal democratic orders than for those who struggle to uphold the latter's values. In other cases, weariness with the entire subject—or lack of stamina—has led to the taking of vulgar short-cuts in treating of it. Auto-pilot reflexes have replaced nuanced responses both in the media and, in consequence, in its audiences. There is also a diminishing distinction to be made—on this as on other, lesser issues—between the 'quality' broadsheets and the 'popular' press; they vary more in the degree of, say, their 'anti-Americanism' or their sensation-mongering than in the refinements of knowledge of their various commentariats.

Resort has also been had in some areas of the Western media, coarsening debate further, to accusations that there is 'censorship' of whatever position a given individual may be seeking to promote. (I have made such accusations, in private, against editors myself.) Thus, Lewis Lapham of New York's *Harper's Magazine* alleged in February 2002 that those, such as he, who opposed what he called America's 'worldwide crusade against terrorism' were being 'muffled' by the 'curators of the national news media'. However, the same type of accusation is made against news organisations, such as the BBC, by those who think they detect a 'liberal' or 'left' bias in their reports upon the conflict between the Islamic and non-Islamic worlds.

The plethora of commentary, speculation and pontification upon all this has certainly not diminished in volume. What can be asserted is that ethical and intellectual confusion in the West about the nature of the Islamic resurgence—a confusion itself signalling a victory for the Islamic revival—has grown. Moral incoherence has made it possible for the 'courage' of youthful suicide-bombers to be saluted at the same time as their acts are condemned; the growing strength of age-old fixations about the Jews has befogged analysis and judgment; hostility to America often serves as an alibi for reasoned argument.

Many of these, and related, phenomena were latent earlier. A strange admiration for the fanatical absolutist was visible in the account in *The Times* in December 1994 of an Algerian Islamist hijacking of an Air France airliner in Algiers, during which passengers were murdered, as the account declares, 'in cold blood'. 'The Armed Islamic Group'—the Algerian Islamist movement—'wants no compromise, just a *jihad* to rid the planet of the infidel', ran the report. 'It was burning devotion to this cause which shone [*sic*] from the Air France hijackers'. 'Shone' was an egregious word to use in the context.

Since then, and despite exceptions, competitive pressures have continued to drive reporting and comment downhill in the direction of excitable falsehood, the further blurring of fact and opinion, and a form of instant punditry which gives little space to those with knowledge of Arab culture or of the history of Islam. Brief squabbles—'I'm afraid I shall have to stop you there' is one of its signatures—make do for television debate, and three sentences of voice-over description and comment upon a lurid scene often serve as 'coverage' of a 'story'. An 'anchor's' lip-gloss or a muscling jaw puts analysis at a discount.

The consequences have been substantial, and not merely in the primacy given to the drama of an event over its wider meaning and truth. Thus, a London *Times* leader in April 2002 declared that 'the news is grimmer every day', that 'the Holy Land seems to be approaching apocalypse [*sic*]' and that 'suicide bombers and synagogue arsonists are making their way to Western capitals', circumstances described as 'the brink'. And when rhetoric is given precedence over fact in this way, measured judgment comes to seem dullness of mind, and knowledge itself suffers.

Academia has also served its own cause ill. This is not only because so many works of scholarly political analysis, on any subject whatever, have ceased to be worth reading and are thus held in contempt. Where there is nothing of illumination to be gained from them, and nothing in them worthy of even being noted or remembered, it is not surprising that the less knowledgeable should also think there is nothing in them. In consequence, where academic works of history—as on Islam—do genuinely shed light on the nature and causes of contemporary disorders, it is their common fate to be ignored. In addition, the independence of Western academic institutions in the field of Islamic studies has been much compromised, especially in the last two decades.

This has been largely brought about by the fact that funds directed to their establishment have increasingly come from Islamic and Arab sources, in particular Saudi Arabia. The donors are deeply *parti pris*, and naturally so, in regard to the matters ostensibly under objective study by scholars whose salaries are paid by such donations. All these factors, and others, have contributed to making rational understanding of the present conjuncture hard to attain. Moreover, the very notion of the need in us for moral and intellectual direction is under constant challenge, or entirely denied, by so many (illiberal) formers of (liberal) Western opinion. It is therefore not surprising that 'the media' should be left to its own devices in punching us senseless with 'breaking news' and strident headlines.

Stupor at the excess of comment and the great tide of 'information' now available through the Internet—not the same as knowledge—is another deterrent to the organisation of our thoughts. Lack of time, absence of concentration, our own prejudices, special interests and special pleading, the gullibilities of open societies and the need felt by many Western politicians and governments to defer to now-sizeable Muslim minorities have also added greatly to our confusions and hesitations. So, too, has the inner struggle between a fear of resurgent Islam and an often equal fear in many individuals of being identified and categorised as 'immoderate', 'hardline', 'neo-conservative', 'Islamophobic' or on the 'far right'.

We also face the repetition of the same political arguments about combating, or not combating, 'terror', and the continuous renewal of media 'shock' at Islamist attacks on fellow-Muslims or on the non-Islamic world—when such attacks have been regular and frequent in the last decades. In these circumstances, the combination of a surfeit of information and sensation, and a paralysis of intellect and will, have (in many in the West) stopped ratiocination altogether. To this paralysis, Western self-doubt and the moral obfuscations imposed on us by both Muslim and non-Muslim apologists for the direst of actions, committed in the name of Islam, have made their own contribution. That events which are related occur without a matching energy to draw the necessary connections between them is itself a demonstration of intellectual failure.

Nearly everything that has so far occurred in this Third World War has gone on, or been known, longer than one thinks or is led to believe. Public satiety dims the apprehending of facts and patterns of facts; an ahistorical temper prevents us looking over our shoulders at what transpired or was said last year, or a decade ago; a false *politesse* inhibits the pointing of fingers; and State Department, Foreign Office and security service calculation bids journalists keep their mouths shut, or hides from them and a wider audience what officialdom secretly knows. Blatant falsehoods, from all directions, also stagger the mind and stop reason in its tracks.

In examining the record of these decades of Islamic revival, of the recovery of Muslim identity and of bloodshed, a serious retreat from the truth by non-Muslim commentators can be detected from around the mid-1990s. In the West, fear of Islam had by then got under the skin of its liberal orders and was turning increasingly into 'anti-Americanism' and Western self-blame. 'Political correctness' increasingly restrained just judgment. The cause of 'human rights' took precedence over the demands of the rule of law. The same paranoias and fixations, and many other reflexes of emotion and argument, came to be shared by Islamists and their Western sympathisers, to the point at which the latter could be found offering defences of Islamist outrages, apologias which Muslims themselves knew to be untrue.

This tendency became more marked from the mid-1990s. It could be seen, for example, in reports on Algeria and its civil war, a war of great viciousness which broke out after Islamists, denied their electoral victory, turned mercilessly on their own people in revenge. Following an Islamist attack on a French embassy compound in Algiers in August 1994, which killed French gendarmes and consular officials, the French, under a 'hardline' Interior Minister, Charles Pasqua—swiftly and in chorus denoted by Islamists and European liberals as little better than a 'fascist'—adopted a tough policy in rounding up suspected Algerian Islamist militants in France. Random identity checks were conducted, road-blocks were set up even on the Champs-Élysées and those held in police sweeps were dispatched to a disused barracks at Folembray—quickly termed by Islamists (and, for example, by the *Guardian* in London) a 'concentration camp'.

From today's standpoint, further epithets used about these events in the mid-1990s were to become the familiar ones; the level of debate reached during the Rushdie affair was past. Headlines took what we can now see was a formulaic pattern, truth was at a premium, and rationality itself was disarmed. Pasqua was 'riding a wave of fear', declared the *Sunday Telegraph*, such a 'crackdown' 'could cause a violent reaction' in the French Muslim community, declared the former French foreign minister, the socialist Roland Dumas. Accusations were also made against Pasqua of 'racism', 'over-reaction', 'intimidation' and (by the head of the Middle East Programme at London's Royal Institute of International Affairs) of 'hysteria'. Pasqua in turn accused Britain, Germany and the United States of 'harbouring militants' of the Islamist cause, and of 'doing nothing to curb their activities even when tipped off'. No, declared his opponents in France and beyond: what was required was not the 'tough tactics' of a Pasqua but a 'genuine dialogue of reconciliation' in Algeria—as the massacres of Muslim by Muslim continued without pause—and the encouragement of 'democratic and moderate forces in Algeria'.

Pasqua has long departed the scene. The civil war in Algeria was to continue, as were all the illusions and falsehoods of the mid-1990s debate. That is, we have been here before, time and again in these years of continuous war. Indeed, *le plus ça change, le plus c'est la même chose*. The pattern of events generated by the Islamic advance was clear three and more decades ago. Yet incidents which can only be understood in relation to such established pattern continue to be presented in an ahistorical void, or without context, generally as further acts of 'terror'.

Thus, as long ago as 1979 it was known (to some) that the border areas of Pakistan and Afghanistan were 'provid[ing] Islamic militants with a playground for military training', and that from 1983 to 1993 some '10,000 Arabs' had already 'undergone such training'. Many of them, 'such as the Algerians'—it was reported in 1993, as the West's political and intellectual confusions about Islam and Islamism began markedly to deepen—'have returned to play significant roles in attempts to overthrow their governments at home'. Nevertheless, 'terror' it has remained.

Or, again, by 1994 the Indian High Commissioner in London, L. M. Singhvi, was already complaining that 'a large number of young people' were 'being recruited' at the London School of Economics and the School of Oriental and African Studies by what he euphemistically called 'different organisations'. Indeed, he specifically named in this context Ahmed Sheikh, who was at the LSE in the early 1990s, and who was to be sentenced to death ten years later in Karachi for his involvement in the abduction and murder of the American journalist Daniel Pearl. More generally, Singhvi asserted that 'Islamic fundamentalist groups' were 'turning increasingly to British universities for recruits to train for terrorist acts around the world'. In April 1995—in the sixth year of the Iranian *fatwa* against Salman Rushdie, the sixth year of the war in Kashmir, the fourth year of Islamist control of Afghanistan, the third year of the Algerian civil war, and so on—the *Guardian* was reporting on the 'receiving' of 'foreign Muslims' in Karachi for training in Pakistani-Afghan border camps, who would thereafter be 'sent on to *jihads* of their choosing', as the *Guardian* somewhat jocularly added.

But the report also told, through the words of a link-man in the operation, Mufti Iqbal—described as an 'Afghan *jihad* veteran'—of 'several hundred foreign Muslims' who had 'come to learn'. Among them were 'Arabs', including Algerians and Egyptians, 'Indians, black American Muslims, Filipinos, Kashmiris and even one Canadian'. 'Our main objective', declared Iqbal, 'is to help Muslims all over the world secure their freedom. We have received thousands of volunteers to fight in Kashmir, Bosnia, Tajikistan and Chechenia'. '*Jihad* is an obligation on all Muslims', he was reported as adding.

There was nothing exceptional in this 1995 account. There has been a Niagara of such reports. It spoke both of matters which we know and of matters which, knowing, we have nevertheless come to yawn over. They were also matters which, as soon as referred to, were sought to be obliterated by protest and denial; and matters which, unless made more 'sensational' with every repetition of the same or connected phenomena, jaded appetites were increasingly unable to digest or which aroused impotent rage, even as the momentum of the revival which had given rise to them continued upon its historic course.

It was almost as if, despite the sound-bite reductionism, despite the media caricatures and the pundits' and headline writers' clichés, the subject as 'news' had already been worked to death. During the Iraq War's television coverage, with its 'embedded' reporters riding in American tanks and taking vicarious part in every gunfight and skirmish, there was more overkill on the screen than on the battlefield itself.

Nevertheless, despite all these crudities, we ought by now to have become well informed about Islam's progress. We ought long ago to have known that students from the Far East and Central Asia were being trained in the *madrassas*, or Islamic schools, which nurtured the Taliban, a word which itself means 'students'; ought to have known that many dangerously 'disinherited' individuals—or Marx's old 'lumpen elements'—had been recruited to Islam and Islamism on rundown estates, from prisons, and from the ranks of the unemployed (of all races) in many countries, including the United States, France and Britain; ought to have known long ago that certain Islamic countries, in particular Iran and Saudi Arabia, were octopus-like in their reach and intentions.

At the same time, the issues which all such knowledge sets in motion—and the clamour of denial which automatically greets it—have been and remain of a density beyond the ordinary grasp of individuals and governments alike. The former turn the page or change channels; the latter go round in political circles, or suddenly pull their guns and fire into the darkness. As long ago as February 1989 it was being declared (by Margaret Thatcher)—more or less exactly as has been declared ever since—that there were 'three preconditions' to be met for peace between Palestinians and Israelis: that the United States should show 'resolve *vis à vis* Israel' (and its settlements); that external support was required to bring the parties to their respective senses; and that 'means' should be 'found' of 'choosing who should negotiate for the Palestinian people', in the absence of convincingly pacific interlocutors who might treat seriously with one another.

As with almost every matter in this global conflict we have thus been here before, and many times. In 1991, the French—as since—were insisting that 'divisions in the Arab world' should be settled 'without conflict'; exactly the same position which was to be adopted in 2003 before the Iraq War. Similarly, it has long been argued by the European Union's foreign affairs commissioners that 'war' in the Middle East (as if a much wider war had not been long in progress) 'would threaten ties between the Arab world and the West', and that the European Community must 'go its own way'.

In the repetitiousness of this kind of thing there has been a profound stasis on the one hand, and a widening scope of Islamist operations on the other. They have been coupled with a growing incomprehension about 'what is to be done'. As long ago as October 1994, and accompanied by a 'living martyr' video released to the Western media, a Hamas suicide-bomber took the lives of twenty-two passengers on a bus in Tel Aviv. It was a year after the 'Declaration of Principles' reached between the parties in Oslo and the supposed end of the first Palestinian intifada. In response to the attack—we have been here before, too, and times almost beyond counting—Egypt warned of the 'very serious consequences' if Israel were to retaliate; Israel's foreign minister, Shimon Peres, counselled 'caution'; a British foreign office minister argued that the 'peace process' had to be 'speeded up' in the wake of the attack, and so on.

'Warnings' of this and that, made in like terms (and usually with the same words) in response to like events, and followed by like consequences—and, equally often, with no discernible consequences at all—have been continuously uttered as the wider war has spread. In March 1993, the then Italian Interior Minister was 'warning' that the 'terrorist threat' by 'Islamic militants' was 'more insidious than ever in various continents and especially in Europe', and that its 'global context' was 'very worrying'. Or, choosing at random from my files, in July 1994, a Saudi group of Islamist supporters of Osama bin Laden was reported in the British press in July 1994 to be 'on its way to London' with the intention of installing itself in Britain for purposes of fundraising and recruitment.

In August 1994, the Tunisian president, Zine el-Abidine ben Ali, likewise 'warned' the non-Muslim world, in the clearest and bleakest terms, that 'fundamentalism is your problem.... France, Britain and the US', he declared, 'serve as rear bases for fundamentalist terrorists'. Yet, he exclaimed, these countries 'in the name of liberty and democracy, grant asylum to the enemies of liberty and democracy'. And in November 1994 (again selecting from a host of such instances), Dr. Ahmed Beloufi, an Algerian Islamist sympathiser—with a doctorate from Sheffield University—announced that the situation in Britain was 'unique'. Why? Because 'the British government does not view the Islamic movement as a threat'.

Indeed, in the same year and month, November 1994, it was reported in *The Times* that 'an increasing number of hardline groups intent on combating Western values and influence and setting up Islamic republics in their countries, are operating from London offices, protected by the democratic institutions they are intent on overthrowing at home'. They were said to include Tunisian and Algerian Islamic militants as well as 'members of Hamas'. The Home Office, the paper added, was 'unwilling to change the criteria for admission and is loath to undermine Britain's reputation for fair dealing'.

Again in the same year and month, the 'hardline' Charles Pasqua in France declared that 'networks of fundamentalists' were 'easily able to travel around Europe on false papers'; and also in November 1994, in an interview in *The Times*, President Hosni Mubarak of Egypt 'warned' that 'you have cells of fundamentalists all over Europe'. At the same time, Hamburg—home to Mohammed Atta, future leader of the attack on the World Trade Center—was said to be 'at the centre' of a 'German investigation into Islamic extremism' in Western Europe, with an 'active' recruitment campaign' allegedly being conducted through some of Germany's mosques.

What was thus known to be in place by 1994 was again not abstract 'terror' at all. There were repeated identifications, generally in the form of 'warnings', of the restless criss-crossing movements of individuals and thoughts; movements generated by the Islamic revival and ranging with remarkable freedom from, to and across the terrain of the Western world. By August 1995 it was being said equally freely, and now without notable frissons of surprise, that London—and other British cities (such as Leicester) which had substantial Muslim minorities—was home to representatives of the Muslim Brotherhood, Palestinian Hamas, Algerian Islamists and Pakistani and Asian Jemaah Islamiyah groups, among others. 'The list grows each day, Arab embassies complain', laconically commented the *Guardian*; complaints that were unsurprising, since individuals wanted for conspiring to murder the rulers of their own countries—including the then king Hussein of Jordan—were among them.

By the mid-1990s, much of this was already old hat. Moral insouciance, together with traditions in Britain of 'fair play', also treated it as such. In a 'sermon' given as long ago as May 1989, Iran's then parliamentary speaker, Hashemi Rafsanjani, had openly called on Palestinians to kill Americans, Britons and other Westerners wherever they could be found. There was, therefore, or so it seemed, little left at which to express either moral indignation or media 'shock'. 'If, in retaliation for every Palestinian martyred in Palestine', Rafsanjani had continued, 'they [the Palestinians] kill and execute, not inside Palestine, five Americans or Britons or Frenchmen, the Zionists would not continue those wrongs. It is not hard to kill Americans or Frenchmen', he added, 'there are so many everywhere in the world. Is their blood worth anything?' he rhetorically inquired. He also urged Palestinians to 'bomb Western factories' and to 'hijack planes'.

By 1994, five years on and many tens and hundreds of thousands of deaths later—including in the Gulf War, in Afghanistan, in Algeria, in the Balkans, in the Horn of Africa, in Central Asia and on a dozen other battlefields across the globe—the stage had therefore been set for those rehearsals of Western doubt and self-doubt with which we were to become familiar; as familiar as we were becoming with Islamist methods of warfare, internecine Muslim hostilities, expressions of racist Islamophobia in the West, fulminations against Americans and Jews, and all the rest of it.

Indeed, as I shall seek to show further, it was these 'rehearsals of doubt and self-doubt' which were to become more frequent in the non-Muslim world, and more revealing, as the tide of Islamism—Islam-as-a-politics—advanced. The doubt and the advance have gone hand-in-hand. The more strident the verbal assaults and the more bloody the physical assaults made by Islamists on Western interests, and by Western arms and interests upon them, the greater the equivocation of response (of many) in the West appeared to become.

One example of thousands will serve here for the rest. It again dates from 1994, when such equivocation began to be increasingly noticeable. After the hijacking of an Air France Airbus at Marseilles airport on Christmas Eve of that year, and the 'storming' of the aircraft by French 'anti-terrorist' police, a *Guardian* editorialist described the latter event as (on the one hand) a 'brilliant solution to an immediate crisis' but (on the other) one which 'could provoke even more trouble in the long run'. The prose of convoluted thought then thickened further: 'That does not mean that the French authorities were wrong to storm the plane. On the contrary'. As any regular *Guardian* reader would know, a 'but' was imminent. 'But it does mean that as France rejoices at the outcome, she should also fear'—a key word and a crucial sense from this time on—'the repercussions of an event which will echo back and forth across the Mediterranean for a long time'.

There was no such echo of the event. The only echo, one to resound across the years that followed, was of the collision of the two minds which exist within each doubting individual in the West about almost every aspect of this war of the worlds. The Algerian hijackers, having killed others, had themselves been killed in an act of rough justice. Hence, declared the *Guardian* leader-writer—speaking less to the facts of the case than to his own doubts—'the Marseilles operation is a problem rather than a solution'. It would 'create martyrs to avenge'; it would 'raise the level of inter-communal tension in France'; and, concluded the editorial, 'they [the French police] and we may yet regret their brilliant victory'. None of this was true.

Indeed, as early as October 1984 and referring to 'terrorism', the then US secretary of state George Schultz had 'warned' that 'we cannot allow ourselves to become the Hamlet of nations, worrying endlessly over whether and how to respond'. Leaflets distributed in Manchester's New Century Hall in September 1992, calling on blacks to join the Islamic struggle, were less confused. These leaflets, too, contained a warning: but in this case it was a warning 'not to follow disarming ideologies, philosophies and doctrines', but to 'mobilise for the forthcoming war to be waged by one billion Muslims on the 500-year-old Jewish/Christian, capitalist, racist, imperialist, European-American-Israeli empire'.

'Waging war'? What 'war'? In February 1989, before Western intellectual equivocation and evasion had begun to take hold, the writer John Berger presciently thought that he had the answer, even if the accumulated facts already set out in this chapter would seem, in retrospect, to have made it hard to miss. 'A unique twentieth-century Holy War, with its terrifying righteousness on both sides, may be on the point of breaking out', he declared—but it had already broken out, and long before—'in airports, shopping streets, suburbs, city centres, wherever the unprotected live'.

Of Muslim 'righteousness' at the time, and since, there can be no doubt. Also in 1989, during an address to Islamic seminary teachers and students, Ayatollah Khomeini proclaimed that 'our war'—the Third World War—was 'the war of the right against the wrong', 'the war of faith against deceit'. A dozen years later, President Bush was likewise to promise to 'rid the world of the evil-doers' in a war of 'good' and 'evil'. Even the Rushdie affair was described in January 1991—by Shabbir Akhtar, a British Muslim educated at Cambridge—as merely 'the latest skirmish between a secularised, post-Enlightenment Western humanity and the adherents of the decisive religion, Islam'. With the end of the Cold War and the 'absorption of Russia into the Western bloc', Akhtar added, 'the sole surviving competition is the religion of the prophet Muhammad, peace be upon him'.

This was a confident assertion of the obvious: that 'Western destiny and identity' had been 'brought face to face' not with 'terror', not with 'evil', but with what he called the 'Islamic temper of mind', which is to say Islam. True, 'terror'—or terrorist acts carried out in Islam's name—there has been for decades, and young suicide-bombers too, as now; a suicide-bombing which killed some forty people outside a police station in Algiers in January 1995, for instance, was carried out by a sixteen-year-old youth.

Nevertheless, there has been a staunch official refusal, for 'diplomatic' or prudential reasons, to pick up in its own terms the gauntlet thrown down by Islam at the feet of the non-Islamic world. A 'war against terror' has no true meaning nor, therefore, possibility of being achieved. Not to put too fine a point on it, it is at best a diplomatic lie, and Muslims are justified in knowing and saying so. Moreover, 'terror' is merely a means rather than an end; one of the many used by Islamism, and described by bin Laden as, in al-Qaeda's case, 'good terror'.

Hence, in contrast with Western confusions, indecisions, anxieties to avoid offence, and an unstable media feverishness over individual events, a steadier truth is to be found in Islamist declarations that a 'confrontation' is in progress 'between Islam and world infidelity', and that a 'clear crystallization' is taking place betweem the 'two camps' of Islam and non-Islam. While Western diplomats and politicians generally prefer to pretend otherwise, the notion that a global war between Muslims and non-Muslims is under way is now a commonplace of Muslim, and not simply Islamist, belief. The foreign minister of Egypt himself condemned bin Laden in November 2001 for being 'at war with the whole world'. Conversely, the US intervention in the 1991 Gulf War was described by King Hussein of Jordan—no Islamist he—as a war being conducted 'against all Arabs and all Muslims and not against Iraq alone'. And from Mecca's Umm al-Qura University came the truly echoing cry that it was 'not the world against Iraq but the West against Islam', despite the presence of Saudi troops among the 'coalition' forces. The same cry was to be heard, even more loudly, during the Iraq War of 2003.

That Islam is the 'West's last enemy' seems less a matter of regret for most Muslims than of pride and divine fulfilment. It is so not only for the fulmi-nating cleric or the *mujahid* fighter. It is also the intellectual and ethical (or anti-ethical) premise of the acts of war that are carried out in Islam's name. Thus, 'terrorism' is both a puny and a false name for the varied means which Islam-as-a-politics has brought to bear in this war. This is so whether such means be perceived (by non-Muslims) as acts of offence, or by Muslims as acts of self-defence and righteous anger. Moreover, such anger is seen by Islamists not as a betrayal of their faith, but as its authentic expression. Indeed, 'any faith', according to a voice of Islamism in Britain, 'which compromises its internal temper of militant wrath is destined for the dustbin of history'. Or, as bin Laden put it, 'it is a question of faith, not a war against terrorism, as Bush and Blair try to depict it'.

A former US presidential adviser, Zbigniew Brzezinski, could declare—again for prudential diplomatic reasons—that it is 'wise' to 'eschew' the 'iden-tification of terrorism with Islam as a whole' and to 'stress that Islam as such is not at fault'. But both the original formulation and Brzezinski's gloss upon it were equally wide of the mark. 'Terrorism' is not specific to Islam, and a 'war against terrorism' cannot be fought. In consequence, Muslims have the advan-tage over the non-Islamic world of being free of such muddles about what some of their number are doing to others—other Muslims included—and about what is being done to them. Or, in the words of Salman Rushdie in November 2001, 'let's start calling a spade a spade. Of course this is about Islam'.

In the West's cautions about what *words* it uses to describe its foes is revealed once more the fear, a justified fear, of what it faces. 'Every denunciation of Islam…in the West is seized on', thus trembled a *Times* leader in October 2002, 'as evidence that it is the West, not Islam, [which is] looking for a new enemy'. Indeed, Western (and even Russian, Indian and Chinese) policy-makers, with the aid of the media, have erected a veritable barricade of euphemistic verbiage to conceal the truth—including, now, from themselves—in order, ostensibly, not to frighten the horses of Islam. It is a language of 'terror suspects', 'networks of terror', of 'terrorism' as a 'scourge of humanity', of 'whipping terrorism', of 'rooting out terrorism from the world', and so on. It is also a language which disables thought and which absurdly seeks not to give offence to Islam while acts of offence (or self-defence) against the Islamic world are being prepared.

Islam, and especially Islamism, is not afraid of what it says. On the contrary, it talks itself up with bombast about the 'Great Satan' whom it will bring down, about the 'world arrogance' which it will humble, about the 'World Devourers' whom it will itself devour. It is also unworried by its own incoherences. Thus, the Indonesian cleric Abu Bakr Bashir was able to praise bin Laden for 'destroying the interests of America as America has destroyed the interests of the Muslims', while simultaneously attributing to the United States and to Israel the destruction of the World Trade Center. But of the nature and purpose of the war in which they are involved and of the identities of its parties—a sense necessary to possess in any war—Islamists have a clearer, even if seemingly paranoid, understanding than does the non-Islamic world. Indeed, the West and its allies may be argued to be girding themselves for defeat in seeking to evade what is at issue.

'Al-Qaeda is a worldwide conspiracy', declared the defence editor of the *Daily Telegraph* in December 2001, 'with large reserves of money, weapons and suicidally-inclined adherents'. But over the purposes of such a 'conspiracy'—itself a misnomer—a veil was drawn. At other times, the West's tremulous treading on eggshells on the question of what it is up against gives us the view that 'this is not a war against Islam but against fanatical Islam'; or acknowledges, with English *sang-froid*, that there is an 'Islamic problem'. It may even venture, before beating a retreat for cover, towards referring to 'Islamist terrorism' or even, taking a deep breath, 'Islamic terrorism'. But even here it is the 'grinding down' of the 'networks of terror', or the 'tearing down' of the 'barriers of hate and fear between the Muslim and Western worlds'—so that 'freedom and [Western] democracy' may reign in all nations—which are held (in the West) to be the challenges which must be met.

Instead, it is a long drawn-out struggle for dominion which is in progress, generated by the gradual reawakening of Islam to a sense, God-inspired, of moral entitlement to inherit the world. For its part, America and its allies, with all their fire-power, are squaring up to foes whom they cannot or will not name, and about whose 'sensibilities', or sense of history, they know little.

Indeed, Clio, goddess of history, may not be on the non-Islamic world's side. For the latter is blinder than it can afford to be, or than its peoples deserve. It is also stepping in hobnail boots onto a terrain that is mined; yet has no choice but to go forward in self-defence or offence, on behalf of its own flawed understanding and value-system.

CHAPTER TWO

A Bad Press

T he 'narrative' of Arab nationalism's and Islamism's revival has been presented grimly in the non-Islamic and especially in the Western world's press. It has ensured that the record of what Muslims have done to fellow-Muslims and to others, in the course of this 'reawakening', has aroused disquiet or satiety at best, fear and hatred at worst. It has been sought to be compensated for by varieties of apologia for Islamist actions furnished by Muslims and non-Muslims alike, denials both of allegation and of fact, and exemplifications of counter-offence given to Islam, to Islamism and to Muslims.

The net effect upon non-Islamic observers of the last decades of Islam's renaissance has been negative. Islam has had an overwhelmingly bad press in the non-Islamic world: the latter, notably through the Anglophone media, has been fed with a diet of atrocity and cruelty, of manifold evidences of a mediaeval intellectual closure and of a seemingly continuous capacity for destruction (and self-destruction) which is allegedly peculiar to itself.

Much of what the Western public has been told of acts committed in Arab nationalism's or Islam's name has, of course, been true. Much, however, has been rendered grotesque by the West's sensationalising relish for harmdoing as such, and has been shaped by stereotypes of the 'barbarous'—as the 'civilised' perceive barbarism. Cultural incomprehension, together with the urgent needs of 'on-the-spot' reporters and cameramen to win their spurs on verbal and visual battlefields—sometimes in collaboration with the actors in the dramas they witness—have completed the task of bringing home to the non-Islamic world the sense of the Islamic world's alienness, of its menace and its unreason, but not of its strengths.

Even allowing for a significant proportion of exaggeration, or perverse magnification of that which is calculated to 'disturb'—an end sought by every Western news-room—'material' such as hijacks, hostage-taking, assassinations, suicide-bombings in public places frequented by civilians, civil war killings of Muslim by Muslim or the targeting of foreigners and tourists in order to gain Islamism's goals are barely amenable to being given a *good* press in the coventional sense. Moreover, those who commit such acts are not indifferent to how the non-Islamic world perceives the acts; they often seek notice of them. Gaining such notice, they achieve one of their principal ends, whatever the abhorrence which these acts arouse. Indeed, for them as well as for Western news editors, the more abhorrence the better. Here, as in many other new aspects of this Third World War, extreme interests coincide. At the same time, Muslims who are opposed to the acts and pronouncements of Islamists bemoan the deleterious effects upon Islam of the de facto alliance between Islamism and a media eager for disastrous event.

The reporters (and apologists) who, together with the rescue-workers, crowd around every latest scene of battle are now protagonists in the battle itself. Without such reporting there would be no 'narrative' at all. But with it, only dismay and confusion are created at the sight and sound of horrors committed in faith's name. It is a dismay and confusion which can only be cut through, or short-circuited, by resort on the part of the Western witness to simple, non-rational reflexes; reflexes, generally of prejudiced hostility, which are often as 'primitive' as the acts which provoke them. The output of rivalrous press commentators, ostensibly (and almost always egotistically) 'clarifying' the issues of this or that conflict in the Islamic world—generally with a quick thousand words in which to do it—is often no more than an addition of 'white noise' to the sounds of real battle.

During Islam's latest 'reawakening' Muslims have often behaved with signal brutality towards one another. But in causes which have nothing at all to do with Islam, their protagonists have also acted (to some extent) as Muslims have acted; hijackings, Semtex, assassination and suicide-bombings have not only been the resort of Islamists. Yet the fact that such methods have been used by others has also helped blur the historically necessary sense that a most particular and specific war is in progress, in which Muslims are the warriors and non-Muslims are their foes.

There are, of course, differences of tradition and conflicts of belief between the majority of the world's Muslims who are Sunnis and the 10 to 15 per cent who are Shi'as; and differences again between the 'extreme' Wahhabi sect—or purist Sunni sub-sect—of Saudi Arabia, named after the eighteenth-century scholar Mohammad ibn Abdel-Wahhab, and more 'moderate', or less belligerent, currents of Islamic opinion.

Although a minority among Muslims as a whole, Shi'as constitute the majority in Iraq, for example. Yet the majority community has not necessarily been the dominant one. Thus, Iraq has hitherto been Sunni-led despite its Shi'a majority. Iran is predominantly Shi'ite also, Saudi Arabia and Pakistan are predominantly Sunni, the Taliban were (or are) Sunnis yet there are also several million Shi'as in Afghanistan, and more millions in Pakistan. Moreover, the fact that Sunnis and Shi'as have slain one another in Iraq and Pakistan, for example, or that Shi'as slew Shi'as in the Iran-Iraq war, or that inter-Shi'a hatreds in Iraq have claimed the lives even of their clerics as the Islamic 'reawakening' and its internal tensions have grown, have also served to confuse the sense of what the true battle-lines are.

Abu Musab al-Zarqawi, the Jordanian-born leader of the most intransi-gent resistance-group in Iraq after 2003, and an al-Qaeda 'associate', described not only 'Crusaders and Zionists' but Shi'as themselves as 'the most evil of mankind'. Conversely, in July 2004, a rival group of masked men, calling itself the 'Salvation Movement', threatened to kill him 'and his allies' for 'defiling the Muslim religion', and to 'present them as gifts to our people'. Such internecine conflicts have amorally 'consoled' some in the non-Muslim world who would prefer to see Muslims attack and slaughter one another—as they have, by the million, in the last four decades—than attack and slaughter 'us'.

Clan allegiances, factional rivalries and sectarian differences among Mus-lims in Afghanistan (as between Uzbeks and Tajiks, Pathans and non-Pathans), Chechnya, Iran, Iraq, Kosovo, Pakistan, the occupied territories of Palestine, Somalia, Turkey, Yemen and elsewhere are intense and often lead to violence. Little can be understood of the infighting within the Palestinian political leadership and 'security forces', or between the Palestinian armed groups, without knowledge of its family clans and factions, some of which have their own militias, or gangs, and whose methods and street-feuds are more akin to those of *mafiosi* than of freedom-fighters; no Palestinian leader has been able to bring them under control. These phenomena have suggested, wrongly, that preoccupation among some Muslims with their own (often killing) animus for each other keeps the non-Muslim world safer.

In Saudi Arabia, the conflict between Sunnis and Shi'as was expressed in the killing in July 1987 of more than four hundred people during clashes in Mecca itself between Shi'a Iranian pilgrims and Saudi riot police. In Sudan,

Arab Muslims have killed not only southern Christians but non-Arab African Muslims in the country's civil wars. In Turkey also, Muslim has slain Muslim during the decades of the Turkish campaign against the Kurdish autonomy movement. Saddam Hussein referred to his brother-Muslim Kuwaitis as 'dogs'; the majority of Arab and Muslim nations have in practice, although not in rhetoric, kept themselves aloof from the Palestinian cause.

Likewise with the threats, made by Islamists after the attack on the World Trade Center in September 2001, that fellow-Muslims who condemned the attack would themselves become the targets of 'true' Muslims, and that if the former did not 'listen' they would be regarded as '*kafir*' (unbelievers) like any other 'infidels'; in February 2005, even Wahhabi-inspired Sunnis in Iraq were being described as 'infidels' by local Shi'as. Such latent fratricidal impulses— as well as the historical and other animosities which have, for example, constantly prevented the 'Arab nation' and its collective institutions from achieving unity of purpose—no more promised peace to non-Muslims than they did to the Islamic world itself. The non-Islamic world is not, as some would like to think, 'let off the hook' by inter-Islamic rivalries and hatreds. For the turbulence of the Arab nationalist and Islamic revivals has generated conflicts not only within Islam but in its relations with the 'other', and such conflicts are linked.

A 'bad press'—in a dual sense—has battened, often with indecent relief and even pleasure, upon all evidences of hostility and violence between and among Muslims. These have included death-squad killings of Muslim by Muslim in the Algerian civil war, among whose victims have been civil servants, doctors, teachers, lawyers, journalists, actors and writers. Tens of thousands of 'ordinary' Algerian villagers also fell victim to attacks by Islamists, and—so it was argued by the latter—by out-of-uniform government troops and police seeking to tarnish the Islamist cause; killings which continued in 2005, although on a reduced scale. There was also the slaying, under a shoot-to-kill policy, of 'Islamic militants' in Egypt's internal war; and in the chaotic aftermath of the overthrow of Saddam Hussein little to choose morally between the killing of Iraqi by Iraqi in score-settling or for their conflicting allegiances, and the killing of innocent civilians in the allied bombardments of Iraq's cities.

The use by Iraq of chemical weapons against fellow-Muslim Iran in its war of 1980–1988, and the employment by Hafez Assad of cyanide, among other means, in the massacre by the Syrian army of thousands of Islamist opponents of the Ba'ath regime—the massacre carried out at Hama in February 1992, already referred to—also did not bespeak any special tenderness between brethren-in-faith. No more did the slaughter by the Saddam regime of tens of thousands of fellow-Sunni Kurds at the end of the 1980s and of an estimated 300,000 Shi'as, including by the use of nerve and mustard gases.

So, too, with the murder of thousands of Palestinian fighters by the Jordanian army in the massacres of 1970, and in the Ajloun woods in 1971, despite the fact that the majority of Jordan's indigenous inhabitants are themselves Palestinian. Nor have these and so many other inter-Muslim killings gone without invocations to the Almighty as to their rectitude according the prescriptions of Holy Writ. In Karachi in February 2003, when a Shi'a mosque was attacked and worshippers were killed, a Sunni cleric branded as 'enemies of Islam' not the Shi'as themselves but fellow-Sunnis who had not participated, while those who had taken part were described as 'soldiers of God'.

The Western media have also made great play with—or good copy of—assassinations, executions, and even public lynchings and displays of the bodies of fellow-Muslim 'traitors', 'informants' and 'collaborators', especially in the Palestinian territories. There, 'hundreds' of such 'collaborators' with Israel were said to have been killed during the first intifada from 1987 to 1993, while Albanian Muslim 'collaborators' with Serbian rule were killed in the Kosovo War in the late 1990s. In June 2003, even the then Palestinian prime minister, Mahmoud Abbas, attracted the epithet of 'collaborator', as did the Palestinian governor of Jenin in July 2003 and the visiting Egyptian foreign minister in December 2003. In 2004 masked gunmen in Gaza and the West Bank shot dead Palestinian 'collaborators' even in their hospital beds or attacked them in prison-cells. Some 'collaborators' were bound and shot in front of hundreds of onlookers—'including children', or with 'young and old cheering and chanting around the bloodied corpse', as a grateful media reported—or were found dumped, 'bullet-riddled', in garbage.

Similar accusations from 2003 onwards of collaboration with the occupying forces of Iraq claimed the lives of many Iraqi Sunnis and Shi'as, Kurds and Christians, whether working for the new government's institutions, or for the 'coalition' forces, or for companies engaged in construction and reconstruction. Many officials of the incoming regime were assassinated, some in their homes, some ambushed and shot, some tortured before death and a number decapitated. The dead included members of the interim government, of the National Assembly and of the team drafting a new constitution, ministry officials, advisers and civilian administrators—among them the governors of Mosul and of Baghdad province—mayors and neighbourhood-council members, senior military and police personnel, and army and police recruits. Lawyers, judges, teachers, translators, drivers and others, including the oficials of rival political parties, were also killed. After Arbil's chief of police had been assassinated in October 2004, the 'Army of Ansar al-Sunna' declared that 'God's law' had been carried out and 'the apostate' killed. Among the Iraqi victims were both men and women. The latter included airline employees on their way to the US-contolled Baghdad airport, as well as interpreters, cooks, laundry workers, labourers and cleaners working for the occupying forces.

However, it is less upon the wider political implications of inter-Muslim hostilities of these and other kinds that the Western mass media has principally fastened, but upon their lurid details. This has enabled sensationalising attention to be directed to what are openly or covertly regarded as the 'typical' methods of 'Islamic warfare'; as if, say, attack by lethal chemical agents despatched by post to the unwary was in some way typically 'Muslim' or 'Arab'. Similarly, at the time of the 1991 Gulf War, experts pronounced that Saddam Hussein's sack of Kuwait, which included the firebombing of power-stations, the torching of oil-wells and the scuttling of oil tankers in Kuwait Bay—to the tune of an estimated $173 billion in losses—was a 'traditional' form of Arab warfare. I argued it myself, and was reproached for it. The same argument was heard after the invasion of Iraq in 2003 as a wave of sabotage and looting struck Iraq's utilities, oil installations, public services (including hospitals) and other institutions.

The like view has been taken of ambushes, seizures for ransom and the torture and killing of hostages, crowding out serious examination of the Islamist cause. Thus, in the admittedly complex Sudanese civil war, it was simpler to opt for stereotypes, as in reports of north Sudanese Arab militias storming villages inhabited by African Christians and animists, and carrying off women and children to 'slavery' in the north. Cultural anthropology also aided the process of 'looking down upon' those who adopted these methods as, for example, 'typically Arab'. 'Analysis' was aided by the fact that such methods have been practiced in the last decades by Muslim upon Muslim as well as upon others, even though the same methods were employed in previous centuries, including upon Muslims, by those of other faiths, and in our own times by Nazism. Nevertheless, present Muslim usage has itself given hostages to fortune. Indeed, 'throat-cutting' could be used by Muslims themselves as a metaphor for aggression. In February 2003, the Saudi newspaper *al-Riyadh* thus declared that the United States was preparing to 'cut the throats of the Iraqi people'.

The looting, raping and killing of civilians from 1992 to 1997 by Afghanistan's Northern Alliance, and the counter-massacres and destruction of homes, farmland and irrigation systems carried out by the Taliban in parts of northern Afghanistan from 1999 to 2001 were also readily fitted into this matrix of beliefs about how Muslims conduct warfare, even against those of shared faith. This was perhaps less surprising when many 'terrorist' suicide-bombings and other attacks after 9/11 occurred in Muslim countries, including Egypt, Indonesia, Morocco, Pakistan, Tunisia, Turkey, Saudi Arabia and Yemen, and therefore claimed Muslim as well as non-Muslim victims. Nevertheless, these methods continue to be identified, wrongly, as particularly Muslim. Yet not even 'suicide-bombing' has been confined to Muslims. The Tamils, for example, have used it as a weapon of war—and employed women suicide-bombers—in their struggle for an independent homeland in Sri Lanka. There have also been few crimes committed by Islamists that were not committed in the Second World War on a larger and more brutal scale.

However, by October 2001, familiarisation (made possible by the labours of a 'bad press') with 'Muslim' methods of war—ancient methods, practised at some time in all cultures—led to largely nonsensical 'expert' conclusions: that there are 'quite distinctively different ways of making war', that 'Westerners fight face to face' in stand-up battle—their special forces and covert operations notwithstanding—'and go on until one side or the other gives in'. 'By contrast', declared Sir John Keegan in the *Daily Telegraph*, 'Orientals', here intended to include Muslims, 'shrink from pitched battle...preferring ambush, surprise, treachery and deceit as the best way to overcome an enemy'. The attack on the World Trade Center was 'in absolutely traditional form', the jumbo jets notwithstanding, with 'Arabs appearing suddenly out of empty space like their desert raider ancestors...in a terrifying surprise raid'. Indeed, Keegan declared, it was an incident in a war 'between settled, creative, productive Westerners and predatory, destructive Orientals [*sic*]'.

During the Kennedy administration in the United States, political leaders—Trujillo in the Dominican Republic, Diem in South Vietnam, Lumumba in the Congo—were assassinated. Many attempts were made on the life of Fidel Castro; Salvador Allende and his rule were not overthrown in Chile in a 'face to face, stand-up battle'. 'Targeted assassinations', using methods of 'ambush, surprise and deceit'—with assailants also 'appearing suddenly out of empty space', and with paid informers, skilful undercover agents, booby-trapped telephones and so on—have also been used to lethal effect by the Israeli defence forces and Mossad.

'Anyone who kills a Jew or harms an Israeli citizen or sends someone to kill Jews is a marked man. Period', declared the Israeli prime minister, Ariel Sharon, in April 2004. According to Palestinian sources, over 150 of their 'militants' had been killed by that date in such 'targeted assassinations', carried out by Israel, during the course of the second intifada. They included, most notably, the Hamas leaders Ahmed Yassin and Abdel Aziz Rantisi killed in March and April 2004 respectively, Ghalib Awali, a senior member of Hezbollah killed in Beirut in July 2004, and Izz el-Deen al-Sheikh Khalil, a Hamas military leader killed in Damascus in September 2004. Wherever possible, pitched battle was also avoided by the United States, as by the use of long-range Cruise missiles, unmanned but rocket-equipped Predator 'drones', 'bunker busters' and so forth. The bombs which destroyed Hiroshima and Nagasaki 'appeared out of empty space'; so, too, did the 'shock-and-awe' air attack on Baghdad in March 2003.

Assertions that the word 'assassin' has a special association with historic Arab methods, that it was first used to describe such methods and that it has the additional meaning of 'hashish-taker' were also made commonplaces of report. In aid of this association, demonstration has been offered that assassination of rulers and rivals goes back to Islam's very beginnings, was common in mediaeval times—as if it was not true of other cultures and politics, including that of the Church—and was employed in Arab and Muslim lands during the late nineteenth century's nationalist stirrings, as when the ruler of Persia was assassinated in 1896. Hence, it was held to be by old tradition that the Muslim Brotherhood's 'terrorist wing' in the 1940s and 1950s used assassination of opponents, as in the case of the killing of Nuqrashi Pasha, Egypt's prime minister, in 1948 in order to further its aims. But so, too, did the Jewish Irgun and Stern gangs, or for that matter Al Capone, and as the Israeli defence forces and Mossad have done.

However, the extent to which assassination (and attempted assassination) of Muslim by Muslim has taken place during the last decades of the Arab and Islamic 'reawakening' remains striking enough. In 1959, the young Saddam Hussein and other Ba'athists attempted and failed to assassinate Abdal Karim Qassem, the ruler of Iraq. In Afghanistan it has been common, as when the leader of the anti-Taliban resistance, Ahmed Shah Massoud of the Northern Alliance, was killed in September 2001. Attempts were made on the life of President Karzai in September 2002 and September 2004, and on Iraq's interim prime minister, Iyad Allawi, in April 2005, while Afghanistan's vice president, Abdul Qadir, was assassinated in Kabul in July 2002.

In Algeria, its president, Mohammed Boudiaf, was shot at a public meeting in Annaba in June 1992, as were other Algerian politicians in its civil war; in Bangladesh, its president, Sheikh Mujib al-Rahman, was killed in 1975 in a coup; in Egypt, President Anwar al-Sadat was assassinated in 1981, and leading officials, including the deputy-governor of security in Assiut province, were murdered by Islamists; in September 1982, Lebanon's president, Bashir Gemayel, was assassinated within days of his election. In Syria, also in 1981, an attempt was made on the life of President Hafez Assad. Similarly, many Iranian dissidents living outside the country, mostly in western Europe, were hunted down and killed—on some occasions gunned down in the street—between 1979 and 1993, and the former prime minister, Shapur Bakhtiar, was also assassinated.

Likewise, Iranian Kurdish leaders were murdered in Berlin by a hit-squad in 1992; Sheikh Omar Abdel Rahman, the blind Egyptian cleric implicated in the first bombing of the World Trade Center, repeatedly called for the killing of President Mubarak, upon whose life an attempt—allegedly organised by the Sudanese secret service—was made in Ethiopia in July 1995; while in Teheran, in June 1992, Ayatollah Ahmed Jannati hailed the assassination of Boudiaf of Algeria as an event which had 'made all the people of Algeria happy', further declaring that his death would 'strengthen the Islamic movement'. In Pakistan, two close attempts were made in Rawalpindi within the space of two weeks in December 2003 to kill President Musharraf, as well as to kill Pakistan's prime minister–designate, Shaukat Aziz, in July 2004. In Saudi Arabia, a series of attempts were made by Islamists, in December 2003, to kill the country's leading security officials, and a foiled plot to assassinate the then crown prince Abdullah was disclosed in June 2004. In 2004, there were also attempted or successful killings of prominent political figures in Kashmir, Lebanon and the Palestinian territories, including an attempt in November 2004 on Mahmoud Abbas, the successor to Arafat as PLO leader. In February 2005, Rafik Hariri, the former prime minister of Lebanon and an opponent of its pro-Syrian regime, was killed in a bomb-attack in Beirut.

Muslim clerics have themselves been murdered, sometimes at the instigation of other clerics. In Iraq in 1999, Saddam Hussein's gunmen shot dead the leading Shi'ite cleric, Muhammad Sadiq al-Sadr, as part of Saddam's reprisals for an earlier Shi'ite uprising against his rule. In April 2003 inside the holiest shrine of Shi'ite Islam, the mosque of Imam Ali in Najaf, Hojataleslam Abdul Majid al-Khoei was 'hacked to death'—a favourite media phrase in reporting on Muslim violences—allegedly at the prompting of al-Sadr's son. Mohammed Baqer al-Hakim, a senior Shi'ite cleric, was also assassinated in Najaf in August 2003, and an attempt made on Iraq's most influential Shi'ite leader, Ayatollah Ali al-Sistani in February 2004, while two of his aides were murdered by Sunni militants in January 2005.

Assassination of political and religious opponents has been a historically universal practice. It has taken the lives of an archbishop of Canterbury, Renaissance princes, a nineteenth-century English prime minister, several tsars, Presidents Lincoln and Kennedy, the Indian prime minister Indira Gandhi and the Israeli leader Yitzhak Rabin. Nevertheless, the open expression of satisfaction, as by Ayatollah Jannati at the death of an Algerian president who was an opponent of Islamism, spoke to the unappeasable nature of the emotions generated by the Isalmic advance.

In September 1972, a letter-bomb killed an attaché at the Israeli embassy in London, and in June 1982 Israel's ambassador in London was shot and wounded, an attack blamed on a Palestinian Fatah group. In the allegedly personal ordering by Yasser Arafat of the killing of three diplomats, one Belgian and two American, kidnapped in Khartoum in 1973—an unsuccessful attempt to secure the release from imprisonment of Sirhan Sirhan, the Palestinian assassin of Robert Kennedy in 1968—the taking of hostages for ransom again reminded Islam's foes of its supposedly typical methods of combat. So, too, did the subsequent resort to their assassination when the exercise failed. In 1979, the American ambassador to Afghanistan was kidnapped and killed. In 1984, similarly, the US deputy military attaché in Paris and the second secretary at the Israeli embassy were murdered. They were killings and counter-killings of diplomats of a kind which also occurred during the Second World War, and which were carried out both by Nazis and anti-Nazis; such acts also marked the rise of communism to power in eastern Europe.

This was therefore again neither 'Arab' nor 'Muslim'. Nevertheless, that the war between the Islamic and non-Islamic worlds has brought resort to such methods, and on both sides, is plain. Assassination, and attempted or foiled assassination, of diplomats, consular officials and UN representatives—American, British, Egyptian, Israeli, Jordanian, Spanish and others in Baghdad, Beirut, Buenos Aires, Islamabad, Istanbul, Jeddah, Kabul, London, Nairobi and elsewhere—have been as common in this war as murder of Muslim by Muslim on grounds of political, religious or personal difference, and whether the killings be of individuals or killings on a larger scale.

Sometimes, the instinct to kill has been close to the surface, as in all wars when the restraints of reason have been lost. 'If your Pope doesn't want to kill Rushdie', a woman in a five-thousand strong demonstration in Beirut in February 1989 shouted to a Western reporter, Julie Flint, 'we will kill your Pope'. Likewise, the targeted killing of Saddam Hussein and his sons—'successful' in the latter case—was an early war aim of the Americans in the Iraq War. That Islamists even in Denmark should have produced a hit-list in August 2002 of fifteen prominent Jewish figures in the country, offering 'cash prizes' for their assassination, was again not Muslim or 'Arab' in some cultural anthropological sense. But it was of a psychological kind with other methods in a war which, like other wars, has come to know few moral bounds.

Death-threats against those—the more prominent the better—who offended Muslim scruples were not only commonplaces but well publicised, both to Islamist and media advantage. Still more serviceable were assassinations such as that of the Dutch film-maker Theo van Gogh in Amsterdam in November 2004, in reprisal for a short film he had made on the treatment of women in Islamic societies, a film which contained gratuitously insulting images of naked women with texts of the Koran inscribed on their bodies. At first merely 'stabbed and shot', journalistic elaborations brought a 'butcher's knife', two knives, the victim's cries for mercy and ultimately his throat 'slit through the spinal column' 'according to the primitive rituals of Morocco'. The killing was bad enough. But the worse it was made to seem, the better for a perversely eager press.

Grim and unconscionable in themselves but media-useful were also kidnappings and murders of aid-workers, as in Afghanistan and Iraq, and especially of those who could be justly said to have brought 'love and devotion' to their work. Of similar ethical and media quality was the shooting at point-blank range in September 2003 of two employees of a non-governmental organisation involved in clearing mines in northern Iraq; or, say, Palestinian suicide-bombers who disguised themselves as Orthodox Jews in order to gain access to their targets. When heart-monitors and incubators were looted by Iraqis from their own Baghdad hospitals during the mayhem which followed the fall of the city to American invaders, the media too had a field-day.

Unsurprisingly, celebrations in the Arab and Muslim 'street' of killings and of other blows struck against the non-Muslim world have also received a 'bad press'. Iran celebrated the assassination in 1981 of Egypt's President Anwar Sadat, naming a Teheran street in 'honour' of his assassin, Khalid Islambouli; a mixture of open festivity and silent satisfaction, as well as of anxiety, in the Arab and Muslim world greeted the destruction of the World Trade Center; in early March 2003, Palestinians renamed the main square of Jenin in 'honour' of the Iraqi army officer who carried out the first suicide-attack against the invading US army in the Iraq War.

In August 2003, similarly, 'fireworks' were reported to have 'burst over Hebron' in celebration of a Jerusalem bus-bombing. Islamist militants in their hundreds, their faces covered, triumphantly cried out '*Allahu Akhbar!*' after a bomb attack in October 2003 on a US diplomatic convoy in Gaza, which had left 'pieces of flesh strewn in the street'. But a 'bad press' itself greeted all such

goriness with its own forms of relish. Thus, Daniel Pearl, the American journalist, was said in the *New York Times* to have been 'personally executed' by
Khalid Shaikh Mohammad, a senior al-Qaeda operational commander, in
Karachi in early 2002; and seven Spanish security officials were reported to
have been not only shot but also 'beaten to death' in an ambush near Baghdad
in November 2003.

However, the unrestraint of the media, or 'bad press', in covering the
decades of hostility between the Islamic and non-Islamic worlds could also be
said to have advanced *pari passu* with the deeds it has reported. The seizure of
aircraft—and even of an Italian cruise-liner by the Palestinian Liberation
Front in 1985—the interception of buses, cars and trains (in Egypt in 1994),
and the taking control of passengers on them either for ransom, individual
execution, bomb-destruction or, in the case of the hijacks of 11 September
2001, for use of the aircraft themselves as weapons against civilians, were all
part of this war's unrestraint of method. Thus, Israel shot down a Libyan civil
airliner in 1973, with more than one hundred passengers on board, on the
grounds that it had strayed into Israeli airspace.

At the same time, as Islamists well knew, spectacular event was required if
an impact was to be made upon audiences with appetites already sated by
every form of excess. Since 1968, aircraft belonging to Pan Am, Sabena, Indian
Airlines, Swissair, Air France and Philippine Airlines, among many other companies, have been seized in the notional cause of Islam, and by Algerian, Iraqi,
Libyan, Palestinian or Syrian nationals, again among others. It has involved
bringing down (or planning to bring down) aircraft while in flight—for
example, 170 lives were lost in the bombing of a French airliner over Niger in
1989, for which Libya agreed in January 2004 to pay compensation, as it did
for the Lockerbie victims—destroying aircraft on the ground, and killing or
wounding passengers and airline personnel.

This has sometimes been accompanied by extremes of cruelty, including
by the cutting of throats, as of some of the crews on 11 September 2001. In
1986, the Syrians were foiled in an attempt to use even a pregnant Irish
intending-passenger, an innocent dupe, to blow up an Israeli airliner in mid-
flight. In August 2004, Chechen suicide-bombers, including women, were
more 'successful', hijacking two Russian passenger aircraft in flight which
crashed almost simultaneously near Tula and Rostov. They were acts which
again made both for good copy and, once more, a bad press.

A Sir John Keegan might have it that the use of abduction and hostage-
taking—to which the notion of hijacking may be said to be 'conceptually'
related—was an 'Oriental' mode of conducting war. The truth is that it, too, is

a criminal commonplace in war or peace. The Germans, again, practiced it frequently enough in the Second World War. Moreover, such methods may be perceived as cowardly for evading the challenge of a 'stand-up battle', but it has clearly been a matter of indifference to Islamists; kidnaps and hostage-takings, with or without ransom demands, have been employed as a constant means in their cause, not least because they served the appetite of the Western media for eye-catching sensation. They were carried out in Afghanistan, Algeria, Indonesia, Iran, Iraq, Lebanon, Pakistan, the Philippines, Russia, Saudi Arabia, Somalia and Uzbekistan, as well as by the Palestinians. The latter used the method in 1972 at the Munich Olympic Games, when Israeli athletes were taken hostage and several killed, and at Entebbe airport in Uganda in 1976, when some one hundred Israeli passengers on a hijacked Air France plane were taken hostage.

The Chechens likewise frequently employed kidnap and hostage-taking: of teenagers from a school in 1993; of patients and hospital workers in Budyonnovsk in January 1996; of passengers on a Russian Black Sea ferry also in 1996; of (three thousand) airbase personnel in 1996; of three British and one New Zealander, working in Chechnya, in 1998—whose severed heads were later found by a roadside—of theatregoers, actors, musicians and theatre-staff in Moscow in 2002; and of some one thousand children, parents and teachers in a school in Beslan in north Ossetia in September 2004.

In Algeria, Yemen's ambassador was kidnapped by the Islamist GIA in July 1994. The envoy's freedom and an offer to stop killing foreigners in Algeria were promised in moral exchange for the freedom of an Islamist leader. In February 2003, more than thirty European tourists—one of whom died of heat exhaustion while in captivity—were kidnapped in the Algerian Sahara by the Salafist Group for Preaching and Combat, 'linked to al-Qaeda', some being released after an attack by Algerian commandos and others on payment of ransom by the German government.

However, it was in Iraq that kidnaps, ransom demands and the killing of hostages reached their apogee. By 2005, over thirty countries' nationals—Iraqis included—had been seized, released unharmed on payment of ransom or (seemingly) without it, held with little or no notice of their fate, or executed, sometimes being filmed for the media by their captors as they died. Those taken included contractors, security guards employed by contractors, civil engineers, construction, energy and telecommunications workers, businessmen and diplomats, journalists, translators and many truck-drivers. Here again the media played a major role in encouraging such methods. It gave the kidnappers' political demands the international publicity they sought; it reported the details of their intendedly blood-curdling threats—to turn a country into a 'bloodbath' and to have 'explosives rip through it'; to 'butcher' its leading politicians; to 'sacrifice in blood', 'burn alive' or 'chop up' captives, and so on. When the kidnappers' demands were refused, it was again the media which demonstrated the consequences with images of slain hostages, and even of their severed heads.

The demands made by the hostage-takers in Iraq included ransom, withdrawal of foreign military forces, freeing of prisoners held in Iraq, cessation of certain military operations, the stopping of the transportation of supplies to the occupying forces and the ending of foreign involvement in commercial and industrial activities in the country. Some demands were more specific. In the case of two Italian hostages, among the prerequisites for their release was the staging of a 'big demonstration' in Italy in protest at the presence of its troops in Iraq; in the case of two Indonesian hostages, it was the release of the Islamist cleric Abu Bakr Bashir; in the case of a seized Iranian diplomat, it was the release of five hundred Iraqi prisoners captured in the 1980–88 Iran-Iraq war. Other demands by kidnappers in Afghanistan, Chechnya, Saudi Arabia and elsewhere, including in Iraq, could be much larger: the release of 'all Muslim prisoners' held by the Americans at Guantanamo in Cuba, the release of 'all Taliban and al-Qaeda prisoners', or, say, the ending of all foreign involvement, including that of the UN, in a Muslim country.

In some of the mass hostage-takings, hostages died in bungled efforts to free them. One hundred and twenty-nine lost their lives in the storming of the Moscow theatre; over three hundred and fifty in the Beslan school, where the desperate conditions and fleeing children—'their faces strained with fear and exhaustion, their bodies bloodied by shrapnel and gunshots', as the *New York Times* reported—furnished the media with prose and pictures of which news editors dream. Indeed, Chechen Islamists again showed notable cruelty—matched by the Russian treatment of them in Chechnya—in the treatment of some of their captives. They were subjected to mock executions, rape and beatings, of which the Russian press, in the manner of their west European counterparts, provided gratifyingly graphic descriptions.

But it was again in Iraq that cruelty to captives was most marked and best publicised, even if the 'slicing off' of 'the nose, ears and tongue' of a fourteen-year-old girl in Kashmir for informing to the Indian army in July 2004, or the alleged 'beheading and skinning' of captured fighters belonging to rival warlords' private armies in Afghanistan in September 2004, might have been thought hard to excel. They were not. Accounts of the excesses committed by the Saddam Hussein regime—which included the 'cutting off of ears and tongues of opponents and army deserters' (in a vivid description by the Associated Press)—and of the beheadings of some foreign hostages and Iraqi 'collaborators' after the US invasion in 2003 became for months part of the Western media's regular diet. Similarly, during the capture of the Iraqi city of Fallujah by US forces in November 2004 the publicity given to 'torture rooms' with 'bloodstained walls and floors', 'handcuffs, shackles and blood-encrusted knives' did terror's work for it.

Attempts to enforce the will of Islamists have required, and obtained, the media's assistance. Such assistance was rendered in the kidnap in 1979 in Teheran, and the keeping hostage, of Americans in the US embassy for eighteen months; in 1987 in Beirut, when British and American hostages—who included the archbishop of Canterbury's emissary—were held under Iranian direction until 1992; and in the kidnapping of two judges in north-western Pakistan in 1994 by armed tribesmen who were demanding the imposition of Sharia law.

The press also served in the many abductions by Islamists in the Philippines since 1992, and whose victims included a Franciscan monk—freed on payment of a ransom—a Spanish cleric, an American bible translator, an Irish missionary and numbers of tourists, with murders and further bungled efforts to free them supervening. It helped, too, in the seizing of hostages in Trinidad in the attempted Black Muslim coup in July 1990. Moreover, media notice of such acts created its own narrow version of the morality of the Islamist cause. It was a notice desired, and often carefully arranged, by the hostage-takers themselves. But it made 'terror' rather than the nature of the Islamist cause its most salient (or 'popular') media feature.

It was so, above all, with Islamist attacks on foreigners, attacks which have been long-standing and varied in their circumstances and locations. They were 'warned to leave' (as 'infidels') by Islamists in Algeria and Egypt, Pakistan, Saudi Arabia and Yemen, as well as in Iraq. Denounced and killed in Algeria as the 'enemies of God', among many other foreign victims were twelve Croatian and Bosnian workers stabbed to death in December 1993. In Egypt, from 1992 to 1997, and again in May 2005, bomb attacks were made on visitors—Austrian, British, German, Japanese, Swiss and many others—including at Luxor's Karnak Temple and the Cairo Museum. In November 1997, in Islamism's cause, six gunmen boarded a tourist bus at Luxor, killing fifty-eight passengers with shots to the head.

'They were dancing and singing Allah, Allah', a Swiss survivor declared to an ever-attentive Western press; which reported, with suitable headlines, that some of the victims were also mutilated. (The perpetrators, members of the al-Gama'a al-Islamiyah, were released by the Egyptian authorities in September 2003.) Tourists have also died in Morocco and Tunisia, and foreigners have been singled out and killed in Pakistan, Saudi Arabia and Yemen. But without the media, from the BBC to al-Jazeera, Islamism's excoriations of the 'infidel' would have largely gone unheard in the non-Muslim world; and without the transmission of its threats Islamism's creation of fear in its foes would have been considerably less.

In most of these cases there was a common feature: the objects of attack were taken unawares, they were non-combatant civilians and they were unarmed, while the taking of their lives or maiming was carried out for a purpose known to the attackers but less understood by the victims. For they were often taken—or killed—by way of *demonstration*, not as enemies, even if they be denoted 'infidels', but primarily as evidence of their captors' will. This evidence the print and visual media readily made available to the entire world; without such assistance, once more, the 'demonstration effect' would have been greatly reduced.

Demonstrating such will was also the purpose of the direct attacks by Islamists on the places of worship of 'unbelieving' Christians, Jews, Hindus and others, the wider aspects of which I will come to later. But Muslims, too, suffered physical assaults and vandalistic desecrations of their mosques, sacred places and cultural centres in Australia, Belgium, Britain, France, Germany, Holland, India, Israel, the United States and many other countries. Islamists—often acting in the same manner as local neo-fascists and employing like methods of arson and other destruction—in their turn attacked Christian churches in West Java, Nigeria, Pakistan, Sudan and Holland. In the Philippines, grenades were thrown into Catholic cathedrals in Iligan and Davao in 1992 and 1993 by members of the Abu Sayyaf Islamist group, and a similar attack was made on a Catholic shrine in Zamboanga in October 2002. Islamists attacked Jewish synagogues also, as in Tunisia in April 2002, killing seventeen German tourists, and two synagogues in Istanbul in November 2003, leaving many dead, the majority Christians and Muslims. In some instances, churches were burned to the ground; in others, worshippers were bombed or shot down while at prayer. Hindu temples and Hindu pilgrims have also been attacked by Islamists in Kashmir, as in March, August and November 2002.

Christian holidays, especially in the period of Christmas, were typically chosen for assault, as they have been in some cases of hijack. This choice was again not unlike that made by the Nazis, who on many occasions rounded up Jews (as in Rome in October 1943) on the Sabbath—when they were almost certain to be at home—or took similar advantage of crowded synagogues on Jewish holidays. Attacks by Islamist suicide-bombers in 1986 on an Istanbul synagogue during Sabbath prayers, on a Passover dinner (with 250 guests) in Israel in March 2002 and a similar suicide-attack on a Sabbath lunch in Haifa in October 2003 fitted such pattern, while Syria chose the Day of Atonement to invade Israel in 1973. There have likewise been destructive attacks by Muslims on Hindu temples in India—a practice dating back to the first Muslim invasions of the subcontinent—and on Hindus at worship; just as Muslim mosques, as in Nepal and India, have also been attacked, one of which at Ayodhya in Uttar Pradesh, as mentioned earlier, was demolished by a mob.

Yet Muslims have also attacked fellow-Muslims—in Afghanistan, Bangladesh, Iraq, Kashmir, Iraqi Kurdistan, Pakistan and Yemen, for example—not only outside mosques as they were leaving prayer but inside mosques also, including on Islam's holiest days. Assaults and bombings, claiming many lives, were carried out by Muslims on mosques during Ramadan, as in Saudi Arabia in November 2003, on Kurds in Iraq during the Muslim holiday of Eid al-Adha, the Feast of Sacrifice, and on a mosque in Rawalpindi in February 2004 during the holiday of Muharram. In March 2004, during the Shi'a festival of Ashura, pilgrims were bombed in the holy city of Karbala with heavy loss of life, and Shi'a worshippers similarly attacked inside and outside the Khadimiya mosque in Baghdad, where the courtyard was described, once more, as being 'strewn with flesh and torn limbs'. Even a funeral procession could be attacked by Sunnis, as in Najaf in Iraq in December 2004, with heavy loss of life. In February 2005, also in the Ashura period, Shi'a mosques in Iraq were the targets of Sunni suicide-bombers, while 'pieces of flesh' were again 'scattered around' (in the media) after another suicide-bomb attack inside a mosque in Mosul during a funeral service in March 2005.

In Quetta in Pakistan, where conflict between majority Sunni and minority Shi'a Muslims was particularly fierce, grenades were similarly used in July 2003 by two suicide-bombers inside a 'packed' Shi'a mosque, killing dozens of worshippers during Friday prayers. In reprisal a Sunni seminary teacher was 'hacked to death'—the standard phrase again—by 'angry' Shi'ites. Other suicide-bomb and grenade attacks inside Pakistani mosques took place in 2004 in Karachi, Lahore and Sialkot. Press accounts of these events often ran amuck in company with fleeing congregants, bent on revenge. In a Karachi mosque in May 2004, the Associated Press reported—with suitably purple prose—'the wounded lay screaming for help on bloodstained carpets'.

In Kandahar in Afghanistan, in July 2003, a remote-controlled bomb was exploded at the Akhunzak mosque, injuring the mullah and worshippers 'as they knelt in prayer'; two days later, another Kandahar mullah, a pro-Karzai government supporter, was shot dead—in the words of the luxuriating Western report—'as he sat praying, a book open in his hand'. Outside Iraq's holiest Shi'a shrine at Najaf, a huge car-bomb, containing some 750 kilograms of TNT, was detonated in August 2003 by Muslim assailants, perhaps themselves rival Shi'ites. It killed dozens of worshippers and clerics as they emerged from worship. From 2003 counter-attacks were also carried out by Shi'ites on several Sunni mosques in Baghdad, a city where Shi'as and Sunnis are roughly equal in number.

In such inter-Muslim conflicts, not even the most sacred places in Islam have been safe from profanation by Muslims themselves. Violence of all kinds, from murder to other mayhem has been committed in them, and they have also been used as weapons depositories and as firing positions. In December 2003, the elderly Egyptian foreign minister, Ahmed Maher, was reported to have been belaboured and physically knocked about by angry Palestinians even in Jerusalem's al-Aqsa mosque; he 'appeared short of breath and near collapse amid the clamour', declared an again grateful Western press. Moreover, as has already been noted, Muslim clerics and preachers, Sunni or Shi'a, and including the most august, pacific and pious, have not been spared violence. In Iraq and Pakistan, they were killed in their houses or walking from home to attend prayers, gunned down on the point of entering or leaving a mosque—as was Ahmed Yassin, the Hamas leader, when killed by Israelis—and slain inside the mosque itself. Even a school attended by Shi'ite children was attacked in February 2003 in northern Baghdad.

There have also been time-dishonoured desecrations of cemeteries in this war. They included Muslim cemeteries in many countries. Some sixty Muslim graves in Bradford in west Yorkshire were desecrated in May 1991, forty in south-east London in March 2004 and there were further desecrations in Britain after the London bombings of July 2005. In Mulhouse in France in November 1992, fifty-eight tombstones of French Muslim soldiers were vandalised; in Strasbourg, in May 2004, swastikas were similarly daubed on Muslim gravestones in a military cemetery. British graves (and especially of the crosses upon them) were desecrated in Izmir in Turkey in 1990. In March 2003, the British war cemetery at Etaples in northern France was vandalised, an act thought to have been carried out by French Muslims since the graffiti upon its main cenotaph included the words (in French) 'Saddam will be victorious and make your blood flow'. In May 2004, the British military cemetery in Gaza was similarly desecrated. Jewish synagogues and historic sites were also desecrated and destroyed during the Jordanian occupation of East

Jerusalem; and harms have been inflicted on Palestinian holy places by the Israelis, and by Palestinians on ancient Jewish shrines.

But the commonest choice of 'direct action' for conducting Islamist war-fare was the bombing of places of mainly civilian public resort, and of mainly civilian means of transportation, the bombs being carried in trucks, vans, cars and on the person. Although most frequently employed in attacks on non-Muslims, such method was also used both in internecine conflict in Muslim countries and—without regard to its effect on Muslims—in locations in the non-Islamic world, such as at the World Trade Center. The characteristics of such attacks were that they were often indiscriminate; were sometimes foiled or occurred in the 'wrong' place in a premature explosion; caused deaths to a few or to hundreds, and in New York to thousands; and were variously used to kill and wound, to 'warn' of the Islamist presence, and to create alarm, chaos or economic damage, or all together. The detonation of a bomb, especially the suicide-bomb, became the most media-familiar (and again the most perversely media-attractive) of Islamism's methods of harm-doing to others and to itself.

Bombs have been exploded against military vessels, an oil-tanker and on a 'crowded' ferry, inside aircraft in flight, at airports, in apartment buildings, in buses, at bus-stops and in bus-terminals, in or outside cafés, bars and restau-rants, in or outside cinemas, in a courthouse (at Batna in Algeria), in or near government and diplomatic buildings, in or outside discos and hotels, in mar-kets, malls and bazaars, at industrial plants and power-stations, in or outside office buildings, amid marchers in processions and at rallies, in or near schools and alongside school-buses, on or under trains or beside train-lines, and in or near railway-stations. For example, attacks associated with railways took place in France in July 1995; Israel in September 2001 and April 2003; in Bombay in December 2002, January, March and August 2003; in Chechnya or its neigh-bouring provinces in September and December 2003; on a crowded metro train in Moscow in February 2004 ('arms and legs were scattered around the carriage'), on four commuter trains in Madrid in March 2004—which left more than two hundred dead and some fifteen hundred injured—and on the London Underground in July 2005 when more than fifty people were killed and some seven hundred injured.

Some bombings were as they seemed, with responsibility swiftly and accurately claimed—in the case of Palestinian suicide-bombers, often with a pre-prepared media-pack of video film and other information. Others were deeply covert operations, in which there might be several Islamist interests involved and working together, as in the Lockerbie bombing of December 1998 with the loss of 270 lives. Others again were the work of Islamist opponents of Muslim regimes but which were blamed on others—in Saudi Arabia, during the late 1990s, on foreign expatriates. Some bombings were of the hit-and-run variety; others were skilfully planned and meticulously carried out.

But in some cases, fairly frequent in the occupied territories of Palestine, the operations were botched and only the bombers were killed, sometimes even before leaving their homes. In others there was a considerable 'sophistication', as in Israel where Palestinian suicide-bombers dressed in Israeli army uniforms in order to gain access to their targets, as in October 2001 and February 2002; or in March 2003, when Palestinian gunmen donned the garb of Jewish seminary students.

Three features of Islamism's use of the bomb, whether directed (as most frequently) against ordinary civilians or against police and army targets, and whether in attacks on fellow-Muslims or non-Muslims, stood out. First, it was a standard weapon of choice. Secondly, its use by Islamists was widespread. Uganda, for example, suffered forty-three separate Islamist bombings, killing more than eighty people, between 1997 and 1999; 'hundreds' of 'home-made bombs' were exploded on a single day in August 2005 in some sixty towns and cities across Bangladesh, allegedly by members of the banned Jamaat ul-Mujahideen. Thirdly, once resort to it as a method became 'habitual', 'truces' and 'cease-fires' rarely succeeded in stopping it, or not for long. Thus, attacks in Israel preceded and succeeded (temporary) accords, took place during negotiation, and both before the declaration of an intifada and after its cessation had been announced.

The reasons for this were not far to seek. First, there was the 'demonstration' effect, especially where there was sufficient carnage to attract media coverage. This brought a high political return for relatively little input of resources, save in such elaborate efforts as secured the destruction of the World Trade Center. Thus, in January 2003, Hamas—which carried out many bombing attacks in Israel—recommended to Iraqi insurgents that they should use suicide-bombers in their 'thousands' against American forces. After the fall of Baghdad in 2003, such attacks were carried out inside and outside police stations and police academies, at police checkpoints, at army and police recruitment centres, against hotels and restaurants (including on New Year's Eve in December 2003), against oil pipelines and installations, at the offices of political parties, against US barracks and their occupation headquarters, and against government buildings—including the oil ministry—and against embassies and UN offices. Secondly, the appetite, once whetted for such activities, was hard to sate since the means were relatively easy to secure, gratification was instant and media 'coverage' more or less assured. In May 2005, after a suicide-attack on a police recruitment centre in Erbil in northern Iraq, the *New York Times* had 'pieces of flesh' even 'coming to rest in trees' and 'heads, hands, eyes everywhere.' Thirdly, competition between Islamist factions or in the Arab case between rivalrous clans of bomb-makers, drove the process of bombing upon its own course and according to it own rules.

Bombings, arson attacks and shootings of civilians have varied greatly in scale, in daring and moral baseness. Their reach was wide. Airports, in particular their terminals and check-in counters, were bombed, or attempted to be bombed. They took place in Algiers in inter-Muslim conflict, in Los Angeles in July 2002, at Lod in Israel, in Rome and Vienna in December 1985, in Jakarta in April 2003, in the southern Philippines in the same month, and in Baghdad in June 2005. Apartment buildings or residential compounds were bombed by Islamists in Calcutta in March 1993, in Dagestan and in Moscow in September 1999, where bombs allegedly planted by Chechens—but which was attributed by some to the Russian secret services—killed three hundred people, and in Riyadh in May and November 2003.

Buses, including school-buses, bus queues, bus-stops and bus-stations were targeted with particular frequency in Israel. 'God forgive me, I had no choice but to step on bodies', said the survivor of an attack in Jerusalem in May 2003—a colourful item for a press report—and 'there was a lot of blood on me, bits of flesh, teeth and hair', said another. Attacks on 'crowded' buses also took place, for example, in Karachi in May 2002, in north Ossetia in June 2003, in Kandahar in Afghanistan in August 2003, and in Kashmir in December 2003 and May 2004; in Iraq, ('crowded') bus-stations were attacked in Karbala and Baghdad by car-bombers in December 2004 and August 2005 respectively. In Egypt such attacks were directed against buses carrying foreign tourists, but in furtherance of a struggle of Muslim against Muslim.

Cafes, bars and restaurants, once more preferably 'crowded'—the standard media adjective—have been frequently bombed. Such bombings took place, for example, in Casablanca, in Davao in the Philippines, in Srinagar in Kashmir, in various towns in southern Thailand, in Tel Aviv, Jerusalem and Haifa, and in Sulawesi province in Indonesia. Islamists have also attacked US-owned fast-food outlets in Moscow, Beirut, Karachi and Makassar in Indonesia, as well as restaurants in the Philippines and Turkey, most notably in March 1995 when Islamists, calling themselves the 'Turkish Revenge Brigade' and the 'Greek Eastern Islamic Raiders', opened fire on several Istanbul cafés, killing and injuring moderate Alawite Muslims. Markets, also 'crowded', were bombed in Kabul and Kandahar in Afghanistan in September 2002 and November 2003 respectively; in Bishkek, the capital of Kyrgyzstan, in December 2002; in Korondal in the Philippines by the Moro Liberation Front—'linked to al-Qaeda'—in May 2003; and in Kashmir in June and September 2003. There were similar attacks on markets in Bombay in August 2003, in North Ossetia in February 2004 and in Samara in southern Russia in June 2004, in a 'bustling morning market' in Narathiwat province in southern Thailand in August 2004; and in Tel Aviv in November 2004. Markets in Baghdad—with 'body parts and human flesh on walls near the blast site', according to the Reuters report—as well as in Kirkuk, in Mosul and elsewhere in Iraq were attacked on various occasions during 2004 and 2005.

Similarly, Islamists have bombed both fellow-Muslims and non-Muslims in other places of resort and public entertainment. Fellow-Muslims suffered in attacks on cinemas showing uncensored and 'soft-porn' Western films, for example in Egypt in 1992, Jordan in 1994, Kashmir in 2000 and Iraq in 2004. Non-Muslims and fellow-Muslims alike were struck in cinemas and other public places in Bombay—where there were eleven separate blasts in one day, with 255 deaths—and in Calcutta in 1993, in reprisal for the destruction of the Ayodhya mosque and for the deaths of Muslims in clashes with Hindus. Discos have been bombed in Berlin, in Tel Aviv and in Bali; the latter claimed the lives of more than two hundred people from sixteen different countries. A rock festival was attacked by a suicide-bomber in Moscow in July 2003, and a 'music show' in Aceh in Indonesia in December 2003.

Hotels have been bombed in Egypt—as at Taba in October 2004 and Sharm el-Sheikh in July 2005—in Israel, in Kenya, in Yemen and in Turkey, as in July 1993, although on this occasion it was a hotel in Sivas frequented by Islamists which was attacked by fellow-Muslims, leaving thirty-six dead. Hotels were also bombed, for example, in Mombasa in November 2002, in Casablanca in May 2003, in Jakarta in August 2003, in Islamabad in October 2004 and in Songkhla in southern Thailand in April 2005. Supermarkets and pedestrian shopping malls were also chosen as targets by Islamist bombers in Israel; in Pakistan, as in Rawalpindi in October 2002; on the southern Philippine island of Mindanao in the same month; in Manila in February 2005; and in a Christian area north of Beirut in March 2005.

Embassies, consulates, cultural centres and embassy housing–compounds have also been popular Islamic choices for bomb-attacks, as in Algiers in 1994; in Patras, western Greece in 1991 when two Palestinians attempted to blow up the British consulate there; in 1992, when the Israeli embassy was bombed in Buenos Aires, an attack for which Islamic Jihad claimed responsibility but in which Iran was the moving force; in Indonesia in August 2000 and October 2002 when Philippine diplomatic buildings were attacked, and again in September 2004 when the Australian embassy in Jakarta was damaged; in Iran, where America's Teheran embassy was occupied, as previously mentioned, from 1979 to 1981 and hostages taken; in Lebanon and Kenya, where the US embassies were destroyed in 1983 and 1998 respectively.

In Pakistan, the Egyptian embassy was bombed in 1995; British Council premises in Karachi were attacked in 1989; and a car bomb was detonated outside the US consulate in Karachi in June 2002, killing and injuring almost forty people, while another bomb blast in Karachi in December 2002 wrecked the Macedonian consulate, where three of its employees also had their throats cut. In Tanzania, the US embassy in Dar-es-Salaam was bombed by Islamists in 1998, the combined death-toll of this bombing and that in Kenya in the same year more than 220 people; in the United Kingdom, the Israeli embassy in London was bombed in July 1994; Islamist plans to blow up the American and other Western embassies in Singapore and Malaysia in December 2001, and to bomb the rebuilt American embassy in Nairobi in 2003, were foiled.

In Iraq, after the US invasion, car-bomb attacks took place outside the Jordanian embassy—which was destroyed—in August 2003, and the Turkish embassy in October 2003, while rocket-propelled grenades were fired at the Dutch embassy in Baghdad in January 2004. There was a further attack on the Jordanian embassy in Baghdad in December 2004, outside the Australian embassy in January 2005 and the Slovak embassy in June 2005. In Turkey, a bomb-attack was carried out at the British consulate in Istanbul in November 2003, and the British consul killed. Government and parliamentary buildings of different kinds, police stations, barracks, schools and hospitals have been attacked by Islamists in Afghanistan, Algeria, Bangladesh, Chechnya, India, Indonesia, Iraq, Israel, Kashmir, north Ossetia, Pakistan and elsewhere.

Persistence, repetitiveness of pattern, attacks both targeted and seemingly random on unarmed non-combatants—passengers, shoppers, worshippers, restaurant and disco patrons, envoys, office-workers, school pupils—and, not least, media-appeal were the marks of this form of combat. Charitable and social centres, including in Buenos Aires (with eighty-five dead) and in London, have not been spared. Carnage was wreaked by an Islamist attack on the Bombay Stock Exchange in March 1993; an Islamist car-bomb outside an Algiers police-station in 1995 slew forty-two and injured nearly three hundred fellow-Muslims, leaving 'people with faces and hands bloodied by flying glass' to 'run frantically through the streets', and with 'the wounded crying on the pavement, bodies strewn all over', as the *Guardian* vividly reported.

Here again were media 'colour', particularly spectacular in the telegenic burning and crashing towers of the World Trade Center; media 'shock', as in the burning and sabotaging of more than 'six hundred' schools during the Algerian civil war; media 'horror', as at the killing and injuring of schoolchildren by bombs left outside schools, whether in an Algiers suburb in May 1997 or, say, in Netanya in Israel in May 2001; and combined media 'colour', 'shock' and the arousing of fear, pity and (sometimes) revulsion at the often frenzied funeral cortèges accompanying the many hundreds of Palestinians who have been killed in clashes with the Israeli defence forces. The 'coverage' of such events often involved fastening upon that which was frightening, or upon the worst that human beings were capable of doing to one another, or both. It also generally required a search, often basely motivated, for the 'photogenic' image and the arresting headline, which Islamists became increasingly skilful in providing.

Anti-Muslim violence served the same media ends. The massacre of some one thousand Muslims by Hindu mobs in Gujarat in India in 2002, the slaughter of over seven thousand Muslim men and boys by Serb forces in eastern Bosnia in July 1995, continuous Russian brutalities against Muslims in Chechnya, the gunning down in the street by Macedonian police of innocent Pakistanis in Skopje in March 2002 on the claim (later admitted to be false) that they were planning an attack were all heinous. But where such crimes were spectacular, and offered sufficiently newsworthy images—as of the skeletal Muslim prisoners held by the Serbs—they were quickly noticed by the media. Otherwise, they registered relatively little on Western public opinion, which was in any case better attuned to atrocity committed in Islam's name. Between 2002 and 2005 the accusations and proofs of maltreatment of captives at Guantanamo in Cuba, Abu Ghraib in Iraq, Bagram airbase in Afghanistan and other US detention centres—in Afghanistan and Iraq over one hundred prisoners were reported by March 2005 to have died from a variety of causes while in American custody—weighed heavily in the moral and legal scales. But in media hands the images of sexual abuse and humiliation at Abu Ghraib crowded out profounder responses; while the trials of the malefactors in 2004 and 2005 passed with little attention.

Likewise, and to choose at random, a report in the *Herald Tribune* in December 2001—headed 'Taliban Justice Maimed Many for Petty Crimes'—served ambiguous ends. They included not only that of drawing attention, on sound moral grounds, to brutal acts committed by our fellows but also of selling copies of the newspaper to readers enjoyably (or otherwise) habituated to being 'shocked' by what they read.

The opening paragraph of this report, without preamble, was as follows: 'To the left, Dol Agha saw his two best friends'—betokening the journalist's

intimacy with his informant—'unconscious and bleeding in the back of a Taliban pickup truck in the middle of the soccer field. To the right, he saw their
severed right hands and severed left feet, tossed onto the grass before a crowd
at Kabul Stadium'. Embellishing the gory scene, as told to the reporter, were
'laughing' Taliban soldiers, a doctor 'whose face was hidden under a hood', and
a 'screaming' crowd; while Dol Agha himself, whose left hand was about to be
amputated for 'spying for the Northern Alliance', 'felt an injection of anaes-
thetic go into his arm' before 'everything went black'.

Once more, this was grim stuff. Given what we now know of Taliban rule
and the rigours of Muslim Sharia law, the report was doubtless true in essence.
It also conformed admirably to the gruesomeness which, by December 2001,
the half-informed reader expected. It had also been deftly embroidered with
the detail required: not in black and white but in local Afghan 'colour', in
which Taliban 'laughter' was a constituent part of the weave.

Other newspaper accounts of Islamic cruelties have for at least two
decades expressed similar impulses. In them the necessary and the gratuitous,
the factual and the factitious—but, unfortunately for Islam, infrequently the
wholly fictional—were combined. To take another example from many, the
Independent in March 1989 informed us that an Iranian journalist, Rahman
Hatefi, had been arrested and executed, but not before his hands had been
amputated for having written against Islam and the Ayatollah Khomeini.

The *Guardian* in 1994 told us that three Iraqi thieves had had their right
hands amputated for stealing carpets from a mosque; the *Guardian*, again, that
in the United Arab Emirates in March 1993 the arm and leg of an individual
convicted of 'piracy' had been similarly severed. Indeed, even Hamid Karzai,
the then prime minister of Afghanistan (described as 'suave' by *The Times* foreign editor), was reported to have said in January 2002 that he 'might support
amputation of limbs as a punishment' under Sharia law, 'provided that the
criminals were prosperous enough to know better'.

Public beheadings, particularly those which took place in Saudi Arabia,
also had a long run in the Western media: of Pakistani drug-smugglers (four
at a time in May 1993); of a Filipino housemaid—millions of expatriates
work in Saudi Arabia, including some one million Filipinos—also in May
1993, for murdering her employer; of eight more drug-smugglers in April
1995, 'blindfolded and with hands tied behind their backs', according to the
report, before they were dispatched in public with a sword; of four Turks, in
August 1995, for 'trying to smuggle aphrodisiac drugs into Saudi Arabia'; of
two Filipinos, in May 1997, for robbing and beating a store employee with an
iron pipe; of a Saudi Arabian woman beheaded in December 2003 for killing

her husband; of a Sri Lankan domestic servant, in July 2004, for murdering her employer; and so on, amounting sometimes to as many as three dozen beheadings in three weeks, as in April 1995, fifty-three in total in 2003, and over forty in the first six months of 2005. In one month alone, January 1995, an Afghan, a Nigerian, a Pakistani and a Yemeni were reported to have been executed in public in Dammam, Jeddah and the Saudi capital, Riyadh. In Iran, there were estimated to have been between 75 and 150 executions in 2003 and 159 in 2004, some by public hanging. Thus, in March 2005, a murderer was publicly executed in the town square of Pakdasht, south-east of Teheran, as 'thousands cheered' and his body swung from side to side—in the *Guardian*— 'causing both his shoes to fall off'.

Publication in the West of such items—even without 'shocking' verbal adornment and without pictures of scimitars carving through the air—succeeded in transforming the manifold content of the Sharia law into mere savagery, the savagery of the 'barbarian' who is beyond the 'civilised' pale. Strapping a convicted American criminal into an electric-chair, while ghouls look on, is not less 'barbarous'. But in this war of the worlds, amputations, beheadings, hangings, lashings—of homosexuals in Saudi Arabia and gamblers in Indonesia—canings and stonings were further grist to the reductive media mill, whose interest in such acts often exceeded that of the human rights lobbies. Indeed, the latter largely ignored the majority of these excesses, or greeted them with barely a nod or serious protest. This relative unconcern was a striking phenomenon, since the 'cruel, inhuman and degrading punishments' practiced by the Saudis, and by other Muslim states, were contrary to article 5 of the Universal Declaration of Human Rights; and even more striking when this unconcern was contrasted with the degree of engagement of such lobbies with, say, the issue of Islamists' rights in the non-Muslim world.

A passive, or voyeuristic, interest in the sensational aspects of such abuses dominated responses to them while Western governments for the most part confined themselves to token protests. Meanwhile, leading Islamic scholars, such as the Egyptian Muhammed Ghazali, for example, endorsed extra-judicial killings of those who opposed the implementation of the Sharia law itself. In similar spirit, at Teheran University in May 1989, Iran's chief justice urged revolutionary courts 'not to show the slightest clemency' in ordering the executions of 'bandits, seditious elements'—an elastic category—'and armed opponents' of the regime. And in Saudi Arabia, also, the scope of the death penalty was widened in the 1980s to include not only apostasy but 'conspiracy', robbery with violence, 'sabotage' and corruption. Moreover, Islamic resort to 'cruel, inhuman and degrading' forms of punishment (of both men and women) again rested upon the need for 'demonstrative' acts; that is, acts which disclosed, to Muslims and non-Muslims alike, the unyieldingness of the Islamic will—an impressive and advancing phenomenon—in the face of foes, internal and external, imagined and real.

To whom among non-Muslims, it should have been asked, was such demonstration of the Islamic will principally directed? The answer was to be found again in that force which helped to sustain Islamism: the media empires of the West, competing for 'stories' and for whom the desire for excess-as-such required to be satisfied daily. What was not required was either history or a true account of the Islamic advance, but the same evidences of 'terror' which Islamists were themselves seeking to provide.

There was therefore perverse satisfaction to be gained (on all sides) by the hangings of drug-traffickers in Teheran and twenty-six other Iranian towns on one day in March 1989; the multiple hangings, across recent years, of Islamists convicted of seeking to overthrow the Mubarak regime in Egypt and shouting defiance—for the cameras—at their judges; the flogging and canings meted out to teenage mothers convicted of 'immoral acts' in Bangladesh, as in 1994 and 1995; the 'four thousand' lashes, at the rate of 50 lashes a week, to which an Egyptian worker in Saudi Arabia was sentenced in August 1995, and which were ordered to be carried out upon him (with his legs shackled) in a town market-place in Qaseem province; or the public hanging in August 2004, in the northern Iranian city of Neka, of a sixteen-year-old girl, again for 'immoral acts'. These were precisely the types of repugnant event which were found 'attractive' to the non-Islamic, and in particular to the Western, media. They confirmed the stereotypes which the latter needed, but advanced understanding of the many-faceted nature of Islam barely at all.

In Britain, particular attention was naturally paid, especially by the popular press, to British expatriates sentenced—as in Saudi Arabia—to floggings for illicit drinking or sexual malfeasance. Attention was also addressed between 2000 and 2003 to five Britons and a Canadian who claimed that they had been beaten and tortured by the Saudi authorities into admission of complicity in a wave of bombings in Riyadh in 2000 and early 2001—probably carried out by Islamists—and for which four were sentenced to twelve years in jail and two faced a public beheading. They were 'pardoned' and released in August 2003.

The caning in the United Arab Emirates in February 1995 of an unmarried couple for 'having sex at a party', or the hundred lashes to which a sixteen-year-old Filipino maid was sentenced, also in the United Arab Emirates in October 1995, for stabbing her seventy-year-old employer to death in the act of rape—a sentence commuted after an appeal on her behalf by the president of the Philippines—satisfied a particularly unwholesome cluster of appetites. They were shared in popular Western cultures: appetites for violence and a prurience about sexuality chief among them.

The stoning to death of women for adultery—among such instances, in Bangladesh in February 1994, or in Iran in July 2001, but with similar sentences by Sharia courts in Nigeria in 2003 and 2004 overturned on appeal—is in practice relatively rare. But it nevertheless attained an iconic 'barbarous' significance by dint of the media's work on its behalf. The stoning to death, in Hamedan in November 1995, of an Iranian man for a homosexual act was less media-familiar; so, too, the sentence meted out by a Pakistani judge in Lahore, in March 2000, to a mass killer of some one hundred children that he should suffer the same fate as they, to be strangled, cut in pieces and dissolved in acid, as *The Times* reported. The overturning of this sentence was less noticed, or not noticed at all.

Likewise with the court sentence in Bahawalpur in December 2003 against a jilted man found guilty of throwing acid in the face of, and blinding, his former fiancée; he was himself sentenced to have acid 'dropped in his eyes'. Similarly, in June 2005, in the case of a man found guilty of blinding another, the Iranian supreme court upheld on appeal a sentence that he have his eyes surgically gouged out in turn. The description provided by a Taliban defector, Hafiz Sadiqulla Hassani, and published in a 'quality' British newspaper in October 2001, of the tortures carried out upon those caught 'watching videos, playing cards or keeping caged birds'—forbidden by the Taliban regime—was equally calculated to satisfy a perverse form of curiosity in Western 'culture' about all forms of human aberration, the worse the better. But, like so many other such reports, it also met Islamism's needs that its rigours be known, and marked, in the 'decadent' non-Islamic world.

'We would beat them', declared Hassani to an agog British journalist, notebook at the ready, 'with staves soaked in water, like a knife cutting through meat [*sic*], until the room ran with their blood or their spine snapped'; only the 'laughing' Taliban is missing here. 'There was a man beaten so much, he was such a pulp of skin and blood', Hassani added for good measure (and Western media pleasure), 'that it was impossible to tell...', and so forth.

Torture of fellow-Muslim detainees in Algeria, Egypt, Iran, Iraq—torture which continued to be carried out, by Iraqis upon Iraqis, under the 'interim government' installed after Saddam's fall—Morocco, Pakistan, the Palestinian territories, Syria and Uzbekistan was also well documented. It was the subject of criticisms, albeit modest and rarely noticed, by Amnesty International and other bodies, as were related Israeli malpractices against detained Palestinians. But there was again more at work in the notice of such cruelties by the Western media than was warranted by any duty to disseminate information about them. This was so, even if 'negative' press attention might be said in a minority of instances—as in Nigeria—to have stopped the application of Sharia law in its tracks.

But the boot here was on the Muslim foot. Media mores, audience appetites and technological means together served the developing political instinct of Islamism to manipulate all three. When some three thousand victims were done to death in the burning skyscrapers of the World Trade Center, the filmed delight of Osama bin Laden, watching the spectacle on television, was itself distributed by video to the Western media, arousing exactly the feelings of horror on the part of the non-Muslim which the act was designed to evoke.

Islamist violences, and the transmission of such violences to a 'global' audience, came in the end to inhabit the same sphere. This shared sphere is that of mutual dependency and reciprocal instrumentalisation. When the BBC described in August 2001 how 'suspected Islamist militants' in the town of Poonch in Indian-administered Kashmir 'woke two Hindu priests from their sleep and allegedly beheaded them', the purposes of the 'militants' and of the media were served together. So, too, with the description by Spanish national radio of an Islamist bomb attack on a Spanish restaurant in Casablanca in May 2003, in which, for good measure, a security guard 'had his throat cut with a large knife'. When the bombs detonated, a restaurant employee was typically reported as saying, there was 'flesh, flesh everywhere'; while after a London bus was blown up in July 2005 the 'whole front' of a roadside building was described in a *Guardian* headline—quoting an eyewitness—as 'covered with blood'.

Other accounts matched fierce act with indulgent and self-displaying prose. In a description by Robert Fisk in the *Independent* on 24 April 2002 of the West Bank killing of a Palestinian 'collaborator', Zuheir al-Mukhtaseb, stones 'thumped off the collaborator's bloodied corpse'—which reminded Fisk 'oddly' of the 'martyrdom of Saint Sebastian, all arrows and open wounds'—while Palestinian boys of ten and twelve, 'whooping with glee', 'were stabbing cigarettes' into his 'almost naked torso', which was (for effect) additionally 'riven with stab marks and holes'. Al-Mukhtaseb was, of course, decapitated while an 'awful crowd roared "*Allahu Akhbar*"'. At the last, 'young men with grinning faces'—the recycled Taliban image once more—'hurled', not threw, 'his corpse into a rubbish truck'. The 'savage mob' had done its work, both for itself and for the press; while Fisk was singled out by name for rare praise by Osama bin Laden himself as 'neutral', in a video released four days before the November 2004 US presidential election. 'Terror', after all, is a construct to which many hands can contribute. Or, as another journalist put it in September 2002 in the *New York Times*—also on-the-spot in the Palestinian territories to the benefit of all—'dozens of men have been killed as collaborators, often publicly'; adding that 'in the street there is no pity, no doubt that justice has been done'.

Likewise, the 'ears' of 'several officials' were cut off (in *The Times* in September 1994) by an 'infuriated Iraqi crowd' which had stormed the local headquarters of the Ba'ath Party in the southern city of Amarah, angered by a similar punishment decreed for draft-dodgers. Two Israeli soldiers were not only lynched—and their bodies said to have been mutilated—by a crowd in Ramallah in October 2000, but filmed doing so by an invited Italian television crew, which was ordered back to Rome when the personal relationships between those who carried out the act and those who observed it came to light.

In February 2002, a similar courthouse lynching by a 'mob' in Jenin of three Palestinians convicted, minutes before, for the clan-killing of a Palestinian Authority security officer was similarly well 'covered' by the *Jerusalem Post*. Bodies were 'dragged through the streets' and shots 'fired into the air', together with other images and appurtenances without which such an event would now lack the ring of truth. Fitting this pattern, the descriptions in the Western press in March 2004 of the lynching in Fallujah of four Americans working for a 'security company' were again filled with the 'colour' used in the journalistic trade. On this occasion, 'smouldering bodies' (one of them with its 'feet on fire' in the London *Daily Telegraph*) and 'charred corpses'—or, for those who preferred, 'blackened and mangled' corpses—were again 'dragged through the streets' to cries of 'Revenge, revenge for Saddam Hussein!' and so forth.

This is not to say that the events did not occur, or that the publicity which was given in the Russian press for the mutilations carried out by Chechen Islamists, or which was given in the Western press to the alleged stabbing and throat-cuttings of some passengers and of the pilots of the hijacked aircraft on 11 September 2001, were fabrications. But the war has required a savage and pitiless foe, the more savage and pitiless the better. Moreover, in this war, the media's role has often been not that of reporters but as protagonists 'on the front line'. Its troops have won their battle honours (and press awards) by accompanying—sometimes with camera crews three paces behind them—an Islamist gang as it sallied forth at night on a 'secret' operation in the occupied territories of Palestine, or by being present even at the site of a lynching. All this has had complex ethical and political effects.

For such media attention was again as much a two-edged sword as those which were wielded in public in Saudi Arabia after Friday prayers. It cut both ways. The engendering of fear bloodied the Islamist cause but simultaneously promoted it to disaffected young Muslims, while helping to disable and cow responses to its advance. Furthermore, for every potential Islamist aroused and recruited by the sight of US aircraft under Islamist command striking Manhattan—images repeated *ad nauseam* in the immediate aftermath of 9/11—there were other Muslims (and even liberal Americans) who, as we shall see, believed the whole to have been a plot to discredit Islam itself. Other Muslims felt alarm for the repute of their faith, and were thus divided both against and among themselves.

Indeed, self-delusion and moral evasion in response to such acts induced ethical paralysis and equivocation in many Muslims. But the non-Muslim was also brought to contradictory responses. They included both the blind 'Islamophobia' of the angered and the need felt by many non-Muslims to 'search-for-causes' of the hatred evinced by Islamism for 'the West'. This 'search-for-causes', as we shall see in a later chapter, was often carried out in a spirit of visceral dislike by some non-Muslims for their own societies' histories and present conduct. There was also a sense of helplessness in those who feared that there were forces at work in the worlds both of the Muslim and non-Muslim which could no longer be brought under control.

In particular, the mass-murder and cruelty of the Algerian civil war, and the passivity or disengagement with which its bloodletting was greeted by both Muslims and non-Muslims, disclosed how normal moral responses could be disarmed by such type of confusions. In Algeria, terrorisation of an unarmed civilian population by Islamists, and the government's equally violent resistance to such terrorisation, were to continue for decades on the shore of the Mediterranean, a geographical hand's span from southern Europe and the countries of the European Union. My own files contain an unremitting record, month upon month and year upon year, of events which ultimately sated the press itself; even Western television vacated the scene.

The warring parties were largely left to their own homicidal devices. Diplomacy turned its back on reports of throat-cutting of humans-as-sheep; of decapitations and mutilations; of killings of almost entire villages with axe and knife; of ambushes of transport and executions of passengers; of the slaughter of parents before their children's eyes and vice versa; of teachers' throats cut—eleven women teachers, for example, and a male instructor, in September 1997—in front of their students; and so on.

The Algerian press, despite suffering the killing of many of its journalists, served as the source of (increasingly second-hand) Western report. In *El Watan* or *Liberté* of Algiers, throughout the 1990s, horror upon horror was recorded: as of village women decapitated in Tlemcen province in western Algeria in November 1997; of burnings alive, and in October 1997 even of burials alive, as of a taxi driver, Mahieddine Ahmed, in February 1995 at Tighrine; of 'hackings'-to-death of women and children in the village of Omaria in April 1997; of the July 1997 slaughter in the village of Aonaria in Algeria's Medea province where, according to *El Watan*, even a pregnant woman is said to have been 'disembowelled'.

There were similar reports of burnings, decapitations and mutilations (including of the genitalia) in Siddi Bakhti in western Algeria in September 1994, and at Beni-Slimane, forty-five miles south of Algiers, in September 1997; of the killing by knife, and burning to death, of 'two hundred' women and children at Bentahla on 24 September 1997. A surfeit of horrors had outrun and dulled all capacity to respond to them; and they therefore continued almost without notice. The hijacking of a bus and the cutting of the throats of the passengers, 'most of them young people', at a road-block set up near Sig, 180 miles west of Algiers, in October 1997 was worth no more than a passing mention; similarly when armed men, 'disguised as police', stopped eight motorists near M'Sila, east of Algiers, and 'slit their throats' in November 1997.

With little remission or outside diplomatic intervention, it continued thus. Twenty-one members of the same family, including a three-month-old baby, were stabbed and shot in Ouled Abdullah, in the Chlef region about 125 miles west of Algiers, in October 2002. In February 2003, insurgents opened fire on vehicles at a road-block at Hameur el-Ain, 45 miles west of Algiers, killing twelve civilians; there were more such deaths in the summer of 2003 and in early 2004. In February 2004 the Algerian government refused to lift its twelve-year-long state of emergency, despite some abatement in the killings. But Algeria had been largely forgotten, not least because it lacked the 'attractions' of an Iraq, and of America's entrapment in it.

Pause is also required, since a multiplicity of issues was raised by this record. They were all events related to the thwarting of an Islamist victory at the polls, as earlier referred to; they had been acts of Muslim against Muslim in a Muslim nation; the three worlds, Islamic, non-Islamic and anti-Islamic, largely bypassed these events as if they were not occurring. The international press agencies continued to contain impersonal notice of them on their wires, but Western newspapers rarely made more of it than three- or four-line 'fillers' for their 'Other News' 'round-ups'.

Satiety with and disgust at such reports had bred contempt as well as pity. Even Algeria's official news agency merely remarked of the massacre of October 2002, mentioned above, that it 'bore the hallmarks of Islamic extremists'. Similarly, in December 2002, a US assistant secretary of state, William Burns, declared cold-bloodedly in Algiers that Washington had 'much to learn from Algeria on the ways to fight terrorism'. That is, a sense of the 'routine' had served, in the Muslim and non-Muslim worlds alike, to disable moral response to Algerian violence. The Algerian government seemed to have largely quelled the Islamist movement by 2005. But the latter had also achieved its ends: that of being seen as ready to act without mercy in its own cause.

The relative unconcern outside Algeria with the consequences was in part the product of confrontation with events that seemed to be outside the moral order itself. They were not. On the contrary, they took place within the moral order as it had become in the wake of the Islamist advance. They were also as if 'normalised' by media repetition; and, as noted earlier, they had the power to attract as well as to repel. Thus it was reported in January and May 2002, respectively, that in Britain and Italy videos showing Algerian Islamists murdering and mutilating their foes—principally fellow-Muslim government soldiers and uncooperative villagers in the civil war—had been circulated for the purposes of recruitment to the Islamist cause. In the same 'demonstrative' fashion, certain Hezbollah posters displayed the severed head of an Israeli soldier killed in Lebanon. The killers of the American journalist Daniel Pearl likewise made and distributed to the media a film of his killing and decapitation, as did hostage-takers in Iraq, showing their captives' pleas and tears, and their sometimes ghastly deaths. These videos were found as far afield as Cambodia, in December 2004.

Although in conventional Western psychological terms these were the acts of classical 'sadists', there was again reductiveness in such superficial judgment, as there was in the similar analysis of Nazi motive and conduct in the previous world war. No, these were brutal but sane political acts, guided by their own anti-ethic. They were given purchase and a deformed legitimacy by the knowledge, shared between perpetrator and observer, that the Western media was drawn, until itself glutted, to that which most terrifies and repels, and had little interest—naturally, one might say—in that which had the unnewsworthy mark of the 'ordinary' upon it. Indeed, too much violence 'of the same kind', as in Algeria or Iraq, could become an 'ordinary' matter too familiar to attract more than passing notice. Events more 'shocking' and of larger scale—say, of the scale of the attack on the World Trade Center—were therefore required equally by Islamism and by its observers, as Islamists have again known well. Ever larger-scale attacks, preferably of 'new' kinds, thus had their own logic, a logic with which Western news organisations were in effect complicit, and for whose outcome they must share the blame.

However, light relief could serve as an alternative for the Western media, especially on a 'dull news' day. Frivolity upon serious matters could also be made a saleable device. Here Islam's dress code, for example, has served now and again for a few jocular or mocking column-inches. Certain Teheran shops were closed for selling Western fashions in June 1993, or were told to stop selling 'short coats', or *manteaux*, in the spring of 2003; men were gratefully reported to have been detained by the Iranian authorities, also in June 1993, for wearing 'Western-style' sunglasses; the permitted colours for women's robes were limited to black, brown and dark blue. 'Women-only carriages in the Teheran underground'and plans to 'screen-off' women's sections in the city's parks likewise had their media moment.

Make-up, nail-polish, women's smoking in public, women's watching of football matches ('Women Get Red Card'), women's driving of cars, women's hairdressing and beauty salons, the admission of 'promiscuously dressed' women to restaurants, the holding of hands in public even by engaged couples, and suchlike, have been prohibited under a variety of rules in Afghanistan, Iran, Pakistan, Sudan or Saudi Arabia, but had a good run in the Western press. The Western fun to be had with all this could serve the 'colour' stories of Islam's ways just as well as could Robert Fisk's 'Saint Sebastian'–like Palestinian collaborator hanging by his feet. Even the freer codes which had begun to appear in Iran from 2003 attracted inordinate interest in the 'bell-bottoms', *manteaux* 'slit on the sides up to the armpits', 'glittery see-through scarves worn half-way back on the head', 'black cocktail dresses', eye-liner and nail-polish to be seen in Teheran or Shiraz.

There has been mileage—which has increased as a consequence of Western feminism's saliency in Western public thought—in the media's pointing to the much larger matter of the unequal (and ill-) treatment of women in the Islamic world. This is expressed in their limited rights to seek divorce, their lesser entitlements under Muslim inheritance laws, and the polygamous practices of some Muslim men. But it is generally the lesser matters which attract the Western media's jackdawlike attentions.

These have included the Taliban's removal from state-run Kabul television of female newsreaders in July 1992, and the detaining in September 1997 in Kabul—by armed 'religious police' from the Taliban's office for the 'Propagation of Virtue and the Prevention of Vice'—of the European Commissioner Emma Bonino for the infringement, by photographers in her entourage, of the rule against the taking of photographs of women by men unrelated to them. They were again serviceable 'stories'. So, too, with the declaration by a (post-Taliban) Afghan judge in January 2004 that the lifting of the ban on women singers on state television 'had to be reversed'. 'We are opposed to women singing and dancing as a whole', he told Reuters.

Better still for Western media purposes was the rule introduced in March 1994 in Kuwait (where, unlike in Saudi Arabia, women were permitted to drive cars) against them driving with their faces unveiled; or the Taliban order to white-wash windows lest unveiled women be seen from outside. The order included second-floor windows 'to a height of six feet'; a height to which even *The Times* was prepared to stoop in March 1997. The journalistic gilder-of-every-lily could have a field-day in such conditions. 'Your shoes', reported a Western woman scribe on conditions in Kabul, 'cannot make too much noise lest they incite lust in men'. Even female suicide-bombers had more piquancy, however grisly and tragic, than their male counterparts; while the report that a Shi'ite cleric had told worshippers at a Basra mosque in May 2004 that 'anyone who captures a female British soldier can keep her as a slave' fed stereotype to the hilt.

Accounts of Islamist violence on the one hand, and of what was made to appear comic or sinister folly on the other, when packaged together, made for a complex form of media entertainment. The Associated Press devoted an Internet page—and was followed by many Western newspapers—to the prison sentence handed out by a Spanish court, in January 2004, to an Islamic cleric in Fuengirola for having published a book, *Women in Islam,* urging Muslim husbands to hit their wives 'on the hands and feet using a rod that is thin and light so that it does not leave scars or bruises on the body'. (The cleric was briefly incarcerated, released by a higher court and sent on a 'training course' in order to 'learn about human rights'.)

Amid all this, it was hard for most non-Muslims to keep a balance. For if certain acts, events and pronouncements created anxiety and fear in some, others provoked ridicule, incredulity and incomprehension. Moreover, whenever offence was taken by Muslims at well-publicised harms done by Western insensibilities towards their faith, such harms were immediately available to be seized upon, to both Islam's and Islamism's net moral or political gain. Thus, a report in May 2005 in *Newsweek* of the desecration, or 'mishandling', of copies of the Koran at Guantanamo—the report was retracted, but then conceded by the Pentagon in June 2005 to be in part true—led to fierce anti-American rallies and violence, with injuries and deaths, in Afghanistan, Bangladesh, Egypt,

India, Indonesia, Libya, Malaysia, Pakistan, the Palestinian territories, the Philippines, Somalia and Yemen.

The Muslim taboo which restricts serious ethical or religious discussion of Islam's texts and tenets by non-Muslims has also invited superficial accounts of what Islam supposedly is, as well as mendacious reports of what it finds, or chooses to find, in the Islamic world. Such reports have again reflected a desire for that archetypal, or stereotypical, worst to which much media reporting irresistibly tends.

The denial under the Taliban of access by females to schools, to most hospitals, to universities, to employment and (unless accompanied) even to the local market permitted the Western lily-gilder to declare falsely in October 2001 that in Taliban-ruled Afghanistan women were 'not permitted to go to a doctor at all'. Nevertheless, fidelity to the truth required, in May 1995, that the death-threats made by the Algerian Islamist leader, Abu Abdallah Ahmed, against 'all Algerian women who insist on acquiring an education' be made public. So, too, did the closure and even reported burning of girls' schools in March 2002 in an area of Kurdish Iraq which had come under the control of Islamists 'linked to al-Qaeda'.

The facts were not merely worthy of note but necessary to be known. Similarly, a series of attacks on girls' schools and girl pupils in an Afghanistan ostensibly freed of Taliban influence, or threats made against women seeking to register to vote in Afghanistan's presidential election in 2004, or the murder in June 2005—in her home—of a popular young Afghan woman TV presenter criticised by clerics for her manner and dress, signified that confidence as to the 'final defeat' of the Taliban and its mind-set was premature: attacks on women's education and emancipation were one of Islamism's markers. Yet they were again reductive of the true nature and extent of the challenge to the non-Muslim world represented by the Islamist advance.

The need to report the phenomenon of compulsory divorces, decreed by clerical and legal authorities, and without regard to the wife's wishes or interests, could be said to have been clear also. For example, in Algeria in 1995, women married to male 'renegades' or 'atheists' were ordered to divorce their husbands; in Bangladesh in 1994, husbands were ordered to divorce wives working for foreign non-governmental organisations; in Egypt, the wife of a human rights activist and academic, Hafez Abu Saada, was ordered to divorce him after he had been declared by a Cairo court to be an 'apostate'. As a 'good Muslim', the court pronounced, his wife 'could not' remain married to him. But particular concentration on such issues—which nevertheless barely stirred human rights lobbies or the 'left'—again shrank the dimensions of

Islam and its often grandiose ethical system to what seemed like manageable proportions. It also fed the delusion that the non-Muslim world was merely facing aberrations from a Western norm which 'modernisation' would cure.

At the same time, a grateful Western press seized on such instances of the maltreatment of women. Report of them remained a mixture of grim truth and good media business, of matters reported for information on the one hand and for the tickling of fancies on the other. Here, Muslim pruriences in relation to women coincided with similar pruriences in the Western tabloid press. Each had taken its own route to a single voyeuristic meeting-point, where, in the words of a speaker in the British (and Iranian-funded) 'Muslim Parliament' in January 1992, 'strange men' in non-Muslim societies 'gaze and gloat over' women in 'all-revealing clothes', for example.

These were twin worlds. In them, male tailors and sales clerks in the United Arab Emirates were forbidden in June 1989 to 'measure women clients', while the Western media, with equal prurience, took the trouble to note it with its own salacious nudge and wink. Likewise, the first Islamic Women's Olympics, held in Teheran in 1993—to denunciations by some Iranian clerics that the games were 'perpetuating obscene Western values'—were closed to male photographers, but made it into Western foreign news-pages. Iranian women were prohibited in October 2000 from buying 'lingerie' from male salesmen, as the *Daily Telegraph* found space to announce; while, in May 1991, Jordan's education minister, Abdullah Akaileh, banned fathers from 'watching girls in gym-slips' at school sports days, a *ukase* appealing to obsessions which Islamist and non-Islamist cultures share. When a Kuwaiti religious official, Khaled al-Mathkour, issued his own *fatwa* against 'Barbie dolls' in August 1994—on the grounds that their 'feminine curves' had 'nothing to do with childhood'—or the Turkish Welfare Party in November 1995 pronounced ballet to be 'indecent', or Saudi Arabia in December 2003 banned the import of female dolls, prurience again spoke to prurience across the cultural barricades.

There was, of course, a long-standing and profoundly held Islamic ethic which led to such *diktats*, and to which the non-Islamic world was for the most part a stranger. But there was also a darker side to Islamism's expressions of sexual fear and obsession; as there is—often darker still, and sometimes to demented and homicidal degree—in our own counterpart obsessions. In Turkey, in February 1995, new educational regulations prescribed 'virginity tests' for any schoolgirl between the ages of eleven and seventeen whom a headmaster and his disciplinary board believed to be of 'unchaste behaviour' and to 'have had sexual intercourse'. In his will, Mohammed Atta not merely forbade women to attend his funeral, but specifically prescribed that 'neither pregnant women nor unclean people'—presumably perceived by him to be in the same category—should be present. Similarly, in the Taliban's 'explanation' of the rigorous necessity for heavy veiling of women, their faces were declared to be a 'source of corruption' for men unrelated to them; and in January 2004, the grand mufti of Saudi Arabia, Sheikh Abdulaziz al-Sheikh, pronounced that 'allowing women to mix with men' was 'the root of every evil and catastrophe' and was 'highly punishable'.

The recoil, both real and feigned, in the world of Islam for what is held to be the 'moral degeneracy' of the West is not always of this obsessional kind. It extends—for the most part irrationally in Western eyes—to many other matters of which Islamic ethics disapproves. But for the Muslim's moral or sexual anger to be indiscriminately treated with mockery, or brushed aside as a form of 'barbarism', is at the non-Islamic world's now-evident peril, and likely great cost. At the same time, for homosexuals to be irately described as 'scum' in Trafalgar Square—as in August 1995—and for an open call to be made (in Britain) that 'filthy homosexuals' stop their 'filthy practices' and 'come back to the system of control' invited a counter-anger.

Yet the notions in the Islamic world that there are 'no morals' to be found in Western societies, or that 'if you practice homosexuality, it's all right', or that 'women can go out almost naked wearing just a bikini [sic]'—as a Muslim lecturer in chemistry in a Birmingham technical college, Dr. Mahmoud Jabar, expressed it in February 1989—are ineradicable ones. 'I would expect the worst in this country', Jabar added, after ten years in Britain. When al-Qaeda claimed responsibility for the bombing of a disco in Bali in October 2002, it added 'brothels' to its description of the targets it had attacked.

Here there was also a double-standard in what was considered to be ethical conduct. Thus, the beating in May 2001 with leather straps (by the Taliban's 'religious police') of members of the staff of a Western-funded hospital in Kabul for the 'sin' of permitting males and females to dine together in the canteen passed Islamism's moral test of righteousness. So, too, did the physical assaults upon Algerian women-students by Islamists in the 1980s for wearing 'short skirts', or for consorting with male students not of their families. Likewise with the attack carried out with wooden clubs by students at Pakistan's Punjab University in Lahore in May 2003 on a male and a female student—both Iranians—who had been discovered sitting together on a verandah; or the intimidation, reported in October 2004, of women students at Baghdad's al-Kindi University as Islamists sought to assert their grip on Iraq after Saddam's fall; or, worse, the shooting dead—as at Boudouaou in Algeria, on 30 March 1994—of two unveiled teenage schoolgirls waiting at a bus-stop.

Also in Algeria, a teacher who refused to separate male and female students into different classes had her throat slit in sight of her pupils in November 1994; two teenage Algerian sisters, Zoulika and Saida Boughedou, similarly had their throats cut in November 1994 for rejecting proposals of what are euphemistically denoted 'short-term' or 'pleasure' marriages to members of an Islamist group. In Bangladesh and Pakistan, women's rights groups have likewise reported violent immolations of women—including, in one case, for merely 'sitting next to a strange man'—as well as many suicides, especially among village women, who have preferred to take their lives rather than suffer public punishments for offending Sharia law. Similar self-immolations by women in refusal of arranged marriages were being reported from 'liberated' Afghanistan in November 2002. Such type of fate has also met Hindu women. But the Muslim stereotype has now overshadowed them, borne along into the non-Muslim world's consciousness by the Islamic advance itself.

To flog women for flouting the dress-code in Iran, or to shoot a twelve-year-old in the legs for wearing tight-fitting trousers—as occurred in Srinagar in Kashmir in June 2000—or for four male relatives to kill a woman and her twenty-two-year-old daughter in the Turkish Black Sea town of Bafra in August 1995 for 'dressing immodestly', answered to a moral culture which non-Muslims could not accept. But 'Islamophobia' could also cancel the knowledge that a different set of moral scruples, coupled with substantive protections, has nevertheless failed to prevent increasing domestic and other violences against women in the West.

A Western lawyer might also point to the 'anomaly' that, in a Sharia law system, Muslim women were required, almost impossibly in any real world, to produce three male (Muslim) witnesses if they sought to prove a rape. Indeed, rape of girls and women—itself on the rise in the West—has gone largely unpunished in Muslim societies, not least because the complainant could find herself charged with adultery or 'fornication' in the absence of proof to the contrary. Moreover, feminists who took up such cases in the Muslim world often put themselves at risk. For example, Nabila Diahnine, the president of an Algerian feminist group, was assassinated in February 1995, while the Bangladeshi feminist writer, Taslima Nasrin, accused of insulting Islam' for saying among other things that it 'repressed women', was forced to flee the country in 1994, pursued by a local *fatwa*. Similarly, the Somali Dutch member of parliament, Ayaan Hirsi Ali, was threatened with death in November 2004 for having collaborated with the assassinated Dutch film-maker, Theo van Gogh, in making a film about violence against women in Muslim societies.

In all this the Western media again played a crucial participant role. It did so not only by its predilection for idle sensation, but also, in this instance, by bringing to public notice that which had been done in Islam's name. The independent Human Rights Commission of Pakistan documented more than 450 'honour killings' of women by family members in 2002 alone; in Britain, in June 2004, Scotland Yard announced that it would 'review' more than one hundred cases of what were thought to have been 'honour killings' in an attempt to 'understand and prevent them'. For example, in October 2003 a British Muslim businessman was jailed for life for murdering his daughter's Christian boyfriend. Also in October 2003, two other British Muslim men were sentenced to life imprisonment for stabbing their twenty-one-year-old cousin to death on her wedding day because they disapproved of her choice of husband. 'They left her dying on the floor in her wedding-dress', read a typically lurid account in the British yellow press; the other side of the coin in which the media deals. In Britain there were also reported to be numbers of suicides (and murders) of young Hindu women, who, for example, had refused arranged marriages. But such fates, like those of women-victims of violence in the general population, could not command the responses which report of Muslim misdeeds aroused.

Indeed, without the 'narrative' of it which has been furnished by the Western media's often sickly preferences, the stereotypes of Muslim unreason could not have been so securely established. Their establishment was to the dis-advantage of Muslims, particularly in the diaspora, in arousing prejudice against them. But, as has been argued, it was to Islamism's greater benefit in arousing fear in non-Muslims on the one hand, and attracting increased support across large swathes of the Muslim world for an advancing cause on the other.

The case of a 'strict Muslim father', Abdul Malik, who was charged at Birmingham Crown Court in July 1989 for slitting the throat of his sixteen-year-old daughter in front of her sisters and mother after she had secretly attended Jehovah's Witness meetings—or, better, 'pulling back her hair and slashing her jugular vein with a knife as her sisters and mother watched in horror', according to a typical news-report at the time—perfectly fitted the media's bill. As prosecuting counsel shrewdly put it to the jury, 'Malik sacri-ficed his daughter for his religion'. 'She wouldn't listen, she had to be taught a lesson', the convicted father declared.

In himself Malik was no caricature but a murderer, and was justly sen-tenced. So, too, was a forty-year-old south London Muslim doctor, Hassan Qadri, who 'put out his wife's eyes' (with a claw-hammer and knife) in front of their eight-year-old daughter in August 1992, and was jailed for twelve years at the Old Bailey in December 1992. Yet for counter-demonstrative purposes they both fitted the media's 'identikit', and therefore satisfied, or gratified, its needs. In the end the Muslim who does not have a beard, does not fulminate, and does not slit, or does not wish to slit, throats cannot—in the dress in which he is required by much of the media to appear for recognition purposes—be a real Muslim.

Behind the façade of these Muslim stereotypes there were two figures. There was the Islamist, the most 'desirable' of all representatives of Islam, who foams at the mouth and commits, or urges others to commit, atrocities in Islam's name; and the uninteresting Muslim, insufficiently newsworthy or photogenic, to whom relatively little attention has been paid. He or she might be morally delinquent, or cowardly, in silently approving or glossing over what Islamists do, or aspired to do. But he or she might also disapprove strongly of Islamism's words and actions—and often enough did, as we shall see—yet gain disproportionately small attention.

Above all, in the battles for circulation and ratings, there was always decreasing air-time and diminishing screen-space—or more commonly, no air-time and no screen-space—for the great upsurge of renascent Islamic argument upon moral problems and issues which were common to the Muslim and non-Muslim worlds. It has been an upsurge which has possessed the confidence to hold in increasing contempt, often with justice, those in the non-Islamic world who contemn it; and which sees, or thinks it sees, in the Western value-system only an 'abyss of sexual corruption, psychological disturbance and the swamp of moral disintegration', as a declaration from Cairo's al-Azhar University expressed it in August 1995. In this so-called abyss and swamp, of which many non-Muslims are also aware, 'desires are stimulated which we consider socially damaging and which we wish to contain', a spokesman for Egypt's Islamic Research Council similarly declared in April 1994.

That some Islamists suffer, or seem to suffer, from 'psychological disturbances' of their own is an insufficient rejoinder. First, however cruel the forms it has often taken, the Islamist cause represents a challenge to many of the moral defects and confusions in the non-Muslim world. Secondly and equally important, with the aid of those who make our images of 'reality' for us, Islamism and Islam have already come to dominate the preoccupations of many non-Muslims.

They have indeed had a 'bad press'. But, as I have pointed out, they have also made 'good copy', which Islamists have grown always more adept at providing to a 'communications industry' corrupted by its own need for sensation. Indeed, without the aid of the media—Muslim and non-Muslim alike—the Islamist advance would have made slower progress. Although the attack from the skies against the World Trade Center was bad news for the United States, it was heaven-sent for the news-desks of the world.

CHAPTER THREE

The Hostile Round

Insulting, harming and attacking Islam and Muslims have been historic constants. Such attacks have generally been seen by the aggressors as having been provoked by Islam itself. This is also how today's attacks by non-Muslims on Muslims are perceived by many. Insult to and attack upon Islam as a creed or a cause, and upon Muslims as individuals, have in turn served in the last decades as ground for further reprisal by Muslims. Attacks upon Muslims in the non-Muslim world have also provided the ostensible grounds for their further retreat into estrangement, or for a deeper sense of outrage and victimhood.

Indeed, every offence given to Islamic sensibility, even if it is held by the offender to be morally justified by whatever offence it is intended to requite, may be turned into evidence of an essential malevolence towards Islam. This is easily capitalised upon by Islamists whose violent diatribes depict the non-Muslim as incorrigibly hostile to their faith. In consequence, equally incorrigible ill-intent is discovered by non-Muslims in many of the sentiments, writings and acts of Muslims which are directed against the non-Islamic world. In this hostile round, Muslims and non-Muslims are now trapped together.

Even the worst of slaughters, whether committed by Muslims or non-Muslims, are invested with precedent causes for which the 'other' is held to be to blame. To choose at random, this was as true of the slaughter of Muslims by Serbs at Srebrenica in 1995—'those people must be killed', the Bosnian Serb leader Radovan Karadzic is reported to have said—as of Islamist justifi-

cations for the attack on the World Trade Center, or of the brutalities committed by the decapitators in Iraq. The torture and execution of Islamists by
the Chinese authorities in Xinjiang; the murder in February 1994 by the Israeli
extremist, Baruch Goldstein, of twenty-nine Arabs from Hebron while they
were praying in the mosque at the Tomb of the Patriarchs; or the earlier-
referred to immolation of thousands of Muslims by Hindus in Gujarat after
the destruction of the Ayodhya mosque in 1992 have all been 'justified',
implicitly or explicitly, in this way.

This is now an unbreakable vicious circle. Many interests and energies,
political, military, intellectual, clerical, 'terroristic' and counter-'terroristic,'
are now whirling about in a vortex of action and reaction. The flux of movement of Muslim political refugees, economic migrants and others, also enters
this vortex. Most of these migrants are of innocent purpose, as in the case of
Muslims who are escaping from their own failed Islamic states, dictatorships
and internal conflicts, or from the exploitations and aggressions which have in
turn been directed against the Islamic world. Nevertheless, such migrants
become ready targets, in their now mass-unsettlement, for the suspicion (and
worse) of the societies which receive them.

Towards incomers in any society there have always been complex emotions and responses on the part of existing or 'indigenous' populations. The
latter, for obvious reasons, will generally conceive themselves to have greater
entitlement to be where they are than those who have chosen their country as
a resting-place or even as a utopia. Today, in relation to Muslim migration into
the non-Muslim world, these emotions and responses include generosity of
spirit and 'racist' unease; a desire to protect migrant rights and counter-objection to the supposedly special favours which such protection provides; friendship, and an impulse for 'profiling'; a sense (in some) that societies are
strengthened by diversity or 'pluralism', and a fear (in others) that the existing
civic, social and moral order will be harmed by 'excessive' 'influxes' of 'aliens';
tolerance of difference, and intolerance; a sense that all, whether citizens or
not, possess equal moral and other entitlements, and—at the opposite
extreme—a desire to do violence to, and even to expel, the incomers.

There is 'head-counting' of 'asylum-seekers', whose claims are increasingly doubted, and special registration of individuals from prescribed lists of
mainly Muslim nations, such as were introduced in the United States in 2002.
Tribunals are set up to distinguish between 'genuine' political refugees who
are at risk of their lives, 'bogus' applicants and 'mere' economic migrants.
Clashes take place between the political parties over the justice of the detention, or non-detention, of prospective entrants. 'The other' is admitted,

deported or disappears into his adoptive nation without permission. Housing, education and related services are provided or not provided to incomers, who accept or object to their new circumstances. The instrumentalisation of the 'immigrant problem' for political ends plays a part in this 'vortex'. Argument breaks out between 'right' and 'left'—within the 'left' also—as to whether or not falling indigenous birth-rates and ageing populations in the West make immigration an increasing economic necessity.

Meanwhile, further confusion and hostility are created in the non- and anti-Islamic worlds by every notice of violent Islamist attack upon the non-Islamic world. Counter-charges as to the present humiliation and historic oppression of Muslims are levelled at the corporate, capitalist West by Muslims and morally supportive non-Muslims alike. At the same time, the raw-edged sensibilities of Muslims and openly or latently hostile non-Muslims in such countries quicken to (and sometimes, it seems, are looking for) provocation and offence. They now have no difficulty in finding grounds for it, and for other more serious fears of a spreading conflict.

To be a migrant from any culture, nation or continent is a fraught condition. But the Muslim migrant's already-existing handicaps and dilemmas in the diaspora are not eased when such migrant's compatriots, or co-religionists, believe themselves to be engaged in a war of good and evil with the receiving culture or nation.

Such 'handicaps' for Muslims have increased in the last decades, as a consequence of being seen as an actual or potential danger to others' well-being, with or without evidence of either. It increases the anxieties of already-established and law-abiding migrants, as in the United States and Britain, of being tarred with the brush of suspicion that what the most hostile or violent of their compatriots and co-religionists have done they are planning to do themselves. After the 9/11 attacks, Muslims almost everywhere in the non-Muslim world, as in Britain, reported 'increasing hostility and discrimination'.

This has not abated. On the contrary, as could have been expected, 'our entire community is being castigated and blamed for the crimes of others', complained an official of the American Arab Anti-Discrimination Committee in June 2004, as victimisation, victimhood and media account of Islamist atrocities advanced together. Moreover, if there is strength in numbers, there is danger in numbers. For 'indigenous' inhabitants—whose ranks in circumstances of suspicion will generally exclude the Muslim, even if the latter is native to the non-Islamic country—will then make tallies of the proportions in their societies belonging to this or that ethnicity or faith. Later in this work I shall myself do this, for necessary reasons.

'Projections' as to the future balance of 'immigrant' and 'indigenous' populations are different matters from statistical certitudes. Yet such projections are regularly made into certitudes, or near-certitudes, for polemical purposes. As the Islamic convulsion leaves its mark upon non-Islamic and Islamic societies alike, it is typically said by the demographic expert that incomer 'Pakistanis and Bangladeshis have tended to continue having large families', since 'they keep bringing into the country'—in this case, Britain—'young brides from remote villages who retain traditional values'. In *The Times* in September 2000 it was reported that 'according to one prediction' 'white Britons will be outnumbered' in London by 2010. Similarly, 'experts' are frequently cited as predicting, for example, that 'if present trends in birth-rates and immigration continue', both Britain and America could become 'white-minority states' within the next '60' or, according to other 'top experts', '140' years. Other 'projections', as for France, would have it that up to one-third of the French population will be Muslim by the end of the twenty-first century or, if you prefer, by 2050, and so on.

However, Muslims in Europe often exaggerate their own numbers, and dangerously so, in order the better to argue that the time for disparaging and discounting Muslim interests is past. Thus, where non-Muslim and anti-Muslim 'head-counters' produce tallies of '14 million' Muslims in Europe, an angry Muslim polemicist will insist, as in the *Guardian* in June 2002, that the total is 'over 20 million'. Here, 'head-count' has been pitted against 'head-count' for related political ends. In these number-games it is fears and threats which are again at work on both sides. There is both fear and threat in the assertion that there are 'too many Muslims' for their own well-being in Europe, in the United States or in other parts of the non-Islamic world; and there is warning and threat that the non-Islamic world overlooks, undervalues and assails the Muslim presence at its peril. There is also truth, on both sides of the question.

The non-Islamic and anti-Islamic perception of such matters is formed empirically, by observation or experience. It is also shaped by subjective impressions, above all impressions fostered by anxieties and paranoias. They are anxieties and paranoias which, as noted in the previous chapter, Islamism itself generates and which serve both to its advantage and to its harm. These 'popular' impressions in Britain are of inordinate numbers of mosques in 'once-British' cities and towns. London's Spitalfields area is therefore given the name 'Banglatown', to which a 'Committee for Bangladeshis' Rights' objects in its turn as a 'ghettoising tag'. Or Europe is described as 'fast becoming an Arab-Islamic land of emigration'. It is true that there are projections that 'one in five

Europeans will be Muslim by 2050'; but there is falsehood in today renaming Europe 'Eurabia', as a serious scholar has done.

Further impulses for paranoia are furnished by other popular beliefs, again in part true and in part false. One belief is that the majority of immigrants, refugees and asylum-seekers in the non-Islamic and anti-Islamic worlds are Muslims, which is true. Another is that all 'Asians' are 'Muslims' which, to the distress of Hindus (for example)—who are made to suffer disparagements directed at Muslims—is obviously not true; 'I class them as one thing and that's it, Pakis', declared a police recruit in a BBC documentary shown in October 2003. A third rough-and-ready sentiment is that even if there are differences of origin, of age, of sectarian allegiance, of ethical (and unethical) conduct and of belligerence or passivity among Muslims in response to harms and insults, these differences are of no real significance.

Such differences will obviously be thought to be of no moment if all Muslims are perceived as essentially 'fundamentalist', or essentially 'primitive', and if Islam is depicted as having a 'black heart' in the words of a (sacked) British Council official in the summer of 2004. The case is likewise made out that relatively few Muslims are either able or willing to assimilate to the 'host culture', that they are 'cuckoos in the nest', and so on. In order to get at all Muslims, polemics may be directed at 'despotic, barbarous and corrupt Arab states', 'few' of which are said to have made 'any contribution to the welfare of the rest of the world', and which are held to be populated by 'suicide-bombers', 'limb-amputators' and 'woman-repressors', in the words of a BBC presenter. He 'stepped down', or was pushed, from his job in the ensuing uproar in January 2004. 'I have been overwhelmed by the support from the general public', he added, as he took his hook.

There is no avoiding the fact that some Muslim demands for special or distinctive rights, freedoms and exemptions have strengthened the popular sense that there are differences, ethical and cultural, between Muslims and non-Muslims which can never be overcome. Equally harmful have been the often ill-disguised contempt of Muslims for Western 'immorality' or 'decadence' when at the same time many Muslims seek their educations and livelihoods amidst it. Indeed, a sense of difference is not only insisted upon by Islamism, but shared by most Muslims themselves. Yet it is combined with objections to differences of treatment at non-Muslim hands.

Recoil, insult and the outraging of Muslim feelings in the non-Islamic world are therefore as well established now as are more benign (or passive) responses to the Muslim presence. A readiness to do Muslims harm, or a moral unconcern over such harms done to them by others, is also well established.

Such harms are felt to match what appears to be the Muslim unconcern for, and even approval of, the harms done by Islamists to non-Muslims.

Hostile sentiment, whether seemingly refined or rough, now has deep roots in apparently liberal Western cultures, and explanations for it are increasingly easy to arrive at. First, there is the sense among critics of Islam that a spirit of toleration is itself absent from, and not compatible with, the forms which the Islamic 'reawakening' has taken. Secondly, there is awareness of a substantial inconsistency in the attitudes of Muslims to the ideal, or ethic, of Western cultural 'pluralism'. On the one hand, it is appealed to by discontented Muslims in the West when their customs, values, interests or rights are felt by them to have been overridden or neglected. On the other, the *same* 'pluralist' ideal is selectively refused by Muslims whenever the defence of their values, interests and rights against the operation of such ideal is felt to demand its rejection.

Thirdly, appeals are frequently and justly made by Muslims in non-Islamic societies to the safeguards which the rule of law and the ethic of 'human rights' provide, and which are generally not found in Muslim societies themselves. This appeal will be made whenever due process, or the principle of equal entitlement under the law, is held by Muslims not to be being observed in their cases. Yet some Muslims can demonstrate by their conduct a disdain for the very societies to whose protections appeal is being made. Other Muslims can give moral and financial support to fellow-Muslims who would—if they could—uproot these societies themselves, including by acts of extreme violence.

Here, questions as to the meaning (if any) to Muslim settlers in non-Islamic countries of the concept of 'citizenship' are raised in acute form. In some instances, the demand will be made of Muslims in the West for practical demonstration that their citizenship signifies more to them than the possession of a passport, a right of residence, and the opportunity of gainful employment. But this is a hypocritical demand when it is directed to Muslims by 'indigenous' inhabitants who may themselves be unfit to make it. 'Are there any Muslims in this country', asked a bumptious *Daily Telegraph* reader in October 2001, 'who have read Locke, Mill or Voltaire?'

One consequence is what has been called a 'confused debate' in Western liberal societies over questions of national tradition, identity and 'social cohesion'. In Europe, in particular, this debate focused in 2003 and 2004 upon objection to the wearing by Muslim females of the *hijab*, or headscarf, in state schools, public employments or (in cases of more acute phobia) in any public place; as if, to put it at its absurdest, the baring of the hair and the back of the neck betokened acceptance of the adoptive nation's value-system. There has even occurred in several European countries the forcible removal of scarves by irate teachers, as well as assaults upon, and the suspension and expulsion of, 'wrongly dressed' Muslim school pupils; even the dismissal of a scarf-wearing Muslim juror in mid-trial in France. Elsewhere in Europe the matter has been left to the individual discretion of school principals and of the heads of other institutions. In other European countries, the practice has been accepted with little or no demur.

In Britain, a Luton schoolgirl who insisted on attending school in an ankle-length *jilbab* was prevented by the head-teacher in February 2004 from doing so. With the support of the Islamist group Hizb ut-Tahrir, she took her case to the High Court on 'human rights' grounds, lost, but had the decision reversed on appeal in March 2005, declaring that hers was a 'victory for all Muslims who wish to preserve their identity and values despite prejudice and bigotry'. In Germany, regional governments, each entitled to make its own judgment, decided both for and against the *hijab*. In the north Italian town of Azzano Decimo, the mayor banned the wearing of veils and the 'concealing of the face' by Muslim women on grounds of 'public safety' at a time of 'terrorist' threat; a decree against veils (and 'other headgear') which 'hindered identification in public' was approved by the Italian senate in July 2005.

In the United States, an Oklahoma school district and the Justice Department agreed in May 2004 to permit a Muslim schoolgirl to wear a *hijab* on civil rights grounds, despite a school dress-code banning 'hats and other head coverings'. But a Muslim employee at Florida's Disney World lost her job, also in May 2004, for refusing to remove it. Denmark's High Court in January 2005 similarly gave permission to a supermarket chain to ban its employees from wearing the *hijab* at work, while in May 2005 (male) prison guards in Madison, Wisconsin, ordered a Muslim woman to remove her *hijab* before visiting her inmate-husband. She filed a federal lawsuit seeking damages from the guards and the Department of Corrections on the grounds that her constitutional right to practice her religion had been violated.

In France, where the *hijab* was in any case being worn only by a minority of Muslim schoolgirls, the matter was taken to the limit in February and March 2004, with the passage of a law by overwhelming majority—since it was supported by both 'left' and 'right' political parties—in the National Assembly and Senate. It forbade the wearing in French state schools of 'signs and clothes that conspicuously displayed the pupil's religious affiliation'. Skull-caps, Sikh turbans and 'large' crucifixes were thrown in for balance, but the Muslim headscarf was the true object of the prohibition, which came into force in September 2004.

Advocates of the ban, taking a hammer to smash a nut, described the *hijab* variously and in ascending order of objection as a 'challenge to France's secular values', a 'political not a religious symbol', an 'ostentatious sign of religious proselytism' and a 'flag of Islamic militancy'. Religion could not be a 'political project'; schools were a 'place for learning'; secularism was the 'best guarantee of equality for all'; 'diversity' was acceptable but 'communalism' was not; and, in the words of President Chirac, 'glorifying particular identities would lead to the break-up of France'. In particular, the *hijab* was a badge of 'division', of 'separatism', of 'lack of integration'; while for feminists, Muslim feminists included, it was a 'symbol of women's subjugation to fundamentalist pressures' and to the dictates of Muslim men. Moreover, it was argued, the *hijab* was banned in schools in Muslim Tunisia. In Turkey, the law prohibits women from wearing headscarves not only in schools but in government offices; headscarves were banned at Ankara University in 1990, and even in Egypt attempts were made in 1994 by the education minister to ban headscarves worn by schoolgirls without their parents' permission.

Opponents of the ban in France protested by the thousands in the streets. The prohibition of the *hijab* was 'legally dubious' or 'unenforceable', a 'matter best left alone', an act of 'discrimination', a 'muzzling of religion', the product of 'secular fundamentalism', a 'denial of human rights', an act of 'persecution' and even an 'attack on the Muslim population'. In February 2004, from his hideout, al-Qaeda's Ayman al-Zawahiri denounced the French ban as 'another example of the Crusader's malice'. The release of two French journalists, seized as hostages in August 2004, was made dependent, among other things, upon the revocation of the ban. The ban was not revoked, but the journalists were eventually released. It was also argued by some French imams that there was a 'divine obligation' to wear the *hijab*, come what may.

Yet in the thick of the argument in France, this position was embarrassingly countered by no less a figure than the Grand Sheikh of Cairo's al-Azhar University, Mohammed Sayed Tantawi. He declared that non-Muslim countries had 'the right' to pass any laws they chose, laws 'which I cannot interfere with as a Muslim'. No, again said the ban's opponents, the prohibition was 'counterproductive', would 'drive Muslims even further away from the rest of the country', was a 'boost for French Islamists' and so forth. In other words, it was both a defence and a denial of human rights; both integrationist and anti-integrationist; both well- and ill-intentioned; right and wrong. A large majority of the French population, when polled, thought it was right.

Most Muslim schoolgirls in France removed their headscarves—and Sikhs removed their turbans—when the law came into force. Those who did not were permitted a period of 'dialogue' with school officials. One schoolgirl in Strasbourg removed her veil to reveal a head shaved bald in protest; a few dozen intransigents were expelled and transferred to private schools. As for the European Court of Human Rights, it unanimously ruled in June 2004 that a ban on headscarves in state schools not only did not violate the freedom of religion, but was 'appropriate' when such ban was designed to 'protect the secular nature of a state, especially against extremist demands'.

Indeed, for most anti-Muslims, and even for the benign, the nature of the relationship between the individual Muslim and the Western civic society which he or she had joined was the issue of issues. Given the differences between Islamic values and the values of a plural, liberal, democratic (or 'decadent') non-Islamic society—differences which are perceived by many Muslims themselves to be irreconcilable—how could the inwardly-divided Muslim be truly a citizen of the body politic to which he or she now belonged? When Islam's mosques in Europe not merely received extra-territorial funding from countries deeply hostile to the West, or which were staffed by clerics who were personally at war—and in a minority of cases recruiting for war—with the countries whose citizens they had become, what then? Was it possible or right, as was proposed in both France and Holland in 2004, to 'monitor' the sermons of militant Muslim clerics in non-Muslim countries, or to 'compel' mosques to employ only imams educated in their adoptive countries? Or what of the 'ordinary' Muslim who is a citizen only in name, being in retreat from, and ignorance of, the society he or she has nominally joined?

Those with the desire to accuse, insult or even to assault the allegedly 'incorrigible' 'other' did not wait for answers to such questions. They believed they knew the answers, without need either of inquiry or response. As a British government minister crudely put it in November 2003, 'British Muslims must choose between the "British way"' or 'the way of the terrorists, against which the whole democratic world is uniting'. But the words and deeds of Islamists in both the Islamic and non-Islamic worlds have spurred on those who see in every Muslim a potential 'enemy of the state'. At the least they believe they see an individual who is not, who cannot be and who does not even wish to be a full member of the civic and moral order of which he or she is supposedly a part. 'Welcome to the United States of America', declared a 'blogger' in November 2004 on an anti-Islamist Internet site. 'We're a free nation.... You can stay as long as you respect our laws and our citizens. Understand that it's not our responsibility to adapt to your culture. It's your responsibility to adapt to ours. You're in our house, so follow the house-rules'. Or, as the British prime minister put it in August 2005 after the London bombings, 'coming to Britain is not a right. And even when people have come here, staying here carries with it a duty. That duty is to share and support the values that sustain British life'.

This, for increasing numbers in Western liberal societies, is now the whole truth. But it also makes those on the receiving end of such form of instruction vulnerable, especially to 'indigenous' aggressors who are themselves among the least social members of the 'host' society. They too may have no greater a civic (or civilised) ethic—and often less—than those from whose heads they would remove the veil, or would even cudgel from the land. Yet there also cannot be any real surprise at such aggressions. In October 1995, Hassan Turabi, Sudan's then religious leader, declared that British Muslims 'should have their own laws'; a 'British' (but Iranian-backed) Muslim, Kalim Siddiqi, set up a 'Muslim parliament' to 'legislate for the Muslim interest in Britain'. In such instances, and many others of the same type, the implicit claim that a collectivity or community of Muslims settled in a non-Muslim nation constitutes some kind of polity-in-itself is easily seen as both presumptuous and threatening to the civic order.

Muslims in Britain who have demanded Islamic schooling for their children, or want Muslim prayer-times to be accommodated as part of the normal school or working day, have similarly aroused opposition. So, too, have French Muslims who have demanded to set their own rules as to which doctors or teachers they will permit to treat or teach them in French hospitals or schools, or which lessons they will or will not attend and which texts they will or will not read, When a campaigner for separate Muslim schools in Britain openly declared in November 1991 that 'other religions' would be 'presented' in such schools 'only as they are seen through Islam', the spectre of an incorrigible Muslim 'separatism' was again raised. Once more the question of who may, and who may not, justly be regarded as a 'true' citizen hovered over the scene.

In September 1991, government inspectors of three of the (then) few fee-paying independent Muslim schools in Britain—there were more than one hundred by 2005—found a 'strong sense of community', but 'low standards', 'authoritarian methods', a 'narrow range' of reading material, the teaching of little or no science and (in one of the three inspected schools) the teaching of 'Islamic history only'. In May 2004, it was reported that in a Saudi-funded school in west London, opened in 1985—and with more than 700 pupils, over sixty per cent of them children of British Muslims and the rest of Saudi origin—'up to half' of the lessons were devoted to religious education, with only one lesson in six taught in English, and with boys and girls following different curricula. Much the same was found by German education officials in a

Saudi-funded school in Bonn in October 2003. They reported that 'only one or two hours a week' were devoted to learning German, but 'eight or nine hours' to religious instruction, and that of a 'very narrow' kind. Here was further proof for many, if proof were needed, not only of the impossibility of reconciling a 'primitive' with a 'post-Enlightenment' pedagogy in a Western liberal democracy, but of making 'true' citizens of those who would turn their backs upon their adopted nations' history and culture.

This was, and remains, a large subject for hostility, estrangement and confusion. It is especially so, paradoxically, in 'multicultural' societies which have already demoted national histories, national geographies and national faiths—such as they are—from their old primacy, in favour of eclecticisms which are more 'inclusive'. Despite this outward movement towards the embrace of 'the other', the Muslim who implicitly wishes no more than a limited belongingness and sense of obligation to the society in which he or she has settled remains in difficulty. Such individual is held by many to be open to criticism, and even outright rejection, for a political as well as an ethical ambivalence; for seeking to benefit as a citizen from a society's virtues, protections, opportunities and provisions, while contemning that same society—even to the point of extremes of emotional and social withdrawal from it—for the contagion of its vices; for eating his or her cake, and rejecting it at the same time.

This abstraction from the reality of where one is, a serious civic dilemma, can also be absurdly expressed. In January 1989, Aziz al-Azmeh, professor of Islamic Studies at Exeter University, described the 'majority of Muslim folk' in Britain as not only 'crushed by misery, uprootedness and disorientation' and 'confronted by a hostile society and state', but as 'distracted by foul weather' and 'forced to live in cramped and strangely organised houses'. Twelve years later in October 2001, the Islamic revival (and its successful assaults on the non-Islamic world) had carried a minority of Muslims in Britain entirely beyond the restraint of the law of their new domiciles, or even of recognition of its legitimacy for them. An Islamist in Britain—a British citizen, educated at the University of London—could declare to *Agence France Presse* that any Muslim, British or foreign, who wanted to 'get rid of' the British prime minister and the British cabinet, in reprisal for the bombing of Afghanistan, would 'not be punished but praised under Islamic law'. He added that 'government buildings, including 10 Downing Street' were 'legitimate targets'.

Publicised by the media to the increased risk of the Muslim community as a whole, this kind of thing furnished all-too-easily assimilable 'proof' to the anti-Muslim of what he already 'knows', or thinks he knows, about 'Islam'-as-such. He 'knows' that among Muslim 'half-citizens', with one foot in Islam and the other in Britain, Islamic law and ethics necessarily exert greater moral and political influence over the Muslim than do domestic norms and values. He thinks he 'knows', too, that the Muslim 'half-citizen' generally perceives these norms and values to be personally contaminating; and on this ground the former thinks it reasonable that such individual should be treated as a 'half-citizen' at best.

These feelings have become increasingly widespread, even if left unexpressed and unacted upon by the majority. They are feelings which form only a part of the malaise of a 'multicultural' society composed of large numbers of individuals who appear, or have been made to appear, citizens in name only. Moreover, when such notional members of the body-politic can remain citizens while being thought to be silently applauding, and in more extreme cases inviting or even helping to plan, acts of destruction against it, another solvent is added to the already tenuous bonds which sustain the liberal civic order as a whole.

At issue are also such matters as the use of mosques, and Islamic cultural centres, as conduits by which to educate, and in a small minority of cases even to recruit to arms, mental warriors against the very society whose hospitality, educational system and other forms of public provision have helped to nurture them. More generally, the rages expressed in word and deed by Islamism against the non-Islamic world, and against less militant or wholly pacific Muslims, challenge the very premises of a notionally plural, or 'multicultural', civic society. One such Islamist from Luton could declare, to yet another grateful reporter from a British 'quality' newspaper, that 'we Muslims in Britain view supporting the jihad as a religious duty'. 'All of us'—an exaggerated reference to the Muslim men of Luton—'are ready to sacrifice our lives for our beliefs', he added. The speaker, a twenty-two year-old British Muslim accountant, further declared himself 'jealous of Afzal', a fellow-British citizen who had allegedly died fighting with the Taliban, since Afzal had 'reached paradise'. This represented more than the mere right in a free society to hold a dissenting opinion.

For here again was the implicit and contradictory claim both of an entitlement to live in peace in an adoptive homeland, or (more often) now a birthplace, and to enter into a war with it, for some a 'war to end all wars'. To make or to imply such claim is to do three things. It is to invite trouble; it is to object—often on human rights grounds—to such trouble, whether it be encountered in the streets or in the courts; and it is ultimately to rely for protection from such trouble upon the rule of law of the very land against which a jihad or other hostility has been declared.

The British press can be guaranteed to provide headline-entertainments

over all matters of this kind. It did what it could to incite popular odium
against Muslims in Britain for the scale of their (un-shy) sympathy—albeit
registered in unscientific and sensationalist opinion-polls—for bin Laden. It
did the same with the alleged objections of Muslims to Western efforts to hunt
bin Laden down, and with the justifications for a jihad offered in the 'Muslim
street'. Nevertheless, 'Asian' radio stations in Britain themselves announced in
November 2001, for example, that '98 per cent' of London Muslims under the
age of forty-five would 'not fight for Britain' against bin Laden's al-Qaeda, and
that '48 per cent' would take up arms for him.

Milking these 'findings' to the last drop of ink (or blood), a columnist in
the *Sunday Times* declared that 'we now stare into the abyss, aghast'. But this
was no 'abyss'. The 'findings' were simply local and passing soundings in an
already long-standing war of worlds and words. They indicated that many
young British Muslims, making nonsense of 'multicultural' assumptions,
could see little or no virtue in the civic orders to which they had chosen to
belong, and in which they proposed to remain.

Thus, after the London bombings of July 2005, a poll found that almost
'20 per cent' of British Muslims felt 'little or no loyalty' to Britain, and 'over a
quarter' had some sympathy with the motives of those who carried out the
attacks.

As such and other problems—civic, ethical, political—have deepened on
many fronts in the non-Islamic world, most individuals, Muslim and non-
Muslim, have kept their own counsels. Nevertheless, the signs and tokens of
anti-Muslim feeling, polite pretences notwithstanding, are now clear enough.
Muslims know this better than any. When Cardinal Giacomo Biffi of Bologna
declared to three hundred local priests, summoned to his palace in September 2000, that a 'struggle [sc. with Islam] for the soul of Europe' was
under way, and demanded that Italy should issue 'no more entry visas for
Muslims', Christian *caritas* gave way to a *veritas* which others have preferred
to side-step. This verity reflects popular feelings, especially as they are
refracted through the mass media. 'We have to be concerned about saving the
identity of the nation', he added; and when asked if he was conducting a 'new
Crusade', he replied (with, in *The Times*, 'a smile', not unlike the 'smile' on the
face of the Taliban at an amputation), 'I have never had anything against the
word "Crusade" personally'.

This, too, was grim stuff. But it was the stuff of candour, not make-
believe. So also were the political voices which called in Austria and Italy, in
France, Germany and Britain for the rejection of 'multiculturalism' in favour
of a 'Christian society'. Hostility's fangs have been bared, as in France, at the

details of Muslim dress, as others once did—or do—at the 'Jewish gaberdine' and skull-cap, or as Muslims do at the sign of the Cross or of the Star of David, the very sight of which is forbidden in Saudi Arabia.

The stridency of anti-Islamic political rhetoric, especially in Western Europe, has often been striking. It was strident even before the murder in Amsterdam, in broad daylight and in a public place, of the Dutch film-maker Theo van Gogh in November 2004 had given a further boost to ill-feeling. In Belgium, the Vlaams Blok—pronounced an illegal political organisation by Belgium's judges in 2004 for its racist policies—had already declared itself 'fed up with foreigners diluting Belgium's culture'; demanded that they assimilate or leave', that they speak Flemish, that they know the country's history and laws and that they be 'approved by their Flemish neighbours'. When the leaders of the Vlaams Blok were asked whom they meant by 'foreigners', they bluntly replied that their 'targets' were 'non-Europeans, primarily Muslims'.

Denmark's once-tolerant image was also gradually cast to the winds in response to popular feeling. There, a law was passed in May 2002 which forbade anyone under the age of twenty-four from 'living in Denmark with a non-EU spouse'. It was a law whose purpose was principally to deter the large Muslim community's practice of arranging marriages with spouses brought to Denmark from Islamic countries. 'I think Muslims are a problem', declared the leader of the Danish People's Party. The Netherlands and Sweden, long notable for their liberal immigration and asylum positions, increasingly disowned such positions as their impatient electorates turned rightwards. In the Netherlands, the growingly popular (and populist) Pim Fortuyn, later to be assassinated by a non-Muslim, demanded 'an end to Islamic immigration', castigating Islam for its 'backward culture', its treatment of women, its hostility to gays, and the 'illiberalism' of its 'belief-system'. He described the latter as 'incompatible' with Western 'sexual and social freedoms'. Moreover, it did not require anti-Muslim racists to point to this 'incompatibility', since Muslims themselves declare it to be so.

In September 2002 the mayor of New York, Michael Bloomberg, addressed himself by implication both to the 'terrorists' who had attacked the World Trade Center a year earlier and to those who supported them in the United States. Like many Americans, he too was strident upon the subject of the freedoms which he felt had been assailed by the attack, freedoms exploited by the attackers themselves. 'You may use our very freedoms to disguise your evil aims', he proclaimed, 'but you will not shake our faith in or our commitment to those freedoms'. In 2002 also, the far-right British National Party ran a 'Campaign Against Islam', describing it as a 'monster'; Fortuyn declared Holland to be 'under threat' from the 'incursions of Islam'; Cardinal Biffi saw a 'struggle' against Islam 'for the soul of Europe'; and at the other end of the political scale, street-thugs in Britain carried out 'vigilante actions' against Muslims around slogans such as that of 'Rights for Whites'.

The murder of Theo van Gogh took European-wide criticisms of 'multiculturalism' to new heights or depths. Mosques in Holland were firebombed and desecrated, and Muslim community centres—schools also—were vandalised and daubed with graffiti, 'White Power' slogans and neo-Nazi symbols among them; some churches were attacked in reprisal. Arrests were made for the incitement of hatred against Muslims; even an Internet book of condolences for van Gogh had to be closed down after being swamped by anti-Muslim abuse. In the days following the killing, the changed tone of many who had previously held liberal 'multiculturalist' views was also notable. 'None of the unspoken expectations, such as the idea that integration was simply a matter of time, has turned out to be right', declared a Dutch professor of urban sociology. 'The veil of multiculturalism has been lifted, revealing parallel societies where the law of the state does not apply', said Germany's *Der Spiegel*, commenting on the implications of the murder. The 'notion of multiculturalism' had 'fallen apart', pronounced Angela Merkel, the leader of Germany's Christian Democratic Party.

Voices could be heard across Europe complaining of 'closed Muslim communities' which had to be 'broken open', of 'Muslim fascism', of Western liberal societies which had 'elevated their defencelessness into a virtue'. 'We have been too naive', declared the Dutch immigration minister; 'holy war has come to the Netherlands', said the speaker of the Dutch parliament; and 40 per cent of respondents in a Dutch poll expressed the 'hope' that Muslims no longer felt welcome in the country. 'If you choose radical Islam', an increasingly popular right-wing Dutch politician, Geert Wilders, told Dutch Muslims—and received death-threats for it—'you can leave, and if you don't leave voluntarily we will send you away'. Traditions of Dutch tolerance were said to be 'gone'.

'We cannot allow the basis of our commonality to be destroyed by foreigners', similarly declared the German Christian Democrat Joerg Schoenbohm. 'If you are unwilling to adopt German values as your own, you picked the wrong country', exclaimed the premier of Bavaria, Edmund Stoiber. The fall-out of the murder was also felt in Denmark, where the Social Democratic Party's spokeswoman, Anne-Marie Meldgaard, demanded that Muslim party-members condemn Sharia law if they wished to remain in the party. 'If they place Islamic law above our democratic system, they have no business with us', she added. On the other side of the argument, the Amsterdam Council of Churches pledged 'solidarity with Muslims', while still-benign voices called for 'more understanding' by non-Muslims in order to 'win back Muslim trust', and for 'long-term measures to reintegrate Muslims in Dutch society'. For their part, Muslims kept their heads down, or protested that they would not be 'integrated' by compulsion and at the cost of their identity as Muslims. This was another Gordian knot that could not now be untied.

However, intellectual and ethical discrimination is required between the different forms which are taken by anti-Islamic expression and action. Complaining that 'too many' Muslims do not possess an adequate grasp of English, and arguing that it would be in their own interests in Britain to acquire it, is one thing; street violence against Muslims is another. But the underlying hostility that increasingly marks, and links, responses to the Muslim presence in the non-Islamic world is obvious. More awkward for Muslims, such attitude is not seen by those who express it as an initiation of hostility or aggression, but as a *response* to it, as already indicated. Even in the worst and most violent forms of such response, attacks upon Muslims are perceived as counter-attacks provoked by the actions and 'behaviour' of Muslims themselves.

Here, Islamism—both by design and unintended consequence—reaps its own reward. In the first fifty days after 11 September 2001, American human rights workers recorded hundreds of 'reprisal-oriented' attacks on Muslims in the US, ranging from spitting in Muslim faces to murder. An increase in 'hate crimes' against Muslims was also recorded in Britain in the aftermath of the July 2005 bombings; Muslim women were urged by the head of the Muslim College in London to stop wearing the *hijab* if they felt it could lead to their being attacked or abused in public. In the period after 9/11, the 'European Monitoring Centre on Racism and Xenophobia', based in Vienna, had similarly noted a 'significant' increase in abuse, physical assault and property attacks against Muslims. Indeed, Muslims in Australia, Belgium, France, Germany and Sweden, among other countries, have been the object of increasing levels of abuse and assault, and in Russia of internal expulsions from Moscow and other cities.

During the 1991 Gulf War such assaults on persons and property were relatively common. 'Fear of attack' in the British provincial city of Bolton was already being described in April 1990 as the 'Asian' community's 'great unifier'. In March 2003, on the eve of the invasion of Iraq, fears were again expressed that the Muslim community in Britain would be its 'main victims'. As early as 1994—when non-Muslims were themselves growing more afraid of both Islam and Islamism—61 per cent of Turks in Germany were similarly reported to 'live in fear of attack'.

In Britain, 'harassment, ranging from verbal to physical abuse', as well as more serious forms of physical assault, have long been said to be 'a reality' for many 'Asian people'. In Denmark, the Netherlands and Sweden, as also in Britain, verbal abuse of women wearing the *hijab* has for some years been reported to be common. Mistreatment of Muslim prisoners in US jails was reported by the Justice Department's inspector-general in March 2005. But it is in France that police harassments and even police killings of Muslims—in some cases, subsequently attributed to 'mishaps'—have been most frequently noted. Such harassments and violence have in some places been met during the last decade by immigrant (and mainly Muslim) riot, arson and looting, as in Lille, Lyons, St. Etienne and other French cities; in Burnley, Bradford and Oldham in northern England in the summer of 2001; as well as in Antwerp in Belgium in November 2002 after the murder of a Moroccan teacher.

Moreover, when a French Muslim of Berber Algerian birth, Aissa Dermouche, was named as prefect of the eastern Jura region of France in January 2004—the first Muslim to be appointed to the post of prefect, who is responsible for law enforcement and administration on behalf of the central government—bomb-blasts in Nantes, his home city, greeted his appointment. In Britain, graffiti insults against the generic 'Pakis' and the daubing of tombstones must be counted as anti-Muslim odium's smaller change.

Islamist action and anti-Muslim reaction—or anti-Muslim action and Islamist reaction, according to point of view—now pursue one another across a large part of the globe. But this is not merely a vortex in perpetual motion, or a tit-for-tat consequence of clerical or media incitements. A Muslim of the diaspora, the Egyptian Heshem el-Essawy—whom we will re-encounter in a later chapter—complained in 1991 that it was 'sad and ironic that the West notices Islam only when it takes a violent form, when it practises terrorism, carries out a massacre, or launches a rocket. This is terrible. It tells you more about the West than about Islam'. He was wrong. It tells one equally of both, and not sufficient of either. There was also some truth in the assertion—by David Hirst in the *Guardian* in April 1994—that 'the baggage of Western prejudice ... depicts Arabs indiscriminately as bloodthirsty primitives, with an unholy will to carve up Westerners'. But this too did inadequate justice to the multiple roots of this prejudice, prejudice though it remains.

In its politer 'intellectual' versions, Arab and Muslim 'backwardness' will be held to be the outcome of resistance to 'modernisation', 'globalisation', 'secular education' or 'change', a resistance driven by the priority given to Islamic and Koranic values. As with most prejudices, there is truth in it. But the thesis of 'primitivism' continues to underlie such assertions, at the expense of an understanding of the force of the Islamic revival. Italian premier Silvio Berlusconi's simplistic assertion in September 2001 of the 'superiority of Western civilisation' was governed by the same presumptions. Decapitations and disembowellings of captives do not help here. But the 'primitivist' argument again dangerously excludes a true sense of the moral strengths of renascent Islam. They are strengths which much of the non-Muslim world— for reasons provided to it by Islamists themselves, and discussed in the previous chapter—is in general unable to accept as such.

Base judgments often delivered, as is fitting, from the lower depths of the metropolises of the West—depths often unemployed, uneducated and environmentally ravaged—are another matter again. Here, Muslims in particular tend to be seen as 'welfare-scroungers', 'battening upon' public provision—the dole, a council house, a hospital bed and so on. These same public goods are also, often, the only sources of shelter and survival for the local 'indigenous' and 'white' unemployed, and the once-proud ex-working man and woman. In this underworld of the 'under-class', 'insecurity' is a poor term for a complex of circumstances. These circumstances include poverty of many kinds, vulnerability to crime, and paranoia lest the 'other' 'take' what does not rightfully belong to the incomer, or outsider.

Of such uglinesses of life and mind the 'intelligentsia' and the liberal-minded often know relatively little or nothing. It is a nether world, in which 'the Muslim'—like 'the Jew' of the Nazi period—has come to embody that which others require to hate or fear. In this world, the disclosure that Abu Qatada, a West London 'cleric' and alleged leading agent of al-Qaeda, had combined the master-minding of atrocity with the annual collection of thousands of pounds in housing and incapacity benefits—to the tune of having '£180,000' in his bank account, as the popular press headlines announced— reached directly into the gut of street-level anti-Muslim feeling. Without the 'welfare scrounging', he would have been an inaccessibly alien figure bent on sinister purposes beyond reach. With it, his villainy became for the first time a recognisable crime against the state; or against the welfare state, and its self-perceivedly more deserving 'English' dependants. The same applied to the sums, allegedly as high as 'half a million pounds' in total, which were said to have been obtained from the state welfare system by the London suicide-bombers.

It is at this level, and in the hostilities which rest upon it, that the Muslim of the Western liberal diaspora puts himself at greatest risk. It is a hostility which is engaged less with high crimes—treason, for instance—than with the kinds of 'parasitism' of which the Nazis once accused the Jews. Even *The*

Times in April 2000 could write of thousands of 'asylum-seekers' in Calais looking to reach England as their 'golden dream', in the hope of obtaining 'security, housing and the possibility of combining a black economy job with social security benefits'. Moreover, in picking out only one individual to express this aspiration—a twenty-four-year-old Muslim from Kosovo—the newspaper knew what manner of prejudices it was addressing.

These prejudices take 'analytical' as well as populist forms. Hence, you could discover in August 2002 that in Denmark, for instance, 'third-world immigrants, most of them Muslims, constitute 5 per cent of the population but consume upwards of 40 per cent of welfare spending'. Or, in the manner of Nazi propaganda in the 1930s against the Jews, it was ascertained that the Muslim minority in Denmark 'makes up a majority of [its] convicted rapists'. The same type of assertion about Muslims is commonly bandied about in Sweden. It remains the expression of a dangerous ill-feeling, and not less for being larded out with statistics. When coupled with the notion that potential or actual foes are simultaneously 'living on the generosity of the British people', as a London magistrate put it in March 2000, it is a potent mix. It also fits comfortably into a paranoid schema. It is that of the 'fifth column'. Indeed, in New York's *City Journal* in the autumn of 2001, the Muslim community in Britain was described precisely so by the Indian writer Farrukh Dhondy. Such 'fifth column' is one which is presented as exclusively Muslim, as wishing ill upon all non-Muslims and as therefore having no moral compunction in using and abusing its citizenship to the limit.

There have been some, both Muslim and non-Muslim—among them a former archbishop of Canterbury, Robert Runcie, in August 1989, and Professor Akbar Ahmed of Cambridge in January 1991—who have chosen to describe the governing attitude to 'the Muslim' and to Islam as one of 'ridicule'. Ridicule plays its part, but more than ridicule is at work. The suggestion that the Muslim is a 'fifth columnist', or an idle 'scrounger' or a rapist of flaxen-haired Danish and Swedish virgins is not 'ridicule'.

Instead, a hostile structure of perceptions of the Muslim and of Islam—some of great antiquity, such as that associated with 'invasion' of the West by Muslims—has been built, and in some cases re-built, in European culture. Much of this has been invited by Islamism itself, as I have pointed out. Indeed, many of the latter's acts are of so dire a kind that Muslims themselves, especially those who by their silences and evasions suggest (often wrongly) that what is done by Islamism in Islam's name has their moral assent, are in an ever weaker position to object to the ways in which they are perceived.

Thus, for 'bin Laden's agenda' to be described (falsely) as 'demented', or for the Nobel laureate V. S. Naipaul to speak of the 'madness in the Islamic world', cannot now be complained of with much plausibility by Muslims themselves. Moreover, insulting references to Muslims inevitably come to manifest as little moral restraint as do the acts of some Muslims themselves. Both grow in extremity, and dangerously step-by-step. In the *Independent* in July 1989, Muslim women were described as 'one step above a slave, two steps above a camel'; in 1997, 'underneath their false sheep's clothing', Muslims were held by a Canadian evangelical Protestant to be 'raging wolves seeking whom they may devour'; by 2002, for the hyper-ventilating Italian author Oriana Fallaci, they had come—shamefully—to 'multiply like rats' and to 'piss in baptismal fonts'; and in October 2003, they were described by Lieutenant-General William Boykin, the US Army's deputy under-secretary of defence for intelligence (no less), as 'worshipping an idol'.

These are merely wars of words, but they are often as belligerent as the aggressions and counter-aggressions of the battlefields of arms. This is so whether such words are inscribed in the pages of a popular Western newspaper, or are delivered by a Muslim cleric who denounces the 'infidel', the 'Crusader' and the Jew from the pulpit. Seemingly minor conflicts between Muslim and non-Muslim on the home-front may be as bruising as any other type of wartime encounter, and of equal import in the long run. Much is at stake when the sub-text of domestic conflict with Muslims is the issue of the entitlement to civic rights of those who are held to be 'separatist' in spirit. Other sources of home-front ill-feeling have to do with such matters as the scant regard sometimes shown by Muslims for local scruple, or the related disregard shown by non-Muslims for the sensibilities of Muslims among them.

Hackles may be raised by what are perceived to be insensate Muslim demands expressed in peremptory or clod-hopping fashion. These have included demands for the meeting of particularist needs of a kind which other 'ethnic minorities' have not sought in the past, and which non-Muslims in Islamic lands could not seek at all. In March 1989, the director of the Muslim Educational Trust in Britain, Ghulam Sarwar, 'insisted' (without success) to the Department of Education that Arabic, Bengali, Hindi and Urdu be included in the 'priority group' of languages to be offered in secondary schools under the national curriculum, alongside eight languages spoken in the European Union. In Belgium, likewise, the 'Arab European League' called in 2002 for Arabic to be recognised as a fourth official language, alongside French, Dutch and German. In France, in 2003, Muslim leaders called for paid days-off on Islamic holidays; in Italy, also in 2003, the president of the Italian Union of Muslims objected—as a matter of his 'constitutional rights'—to the presence of crucifixes on the classroom-walls of the state elementary school attended by his children.

The same form and manner of moral claim—with complaint of 'discrimination' when it is refused—characterised the 'sit-down protests' by Asian parents inside a Birmingham school in September 1989, after the city council had appointed an education liaison-officer who could not speak Urdu. Seventy per cent of the parents involved were from Mirpur, in the Urdu-speaking and Pakistani-controlled part of Kashmir. The chairman of the school's governing body, Mohammed Yussouf, also objected that although the school's pupils were 'virtually all Asian', the great majority of their teachers were not. A Muslim parent joined the press fray, complaining (again in insensate mode) that his wife, along with 'lots of other parents', being unable to speak English, would be unable to communicate with their liaison-officer. A Tory government minister's tough response to this fracas—that the protesting parents 'should learn English'—was then hot-headedly taken as evidence of 'racism'.

From one point of view these are no more than Clochemerles, or local sound-and-fury signifying nothing. From another, they may be said to merit close consideration for what they reveal about the problems of a 'plural' culture. Matthew Arnold would have regarded them as important, and with reason. Moreover, demand upon demand of related cultural kind has been made across the decades of Muslim migration and settlement. They have been decades of Islam's growing arousal, and of the increasing confidence among Muslims as to their entitlement in the non-Muslim world. Such arousal, confidence and demand have also coincided with the widening influence of the politics of 'human rights', a fortuitous development both for Muslim and Islamist causes.

What of a 'demand for 'mother-tongue' teaching in Lancashire schools in April 1990? Or the removal by Muslim parents of their children from a Church of England primary school in September 1990 in protest that the school, near Manchester, was failing to meet their needs for 'Islamic teachings and values'? Or accusations (by the Committee for Bangladeshis' Rights in the United Kingdom), also in September 1990, that a London borough's bureaucracy was 'racist' for failing to recruit Sylheti-speaking teachers who 'understand Bangladeshi culture and history'? These were not only matters for a latter-day Arnold, but symptoms of a much wider ferment: the ferment of an intensifying Islamic (and Islamist) consciousness, and one ready for head-on engagement with those who stood in its way. Furthermore, for some Muslims the price to be paid in hostility was clearly a matter of indifference.

Demands for state-funded Muslim schools in Britain, and complaints of 'racism' made when these and other demands were refused, have led to many exchanges of asperities on both sides of the argument, and sometimes to fisticuffs, boycotts and writs. In these domestic wars, not arms or bombs but verbal abuse, the pillorying of officialdom, the forcing of resignations, the demanding of 'inquiries' and occasionally the uttering of death-threats have been among the weapons of conflict. In an East London dispute of great intensity in 1992, a female head-teacher was accused—falsely, as it turned out—of 'intimidation', 'racism' and even 'assault' upon a Muslim faction-leader. Members of the National Association of Head Teachers, which defended her, were declared by a certain Muhammed Haque to be 'liars' and, again, 'racists'. The Muslim governors of the school at the centre of the conflict were dismissed from their posts by the Education Secretary; the Education Secretary was in turn denounced by Haque as a 'bully boy' who was 'behaving like a colonialist'; the minister, Haque declared, could not 'force' Muslim protesters into 'submission'.

This culture-war in education, or *kulturkampf*—which has deserved more careful attention than it has been given—has been a fierce one. The angers it has generated, often knowingly on both sides, have been acute. Some militant Muslims and some hostile non-Muslims have perceived such contests as matters of cultural life and death. It was an additional irony that non-Muslim 'multiculturalists' have sometimes been more in favour of 'separatist' educational provision for Muslims—as in state-funded Muslim schools—than were many Muslims themselves. Equally, in March 1992, when the (Iranian-supported) British 'Muslim Parliament' 'demanded' state subsidies for 'religious and moral instruction by mosques'—aid which was provided in certain other European countries—warier Muslims felt this was a demand too far. The related demand for state-aided, single-sex Islamic schools has commanded wider, but nevertheless still minoritarian, Muslim support in Britain and elsewhere; by June 2004, there were still only five state-funded Muslim schools in the British education system.

In making a demand for them, Islamists in Britain—a minority among a minority, but capable of striking majoritarian poses—had been ready to push their case to extremes, courting anti-Islamic hostility with the same relish as that with which the mass media fan any available flame. These Islamic schools, their supporters declared in March 1992, would not merely be schools 'with an Islamic ethos'—no more or less objectionable, depending upon point of view, than schools with a Catholic or Jewish 'ethos'—but would also 'avoid a primarily Eurocentric perspective' in teaching the national curriculum. In an Islamic school in Britain, it was stated, the First World War would be renamed the 'First European War'—despite the engagement in it of the Ottoman Empire. There would also be other 'adjustments' of perspective and curriculum content.

Although minoritarian, such Islamist candour of intent was a serviceable because instructive thing. For here was a larger matter for disputation than issues to do with school uniform for Muslim girls, or with the ethically-dictated refusal of mixed-sex physical education and swimming lessons, or with the wearing of a headscarf in class. Now, Islamists were objecting to what they (and their non-Muslim supporters) called a 'primarily Eurocentric perspective' in teaching in Britain. What was required instead was the teaching of a 'primarily' Islamic, or Islamist, worldview to the Muslim citizens of a European nation. From one standpoint it was a gratuitous further provocation of anti-Islamic sentiment. From another, it was well calculated both to appeal to, and to unsettle, 'indigenous' 'multiculturalists', many of whom have a distaste for their own history and their own cultural traditions. But as public policy began to change in the wake of the London bombings, the British government, far from conceding Islamist demands, in August 2005 proposed to bring under state supervision the over one hundred independent Muslim schools in order to exert control over the curricula being taught in them.

In 1984, in Bradford, an earlier round of fierce conflict had taken place over what should and should not be taught in those British schools which had a high proportion of 'Asian' children on their rolls. Here, the 'multicultural' intentions of the local education authority, seeking to satisfy the cultural needs of 'Asian' school pupils—often without such needs being expressed, and sometimes against the wishes of 'Asian' parents themselves—were met by the intransigence of a headmaster, who was ultimately removed in a storm of ill-feeling on all sides.

The headmaster, Ray Honeyford, refused to truckle to what he regarded as a 'highly tendentious race lobby' which mobilised against him, with many Muslims among its leaders. He declared with notable firmness and some belligerence that it was 'not the job' of English schools to 'preserve and transmit' what he called 'immigrant culture'; colourfully denounced 'multiculturalism' as 'the work of post-imperial liberal guilt'; and stated that 'the price to be paid for emigration to Britain' was the 'pain of change and adaptation'. And so saying, 'the English language' was proclaimed by Honeyford—as (multicultural) protest processions marched against him in the streets of Bradford—to be 'the key to every child's future, Asian and non-Asian, in Britain'.

His opponents, Muslim and non-Muslim, would have none of this. He was 'forcing Asian children to accept the majority culture'; and his view that a mastery of the English language and a knowledge of Britain were the true needs of 'Asian' pupils—a very large majority in his school—was held to be no more than a 'camouflage' for 'racism'. The local authority refused him its support, and Honeyford departed his post. Two years later, a Bristol teacher who had the temerity openly to support Honeyford's pedagogical, cultural or 'racist' positions was himself told not to return to his school, since his colleagues 'no longer wished to work with him'.

The 'battle of Bradford' and the arguments, hostilities and outcome of it, were again of high Arnoldian importance. For here was a seminal conflict, on a domestic front of the war of the worlds, in which a local form of Islamism was a protagonist in the battle. At its heart were notions that there is a 'distinctive British cultural heritage'; that such 'cultural heritage' is an obligation of British teachers to pass on; and that their pupils—whatever their origins—need to have knowledge of it if they are to make their way in Britain.

Against these notions was pitted the view that to attempt to disseminate such knowledge to children of different cultural origins was to promote a 'divisive, monolingual, discriminatory, unfair, unlawful, undemocratic, backward-looking and partial education', as it was put by one of the directors of the Commission for Racial Equality in December 1988. Honeyford himself declared that he was 'colour-blind'. But in a confused and disorientated liberal society his view of matters was rejected, his headship lost.

Equally important, Muslim agitation confidently rode out the anti-Muslim feeling provoked by it. Muslims believed that, with Honeyford's defeat, they had gained their 'rights': the 'right' to refuse whatever did not meet their view of their cultural needs; the 'right' to choose whether to tolerate or to reject values which were being attempted to be transmitted, as by a Honeyford, through the state education system; and the 'right' to expect support from non-Muslims in identifying their opponents in this culture-war as 'racists'. In the 1980s it was support which in Bradford, and beyond, they gained to a decisive degree.

While (mainly) Muslims were locking horns with Honeyford and with his view of educational purposes in Britain in one part of Yorkshire, in another—Dewsbury—'white' parents were refusing to send *their* children to a school 85 per cent of whose children were 'Asian'. In addition, they had taken the council to court for failing to allocate their offspring to predominantly 'white' state schools of their choosing. Here was a further outbreak of cultural hostility and conflict between 'whites' and 'Asians' to which a Matthew Arnold would have given his attention. This time, however, the initiative for the confrontation had come from the other side of the barricades, where 'white' parents—whose position was the mirror-image of that of Muslim activists in

Bradford—were demanding that their children be educated 'in a traditional English and Christian environment'.

This was the very 'environment' which Honeyford had wished to provide for 'Asian' and English pupils alike. Six months later in Wakefield, again in Yorkshire, battle erupted over the same desire on the part of one family to avoid a majority 'Asian' school. 'We are not racist', they declared, 'we are a Christian Church of England family and we want a traditional, Christian, English education for our children'. They did not want their own young child 'taught to speak and write her name in Punjabi', they added. In a more ignorant version of this objection, 'I don't think it's right when she comes home singing in Pakistan [*sic*]', said another mother about her daughter.

As in the wider war of the worlds, there were thus many cross-currents in these local conflicts. The official ethos of 'multiculturalism' notwithstanding, both 'white' and 'Asian' parents could be found insisting on their own particularisms. Indeed, the concept of a 'British cultural heritage' had become for many, both 'Asian' and 'British', a particularism itself. Teachers like Honeyford who insisted upon a 'British education' in Britain, regardless of the native or home culture of the pupil, tended to go to the wall. And in schools with a large majority of 'Asian'—or, in effect, mainly Muslim—pupils, pressures also grew, often propelled by Muslim school governors, for such schools to become exclusively Muslim institutions, but state-funded. The ruling assumptions of the time might be 'multiculturalist'. But as a consequence of mutual antipathy, accident of catchment-area and particularist cultural demands, a *de facto* educational apartheid was being 'spontaneously' created, by choice or by demand. The choice or demand might be mosque-supported and Islamist, or (allegedly) Christian 'racist'. Yet the desired cultural outcome of such seemingly opposed choices—separation—did not materially differ.

Nevertheless, the actual outcomes did differ, and discrimination against Muslims in arriving at the decisions was clear. White parents who had sought the help of the law in extracting their children from allocation to predominantly 'Asian' schools were generally victorious. Muslim parents—by the many hundreds in one or two towns—who temporarily withdrew their children from the system in the 'struggle' to secure an Islamic education in all-Muslim schools, failed. Tory education ministers declared that the core of the study of history in all schools should be the history of Britain; but agitated 'multiculturalists' maintained that a 'concerted assault' was being mounted upon the 'cultural and religious traditions of minority groups'.

Some Muslims argued that they were being expected to compromise, and even abandon, their values by having their children educated (in a non-Muslim land) in non-Muslim institutions. Injunctions to the Muslim community to 'learn English and recognise where you are' were met by injunctions to the faithful from the Muslim pulpit to 'remain Muslims or lose your souls'. Muslims were also accused of possessing an 'unhealthy ghetto mentality', an accusation with undertones of older objections levelled at Jews. Yet for Muslims, this same 'mentality' was dictated by the felt need for self-protection against the contagions of a culture of which many not merely disapproved but to which they were opposed on principled grounds, those of faith and its value-system.

The battles of the 1980s in Britain have not been resolved because they cannot be. Instead, they repeat themselves in one form or another. Muslims' sense of their rights in the non-Islamic world has grown stronger; by 2005, in the earlier-mentioned town of Dewsbury—from which one of the London suicide-bombers came—an independent 'Islamic academy', catering to 'children, teenagers and young adults', had been set up by a Dewsbury-born Muslim teacher. He was an open advocate of 'physical jihad' who, according to *The Times* in July 2005, was allegedly telling parents that they betrayed their children if they allowed them to associate with non-Muslims. In addition, the proneness of many Muslims to detect racist insult or offence against Islam is quicker off the mark; the confusions of non-Islamic societies over their own value-systems have become more profound; and disillusion with 'multiculturalism', even among the liberal-minded, has deepened. Moreover, political invocations to a sense of 'common citizenship' have diminishing weight as the numbers, and proportions, of Muslims in the non-Islamic world increase. The insistence that incomers to Britain adhere to what the Home Secretary in December 2001 called 'norms of acceptability' now has less chance than ever of being attended to by Muslims as the war of the worlds spreads.

Indeed, many Muslims now believe themselves to be entitled to moral autonomy in non-Islamic countries. This belief is itself an expression of the force of the Islamic 'reawakening' in the world. On the wider stage, and despite their divisions, it has given Muslims (Arabs included) feelings of potency in relation to an uncertain non-Islamic world, whose own divisions, fears and doubts are such that a free and competitive media could not conceal them even if it wished to. Moreover, Western social and 'human rights' policies have provided impetus for the sense of special Muslim entitlement in non-Muslim nations.

Moral recoil from racism has also made for many special efforts in Britain to compensate for the disadvantages of the incomer. Later to be objected to as insufficient—when the Muslims' sense of entitlement had grown—these efforts included the much-mocked impulse in the 1980s to provide 'race-awareness' training for teachers and other public administrators, in order to counter racist discrimination against both Afro-Caribbeans and 'Asians'. Among the latter, it was generally held that Pakistanis, the catch-all 'Pakis' of racist abuse, were the largest category of victims.

In 1987, the cross-party Home Affairs Committee of the House of Commons called for a statutory duty on local authorities to make English-language teaching available to all immigrant adults who wanted it. Special funding was likewise recommended for the nursery education of children from 'linguistic minorities'. The committee also approved the teaching of Bengali in schools on the grounds that it promoted the 'parallel learning of English'. Two years later, the Adult Literacy and Basic Skills Unit again called for greater funding of language courses, in particular for (mainly Muslim) Bengali and Urdu speakers. They were described as 'experiencing the greatest difficulty', while the 'cost in human terms' of 'neglect' of the problem was called 'staggering'.

On other fronts, local authorities in various parts of the country were providing *halal* food in schools by the late 1980s, had appointed interpreters to social service departments and were providing land, building grants and permissions for mosques, Muslim cultural centres and Muslim youth clubs, often against local opposition. In teacher-recruitment in London, for instance, there was also discovered to be what was called 'institutional racism' as early as March 1988. (It was a problem which was rediscovered a decade later—this time in the British police force.) 'Anti-racist awareness training', Government-funded language education, appointment of liaison-officers and interpreters, and multilingual information services in hospitals and in other sectors of public provision have all been part of this effort.

Yet 'anti-Muslim behaviour' continued to be denounced, with and without justice, by Muslim organisations. It was said to exist, for example, among 'pupils, teachers, governors, heads and local authority representatives on school governing bodies'. Not in doubt is that offences to Muslim religious sensibilities—the most serious being those provoked by the Rushdie case, from 1989 onwards—often cut across the hopes of well-intentioned non-Muslims, or the naive, for 'greater understanding'. Mutual antagonisms deepened in the uproar over *The Satanic Verses* while voices of pacification were lost in a babel of accusations. Islamist fervour and hostility towards Muslims advanced together, their need of one another ever more obvious.

Notwithstanding all the financial grants, proliferating 'programmes' of special aid and so on, the inequality—in law and life—which affects Muslims in Britain and elsewhere in Europe has also been clear. The extension of the English law of blasphemy to protect Islam from vilification was refused by the courts in 1990; the rate of unemployment among Muslims has been discovered in many European countries to be persistently higher, and often sharply higher, than among other minorities; claims that 'Asian' children were being 'dumped' in under-subscribed schools in Britain with poor standards—from which 'white' parents had fled in the fashion earlier described—were rejected by the High Court in 1993.

A decade later, Pakistanis and Bangladeshis in Britain were still found by researchers to be disproportionately unemployed, as the result both of discriminatory 'exclusion' from jobs and by their own choice, and often received low pay when in work. In February 2002, less than a fifth of Bangladeshi women were reported to be economically active; Muslim youth unemployment—a pool of recruitment to Islamism's angers—was as high as 50 per cent in some English towns, and as high as 70 per cent in some parts of France. In the Muslim community in Britain it is also believed, again with some justification, that there is disproportionate custodial sentencing of Muslims by the courts and that young Muslims convicted of criminal offences tend to be given longer sentences in gaol than are others. An increasing rate of street-searches of 'Asians' by the British police—like the increased 'profiling' of Muslims in America—was also reported after both the 9/11 and the London attacks. In a poll conducted in the United States in December 2004, no fewer than 44 per cent of respondents believed that the civil liberties of Muslim Americans should be curtailed. But when a bill was introduced in the House of Commons in June 2005 to do the opposite—to protect Muslim sensibilities and to prevent 'incitement to racial and religious hatred'—it was itself condemned by civil libertarians as a limitation upon freedom of speech and opinion.

Nevertheless, the notion that Islam is a threat and that Muslims are inherently 'separatist' and potentially violent weighs heavily against the interests of the diaspora Muslim. This is so whatever be his or her individual religious and political standpoint. In January 1991, the co-editor of the *Muslim News*, Musadiq Dhalla, had already declared it to be 'strange and inequitable' that while the representative Jewish body in Britain, the Board of Deputies, was 'seen as being acceptable', 'Muslim equivalents' were 'derided'—the 'mockery' thesis again—'as separatist in nature'.

It is a sense that diaspora Muslims cannot now live down. Furthermore, long before Islamist attacks upon the non-Islamic world had (for some) discredited Muslim values as such, the 'exclusion' of Muslims for their own perceived exclusivism had already cost Muslims much in Britain. Moreover, the intensest cultural battle has often been over education, as has already been shown. For it is here, in the question of what will be the value-system of future generations of European-born Muslim citizens, that the hopes of the 'assimilationist' and the fears of the pious collide. For example, as Akbar Ahmed put it in August 1990, 'while other religious groups are able to maintain their cultural identity through their own schools Muslims are discouraged from doing so', the reigning 'multiculturalist' orthodoxy of the 1980s and 1990s notwithstanding. Indeed, it is another minor irony that in Belgium, for example, it is the extreme right which has wanted Muslims educated in separate schools, its motive that of drawing a cultural ring-fence around an educational ghetto for Muslims.

Muslims have protested that they constitute the 'largest religious minority in the United Kingdom', as they are. There are some seven times more Muslims in Britain than there are Jews. Yet the argument for the discriminatory (or 'racist') refusal of Muslim demands has been made painfully, or unjustly, clear: 'Catholic, Protestant or Jewish children', declared *The Times* in November 2001, 'will not return from school to a home life which is also physically or culturally divided from most other parts of society'. That is, the reconciliation of Islamic demands with a supposedly liberal and 'pluralist' order was held, paradoxically, to be impossible to attain.

This was a moderate version of a more pugnacious 'progressive' or 'left' argument which has been heard at least since the 1980s, including from Muslim feminists. It is one in which 'separatism' is rejected on the grounds that it is intended by some Muslim community leaders as a means of promoting 'reactionary' and, in particular, 'patriarchal' Muslim values. In April 1989, the few permissions then being given by British authorities for the creation of separate Muslim schools were described as 'capitulation to the increasingly fundamentalist power of the mullahs'; or as 'backing the mullahs against the legitimate and legal rights of Muslim women'; or, by the head of the Inner London Education Authority, as the creation of 'educational apartheid in Muslim schools, to which very few non-Muslim parents are likely to want to send their children'.

Indeed, research findings showed that the great majority of Muslim girls, and half of all Muslim parents, themselves did not want single-sex Islamic schools, whether state-funded or independent. Islamists persisted in their demands. A London Muslim schoolteacher, Iftikhar Ahmed, asserted in November 1991 that non-Islamic schools were 'not suitable for our children', since in such schools they 'learn nothing [*sic*] but to question the fundamentals of our religion'. Contrarily, leading 'liberal' Muslims, such as the principal of the Muslim College in London, Zaki Badawi, declared themselves against the 'ghettoising of the Muslim community', holding that separate schooling would be a 'disaster for our children'.

But the growing strength of the Islamic sense of collective identity in the world has survived all that has been thrown against it. The education and experience of Muslims in non-Muslim societies has confirmed, rather than undermined, such sense of identity. Despite the backsliding of a minority of Muslim youth, the hostility felt by the majority of the younger generation of European Muslims towards the non-Muslim world has also been held in place by 'Islamophobia' itself, just as anti-Semitism helps confirm the identity of Jews. Whether it be in the countries of Muslim settlement, or in the wider theatres of battle which have been joined among Muslims and between Muslims and others, this process of action and reaction cannot now be halted.

On the home-fronts of Western liberal democracies, 'multiculturalists' have been hoist with their own petards. Having espoused parity of esteem between one culture or faith and another, they find themselves faced, in Islam's case, with the judgment made by many Muslims that only a form of moral and cultural 'apartheid' can safeguard it. Moreover, a 'multicultural' educational philosophy which encourages children to look at the world's religions 'objectively', or as mere 'subjects of study', is itself offensive to devout Muslims. What such Muslims have demanded, as the *Independent* paraphrased their position as long ago as February 1989, is the transmission of the 'dictates of Islam' 'without criticism' and by 'committed Muslim teachers'.

In all this there has been a dialogue between the deaf. It is a dialogue in which one participant, gulled by wishful thinking, has aspired to be amiably accepted by the 'other' in a benignly 'inclusive' and plural order. But the 'other' increasingly rejects such incorporation, and asserts the 'right' to choose whether or not to accept the extended hand of a society perceived to be in turn increasingly hostile to Islam, as Islam is hostile to it. This has increased the dilemmas of those who seek to do the best they can in the name of social peace or good 'race relations', at the same time as the sense of Islamic 'separatism' deepens.

Existing patterns of insult and offence given to Islam and to Muslims in the non-Islamic world are also being continuously reinforced. In 2001, the French writer Michel Houellebecq thus described Islam as the 'stupidest of religions'—itself a foolish judgment—declaring that 'when you read the Koran you give up'. He even has the main character in his novel *Plateforme* say that he experiences a 'frisson' of pleasure each time a 'Palestinian terrorist is killed'. In August 2002, a Fox News 'talk-show host', Bill O'Reilly, described the requirement at the University of North Carolina that incoming students read an academic study of the Koran as comparable with 'teaching *Mein Kampf* in 1941'. Islam, he added, is 'our enemy's religion'. There has also been intemperate and vulgar insult of the prophet Mohammed by American television evangelists, by Baptist pastors, by leading British media commentators and others.

Expressions of contempt for the creed of Islam in the last decades have not been the work of non-Muslims alone. Indeed, the Islamic 'reawakening' could be said to have stimulated conflict not only on the battlefield of arms and bombs but in intellectual and literary arenas also: a sign of life. Giving great offence, it was a Muslim, Salman Rushdie, who had a character in his fiction named the Prophet 'Mahound', as Mohammed was called in mediaeval Christian caricature. Exercising his freedom as a writer, Rushdie also permitted an invented fictional character to give the name of 'The Curtain'—or *hijab*, the female veil of modesty—to a brothel, each of whose inmates is further given the identity of one of the Prophet's wives. In similar mode, although it remains that of fiction not fact, he suggests that it was Satan, rather than the Angel Gabriel, who dictated the Koran to the Prophet; and, lest there be any mistake about it, Rushdie made this suggestion the title of his book, *The Satanic Verses*.

The violent acts of armed Islamism have often seemed to non-Muslims also to be works of the Devil, at least metaphorically so. That the Koran itself should have been denoted thus by a Muslim was another matter. Those who sought to protect Salman Rushdie from an ayatollah's death-sentence—or from one brutishness directed against another, in the characteristic fashion of so many inter-Muslim disputes—correctly pointed out that his novel had not called the Prophet himself a devil, nor had in terms called his wives whores. They explained, on the author's behalf, that all is made a fantasy in the fiction's structure, and even a dream within a dream; and that fiction is not fact. Nevertheless, on that front where Islam is engaged in a war with itself, as well as with the 'infidel', there was a heavy exchange of fire.

In return for the calculation and pungency with which the recoil from Islam was expressed in his book, an Iranian *fatwa*, in this case a sentence of death, was pronounced against its author, and a cruel bounty repeatedly offered for his head. There are few in modern times who have troubled to ascribe the Hebraic Pentateuch or the Christian Gospels to the Devil's hand; and if they did, few Jews or Christians would be greatly ruffled, or be ruffled for long. Nor would the author of such a notion have a contract taken out on his life. But the insult to Islam and to Muslims offered by *The Satanic Verses* was real. This was not least because—or particularly because—it was an 'apostate' Muslim's work.

Compounding the author's problems, some Christian leaders joined in the witch-hunting of him. To the archbishop of Lyons, Cardinal Decourtray—who, in common with most Muslims, had not troubled to read the book—it was an 'offence against religious faith' as such. Billy Graham, the American evangelist, declared against it. Christian scholars—many of them, doubtless, closet 'Islamophobes' themselves—shed crocodile tears over the hurt done to Muslim sensibilities by *The Satanic Verses*. 'Those in the West who have no religious belief', opined one, 'are oblivious to the depth of pain caused to those who have [such belief]'. Of this kind of sententiousness there was no shortage.

Many, or most, Jewish intellectuals objected more to the *fatwa* than to the novel, or did not object to the novel at all. But there were Jews—and Japanese—who took insulted Islam's side. The writer John Berger, describing his fellow-novelist's work as 'irresponsible', expressed his sympathy for those who 'lived by a book', the Koran, which 'has helped, and still helps, many millions of people to make sense of their lives and their mortality'. The Japanese foreign minister objected to the *fatwa,* but thought that 'proper consideration' had not been given by Rushdie to the feelings of the 'Islamic people'. As could have been expected, only a minority of Muslims sought to pass a considered literary—rather than an outraged religious judgment—on a book which they generally could not bring themselves to read. They consigned it to outer darkness, or to the flame, without soiling their minds or harming their souls by examining the work itself. To the Inayatullah Zaigham (of Gravesend in Kent) the book was a 'prostitution of intellect'; to the Bishop of Bradford, with Muslim book-burners at large in his own city's streets, it was no more than a 'fairly crude piece of work'; to Berger, it was a 'rather arrogant fiction which would be forgotten in a few years'.

Other intelligences took more care with, but also did more harm to, the author's claims to innocence of intent. Such care was warranted, since insult to Islam is a serious business. In February 1990 Bhiku Parekh, a professor of political theory at Hull University and leading figure in the 'race relations industry', perilously wanted to know why, in what was presented as (and is) a fiction, Rushdie had remained 'so recognisably close to historical facts which they [sc. Muslims] remember and recite daily'. Why, he asked, was the writer's 'level of abstraction' 'so low', a telling question. Parekh also wanted to know 'what gives the artist the right to plunder and reduce the deepest experiences and memories of a community' to 'raw material to be used as he pleases.... They deserve answers'. To questions of this quality Rushdie could give, and gave, no coherent responses.

Also in February 1990, the British Muslim writer Shabbir Akhtar took matters quite beyond Rushdie's intellectual reach. 'The mockery'—the 'mockery thesis' once more—in *The Satanic Verses* was not only 'unprincipled' in a Muslim but 'uniformly supercilious', 'dismissive' and 'shallow'. There was 'nothing' in the work which helped to 'bring traditional Islam into a fruitful confrontation with modernity, nothing that brings it into thoughtful contact with contemporary secularity and ideological pluralism'. This might be regarded as a criticism made more from cunning than for truth's sake, but it was unanswerably to the point. For the book was published in a period of the increasingly rapid advance of the Arab and Islamic revivals, and of their growing challenges to the non-Islamic world. In such context, *The Satanic Verses* could be seen as having been little more than a blunt instrument of further insult to Islam at a time of great moral and political intricacy (and growing violence) in the relations between Muslims and non-Muslims, and among Muslims themselves.

Muslims took near-universal offence, able to unite in a cause which transcended their internal divisions. Their organisations in Britain expressed 'anguish', 'bitterness' (even 'permanent bitterness'), 'suffering' and 'hurt' at what had been inflicted upon them by a 'blasphemous' and 'obscene' book. The knowledge that hundreds of thousands of copies of it had been sold in many languages did not help. 'You have vilified, quite gratuitously, those who are dearest to me, dearer to me than my own life', cried a typical and despairing Muslim voice, addressing himself through the press to the terrified author, now in hiding.

In all alleged 'crimes' the question of intent, or *mens rea*, is central to determining the culpability of a defendant. On the instant, some asserted that Rushdie's was an 'intentional blasphemy'. That is, he had set out with malice aforethought, and intellectually armed, to commit 'blasphemy' and had carried out his purpose. It was a position adopted by some censorious (and again sententious) non-Muslims, as well as by most Muslims themselves. Other non-Muslims, more numerous, argued in different ways but to the same moral conclusion that Rushdie 'must have known' what the effects of his work would be; or, as in the case of André Frossard in *Le Figaro*, that it was 'illogical' of the author implicitly to criticise Muslims for their propensity to 'violent reactions', to 'wound them in their deepest convictions' and 'then complain about the consequences'.

To similarly harmful effect for Rushdie—and arguing like a Muslim—Berger held that the writer had 'knowingly defiled the Holy of Holies'. In an 'open letter to Salman Rushdie' in February 1990, and hot-under-the-collar on wounded Islam's behalf, Michael Dummett, an Oxford professor of philosophy, likewise told Rushdie, 'You protest the falsity of the accusation "He must have known", but I incline to think that, if you really did not grasp the offence you would give to believing Muslims, you were not qualified to write upon the subject you chose'.

This proposition was an entire *non-sequitur*, but in his agitation even an Oxford logician was capable of it. However, the issue of Rushdie's 'knowing-ness' remained. And here the writing was on the wall, or on the page, in the book itself. For Rushdie's fictional *alter ego*, 'Salman the Persian'—to whom Rushdie ascribes the blasphemies in his fiction—is actually made to anticipate death at the hands of the Prophet for his offensive words. 'Your blasphemy, Salman, can't be forgiven', Rushdie has the Prophet declare, as sentence is pro-nounced against 'Salman the Persian'—a *fatwa* before-the-fact. 'Do you think I wouldn't work it out? To set your words against the Words of God', the Prophet declares. 'Why are you sure he will kill you?' Rushdie has his char-acter Baal similarly ask of 'Salman the Persian' a few pages earlier. 'It's his Word against mine', 'Salman the Persian' (and Salman Rushdie) reply.

It could thus be argued that, far from being 'unknowing', Rushdie's antic-ipation of punishment for what he had written was among the most imagina-tive aspects of the work. Indeed, on the penultimate page of *The Satanic Verses*, another *alter ego* of the author—with the variant first name of 'Salahuddin'—is described as 'thinking... about how he was going to die for his verses'. More revealing still, 'Salahuddin', writes Rushdie, 'could not find it in himself to call the death-sentence unjust'.

In other words, the consequences of writing *The Satanic Verses*—including the accusation of 'blasphemy' and the death-sentence visited upon the author—were foreseen by the author himself (in fictionalised form), even to the extent of finding such death-sentence just. Here, therefore, was neither naivete nor 'unknowingness'. Yet his authorial act could have been considered a capital offence only under Islamic law, and even that was to became a sub-ject of dispute among Muslims. Nevertheless, it remained a case of gratuitous insult, consciously given, to Muslims. Its only true distinctiveness from the ordinary run of anti-Islamic acts, apart from the presentation of it in literary guise, was that it was the act of a Muslim.

The response of fellow-Muslims to it may be thought to have been extravagant, but Rushdie was right to have anticipated such response. It was a response of Islam *redivivus*, of Islam (and not only Islamism) on the warpath, of Islam ever quicker—as earlier noted—to be insulted, and to respond to such insult with anger and threat.

Moreover, there are no boundaries in this battle on home-fronts and foreign fields. Nor can there be, since Islam is a near-global force. Action and reaction, the world over, have been of like vigilance and often of like violence. The front upon which Palestinians and Israelis have for decades stood with daggers drawn is merely one front among many, even if many believe it to be the eye of the storm. Here, the Islamic and non-Islamic worlds, Arab and anti-Arab, Sir John Keegan's 'Oriental' and the long-occidentalised Judaic, have stared one another in the eye with singularly little mercy or compassion on either side.

The Arab-Israeli conflict has been conducted on a small terrain with the battle-lines permanently close. Here the issues, although a microcosm of others, are writ large. Hatreds and paranoias—as well as more rational dispositions among a minority on both sides—have been acute, and the resort to aggression and counter-aggression swift. After decades of conflict of many kinds, each side has become equally inured to exchanges of offence and fire. Indeed, the establishment of Israel in 1948 and the Arab nationalist and Islamic 'reawakening' were more or less contemporaneous; many have been disposed to find a causal relation between them. Each side claims both a moral and juridical entitlement to the same land; Islamism has sunk deep roots in its fertile soil; and anti-Arab and anti-Jewish 'racisms' have confronted one another with matching venom.

In consequence the physical integrity of persons, lives, livelihoods, dignities, homes—and in Israeli assaults on the Palestinians, even trees and crops, contrary to the Hebraic code—have been treated cheaply and without mutual respect. But the suicide-bombings and targeted assassinations, the disproportionate responses, and the routine attacks upon non-combatant civilians do not make this (miniature) battlefield between the Islamic and the non-Islamic worlds *sui generis*. On the contrary, as we have seen, such acts correspond to the now characteristic patterns of the wider conflict. The asperity of the intent to dominate, expel and even extinguish the respective 'other'—Israeli or Palestinian—is no aberration. At worst, it may also have represented the larger shape of things to come between Muslim and non-Muslim.

This mutual asperity is heightened in respect of Jew and Arab—each an exemplar of the non-Muslim and Muslim worldviews—by one particular. The Arabs were not responsible for the plight which drove the Jews to make Israel their redoubt. But insofar as they deny or minimise the facts of the Holocaust, as some Arabs and Muslims do, or deny the Jews' entitlement to be in Israel at all, they align themselves in Israeli minds with the worst of their oppressors. In historical terms they are not. Nevertheless, 'the Arabs'—who in their tens of millions surround Israel—more than fulfil the role of being seen by the Israelis, and by many Jews, as their permanent foes.

Here, the cultural contempt felt by many Jews for 'the Arabs' plays its part in creating a gulf which can barely be bridged. The notion of 'fencing-off' Arabs from Jews expresses it. Indeed, in rabbinical writings as early as the third century, 'the Arabs' were already being described as the 'lowest of all peoples', as they are felt to be by many Israelis today. It is a perception, matched by stereotypes of 'the Jew' in Arab minds, which permits war-crimes to be carried out with little conscience by each upon the other, as Amnesty International reported in 2002. Illegal Israeli settlement on Palestinian lands is a rank injustice. So, too, has been the deliberate Israeli strangulation of the Palestinian economy, the latter made more threadbare by corruption and inertia. They are injustices matched by the injustice of desires to end the existence of Israel entirely.

Several local wars have been fought both in pursuit of such desires and in objection to Israel's own conduct. They are no more than illustrative and highly visible instances—because continuously publicised—of an often less colourful but wider world conflict. When Israelis argue, *in extremis*, that there is no place for Arabs in Israel, or Arabs that there is no place for an Israel in the region, they express openly what is elsewhere declared in private: that there is no place for Muslims in the non-Muslim West, or no place for the 'infidel' in Muslim lands. When Israelis perceive, as they often do, all Palestinians—and even all Arabs—to be potential or actual 'terrorists' and 'extremists', they speak to a popular (and once more populist) prejudice which now knows no geographical limits.

Indeed, hostile generalisations in the non-Muslim world about the 'essential' nature of Islam and of Muslims have become the norm. That this is so is unsurprising, as Islamism lashes out in turn against the non-Islamic world. However, the common Israeli epithet of 'dirty Arabs'—an immoral correlate of the racist 'dirty Jews'—is of unpleasantly long standing. Indeed, as mentioned, it derives from Jewish sentiments which predate by at least sixteen hundred years contemporary grievances over the repeated Arab invasions of Israel since 1948. But such crudities of view have matched the crudities of means used to harm the other during the past decades of conflict.

Upon one front after another of this small-scale Middle Eastern war, the room for humanity of thought and act has narrowed. As the editor-in-chief of the Israeli newspaper *Ha'aretz* declared in May 2002, 'some of our readers have found it difficult to accept an Israeli reporter who shows sympathy for Palestinian casualties of the situation.... Antipathy has grown towards those reporters who continue to describe the suffering on the other side'. But not even this is unique. A similar 'antipathy', equally amoral, has been demonstrated in many countries to the mere giving of shelter to needy refugees from the latest Islamic upheaval, as if every refugee were a potential suicide-bomber.

Such attitudes represent an increasing danger for Muslims in the non-Muslim world. Islamists bear—but disown—large responsibility for this danger. Instead, Islamic militants (and their non-Muslim sympathisers) choose other points in the chain of causation at which to begin their 'narrative' of justification for what they do. However, they can be less faulted for this evasion than anti-Muslims might wish. For mankind has been as cruel to Muslims as Muslims have been to others, and in many places more cruel. Unconcern over the death of Muslims has for centuries been the mark of assaults upon them, just as it now is of Islamist attacks on non-combatant civilians, both 'infidels' and Muslims. From the mass-killings of Muslims in the Crusades to, say, the mass-killings of Muslims by the French during the Algerian War of Independence, ethical unconcern has been among their characteristics, as during the genocide of the Jews or in the pursuit of jihad.

The killing of some one hundred Algerians who had been taking part in a demonstration in Paris in October 1961 was of typically great cruelty and without serious moral consequence; their bodies were found floating in the Seine at a time when Maurice Papon, former high functionary in the Vichy government's wartime deportations of the Jews, was chief of police in Paris. Relatively small in scale as such killing may have been, especially when compared with the massacres of Muslim by Muslim in recent times, it was of a signal brutality nonetheless. So, too, was the slaughter of Muslims by the Lebanese Christian Falange in Sabra and Chatila in 1982 during the Israeli occupation of Lebanon. Killings in India of Muslims by Hindus (and of Hindus by Muslims) in 'communal riots', most notably in the states of Gujarat—earlier referred to—as well as in Bihar and Maharashtra, largely go by on the nod.

As with the mass-murder of blacks in 'remote' parts of Africa—Rwanda, for example—the leaving of Muslims to their fates, whether they are killing one another or being killed by others, has thus been a distinctive aspect of their recent treatment in the world, as the Islamic 'reawakening' has advanced. It was 'hard' to 'leave the Algerian population to their lot', Kofi Annan, the UN secretary-general, was meekly to declare of the Algerian civil war. But they were so left; and died in Algeria by the tens of thousands, largely unlamented in the Muslim and non-Islamic worlds alike.

In all these separate and varied hostilities, from the relatively minor pin-pricks of insult to discrimination or even murder on the grand scale, there are large differences in degree of offence to the moral order. However, each form and act of anti-Muslim hostility, small as well as large, have added to the sense in Muslims that it is the 'other', the non-Muslim, who is at fault for the pass which has been reached in the relationship between them. It is a relationship in which Muslims see themselves as victims. Yet, despite (or because of) such victimhood, both real and imagined, Islam's élan and Islamism's belligerence have grown. Once more, Muslims have been harmed and served by what the non-Muslim world has done to them. They have harmed others, and themselves, in turn.

CHAPTER FOUR
Beyond Reason

For a decade and longer the Western media has made play with, and fun of, whatever gives the clearest indications of the 'closure of the Muslim mind'. This includes 'closure' in relation to the minutiae—or what the West thinks to be the minutiae—of daily life. Muslim responses to these matters are taken to be the products of aberrant reflexes and obsessions, for which the rationalist (in his or her self-estimation) can feel an enlightened disdain.

In March 1991 in the French city of Valence, some one hundred Muslim youths sacked a local butcher's shop, after a dispute over the presence of pork in a pizza, and set cars alight. In June 1992, Islamists—later to be known as the Taliban—used a tank in Kabul to crush four thousand bottles of vodka, forcing shopkeepers who had stocked it to watch the destruction. Far away in Tanzania, in April 1993, Islamists were reported by Reuters as having gone 'on the rampage', attacking shops which sold—once again—pork. In 1995, in the Turkish city of Marmara, and during Ramadan, non-fasting students were attacked in the university's dining-hall by Islamists armed with knives and iron bars. Other faiths, cultures and cults have their own (and sometimes very similar) taboos and scruples, many of them incomprehensible to those who are not of their party. But in Islam's case, their reach, the sensibilities which attach to them and the will to resort to violence in 'defence of the faith'—in societies as disparate as Afghanistan, France, Tanzania and Turkey—could be held to be distinctive.

127

So, too, with the speed of response to religious insult, sometimes unintended. In April 1992, the vice-chairman of the Nottingham Islamic Centre, Haji Mohammed Asmat, expressed 'outrage', on behalf of the city's 12,000 Muslims, with the owner of a Nottingham fashion-shop among whose wares were 'gold dress-shoes'. By mischance these shoes had—or appeared to have—a phrase from the Koran in the design upon them. It was 'more serious than Salman Rushdie', declared Asmat; Rushdie's was a book which 'you carry in your hand', but here the offence, or insult to Islam, was 'on the feet'. The owner—'I'm a Catholic and my husband is Church of England, but we don't clash'—refused to withdraw the shoes from sale.

In July 1992, far afield in Saudi Arabia, similar offence was found in the design of an imported Japanese car-tire, whose tread was said to 'resemble a verse in the Koran'; gunmen fired three shots into the Tokyo home of the tire-company chairman, Hisaaki Suzuki, and protest spread to Brunei and other Islamic countries. In January 1994, the German couturier Karl Lagerfeld was said to have been made afraid for his safety after (what appeared to be) words from the Koran were declared, by Muslim groups in France, to have been embroidered across a Chanel dress worn by Claudia Schiffer in a Paris show. Nottingham, Tokyo and Paris had not only offended, but the 'guilty' parties were put under varieties of pressure and, in two of the cases, had their lives threatened. Clerics in Saudi Arabia also objected to the Starbucks logo on the ground that it was 'un-Islamic'.

In the larger scale of things, these instances and responses might be considered trivial, and media-driven trivia at that. But they derived from a comprehensive, and comprehensible, 'thought-system'. It is one which now stands outside the bounds of what is generally held to be 'rational' and 'enlightened' by the average Western 'rationalist', even if such 'rationalist' is often enough in unreason's grip on other matters. Moreover, Islam's 'thought-system' has its own logic, its own cultural values to defend and its own ethic, whether or not knives, iron bars, a tank and hit-and-run gunmen are pressed into their service.

From the widest intellectual perspectives, all such expressions of faith's self-defence—the defence of taboo—may be considered forms of mental 'closure'. But a structure of religious belief necessarily makes certain acts, objects and persons profane in order that other persons, acts or objects be made the more sacred or holy. A Satan is God's *alter ego*. Hence, quickness of objection to a tire-mark, or the design of a dress, or a shoe or a logo is not mere paranoia, even if paranoia may play its part. It is also a willed 'closure' to that which faith makes impermissible, so that faith may thereby be demonstrated and, having been demonstrated, be defended.

Media jokes and sensations over the moral excesses and intellectual follies of the Taliban movement, or Iranian *ayatollahs*, have served to prevent true judgment about what is at issue. In Afghanistan under the Taliban and in Iran, the activities of their respective squads of moral police for the 'Prevention of Vice and the Fostering of Virtue' were greeted in the non-Islamic world with an uneasy mixture of ridicule, incomprehension, fear and counter-outrage. In Afghanistan the Taliban allegedly banned, or sought to ban, not only 'all music' except marching-songs of the Taliban movement itself, but the cinema, television and video-watching also. It banned, as well, the portrayal of all living things, including animals, to the length of destroying anatomy text-books and the depictions of the human form therein; banned the playing of musical instruments and card-playing too. Such prohibitions invited recoil in the West. They also earned a foolish media welcome for what could again be presented as aberration, the more 'primitive' or 'uncivilised' the better.

The Taliban's warning to men that their beards were 'too short', or the forcible cutting of their hair for being 'too long', became markers of the nature of Islam itself. 'When you pray', declared the authorities in Kabul, long hair 'gets in the way of your forehead touching the ground'. In such circum-stances, they pronounced, 'the Devil', that necessary Devil of faith, 'stands between you and God'. But such ridiculed media 'items' themselves obstructed the non-Muslim world's view of what these excesses might signify. During the 1990s, Iranian clerics similarly issued condemnations and prohibi-tions of 'decadent Western music', 'indecent Western television programmes', 'obscene Western values', video-films, horoscopes, satellite-dishes and so on. In July 1994, even 'ties and bow-ties' were declared by Ayatollah Ali Khamenei to be 'offensive' to Islamic culture. In Kashmir, in Kuwait and in Saudi Arabia, 'warnings' respectively against MTV, or fashion-shows, or (again) the spread of satellite-dishes, were of like kind.

Again one should beware. It is at some risk that the offended Muslim is taken by the non-Muslim to merit the world's scorn or, worse, laughter. The charge of hypocrisy—Iranian clerics and officials were gleefully reported in the West to own satellite-dishes themselves—cannot deter the Muslim's sense of moral danger. That Saudi Arabia and other Muslim countries have stakes in the satellite technology used by the Western media, as well as in Western television organisations, does not lose its significance—on the contrary—in the larger scheme of things: the war of worlds. Moreover, what appears to be the petty product of a deformed ethic is not more so than the disavowal of meat-eating on Fridays, the sanctification of the cow or the transfer of one's sins to a scapegoat.

In Islam's fiats and refusals, and in its readiness to punish those who hold
its worldview at naught, there is more at issue than 'fundamentalist' rigour. For
Islam—and not merely Islamism—combines seeming intellectual 'closure'
with a formidable moral certitude. Its forms of thought often appear tortured
(and torturing), but they are contained within and compose a coherent moral
system. Muslim logic, like the logic of other faiths, also possesses a capacity to
entrap others in labyrinths of unmeaning and untruth; its energy of word and
mind can coexist with an atrophy of intellectual invention; and its accelerating political self-confidence goes hand-in-hand with fear-driven assaults on
those, Muslims and non-Muslims alike, who would question its beliefs and
conduct. But none of the intellectual and moral demands which these complexities pose can be reductively met by scoffing or aggression.

Too serious for satire, as well as for the simplicities of counter-assault, are
modern Islam's refusals of criticism. So, too, its harshness with 'apostates' and
'blasphemers'; so, also, with its use of threat (and worse) against its own intellectuals when they are of independent cast of mind, and its widening abandonment of the principles of balance and compassion, proclaimed by other
Muslims to be 'central features' of Islam. Scholarly historical 'explanations'
that Islam was either always thus, or never thus in the past, are no longer of
much service. Both 'explanations' are simultaneously proffered to us by
'experts', and cancel each other out.

There are those—again Muslim and non-Muslim alike—who point to an
Islamic 'golden age' of learning in mediaeval times. It was a period when
Muslim Aristotelians, neo-Platonists and others are held (by some) to have
helped transmit Greek, Hindu and other systems of knowledge to the Christian West. Their freedom of speculation is perceived (by some) to have added
independently to the store of human wisdom. However, there are also those
who argue that such Muslim thinkers did no more than pass on what was discovered and known by others; that, being Muslims, a free spirit could not be
theirs, and that they were incapable of disinterested enquiry. There is a third
party which would have it that, insofar as Muslims in the past thought cre-
atively and independently, they did so despite (and against) Islam's constraints,
and at risk to themselves. Yet another party sees a record of Muslim intellectual inventiveness in the past, but an inventiveness without possibility—in the
confines or straitjacket of the Islamic world—of being applied practically to
science, to technology or even to political thought.

Whichever of these broad historical judgments is most just, the evidence
of a renewed Islamic militancy and of a renewed insistence by Muslim clerics
that Muslims avert their gaze from the seductions of the non-Islamic world is

clear. Within this self-enclosure, but only within it, there is again an entire logic, obnoxious as it may seem to those outside Islam's pale. In the sentencing to death or to long terms of imprisonment of writers accused of 'blasphemy' or 'apostasy', and the extra-judicial killings of, or threats to kill, those who have aided their endeavours, this logic—the logic of a powerful moral code, like it or not—is at work.

The writers who in the last decades have earned the disapproval of Islam have included, among many, Salman Rushdie in February 1989 (with his Japanese translator murdered, and his Norwegian publisher and Italian translator wounded in attempted assassinations); the Egyptian novelist Alaa Hamid, sentenced to eight years' imprisonment in December 1991 for a satire on the lives of the prophets; ten Indians condemned to six years' jail in the United Arab Emirates in October 1992 for participating in a theatrical production deemed blasphemous; the Cairo scholar Nasr Hamid Abu Zaid, charged with apostasy in 1993 for his writings on early Islamic jurisprudence; and the Bangladeshi novelist Taslima Nasrin, ordered to be arrested in June 1994 for 'offending religious feelings' in a fictional work which described a Muslim's rape of a Hindu girl.

Nasrin was described by one of the leaders of Bangladesh's Jamaat-e-Islami as 'shameless' and 'rotten'; 'we must keep her death-knell ringing', declared another. This sense of the death-deserving 'shamelessness' and 'rottenness' of the too-freethinking Muslim may again be held to derive from a 'closed', or confined, thought-system. But it now reaches, or bids to reach, across the world in pursuing its various quarries.

The speed with which in November 2002 a *fatwa* for 'insulting the Prophet' could be issued against a *non*-Muslim Nigerian journalist, Isioma Daniel, and in her case not by a clerical body but by an Islamist state government in northern Nigeria, was also an indication of such will. 'Like Salman Rushdie, the blood of Isioma Daniel can be shed', the deputy-governor of Zamfara state, Mamuda Aliyu Shinkafi, declared. It was a 'religious duty binding on all Muslims' to kill her; Islam 'prescribes the death penalty on anybody, no matter his faith, who insults the Prophet', announced the minister of information. Nigeria's supreme Islamic body rescinded the *fatwa* on the grounds that a politician had no authority to issue it. But his initial assumption that he was entitled to do so was telling.

In all such accusations, it is not the accused person alone who is under charge. The decadent non-Muslim world in general is charged with influencing—or even masterminding—such 'shamelessness'. The Muslim 'apostate' and 'blasphemer' become representatives, in Muslim eyes, not merely of the non-Muslim world's various degeneracies but agents of its designs against Islam itself. It is therefore again insufficient to ascribe such phenomena to Muslim intellectual 'closure'. The opposite could even be said to be the case, and on a near-global scale.

Some have pursued the 'infidel' world with sword-in-hand. Others, armed only with their wallets, have invested in Western enterprises, in its education and in much else besides. Others again, in millions, have sought residence or refuge in 'infidel' lands. In this respect, Islam is not in the least enclosed; and particularly not when bent upon purchasing or otherwise finding its place at the heart of the non-Islamic world itself. It is not enclosed when set upon avenging, anywhere or everywhere, harms—many of them real—which have been done by non-Muslims to its *amour-propre* or belief-system. Moreover, the rooting out of 'shamelessness' in its own ranks is pursued with a sense of pride, not embarrassment, at the means used to restore Islam's honour in non-Muslim eyes. Once more, such posture is coherent and self-validating. Moral criticism, Muslim or non-Muslim, cannot touch it, since not to seek to extirpate that which is held to be 'rotten' would itself be 'rotten' to the same or even greater degree. A death-penalty for apostasy or blasphemy, or a warning—for example, that issued by Islamists in Algeria in May 1995—that women who married 'atheists' risked death, is easily pronounced, because they are decrees determined by an internally consistent logic.

Ethical handwringing in the non-Islamic world over this logic avails nothing. Indeed, such handwringing is itself seen as betokening a desire to seduce Muslims from faith's morally immune or autonomous dictates. When the promotion of any other religion than Islam was made a capital offence by the Taliban in Afghanistan in November 2000, it was not the right of the non-Muslim which was being infringed, but a Muslim's duty to Islam which was thought to be being fulfilled. Likewise, when an Iranian 'charitable trust' in February 1997 raised the head-price on Salman Rushdie to $2.5 million, and specifically made it payable to his Western bodyguards, the Muslim view of what was meant by 'charity' took no account—in its own terms rightly—of what might be thought by non-Muslims of such an offer.

Again, when a Pakistani professor of physiology, Mohammed Younus Shaikh, was sentenced to death for blasphemy in August 2001, for (among other things) declaring in a college lecture that the Prophet's parents were not Muslims—his grounds being that they could not have been Muslims before the fact—Professor Shaikh's notion of reason was not reconcilable with that different type of reason which governs, and is defended by, faith. He appealed against his death penalty, but was shot dead in jail by a fellow-prisoner who, it

seems, had been supplied with a pistol. Nor does it serve for the Muslim rationalist, such as Fouad Ajami, a professor of Middle Eastern studies at Johns
Hopkins University, to seek to explain what appears to be 'unreason' in terms
of 'political Islam's anti-modern approach', as he did in October 2003. For
faith has reasons of which faithlessness knows nothing.

As the history of Christianity shows, clerical establishments—let alone
books of holy scripture—may also not have their authority lightly questioned
by the lay. A death-sentence for 'blasphemy' was pronounced in November
2002 at Hamedan in Iran against Hashem Aghajari, a professor of history,
principally for questioning in a speech in June 2002 the exclusive entitlement
of clerics to interpret the meaning of Islamic teachings, and for arguing that
such meaning should be reinterpreted by each new generation. His were positions held to be an insult to Islam itself.

The sentence was greeted with an unusual degree (for Iran) of public dissent and, despite threats by hard-line clerics that they would execute Aghajari
themselves if he was spared, the sentence was set aside by the Iranian supreme
court in February 2003. Yet within days it was announced that he would be re-
tried. Meanwhile he remained in jail, much of the time in solitary confine-
ment. In May 2004, the Hamedan court reinstated the death-sentence against
Aghajari, a one-legged veteran of the Iran-Iraq war of 1980–88. He declared
that he would not appeal the sentence, challenging his tormentors to execute
him; and in a new trial held in Teheran in July 2004 he was sentenced to five
years' imprisonment on a lesser charge of 'insulting Islamic values'.

It was the original sentence which was the more revealing: an attempt, in
effect, to confine the intellectual proprietorship of the meaning of Holy Writ
to its priestly guardians. Here, for those who wished it, was evidence of that
intolerance, and even outright denial, of free thought in the Islamic tradition
to which is attributed its larger atrophies of intellect and imagination. Indeed,
book-burning and death-threats as modes of literary criticism—as the writer
Farrukh Dhondy has put it—invite being ascribed to fear of thought itself.
But this assertion is too simple, or simplistic, by half.

It is often repeated, sometimes by Muslim intellectuals themselves, that
Islamic culture has fallen back into, or never left, a 'wearisome Dark Age', as
Ishaq Husseini expressed it in October 1956. Yet the mid-1950s were also the
time when Arab nationalism and Islamic revivalism were beginning to make an
increasing impact on the Muslim and non-Muslim worlds. Husseini's judgment, or cliché, was shallow, as in hindsight is apparent. To repeat it now is
shallower still. For Islam's militancy is no regression. Its logic and reason are
its own, call them illogic and unreason as the non-Muslim may; and its cler-

ical custodians, its hanging judges, its meeker followers and its suicide-bombers or 'martyrs' all know what they are about.

Historians have pointed out with intellectual disdain—the disdain of the Western 'enlightenment' tradition—that there was a 'total ban' on printing in the Islamic world until the nineteenth century. Others, a few daring Muslims included, have asserted, heaping cliché upon cliché, that rote-learning of Koranic texts, whose authority and infallibility may not be questioned, is of a piece with the stifling of mind itself. Or, putting the same point in variant fashion, they argue that since Muslims believe that all truth is to be found in the Koran and Sunnah, nothing other—or more—is required for the possession of wisdom; and that the cerebral impulse itself is therefore stopped dead in its tracks. Others have argued the contrary. They have found a continuous examination of Islam's tenets inscribed in the works of its theologians, the twelfth-century El-Ghazali greatest among them; or, pointing to the inventiveness and intellectual freedoms of the Sufi tradition, have discerned no qualitative difference between such tradition and that of Talmudic self-questioning, or the disputations of Christian theologians upon their articles of faith.

But little of this is now germane. For Islam is again insisting, in our times as in its past heyday, that none stand in the way of the advance of its self-belief, whether or not this meets with the approval of the non-Muslim ethicist or the belligerent Westerner with his own finger on the trigger. When the Iranian president issued a death-threat during Friday prayers in Teheran in March 1989 against 'any writer who criticises Islam', an editor of the *New York Review of Books* might blench. Likewise, a former English-teacher in Saudi Arabia declared in January 1991 that he had been 'shaken' by statements put to him by his students 'in absolute certainty', and 'with no question about other view-points'. For such certitudes are not in accord with the conventions of 'liberal learning'. They cannot be squared with the latter's distinctions between fact and opinion, and show a quite different kind of zeal-for-truth (and a different understanding of what truth is) from that which the Western intellectual and scientific revolutions taught.

In August 1994, Algerian Islamists led by Abou Abed Ahmed even sought to 'ban all teaching' in schools and universities in Algeria, on the grounds that *education itself* was a 'hindrance to the task of *jihad*'. They threatened (and carried out) 'severe punishment' of students who ignored the ban. 'Any teacher who arrives at their place of work, or any head-teacher who opens the door of their building', the order specified, 'will be equally punished'. Hundreds of schools were reportedly burned to the ground and many teachers—sixty within the first three months of the 'ban'—were killed. Some were shot out-side their schools, some on their way to them, others in the classroom.

Physical assaults upon, assassinations of and judicial processes brought against intellectuals, especially teachers, writers and journalists, have been a feature of the Arab and Muslim revivals in many countries, including in Algeria, Bangladesh, Egypt, Iran, Iraq, Pakistan, Saudi Arabia and Turkey. In Egypt a Nobel laureate, the eighty-three-year-old Naguib Mahfouz, was stabbed by Islamists in October 1994; the liberal intellectual Farag Fouda was shot dead for poking fun at Islamism's preoccupation with issues of sexual morality. In Turkey in July 1993, thirty-six intellectuals and artists were burned to death in an arson attack—already referred to—on a hotel, an attack whose principal target was Aziz Nesin, the translator and publisher of extracts from *The Satanic Verses*.

To attribute acts like these merely to 'fanaticism'—and to reduce Islamism to 'terrorism'—is the error of errors, an error for which Western 'rationalists' and aggressors alike have already paid dearly. For such acts, like the acts of suicide-bombers, are not only demonstrative acts of will, as already discussed, but acts of knowingness and rational calculation, however abhorrent such reason may be to others. Moreover, they are acts with deter-minate political ends in view, ends which are generally pursued not only with little mercy but also without moral self-doubt. The authors of such acts have faith as their prompter, and in most cases are without other intellectual or eth-ical censor.

In consequence, and in a secular age in the West, Islamism's acts of phys-ical violence and cruelty are difficult for most non-Muslims to understand, and therefore to counter. But so too are the means employed by Muslims in the combat of argument and polemic. Here, the absence of an inner censor plays havoc with 'conventional'—which is to say, Western—understandings of what truth is. Indeed, the meaning of a gun-shot or a bombing in a place of public resort is generally clearer than are words which have no such plain import. And when their meaning is opaque, or duplicity their intent, a special form of difficulty is created. A foe may be stabbed in the back or a throat be cut with a knife. But the 'lie direct', the half-truth, the morally evasive side-step, the logical contradiction, and what often appears to the non-Muslim to be the standing of verity upon its head are also weapons.

The darker, falsifying arts are practiced in the political discourse of all cultures, and propaganda and disinformation have always been arms of war. In October 2002, as the US was preparing for its invasion of Iraq, it was declared by President Bush—and was repeated by 'coalition' representatives at the

United Nations—that Iraq possessed and was producing chemical and biological weapons, and was also 'seeking nuclear weapons'. Therefore, a preemptive strike on the Saddam regime was argued to be warranted. It was to remain possible (and was so claimed by US intelligence officers and others) that some of these weapons, 'weapons of mass destruction' as well as 'mobile chemical laboratories' and other equipment, had been moved to Syria, Iran, Lebanon's Bekaa Valley and elsewhere both before and after hostilities had begun. However, the 'stockpiles' of such lethal armament were not found, or had not existed.

In many displays of special pleading, the best was attempted to be made of this. For example, Western intelligence agencies had been misled—in part true—by Iraqi opponents of the Saddam regime who had an interest in its fall, and who had therefore talked up the existence of 'weapons of mass destruction' in order to induce the US to act. Or, the dictator had 'idle programs' which he intended to 'revive'; or, at the very least, looters 'could have sold' Iraq's lethal weapons to 'militants' in other countries and so on. Nevertheless, thousands of pages of official reports commissioned by the American and British governments, and published in 2004 and 2005, found the intelligence assessments on the basis of which Iraq was invaded to have been 'flawed', 'unreliable' or even 'dead wrong'. That such assessments had also been manipulated in order to justify political and military decisions which had already been taken to invade Iraq was asserted by some and refuted by others. Similarly, evidence for a link between the Saddam regime and al-Qaeda was clear to some and unclear to others, was asserted as a fact, was denied, and was ultimately clouded over in the 'fog of war'.

The promotion of Arab and Islamic interests in their current resurgence has equally involved assertions of 'fact' which are fictions, or which bear only a strained relation to truth. There has also been resort to modes of reasoning and forms of logic bewildering to others. It is too easy to suggest that explanation for these labyrinthine forms is to be found in the absence of a culture of self-questioning, or of space for doubt in matters of belief, since the same phenomena were at work in Washington and London. Nevertheless, the non-Muslim world is predisposed—at its risk—to think itself largely immune from such defects, and that when they occur they are aberrations. Conversely, 'experts' on Islam in the West can be found to argue that deception, or *taqiyya*, is not merely a Muslim norm of behaviour but 'sanctioned' and enjoined in the Koran itself.

This is overstated: the texts these 'experts' cite give no such legitimacy to deception. Instead, they refer to the practices of 'hiding' one's true purposes in one's heart and of misleading those who 'have no knowledge', but the texts do so without approving (or disapproving) of them. However, it is also obvious that where the mind is forbidden, or deterred from, the freedoms of open scepticism or dissent, obfuscations of meaning as well as deceptions of self and therefore of others may become habitual; the construction of elaborate edifices of make-believe and falsehood, and even delusion, also.

But the world of Islam has no monopoly in the matter of falsehood in word and deed; the confrontation of the non-Muslim world with it has led to the telling by Western policy-makers and politicians of lies aplenty. Moreover, in this war of the worlds the falsehoods which the West tells itself, and others, about its motives and actions are generally born of more self-doubt and con-fusion than those which Muslims tell themselves and others. However, although they often have their close parallels on the 'other side', the devices of Arab and Muslim argument are of a distinctive complexity.

I have here attempted to identify twelve of these devices which have been employed in the last decades, both in the course of 'diplomacy' and of combat. This is an analytical schema only. The devices overlap, are related, may be employed serially, and with greater or lesser consistency and persis-tence. Each device is illustrated with brief examples, from a choice of many.

****

FIRST DEVICE: *To appear, in your own interest, to be sympathetically disposed to the non-Islamic world, while continuing covertly to act against it, as by condemning hostili-ties against it in which you have had, and continue to have, a hand.*

This device has been best exemplified by the conduct of the Saudi royal household. Thus, while members of it have continued covertly to support and fund Islamist assaults on the non-Islamic world, the Royal Embassy of Saudi Arabia in Washington declared in full-page advertisements in the *New York Times* on 19 September 2001 and 21 September 2001, respectively, 'America, We Grieve With You' and 'We Stand With You, America'. In the first text, Saudi Arabia—from which fifteen of the nineteen hijackers of 11 September 2001 came—described the 'terrorists' as 'shameless'. It also professed, in accord with this first device, to 'share' with America the 'devotedly held values that those unspeakable acts are reprehensible and must be condemned'. While continuing to abet and finance groups carrying out such 'unspeakable' acts, the 19 September declaration ended with the call to 'vow together that such ter-rorism will never happen again to any nation'.

On 21 September 2001, the Royal Embassy of Saudi Arabia in Washington reinforced its resort to the First Device. 'America', it proclaimed, 'we stand with you in the battle against global terrorism', and announced that it had cancelled its own National Day celebrations scheduled for 23 September. It called the events of 11 September 'barbaric'—adopting the terminology used in the non-Islamic and anti-Muslim world—and cited the judgment of a senior Saudi cleric that these events were 'not tolerated by Islam'. In July 2003, the Saudi ambassador to the United States, Prince Bandar bin Sultan, repeated that 'the Kingdom has been one of the most active partners in the war on terrorism'.

Similarly, Syrian spokesmen on several occasions in 2003 declared Syria not to be an adversary of the United States, and to be actively cooperating in the struggle against 'terrorism', while continuing to support it in the Middle East and elsewhere.

SECOND DEVICE: *To condemn acts or abuses by others which are as bad as, or less bad than, those which you yourself have committed or are practising, assisting or condoning.*

Examples of this device include the condemnation in December 1997 by the Ayatollah Khomeini of the 'gruesome crimes' committed by Islamists in Algeria; the condemnation by Yasser Arafat of the attack by Islamists on Western tourists at Luxor, also in 1997; and the condemnation of the same attack by Sheikh Ahmed Yassin, the then 'spiritual leader' of Hamas. In the same category were the condemnation by the Syrian Ba'ath Party newspaper of the 'flagrant occupation' of Iraq by US and other military forces, and the assertion by the secretary-general of the Arab League that 'Arab countries do not take part in the occupation of another Arab country', despite the presence at the time of thousands of Syrian troops in Lebanon.

Similar were the declaration in June 2003 by the leaders of Saudi Arabia and the Palestinian Authority, among others, of intent to 'use all the power of the law to prevent support reaching illegal organisations', and the decree issued by the Palestinian Authority in July 2003—the same as one issued in 1998—banning 'incitement' which 'encourages the use of violence' and 'outlawing' groups which 'agitate for change through force'. Of like kind were the terms of Yasser Arafat's condemnation of a bomb-attack at a Tel Aviv bus-stop in July 2004. 'We condemn this act', he declared, 'as we always condemn these acts'.

In the same category were criticisms by Arafat in December 2003 of a lack of democracy in Israel, and condemnation by Sheikh Ahmed Yassin in August

2003, shortly after the suicide-bombing of a Jerusalem bus by a Hamas militant, of the Israeli assassination of a Hamas leader as a 'crossing of all red lines'. A 'crossing' or 'breach' of 'all red lines' is a phrase of condemnation commonly used by Islamists in respect of violent acts of the same kind as, or of lesser gravity than, they themselves have committed or are planning to commit.

Also common is the condoning, or cancelling from mind, of violent acts carried out by Muslims, including against fellow-Muslims, while condemning similar or lesser acts carried out by non-Muslims. 'I never could have imagined such violence would take place in my country', thus declared *vox pop* in Baghdad in May 2004, of the decapitation of a US hostage. By dint of such cancellations, it could be held that the harms done in Iraq to civilians and detainees by the 'coalition' forces from March 2003 onwards were without precedent. They could thus come to overshadow morally the violences of the Saddam regime or subsequent Islamist atrocities in Iraq, including against the Iraqis themselves. In the same way, and as if the World Trade Center had never been attacked, the Iranian foreign minister in November 2004 objected to the 'bombing of towns' in Iraq by US forces.

THIRD DEVICE: *To praise, or even recommend to others, what you do not do, have never done and do not intend to do yourself.*

Model examples of this were furnished during the debate in 2003 and 2004 on attempts to transform Iraq's political institutions and to 'bring democracy' to Iraq. Thus, the Arab League, on behalf of its twenty-two members—none of which is ruled with genuine democratic support—called in August 2003 for a 'legitimate government' in Iraq. In March 2004 Iran, no less, hailed moves towards holding 'general and popular elections', while Saudi Arabia, which knows nothing of such elections and has no constitution, praised the signing of the new interim Iraqi constitution paving the way towards elections.

In April 2004, the *Teheran Times* similarly called for an end to the 'suppression of the Iraqi nation' and for the holding of 'free elections'. An editorial in the *Jordan Times*, looking for an 'indication' of 'the way' Iraq might go, raised its hands to heaven and prayed 'May it be towards democracy', a democracy which does not exist in Jordan itself. In November 2004, the Jordanian foreign minister, Hani Mulki, went further. 'What's sacred in the democratic process', he pronounced, 'is the full participation of all segments of the population.... The dates are not sacred. The process is the only sacred thing', notions not respected in Jordan, let alone regarded as 'sacred'.

In the same month, the Syrian foreign minister told an international conference, in regard to US conduct in Iraq, that 'we cannot overemphasise the need to refrain from shelling civilians, destroying cities and killing innocent people'. In cancelling Syria's own internal history he thus employed the Second Device also.

FOURTH DEVICE: *To condemn in public acts which you support or condone in secret, including for reasons of self-protection from the actors.*

Acts against the non-Islamic world are often covertly inspired and supported, as in Pakistan, Sudan, Syria and Saudi Arabia, by state bodies, intelligence services, para-state organisations—such as 'charities'—or individuals acting in complicity with them. This support is generally dictated by these nations' own *raisons d'état.* Among such 'reasons' is that to refuse support to violent Islamist groups is to invite a threat to themselves. This is perhaps the most precarious of the Twelve Devices. Even cosmetic public condemnation—for diplomatic purposes—of those whom you have reason to fear carries a risk of reprisal by those whom you are covertly supporting. Nevertheless, such diplomatic condemnation is often required where there is simultaneous resort to the First Device. However, to condone acts provided that they are directed only against others has proved—as in Saudi Arabia—an unreliable insurance against attack, since the covert protection and support given to Islamist groups enables them, sooner or later, to turn on their former protectors.

FIFTH DEVICE: *To adopt, conceal or change policies, to reverse stated principles and to switch loyalties according to the need to gain, or regain, favour whether from Muslims or non-Muslims.*

On 5 May 1989, President Rafsanjani of Iran called on Palestinians in a 'sermon' to hijack aircraft and 'bomb Western factories', and for 'every martyred Palestinian' to 'kill five Americans or Britons or Frenchmen'. 'God knows', he declared on that occasion, 'there is a solution [to the Palestinian problem] if you [sc. the Palestinian leadership] threaten American interests throughout the world'. A mere nine months later, in February 1990, Rafsanjani was indicating a contrary desire to temper Iran's image in the West in order to attract foreign investment. In the same way, and for similar reasons—including in order to secure the lifting of Western economic sanctions and embargoes against it—Libya in 2004 reversed, or appeared to reverse, its long-standing state policy towards the non-Muslim world with an implicit disavowal of support for violence against it.

In order to protect its nuclear development programme as it progressed towards a critical stage, Iran likewise denied it had such a programme, while engaging in prolonged diplomatic manoeuvres with European powers so that it could covertly continue with it. Such 'twin-track' approach can be seen as a token of confidence, not weakness or vacillation.

In the turmoils of the Arab nationalist and Islamic revival, shifting policy and allegiance have also played a large role in inter-Muslim conflicts. Knowledge of the usages of 'conventional' diplomacy is often no guide to the speed and complexity of such changing loyalties, enmities and alliances. Thus, after a decade of war between them—which included the use of chemical weapons—Iran gave help to Iraq after the 1991 Gulf War in the breaking of UN sanctions; Jordan, ostensibly allied with the Western powers, did the same. Saudi Arabia helped to fund Iraq's weapons ambitions before the Gulf War, only to turn against it. Conversely, the PLO and Yasser Arafat, having been funded in the 1980s by Saudi Arabia, were in the 1990s calling on the Saudi people to 'rise up' against the House of Saud in retaliation for the latter's opposition to Saddam Hussein.

The ready ability to change, or to seem to change, stance and direction has also been a feature of Muslim diaspora politics. Of many examples, the Bradford Council for Mosques in January 1989 organised the public burning of *The Satanic Verses*. In the following month it called on Muslims to 'ignore the directions of foreign governments'—that is, Iran—and to 'obey the law'. Likewise, Salman Rushdie's decision to restate his loyalty to the letter of Islam in December 1991, a decision declared to be 'in good faith' but dictated by necessity, was speedily followed by his expression of moral regret that he had done so.

SIXTH DEVICE: *To initiate, support or carry out acts condemned by others, to deny having done so, and/or to express surprise and indignation when accused of it, and/or to blame others for it.*

This device is a commonplace. 'No's, 'nevers', 'nothings' and 'not-me's play a standard part in this discourse. In Indonesia, the Jemaah Islamiyah leader Abu Bakr Bashir throughout 2004 dismissed charges of implication in 'terror' as 'laughable' and 'disgusting', while the head of the Islamist Justice and Prosperity Party declared that there was 'no evidence' that justified such charges, despite evidence to the contrary furnished by members of Jemaah Islamiyah itself. In November 2003, Iran likewise asserted that there was 'nothing' to suggest that Iran was pursuing nuclear weapons in the teeth of evidence to the contrary about its bomb-grade uranium-enrichment and missile programmes. In March 2004, Iran's chief delegate to the UN atomic agency again insisted that 'we have never been involved in any nuclear weapons programme'; and in March 2005 Iran's Supreme Leader, Ayatollah Ali Khamenei, not only declared it to be 'a fiction' that Iran was engaged in such activity but described the allegation itself as part of a 'conspiracy against Iran'.

In detention in Iraq, Saddam Hussein similarly claimed at the end of June 2004 to have had no involvement in the killing of thousands of Kurds, at his orders, in poison-gas attacks in 1988. In December 2003, a Syrian minister likewise declared that his country had 'not done anything' to merit being placed on the list of 'terrorism'-sponsoring states, while in May 2004 President Assad asserted that there were 'no leaders' of Hamas and Islamic Jihad in his country, and 'no evidence' of foreign fighters crossing the border from Syria to Iraq. On trial in Turkey, the Islamist militant Metin Kaplan similarly claimed in December 2004 that 'no Muslim can be a terrorist', one of the commonest of Sixth Device assertions. The same arguments have been brought to the Muslim diaspora. Thus, in March 2004—from many such examples—the secretary-general of the Muslim Council of Britain asserted that 'hatred and violence' had 'nothing to do with Islam'.

Profession of innocence is frequently accompanied by blame of others for the same acts, and by the self-presentation of the accused as not morally responsible for such acts, being a victim of others. It is a device that has been continuously adopted since the beginning of the Arab nationalist and Islamic revivals, and has many variants.

Thus, on 16 February 1990—when the uproar over the Iranian *fatwa* against Salman Rushdie was at its height—President Rafsanjani expressed surprise at such uproar. Declaring that there was 'no need for the kind of ruckus which has been raised by the enemies of Islam', he by implication disclaimed Iranian responsibility for having caused it, and blamed others. From many such instances, in July 2003 the Saudi ambassador in London declared himself to be 'frankly appalled' that his country was being implicated in the 'spreading of hatred of the West', and that 'nothing could be further from the truth' than the suggestion that 'Saudis finance terror'.

The same forms of denial of culpability were demonstrated by much of the Muslim world in the disowning of responsibility for the attack on the World Trade Center, and the transfer of blame for it to others. So, too, in Iraq—and choosing at random—it was Americans, not Iraqi looters, who had 'stolen Iraq's national archaeology' and 'destroyed the Iraqi National Museum', according to taped messages from the overthrown Saddam Hussein in May and June 2003. Likewise in Karbala and Baghdad, the attacks of March 2004 on Shi'ite festival celebrants were blamed on American forces. Iran's Supreme Leader, Ayatollah Ali Khamenei, was 'sure' that similar attacks in December 2004 on Shi'ites in Karbala and Najaf were the work not of anti-Shi'ite Muslims but of 'Israeli and American spy services'. According to the *Teheran Times* in April 2004, there was 'only one cause'—'US incompetence'—for the unrest in Iraq. Even Abu Musab al-Zarqawi, the leader of the al-Qaeda-linked group of fighters and decapitators in Iraq, was proclaimed from the pulpit in Baghdad to be a 'myth created by America'.

SEVENTH DEVICE: *To accuse others of having carried out acts of which you ostensibly disapprove, to deny sympathy for the perpetrators, but simultaneously to celebrate such acts as aiding your cause or as redounding to your credit.*

The *locus classicus* for the use of this Seventh Device was in the expressions of disapproval by many Muslims of the attacks of 11 September 2001. However, this disapproval could be combined with the insinuation, according to the Fifth Device, that the attacks were carried out by the Americans and/or the Israelis. The denial that any Muslim would (or could) have carried them out was also accompanied in the Muslim world by expressions of satisfaction at, and in a few documented instances by public celebrations of, a Muslim 'success'.

A variant of the Seventh Device was employed in July 2005 by Hani al-Siba'i, the Egyptian director of the London-based 'al-Maqreze Centre for Historical Studies', immediately after the suicide-attacks on the city. Using the device, he was able to argue simultaneously that the British prime minister would 'pay the price' for the 'grave error' of attributing the attacks to Islamists and suggested that they could have been the work of 'Zionist Americans', but that 'if al-Qaeda indeed carried out this act, it is a great victory for it' and had 'rubbed the noses of the world's most powerful countries in the mud'.

EIGHTH DEVICE: *To act the peacemaker and conciliator when under criticism or suspicion as an open or covert belligerent, as an untrustworthy ally or as an increasing threat to the non-Islamic world.*

The suspicions aroused by the scale of participation by Saudi nationals in the 11 September 2001 attacks can be argued to have led logically—according to the forms of logic earlier discussed—to the presentation in March 2002 of the Saudi 'peace plan' for the Middle East. It thus represented less a search for 'common ground' between the combatants in the region than an act of conciliation between Saudi Arabia and the United States.

The particularity of this logic was understood by Arab and Muslim states who absented themselves from 'pan-Arab' discussions of the plan. Being habituated to the style of this Eighth Device, they were able to recognise that its principal purpose was the deflection, or distraction, of attention from the Saudi role in the attacks on the United States. According to circumstance and audience, other Arab and Muslim nations and organisations—including Egypt, Jordan, Pakistan, the Palestinian Authority, the Organisation of the Islamic Conference, the Arab League and Syria—have presented themselves simultaneously to the Islamic world as standing with it in co-belligerence and to the non-Islamic world as neutral honest brokers, and of pacific intent.

NINTH DEVICE: *To pretend to others, and to yourself, that you are not merely not a foe but an exemplary friend, and more to be relied on than others who merely profess to be so.*

This is an elaboration of the Eighth Device. Some of the most striking examples of its use have been Palestinian. On 13 November 2001, Yasser Arafat called publicly on Arab states to declare their readiness to join the 'international coalition against terror'. On 16 November 2001, the Palestinians' chief negotiator, Saeb Erakat, went further. Describing the circumstance after 11 September 2001 as a 'new kind of war, a new kind of battlefield'—repeating the formulas of President Bush—he argued that 'the United States will need the help of Arab and Muslim countries'. Ten days later on 18 November 2001, he declared with increased energy that 'the Arab countries' were 'more needed in such an alliance' than Israel. The latter 'can't be part of the alliance', he added. The Palestinians, that is, were *'plus royales que le roi'*; the Ninth Device.

TENTH DEVICE: *To invite the very foes against whom you are fighting, have been fighting, or to whom you are deeply hostile, to ally themselves with you against a supposed or actual common enemy.*

Here one enters further into a moral and intellectual wonderland where few who are not habituated or privy to its forms can follow. Thus, in January 1997, Yasser Arafat called on Israel to join the Palestinian Authority in a joint struggle against the Iranian regime. 'I understand your suspicions and the suspicions of the people in Israel', he declared, referring to awareness of Iran's role in providing armed support for the Palestinian struggle against Israel. 'We also have our suspicions.... We must fight against them, win and strengthen the peace', he told Israel.

In December 2002, Saddam Hussein similarly called on 'brother' Kuwaitis—whom he had attacked and pillaged in 1990 and called 'dogs'—to join hands with 'your Iraq' and 'your Baghdad' in resisting the United States. At the same time, he apologised for the Iraqi invasion of Kuwait; declared that the harms done to it were done 'unknowingly'; and claimed, in accord with the Ninth Device, that the same invasion was carried out to protect Kuwait from external aggression and occupation.

Likewise, on 19 December 2002, the Syrian foreign minister suggested in a BBC television interview that the British join Syria in combating the activities of Islamist organisations which Syria was itself supporting. In August 2004, the Iranian president, Mohammad Khatami, also employed a form of the Tenth Device in warning Washington that the US could 'not succeed in Iraq and Afghanistan without an Iranian presence'.

ELEVENTH DEVICE: *To give an undertaking that you will pursue a certain course, or assume a moral (or other) responsibility, in order to gain time or opportunity for the continued or accelerated pursuit of your existing ends.*

This device, employed in all cultures and ages and particularly at times of preparation for war, has again been a commonplace of the Arab nationalist and Islamic revivals. It has been widely used by all parties to the Middle East conflict, as well as by Iran in its manoeuvres to protect its nuclear development programme, earlier mentioned. It was also used by Iraq before the US-led invasion of 2003, and in response to adverse United Nations resolutions, condemnatory reports on breaches of human rights and the like. Under cover of truces, 'peace settlements' and other seeming accords, the Eleventh Device has equally served Afghan factions, Chechens, Indians and Pakistanis in the dispute over Kashmir, Israelis and Palestinians, Somalis and Sudanese, and Islamists in Indonesia and the Philippines. It has been used in matters of differing degrees of gravity, from local conflicts to those which threaten the peace of the world.

TWELFTH DEVICE: *To pretend to be acting in ways you would wish others to believe that you are acting, or to have changed the ways in which you were formerly acting, while continuing to do what you were doing before.*

Closely related to the Second and Eleventh Devices, this has also been a commonplace in the conflicts, internal and external, generated by the Arab and Islamic resurgences. Its use has extended across the gamut of political, military and other actions. It involves the deception of others and, equally often, self-deception. In the latter case, an entire disjunction can sometimes be observed between an act and the perception of such act by the actor himself.

Acts which have not taken place can be believed to have occurred merely by insisting upon it. Similarly, unmet promises can be believed to have been fulfilled merely by the saying so. Conversely, acts known to have been carried out can be flatly denied to have been done and even be cancelled from the mind, as earlier mentioned.

Here, the lack of toleration of free intellectual activity in most Arab and Islamic societies may go some way towards explaining the ease of resort to double-think and self-delusion in such and other pretences. To claim to be engaged in purely welfare activities while simultaneously engaged in procuring acts of armed warfare, or to be pursuing charitable ends while collecting funds for weapons, or to be democratising your institutions and observing the rule of law when the opposite is the case, are all instances of resort to the Twelfth Device.

****

Although the use of these and related devices may intermittently rebound against the user, they have between them posed substantial and growing problems to the non-Muslim world. The adoption in the non-Muslim world of related devices of deception and self-deception, including in the 'misnaming' discussed earlier in this book, has further deepened the 'fog of war'. Nor is there a particular 'Arab mentality'—a racist notion—from which the non-Arab, and non-Muslim, is exempt. Telling lies, obscuring the real issues and pretending innocence of crime are the monopoly neither of Muslim nor non-Muslim. Nevertheless, recourse to these devices has been so marked, and repetitious, in the last decades of the Muslim advance that they have sometimes taken on the appearance of reflexes.

In the struggle of Islam and Islamism to make their further way, even the seeming belief that, say, falsehood *is* truth has played a large part. This has again not been the exclusive characteristic either of the Arab or non-Arab, Muslim or non-Muslim. There has been swearing to the truth of what is half-true, or down-right untrue, in all camps. Thus, in March 2003 Saddam Hussein asserted that Iraq was a 'democracy', while the US and Britain claimed that Iraq possessed weapons of mass-destruction ready to be used against its foes 'at forty-five minutes' notice. Unless such weapons be found, there was not much to choose between the claims.

However, there have been peculiarities, as well as complexities, in the manner in which the Arab and wider Muslim worlds have addressed themselves to the West, and especially to the United States. One such is the moral (or psychological) contradiction, already adverted to, between the desire in some Muslims to see America punished, suffer, or even be destroyed, and the desire—often enough in the same individuals—to live there, to be educated there, to work there, to holiday there, to invest there, to be accepted there and so on. This ambiguity, found in the Muslim intelligentsia as well as in intending killers, can take the absurdest forms. Thus, when accused of practising torture in interrogations, the Palestinian Authority defended itself by arguing not merely that its interrogators were 'experienced and qualified intelligence men' but that they had been 'trained in Britain and the United States'.

In contrast with such 'psychological' convolution, outright lies possess an almost refreshing simplicity, even if—like so much else in this war of words and worlds—they know no bounds. Again choosing at random, Dubai described itself in its television advertising during 2003 and 2004 as 'a place where the mind is free'; the president of Syria, a country in which political activity is tightly controlled and where demonstrations of dissent frequently lead to detention, claimed in November 2003 that Syrians felt under 'no constraint' in criticising the regime; and after the rigged Iranian elections in February 2004, from which many hundreds of reformist candidates were excluded, Iran's Supreme Leader, Ayatollah Khamenei, declared that the poll had been 'totally free'.

Iraq, declared Saddam Hussein's ambassador to the United Nations in November 2002, mentally cancelling the long war with Iran, the invasion of Kuwait, the gassing of Kurds and the slaughter of Iraqi Shi'as, had 'always opted for the path of peace'. There was 'no proof or evidence' of 'strategic weapons deals' between Pakistan and North Korea, declared President Musharraf in September 2003, and 'no basis for' and 'no question of' Pakistani involvement in 'nuclear proliferation activity', asserted Pakistani officials in January 2004. Likewise, Pakistan's 'Information Minister', Sheikh Rashid Ahmed, also in January 2004, denounced the report of Pakistani assistance to Libya in the transfer of nuclear technology—assistance which the Libyans themselves acknowledged—as 'total madness'; Pakistan had 'never proliferated', he repeated.

However, even the simple 'lie direct', although free of the often self-entrapping intricacies and torments of logic found in the Twelve Devices itemised above, has its oddities. The most notable is the readiness of those who employ it to declare to be true what is known by the liar himself not to be so, and is also known by the liar not to be believed by those to whom the lie is addressed. Nevertheless, it gives no pause. Choosing from many examples, such predisposition permitted the Sudanese Islamist leader, Hassan Turabi, to assert in October 1995 that 'Christians in Sudan' had 'more rights than the Muslims in Britain'. Similarly, the 'Voice of the Republic of Iran'—Iranian state radio—claimed in May 2004 that the issue of the torture and other mistreatment of Iraqi prisoners by their American captors had been 'totally ignored' by the 'Western media', when the opposite was the case and to perverse degree.

Such habits have again been carried over into the Muslim diaspora. They permitted British and American Muslims trained in al-Qaeda camps in Afghanistan to insist that they had been in Pakistan 'visiting relatives', or 'working for charities' or had strayed over the border with Afghanistan 'by mistake'. The opening of a Muslim high school in the northern French city of Lille in September 2003 was described as a 'great day for secularism' by Amar Lasfar, head of the local al-Imane mosque; and in January 2004, Mohamed Halhoul, director of the Islamic Council for Catalonia, asserted that 'in Islam, there does not exist any type of call for aggression'. As we shall see, this predisposition can also translate defeat in battle into 'victory', and so on.

Such falsehoods are not all of the same nature. Some are free-standing, others adjunct weapons in the deployment of one or other of the Twelve Devices. Others again are more easily understood in the non-Islamic world than untruths which have the character of actual delusion. Nevertheless, they possess several features in common. Chief of them is lack of embarrassment in their telling, since an inner moral and intellectual censor appears to be absent. Another is the often 'sincere' belief, or earnest self-persuasion, not only that the untrue is true but that those who deny it are themselves lying. A third is the capacity for embroidery of falsehood with further falsehood, however contradictory such further falsehood may be.

One example of this last (again from many) must suffice. Four days after the attacks of 11 September 2001 on the United States, some fifteen hundred celebrating Palestinians were reported by the Associated Press to have marched in Gaza, bearing at their head a large portrait of Osama bin Laden. After the rally, Palestinian police questioned journalists and confiscated news-videotapes and other film of the proceedings; in Nablus, where an even larger rally of several thousands of Palestinians had celebrated the attacks on the United States, the Palestinian police stopped camera-teams and photographers from covering the event, as the Associated Press reported.

That there had been such public celebrations *at all* was categorically denied. This was despite the fact that some images of these and other celebratory rallies had already reached the non-Islamic world. 'It was less than ten children', declared Yasser Arafat, of one such celebration in East Jerusalem, adding—in almost the same terms as had the Saudis in their *New York Times* advertisements—that 'our hearts go out to the people of the United States during this tragedy, our prayers are with them'. Yet, in December 2001, in Lebanon's *Daily Star*, for example, no bones were made—however contradictorily again—over the fact of celebrations of this kind. 'It must not be a pleasant thing for Israelis to watch Palestinians hand out sweets to celebrate the murder of almost thirty Israelis', the paper candidly admitted of Palestinian responses to a suicide-bombing. In July 2002, some ten thousand Palestinians again marched through Gaza City, on this occasion to celebrate the bombing of a restaurant at the Hebrew University campus. Again, at the end of November 2002 after the bombing of an Israeli-owned hotel in Kenya, seven thousand people at a Gaza rally cheered as a speaker declared, 'Today, we struck again in Mombasa'. Similarly, the family of a Jordanian suicide-bomber celebrated publicly after 125 people were killed in an attack carried out in the Iraqi town of Hilla in February 2005.

Here it was not the 'celebrations' themselves which were worthy of remark. Rather, it was the blank denial that they had occurred. The outright denial that, say, 'crimes against humanity' have been committed is to be expected of those who are accused of them, whether they be Nazi, Serb, Arab or Jew, since such crimes are matters of legal definition, and of judicial inquiry or process. The denial that publicly-witnessed, non-violent and even filmed events took place at all occupies its own order. It is one which may be called 'beyond reason'. Yet here caveats are again required. For even in holding truth to be falsehood and falsehood truth, there are reason and logic of a quite determinate kind. They are those of an advancing cause which is exercising its strengths in whatever ways it chooses, and will not have such choices dictated or obstructed by the non-Muslim.

Thus, all the devices, ruses and untruths which have been noted have their purposes and meanings, complex and even incomprehensible as they might often seem to be. Such incomprehension is also mutual: abuse of language—especially of the language of ethics—has been practised on large scale, while *suggestio falsi* and *suppressio veri* have ruled the intellectual roost on all sides.

When Sheikh Abdel Rahman—charged with taking part in planning the first attack on the World Trade Center in February 1992—declared that its bombing 'could not have been done by a true Muslim', violence was being done to the truth itself, and such as would seem capable independently of bringing down the world. Hence, the struggle with Islam's belief-system and with its modes of expression is as much epistemological as military, as much a war of falsehoods as an exchange of fire. The historical record—of Islam's birth and nature, of Western imperialism, of the facts of the Arab-Israeli conflict or of inter-Muslim wars and so much else—has also been buried under a mountain of disinformation. The non-Muslim, or anti-Muslim, might turn away in disbelief from the claims made in March 2003 by the Taliban leader, Mullah Mohammed Omar, that the United States—but not the Taliban—was a 'symbol of terror'; but Islamists, and many Muslims, turn away in disbelief from America's hymns to itself and its virtues.

The disbelief of the non-Muslim at what is told him evidently cannot check false assertion in its stride. Thus, Yasser Arafat was again able in October 2002 to condemn, without embarassment, 'all terrorist attacks that target civilians anywhere in the world', and to assert that this was an 'ethical stand based on our values'. Some of these assertions were closer to wishful thinking than to delusions or lies. Others demonstrated a moral myopia which was also shared in this war by the foes of the Arab and Islamic worlds. Riduan Isamuddin, alias 'Hambali' and alleged to be the 'operations chief' of Jemaah Islamiyah—the organisation behind the Bali bombing—was described by the cleric Abu Bakr Bashir in August 2003 as a 'good man'. Yet apologists for American and Israeli policy have been equally capable of dislocating and inverting the ordinary meaning of words and the stability of moral categories, by investing wicked acts with high purpose. They were also capable of harming the innocent with a degree of disregard which they were swift to denounce as 'barbarous' when done to them.

As well as moral delinquencies of every kind, paranoia has played a role in bringing the Islamic and non-Islamic worlds to their present relation. In predominantly Muslim northern Nigeria even a polio vaccination programme of the World Health Organisation was asserted in 2003 to be part of a 'US plot' to make Muslim women infertile. 'The British design', I was told in July 1990 by Kalim Siddiqi, leader of Britain's 'Muslim Parliament', was 'to destroy Islam'. In August 1990, a 'senior Muslim diplomat in London' was cited by the Cambridge professor Akbar Ahmed as believing that there was an 'international conspiracy'—and not merely a common interest of news-desks—to construct a 'stereotype of Islam' composed of its 'worst images'.

The mass-murder of Muslims in Bosnia was likewise said in January 1993 to be 'part of a plannned Western Christian crusade against Islam'. Similarly, Ayatollah Khamenei declared in October 1994 that the 'US president and administration' were 'directly involved' in every death of a Palestinian; and, in a deepening of such expression of delusion, the crimes being committed in Algeria—by Muslim against Muslim—were held by Khamenei, in December 1994, to be the work of 'covert hands' which were bent upon 'defiling Islam'.

Khamenei's assertion was again that of the Sixth Device, by which blame for the acts of Muslims is transferred to the non-Muslim. Yasser Arafat could thus declare in September 2001 that 'fanatic groups' among the Palestinians had 'been established by the Israelis', and in October 2001 that the killers of the Israeli government minister, Rehavam Ze'evi, were 'collaborators with Israel'. In 2001 and 2002, bomb-attacks probably carried out in Riyadh by Islamist militants—in which British and other Western expatriates were killed—were blamed, as we have seen, on the expatriates themselves. In yet another form of self-exculpation, Farouk Kaddoumi, speaking for the Palestinian Authority, declared in December 2003 that physical assaults (by Palestinians) on the Egyptian foreign minister in al-Aqsa mosque, referred to earlier, had 'nothing to do with the Palestinian people'. Also in December 2003, Saddam Hussein, under questioning in captivity, described his own use of chemical weapons against the Kurds of Halabja in 1988 as the 'work of Iran'.

In November 2001, far away in the Muslim diaspora but near-at-hand in moral style, Dr. Ghayasuddin Siddiqui, a British Islamist, claimed that the 'catastrophic humanitarian disasters of the Middle East' were the 'responsibility' of the United States: a characteristic moral transference which absolved all other actors of blame. Such procedure also permitted the attribution, both by Muslims and non-Muslims, of greater responsibility for the London suicide-bombings of July 2005 to 'Bush and Blair' than to the bombers themselves and their instigators. Sometimes, particularly heinous acts such as the attack on the World Trade Center will be asserted to be not merely the acts of others but to be beyond the ability of Muslims to carry out. As the father of Mohammed Atta—the leader of the attack on the World Trade Center—put it, 'Israel's intelligence agency had the capacity to organise such an attack, but my son did not'. This argument is more devious than a mere denial of responsibility and its transfer to the 'other'. Here, a profession of innocence was couched in terms of self-deprecation, even to the point of abjection, in order that blame be attributed to others.

One step further is to allege that acts which might *seem* to have been the work of Muslims were carried out by non-Muslims in an effort to discredit Muslims themselves. As the pupil at an Islamic boarding-school in Jakarta put it in May 2002—characteristically after 'credit' for the attack had already been claimed by Islamists—Muslims had been 'blamed for something that they have not done'. And if that was not the explanation there could be no other. Thus, immediately preceding the violent American counter-assault on the Taliban regime in the autumn of 2001, Taliban spokesmen claimed that they had 'done nothing to deserve it'. Denial of Muslim culpability was also implicit in the incomprehension of a Jordanian political scientist—Radwan Abdullah, in February 2002—over the measures taken by the United States after the attacks of 11 September 2001. 'Nobody understands US policy', he declared, and 'everybody is baffled'.

Thus, both ethics and intellect may be thrown to the winds in the face of challenge. At other times, reason in argument can appear to collapse altogether in welters of mere words, or formulaic statements without meaning or logical connection. 'Although 11 September changed the Western world', the editor of the London Arabic newspaper *al-Quds al-Arabi*, Abdel Bari Atwan, declared in March 2002, 'the effect on the Islamic world has been far greater. The gulf between the two is widening. Today, many in the Islamic world are convinced that the US administration harbours real enmity for Islam and the Muslims'. Behind this logical inconsequence—or succession of words which appeared to be sequential—a deformed meaning could just be made out: the American response to the attack by Muslims on the World Trade Center signified that the United States harboured enmity for Islam, and it was the *response* not the attack which had 'widened the gulf' between them.

Such convolution was also present in Atwan's argument that 'as Arabs and Muslims we have been terrorised by the campaign launched in Afghanistan, the Philippines, Yemen and Georgia. The supposed potential dangers facing the West have not been eliminated. This campaign has given the mistaken impression that Muslims are the source of terrorism in the world, creating tensions and providing Islamic radical groups with the ammunition to recruit thousands of young Muslim men and women'. Otherwise put, it again meant—or appeared to mean—that it was the *responses* to Islamism and Islamist attack which justified Islamism and Islamist attack in the first place.

To attend to such forms of argument was itself brain-scrambling. The closer examined, the less the words meant on the page, and the more (and worse) they meant when decoded. Similarly brain-scrambling was the response in November 2002 by a Jordanian analyst, Labib Kamhawi, to the bomb-attack, already referred to, on an Israeli-owned hotel in Mombasa. He suggested that Israel would now 'join the war on terror'—as if they had not been part of such war for years—but if they did join it, declared Kamhawi, it would 'confirm all the suspicions that Israel and the US are in cahoots and that the war on terror is a war on Arabs and Muslims'. That is, it was again the nature of the *response* and not the attack itself to which Muslims should attach the greater moral significance. For this response would disclose the essential ill-intent of non-Muslims towards them.

Nevertheless, one must again take care. For reason and logic were at work in what appeared to lack both. They were the reason (in seeming unreason) and the logic (in seeming illogic) of an awakened and excited intellectual and physical force. Moreover, it is a force which now declares its meaning without need or obligation to explain itself to the non-Islamic world. It has even less sense of obligation to abide by ethical principles which themselves go unobserved by the non-Muslim world when its own necessities dictate. Hence, there was neither intellectual nor moral obstacle in the way of the declaration in August 2002 by the Saudi foreign minister, Prince Saud al-Faisal, that bin Laden had 'chosen 15 Saudi citizens among the 19 hijackers on September 11 [2001] in order to drive a wedge between the US and Saudi Arabia'.

Truth was quite unnecessary to such assertion. It was governed by other criteria. Chief among them, once more, was the divestment of moral responsibility for the act. Likewise with the assertion in September 2002 of another Saudi prince, Khalid al-Faisal al-Saud, the governor of Asir province (home to four of the hijackers), that 'the Zionist movement' was 'using the opportunity'—that is, the 'opportunity' of the events of 9/11—'to make Islam and the Arabs the enemy of the West. This is entirely wrong'.

In only two sentences were several features of that special form of reasoning which has been adopted by Islam in its advance. Chief of them, here, was an emphasis on the 'wrongness' of what was being done to Muslims rather than by them, and with it an implicit claim that violent acts carried out by Muslims are justifiable in a way that the violent acts of non-Muslims are not. Such argument has also been a constant in the Arab-Israeli conflict. However, there is again not much to choose, morally, between Muslim positions of this kind and, say, the falsely ingenuous 'apologies' by Americans and Israelis for civilian killings. But there remains no correlative for the Arab and Muslim argument that the non-Islamic world's *responses* to attacks made on it by Muslims represent the 'demonising' and 'persecution' of Muslims themselves; and no correlative for the further argument that retaliations by Muslims—whatever form they may take—are therefore prima facie just, since Muslims are the innocent parties to the conflict.

Even these moral self-exculpations, or claims to moral immunity, have not been sufficient for some. Abu Bakr Bashir, already mentioned as one of the leaders of Indonesia's Jemaah Islamiyah—which has 'links to al-Qaeda'—not only denied in November 2003 that Jemaah Islamiyah existed at all, but declared on 15 October 2002, to the BBC, that the very existence of al-Qaeda was an 'American invention'. 'What is al-Qaeda?' he asked, as if in innocence, 'does anyone know?' In January 2004, the Syrian president similarly asserted that there was 'no indication' that there was an 'entity called al-Qaeda'. Here, self-absolution went beyond the device of asserting that an act carried out by Muslims was carried out by non-Muslims, and that the covert purpose of such act was to justify attacks by the latter on the former. For Bashir and al-Assad had in effect implied that the foes identified by the non-Islamic world were phantoms.

The arms of this 'innocence' have now been spread wide across the world. It is an 'innocence' to which the non-Muslim world also lays claim, as when it justifies 'pre-emption' on moral grounds, or takes oil from Arab and Muslim countries as if such oil were the common property of humankind. Indeed, a state of denial in this war of the worlds often appears to be something close to a first moral choice for all the combatants in it. The main exception to this is where practical benefit, such as the creation by Islamists of fear in others, is thought to reside in admitting or claiming responsibility for a heinous act, such as a suicide-bombing or a decapitation.

In general, however, refusal or denial of responsibility has remained the commonest Muslim response to moral challenge, on the home-fronts of conflict as well as further afield. For example, after having expressed approval of the *fatwa* against Salman Rushdie, the president of the Bradford Council for Mosques, Sher Azam, declared—in reference to Muslims in Britain, and in Bradford, who appeared to be bent upon hunting Rushdie down—that 'Islam does not ask us to take the law into our own hands. If any individual takes the law into their own hands, whether they are Muslims or not, we do not feel responsible'.

Such type of moral disclaimer has been reiterated from one end of the Islamic world to the other. Indeed, the more serious the issue the speedier (in general) the divestment of responsibility. 'You speak of the intolerant face of Islam. Here you may be referring to the heinous crimes that are committed in Muslim countries by their Muslim governments. These crimes have nothing to do with Islam', a Shaikh Mohammed of Croydon told the *Independent* in January 1989. It is plainly untrue that inter-Muslim conflicts have 'nothing to do with Islam'; as untrue as would be the assertion that inter-Christian conflicts had 'nothing to do' with Christianity.

Yet the statement in question was not principally concerned with truth as conventionally understood. For all such assertions are acts of defiance against an overweening non-Islamic world, whose notions of truth, reason and morality Muslims increasingly refuse to accept as their advance progresses. It remains the case that the complexity of some forms of Arab and Muslim retreat from acts of which they have knowledge, or in which they are directly or indirectly implicated, is also a powerful weapon of deceit. But deceit is itself an arm of war, and is universal.

When Imam Waheed Rana of St. Louis, Missouri, thanked Americans on 11 September 2002 for what he called their 'tolerance' following the attacks of the year before, he declared 'Our community is like a body. When one part of the body is injured, the whole body feels the pain'. Here was ambiguity worthy of analysis by a William Empson. Which 'community'? Whose the 'injury' and whose the 'pain'? It was not wholly clear. In such uncertainty, in the lack of direct expression of regret or responsibility for such 'injury', and in the ambivalence as to which 'part' of what 'community' had in fact been 'injured'—Muslim or non-Muslim—a labyrinth was created. It is a labyrinth which is both intellectual and moral. Similarly, at a multi-denominational ceremony in Washington's National Cathedral three days after the 11 September attack, Muzammil Siddiqi of the Islamic Society of North America pronounced that 'to those that lay the plots of evil, for them is a terrible penalty'. The most seemingly forthright and absolute of declarations, it once again left open—even on such a solemn public occasion—the question of precisely whom it was condemning. Equally opaque was the statement by the Muslim Association of Britain in the wake of the London bombings in July 2005 that 'we cannot rule out the possibility of a conspiracy to carry out more attacks in the future'; 'conspiracy' by whom was characteristically left unclear.

Cynicism, fear by freer-thinking Muslims of rejection by the Islamic constituency itself, the absence of an 'inner censor', the habit of moral divestment and the transfer of responsibility to others, together with a proud refusal to truckle to non-Islamic expectations of the Muslim, have each contributed to this kind of obfuscation. Moreover, the devices employed by Muslims against non-Muslims are also employed by Muslims against each other.

In addition, these intellectual deceptions and moral evasions contain large elements of delusion, as already suggested. 'Oh Iraqis, Oh Arabs, Oh Muslims who believe in justice', proclaimed an Iraqi Radio army communiqué in January 1991 during the Gulf War, and in the toils of grim defeat, 'your forces have moved to teach the aggressors the lessons they deserve. They have launched their lightning attack and crushed the armies of atheism as they advance, routing those who could run away while cursing the infidels and heathens'. The following day, according to Baghdad radio, the 'forces of Saddam Hussein' were 'wiping out the renegade invaders'. In *al-Quds*, a 'thunderous storm' was sweeping the foe from 'the Arab desert'; in *al-Thawra*, as Iraq's armies were being brutally slaughtered, they had gained 'superiority on the ground during field-battles'.

By 13 February 1991 the Saddam regime, defeated, had 'triumphed'. At its surrender, it described itself as having 'refuse[d] to comply with the logic of evil, imposition and aggression'. A rout—warranting the world's pity for the scale of death visited upon the Iraqi soldiery by 'coalition forces'—was turned, by words alone, into a battle which would be 'recorded by history in letters of light'. In defeat and retreat Iraq pronounced itself not simply to be victorious, but 'master of the whole land and the leader of the Muslims in the whole world'. In December 2002, Saddam Hussein was still declaring that Iraq had been 'graced' by the deity with 'victory over those who waged that war'.

In January 2003, faced with the prospect of a US invasion, Saddam warned that the 'Mongols of our age' would be 'forced to commit suicide at our gates'. Iraq, similarly declared Saddoun Hammadi, its National Assembly speaker, would be a 'graveyard for all aggressors'. In March 2003, on the eve of the Iraq War, Saddam warned that 'if attacked, we will strike back wherever there is sky, land or water in the entire world'. 'Cut the throats of the Americans', he further instructed in language more than metaphorical, and hallowed by custom.

Victory was 'near', was 'certain', announced Saddam Hussein and his information minister, Mohammed Said Sahhaf, as the US bombardment began; victory was 'in our grasp', the advance of the US forces was an 'illusion', 'most of the infidels' had had 'their throats cut' (again) and God would 'roast their stomachs in hell'. The enemy was (again) 'committing suicide' and was 'not even one hundred miles from Baghdad', announced Sahhaf as the city was surrounded; and, as Baghdad fell, the 'American command' was described as 'under siege' while the Iraqis were in 'full control of the situation'. It was a battle which was being fought—by Iraq—not only to 'defend the values of all mankind' but the 'freedoms of Europe, Africa and Asia' in the words of the Iraqi foreign minister, Naji Sabri.

There was nothing in this, nor in Saddam Hussein's meek surrender in December 2003—despite his calls to Iraqis to fight to the last—to chuckle over. Moreover, the celebration by Muslims of defeat-as-'victory' has a resonance deeper than that of self-delusion. For it speaks to the historic sense, perilous to non-Muslims, that victory is secondary to 'martyrdom', and that martyrdom is victory itself. 'To Jerusalem we will go as martyrs by millions', proclaimed Yasser Arafat in September 2003 from his ruined headquarters in Ramallah.

The idea of martyrdom is also associated, again to the danger of others, with something that appears close to a necessity to shed blood; the rhetoric of Arab and Muslim bellicosity, both in poetry and prose, is often profoundly sanguinary. Even lesser-order rhetorical excesses are *sui generis*, and have again been carried over into the Muslim diaspora. Thus, Britain's Muslims were said by Fuad Nahdi in the *Guardian* in April 2003 to be 'living on a diet of death [*sic*], hypocrisy and neglect'; in December 2003, also in the *Guardian*, Sami Ramadani, a lecturer in sociology at a British university, felt no intellectual hesitation in describing Paul Bremer, the US administrator in Iraq, as a 'tyrant'.

In the darkest thickets of Muslim and Arab prose, 'lions devour their prey', as Ayman al-Zawahiri, one of al-Qaeda's leaders, urged the Iraqis in September 2003 to do to the Americans; it was also a 'lion'—from a 'martyrdom brigade'—who was claimed to have carried out the suicide-bombing (against 'apostate volunteers') at a Baghdad police headquarteres in September 2004. On the wildest shores of Muslim rhetoric, you drown in blood-and-gore, and indifferently whether the blood shed be that of the martyr-to-faith or of the foe. Amid the delusions of the Gulf War, the 'invaders' (of Iraq) would be made to 'eat fire', according to Baghdad's *al-Jumhuriyah* in January 1991, while the Iraqi defence ministry newspaper, *al-Qadisiyah*, warned that 'all Bush's troops' would 'turn into scattered bits and pieces, swimming in pools of blood'. On 3 February 1991, the same paper promised its enemies that they would not be given the opportunity to 'remove their dead from the pools of blood in which they will float'.

As the Iraqi army sank to defeat while simultaneously proclaiming that Iraq's foes were 'wallowing' and 'staggering' in their own blood and their 'failed cohorts' were being turned into 'torn fragments of flesh', Baghdad radio was calling on Iraqi forces—with ever greater excess of delusion—to 'smite the evil invaders and tear them to pieces'. 'O glorious Iraqis', it declaimed, using the language of the Koran itself, 'strike at their necks, chop off their fingers' and so on. Twelve years later, as the second US invasion neared, Saddam Hussein's son, Uday, declared that the 'wives and mothers of US soldiers' would 'weep tears of blood'; and after he and his brother Qusay had been killed by US forces in July 2003, 'Our blood, our souls, we'll sacrifice for Saddam!' chanted the crowd at their funerals in Awja.

This was not merely sanguinary, and even less was it dismissible as hysteria. It was again that mode of expression by which a 'victory' is proclaimed even in the midst of defeat. To the non-Muslim mind, truth has been lost from sight in a haze of near-insane verbiage. This is a misjudgment on several grounds. The language of 'blood', 'fire', 'hell' and 'death' is a cultural convention. Moreover, in the war of the worlds, such rhetoric has often been translated into cruel fact, while the language of it itself betokens not weakness but advancing confidence and strength. A sacrificial readiness to shed blood—whether one's own or that of 'the other'—is also perceived as heroism. The self-slayer, or suicide-bomber, is both martyr and hero; and the more who are seen (or imagined) to 'stagger' or 'wallow' in blood after the suicidal deed is done, the more heroic the act. To most, but not all, non-Muslims it is the reverse of 'heroic'. Yet it is rightly perceived by Islamists as a form of warfare difficult to defeat.

In November 2000, even the director-general of the Palestinian Authority's 'ministry of information' pronounced the 'blood' and 'sacrifice' of 'our martyrs' to be 'inevitably' the 'only way to impose our conditions'. 'Israel has the Dimona nuclear plant', the Palestinian cleric Abdullah Nimr Darwish similarly stated in August 2001, 'but we Palestinians have a stronger Dimona, whom we can use on a daily basis—the suiciders'. In the words of the then leading spokesman of Hamas, Abdel Aziz Rantisi, in August 2002, 'we don't have F-16s, Apache helicopters and missiles, but we have a weapon they can't defend themselves against. It creates a kind of weapon, because it is like an F-16'. 'The weapon of martyrdom is easy and costs us only our lives', likewise declared the secretary-general of Islamic Jihad, Ramadan Salah, in 2000.

At the same time, verbal pledges to shed one's own 'blood' or to take the 'blood' of others are tokens of true, or sincere, purpose and righteous determination. Thus, the sacrifice of 'blood and soul' was once more promised by militants after the Israeli assassination of the Hamas leader Ahmed Yassin in March 2004, while in August 2004 a crowd in the centre of Kufa, near Najaf in Iraq, professed 'by soul and blood' their 'worship' of Moqtada al-Sadr, the militant Shi'ite cleric. To non-Muslims, much of this is 'barbarism'. But to march in a Hamas-organised funeral procession in Gaza dressed head-to-toe in burial coverings—a sign of readiness to die in a suicide-attack—is obviously not 'barbarous' in the eyes of Islam. Nor is the cry 'Make a bomb of me, please!' which has been heard on such occasions from Palestinian women too, dressed in the white shrouds of the grave.

Most of this is simply seen by non-Muslims as indicating a 'bloodthirsty' readiness to take life. Instead, 'bloodthirstiness' is attributed to the non-Muslim foe. In August 2004, as US troops were besieging Najaf, Ayatollah Ahmad Jannati at Friday prayers in Teheran described them as 'bloodthirsty wolves'. It was they, promised Ayman al-Zawahiri in September 2004, who would 'bleed to death'. After the Madrid bombings in March 2004, al-Qaeda gave further warnings that it would 'make blood flow like rivers' in Spain; in July 2004, Australia was warned, also by al-Qaeda, to withdraw its troops from

Iraq 'before your country turns to pools of blood'. In the same month, the Abu Hafs al-Masri Brigades, 'linked to al-Qaeda', threatened European countries which had forces in Afghanistan and Iraq with 'waterfalls of blood that will drag you to their depths' if they were not withdrawn. 'The language of blood is on its way to you', the Italians were told in August 2004, while the testament found in November 2004 in the pocket of the assassin of Theo van Gogh was entitled 'Drenched in Blood'.

However, invocations to 'blood' and commitments to shed 'blood', one's own or that of others, are of a character which is not confined to Islam. The 'blood' of Christ, the image of sacrifice upon the Cross, belief in the 'transubstantiation' of wine into 'blood' at the Eucharist, and the sanctification of Christian martyrs who died for their faith—to say nothing of the blood-letting carried out against Muslims and Jews during the Crusades—stand at the very heart of Christian faith, history, iconography and rite. Hence, much non-Muslim objection to the use of similar imagery by Muslims, or its translation into deed, is on historically weak ground. Islam is no more conceivable without its metaphors of 'blood' and 'sacrifice' than is Christianity itself. Nevertheless, the frequency and intensity of reference to them in current Muslim discourse, in country after country, and by most militant Islamist groups, is distinctive.

In an address to instructors and students of religious seminaries on 22 February 1989, broadcast by Teheran radio, Ayatollah Khomeini's incantatory summoning up of images of blood was culturally akin to that of Baghdad during the Gulf War. Here it was future clerics, not troops-of-the-line, whose ardour was intended to be incited. The 'martyred custodians of prophethood', Khomeini declared, had shown their 'crimson and bloodstained commitment' to the 'greatness of the Islamic Revolution'; the clergy had 'written their theoretical and practical epistles with the crimson of martyrdom and the ink of blood'; and as 'sentinels' of the nation, their 'sincerity' had been 'attested' by the 'drops of their blood and the torn-off pieces of their bodies'. There was no significant ethical difference between this clerical 'crimson', body-parts included, and the 'pools of blood' and 'torn fragments of flesh' to which Baghdad radio, two years later, was reducing the invading foe.

In what Khomeini openly called the 'cult of martyrdom', stress was laid once more on the heroic nature of blood-shedding. It was as if 'crimson' were the colour of strength itself, and life-blood was sanctified by being shed in killing, or in being killed. Bin Laden's frequent evocation of the sanguinary as a token of courage and victory (even in self-martyrdom's seeming defeats) has drawn on the same Arab or Muslim 'poetry' of blood-letting. It is a language which can be employed equally in an Iraqi army communiqué or by a Muslim 'man of the cloth'. In his Afghan cave-video of October 2001, bin Laden lyrically conjured up a 'vision' of Saladin, the twelfth-century Kurdish Muslim who liberated Jerusalem from the Crusaders, 'coming out of the clouds carrying his sword, with the blood of unbelievers dripping from it'. Without dripping blood, the 'vision' would no doubt have had less cultural impact upon the 'ordinary' members of his Muslim audience. 'I want to see your swords dripping with the blood of your enemies', Abu Musab al-Zarqawi, leader of the Iraqi insurgents, likewise told his followers in April 2005.

Indeed, all manner of ghastly fates has regularly been promised to Islam's foes. 'The earth' would be 'shaken under the feet of every Italian' if Italian troops were not removed from Iraq, Islamist militants declared in August 2004. 'All of Palestine' would 'turn into a volcano' in revenge for the murder of Ahmed Yassin in March 2004. The 'blood' itself of Yassin and Abdel Aziz Rantisi, the Hamas leaders, would similarly 'force the eruption of new volcanoes' in the occupied territories of the Holy Land, while in April 2005 the al-Aqsa Martyrs' Brigade promised a 'reaction like an earthquake' after one of its combatants was shot dead in Nablus by the Israelis. In August 2005, both 'blood' and 'volcanoes' were invoked by al-Qaeda's Ayman al-Zawahiri when claiming that the British prime minister—rather than Islamist suicide-bombers—had brought 'destruction to Central London'. 'You shed rivers of blood in our land', he declared, 'so we exploded volcanoes in your land'.

'Fire' (in April 2004) would turn Spain into an 'inferno', 'scorch the land' of Italy (in July 2004) and 'burn the hearts of Silvio Berlusconi and the Italian people' (in September 2004). 'May God burn and slaughter him!' was the imprecation of the Islamist group Ansar al-Jihad in November 2004 against Iyad Allawi, interim premier of Iraq under the US occupation. Aggressors against Iran were similarly threatened by President Mohammad Khatami with 'burning hell' in February 2005.

'Hell' and 'unbearable hell' have also been widely promised to 'infidel land'. 'When explosions hit your towns and their light turns night into morning, we swear you will see hell with your own eyes', the al-Qaeda-linked Tawhid Islamic Group warned Italy in July 2004. Likewise, non-Muslim enemies are frequently warned that they have 'opened the gates of hell' by their actions; and having been 'opened', as was declared by Palestinian organisations after the assassination of Yassin, 'everything' was 'permissible' in order to avenge what had been done.

Metaphorically and in literary convention, 'the sword' has always been invoked as the instrument of Islam's meting out of a deserved justice to those who threaten it, who hold it in disrespect or who usurp its claims on earth; the name of the Filipino Islamist group 'Abu Sayyaf' means 'Father of the Sword'. 'Nothing will stop us cutting off his head', declared a Hamas leader referring to the Israeli prime minister, Ariel Sharon, in March 2004; 'Israeli hands we will cut off, God willing', proclaimed Sheikh Hassan Nasrallah, after the assassination in Beirut in July 2004 of a leading member of Hezbollah. Such rhetoric can also be applied to fellow-Muslims. Ali Hassan al-Majid, the cousin of Saddam Hussein and known as 'chemical Ali' for his role in the gassing of thousands of Kurds in 1988, threatened to 'cut open' the regime's foes 'like cucumbers'. And after Saddam's fall, even the new interim president of Iraq, Ghazi al-Yawer, promised in July 2004 a 'very sharp sword' for those who threatened the security of the country. But he was outdone in September 2004 by Abu Musab al-Zarqawi—the 'sheikh and commander of slaughterers'—who warned that 'bringing principles' to Iraq would cost 'a lot of torn limbs and blood'.

All such threats point to the grave. 'God willing', declared the Taliban's still-active military commander, Mullah Dadullah Akhund, in September 2004, 'we will make Afghanistan a burial ground for the Americans'; 'we will send death to every home, every city, every street in Israel', loudspeakers similarly proclaimed in Gaza in March 2004 after Ahmed Yassin's death. 'Dig deep into the ground mass graves prepared for the Crusaders', instructed the 'Army of Mohammed' in July 2004, in anticipation of 'infidel' intervention in Darfur, in western Sudan.

'Our choice is between death and death', declared Khaled Mashal, the political leader of Hamas, in May 2004. This was again an invocation of martyrdom. Yet to identify it as exclusively a mark of Islam at war remains wrong: '*patria o muerte*' has been an historically universal slogan, in one form or another. Not even the deliberate committing of suicide in attacking a foe is unique to Islam. The *kamikazes* were not Muslims, nor the Tamil Tigers, whose suicide-bombers—men and women—wrought havoc during their struggle from the 1980s for an independent Tamil homeland in Sri Lanka. Nevertheless, there is a cultural particularity in holding that 'paradise lies under the shade of swords', in the words of an Abu Sayyaf movement leader in the Philippines in April 2004. Or, as a Hamas leader told a crowd in Nablus in January 1997, 'our point of strength is our faith in paradise'.

That funds, and free trips to Mecca, should have been awarded both by Ba'athist Iraq and by the Saudi Arabian royal regime to the families of 'martyrs' after each attack on Israel is, therefore, not to be wondered at. However, assertions that suicide is 'easy', costs 'only lives' and is usable 'daily' spoke to a moral and military code that went beyond that espoused by Japanese fliers in the Second World War. Even the Saudi ambassador to London, Ghazi Algosaibi, could publish a florid poem in praise of an eighteen-year-old female Palestinian suicide-bomber. 'You died to honour God's word', hymned Algosaibi. 'May we all be accepted to be martyred', a Palestinian commander of such acts also declared; 'we are happy to die', announced nine Egyptian Islamists, sentenced to death in March 1994 for attempting to assassinate Egypt's prime minister, Atef Sedki. 'We love death, the US loves life, that is the big difference between us', bin Laden was quoted by a Pakistani journalist as saying in November 2001.

But, once more, to associate feelings of 'happiness' with dying is not confined to Islam. It plays its part, too, in Christian ethics, and is a prominent theme of the 'ecstasies' of its saints. Satisfaction at the dealing out of death to a foe is also not confined to Muslims. Gratification is clearly felt by many non-Muslims when leading members of Islamist groups are killed, and limited grief is aroused even when innocent civilians die in Afghanistan or Iraq. Yet when bin Laden was seen and heard, in a video-film circulated in November 2001, to declare of the attack on the World Trade Center that 'They were overjoyed when the first plane hit the building, so I said to them, be patient', and, again, that 'the brothers who heard the news [of the second strike] were overjoyed by it', the expression of such 'joy' appeared to most non-Muslims to be yet another deformity of mind.

Indeed, the non-Islamic world's inability to understand such sentiments has led to further errors of judgment about what it is facing. 'It should not be hard to agree', opined a leader in April 2002 in the *Washington Post*—from a great ethical and intellectual distance—'that a person who detonates himself in a pizza parlor or a discotheque filled with children, spraying scrap metal and nails in an effort to kill and maim as many of them as possible, has done something evil'.

Such acts are indeed evil. But the *Washington Post*'s imaginary moral 'agreement' on such matters was not to be expected between Islamists and the non-Islamic world. For Islamists can by political argument justify these deeds as acts which it is entitled to commit against an occupier, or a colonialiser or an imperialist, and can also sustain such argument by appeals to Holy Writ itself. Expostulations, whether by Muslims or non-Muslims, against the same acts as perversions of the teachings of Holy Writ do not and cannot touch them. 'The scenes of mothers celebrating the self-immolation of their sons' were 'incomprehensible' to an English editorialist; the wish of Palestinian parents, who had already lost one child in a suicide-bombing, that their other children might die in the same way, was described by a rabbi as 'madness'. An American commentator, shaking his head in the same fashion as the others, in turn asserted that those who had 'embraced a death-wish' possessed 'no capacity to ponder the serious philosophical questions about the meaning of life'.

However, they were again wide of the moral mark, despite the truths they told. That there was an egregious readiness-to-die among Islamist suicide-bombers was not in doubt. Farouk Kaddoumi, a close associate of Yasser Arafat, could even describe it in March 1997 as a 'normal reaction' to the 'provocative policies' of the Israelis. But without an understanding of the sense of Muslim righteousness and of the growing strength of the Islamic resurgence, meaning cannot possibly be made of such stances. Self-belief in Islam's mission in the world has passed beyond the confines of non-Islamic 'reason', and proceeded ever more deeply into the recesses of its own logic. From these recesses it can be extracted neither by force nor by persuasion, neither by bombs nor bribes, although the non-Islamic world has been left with little choice but to attempt it. Moreover, Islam's moral certitudes are no more capable of being translated into the non-Islamic world's terms than its delusions—including its delusions of grandeur—can be cured by self-defeat.

Even where the beliefs and methods of the Islamic world in its relations with 'the other' are auto-destructive—suicide-bombing is a fitting symbol of it—the compulsions which underlie them are too strong to be set aside. Disjunctions from reality may even be considered functional, not dysfunctional, in their contexts. Dislocations of the truth, as the non-Islamic world perceives it, are not felt to be harmful to the degree that the non-Islamic world expects. Refusal to respond to moral criticisms by the 'infidel' foe might also be plausibly considered part of Islam's strength, especially at a time when Western liberal democracies have lost much of their own sense of moral and political direction.

Islamist assault upon liberal and open-minded Muslim intellectuals—for various forms of insubordination towards God and man—might again be said to disclose the strength and not merely the 'alienness' of Islam's own forms of reason. In May 1993, Saudi Arabia's leading cleric, Sheikh bin Baz, declared that criticism of an Islamic ruler, since it had the tendency to lead to destabilisation, constituted unacceptable 'revolt' in the eyes of Islam. He added that 'disobedience' was tolerable only when a Muslim sovereign took a decision which was 'evil in the eyes of God'. Bin Baz might also believe that the earth is flat, as he did in fact. But here, like it or not, he spoke to a concept of the polity with deeper historical and cultural roots than those to be found in a Jefferson or a John Stuart Mill.

Such polities may turn to the non-Islamic world for material aid in suppressing their internal oppositions. They may insist to the West that their royal households or military dictatorships, as in Saudi Arabia or Pakistan, can guarantee the security of non-Islamic interests in their respective regions. They may simultaneously deflect the hostilities of their restless populations by condemning, generally through the pulpit, the value-systems of the Western countries which sustain them, while themselves covertly sustaining Islamism. Yet these complexities are again integral, or organic, features of the Arab and Islamic worlds. Western conceptions of what constitutes a rational order of things, or Western hopes of a gradual democratisation of such labyrinths, cannot radically affect them.

As we have seen, numerous devices in the Islamic world mask motive, erase a sense of culpability, and cancel fact. But misjudgments in the non-Islamic world about Islam's nature, purposes and powers make as large a contribution to the confusions of this war. Those who think that a culture of 'human rights', for example, can be introduced into Muslim polities, or who believe that Western Enlightenment notions of freedom of thought, conscience, religion and expression are compatible with Islam in its revival and advance are themselves guilty of delusion.

In the case of Islamists, their lack of hesitation in resorting to violent methods in the defence of the interests of Islam—as they see them—is a just object of non-Muslim abhorrence. But readiness to kill a foe with little or no scruple—as Israel has also demonstrated—is a powerful caution to critics. To pronounce that Saudi Arabia 'cannot be considered part of the international community' for its 'flouting of international law' in the conduct of trials, is likewise a mere whistling-in-the-wind when Western economies are dependent upon its oil. The means of defence of the faith of Islam, of an Arab 'feudal' kingdom, or of a Muslim military regime are governed by rules from which the Western world may recoil, but which it is powerless radically to change. When a Pakistani Christian, charged in Lahore with 'blasphemy', was shot dead as he emerged from court—with the trial incomplete—or when Islamists charged before a military tribunal in Tunisia with 'conspiracy to overthrow the state' were observed having difficulty in walking, the infractions of Western notions of 'human rights' counted for little or nothing.

For Islamists are well aware of the greater crimes—including genocide and slavery—which went to the creation of the West's Great Powers, and which served them further in their colonial and imperial phases. The 'Crusader' has also been a figure at whom it has been easy for them to point in the bypassing of criticisms of their own breaches of the moral code; it is as if the cruelties of Muslim rule in India or Ottoman excesses, for example, had never occurred. But most Muslims know, to their own advantage, that in any contest of rival hypocrisies and corruptions those of the non-Muslim world are great enough to lend a spurious legitimacy to almost any Muslim transgression, whether great or small.

Abdurrahman Wahid, the former cleric-president of Indonesia, was thus fully entitled—in his own estimation—to declare in September 2001 that the United States had 'no moral right' to retaliate for the attacks upon it. When a Palestinian 'parliamentary committee' in July 1997 called upon Yasser Arafat to dissolve his cabinet, and to bring to justice its corrupt members—whom the committee named—for the embezzlement and misapplication of up to half the Palestinian Authority's budget, nothing was done. Nothing could be done short of the removal of the Palestinian Authority itself, and of most of those who served it. But corporate America has itself nothing to teach others in the matter of corruption.

Indeed, Islamism's judgments delivered against the West, such as those by a bin Laden, can be described as deriving from their own morally secure sphere. It is a confidence which has advanced in step with Islam's growing faith in its own cause. This faith is more than capable of resisting the claims to superior virtue and justice made by its critics. After a senior UN investigator had condemned the Islamist Sudanese regime's human rights record, he was himself branded by Sudan a 'promoter of the morality of Satan'.

The sense of the justice and truth of Islam, and of the injustice and falsity of its foes, creates the confidence in Arab or Muslim eyes that even its falsest arguments are true. This confidence could not be sustained without the defence of its own mental procedures, the readiness to counterpose one logic to another, and the refusal to accept the non-Muslim's structure of truth-values and ethical norms. For this refusal, Muslims again have many excuses; not least when they observe the relative unconcern with which most of the non-Islamic world regards the fate of innocent Muslims caught up in conflict. Their lives are almost always considered cheaper than those of non-Muslims. It is a valuation which makes nonsense of the 'Judeo-Christian' West's claims to possess a superior respect for the sanctity of life itself.

Moreover, in an exchange of prisoners, Israeli captives will be thought (by the Israelis) to be equal in human worth to two hundred, or even more, 'Arabs'. Likewise, the killing of Muslim civilians during efforts to save them from themselves will be ascribed to the category of 'collateral damage' without much sign of true remorse. Given such degree of contempt, it is unrealistic to expect the giving of much quarter to the 'infidel' in battle, as the force (and forces) of Islam advance.

However, in order to maintain such stance of belligerence, it has also become necessary for some (or many) Muslims to believe that they are 'persecuted everywhere', as the Imam of Regent's Park mosque in London, Sheikh Zah'ran, put it to me in March 1991 during the Gulf War. More egregious morally was the formulation arrived at by Faisal Bodi in the *Guardian* on 6 November 2002—described by the paper as a 'writer on Islamic affairs' but who was also working for al-Jazeera, the Arab news channel—that 'in one sense it does not matter who the Bali culprits are. Ultimately, the victims, as with the events following September 11, will be Muslims'.

Once more, the unexpressed corollary of such assertions is that not merely issues of responsibility but facts are subordinate to the justice of the Islamist cause. Indeed, an increasingly thick-skinned sense of immunity from ethical criticism has been acquired throughout the Muslim world. This sense of moral autonomy is strengthened by the bewilderment created in others—non-Muslim intellectuals above all—by the complexities, evasions and inversions of so much Muslim and Arab discourse. Yet such discourse has an organic role in Islam's revival, and gains further impulse from the necessity for it. The sense of a just cause may—and often must—sweep aside all scruple, whether intellectual, political or moral, if such sense is to be sustained. It is the lesson that the Jacobins taught.

Among the tens of millions of the unemployed and disaffected in Muslim and Arab countries, as well as in the Muslim diaspora, the reach of Islamism is therefore growing wider. For it is Islamism's fierce and unyielding pride in its cause which appeals to what might once have been termed the Islamic world's 'lumpen' or 'marginal' elements, including among the unemployed intelligentsia. The assassin of Theo van Gogh was on welfare—after interrupting his studies—and had a history of petty crime, while among the bombers and would-be bombers in London in July 2005 were not only a teaching assistant but benefit-dependants and a former criminal gang-member with a prison record. Millions of young Arab men in the Maghreb between the ages of fifteen and twenty-four, for example, are without work; the unemployment rate in the most populous parts of Morocco—with the coast of Spain only eight miles from Tangier—is as high as 30 per cent. In Algiers at least half of those under the age of thirty were estimated in 2003 to be jobless. The leaderships of a succession of violent Islamist movements in Algeria have included militants in their twenties, with many of the recruits coming from the poorest sections of Algerian society. Many Muslims of Arab origin in France are also young, poor and unemployed; and there is a disproportionate number of Muslims in the jails of both Spain and France. In France,

more than half the prison population is said to be Muslim, and a high percentage of Muslims in Holland is without work.

Two-thirds of Iran's more than 65 million population is under thirty, and
more than half under twenty-one, with an unemployment rate (unofficially)
declared to be in the order of 25 per cent; three-quarters of a million new jobs
are required each year to provide work for the rising generation. Significant,
too, in Iraq was that some 60 per cent of men in Baghdad's poverty-stricken
Sadr City, the stronghold of the Islamist cleric Moqtada al-Sadr and his private army, were estimated to be jobless. In Libya more than 60 per cent of the
population is said to be under fifteen, with an unemployment rate of some 30
per cent. Of Malaysia it was reported, in November 2003, that increasing
numbers of the educated young were failing to find jobs; more than a third of
young men in Malaysia's southern provinces, where 80 per cent of the population is Muslim, were reported in January 2004 not to have completed their
primary education. In Muslim-majority Indonesia, some 30 per cent of those
of working age were estimated in 2004 to be jobless or underemployed. In
Pakistan, two-thirds of the population—increasing at the rate of 2.6 per cent
a year, and with many millions living in abjection—is illiterate.

In the Palestinian territories, the rate of unemployment among youths
aged between fifteen and twenty-four was said in 2004 to be some 40 per cent,
with over half the population in the West Bank and four-fifths in Gaza living
below the poverty-line of $2 a day. '60 per cent' of the population of Saudi
Arabia was said in 2003 to be under the age of twenty, and 'three-quarters'
under forty. There were twice as many new job-seekers each year as there
were new jobs, and an estimated unemployment rate among young adults—
aged between twenty and twenty-four—of up to 30 per cent. In Syria, only
about one-third of the 300,000 students graduating each year can find work,
while some of those implicated in the bombings of synagogues and British
targets in Istanbul in November 2003 came from areas of eastern Turkey
where the unemployment rate was estimated to be as high as 70 per cent.

In this vast Muslim constituency of the disenfranchised and discontented,
the urgent search for redemption from the ills of life cannot be expected to
make for any great tender-heartedness towards the 'infidel', nor for patience
with the fellow-Muslim who is accused of serving the interests of the non-
Muslim world. Regard for the 'infidel's notions of justice, reason and logic is
in general no match for the superior claims of faith and the felt need to strike
blows against those who show insufficient respect for Islam itself. Moreover, in
Britain, France and the United States, and in many other Western countries
where Muslims have often prospered less than other minority groups, a sig-

nificant proportion of those who have been attracted to Islamism—including those who attended al Qaeda training camps in Afghanistan—appear to have had chequered histories of disaffection, unrootedness and sometimes of crime, before they discovered a personal cause in militancy of faith.

Nevertheless, many leading Islamists in the world have privileged social and educational backgrounds, including education in the West. The increasing numbers of Western converts to Islam (and Islamism) likewise contain individuals of all social origins and levels of education. But it is to the statistics of unemployment and 'marginalisation' in both Islamic and non-Muslim countries that one must again look for at least a part-understanding of Islamism's appeal. In the United States, for example, African-Americans constitute some one-quarter of the American Muslim community; in 2003 it was even asserted that Islam could become the 'dominant religion among urban blacks'. A convert-member of al-Muhajiroun ('the Emigrants')—one of the most radical of Islamist groups in Britain, which 'disbanded' itself in October 2004 in order to 'link up with other groups'—was reported as saying in 2002 that he had converted to Islam because he had never felt that he 'belonged anywhere'. 'The mosques are full', he added, 'so Islam obviously has something'. In Egypt, such form of appeal was noted in the mid-1990s to be strong among its army of unemployed graduates in the cities. In France, Islamism has drawn much of its strength from jobless youths in bleak, peripheral urban estates, where school failure, drugs, drug-dealing and police harassments parody the possibilities of life.

In Britain, where the 'shoe-bomber' Richard Reid converted to Islam behind bars, Muslims are again disproportionately the fourth largest group of prison inmates, some 10 per cent. 'They [sc. other Muslims] tell you [in prison]', Abdul Haqq Baker, the chairman of London's Brixton mosque, declared in December 2001, 'how you are having a bad time because the authorities in Britain don't want Muslims to succeed. These are the ones that the extremists prey on, the weak characters. They are very persuasive. We have a lot of converts and ex-convicts', he added. Similarly, converts to Islam in Australia, in France, in Spain, in the United States and elsewhere, drawn—in company with Muslims from birth—to Islamist activism, have been found to include a significant proportion who for the first time found their identity and sense of purpose in militancy on behalf of their adopted faith.

Indeed, when converts to Islam who have known disadvantage in prosperous non-Muslim societies denote their own countries as 'places of war'—according to the dichotomies of Islam—it is as explicable as was the adoption of doctrines of class and 'class war' by some of their predecessors. In the west

Midlands town of Tipton, those who were said to have been recruited to fight with the Taliban had convictions for gang violence. As the Runnymede Trust reported in October 1997, 'there are trends amongst young British Muslims, particularly those who are unemployed or who expect to be unemployed, towards territoriality and gang-formation and towards anti-social conduct, including criminality'.

Similarly in the United States, where a disproportionate 40 per cent of its prison population of over 2 million is black, many black recruits to Louis Far-rakhan's 'Nation of Islam' were converted to 'atonement and responsibility' in prison, or were rescued from addiction. In Eastern New York's 'correctional facility' in September 2002, for example, one-quarter of its one thousand inmates were said to be Muslims. Nevertheless, estimates by evangelical Christians in the United States of an annual rate of prison-conversions to Islam as high as '30,000 to 50,000' are likely to have been exaggerated even if Muslim sources in the US, such as the National Islamic Prison Foundation, which actively proselytises in American jails, claim an even higher annual rate of prison conversions, the large majority African-Americans.

However, disparagements of 'jailhouse Islam' are morally short-sighted. For although the appeal of Islamism to the 'lumpen', both in the Islamic and non-Islamic worlds, is evident, the fact of it has led many non-Muslims to make further mistakes of judgment. Thus, Islamism could be condescendingly seen as providing 'militant fellowship and exalted meaning to otherwise mean and meaningless lives', as David Hirst put it in July 1992; or—in another disparaging view—it could be presented as nothing more than an instrument for those 'seething with resentment at the West'. This was again too arrogant and simplistic by half. That Islam is 'increasingly attracting the drifters, petty criminals and underdogs', as *The Times* put it in December 2001, may even be true in its fashion. But such pronouncements took insufficient account of the fact that, for growing numbers, Islam's overarching 'thought-system' provided a structure of belief not only to those who had experience of the anomic wilderness, unemployment, or other personal failure, but to others with an entirely different experience of life.

For ardent Islam is an advancing cultural, political and ethical force, the violences committed by a minority of its faithful notwithstanding. It sees truth, good, God and justice as on its side and, as its confidence grows, increasingly attributes falsehood, evil, devilry and crime to all that is not-Islam. Each—Islam and non-Islam—has also come to be perceived by the other as standing beyond the pale of reason itself; and sometimes with reason by both.

CHAPTER FIVE

Israel and Jews

Neither Israel nor the Jews are seen, whether by themselves, by their friends or by their foes, as a nation and a people like others. They are 'particular', distinct from others in their own and allegedly in God's eyes, embodiments or fulfilments of a supposedly transcendent purpose. For many others, evangelical Christians and Muslims alike, Israel is also more than it is. For the former, as for the Jews, it is the 'Zion' of prophecy, part of 'God's plan'; for Muslims, it has been elevated into a symbol of oppression. For many others, it furnishes justification for Muslim angers, since, with the West's support, it is held to have usurped the rights of the true proprietors of the same land.

To most Jews Israel is perceived as a land of promise, although they disagree over whether this promise has been achieved. There is a further division among Jews. That which most (but not all) see as a last secular refuge from exterminating twentieth-century foes, other Jews (a minority) see as belonging to them by biblical entitlement and divine right. A further minority, awaiting a higher, Messianic deliverance from the world's travails, disowns the very idea of a 'state of Israel' and, although living in it, refuses to defend it. All face the extreme counter-claim of many, perhaps a majority, of Muslims and a minority of non-Muslims alike, that Israel has no right to exist at all.

Nevertheless, by section 13 of its 1994 penal code, Israel—which describes itself as the 'state of the Jewish people'—has assumed a unique extraterritorial obligation to protect all Jews as if they were citizens of Israel,

171

and as if any crimes committed against them were committed within Israel's state borders. Israel thus considers all Jews to be within the purview of its jurisdiction, should they be threatened or otherwise put at risk merely on the ground that they are Jews. It has even given itself the right to demand the extradition to Israel of offenders against Jews-as-Jews, wherever the latter may be.

Israel, which has had an inevitable fight on its hands since its founding in 1948, is for some an initiator of aggression, and for others a continuous object of it. It is simultaneously holy and unholy (including, in the latter case, to a minority of Orthodox Jews themselves); a locus of redemption, actual or potential, and a focus of hatred; an institutionalised expression of injustice towards the Palestinians, or the historic requital of injustices committed against the Jews themselves, or both. 'Fascist' to some, it is the 'only democracy in the region' to others; according to judgment, the dream-child of utopian socialists, or the settlement of Zionist colonialisers. Above all, for many (or most), it is less a humdrum and functioning social order, or small-scale polity and economy, than a projection of what it is required to be by all the parties.

In consequence, a land smaller in area than the island of Sardinia, or Wales or San Bernardino County in California has been invested by its inhabitants, by its supporters and by its enemies with greater significance in the general scheme of things than it has merited. The nature of its powers (like the supposed powers of the Jews), real as they are, has also been magnified as in a distorting mirror. Indeed, the paranoias of Jews and Israelis, and of the foes of Israel and the Jews, are of similar dimension. Exaggerations glorify its history, minimisations reduce or dismiss it. To Arnold Toynbee, the Jews were merely the anachronistic survivors of a long-dead Levantine sub-culture. As for Judaism, it is dismissed in a footnote to Samuel Huntington's *The Clash of Civilisations* as no more than a 'historical affiliate' of Christianity and Islam, rather than as a progenitor of both.

Yet at the same time the Jews-as-such are seen by many as constituting a conspiracy with designs to bring down everything from Islam to the globe itself, while Israel is made over into the political expression of such intent. Then it becomes conspiracy's right arm, and the spider at the centre of the world-wide ('Zionist') web.

Thus, although the Jews have been made out to be less than they are, it has been historically commoner for Jews, 'Jewry', Judaism and Israel to be invested with an iconic (or fetishistic) significance. In the case of the Jews, they are variously a 'chosen', or self-chosen, people, the hidden controllers of the world's affairs, the 'source of all the trouble in the Middle East' and elsewhere, and so on. These representations are not required to be true in order to serve the purposes of those who believe them, or make use of them. By the same token, such representations do not become less potent where they are false. It is sufficient that they seem to have sufficient truth about them to be plausible, or if false that they are believed.

Even in the lacerating conflict between Israeli and Palestinian, where the one knows the other face-to-face, these representations cast their shadows equally over both historical facts and the true proportion of things. That which reveals a truth inconvenient to one or other party is denied. Events are held not to have taken place; like the earth of the Holy Land itself, the very ground upon which argument seeks to stand is disputed. The loyalties of Palestinians and Israelis to their respective interests are reciprocally held to be illegitimate or factitious; their histories to be fabrications; their claims to nationhood, myths; their vitiated natures incorrigibly this or that.

In further consequence, that which is held to be so by a Jew or Israeli ceases to have a truth-value to a Palestinian Arab or Muslim, and vice-versa. Such is equally the case whether a claim be true, half-true or false. Moreover, habituation to the employment of falsehood, in order that the case of one against the other be the more persuasive, makes every assertion suspect. Exaggeration of the strength or of the diabolism of the foe justifies a sense of victimhood or an act of aggression, or both; magnifications of the vocabulary of hostility inevitably become the *lingua franca* of all parties; and measured judgment of that which has been made to appear measureless becomes impossible.

Attribution to the Jews of inordinate powers, for instance, is of cultural long-standing. It has been carried down the ages, and is found in non-Muslim and Muslim discourse alike. It is also a characteristic compound of fact and fancy; or of truth and (once more) magnification of truth to the point at which such magnification turns to falsehood.

Most such arguments as to Jewish powers would be more persuasive were there not so few Jews in the world. At an estimated total of 12.9 million, a total which is falling—and comparable, in order of magnitude, with that of the Mormons, whose numbers worldwide are some 10 million—there is therefore one Jew on the planet to some one hundred Muslims, whose total is quickly rising. The disproportion in relation to the number of Christians is even larger; it is estimated that by 2050 there will be three billion Christians in the world. There are fewer Jews in the world than there are, say, Swiss or Dutchmen.

Of Israel's estimated population in 2004 of 6.8 million, some five and a half million were Jews. They were outnumbered more than tenfold by the combined populations of its four contiguous Arab neighbours, Egypt, Jordan, Lebanon and Syria, while the Arab League's more than twenty members had a combined population of 270 million. The number of Jews in Israel, with its rate of immigration falling, is roughly the same as the population of Rio de Janeiro, half the population of Mexico City and one-thousandth of the world's population. In the United States, which (for some) is commanded by Jews, they make up only some 2 per cent of the populace, a percentage which is slowly shrinking.

In its concealed arsenal of nuclear, chemical and biological weapons—it has perhaps the sixth-largest stockpile of nuclear weapons in the world—Israel of course possesses real power, and also has the highest defence budget as a percentage of GDP, at 9.5 per cent, in the Western world. It possesses power, too, in the extent of the support, political, economic and military, which it receives from the United States; some two billion dollars a year in military assistance alone. Moreover, its per capita GDP is more than thirteen times that of Egypt, a land fifty times larger in area than Israel and with more than ten times its population. Israel's GDP is also more than three times that of oil-rich Libya and of Syria, the latter of which is nine times larger in land-area. It is also one of the world's leading weapons and defence exporters, behind only the United States and Russia. In 2003 its exports of 'defence goods' accounted for 10 per cent of the world total.

India, China, Russia, Singapore, Turkey and the United States, among others, have a variety of military supply, joint training and security relations with Israel. With the US, among other countries, there are regular bilateral exchanges in fields of 'strategic cooperation'. In 2004, Israel and the United States jointly tested anti-ballistic missiles, US forces were trained in Israel in counter-insurgency tactics and Israeli forces were reported to have received training in the United States. Long-range US F-161s were beginning to be provided to Israel, and in the summer of 2004 the Pentagon agreed to supply Israel with satellite-guided bombs.

Nevertheless, Israel is no Goliath. Its four contiguous neighbours, whose combined land-area is more than sixty times that of Israel's some twenty-thousand square kilometres—excluding wrongfully-occupied Palestinian lands—are equally no David. When three non-contiguous but not very distant Muslim nations—Iran, Sudan and Saudi Arabia—are taken into account, the disproportions of scale in territory and in population grow greatly. These seven nations together possess more than three hundred times the land area of Israel. Iran alone is eighty times larger than Israel, and has eight times its population.

The Jewish diaspora in the West is also dwarfed in numbers by that of the (increasing) Muslim diaspora in the non-Muslim world. Support for Israel, as in the United States, may be held to compensate for its small absolute size and the relatively few Jews in the world. Israel does not belong to anything which might be compared with the Arab League or with the fifty-seven-nation Organisation of the Islamic Conference, disunited as these organisations are. Jews may speak and think in terms of the 'Jewish people' as a whole, but the 'Arab nation'—to which Arabs similarly refer—and the Islamic 'world community' of some 1.3 billion Muslims are of a different order of magnitude.

Yet fancy, Muslim and non-Muslim alike, has the power to annul these different orders of magnitude—of population, of scale of belongingness to a faith or culture, of territorial possession. Such type of fancy has long made of the Jews and of Israel whatever they are required to be. 'The Jew' in particular has a crucial role in those constructs by which we organise our perceptions of reality, so that such perceptions may 'make sense' to us, whether or not they be out-of-correspondence with fact. In its 'thought-system' the refusal of Christ's divinity by 'the Jews' has helped Christianity to sustain its Manichean distinction between those who are 'saved' and those who are not. Similarly, the 'Crusader' and the 'Zionist' have between them helped to carry Islamism into battle.

In conceptions of Israel, or of the 'Israel' which fancy requires, much of this Manicheism is translated into political terms; Israel becomes the anti-Christ among the nations. The simplification of complexity must also ride roughshod over disorderly facts, if 'Israel' is to remain the single-minded 'Zionist totality' which polemic and warfare require it to be. In 2004, more than one million, or at least 16 per cent, of Israel's population—and one-quarter of its population of children—was Arab. There are Arab members of Parliament, Arab political parties, and an Arab supreme court justice. Moreover, there is an increasingly heterogeneous population in Israel, as the proportion of Arabs and non-Jewish immigrants among its citizens increases. But for the notion of 'Israel' to retain its value as a simplified and unitary abstraction, its actual composition, the contradictions of its nature and the deep political divisions among its Jewish population need to be discounted, or otherwise transmuted.

In many respects, it is a modern Western polity with democratic institutions, an independent judiciary and a free press. There is also discrimination against Arabs, who suffer from higher rates of poverty and infant mortality, less access to public goods and small representation in many areas of Israeli life. In addition, intransigent fundamentalists hold racist views of 'the Arabs'.

'It is forbidden to be merciful to them. You must send missiles to them and annihilate them. They are evil and damnable', declared Rabbi Ovadia Yosef, a leading religious figure, in 2001. It was a view morally indistinguishable from the more extreme pronouncements of Islamist clerics. At the same time, a significant proportion of the Jewish population of Israel is hostile to the policies and purposes of the Israeli state, and hostile to such views.

However, settlers on Palestinian lands regard their rights as God-given. To vacate these lands, pronounced the former chief rabbi, Avraham Shapira, in October 2004—as Israel made plans to withdraw its settlers from Gaza— was morally equivalent to 'desecrating the Sabbath'. But there were again Israelis, and Jews, who strongly objected to such notions, believing that the settlements were no more than predation. Moreover, road-blocks, barriers, security fences, travel restrictions and other state policies—including rules making it difficult for Palestinians who marry Israelis to acquire citizenship rights in Israel—were separatist in effect. A proposal even to construct 'alternative' road networks for Palestinians and Israelis in the West Bank was put forward by the Israeli government in 2004. Damaging to the livelihoods and general well-being of the Arab population within Israel and beyond its borders, these measures were also held to be so by other Jews, for whom they represented a breach of Hebraic ethics and an abandonment of its concepts of justice.

Thus, the Israeli newspaper *Ha'aretz* declared in December 2004 that there was 'no more serious aberration in Israel's democracy than its control over 1.5 million Palestinians [in the West Bank and Gaza] to whom that democracy does not apply'. Yet Israelis could also correctly claim that the construction from August 2003 of its West Bank separation barrier served to reduce attacks on their state. But its line incorporated further Palestinian lands, and was held by the International Court of Justice in July 2004 to be a violation of international humanitarian law and human rights law. This was despite the existence of similar security barriers between India and Pakistan, between Saudi Arabia and Yemen, between Turkey and Syria, between the Turkish and Greek sectors of Cyprus, and between Morocco and the Western Saharan region claimed by the Polisario Front guerrillas.

To a significant section of Israeli opinion, too, the security barrier was 'invasive' and 'forcibly annexationist'. But other Israelis and Jews were untroubled by any measures, however inhumane, which they believed to protect them from attack. Hand-in-hand with the continuation of the construction of tens of thousands of housing units on Palestinian lands, these measures included punitive demolitions of several thousand Palestinian homes in the West Bank. They created homelessness and were described as 'war crimes' by

Amnesty International in May 2004, but were declared by the Israelis in February 2005 to have been 'stopped'. Israel also engaged in the wanton churning up of Palestinian agricultural land, and the cutting down of a reported quarter of a million fruit and olive trees belonging to Palestinian farmers. This damage was carried out both in order to create 'buffer zones' and as reprisal punishment for attacks across Israel's borders or on its settlements. There were also allegations of the shooting of injured non-combatants by Israeli forces, and even, as in June 2004, of isolated abuse of corpses of Palestinian fighters, acts described by the chief rabbi of the Israeli army as 'immoral' and 'inhuman'.

The numbers both of Palestinians and Israelis are very small, but they loom large in each other's perceptions, as they do in the perceptions of much of the rest of the world. They have also suffered disproportionately from the harms and deaths which they have inflicted on one another, while their reciprocal demonisation has also served to make the lives of both seem cheaper than either could afford. One month's killings in an average month, as in March 2002, represented proportionately greater losses to each side than did the deaths of Americans at the World Trade Center in September 2001, in relation to the American population as a whole.

As with Jewish numbers and powers in the world, so Israel's size and strength are magnified in fancy. The Israeli armed forces, less than 200,000 strong, are one-fifth of the size (on paper) of the combined forces of its four contiguous neighbours. Yet the effect of myth-making, together with actually superior armament and tactical skill, is to make this army seem—to both Muslims and non-Muslims—an invincible force, and Israel a colossus.

In September 2004, Sheikh Hamad bin Khalifa al-Thani, the ruler of Qatar—one of the Gulf states with which Israel maintains limited relations—referred to the 'might' of Israel. 'Bombs, missiles, delivery systems, gases, germs? Tel Aviv has the lot', similarly wrote a *Guardian* columnist in December 2003. Israel, declared an Anglican peace activist, calling in September 2004 for a 'boycott' of the country, was 'one of the most wealthy and incredibly powerful nations'. The Israeli defence forces had thus undone the older image of 'the Jew' who shambles unresisting into the jaws of death. But whatever its armament and the extent of its external support, Israel remains a minuscule nation with a small population, and is only some ten miles wide at its narrowest point.

This combination of Israeli potency and vulnerability, of strength and weakness—but not a vulnerability or weakness as great as that of the Palestinians—is a further complexity. It has made for a matching confusion of judgment. Those who are hostile to Israel and to Jews tend mentally to aggrandise their strengths; Israelis and Jews tend to imagine their vulnerabilities to be larger than they are. This latter sense owes much to the argument, expressed by Islamists in extreme terms, that the Jews have 'no right' to be in, or have no claim upon, the Holy Land at all.

Historians of varying persuasions—driven by competing religious and national interests—have worked hard to prove or disprove the longevity and rootedness of the ancient Hebrews and Philistines (or Palestinians) in what was once the land of 'Canaan'. Some have argued, for example, that the Philistines were not autochthons but a maritime people who were relative latecomers to the eastern Mediterranean's shores, and that the Palestinian claim to distinct nationhood has no historical foundation. Or, it is held that invading Hebrews expropriated the indigenous Canaanite tribes two and a half millennia ago, and have simply repeated the procedure in modern times. Thus, Arab and Muslim revisionist historians of Jerusalem have maintained that the biblical Jebusites were the true first rulers of the city, that they were an Arab tribe, and that the Palestinians are their natural heirs.

At Camp David, Yasser Arafat is said to have denied that Solomon's Jerusalem Temple had ever existed. In December 2003 he conceded 'the Jewish historical attachment to Palestine', but in June 2004 again implied that the biblical account of the building of the First Temple was a myth. Alternatively, or in addition, the sack of the second Jerusalem Temple by the Romans in 70 AD, and the massacre and scattering of the Jews, have been held to have cancelled their 'right of return'; as the Jews were to cancel that of the Palestinians after 1948. Moreover, the revival by Jews of the claim to a state of their own, and in a region from which all but a relatively small number of them were 'exiled' for two thousand years, is held in turn to have usurped Arab and Muslim claims upon Jerusalem and the land associated with it.

It is thus argued that, despite the religious primogeniture of Hebraism in relation to Christianity and Islam—by at least a millennium in one case, and by a millennium and a half in the other—Jews have no precedence of entitlement over Muslims (or Christians), and for some no entitlement at all, to be installed or re-instated in the midst of the Levant. Jews and their Christian evangelical supporters insist, on the contrary, that not only Jerusalem but the 'land of Israel from the river Jordan to the sea' was bestowed on 'the Jewish people' by God, and can belong rightly to no other.

In late 2001, a number of Christian organisations in the United States formally declared the Palestinian intifada a 'travesty'. They approved of Israel's refusal to negotiate while attacks upon it continued, and even 'acknowledged'

Jerusalem as the 'undivided capital of the Jewish state'. In March 2002, Senator James Inhofe called on 'Jews' to maintain control of the Palestinian territories 'because God said so'. 'Look it up in the Book of Genesis', he added. American Christian evangelical leaders were reported to be 'praying for peace and protection for the Jewish people'; 'dozens of Christian television stations' held a 'telethon' in August 2002 to support Israeli casualties of the intifada; a prominent 'born-again' Christian from New Mexico disclosed that he had been 'observing the Jewish Sabbath for the past two years'. Christian evangelical groups were also said in *Time* magazine in June 2002 to be 'spending millions on everything from armored school-buses for Israeli children to halogen lights for the Israeli army's emergency-reserve service'.

In October 2004, the American evangelist Pat Robertson sent 'notice' to 'Osama bin Laden, Arafat and Palestinian militants' that they would not 'frustrate God's plan to have the Jews rule the Holy Land until the Second Coming of Jesus'. The purpose of of the 'rise of Islam' was to 'destroy Israel and take the land from the Jews. I see that as Satan's plan to prevent the return of Jesus the Lord', Robertson declared; 'God says', he added, 'It's my land, keep your hands off it'. Other Christians thought differently. For example, in June 2004 the American Presbyterian Church decided to divest its funds from companies 'doing business with Israel', and took a stand towards it sharply distinct, both theologically and politically, from that of much of the evangelical movement; in June 2005 an Anglican consultative council unanimously recommended a similar policy of 'disinvestment' to the Church of England.

The presence of one of Islam's most sacred shrines upon the site of the Jerusalem Temple is a physical symbol of such contentions. To Jews it signifies that latecomer Muslims wrongfully occupy an ancient Jewish holy place; to Muslims, that today's Jews wrongfully occupy an ancestral Arab city sacred to Muslims; or it may be asserted that Jews also occupy Christian holy sites. In these polemics, a Muslim scholar has asserted that Israel's 'disposition to assert dominion' in Jerusalem is 'almost atavistic'. Indeed it *is* 'atavistic'. That is, it is a claim, given political form in 1948 and subsequently defended tooth-and-nail, to what is held to be a biblically-derived entitlement. Hence, to most Jews—and clearly to many Christian 'fundamentalists' also—the term 'atavism', far from being the reproach that was intended, is a fair description of what is held by them to be a just impulse.

One consequence of such conflict was that in nearly six decades only a tiny handful of Muslim nations—Egypt, Jordan and Mauritania, whose government was overthrown in August 2005—gave formal recognition to Israel's existence; Iran's refusal was described in April 2005 by its president,

Mohammad Khatami, as both 'logical' and 'moral'. But such attitudes were not confined to the Muslim world. Israel was recognised by Spain, for example, only in 1986, while the Vatican did not agree to recognise Israel until the end of 1993. This was forty-five years after the foundation of the state; or as Pius X (1903–1914) once put it, 'the Jews have not recognised Our Lord, therefore we cannot recognise the Jewish people'. Yet by May 1989 almost one hundred countries in the world had formally recognised the PLO as a presumptive political entity, contrary to international legal practice. Moreover, although a member of the UN since 1949, the destruction of Israel remains the avowed aim of some of its fellow UN members, contrary to the UN charter.

But if the very creation of Israel was anathema to most of the Arab and Muslim world, matters were to become ethically and politically more serious with each succeeding war, fought from 1947 onwards, over the territory of which it was composed. The 'atavistic' impulse was extended, in breach of the Fourth Geneva Convention, to the re-settlement by Israelis of militarily-occupied lands in the West Bank, lands which they considered to be a part of the same biblical patrimony, and which were renamed Judea and Samaria. This in turn gave rise to the charge that the Jewish settlers were an 'alien population', as it was put (to *The Times*) by a Cambridge professor of political theory, and by other leading English intellectual and political figures, in July 2002. Similarly, Israel was described as a 'settler state' by David Hirst in the *Guardian* in December 2003.

It was likewise asserted at a conference held by the United Nations in Durban in September 2001 that the Palestinian people were 'under foreign occupation'; or were living under a 'foreign power' and 'foreign subjugation', as *Guardian* editorialists declared in December 2001 and January 2004; or, in its Islamist variant—which is not greatly different—'the enemy [sc. Israel] is present in a Muslim land', as a text-book in use at the UNRWA-sponsored teachers' training college in Ramallah has it. In April 2004, Saeb Erakat, a senior member of the Palestinian cabinet, described the prospect of conceding a permanent Israeli presence on the West Bank as 'like giving a part of Texas to China'.

Thus, such charges of being 'alien' can be brought equally against Jews who live within the borders determined by the UN in 1947 and those who have wrongfully settled outside them. Indeed, many of the charges carry the imputation that Jews are figures extraneous even to the Old Testament's lands. Early European Zionists had themselves recognised that a reconstituted Israel in the Middle East would have an uncertain fate as an 'island in a Arab sea', as

Theodor Herzl put it. Since 'most Jews' were 'no longer Oriental', he confided to his diary, 'a transplantation' of them to Palestine would be 'difficult to carry out'. Nevertheless, the argument that Jews are 'aliens' in Israel is no more rational a contention than the assertion by some Jews that Palestinians 'do not belong' in Israel, or that their aspiration to statehood is of a lower moral order than was that of the Jews. Moreover, the attribution of 'alienness' to the Jewish presence, whether in Israel or in its settlements, has the nature of yet another projection. Under it, the sense (in some) of the 'foreign'-ness of 'the Jew' in the diaspora has been transposed to the Jew wherever he might be, even when he is in the 'land of Canaan'.

There are few facts or fictions related to, or projected upon, Israel and Jews which are free of complexity and of feverish sentiment. The history both of the Jews and of Israel is a battleground of rival interpretation and reconstruction, whether in respect of occurrences millennia ago or during the last decades. Compounding all this has been the contribution made by the muddled and contested circumstances of Israel's creation. In 1915, in the course of a world war in which the Ottoman Empire, then masters of the 'Holy Land' and the Levant, joined the Axis powers, the Arabs were assured by Britain that the 'independence of the Arabs' in the Levant would be upheld when the war was won. But in 1916, as the anticipatory carve-up of the Ottoman Empire was being planned, 'Palestine' was allotted to Britain. In 1917, again before the Axis powers had been defeated, Britain's foreign secretary Arthur Balfour was 'looking with favour' on the establishment of a 'Jewish national home' in the same 'Palestine', provided that the civil and religious rights of 'existing non-Jewish communities' in 'Palestine' were not 'prejudiced'. From the outset this was a proviso to confound matters further.

Moreover, selective short-cuts in accounts of the past have been taken by all parties, as well as by bystanders, to the Israeli-Palestinian conflict. Thus, the 'influx' of European Jews into Palestine in 1945 could be discussed in *The Times* in November 2001 without any reference to the circumstances which brought it about. Conversely, Jews continue to make much of the enthusiastic support of the Grand Mufti of Jerusalem, Haj Amin al-Husseini, not only for the Palestinian national cause but for Hitler's Germany. He spent part of the war years in Nazi Berlin, where a 'pan-Arab government' in exile was formed, a forerunner of the Nasserite pan-Arabism of the postwar years. 'Slaughter the Jews wherever you find them', al-Husseini declared in a broadcast from Berlin in 1942, 'their spilled blood pleases Allah'. The widespread denial in the Arab and Muslim world of the scale, and sometimes even of the fact, of the Holocaust ties the knot of odium between Jew and Arab still tighter. So too does the record of the asylum given in Arab countries, such as Syria and Egypt, to German Nazis, as well as to several leading post-war neo-Nazi 'revisionists' who fled prosecution at home.

The United Nations decision on 29 November 1947 to partition Palestine, to the perceived disadvantage of the Palestinians, contributed to the confusion and bloodshed which were to follow. It also ensured the hostility which the very existence of Israel was to arouse. In their pro-Israeli partiality, some historians and commentators have sought to ignore the implications of the disproportions in territorial allocation in the UN partition plan. Others, in their pro-Arab partiality, have sought to cancel the implications of the invasion of Israel on 15 May 1948—within a few hours of the proclamation of the new state on 14 May 1948—first by Egypt and then by the armies of Iraq, Transjordan (as it then was), Lebanon and Syria.

Others have elided the complexities of the passage of events from 1947 to 1949. A *Guardian* commentator in January 2004 could therefore reduce these events to 'the war that gave birth to the state of Israel in 1948', which by omission contains its own falsehood. Others have translated the flight of Arabs in 1948 and 1949—thousands fled even before hostilities had broken out—into their 'expulsion'; or, better still, into their 'deportation' by the new state as it was attacked. Some of those who were intended to be assisted by the attack—the local Arab population—stood their ground, fighting alongside the invading armies so that in certain sectors they for a while gained the upper hand. Others cut and ran, led in their flight by their own communities' heads; many other tens of thousands of Arabs were driven from their ancestral homes and terrains at the hands of the Israelis.

In some villages and cities, including Haifa, Jaffa and Tiberias, the exodus appears to have been ordered by Arab community leaders themselves; often they were among the first to flee, having the means to do so. As the then British High Commissioner for Palestine, General Sir Alan Cunningham, reported, 'the collapsing Arab morale in Palestine' was attributable in part to what he called 'the increasing tendency of those who should be leading them [sc. the Arabs] to leave the country'. Furthermore, 'in all parts of the country the *effendi* class has been evacuating in large numbers over a considerable period, and the tempo is increasing'. As Hussein Khalidi, one of the Palestinians' leaders complained, 'Everyone is leaving. Everyone who has a cheque or some money—off he goes to Egypt, to Lebanon, to Damascus'.

Even before the invasions of May 1948 Israeli militias had acted brutally against the local Arab population, as at the village of Deir Yassin on 9 April 1948, when more than one hundred villagers were killed. But in the repetitions of the history of this period, the numbers of those who fled, who were expelled, who were deported or who were 'ethnically cleansed' have often been exaggerated. Perhaps 700,000 fled the fighting in search of safety, or were driven from their homes as the Israeli army conquered; '600,000' were displaced according to the British Foreign Office estimate at the time. In addition, from 1948 to 1951, hundreds of thousands of Jews also left, or were driven by expropriation and attack from, their homes in Egypt, Iraq—where 118,000 of the total Iraqi population of 4.5 million were Jews—Lebanon, the Maghreb, Syria and elsewhere in the Arab world; in August 2004, the Libyan leader offered compensation for their losses.

The fate of the Arabs in a conflict which lasted until the uneasy truce in 1949 was a many-sided matter. So, too, was the multiple invasion of Israel—which at the time had an army of only 30,000—by neighbouring Arab nations. Nevertheless, a simplified history of complexity, war, fear, crime and flight has reduced the events, for many, to the victimisation of Arab by Jew. Contrariwise, and with related simplification of the truth, it has been asserted by a Jewish historian that 'had the Palestinians and the Arabs refrained from launching a war to destroy the emerging Jewish state, there would have been no refugees and none would exist today'.

On both sides, varieties of misrepresentation of these tangled events have made their contributions, often knowingly, to the intractability of the issues. Worse, the refugees—with the assistance both of international organisations and of the same neighbouring countries which attacked the new state—have remained refugees. In conditions of economic and political stasis they are to be found in almost sixty 'camps' in Gaza and the West Bank—conquered by Egypt and Jordan in the 1948–49 war—as well as in Jordan, Lebanon and Syria. The displaced Palestinians have grown in number to a population of some four million, many marooned in limbo in the Arab states where they are housed, and often with their rights curtailed by their 'hosts'.

Their condition is a continuing injustice. (This has made it possible for some crudely to ask, 'Why can't 200 million Arabs feed four million Palestinians?') They also fulfil the need for a *casus belli*; a need met by the instrumentalising of their crying grievances by Islamists in the region and far beyond. Moreover, in the eyes of Muslims and many non-Muslims alike they are grievances which have served to give legitimacy to acts which would otherwise be morally indefensible. Even the United Nations has been party to this process. Its relief agency UNWRA, set up expressly to cater to the needs of the 'camp' inhabitants—but not to resettle them—has helped to ensure that yet another Gordian knot cannot be untied.

The unjust terms of the 1947 partition—rejected by the Palestinians and for the same reason accepted by the Israelis—together with the violence and counter-violence which followed have also been placed within an Arab, and now wider Muslim, 'narrative' of humiliation and affliction. It discomfitingly mirrors the historical 'narrative' of the Jews themselves, with each people self-perceived as singled out for special maltreatment. However, they are unable to make common cause even on such wretched ground. For Islam—like Christianity before it—has singled out the Jews and Israel as its particular foes.

The injustices done to the Palestinians have been worsened by the acts which they and their fellow-Arabs have taken to correct them. The 1948 invasion of Israel and the subsequent Arab defeat led to Israel's possession of larger tracts of land than it would have occupied had it been left in peace. The Six-Day War of 1967, in which Israel faced down Egypt, Jordan and Syria as they mobilised for a joint attack, similarly led to the capture of the whole of Jerusalem and the West Bank, the Golan Heights and part of the Sinai desert, the latter subsequently returned to Egypt. It also added a further chapter to the 'narrative' of self-inflicted Arab humiliation. This time it was swift and real, as well as saddling Israel with intractable problems—diplomatic, military, demographic, ethical and economic—which were to come to haunt it.

These conflicts have had abasing effects far from the theatre of events. They have been effects which are not physical or territorial, but intellectual and moral. They have made falsehood and simplification the common coin of apologia, whether on Israel's or on anti-Israel's behalf. Untruths have become as much settled and commanding features of the terrain of argument as are the settlements of American and other Jews on the hill-tops of 'Judea and Samaria'. 'In 1948', thus declared John Pilger in September 2002, 'the Arab world rose up when Palestinians were forced to flee from their homes in a blitz of fear and terror'.

This was not merely prose of high colour but itself a form of aggression. Other elisions of facts—such as those required for a full accounting of how the 'occupied territories' came to be occupied in the first place—add intellectual to physical violence. To assert that the 'root of the problems facing the Israeli nation is the continuing occupation of most of the Palestinian territories captured by force of arms in 1967' is a half-truth, since it excludes the precedent causes of the occupation. Even the gross murder in 1991 of eight hundred Palestinian refugees in Sabra and Shatila in Lebanon, at a time when Israeli forces were in occupation of part of the country, was carried out not by Israelis but by Lebanese Christian militiamen in reprisal for the assassination of the Lebanese president Bashir Gemayel; subsequent attribution to

Israel of 'direct responsibility' for the massacre therefore overstated its culpability, as both the Lebanese and Palestinians themselves knew.

Habituation to untruth also undoes intellectual integrity and judgment. In January 2002 Edward Said, the Jerusalem-born Arab-American scholar, could thus describe Israel's military occupation of Palestinian lands since 1967 as the 'longest such occupation in history'. It was an assertion which any history of colonialism and imperialism—including of the Ottoman Empire—refutes on the instant. Abuse of truth and misuse of language could also permit the claim that the dispute between Israelis and Palestinians 'led Israel into open war in 1956, 1967, 1973 and 1982', as a commentator in *The Times*, Simon Jenkins, misleadingly put it in December 2001.

Under international law, territory which has been used for hostile attacks upon an ultimately victorious power need not be surrendered until a peace treaty has been made with the former foe. It is a principle, one might argue, of natural justice and reason. But such principle is irreconcilable with the schemata to which causation and complexity have been reduced. It is therefore generally omitted from the reckoning also. Conversely, the intellectual and ethical violence by which biblical lands are claimed by Jews to be eternally their property, and by supposedly divine fiat, is not less than the other violences which cancel inconvenient fact. Jews have no prescriptive (or divine) lien on the territory of the ancient kingdoms of Israel and Judah. The notion is absurd. Suicidal and other attacks on Israel also cannot be described simply as responses to the latter's 'occupation of Palestinian and Arab lands since 1967'. There were many ambushes and killings of Israeli civilians, farmers, shepherds and policemen before the Six-Day War of 1967 and the occupations which resulted from it.

There was also a different form of cruelty, but cruelty nonetheless, in the Jewish denial of the trials endured even by an Arafat, however cruel was his own implication in the suffering of others, Palestinians included. His unremitting desire to see the creation of a Palestinian state was not less admirable in principle than was the same desire of the Jews. Most of his fellow-Arabs gave him relatively scant aid, and others expelled him from their midst; in the Jordanians' case, accompanied by mass killings of his followers, despite the fact that the majority of Jordanians are themselves Palestinians, as already noted. They watched him proceed from operational base to base in Syria, in Jordan, in Lebanon, in Tunisia, in the West Bank and at the last to a destroyed bunker in Ramallah. In this itineration, much of it for bloody purpose and with self-defeating outcome, tragedy was inscribed as well as farce.

The cancellation of the sense of it has served no more than, say, the reciprocal cancellation from the moral record of the attack on Israel in October 1973 by the Egyptian and Syrian armies, again acting in co-ordination. It brought Egypt once more across the Suez Canal into Sinai, and Syria into Galilee. But for most Muslims and many non-Muslims more blame attached to the invaded—for having provoked the invasion—than to the invaders.

'Authoritative' or scholarly commentary which cancels or misrepresents past and present has made a perverse contribution to the prevention of accord and peace in the Middle East. So, too, has media preference for sensational effects over the painstaking exploration of causes. The lie or half-truth often serves only to provoke or to justify a conflict, and therefore to prolong it, often in the interests of the media itself. Moreover, on the barricades, the falsehoods of one side serve the falsehoods of the other.

Thus, it has been made easy for most Israelis and many Jews, like many Muslims, to avert their gaze from what has been done in their names. Alternatively, where the truths of the Middle Eastern conflict are awkward—because thay do not square with some pre-existing structure of 'explanation'—only the most fitting facts will be admitted by protagonists and commentators alike. For example, the decades-long Syrian occupation of Lebanon, and the subordination of the latter to the former's diktats, could be reduced in 2002 to that of a 'locally enforced peace' which had 'held' since 1983. A true account of the years of Lebanon's occupation both by Syrian and Israeli armies could thus be 'covered' by a glib phrase and a few casual words. Abolition of unwelcome truths or difficult facts can take many forms: in July 2002, an exhibition in China on Albert Einstein was cancelled by the Israelis after the Chinese had demanded the removal of references to Einstein's Jewishness and to his support for the creation of a Jewish state.

Truth is ill-served, too, by seeming innocence of perception in relation to matters where naivete has no place. 'It never seems to occur to the Israelis', declared a commentator in the *Guardian* in July 2001—on the subject of the building of a wall by the Israelis between themselves and the Palestinians— 'that there are simpler and more obvious ways to allay their [sc. Israeli] fears of the Palestinians, such as learning to live alongside them'. Or, also in the *Guardian* in February 2002, 'the question of why this war, for this is what it is, . . . is being fought is truly a rather mysterious one'.

To reduce to simplicities that which is not simple on the one hand, and to make 'mysteries' of that which is no mystery on the other, sets its own moral and intellectual puzzles. But they are less worth pursuing than related disservices to the truth which have been of larger significance. The most important has stemmed from the desire to separate the conflict between Israel and the

Palestinians from the broader collision between the Islamic and non-Islamic worlds; as if it were a lethal but 'private' quarrel which could be settled by negotiation between the parties, rather than a fierce confrontation upon one of the many front-lines of a larger war.

That such simplifications are another form of falsehood is clear from the affiliations of the parties in the Middle East conflict, whether they be expressed in the form of aid to Israel from the United States, or Muslim support to Islamist groups hostile to Israel's existence. Why, then, has the long Palestinian-Israeli belligerency been so detached from its wider context? The principal reason derives from the desire, shared by Muslims and many non-Muslims, that the Middle East conflict—and especially Israel's role in it—be seen not as part of the wider war but as the cause-of-causes of it. A point of convergence with Islamist perceptions, in its most pungent expression it holds that Israel is the *fons et origo* of 'the trouble'.

This notion of Israel's centrality, like assertions as to its power or 'might', is presented in various forms. The first is that the war in the Middle East is essentially Israel's doing. The thesis appeals to many. Thus, Tim Llewellyn, a former BBC journalist in the region, declared in September 2002 that Israel bore 'overweening [*sic*] responsibility' for the 'disaster' in the Middle East. Similar was the assertion by the Palestinian Anglican bishop of Jerusalem, Riah Abu el-Assal, that any attack upon Israel should be laid at the door of 'the Jews' themselves. 'This region', declared Prince Khalid-al-Faisal al-Saud of Saudi Arabia in September 2002, referring to 'Palestine', 'has been politically disturbed for more than 60 or 70 years and the reason is Israel'. In the words of Yasser Arafat's aide Nabil Abu Rudeineh, the Israelis were 'responsible for every single act of violence in the region'.

A second version of the 'Israel-as-source-of-the-trouble' thesis has it that the 'war on terrorism' cannot be won 'without peace and stability in the Middle East', and that the Israeli-Palestinian war therefore 'ought to be at the very top of the agenda'. A typical expression of this view—again shared by Muslims and many non-Muslims, by Western peace-brokers and Islamist militants—is that the 'Palestinian issue is the centre of everything', as President Mubarak of Egypt insisted in March 2004. A rougher third version is that Israel's policies, being an 'unqualified disaster', threaten disaster to others in the region.

A fourth version of the argument, common in the aftermath of the 9/11 attack and heard from 'left' to 'far right', holds that 'our support for Israel is what got us into this mess'. According to William L. Pierce, leader of the neo-Nazi National Alliance in the United States, speaking to the press in September 2001, this support had 'provoked' the attack on the World Trade Center. Similarly, America's 'unilateral support for Israel' was the 'central running sore'—an image of infection—in Muslim relations with the non-Islamic world, according to the *Guardian* in October 2001. In a fifth, 'sophisticated' form of this populist fourth version, Zbigniew Brzezinski, President Carter's national security adviser, argued in September 2002 that 'the defeat of the Arab effort to prevent the existence of Israel and the subsequent American support for Israel and its treatment of the Palestinians' had helped to shape Arab 'political emotions'.

These assertions coincided in essence with some of Islamism's principal rationalisations for attacking the West. They were assertions which cumulatively represented Israel as not much less of a threat to world peace than, say, Iran or North Korea. Indeed, in the eyes of '60 per cent' of Europeans—according to a much-disputed poll in October 2003—Israel was the 'greatest threat to peace in the world'. 'This small nation', added the Greek composer Mikis Theodorakis in November 2003, is 'the root of evil'.

Here, many of the combatants in the conflicts between the Islamic and non-Islamic worlds come to a point of agreement. It is a concordance of view on Israel's culpability which would in logic justify the taking up of arms by Islamism against the West, and for a minority of non-Muslims in the West does actually justify it. But the 'root of evil' argument also helps to sell the strategic pass to Islamism's endeavours, as Islamists plainly know. In assailing Islamism for its attacks upon the West while sharing much of the former's preoccupation with Israel, non-Muslims invite what they seek to prevent: Muslim attack upon them for their moral double standards. Moreover, if at least part of the non-Islamic world itself believes what many Muslims and Islamists together believe about Israel (and the Jews), Islamism's assaults upon Israel and the nation that principally supports it cannot be objected to on principle, but only on the ground that the wrong means are being used.

The historical precedents for attributing 'this mess' to Israel and abstracting it from the world's larger dilemmas, are clear enough. In the Second World War some believed—both on 'left' and 'right'—that the *casus belli* in that case too was not the terms of the Versailles Treaty, nor Hitler's aggrandising intent for Germany, but was in some way attributable to the Jews, whose supposed interests in world dominion were allegedly served by war itself. Indeed, there was, and on the 'far-right' still is, a current of opinon which would have it that the Second War was actually fought 'for the Jews' or, in a more fanciful variant, was a 'Jews' war'. Broadly speaking, past preoccupation with 'the Jews' is today's preoccupation with 'Israel', although 'the Jews' as such also continue to play their historically-allotted role.

The note pinned, by knife, to the chest of the assassinated Theo van Gogh in November 2004 complained that the Netherlands was controlled by Jews. The Greek composer Theodorakis—who wrote the Palestinian national anthem—declared in August 2004 that Jews 'hold world finance in their hands'. In December 2004 a Turkish cleric, Imam Gecgel, asserted that 'higher powers', Jewish and American, had even the Turkish government in their 'control'. At its extreme, as expressed by the deputy-editor of the Egyptian government daily *al-Gumhouriya* in April 2004, Jews have carried out 'all terrorism worldwide'. In November 2004 the Danish Muslim cleric, Nabil Shaker al-Talegani, even suggested that terrorists were Jews pretending to be Muslims.

The bombing of a disco as far away as Bali was therefore attributed by some Islamists to Israel. The 'American people', said the Jemaah Islamiyah leader Abu Bakr Bashir in September 2003, were being 'manipulated by Jews to fight against Islam'. In Iraq, bombings of Shi'ite mosques, the maltreatment of Iraqi prisoners and 'attempts to penetrate' or 'infiltrate' Iraq were blamed on 'Israel', 'Zionists' or 'Jews'. The Iraqi opposition to Saddam Hussein, thought Ahmad al-Kebeisey, speaking in April 2003 from the pulpit of Baghdad's Abu Hanifa mosque—a Sunni place of worship—was similarly composed of 'traitors and stooges of America working to realise Jewish aims'. The car-bomb attack in the Iraqi city of Najaf in August 2003, which killed the Shi'ite cleric Ayatollah Mohammed Baqer al-Hakim, was carried out by 'Americans and Jews' according to an al-Qaeda spokesman, Abdel Rahman al-Najdi.

In a sermon in November 2004 at the al-Shahid mosque in Khartoum, the Sudanese cleric Abd al-Jalil al-Karouri—who three months earlier had described 'the Jews' as a 'malaria microbe which the US carries in its stomach'—likewise alleged that there were 'one thousand Jewish soldiers', including 'thirty-seven rabbis', among the US forces besieging Fallujah. Even the Kurdish political parties were described by the 'al-Qaeda-linked' Ansar al-Islam in February 2004 to be 'Jewish'. In May 2004, the then Saudi crown prince Abdullah was '95 per cent' certain that 'Zionist hands' were behind the (al-Qaeda) attacks in Saudi Arabia. Osama bin Laden, for his part, asserted in February 2003 that there was a 'new crusade' in process in order to prepare the 'whole region' of the Middle East for 'rule by Jews', while the Saudi defence minister, Prince Sultan, claimed in February 2005 that bin Laden himself had been 'sent by the Jews'. In September 2004, Sudan's Islamist president, Omar Hassan al-Bashir, denounced the party of his political opponents, also Islamists, as being sponsored by 'Zionists and freemasons'; and the Bahraini scholar Ali Abdullah had 'no doubt', again in September 2004, that the seizure of hundreds of hostages at the Beslan school in North Ossetia was 'the work of the Israelis who want to tarnish the image of Muslims'.

Such obsessions have their roots in much older Christian demonisation of the Jews. In September 2004 Maurizio Blondet, a columnist and special correspondent of *Avvenire*, the newspaper of the Italian bishops' conference, alleged that one of the authors of the Madrid bombings in March 2004 'seems to have been a Jew'. But Blondet's reach was wider. 'Israel', he declared, 'uses other human beings like flesh to be gnawed upon, because that is what its religion teaches'.

It would thus appear (to some) that little has occurred during the current struggle between the Muslim and non-Muslim worlds which is not covertly in the Jews' interests, or being manipulated by them. It is a view put equally by Muslims, 'moderate' or 'extreme', and by non-Muslims whether of 'left' or 'right'. Even the idea that there is a 'clash of civilisations' between the Muslim and non-Muslim worlds was described in sections of the Arab press in 2002 as a 'Zionist fabrication'.

There is therefore nothing, once more, which (for some) is beyond the reach of 'Israel', 'Zionism' or 'Jews' to achieve. In May 2003, the 'left-wing' British parliamentarian, Tam Dalyell, was pointing to the 'Sharon-Likudnik agenda' of the 'cabal' which allegedly determined American foreign policy, while in Indonesia, Abu Bakr Bashir was declaring at his trial, also in 2003, that the charges against him had been 'fabricated' by 'the United States and Israel'. The invading US troops in Baghdad, according to Thaer Ibrahim Shomari, preaching at the Mother-of-All-Battles mosque in Baghdad in June 2003, were again mainly Jews, who were 'buying real estate, homes, shops and agricultural fields, using fake names, to do to us what they did with Palestine'. 'Spill the blood of any Jew who attempts from now on to own land or homes in Iraq', an edict from Ayatollah Kadhim Husseini Haeri, a senior Iraqi cleric, commanded in the same month.

Similarly, such was its 'strength', Israel was described as a 'behemoth' in a *New York Times* editorial in September 2003. Israel was 'fueling the war against Islam', declared the Syrian president in October 2003. The Jews 'rule the world by proxy', 'getting others to fight and die for them'—another echo of the 'Jews' war' argument of the 1930s and 1940s—but '1.3 billion Muslims cannot be defeated by a few million Jews', proclaimed the Malaysian prime minister Mahathir Mohamad to the leaders of fifty-seven Islamic nations, gathered at Putrajaya in October 2003, to a standing ovation. (At Mahathir's annual party conference, held in June 2003 in Kuala Lumpur, each delegate was given a copy of Henry Ford's *The International Jew*, first published in the 1920s.)

Agreeing with Mahathir, Yemen's foreign minister declared that 'Israelis and Jews control most of the economy and the media in the world'; the Egyptian foreign minister called Mahathir's views 'a very, very wise assessment'; they were 'very correct', concurred the Afghan leader, Hamid Karzai. In May 2003, Saddam Hussein had also told the Iraqis that 'you know very well that the mass media in the whole world is controlled by the Zionists'. Over one-third of Italians polled in January 2004 agreed 'totally' or 'substantially' that the Jews 'secretly control economic and financial power and the media', with a further 18 per cent 'undecided'. But few could have believed the Libyan leader's allegation, made to the Italian daily *La Repubblica*, also in January 2004, that the Israelis were 'spreading hashish along the Egyptian coast, in Syria and in North Africa', even if Gaddafi himself was 'certain' of it.

From 'far right' to 'left', and from the world of Islamism to the world which seeks to oppose it, such concord of opinion has more of neurosis about it than considered judgment, for all the wrongness of Israel's acts. At its prompting it becomes possible to argue, from 'neo-Nazi right' to *bien-pensant* 'left', that 'anti-US hatred' derives principally from the failure to meet Palestinian grievances against Israel. It can be simplistically asserted, as by Sir Henry Marking in *The Times* in February 2002, that 'terrorism has its roots in the Palestine question'—which is to say, the Israel question—and that once resolved, 'tensions between Muslims and those of other faiths' will be 'dissipated'.

The short-hand version of this argument, and the commonest, is that 'Palestine', which is to say Israel, should be 'tackled first', as a former British ambassador to Saudi Arabia expressed it in the same month, and as many others, Muslim and non-Muslim, also think. Why so? Because, in the words of the UN secretary general Kofi Annan in September 2002, 'the Palestinian-Israeli conflict is the number one threat to world peace'.

This fixated assertion as ever abstracts the conflict from the long process of the Arab nationalist and Islamic revival. Its corollary is that once such conflict is 'resolved', the 'effect throughout the Arab world' would be 'enormous'. Indeed, 'the situation would be transformed', in the words of a group of signatories of a letter to *The Times* in July 2002—who included a former permanent secretary at the Foreign Office. Welcome as such 'transformation' would be, the element of delusion in such prognosis is almost as great as that of Baghdad's war communiqués in 1991 and 2003.

For even if such 'resolution' of the conflict could be found, it would have minimal 'transformatory' effect, or no effect at all, upon the warring parties in other conflicts generated by the Islamic 'reawakening' from Algeria to Sudan, Iraq to Indonesia, and the Philippines to Nigeria. During the last decades most

Islamist attacks on the non-Islamic world, attacks on Israel apart, have not made the Palestinian issue their first cause, or made it their cause at all. Yasser Arafat, in an interview with the *Sunday Times* in December 2002, even accused Osama bin Laden of having 'work[ed] against our interests'. 'Why is bin Laden talking about Palestine now?' he asked. 'Bin Laden never stressed this issue [sc. in the past]. He never helped us'. And when Egypt and Jordan themselves ruled Gaza, the West Bank and much of Jerusalem, neither gave thought to ceding control of those areas to the Palestinians, let alone to creating a Palestinian state.

Nevertheless Israel, and America's support for it, have increasingly been singled out by both 'left' and 'right'—in concurrence, sometimes to the letter, with Islamism's own pronouncements—as the principal ground, or reason, for attacks on the West. From the 'left', a *Guardian* journalist could speak in December 2001 of the need for the 'screws' to be turned on America's 'Israeli ally' in order to 'draw the poison of Muslim rage'. Eighteen days later in *The Times*, a former British diplomat of the 'right', Sir Andrew Green, was writing in almost the same terms of America's 'unquestioning support' for Israel as having 'fuelled a fury in the Arab world'. A mere two days later, it was the turn of a Labour cabinet minister of the 'left', Clare Short, to refer to the 'hurt' caused to the 'hearts of the people' by the 'unresolved conflict in the Middle East'.

'Rage' and 'hurt' there are. At the same time, simplistic identification of their etiology with one, or one principal, source—Jewish misdeeds—has historical roots in reflexes which long predate the events of 1947–48. There were familiar, and even mediaeval, resonances in the description of Israel's conflict with the Palestinians as 'polluting' the politics of the region with its 'insidious poison', in the words of an editorial in the *Guardian* in November 2003; and in the similar description of Israel's policies as 'the big poison' by Lakhdar Brahimi, a former Algerian foreign minister and UN envoy, in April 2004.

Despite the absence of any medical evidence for it, Israel was similarly accused in November 2004 of having 'poisoned' Yasser Arafat. The political leader of Hamas, Khaled Mashal, had 'no hesitation' in making the charge; a month later, in December 2004, despite the insistence by French doctors who had treated Arafat that he had not been poisoned, Mashal remained 'convinced' of it.

Indeed, intemperance of judgment has afflicted both Muslims and non-Muslims when the subject has been Israel and Jews. Thus, Israel and its 'lobbying power over Congress' was blamed by Robert Fisk in the *Independent* in May 2002 for 'turning' Muslims into 'enemies of Europe, and Westerners into enemies of Islam'. The implicit argument, presented in different forms across the centuries, was again clear: that of the inordinate influence of 'the Jews'. This is made of the same stuff as that of the *trahison des clercs* in the 1930s. However, not all of its present ways are familiar. For, as well as falsehood, a vicarious relish for disaster can be found in it. It is a relish which is of our own media-driven times. If Israel were to remain in occupation of Palestinian territory, thus wrote a correspondent in *The Times* in April 2002, 'the whole Islamic world will unite against us, and rightly so'. This was not only perverse but in essence bin Laden's view also, even if the latter's has been more floridly expressed.

False reporting of events is an inevitable consequence of such emotions as these. On 17 April 2002, Janine di Giovanni of *The Times* was able to inform readers that what she had seen, after an incursion of Israeli forces into the West Bank town of Jenin, was a 'wasteland of death' in a camp which 'once housed 13,000 people'. The witnesses she interviewed 'were not lying. If anything', she asserted, 'they underestimated the carnage and the horror. Rarely in more than a decade of war reporting from Bosnia, Chechnya, Sierra Leone, Kosovo', declared *The Times*' senior foreign correspondent, 'have I seen such deliberate destruction, such disrespect for human life'. One of her informants, whose veracity was not doubted, 'saw them [sc. the Israelis] pile bodies into a mass grave, dump earth on top, then run over it to flatten it'.

In Rome's *Il Messaggero*, on 18 April, as in many similar reports in the non-Muslim and Muslim worlds, the 'stench of corpses' hung in the air over the town. Nabil Sha'ath, a senior member of the Palestinian Authority, was equally able to confirm everything that Western reporters, such as di Giovanni, thought and said they had seen—the aftermath of a 'massacre' of grim proportion. Instead, subsequent testimony showed that there had been a vicious fire-fight, the razing of buildings and a total, according to the UN's final report, of seventy-five dead, of whom fifty-two—many of them combatants—were Palestinians, and twenty-three were Israelis. The Israeli forces, in the midst of a hornet's nest of armed men and booby-trapped buildings, were later held by human rights' workers to have acted with disregard for civilian well-being, to have used innocents as 'human shields' and to have wrecked their homes. But it was not a 'massacre', let alone a massacre of Bosnian or Chechnyan scale.

To Sha'ath, however, the Israelis (or 'Israel') had carried out summary executions—of which there was no evidence—and had thereafter removed the victims' corpses in refrigerated trucks. According to the Palestinians, and those Western journalists ready to accept their assertions without enquiry, 'five to six hundred civilians' had been killed. Amnesty International called for an immediate investigation into the killings of 'hundreds of Palestinians'. Still wilder reports had it that there were thousands of deaths; for those who wrote such reports it was a 'blood-bath'. *La Stampa* of Turin—whose correspondent was immediately on the site in Jenin—was a rarity among European newspapers in referring on 17 April 2002 to 'lies'; even the refrigerated truck seen in the area was found to be that of a vegetable wholesaler.

The *Washington Post* was cautious on 18 April 2002, sceptical of Palestinian 'eye-witness' reports, sceptical of local political numerations of the dead, sceptical of the estimates of many Western journalists and commentators. 'No evidence', it declared, 'has surfaced to support allegations of large-scale massacres or executions by Israeli troops'. Nevertheless, on 17 April 2002, the European Union Commisioner Chris Patten—without benefit of knowledge—was aggrandising the occurrence as a 'calamity'. With similar hyperbole a junior Foreign Office minister, Ben Bradshaw, considered the refusal by Israel of a UN fact-finding commission—on grounds, among others, that there was no massacre to investigate—to be a 'cataclysmic public relations mistake'.

Yet, months earlier on 25 September 2001, the town of Jenin had been described with pride by the Palestinian Fatah movement as 'characterized by an exceptional presence of fighting men'. They were 'ready for self-sacrifice with all the means' and it was therefore 'not strange', the Fatah internal report continued, that Jenin was 'termed the suiciders' capital' by Palestinians themselves. In contrast with this description—from the horse's mouth—some Western reporters' views of Jenin, and of the fighting which had taken place there, were deeply revealing of the power over eye and mind of the 'foregone conclusion', whether such conclusion occurs or not.

It was again plain that expectation of, and even a perverse desire for, a further 'disaster', or a greater 'pollution' or a more exemplary brutality attributable to 'Israel' were powerful impulses in many reports. For those with such expectations (or even hopes), there had necessarily been an indiscriminate 'massacre', a 'calamity' and even a 'cataclysm' in Jenin. For those observers with a less febrile sense of 'Israel' as the stereotypical source of others' woes, there had been no 'massacre of the innocents', even if the Israeli assault were held to have been contrary to the the laws of war.

Nevertheless, despite the increasing awareness on all sides that 'the-worse-than-Bosnia' mass-murder reported by *The Times* and other Western and Arab newspapers had not taken place—the Palestinians themselves revised their figures of '500 to 600' dead to fewer than 60—the desire for a 'calamity' to have occurred persisted. On 25 April 2002, the *Independent* thus claimed to have 'unearthed compelling evidence of an atrocity'; the United Nations Middle East envoy, Terje Roed-Larsen, described what he saw, or thought that he saw, as not only 'horrifying beyond belief' but, more tellingly, a 'blot that will forever live on the history of the state of Israel'. Justin Huggler and Paul Reeves told *Independent* readers that an 'Orwellian attempt', no less, was being made by Israel to 'alter the hard, physical facts on the ground'. The Saudi Arabian ambassador in London declared that the 'destruction of Jenin' would have 'made Attila the Hun proud'.

'There is simply no evidence of a massacre', reported Peter Bouckaert of Human Rights Watch on 29 April 2002. On the same day, Major David Holley, a British military adviser to Amnesty International, stated, 'I did not see any evidence of a massacre. The Israeli army was fighting against some desperate [Palestinian] fighters here'. Yet nine days later, at a rally in Trafalgar Square, Massoud Shadjareh, the chairman of the Islamic Human Rights Commission, insisted that there had been 'massacres'—now in the plural—in Jenin; multiplication was being added to the earlier magnification of the violence. As late as September 2003, the Indo-Arab Islamic Association, meeting in New Delhi, was still denouncing the 'Jenin massacre'.

For those belonging to the school-of-the-foregone-conclusion there must have been a 'massacre' even if there had not been. The wickednesses of what the Israelis had actually done to the Palestinians in Jenin on that day, and the Palestinians had done to the Israelis, had been insufficient in themselves. Both a 'massacre' and the 'stench of corpses' were needed for a 'calamity' worthy of the name. On 21 May 2002, when the stench had abated, a senior news analyst at United Press International was to speak of how 'most of the major press and broadcasting outlets in Western Europe' had 'uncritically gobbled up the Jenin Massacre Myth with self-indulgent abandon. Much of the coverage', he declared, 'was exaggerated, wildly inaccurate and reflected a sweeping rush to judgment'. Journalists who had had no means of verifying local testimony had nonetheless reported it as fact, or as presumptively true.

Moreover, the reports of 'massacre' were sufficient to bring a wave of attacks, including arson and physical assault, on Jewish targets, especially in western Europe. Much of the press remained silent on its own misreporting, making no retractions. Other newspapers produced apologias which contained defensive half-truths. The *Guardian* claimed on 18 May 2002 that it had 'not at any time applied the word "massacre" to the events at Jenin'. Indeed, it had kept the word in quotation marks in its 17 April 2002 headline, 'Israel faces rage over "massacre"'. Yet in its editorial on the same day, under the title 'The

Battle for the Truth', it had gone further than assert a massacre. It had declared not merely that the events in Jenin had 'that aura of infamy that attaches to a crime of especial notoriety' but that Jenin's 'concrete rubble and tortured metal evokes another horror half a world away in New York, smaller in scale but every bit as repellent in its particulars'.

Before-the-fact (and even after-the-fact) presumptions had therefore done their harms, all of them predictable and some seemingly willed. Here, the media's general culture of 'catastrophism'—in which a 'massacre' is always preferred to a non-massacre—requires to be analytically separated from the associations-of-ideas which had been at work in Jenin. Once more the latter had to do with an Israel, or 'Israel', as a source of 'fury' in others, as a 'threat to peace', as the 'root of evil', as the single most important cause of Muslim enmity for the non-Muslim world and so forth.

This episode was therefore not simply a matter of 'self-indulgent' jour-nalistic and political 'abandon', as UPI had expressed it. Rather, it expresssed a species of negative investment in Israel, or 'Israel'. It is an investment which (for some) appears to require continuous emotional renewal. Moreover, it seems to be a matter of indifference for many commentators whether it be the real Israel or the 'Israel' of projection which provides these gratifications. Such gratification can also be gained from the distortion of small matters as well as of large. When a campaign of 'disinvestment' from Israel was initiated at Harvard in 2002, the American press was attracted to the fact that there were four hundred signatories supporting the campaign. That there were almost six thousand signatories against it was barely mentioned, and in many reports it was not mentioned at all. The four hundred signatures plainly met a need which the six thousand did not.

The suggestion that Israel exaggerates the dangers it faces—as it some-times does—can evidently be as satisfying as the argument that it is a menace to others. Here, once again, most Muslim and some non-Muslim arguments join hands. In January 2002, Israel asserted that 50 tons of Iranian weaponry had been intercepted aboard the *Karine A*—weaponry which included 345 rockets of twenty-kilometre and eight-kilometre range, and which the Israelis claimed had been purchased from Iran by the Palestinian Authority. This claim was rightly subjected (as in the *Guardian* on 21 January 2002) to critical examination, but of a kind not found in credulous reports of the Jenin events. The 'official version as told by Israeli spokesmen' had been 'spoon-fed to selected journalists', declared a *Guardian* reporter, implying that such version was false. The account 'failed to substantiate its case'; it made 'little sense'; there were 'many pieces in the jigsaw' which did not 'fit' and so on. But the 'official version' was subsequently found to have been as true as press descriptions of a 'massacre' at Jenin had been false.

A negative emotional investment in 'Israel' can plainly be emotionally demanding, since it drives some to exhaust the vocabulary of excess. This demand was visible when Robert Fisk in the *Independent* in May 2002 wrote of what he called the 'filthy war' in the Middle East. In this 'filthy war', it followed that 'mass looting' by Israeli troops in Ramallah was, for Fisk, of 'epic proportions'; that 'much of the building' of the Palestinian ministry of culture was not merely wrecked, as it was, but 'left soiled with excrement and urine'. Likewise, according to the Italian daily newspaper *Il Manifesto* in April 2002, there had been burials of Palestinians in 'mass graves' in Ramallah; Bethlehem, it declared, had been 'crushed' or 'flattened', while 'Israeli aggression' was 'becoming an extermination'.

These responses were striking for the needs which they expressed. In their excesses and abuses of language—Bethlehem was not 'flattened', looting was not on an 'epic' scale, an 'extermination' was not in progress—they even had something in common with the rhetorical dislocations of truth which allowed Saddam Hussein to see his foes, in another 'epic', as drowning in their own blood. In both sets of cases, yet deriving from quite different cultures, those who think they see such things cannot be expected to give the right names to whatever, or whomever, has a fixed place in the observers' structures of perception.

Given their needs, it also could not be expected of Western media organisations that suicide-bombers in Israel would be denoted 'terrorists' without resistance, or be denoted 'terrorists' at all, the 'war against terror' notwithstanding. Hamas, Hezbollah and Islamic Jihad can therefore be presented as mere 'Islamist groups'. For the Israel against which the latter strike is also the 'Israel' of many journalists' and commentators' negative projections and emotional investments. Moreover, this is a world of Western perception and language which, as in the Twelve Devices of Muslim and Arab argument, possesses its own internal coherence. It is a coherence which does not depend upon correspondence with external events, as the case of Jenin demonstrated.

Like Saddam Hussein's world, it is a world of perception which, from a moral and intellectual point of view, is deeply shadowed. In it, Israel was conducting a 'war of annihilation' against the Palestinians, according to Norbert Blüm, a former Christian Democrat minister in the German government, in April 2002. Such projections have known few political or party boundaries. Thus, also in April 2002, the Free Democrat Party's deputy chairman, Jürgen Möllemann, openly declared his support for Palestinian 'force'. From the left,

a *Guardian* commentator held that the 'violent resistance' of the Palestinians—and, by implication, whatever the means employed in such resistance—was a 'right'. In May 2002 the British Labour MP, George Galloway—
who had greeted Saddam Hussein in 1994 with the words 'Sir, I salute your
courage, your strength, your indefatigability'—expressed in synthesis the logic
of the foregoing: the 'suicide-bombers' in Israel were 'not terrorists' but
'heroes'.

Such sentiments, whether considered true or false, possess a notable
quality: they are those of Islamism itself. Under the terms of this shared perception, the 'Israel' that others need is not facing 'terrorism' but punishment
for its own misdeeds. From here, it is a short step, taken by many of all prove-
nances and persuasions, to pronouncing it not merely guilty itself of 'terrorism' but of being a 'terrorist state', if it is a state at all. It may also be
asserted that Israel has been so since 1948, having been created by 'terrorists'
using 'terrorist' means.

According to the elements that make up this perceptual structure, 'Israel'
is facing 'heroes' celebrated (even by some non-Muslims) for attacking a
state—if it is a state—which is carrying out a 'war of annihilation' against
others. Indeed, when counter-violence committed against it is perceived,
including by 'peace activists', as a human right, Israel can with intellectual and
moral comfort also be regarded as guilty of offences which are graver than
those of its attackers.

At the very least during the last two decades, the epithet 'terrorist' has
been transferred from one side to the other, or assertions made of the equally
'terroristic' nature of both. Thus, when Israel carried out a pre-emptive attack
on Iraq's nuclear reactor at Osirak in June 1981, on the eve of the arrival there
of a shipment of enriched uranium sufficient to build four or five Hiroshima-
sized bombs, the *New York Times* declared that Israel had adopted 'the code of
terror'. For many, Israel's targeted assassinations, mass-arrests, the bulldozing
of homes in areas under its occupation and the killing of innocent Palestinian
civilians in 'cross-fire' and other 'regrettable incidents' have not merely given
it a position of ethical symmetry with those who have attacked it since its
foundation; for many, its acts are considered to be worse.

In the Teheran Declaration of December 1997, Israel—but not Iran—was
thus condemned as a 'terrorist state'. Outside the White House in October
1999, at a rally jointly called by the mainly Saudi-funded Council on American Islamic Relations, the American Muslim Council and the Muslim Public
Affairs Council, the same epithet was chanted by the crowd. Likewise, in
Trafalgar Square in May 2002, Massoud Shadjareh, the chairman of the

Islamic Human Rights Commission, pronounced Israel 'guilty of state terrorism'. A month later CNN's founder, Ted Turner, declared Israel to be engaged in 'terrorism' against the Palestinians. In September 2001, the Islamic Iran Participation Front, the main Iranian reformist party, had gone further, describing Israel—or the 'Israel' of such necessary transferences—as 'terrorism's greatest sponsor'; in September 2003, Syed Ahmed Bukhari, the Imam of New Delhi's great Jama Masjid mosque, also called Israel a 'terrorist state', as did Syria's president in the following month. In June 2004, in the view of the Turkish prime minister Recep Tayyip Erdogan, Israel was practising 'state terrorism'.

The same arguments can thus be heard from Islamists, from European liberals and from the parliamentary 'left'. 'The Muslim world', declared Iran's foreign minister Kamal Kharrazi in October 2001, 'cannot close its eyes to terrorist actions committed by Israel'. Actions against Israel, many funded and encouraged by Iran, clearly possessed a different moral status. This status belongs to those with a 'right of violent resistance' to the 'violence of the oppressor', as a *Guardian* commentator put it in March 2002. Three weeks later, a British foreign office minister, Peter Hain, was also referring—on 25 October 2001—to Israel's 'terrorist acts'. In February 2002, the attempted delivery by Iran to the Palestinians of 50 tons of arms, including the 300 missiles earlier referred to, was declared, in the *Guardian*, to be 'not in itself' a 'terrorist act'. In 2002, the editor-in-chief of the *Oxford Encyclopaedia of the Modern Islamic World*, John Esposito of Georgetown University, similarly condemned attempts to associate Hamas with 'terrorism'.

Such views largely depend, again, on the abstraction or extraction of Israel from the general circumstance of other nations—if it is conceded to be a nation or held entitled to exist at all. Even when perceived as an actual polity like others, it is placed at some distance from the (supposed) comity of peoples. It is therefore subjected, or is attempted to be subjected, to different rules, constraints and expectations from those applied elsewhere. Hence, while the United States and other nations have professed themselves to be engaged in a 'war against terrorism', with the use of the roughest methods on both sides, Israel has been frequently told by Western politicians and diplomats that 'military means' cannot 'solve the problem of terrorism'.

In a *New York Times* editorial in March 2002 entitled 'The Limits of Force', Israel's counter-measures against Palestinian 'militants' were described as 'fanning the flames of anger and resolve'. True, the paper conceded, Israel faced a 'Palestinian terrorist infrastructure' and 'Palestinian terror groups', but it was in effect being advised not to respond militarily. Others could be heard arguing in Washington in September 2002 that 'we can't say that we have to defend our national security interest and tell the Israelis they cannot defend their own'. But this position, advanced by the American Enterprise Institute, was quickly identified as the position of US 'hawks' and as the work of the American 'Jewish lobby'.

'The moment that Israel strikes back against Iraq, what happens then to the ability of any Muslim nation to continue to support...our efforts?' Senator Joseph Biden inquired anxiously in September 2002, posing a hypothesis current at the time. In the same way, Israel was warned by the State Department in October 2002—after a wildly misjudged assault on Khan Yunis had left fourteen Palestinian civilians dead, and more than one hundred wounded—that Israel's 'right to defend itself' should be confined to 'ways that do not harm civilians'. The secretary-general of the UN went further: 'such actions', he declared, had 'no legal or moral justification'. But there are no such 'ways' in which civilians can escape harm in war. Moreover, there is some justification in law and morals—on both sides, Israeli and Palestinian—for lashing out in self-defence against those who are considered to be, or who are, a threat to oneself.

Modern Israel, like its biblical forerunner, has the blood of the Philistines upon its hands. History here repeats itself, but not as farce. Indeed, the real Israel has more heinousness to answer for than its own large minority of moral know-nothings, inhabitants of an ideal Zion placed outside the bounds of normal judgment, can or will admit. Nevertheless, an 'exceptionalism' which makes Israel a 'special case'—and which is therefore a mirror-image of Israel's perception of itself—appears to be at work in the standards of morality expected of it by others. As observed earlier, there is also exceptionalism in the magnifications of Israel's size and significance in the world, matching the magnifications of the numbers and powers of 'the Jews'. It is placed in an exceptional double-bind even by those who befriend it; while worldwide non-Muslim hostility to Israel has continued to serve Islamism's cause.

Under the dictates of this exceptionalism, questions such as 'If someone came here [sc. to the United States] and blew up a bus, what do you think we would do?' or 'Is it permitted to be the objects of terror but forbidden to fight it?' have often been passed over in silence. Or they may be given an answer which has been implicit in much of the foregoing: that the object of attack, having provoked or invited it, is in no ethical position to respond, and will merit condemnation when it does.

Few states, if any—supposing 'Israel', for the sake of argument, to be a state like others—are expected not to respond, nor in fact fail to respond, to assault. This has been notably so in the case of Arab states attacked internally by Islamists—Algeria, Egypt, Saudi Arabia and Syria, for example. They have not hesitated to use extra-judicial killings, executions, army assaults and even the razing of entire towns in order to meet and crush such threats to themselves. Moreover, they have generally had little or no thought of negotiating with those who have attacked them. Yet an openness to negotiation with its assailants has been demanded of Israel, a demand to which most states making it would not themselves accede.

'Neutral' pacifists, as in Italy, could also march in protest not against the violence of all parties to the Middle Eastern war, but against Israel alone. It could lead other 'pacifists' to try to intercede with the Israeli military as 'human shields' of the Palestinians, but to make no comparable moral effort with suicide-bombers, nor with those who dispatched them. It could also lead a Nobel committee to consider the withdrawal of the peace prize awarded to the Israeli foreign minister, Shimon Peres, but not its withdrawal from his co-laureate Yasser Arafat; nor, more equitably, its withdrawal from both.

Such exceptionalism has in turn invited the most aggressive Israelis to perceive themselves as morally justified in doing whatever they see fit to do in their own interest. Historically it has always been so. The 'moral autonomy' already noted as a common characteristic of Arab and Muslim actions—in the form of a sense of exemption from criticism by the 'other'—has been matched by a similar autonomy arrogated to itself by Israel, and by many Israelis. This has in turn invited the world's censure, another vicious circle. Moreover, an amoral sense of entitlement, egged on by rival partisans of their respective causes, has governed many of the actions of both Israelis and Palestinians. In these circumstances of moral free-for-all, the law of the jungle must take over on both sides, failing a just peace for all.

Even international organisations, such as the European Union, contributed to the free fall, with their open financial and covert political support for Palestinian paramilitary organisations. The UN's refugee relief organisation, UNRWA—which had itself received funding from al-Qaeda-supporting Islamist charities—was said at the time of the 'Jenin massacre' to have permitted Palestinian refugee-towns to become bases of armed activity, contrary to the UN's own resolutions and rules. It was accused of having failed to 'maintain the neutrality and humanitarian character of the camps', and to keep them 'free from any military presence or equipment, including arms and ammunition', as it was required to do. In moral, or immoral, consequence, Israel itself failed to respect the integrity of the 'camps' or the safety of the UNRWA officials who work in them, several of whom died in Israeli military actions.

In such void, international law, the Geneva Convention and UN resolutions—to say nothing of the Decalogue and the Golden Mean—were flouted without ethical embarrassment. In a moral free-for-all, the wills of the militarily superior, the Israelis, confronted the wills of the physically and politically suicidal in forms of combat invented by the parties. From this, Islamism has gained while both Palestinians and Israelis have suffered. The former have suffered, particularly since 1948, from expropriation and displacement, the use of excessive violence against them, and continuous evasion of their claims to statehood; and the Israelis have suffered from repeated invasion, subjection to suicide-attacks, and the view that Israel was not a state like others. The various non-state names given to Israel in the Muslim world have been tokens of it.

Of these the commonest—used by Iran, by the Saddam Hussein regime, by Hamas, by the Lebanese Shi'ite movement and by many others—has been the term 'Zionist entity', or non-state. In 1991, during the Gulf War, the Iraqi army newspaper described Israel—avoiding its very name—as the 'bastard entity of the Zionists', to which it vowed 'complete annihilation'. The same term, 'Zionist entity', was used by both the Syrian and Iraqi ambassadors to the United Nations in the Security Council debates in February and March 2003, which preceded the invasion of Iraq. At other times, it is a 'criminal entity', or some variation upon this. In April 2003, a statement from the deposed Saddam Hussein called it the 'deformed Zionist entity on our Arab land'; in August 2003 it was 'so-called Israel' to a Hamas spokesman addressing a Gaza crowd; in March 2004, it was a 'cancerous entity' to the leader of Lebanese Hezbollah, Hassan Nasrallah. Even Yasser Arafat's successor, Mahmoud Abbas, at the very time in January 2005 when he was attempting to negotiate a peace between the parties, reduced Israel to the 'Zionist enemy'.

In July 1994 Ayatollah Ali Khamenei—who has also called Israel a 'cancerous tumour'—elaborated upon epithets which have been in use for centuries, describing Israel as having 'gathered together groups of Jews with records of murder, theft, wickedness and hooliganism from throughout the world'. It was a description of Israel given in the aftermath of the bombing on 18 July 1994 of a Jewish community-centre in Buenos Aires, in which Iran was later found to have been implicated. 'Under the name of the Israeli nation', Khamenei added, the 'Zionist regime' had 'created an entity' which 'only understands the logic of terror and crimes'.

Yet it has not taken an Iranian ayatollah, Arab diplomats or jihadist warriors to deny Israel's statehood in such fashion. Even a letter to *The Times* on 4 April 2002 referred to the Israeli 'state' in quotation marks. Two days later, the Palestinian Authority's Ali Rashid, speaking at a conference in Italy of

Rifondazione Comunista, was more moderate than this. Unlike *The Times* letter-writer, he felt able to refer to Israel as a state—without the use of quotation marks in his published text—while adding that it was a 'strange creature'. That is, it was a state, but again not a state like others.

In the few cases where a Muslim nation has given formal recognition to Israel, as did Egypt after the peace treaty reached in 1979 between them, the Egyptian media, Egyptian school text-books and Egyptian public opinion continued to address themselves to Israel as if the two nations were at war. Rigid boycotts of Israel by academic, professional, cultural and sporting Egyptian organisations were also maintained despite the formal peace. 'We have a peace agreement', declared President Mubarak in March 2001, 'but does that mean I have to talk with him [sc. Ariel Sharon]?' It was not until February 2005 that a (fragile) decision was taken by Egypt and Jordan to restore diplomatic relations.

This refusal, or unwillingness, in both the Muslim and much of the non-Muslim worlds, to recognise Israel as a state like others served to weaken the scruples of many Israelis themselves, as already mentioned. If they were not perceived as citizens of a legitimate state, there was less inducement, and for some no inducement at all, to abide by the rules of the 'international community' in defending themselves. Just as Muslims, and Islamists acting on their behalf, have been increasingly driven by the contempts and hostilities of non-Muslims towards Islam to live by their own law, so Israel did the same; as with Islamists, they decided for themselves what was just and unjust. In August 2002, the British chief rabbi declared that there were, in consequence, 'things' which 'happen [in Israel] on a daily basis which make me feel very uncomfortable as a Jew', and that Israel was being 'forced' into 'postures incompatible in the long run with [Judaism's] deepest ideals'.

The price Israel (and Jews) have paid has been high; another vicious circle. In June 2004, the 'people of Israel' were even accused by the Turkish prime minister of treating the Palestinians 'as they [sc. the Jews] were treated 500 years ago at the time of the Inquisition'. With a remarkable congruence of opinion, Israel's conduct was termed 'barbarous' by (for example) Italy's 'Action for Peace' in April 2000, by the Lebanese foreign ministry in March 2002, by the *Jordan Times*, by the leader of the Italian Rifondazione Comunista and by a Labour member of parliament, Gerald Kaufman—a Jew himself—in the House of Commons, all in April 2002. Also in April 2002, to the Tory MP Sir Patrick Cormack, the 'Israeli regime' under Ariel Sharon deserved to 'stand condemned in the eyes of all who call themselves civilised', while in 2001 a former British defence secretary also described Israel as an 'affront to civilisation'. To the Italian Islamist group Ahl al-Bait in March 2004, Israel was even worse: a 'bloodthirsty animal' which 'for fifty years has massacred, deported, tortured and humiliated an entire people'.

To a commentator in the *Guardian* in December 2001, the Israeli prime minister Ariel Sharon—frequently described as a 'war criminal'—was (in the same spirit) 'the man of blood'. In an editorial in the same paper in February 2002, he was 'rooted in his own bloodied past'. To Lord Rees-Mogg, in *The Times* in August 2001, Sharon's 'policy of targeted killing' made Arabs see him as 'quite simply, a murderer'. In November 2001, to 'take reprisals against bin Laden without demanding major concessions from Israel' made 'the blood' of the political editor of the *Spectator* 'run cold'. By March 2002, Sharon was for the *Guardian* 'beyond the pale', 'an enemy to peace and to his own people'; worse, in April 2002, he had only a 'talent for wanton destruction'. 'He likes aggression', declared another *Guardian* commentator in October 2002. In September 2003 and May 2004, Muslim demonstrators in Bombay and Italian Islamists in Rome were of like mind: he was 'the enemy of the whole of humanity'. In other words, such views again knew no boundaries, Muslim or non-Muslim, 'right' or 'left'.

In more general terms, Israel came to be denoted by its foes as a state which was based on race—when it was acknowledged to be a state. It has been further described, by some, not simply as discriminatory, which it is, but as an 'apartheid state' or 'second South Africa', and has been subjected to boycott as was the latter. A minority of Jews also espoused this notion. 'Economic sanctions and an arms ban against Israel are the only way of breaking the impasse. Such a policy brought down apartheid', wrote the Labour member of parliament, Gerald Kaufman, in July 2004, making the analogy obvious.

In the view of Geoffrey Wheatcroft, expressed in the *Guardian* (once more) in August 2001, Israel had an even 'deeper problem' than merely being regarded as an 'apartheid state'. 'The truth', he declared, 'is that Zionism is not racism, it is colonialism'. This argument was also implicit in the suggestion, referred to earlier, that the Jews were 'aliens' in the Middle East. Likewise to Robert Fisk, in the *Independent* in May 2002, Sharon was ('hopelessly') attempting to 'suppress a vicious anti-colonial war'. As Professor Robert Alter of Berkeley also explained in August 2002, 'the Arabs in general and the Palestinians in particular are perceived as people of the Third World and as victims of colonialism'. To the French foreign minister Hubert Védrine in February 2002, Israel's policies were those of 'pure repression'; to a former British diplomat, writing to *The Times* in the following month, the 'situation' was 'rather analogous to that of France in Algeria', which was to say one of colonial rule; to a *Guardian* writer in January 2003, it was simply a 'tyranny'.

But these were themselves mild reproaches when set against allegations, as in the *Independent* in October 2000, of Israel's 'constant use of torture and ethnic cleansing', or of its 'ethnic cleansing programme' in the words of George Monbiot, again in the *Guardian* in August 2001. They were also the charges, made two weeks later in the same terms, of an Arab declaration to the 'United Nations World Conference on Racism' in Durban. There, the Arab and Islamic nations also described Israel as a 'racist occupying power'. Worse, Israel (or 'Israel') could be accused, as by A. N. Wilson in London's *Evening Standard* in April 2002—and eight days later by the Algerian president Abdelaziz Bouteflika—of the crime of 'genocide'; albeit a 'kinder, gentler genocide' than that carried out by Hitler, in the judgment in June 2002 of Michael Neumann, a (Jewish) professor of philosophy at a Canadian university.

Barbarous and bloodied, genocidal and an affront to civilisation—with its 'acts of ethnic cleansing well documented', according to Khader Shkirat, a Palestinian human rights activist and visiting law fellow at Harvard, once more in the *Guardian* in March 2002, and its expansion one which 'includes ethnic cleansing', according to London's mayor in March 2005—these were heavy charges. Moreover, there were again few, if any, moral bounds to such accusations. Although the 1975 UN General Assembly's equation of Zionism with racism-as-such was withdrawn in 1991, it was transcended by a charge heavier still: that Israel—in a supreme moral inversion—was a 'Nazi' or Nazi-like regime.

At a meeting of Arab leaders in Jordan in March 2001, President Bashar al-Assad of Syria described Israeli society as 'even more racist than the Nazis', repeating this description in the presence of the British prime minister at the end of October of that year. Also in 2001, the Egyptian newspaper *al-Akhbar*—whose opinions usually reflected those of the government—similarly described Israel as 'worse than the Nazis' and in August 2004 as having been 'revealed to the world as a Nazi country'. In May 2001, a columnist in the Egyptian *al-Arabi* even held that Zionism was 'a double Nazism'. Nor, once more, has this kind of view been confined to Arabs and Muslims. In February 2001 and in April 2002 (in an interview with the Egyptian newspaper *al-Ahram*), the Oxford academic and poet Tom Paulin referred to Jewish settlers as 'Nazis' and the Israeli army as the 'Zionist SS'; and when accused of 'anti-Semitism', complained in a poem that he had been 'dealt the anti-Semitic card' with its 'usual cynical Goebbels stuff'.

In Spain, in May and June 2001, the liberal daily *Cambio 16* depicted Sharon as a swastika-wearing Nazi. *La Vanguardia* described the treatment of the Palestinians as a 'holocaust'; and *La Razon* as (again) a 'genocide'. The treatment of the Palestinians was also a 'genocide' to a columnist in the Greek daily paper *Apogevmatini* in March 2002. Even in Germany, a legislator in the state assembly of North Rhine-Westphalia referred to the 'Nazi methods' of the Israeli army, while an editorial in *Der Spiegel* in December 2001 likened the policies of Ariel Sharon to those of Adolf Hitler. In January 2003 Greta Duisenberg, the wife of the Dutch head of the European Central Bank, went further, declaring that the Israeli occupation of Palestinian territory was 'worse' than Nazi Germany's occupation of the Netherlands. This was more than the Malaysian prime minister, Mahathir Mohamad, himself claimed in October 2003: 'the Jews' were behaving towards Muslims 'exactly' as 'Europeans' had behaved towards them. But the Saudi ambassador in Britain held the same position as Duisenberg: the Israeli occupation of the West Bank and Gaza was 'far more severe than anything the Germans did'.

A small minority of Jews took a similar view to that of Mahathir. In June 2003 a British Labour MP, Oona King, herself Jewish, conceded that Palestinians were 'not being rounded up and put in gas-chambers' but described Gaza as 'the same in nature' as the Warsaw Ghetto. (To the Polish and Spanish representatives at a Council of Europe meeting in April 2002, the 'Palestinian resistance' at Jenin was also comparable with the Jewish revolt in the Warsaw Ghetto.) In the view of a morally embarrassed Anglo-Jewish scientist—who declared herself in April 2002 to be ashamed of being Jewish—Israeli settlers were now behaving in a manner which 'in many ways' was 'similar to that of the Nazis in Hungary in 1944'. Even Israel's Justice Minister, Yosef Lapid, ventured in the same direction in May 2004: a picture of an elderly Palestinian woman in the rubble of her home reminded him of 'my mother in the Holocaust'. Facing protest, he himself protested that he was not comparing Israel with the Nazi regime, but there was 'no forgiveness for people who treat an old woman in this way'. Ultranationalist Israelis used the Nazi analogy in a quite different fashion in 2004. Plans to evacuate settlers from Gaza were denounced as equivalent to the Nazi 'relocation' of Jews in the Second World War.

The callousness and cruelty, large and small, of Israeli attitudes towards and actions taken against the Palestinians have demanded redress. But the making of Israel, or 'Israel', into a Nazi or Nazi-like regime has been a logically consistent last step in magnifying the scale of its wrong-doing. It has been a need evidently felt by a variety of individuals with seemingly little else in common. An Oxford poet, a leading German editorialist, a Saudi diplomat, an English-Jewish academic and a Syrian Ba'athist could all concur with Yasser Arafat, who in March 2002 asked rhetorically—of Israeli army conduct in Tulkarm—'Is this not what they said the Nazis did to the Jews?' 'Why not the swastika?' also enquired Cornelio Sommaruga, a former president of the International Red Cross—to which Israel was the only nation, if it is a nation, not to be admitted—when asked to explain the Red Cross movement's refusal to recognise the symbol of the Star of David. But 'Hands Off Palestine! No German Weapons for Israel!' shouted neo-Nazis as they marched in December 2002 in protest at the presence in Berlin of the Israeli president. To the neo-Nazis at least, the latter was not a fellow-Nazi.

In April 2002 Amos Luzzatto, the leader of Italy's small Jewish community, saw the charges against Israel differently. It was a 'way of freeing the conscience for what was done in Europe'. How so? Because, replied Luzzatto, it makes it possible to say, 'Do you see? They [sc. the Jews] do the same themselves'. But even if this were so, attributions of barbarism, colonialism, racism, tyranny, ethnic cleansing and Nazism to Israel have all served to suggest that it is not the state it thinks it is, if it is a state. It might declare itself to be a parliamentary democracy living under the rule of law, or to be the only such democracy 'in the region', or claim that Arabs in Israel had more political rights than they would possess if they lived in Arab countries. Whether such claims be true or false, they did not avail. For Israel faced a belief among many of its foes, and perhaps among some of its friends also, that it would have been better for everyone (including the Israelis) if it had not existed at all.

This belief has been explicitly expressed. 'Israel Must Not Exist!' shouted protesters outside the White House in October 1999 at the earlier-mentioned rally organised by three of America's leading Muslim organisations, at least one of which has been shown to have connections with violent Islamism. 'There is no moral case for the existence of Israel', declared Faisal Bodi in the *Guardian* in January 2001. Moreover, this absence of right to exist was not only described as a 'fact' but was held by Bodi to be 'central to any genuine peace formula'. Nor was this view confined to Muslims. Tom Paulin, a self-described 'life-long opponent of anti-Semitism', asserted in April 2002 that he had 'never believed that Israel had a right to exist at all'. There were also less explicit ways of making the same point. In the *Guardian* in November 2003, Fiachra Gibbons declared that 'of all the trials that have befallen them [sc. the Jews] over the last five hundred years, none has brought more threat than the existence of Israel'. There was no such circuitousness of argument in bin Laden's declaration, in his 'Letter to the American People' of November 2002, that 'the creation of Israel' was a 'crime which must be erased'. Nor was there anything covert in Ayatollah Ali Khamenei's assertion in December 1990 that 'in the Palestinian issue the goal is the obliteration of Israel'.

Quite apart from its 'non-recognition' by the great majority of Muslim countries, the conditionality of Israel's existence has been a premise of much Arab and Islamic—and not merely Islamist—polemic against it. 'All of Jewish society [sc. the whole of Israel] illegally occupies an Islamic land. All Palestine is a territory of war', declared Abdel-Samie Mahmoud Ibrahim Moussa, the imam of Rome's main mosque in June 2003. 'Does Syria feel threatened?' President Bashar al-Assad was asked during the Iraq War. 'As long as Israel exists, the threat is there', he replied.

In discussion with UN inspectors, Tariq Aziz, former foreign minister of the Saddam regime, is said to have 'explained' that the Iraqis had earlier designated their chemical weapons 'for the Jews'; in March 2004, after the abandonment by Libya of its advanced weapons programmes, the son of Libya's leader admitted that they had been 'developed for a battle' in aid of the Palestinians. After his fall, Saddam Hussein, in a letter from hiding addressed to the Iraqi people, similarly adopted the Islamist slogan of 'Long live Palestine, free and Arab from the river to the sea!'—that is, from the Jordan to the Mediterranean—implying the dissolution of Israel by its incorporation into an Arab state. 'There is no Israel, there is only Palestine', Mounir el-Motassedeq, accused of helping the 9/11 hijackers, was alleged at his trial in August 2004 to have said.

Similarly, after the Istanbul bombings of synagogues in November 2003, a statement issued by the Abu Hafs al-Masri Brigades declared that 'Jews around the world' would 'regret that their ancestors even thought about occupying the land of Muslims'. In a related conflation in October 2000 between 'Israel' and all Jews, a poster and leaflet campaign by the Islamist group al-Muhajiroun, which exhorted British Muslims to 'kill the Jews', was 'explained' by its leader as 'merely a warning not to support the state of Israel'. Nevertheless, imprecations against Israel have often been indistinguishable from threats to Jews as such, while many Islamists have had Jews on their minds rather than merely Israel itself. When the Indonesian al-Qaeda militant Amrozi was found guilty in August 2003 of participation in the Bali bombing, the few words he shouted from the dock, as he was sentenced to death, included 'Burn, burn the Jews!' 'The Jews should be annihilated', a member of the crowd at the funeral of Ahmed Yassin in March 2004 told the *Herald Tribune*. 'The fingernail of Sheikh Yassin is worth all the Jewish people', he added.

Moreover, where there has been an undifferentiated cursing of Israel, Zionism and Jews in many Islamist slogans, they have often expressed a death-wish for all of them, as well as for their supporters. The term 'Zionist' has also been used as a term of generalised denunciation, and harm wished upon whomever is thought to have earned the epithet. 'Death to Chirac the Zionist!'

shouted students in Teheran, protesting in December 2003 outside the French embassy at the ban on the *hijab*. Muslim and Arab expressions of a terminal hostility to the existence-as-such of Israel have been routine. 'We will not rest, we will not sleep, until the last Zionist leaves our territory', Mohammed Mahdi Atef, the leader of Egypt's Muslim Brotherhood, declared. 'Death to Israel!' read signs at Iranian-Iraqi border posts. In March 2004, the Iranian leader Ali Khamenei pronounced that Israel was 'doomed to extinction'. 'Death to Zionists!' shouted an irate crowd of Shi'ites in February 2004 at the Imam Kadhum mosque in Baghdad, after an attack on the mosque. In May 2004, the Arab League even protested to the Austrian authorities at plans to name a square in Vienna after the founder of Zionism, Theodor Herzl, on the centenary of his death. It would 'not serve the cause of good relations between Austria and the Arab-Islamic world', the League declared.

Moreover, from disparagement of the Jews as, say, 'sons of monkeys and pigs'—a description sanctioned by a Koranic text, and often enough heard from the mosque pulpit—it has been a small next step to hope for, or even to demand, physical measures to be taken against them, and not merely against Israel. When Imam Fawaz Mohammed Damra, the Palestinian-born head of the Islamic Center of Cleveland, Ohio, employed the description of Jews as 'monkeys and pigs' in a 'sermon', he called in the next breath for 'rifles' to be 'directed at' Jews. Supporting and accompanying such notions has been a bitter sense that the creation of Israel in 1948 was a 'catastrophe' for the 'Arab nation'—even for the entire Islamic world—and not merely for the Palestinians.

Its establishment, declared the then president of Iran, Hashemi Rafsanjani, in December 2001, was the 'worst event in history'. But it is often Jews as such, not Israelis nor even 'Zionists', who are pronounced guilty of Israel's sins. Thus, it was 'Jewish aggression', not Israeli aggression, which was denounced from the Grand Mosque in Mecca in April 2004. Asked in December 2003 if there was any place at all for the state of Israel, the Hamas leader, Sheikh Ahmed Yassin, replied 'they could set up a state in Europe'. The 'they' were clearly Jews, not only Israelis; or, according to Gaddafi's proposal at the non-aligned summit in Belgrade in 1989, the Jews should establish a 'new homeland' in 'Alsace-Lorraine, the Baltic states or Alaska'.

Although the death of Yasser Arafat brought a renewal of hope, again naive, that the Palestinian-Israeli conflict could be 'finally' resolved, the 'Covenant' of the Palestinian Authority makes the extinction of Israel a primary aim. The emblem of the Palestinian Fatah movement shows the entire state of Israel—if it is a state—as Palestinian. Similarly, in some of the public art in Iraq during the Saddam regime, the Ba'athist leader was set against a background of Jerusalem's Dome of the Rock; the statue of him which was demolished in Baghdad's al-Furdus (or 'Paradise') Square in April 2003 had its arm pointed towards Jerusalem. Even the late Faisal al-Husseini, regarded as a moderate member of the Palestinian Authority, declared in March 2000 that 'We may win or lose, but our eyes will continue to aspire to the strategic goal', which he described as 'a Palestine in place of an Israel'.

Thus, when Sheikh Yassin asserted in January 1993 that the organisation's purpose was the 'establishment of an Islamic state in all of Palestine to replace Israel'—regarded as occupying the 'religious inheritance', or *waqf*, of Islam—he was speaking not only to the agenda of Hamas but arguably to the aspirations of most Muslims. Indeed, Yassin's was the same position as that adopted by Yasser Arafat in his 1975 speech to the United Nations; and the same, in turn, as the position adopted by Ayatollah Khamenei, the 'moderate' Faisal al-Husseini, or the immoderate bin Laden. The outcome of the 'single state' solution, advocated by some Muslims and non-Muslims alike—and even by a very small minority of Jews—would again be the disappearance of Israel.

Despite the fact that the dissolution of Israel is not the same as the Nazi 'project', the rhetoric with which the desire for the former has been expressed has sometimes gone beyond merely political aims. 'Israel', announced a Hamas leader, Mahmoud al-Zahar, at a rally in Gaza in January 1994, 'will be destroyed in March 2002. It is sufficient to study the Koran carefully. First, there will be a great battle which will bring about the birth of a unified Islamic state in the whole of the Middle East. Then, we will conquer Jaffa, Tel Aviv and Haifa until we arrive at the holy sites of Jerusalem'. In December 2002— nine months after Israel should already have been 'destroyed'—Sheikh Yassin, also at a Hamas rally in Gaza, gave Israel 'less than twenty-five years left to live'.

But what is it which will be 'destroyed'? The answer lies in the promise of Israel's 'eradication as a Jewish state', an aim repeated by Hamas (and al-Zahar) in April 2002, and which called for 'daily attacks' upon it. In an 'appeal from the heart', the urgings of Abdel Aziz Rantisi of Hamas in October 2002 made the scope of such intent both wider and more specific. He called on Israel's foes to 'strike everywhere, kill every Zionist wherever he comes from, whether from America or Russia. They are all murderers and criminals', he cried out, 'and not a single one of them is an innocent'. Moreover, 'anyone who call[ed] for negotiations with Israel' was 'a criminal' also; Palestinian politicians included.

Such calls to 'destroy' and 'kill' have echoed far and wide in the Muslim

world. In Lebanon in October 2000, Hezbollah's leader, Sheikh Hassan Nasrallah, called on all Palestinians to launch suicide-attacks to 'kill as many
Israelis as possible'. Outside London's Central Mosque, in March 2002,
emerging worshippers chanted calls for a jihad against Israel; in October 2002,
the British Islamist organisation al-Mujahiroun declared that 'the message
from Muslims remains loud and clear that we will keep on striving until . . .
Israel is permanently exterminated'. Even non-Muslims, whether on the 'right'
or the matching 'left', and speaking out when greater discretion held its
tongue, could occasionally join in. 'We must support the Palestinians',
declared the Labour MP George Galloway at a London University meeting in
May 2002, 'and assist them in wiping out the Zionist entity'; the same non-
state term which had been adopted by Saddam Hussein, among others.

The language of 'replacement', 'destruction', 'erasure', 'obliteration' and
'extermination', whatever else it is, has not been the language of peace. Moreover, the use of such terms by Islamists was clearly not directed to issues of
territory alone. There have always been persons—whether Israelis, 'Zionists'
or Jews—who were implied to stand in the way of their fulfilment. For a
common feature of the impulses which the words expressed has been, at the
least, an intense desire to see Israel, or 'Zionists' or Jews worsted, or 'taught a
lesson'. The means are also largely a matter of moral indifference, as in the
wider battle with the non-Muslim world.

The founder of the American Muslim Council, Abdurrahman Alamoudi, thus described the attack in 1994 on a Jewish community centre in
Buenos Aires—which killed eighty-six people—as a 'worthy operation'.
Abubakr Awadh of the Supreme Council of Kenya Muslims similarly
declared in November 2002 that the killing of Israelis in a bomb-blast in
Mombasa had been a 'worthy cause'. However, it is also true that there was
no great moral distinction between such sentiments and the language of
some Western journalists who have written of 'successful' raids by Palestinian suicide-bombers into Israel, or of the 'increasingly effective violence
and terror' brought to bear against it, or of Hezbollah as the 'most successful
of anti-Israeli insurgencies'.

Nevertheless, the language with which Islamism has expressed its purposes has been its own. In a tape released in November 2001, Osama bin Laden
declared that 'killing Jews is a top priority'. In a further tape released in May
2002, he asserted that 'the war is between us and the Jews. Any country that
steps into the same trench as the Jews', and not merely the 'same trench' as
Israel, 'has only herself to blame'. In October 2002 Fadi Abdullatif, a
spokesman for the Danish section of Hizb ut-Tahrir—Saudi-backed, founded

in Jerusalem in 1953 and banned in Germany in January 2003 for 'promoting anti-Semitism' in universities and elsewhere—called the Jews 'people of slander' and similarly declared that they 'should be killed'. In August 2001, the Palestinian television service invoked 'blessings upon him who shot a bullet into the head of a Jew', and urged that 'all weapons must be aimed at the Jews'.

Here, there could arguably be heard the accents not of political resistance to a 'colonial occupier' or 'settler state', but those of hatred of the members of an entire race, wherever they might happen to be. Those who decapitated the American Jewish journalist, Daniel Pearl, in Karachi and made him declare 'I am a Jew' to a video-camera before his throat was cut, appeared to be acting in the same spirit. Similarly, Zacarias Moussaoui, charged with conspiring in the attacks of 11 September 2001, told a Virginia court in April 2002 that he 'prayed to Allah for the destruction of the Jewish people'. Likewise in Riyadh in September 2002, a Saudi cleric prayed 'O God, destroy the tyrant Jews'— not merely Israel—'O God, oppress the Jews'. When the British Islamist group al-Muhajiroun in October 2002 called not only for the 'permanent extermination of Israel', as noted earlier, but declared that 'the final hour will not come until the Muslims kill the Jews', this was again to stand on ground occupied in the non-Islamic world only by the most extreme. Thus, America's World Church of the Creator, which claimed to have 70,000 to 80,000 followers and to be the 'fastest growing white racist and anti-Semitic church [sic] in America', declared that the Jews were a 'form of vermin'. 'Judaism Must Be Destroyed' is among its slogans; not greatly distinct, morally or practically, from bin Laden's 'top priority' of 'killing Jews'. Hence, the establishment of common cause between European neo-Nazis, for example, and local Islamists would have its own logic; during 2005, it was asserted (by some) that such alliances already had an embryonic existence.

Indeed, the Hamas 'Covenant'—its statement of aims—even cites the 'Protocols of the Elders of Zion', while in March 2002 the Saudi government daily al-Riyadh told its readers that Jews used human blood during their religious festivals, in this case 'drying it into granules and blending it into pastry dough for holiday consumption'; a version of the mediaeval Church's 'blood-libel'. There have been many such historically familiar assertions about the Jews as the Muslim advance has accelerated. The Jews, proclaimed the Egyptian government daily al-Ahram in May 2002, 'are accursed in heaven and on earth, a catastrophe for the human race. They are the virus of the generation, the plague of the generation, and the bacterium of all time'; Hitler thought the same.

Nocmettin Erbakan, leader of the Turkish Welfare Party, was described in 1995—as if it were a token of (Islamist) virtue—to be 'vehemently anti-Jewish'. In London, in October 1995, the Islamist group Hizb ut-Tahrir even declared that Jewish students had 'no place' in the British education system. The Saudi-trained Jamaican Muslim cleric, Shaikh Abdullah el-Faisal, sentenced at the Old Bailey to nine years' imprisonment in February 2003 for inciting murder, toured Britain during 2001 and 2002 proclaiming the 'filthy Jews' to be 'evil to the core'. Another British Islamist cleric, Sheikh Abu Hamza, employing rhetoric also made familiar in Europe by the mediaeval Church, equated Jews with 'Satan' in his pulpit orations during 2002; and at the UN World Conference on Racism in Durban in August 2001, copies of the 'Protocols of the Elders of Zion' were being sold as a 'non-government exhibit'. Marches in Durban, attended by what were described as 'pro-Palestinian activists', carried slogans—once exclusively neo-Nazi—that 'Hitler should have finished the job'.

'I was ready to kill 100 or even 200 Jews', declared Saber Abu el-Ulla, an Egyptian tried in October 1997 for killing nine German tourists, and who expressed his regret to the court that his victims had not been Jews. In September 2002 a Turk, Osman Petmezci, suspected of plannning an attack with others on the US army's European headquarters in Heidelberg, was described as having made 'little effort to hide his hatred of Jews'. 'It was a real sickness, I felt', declared a neighbour. 'He hated them'.

With those who feel such hatred, Israel, being perceived as 'the Jew' writ large, has attracted odium less for what it does than for what it is. 'Islamophobia' demonises 'the Muslim' in the same fashion. Moreover, where Israel was held to be no more than a usurping 'Zionist entity' composed of Jews, the Israeli victims of Islamist suicide-bombings could be perceived not as citizens of a state but more simply as 'Jews'. In a 'sermon' broadcast in June 2001 by the Palestinian Authority's television channel, Sheikh Ibrahim Madhi thus prayed that the Knesset, the Israeli parliament building, would 'collapse over the heads of *the Jews*'; Arab members of the Knesset would presumably be spared. In the same broadcast he also 'blessed' 'whoever has put a belt of explosives on his body or on his sons', and plunged into the midst of *the Jews*'. Likewise, the British academic and poet Tom Paulin admitted to the Egyptian newspaper *al-Ahram*, again in April 2002, that he felt 'nothing but hatred' for 'Brooklyn-born Jews' who had settled in the occupied territories; they 'should be shot dead', he added.

For 'Jews' as such to be objects of preoccupation or obsession has always hitherto been the distinctive mark of the 'far-right'. Shortly after the attacks of 11 September 2001, the leader of an American 'hate-group', the National

Alliance, declared that 'anyone who is willing to drive a plane into a building to kill Jews [*sic*] is all right by me'. As we have seen, many Muslims also appeared to believe that the attack was carried out not merely by Mossad (or the CIA) but by Jews, or 'the Jews'. The Imam of Valencia, addressing worshippers on 23 September 2001, asserted that 'all the evidence shows that the Jews were guilty'; Baluchistan's information minister, Hafiz Hussain Ahmed Sharodi, likewise claimed that 'a conspiracy by Jews to start a war between Muslims and Christians' lay behind the events.

'Who told 4,000 Israeli workers at the Twin Towers to say home that day?' inquired Amir Baraka, New Jersey's 'poet laureate', in a poem written in October 2001. And 'didn't a Jew company have the control of the security of the airport from where these airplanes took off?' asked an article in the Pakistani newspaper *Ausaf* in September 2002. The logical corollary of such views is that attacking or 'destroying' Israel is not enough. In a 'promotional' audio-tape which was circulating in Islamic bookshops in Britain in 2002, the already-mentioned Muslim cleric Abdullah el-Faisal (previously William Forest) pronounced of the Jews, 'You have no choice but to hate them'. 'How do you fight the Jews?' he asks on the tape. 'You kill them', he answers.

In April 2002, in a Gaza kindergarten halfway across the world, a teacher, Samira Ali el-Hassain, was at the same time asking her class of five-year-olds—as reported in the *San Francisco Chronicle*—'Who are the Jews?' 'The enemy', they replied in unison. 'And what should we do to them?' 'Kill them!' the children cried.

Logically, too, it is not only the most radical of Islamists who deny or minimise accounts of past killings of the Jews. Mahmoud Abbas, Yasser Arafat's successor as leader of the Palestinian Authority and approved by many for his moderation, argued in 1983 in his book *The Other Side* that the Holocaust had claimed 'only a few hundred thousand lives', and that the figure of six million had been 'inflated' 'in the interest of the Zionist movement'. 'All the data regarding the killing of the Jews' were 'exaggerated', he asserted, 'as an expedient to smooth the way for the occupation of Palestine and the justification of Zionist crimes'.

The official Palestinian *al-Hayat al-Jadida* went further on 13 April 2001, Israel's Holocaust Remembrance Day, describing the Holocaust as a 'fable'. Figures of the Jewish dead were a 'lie', their dissemination a product of 'international marketing' by Jews. In France in February 2004, teachers similarly reported that Muslim pupils had for some time been interrupting history classes in order to object to accounts of Nazi policy and actions in the Second World War. In the Egyptian government-sponsored *al-Akhbar*, however, the fact of the Holocaust was not denied but lauded in April 2001. 'Thanks be to Hitler of blessed memory', wrote one of its columnists. 'On behalf of the Palestinians he took revenge in advance'—a notion not to be found even in the Twelve Devices of argument—'on the most vile criminals on the face of the earth. Still, we do have a complaint. His revenge on them was not enough'.

Nevertheless, in December 2002 Osama el-Baz, one of President Mubarak's advisers, warned Egyptians in *al-Ahram*—which in 2000 had accused Jews of being vampires who used the blood of non-Jews in their baking—not to espouse 'racist views'. He conceded that Jews had been 'exposed to the most brutal mass slaughters by Hitler'. 'I wonder', he added, 'how some Arab writers and politicians could support his Nazi movement'. His wonder was misplaced. The attractions of the thesis that the scale of the Holocaust has been exaggerated or is a fable have been too strong, judging by the frequency of its repetition in the Arab press. Thus, in May 2001, yet another columnist in *al-Akhbar* declared the Holocaust to be 'no more than a fabrication, a lie and a fraud'. Addressing Hitler, he exclaimed, 'If only you had done it, Brother, if only it had really happened, so that the world could sigh in relief without the Jews' evil and sin'.

From all this, it is clear that Israel cannot be considered by Muslims a state like others, whatever passing moves may be made towards an accommodation with it. This appears to be so even among those for whom the legitimacy of Israel's existence is not in question. It is a problem to which the Jews, beginning with the Old Testament's authors, have contributed by arrogating to themselves the status of a 'particular' people. Moreover, the 'particularity' of Israel's history, circumstances and self-view as the 'Promised Land' has been increased by the inordinate favour shown to it by the United States. Indeed, some evangelical supporters of Israel even call themselves 'Christian Zionists'.

This partiality has generally been explained by Israel's foes as the work of a 'Jewish lobby'. Conversely, to many Jews hostility towards Israel has tended to be perceived as an expression of 'anti-Semitism'. The accusation of 'anti-Semitism' could be held to be a moral catch-all, by means of which disapproval of what Jews do is sought to be disqualified at source. Nevertheless, in the swirl of cross-currents on this subject, those who are critical of Israel have been regarded as closet 'anti-Semites' by many Jews. The latter's sense of threat—whether in the form of a threat to them, or a threat to the existence of Israel—might be regarded as excessive and, in common with much else in this war of the worlds, even paranoid; France's ambassador to Israel, Gérard Araud, was reported in September 2003 to have described Israel as a 'paranoid' state, if it is a state. But with attacks on Jews and Jewish institutions taking place from Australia to Belarus, and Belgium to New Zealand, a sense of threat was increasingly aroused, especially in France. When Jean-Marie le Pen made ground in the French elections in April 2002 queues formed outside Jewish travel agencies, and the rate of French immigration to Israel rose. In France, in the decade to 2002, there was reportedly a ten-fold increase in attacks.

In January 2003, a poll published in *Le Monde* revealed that no less than 77 per cent of French Jews feared for their personal safety. The French-Jewish lawyer Arno Klarsfeld declared that the moment was 'fast approaching' when the Jews would have to leave Europe or live as 'political Marranos', their identities and opinions concealed. 'Things cannot improve', he repeated in June 2004. Attributed both to 'neo-Nazis' and to 'Arab youth', there were further increases in 2004 in physical assaults, threats against individuals, arson and other acts of vandalism against synagogues, lycées, community centres and cemeteries; but attacks on Muslims by 'far right' supporters also increased. In July 2004, the Israeli prime minister angered the French government by calling on French Jews to 'move immediately' to Israel in order to escape what he called the 'wildest anti-Semitism'. Jewish organisations in France and elsewhere in Europe blamed the attacks on the 'promotion of anti-Semitism by the Arab media and Islamist organisations', and its effect on the 'attitudes towards the Jews of Muslim communities around the world'.

The notion that criticism of Israel, or of acts done by Jews, is per se 'anti-Semitic' is foolish. But in some Jews such notion can become an almost overwhelming preoccupation. 'We cannot even say one word about the Jews without being accused of being anti-Semitic', complained Mahathir Mohamad in October 2003, having just described them as 'ruling the world by proxy'. 'A single critical mention of Israel's treatment of Palestinians will do it', similarly asserted a *Guardian* journalist in February 2002. 'Criticise Israel and you are an anti-Semite just as surely as if you were throwing a pot of paint at a synagogue in Paris', wrote the diplomatic editor of the *Observer*. The subject of Israel as such—like the subject of 'the Jews' as such—can drive rational and irrational commentators alike to excess; in August 2004, Theodorakis could even claim that the Jews 'like to be victims'. Easily crossed have been the boundaries between analysis worthy of the complexities of which it treats, and reflexes which have revealed more about the commentator than about the object of comment.

Accusations of 'anti-Semitism' have been met in a variety of ways. In May 2002, the *Guardian*—which had given space in its columns, as was noted earlier, to the headlined assertion that Israel had 'no moral right to exist'—

revealed that it was being seen as 'a paper that is hostile to the Jews, one which even liberal Jews cannot read any more'. Its response was defensive. 'The *Guardian*', it stated, 'is a progressive paper with a noble history'. It was 'the first in the British press to realise the persecution of the Jews in Nazi Germany', and was 'an early backer of the Zionist project'. In January 2002, four months earlier, it had already been driven to declare that it had 'no doubt that the perception of the *Guardian* as anti-Semitic' was 'genuine among those that hold it'. Such perception 'deserved' to be 'taken seriously' but, the paper believed, it was unfounded. In February 2002, the *Guardian* had also sought to turn its defensive argument round: pronouncing in an editorial that 'fears about a rising tide of anti-Semitism in western European countries' stemmed from 'over-defensiveness' among Jews themselves, who 'resent the current torrent of international criticism' of Israel.

There were other types of response both to the 'anti-Semitic' charge and to Jews who declared their sympathies for Israel. 'Extreme Zionism', declared a writer to *The Times*, also in February 2002, 'may be considered as racist as anti-Semitism'. In an account, once more by a columnist in the *Guardian*, of the political views and personality of the Nation of Islam's Louis Farrakhan, it was said that his 'Jew-baiting' might be 'deplorable', but it was part of a 'racist discourse in America' which Farrakhan 'didn't invent'. That is, he was less culpable than he might appear. Or a commentator in the London *Observer* could admit that 'when confronted by letters to the editor in support of the Israeli government', he had 'developed a habit' to look at the signature to see if 'the reader has a Jewish name. If so, I tend not to read it'.

Alternatively and in rare non-Jewish sympathy with the 'anti-Semitic' charge, Daniel Johnson in the *Daily Telegraph* in October 2001 thought that there was a 'subliminal anti-Semitism at work in the persistent desire of the West to identify with states and movements that deny Israel's right to exist'. Boris Johnson, editor of the *Spectator*, was more forthright. 'It is true', he wrote in April 2003, 'that those who carp at Israel are often motivated by anti-Semitism; and it is true that those who attack Israel often wish to destroy her and drive the Jews into the sea'.

But such views were overshadowed by those who objected to being regarded as 'anti-Semites' merely because of their criticisms of Israel. 'Especially pathetic on the part of our apologists for Israeli oppression is their bleating about anti-Semitism', declared Paul Foot in the *Guardian* in March 2002. To the Australian journalist John Pilger, in September 2002, there was even a conspiracy to have non-Jews believe that any criticism of Israel was anti-Semitic. To Fergal Keane of the BBC, it was 'contemptible' that a spokesman for the Israeli foreign ministry should allege that the BBC's coverage of Israel was 'tinged with anti-Semitism'. To Robert Fisk, writing in the *Independent* in May 2002, such charges were 'dishonest', while to a senior *Guardian* journalist in May 2002, accusation of 'anti-Semitism' in coverage of Israel was both 'orchestrated' and 'blackmail'.

In the *Independent*, in December 2001 and May 2002 respectively, Deborah Orr—who had expressed her agreement with the French ambassador in London when he described Israel as a 'shitty little country'—and Robert Fisk declared themselves to be 'fed up' with, and 'tired' of, being called 'anti-Semites'. In March 2003, after Richard Perle, chairman of the Pentagon's Defence Policy Board, had referred to the '*sotto voce* anti-Semitism' in criticisms of US administration policy, Patrick Buchanan—the American conservative, and former presidential candidate—not only described Perle as 'like a squid, emitting this inky fluid of alleged anti-Semitism' but suggested that he was an 'agent of influence of a foreign power'. Likewise, when the Labour MP Tam Dalyell was criticised for accusing the prime minister in May 2003 of being 'unduly influenced by a cabal of Jewish advisers', he declared—hot under the collar—'I am not going to be labelled anti-Semitic, but the time has come for candour'.

Meanwhile, Jews who expressed support for Israel were called 'Zionists' even if they were not Zionists, 'right-wingers' even if they were 'on the left', and members of the 'Jewish lobby' even if they were thinking and acting on their own initiative. If they were Christian supporters of Israel's existence they were likely to be similarly accused of being 'right-wing fundamentalists', whether they were so or not. Here, the view of many non-Muslims, both of 'right' and 'left', that there was a Christian-Jewish alliance centred upon the US converged with that of Islamists themselves, again to the latter's advantage as Islamism made its way in the world.

Moreover, the instinct to magnify the power of 'the Jews' was at full stretch in attributing US policy to their influence. But this too was unsurprising. If Israel could be invested—as in *The Times* in October 2000—with a 'vast' military superiority over 'all of its neighbouring countries together', or the economic aid it received from the United States could become 'massive' in the *Guardian* in March 2002, the wealth and influence in the United States of the 'Jewish lobby' could only be of proportionate scale. In *The Times*, in April 2002, such influence was duly said to be of 'almost mythical proportions'; and again in *The Times* in May 2003, 'Jewish money' was said to play a 'huge role' in American presidential campaigns.

Similarly, in July 2004, President Khatami of Iran declared America's capital to be 'Tel Aviv, not Washington'. 'It's the Zionists who dominate the United States', he asserted. But if the support, political, military and financial, for Israel in the US could be exaggerated, there were no grounds for minimising it. In May 2002, both the House of Representatives and the Senate not only declared, by very large majorities, that the US and Israel were engaged in a 'common struggle against terrorism', but expressed solidarity with Israel 'as it takes necessary steps to provide security to its people'; and in July 2002 the US approved a grant of $200 million to Israel for the specific purpose of assisting it in its 'war against terror'. 'We will never leave their side', proclaimed the majority leader in the House of Representatives, the Republican Tom DeLay, speaking of Israel in May 2004. 'Israel's fight is our fight', declared the House Democratic whip, Steny Hoyer, also in May 2004.

In June 2004, both houses of the US Congress voted overwhelmingly— by 407 votes to 9 in the former, and 95 to 3 in the latter—to reject the principle of the 'right of return' to Israel of Palestinian refugees, as well as the demand that Israel return to the borders which existed before the 1967 war. Moreover, the defeated Democratic contender for the US presidency in 2004, John Kerry, described Israel's security barrier as a 'legitimate act of self-defence'. He also supported the notion of moving the US embassy in Israel to Jerusalem, and was in favour of US assistance to Israel in order that its 'military supremacy' in the area be maintained. More specifically, President Bush in February 2005 pledged to support Israel were its security to be 'threatened' by Iran, while in May 2005 the US House of Representatives even voted $50 million to Israel for construction work at checkpoints surrounding Palestinian areas.

But if 'the Zionists' 'dominate' the United States, they do so with a proportion of Jews in the American population, according to a University of Chicago survey of religious affiliation published in July 2004, of just under 2 per cent, as already mentioned, compared with some 25 per cent who are Catholic and 52 per cent Protestant. Moreover, despite almost unqualified Republican Party support for Israel, only 19 per cent of Jews voted for President Bush in 2000—against 79 per cent for his Democratic opponent—and only 24 per cent even in 2004. Moreover, two-thirds of Jews, a higher proportion than in the rest of the population, disapproved of the 2003 invasion of Iraq.

The presence of Jews in the ranks of 'public intellectuals', in the legal profession, in the higher reaches of the civil service, in the press, in the broadcasting media and in academia is a significant one. It is also disproportionate to their small numbers in the US population. In addition, they have been described as 'among the wealthiest groups'—or minority sub-groups—in America. Furthermore, only some two-fifths of the general American population of college age are enrolled in higher education, while over 80 per cent of Jews are so. Their influence could therefore be said to be a function both of education and money. But, in the last analysis, it appears to be education which is the decisive factor in the positions which Jews have come to hold in American life.

Nevertheless, their influence as a 'lobby', despite such 'lobby' being held to be of 'almost mythical' impact, has its limits. These limits are determined by many factors. They include rivalrous hostility to such influence itself, and—more important—the impossibility of overriding whatever America considers to be in its own larger strategic interests. They are interests which have made the 'oil lobby' a greater influence than any which a 2 per cent minority could wield. To regard the Jews' supposed influence over the American polity as an absolutely determining one is also to reveal scant knowledge of America itself.

As the religious historian Philip Jenkins expresses it in his book *The Next Christendom,* 'Americans still take biblical arguments very seriously, and therefore give credence to the Zionist project that Europeans do not'. These 'Hebraic' sympathies and moral reflexes in American culture and politics derive principally from the influence of the Puritan heritage, and therefore of Christian nonconformist beliefs, rather than the pressure of a conspiratorial Jewish 'lobby'. In addition, the number of those in the US population who describe themselves as 'Christian conservatives' is some nine times larger than the number of Jews.

Nevertheless, the Islamic advance has brought with it increasing insistence upon Jewish 'conspiracy' and 'power' in the world. In February 1989, Ayatollah Khomeini declared that the defence of Salman Rushdie was being 'masterminded' by 'Zionist, American and British institutions'. In 1990, *International Guerrillas*, a Pakistani-produced film widely shown in Muslim countries, similarly made a 'Jewish conspiracy' against Pakistan and the wider Islamic world a central theme. In 1993, Egypt even blamed the fall in its revenues from tourism upon negative reports by journalists 'working for the world Zionist movement'. Or, from a host of other such instances, the Islamist movement Hizb ut-Tahrir warned its audiences at public meetings in Britain in 1994 to be on their guard against 'the Jews, policemen and spies for the Western media'. Or, in related magnification, the Egyptian Islamist party al-Gama'a al-Islamiyah declared in January 1995 that the Egyptian government had 'mortgaged the will of the nation to Jewish enemies and the Americans'.

Indeed, in many of these Islamist declarations, the interests of 'Jews' or 'Zionists' can be given precedence over American interests themselves, not least since the latter are held to be in the hands of Jews. In other diatribes, the Americans come first. Thus, in October 2002 Abu Bakr Bashir, the leader of Jemaah Islamiyah, attributed accusations of his involvement in the Bali bombing to 'a lie made up by America and Jews'. In the same month, Saddam Hussein was counselling the Chechens against continuing with their Moscow cinema hostage-taking, on the grounds that it would give 'Zionism and America'—in that order—further cause to 'undermine Islam and Muslims'. But whichever is given primacy, it is clear that 'Jews'—a small minority people invested with world-conquering powers—play a vital ideological role for Islamism, as they did for their 'Judeo-phobic' European and Christian predecessors, and for Nazism.

Moreover, since sufficient numbers of non-Muslims share, usually covertly, the Islamist view of Jewish influence, the West's response to Islamism has—for this reason among others—sounded an uncertain note. While a Bashir and a Saddam Hussein were blaming the Jews for seeking to undermine Islam, a prominent 'left'-wing weekly in London was implying that there was a 'kosher conspiracy' in Britain, the magazine's cover depicting the sharp point of the Star of David piercing the Union flag. Indeed, when bin Laden pronounced in his 'Letter to the American People' in November 2002 that 'the Jews have taken control of your economy, through which they have taken control of your media, and now control all aspects of your life', he spoke to a sense shared by many, whatever their other political beliefs or faith.

In 1972 Richard Nixon, as recorded on a White House tape, could be heard in the Oval Office complaining of the influence in the Justice Department of a 'terrible liberal Jewish clique'. In the subsequent phase of such assertions it was not of liberals but of 'neo-conservatives', and of the influence of 'Jewish hawks', that complaint was to be made. Or, as the French foreign minister Dominique de Villepin put it in March 2003, 'the hawks in the US administration are in the hands of Sharon'. Also in March 2003, Patrick Buchanan in *The American Conservative* 'charged' that a 'cabal of polemicists and public officials' in the United States was not only seeking to 'ensnare' America in a 'series of wars', but to 'conscript American blood to make the world safe for Israel'. When the Islamist Abu Bakr Bashir asserted in October 2002 that 'Israel is in control of America', the burthen of the objection was the same.

'It is common talk that some of them', declared Hugo Young in the *Guardian* in November 2002—writing of the 'hawks' in the Bush administra-

tion—'are as much Israeli as American nationalists'. 'Behind nervous con-
fiding hands', he reported from Washington, 'come sardonic whispers of an
American outpost of Likud'. 'East Coast Zionism', Ed Vulliamy called it in
February 2003 in the *Guardian*'s sister paper, the *Observer*. 'The aura of a dirty
little secret', Young added, 'surrounds the possibility... that the emotional
thrust of the anti-Saddam campaign from the most hawkish hawks contem-
plates the security of one country Israel... more than that of another, the US
itself'. As in related arguments before and during the Second World War, this
was to imply that war was being joined for the sake of, and even at the behest
of, 'the Jews'.

A commonplace stereotype determined such judgment. In Young's case, it
moved easily from the notion of a 'Jewish lobby'—now 'liberal', now
'hawkish'—to the very nouns and adjectives, including 'tightly-knit' as well as
'secret' and 'dirty', which have been typical of such forms of perception. In
December 2002, Young also had one of his Jewish hawks, Paul Wolfowitz, the
American deputy-defence secretary, 'ceaselessly deferential' to the president,
an old adjective for the comportment of 'the Jew'. To the Arab-American literary critic Edward Said, in the *Guardian* in April 2003, 'reactionary Washington institutions' had not only 'spawned' 'Wolfowitz, Perle, Abrams and
Feith'—thus singling out only the Jews, while using the verb 'spawned' as did
T. S. Eliot of a Jew in his notorious poem 'Gerontion'—but the four had produced an 'unhealthy intellectual and moral atmosphere' around them. To
Young, returning to the subject in December 2002, Wolfowitz was a 'prince of
darkness', an old trope for the imagined 'Satan' in 'the Jew'.

Given the historic nature of these reflexes, it was inevitable that epithets
traditionally employed in descriptions of Jews should also have been
employed in descriptions of Israel and Israeli politicians. Ariel Sharon and
Shimon Peres were thus described in the *Economist* in May 2001 as Fagin-like
'artful dodgers'; to Martin Woollacott, in the *Guardian* in August 2003, Ariel
Sharon was in Jewish character as a 'flatterer', 'Machiavellian' and 'wily'; in
mediaeval fashion, in April 2002, the Israeli government was charged by A. N.
Wilson in London's *Evening Standard* with 'poisoning the water supplies' of the
Palestinians. This kind of thing again made Israel into 'the Jew among the
nations'.

To accuse Israel of 'revenge'—in preference to 'retaliation' or 'response'
to attack—was again to make the state, if it is a state, the Jew-writ-large. To
the *Guardian* in February and November 2002, respectively, the ostracism of
Yasser Arafat by the Israelis was '*vengeful*' and the Israeli government's policies
'offered *revenge* but no resolution'. In April 2002, Israel's leaders were 'bloody

and *vengeful'* in the view of the Grand Mufti of Marseille, Soheib Bencheikh; to the Vatican spokesman Joaquin Navarro-Valls, they were guilty of carrying out '*revenge* attacks'. In its turn, the Foreign Office in March 2002 urged Israel 'to choose restraint rather than *revenge*'. And after the attack on an Israeli-owned hotel in Mombasa in November 2002, the Israelis—in the *Daily Telegraph*—were planning '*retribution*', while Ariel Sharon had 'left Israelis in no doubt that Mossad... would wreak *vengeance* soon or later'.

The features of this world of 'princes of darkness', of 'dirty secrets', of 'Jewish lobby' powers, of Jewish control of economies and of media 'empires', and of variously deferential, vengeful, wily and well-poisoning Jews are culturally familiar. Moreover, there was again an almost seamless web between non-Muslim and Muslim, and 'right' and 'left', views of the 'eternal Jew' and his ways. In Jenin, therefore, bodies were not only 'piled in the streets' but, according to Richard Ingrams in the *Observer* in April 2002, 'removed for secret burial'. 'In the 'nightmare of Israel'—as Peter Preston described it in the *Guardian* in December 2001—'Jews' were almost bound to act in this fashion.

Beyond, or below, were other depths. They were those of 'Israel' as a '*cancer* of the Middle East', according to the chants of Muslim protesters at the White House in October 1999. They were those of an 'Israel' guilty of the '*desecration* of the birthplace of Jesus Christ', again according to Richard Ingrams in the *Observer*, or of an 'Israel' '*defiling* the streets of Bethlehem', according to William Abercrombie in a letter to *The Times* in April 2002. To Yasmin Alibhai-Brown, writing in the *Independent* in April 2002—and awarded British journalism's Orwell Prize—the mark of the Israeli government under Sharon was 'depravity'; to the British section of Hizb ut-Tahrir, the extreme Islamist group, 'every inch' of the 'land of Palestine' required to be 'purified from the filth of the occupying Jews'.

The association between 'the Jew' and 'depravity', 'defilement' and 'dirt' have been of long durance, leaping cultural boundaries from Western Christian polemics—as in Chrysostom and Luther—to the world of the Islamic revival. Saudi princes were reported in April 2002 to speak ('among themselves') of 'the Jews of Israel' as 'ants on a dung-heap'. Tariq Aziz, Iraq's foreign minister, was reported by Richard Butler, the head of the UN's arms inspectorate, to have described Palestine as 'occupied by dirty Jews'. Even to the president of the French Red Cross, Marc Gentilli, it was 'disgusting' to contemplate Israel's admission to the international movement. Moreover, the 'danger' of the 'Judaisation' of Jerusalem—as Yasser Arafat and Saddam Hussein expressed it in March 1997 and December 2000, respectively—appeared to arouse the same frisson of recoil among both Christians and Muslims.

The cumulative force of this type of perception has been large indeed. It is a force which has gained in potency during the years of the Arab and Islamic revivals. The confident reassertion of Muslim hostility towards the Jews and Israel, without discrimination between them, has found an answering echo in the non-Islamic world. Even Jews could sometimes be found using its language, perhaps from that 'self-hatred' of which Freudians wrote a century ago. In February 2002, a letter to *The Times* from a Jewish reader referred to the policies of the Israeli government as not merely 'repressive' and 'unenlightened' but 'unsavoury'. In September 2002, the Labour MP Gerald Kaufman found Jerusalem to be 'infested' by ultra-orthodox Jews; in the *Guardian* in the same month, the Jewish actress Miriam Karlin attributed Ariel Sharon's (and George Bush's) actions to motives of 'revenge'.

In such circumstances, compounded by Israel's own moral misdeeds, both the 'Israel' and 'the Jew' of conventional magnification, emotional projection, and ideological need have flourished. By the same token, *verus Israel* and actual Jews cannot.

CHAPTER SIX

Into the Moral Labyrinth

In May 1991, during the second year of the *fatwa* against Salman Rushdie, now-familiar moral questions were posed in Britain. 'Where', asked a writer in the *Independent*, 'are the British Muslim leaders who can rescue the good name of their community by articulating a dissenting view among their people? And, if there is no such widespread view, how will non-Muslims be able to resist the conclusion that our Muslim community generally is prepared to condone the crime of murder in the name of their religion?' A decade later, in the wake of the attack on the World Trade Center, Margaret Thatcher told *The Times* that 'the people who brought down those towers were Muslims, and Muslims must stand up and say that that is not the way of Islam. ... They must say that it was disgraceful. I have not heard enough from Muslim priests'.

On the contrary, whether in 1991 or 2001 or 2004 and 2005, much was heard from 'Muslim priests' as well as 'ordinary' Muslims about acts carried out in their names. A minority openly and forcefully objected, both in general and specific terms, to a wide variety of Islamism's deeds. They did not mince their words. In May 2004, the deputy-editor of the Italian *Corriere della Sera*, Magdi Allam—one of the most outspoken critics of Islamism—denounced what he called 'globalised Islamic terrorism'. This 'terrorism', which had 'contempt for the logic of compromise' and the 'principle of peaceful coexistence', had 'unleashed a war against the West and the free world, a war that can and must be won'.

A 'culture of destruction' had 'taken root in our society', the Qatari scholar of Sharia and cleric Abd al-Hamid al-Ansari stated in August 2004. 'No one' had 'enticed' the 9/11 hijackers, he continued, 'and they did not suffer from oppression, repression or poverty. They were our young people and our sons, and they were our responsibility', and had been 'incited to die for the sake of Allah' by 'our harmful religious views'. Similarly, 'our terrorist sons are an end-product of our corrupted culture', a culture in which 'violence' was 'preached in the name of religion', declared Abdel Rahman al-Rashed of the al-Arabiya television network in September 2004. 'Most perpetrators of suicide operations in buses, schools and residential buildings around the world for the past ten years have been Muslims. What a pathetic record, what an abominable achievement', he exclaimed.

Indeed, in March 2005 the Islamic Commission of Spain, one of the principal bodies representing the country's Muslims, issued a fatwa against Osama bin Laden, pronouncing that his acts and those of al-Qaeda were to be 'roundly condemned'; in May 2005, the Australian Muslim leader, Sheikh Taj al-Din al-Hilali, offered himself to Iraqi insurgents in exchange for the release of an Australian hostage; in June 2005, a mosque's board of directors in Lodi, near Sacramento in California, unanimously voted to sack its imam—earlier detained during an FBI 'terror investigation'—for 'speaking against the United States'; and in July 2005, in a fatwa, the Sunni Council in Britain condemned the London suicide-bombings as the work of a 'perverted ideology'.

But many Muslims, al-Hilali included, adopted a variety of ethically ambivalent, qualified or evasive positions. Others appeared by their silence to approve, or made it sufficiently clear that they did approve, of most of the actions of which the majority of the non-Muslim world disapproved, or at which it stood aghast. The sum of these responses was that of moral ambiguity. Arguments therefore broke out about 'where Muslims stood'. 'Poll' findings were disparate and contested. Implied and express demands that diaspora Muslims should condemn acts of which non-Muslims disapproved were met by counter-assertions by Muslim spokesmen that they had already done so. These counter-assertions were in turn generally treated with scepticism, or otherwise found wanting. 'There are reasons why people don't seem to register your condemnations', declared one critic on an Internet Web site in October 2004. 'People are sceptical of them because there is no significant anti-terrorist movement within Islam, and there don't seem to be any efforts within the Islamic community to stop the growth of Isalmic terrorism'.

Such reactions were evidence of the degree of ambiguity perceived to characterise Muslim positions. Indeed, the dissatisfied non-Muslim world continued to insist that it was 'incumbent' on Muslim leaders, clerical and secular alike, to condemn 'unreservedly' the 'terroristic acts of fellow-Muslims'. Muslim leaders in the diaspora, for their parts, routinely claimed that mosque sermons had unequivocally castigated the attacks of 11 September 2001, for example. Their spokesmen irately asserted, as in Britain, that 'all the major Muslim organisations' had registered 'immediate condemnations' of what had occurred. Yet in November 2003, a British foreign office minister urged imams and other Muslim leaders to use 'clearer, stronger language' in condemning 'terrorism'; and in March 2004, a former archbishop of Canterbury, George Carey, again asserted that 'very few Muslim leaders condemn clearly and unconditionally the evil of suicide-bombers'.

Such type of criticism was regularly rejected by Muslim spokesmen, the more dismissively as Islamist attacks grew more frequent and more violent. The Muslim community had 'consistently condemned terrorism', declared Inayat Bunglawala, of the Muslim Council of Britain; Carey's charges were 'nonsense', pronounced Manzoor Moghal, chairman of the Federation of Muslim Organisations. But even Arab politicians, albeit a minority, conceded—as did Jordan's foreign minister, Marwan Muasher, in January 2004—that 'we have not publicly, clearly, unequivocally taken a stand against suicide-bombs'. Nevertheless, Muslim spokesmen continually insisted that Islam forbade the killing of innocent non-combatant civilians, as the scale of such killings by Muslims, including of innocent fellow-Muslims, spread across the world. Such practice, characteristically asserted Sheikh Husam Qaraqirah, a Lebanese cleric, in July 2003, had 'no relation whatsoever to Islam'.

Almost everywhere in the Muslim world, equivocation also accompanied or shadowed that which purported to be categorical. Qualification modified that which presented itself as unqualified; and, despite the exceptions, abbreviated ethical response turned, in many cases, to minimisation or silence. By January 2003 the Pakistani foreign minister, during a visit to the United States, had reduced the destruction of the World Trade Center to an 'unfortunate' event.

At the time of Margaret Thatcher's criticisms, Iqbal Sacranie, chairman of Muslim Aid, had found unwarranted her demands that Muslims in Britain 'stand up' and declare the attacks on the World Trade Center and elsewhere to have been 'disgraceful'. Condemn the attacks they had done, he declared on 3 October 2001, but it was 'outrageous' for her to 'relate' them to Muslims. There was no proof for Sacranie—who became 'Sir Iqbal Sacranie' in June 2005—that Muslims were involved at all, until bin Laden himself claimed it as al-Qaeda's doing. Typical also was the statement in Britain of Syed Aziz

Pasha, general-secretary of the Union of Muslim Organisations, after the events of 9/11. The Union's 'board of Muslim scholars' had 'issued a very clear statement condemning the terrorism', he stated; Islam was a 'religion of peace'; and he therefore had 'reservations' about assertions that the attacks were the work of Muslims.

As in resort to the earlier-discussed Twelve Devices of argument, the ground had therefore been laid for complexity: the ambivalent 'yes-and-no' in response to the 'question direct'. Muslims complained (with some justice) that the Anglo-American media paid more attention to the signs of approval by Muslims of the attacks on the United States, or to their silences, than to what Muslims described as their 'denunciations' of the 'atrocity of 9/11'. Indeed, the open declaration in November 2001 by Syed Ahmed Bukhari, chief imam of the Jama Masjid in Delhi, India's leading mosque, that he had 'no regrets' for the deaths in the attack, also made for 'better copy' than any Muslim criticism of the events of 11 September 2001, especially criticism which was morally qualified or ambiguous. Bukhari's assertions that 'Americans should know what it means to lose close relatives, sons and brothers', and that 'for the last 50 years' America and Israel had been 'bleeding the Muslims', were further grist to the media mill. So, too, was the description of 9/11 by the earlier-mentioned Sheikh Taj al-Din al-Hilali, the mufti of Australia, as 'God's work'.

Nonetheless, there have been outright statements by Muslim leaders, religious and lay, of moral objection to insensate violence carried out on Islam's behalf. At Alexandria in January 2002, Mohammed Sayed Tantawi, the Grand Sheikh of the al-Azhar Islamic university in Cairo, put his name to a joint Muslim, Christian and Jewish declaration that 'killing innocents in the name of God is a desecration of His Holy Name, and defames religion in the world'. It was a declaration with which the Egyptian president, Hosni Mubarak, expressed his agreement. Nor was this morally exceptional. A decade earlier in February 1991, Tantawi, Egypt's chief religious jurist, had declared in Riyadh that the overthrow of Saddam Hussein was a 'religious duty' and that, as 'chief of the wrongdoers and aggressors', Saddam deserved the severest punishment, 'possibly crucifixion'.

The beheading by Islamists of captives in Iraq showed 'how base and vile those who wear the robe of Islam have become', also declared Abdullah Sahar, a Kuwait University scholar, in May 2004. Even Lebanese Hezbollah condemned the decapitation in Iraq of the US telecoms engineer, Nick Berg, as a 'horrible act'. A similar beheading of an American hostage in June 2004 was described by an official of the American Arab Anti-Discrimination Committee as 'repulsive', while the militant Iraqi Shi'ite cleric Moqtada al-Sadr himself denounced as 'criminals' 'those who decapitate prisoners. Islamic law', he added, 'does not permit them to do this', an assertion which could itself be contested.

Likewise, bombings of churches in Baghdad, as in August 2004, were described as 'criminal actions' by Grand Ayatollah Ali al-Sistani, the Shi'ite leader; while Ali el-Messery, one of Spain's leading imams, called the bomb-attacks in March 2004 upon Madrid 'a crime that not even animals would commit'. In September 2004 the abduction and execution of foreigners in Iraq was also condemned (as 'not Islamic') by Iraq's senior Sunni religious body, its committee of Muslim scholars or *ulema*. In the same month, the Libyan leader described as 'terrorism' the kidnappings of foreigners in Iraq; and even Hamas and Hezbollah in August 2004 criticised the seizure of two French journalists, although less on grounds of principle than in recognition of what was described as the 'understanding' of France for the Arab cause.

The school siege and hostage-deaths in Beslan in North Ossetia in September 2004 aroused wide recoil in the Muslim world, not least for the harm done to the 'image' of Islam, a subject to which I will return. Those responsible had 'taken Islam as a cover' and their acts were those of 'criminals, not Muslims', Tantawi reiterated in a sermon in September 2004. To Egypt's semi-official *al-Ahram*, the events at Beslan were an 'ugly crime against humanity'; the Egyptian government daily *Okaz* called the perpetrators 'butchers in the name of Allah'.

In the face of Koranic and other sacred Muslim writings which allegedly demonstrated the contrary, even 'hate for the Jews' was declared in May 2002 by the writer Tariq Ramadan to be 'not Islamic'. 'Nothing' in Islam legitimised it, Ramadan characteristically asserted. Again, when Mahathir Mohamad had claimed in October 2003 that Jews ruled the world and had their wars fought for them by proxy, voices of dissent—but decidedly minoritarian—could be heard from within Saudi Arabia itself. Mahathir had been 'swept along by hyperbole and exaggeration', declared *Arab News*, an online daily; 'Jews no more control the world than do Muslims or anyone else', and it would be 'tragic and wrong' should Mahathir's words be 'taken as an invitation for hate crimes and terrorism against Jews', it added.

However, one of the commonest marks of Muslim objection to the actions of fellow-Muslims is the side-stepping of such moral categories. 'Condemnation' of an act may therefore be offered without straightforward attribution of wrongdoing to the acts and actors 'condemned'. 'It is really very sad and unfortunate', the imam of the London Mosque, Ataul Mujeeb Rashed, declared in January 1991, that 'ignorant Muslims, by their actions and statements which run contrary to Islam, are helping the Western media to depict a blood-soaked picture of Islam'. But 'ignorance' is not a moral category. Indeed, culpability is lessened, or absent, if mere 'ignorance' is at work. Similarly, the London bombings of July 2005 were evasively described as a 'tragedy' by a group of British Muslim leaders. Moreover, they were a 'tragedy' which demanded that 'all of us'—signifying both Muslims and non-Muslims—'both in public life and in civil and religious society, confront together the problems of Islamophobia, racism, unemployment and social exclusion'. However true, it was also a deft shift of focus from crime to 'tragedy', and sought to keep the responsibility for it at a moral distance. Moreover, crimes and offences committed against Muslims—at Guantanamo or Abu Ghraib, for example—may earn severer condemnations than do equally serious, or more serious, acts carried out by Muslims. Nevertheless, the presumption among most non-Muslims that Muslims do not speak out against malfeasances carried out in their names, or do so with ethically forked tongues, is often enough unjust.

'When I speak against the Taliban and Osama', the imam of New York's Hazrat-I-Abubakr Sadiq mosque, Mohammed Sherzad, complained in September 2001, 'they [sc. his congregants] harass me, so many times they harass me. They say, "Why do you speak against Osama bin Laden? He is a good Muslim"'. Indeed, Sherzad had not only condemned the Taliban but, accusing a group of his mosque members of funnelling donations to it, had ejected them; the latter fought back through the courts, won their battle in June 2004 and had the imam himself ejected.

The sceptical non-Muslim might consider Sherzad's stand to have been that of a small 'unrepresentative' minority of diaspora Muslims. But non-Muslim accusations of a morally complicit silence among Muslims have been too sweeping. In May 2002, for example, some half a million Moroccans demonstrated in Casablanca against 'terrorism'; in June 2003, Sayed Safavi, an Iranian Sufi cleric, condemned suicide-bombing as a 'crime'; Cairo's Grand Sheikh Tantawi described 'extremism' as the 'enemy of Islam'; in November 2003, the Turkish government ordered the imams of mosques across the country to denounce 'terrorism'; and when Saudi Arabia itself began to be struck by al-Qaeda-inspired bombings, even a radical cleric, Sheikh Nasser al-Fahd, was 'persuaded' in November 2003 to recant his support for violent Islamist acts, and to describe 'blowing oneself up' as 'not martyrdom but suicide'. 'Fear God and repent', he added, before being taken back to jail. And as the rate of attacks within Saudi Arabia increased during 2004, leading Saudi clerics—most of whom had been silent about 9/11—found the bombings (in

Saudi Arabia) 'dastardly', 'devastating', 'criminal', 'heinous' and 'evil', described their perpetrators (in Saudi Arabia) as 'deviants' and called on them to 'return to the true path' in order to obtain 'forgiveness'.

More courageous in the circumstances was the imam of the al-Madina mosque in east London, Mohammed Saddique, who disclosed in November 2001 that worshippers had demanded that a 'stronger stance' be taken against the activities of local Islamists. Immediately after the events of 11 September the latter had sought to make an announcement in the mosque calling for a jihad, and for recruits from the community to join it. 'I immediately told them to leave', declared Saddique; 'we did not want anything to do with them'. In March 2004, Abdulwahab Hussein Gomaa, the Egyptian imam of Rome's Great Mosque, similarly refused to accede to the demands of militant Islamists in the congregation that he conduct memorial prayers for the assassinated leader of Hamas, Sheikh Ahmed Yassin.

Likewise Abdul Haqq Baker, chairman of the Brixton mosque which had been attended by the 'shoe-bomber' Richard Reid, spoke out against Muslim 'extremists' who had been active among his congregants. He too had the courage to disclose that he had been 'threatened with having my legs broken simply because the extremists were angry that they could not get a foot in the door'. He was afraid for himself, his family and his friends. 'If this place gets a firebomb', he declared, 'it will be other Muslims behind it', but he intended to continue with his teaching. In December 2001 the principal of London's Muslim College, Zaki Badawi, called on the British government to stop giving priority-entry to foreign clerics who, he said, were 'unable' to prevent extremists taking over their mosques. He also urged the government to close after-hours schools run by militant Islamist groups where there was little oversight of what was taught. Yet Badawi himself was among those who expressed doubt that the attack on the World Trade Center was carried out by Muslims.

There was moral complexity in this latter species of ambiguity. A minority of individuals, including certain imams, might declare themselves to be against what had been done in Islam's name, but again without direct use of the terminology of moral condemnation. When they did use such terms, it was often only when the significance of heinous acts could no longer be side-stepped, or after a serious reverse for Arab and Muslim interests, such as the fall of Baghdad. 'We were never candid enough to stop blaming the outside for our ills and failures', declared the Egyptian scholar, Saad Eddin Ibrahim, in April 2003; or, 'we are responsible'—a rare word and sentiment—'for all that is happening to us. The problem is in us, not imposed upon us', concluded a Saudi journalist, Anas Zahid, writing in the pan-Arab newspaper *Asharq al-*

Awsat in the same month. And in March 2004 the Libyan foreign minister, Mohamed Abderrhmane Chalgam, described al-Qaeda as a 'real obstacle against our progress, against our security, against women ... against any change in our region'. In the same month, the Muslim Council of Britain urged mosques to take to the police any evidence they might have of 'criminal activity or wrongdoing' by community members.

Those who were forthright were rarely persistently so. Or, as we have seen, they might qualify their forthrightness with intellectually bewildering reservations. In addition, factional and other divisions within Muslim communities generally prevented their leaders and spokesmen from taking exposed and unilateral public positions for long, or at all. If they did, or were minded to do, they might also be threatened; the Muslim Council of Britain's advice that Muslims take their 'suspicions' to the police was immediately condemned by British Islamists as an invitation to Muslims to 'cooperate with local authorities against other members of the faith'. Moreover, habits of intellectual evasion, similar to or identical with the type of thing noted in the Twelve Devices, led to logical contradiction and moral incoherence in response to unwelcome interrogation by non-Muslims. The latter looked, often naively, for directness and consistency of judgment from Muslims, and equally often did not find it.

Despite all this, it was wrong of non-Muslims to assume, and continually to repeat, that objection to Islamist excesses was not to be found in the Muslim world. Again taking examples at random, the National Federation of Muslims of France expressed 'stupor' in December 1994 at the 'odious assassinations' of four Christian missionaries at Tizi Ouzou in Algeria, carried out in reprisal for the earlier killing of four Algerian hijackers by the French; adding, however, that the missionaries had been murdered by 'we know not what devil', a lurking qualification. But the condemnation was plain enough.

Likewise, after Islamist car-bombs killed 42 and injured 286 in Algiers in January 1995, Algeria's president Zeroual described the act as one of 'barbarism', and its perpetrators as 'monsters'. 'One does not have to kill', declared an Algerian medical student about another act of violence carried out by Islamists a few weeks later. But she could not give her name to the journalist who reported her views, since it would have been perilous to do so. 'They are criminals not Muslims, and this is barbaric justice', she added. The Indonesian Ulamas Council, the country's highest authority on Islamic matters, similarly made no bones about the death-sentence handed out to the Islamist Amrozi for his part in the Bali bombings of October 2002. He 'deserved the penalty', the council stated. Again, after the assassination in March 2004 by the Israelis of the Hamas leader, Sheikh Ahmed Yassin, some seventy Palestinian intellectuals and officials rejected calls by Yassin's successor for revenge, and urged restraint.

Indeed, during the years of the Islamic 'reawakening' it has been rare for events which have aroused non-Islamic criticism, or recoil, not to have somewhere aroused similar responses in Muslims. Aziz al-Azmeh, a professor of Islamic studies at Exeter University, went as far in February 1989 as to refer not only to the Islamic 'seclusion and subordination' of women, but to the 'prurient imagination' which 'reduced' them to mere 'causes for temptation'. To most non-Muslims, this was precisely the kind of criticism of the prohibitions and restraints, discussed in an earlier chapter, which they hoped to hear. Moreover, it was not a non-Muslim but a former student of Khomeini, Ayatollah Jalal Ganje'i—a participant in the 1979 Iranian revolution against the Shah—who termed the former's divinised ten-year rule as no more than 'another form of dictatorship' over Iran.

Likewise, in January 2004, the 'reformist' Iranian president, Mohammad Khatami, and the speaker of the Iranian parliament, Mahdi Karroubi, themselves denounced—as a denial of 'Islamic democracy'—the rigging of the Iranian general election by the country's 'Guardian Council' of Islamists. In June 2003, Iraq's senior Shi'ite cleric, Grand Ayatollah Sistani, did not think that 'religious scholars' should hold 'positions of administrative and executive responsibility', let alone—as in Iran—wield absolute power. In August 2003 an Iraqi Shi'ite cleric, Sayyid Iyad Jamaleddin, even declared categorically that 'secularism is not blasphemy. I am a Muslim. I am devoted to my religion, but I want to get it back from the state. That is why I want a secular state'.

Non-Muslims also have no monopoly in criticisms of the Islamic world for its alleged 'backwardness'. In February 2002, President Musharraf of Pakistan went further than any non-Muslim would have dared in describing Muslims as 'the poorest, the most illiterate, the most backward, the most unhealthy, the most unenlightened and the weakest of all the human race'. The 'Islamic world', he pronounced, was 'living in darkness'. In May 2004 he added to these charges. In Pakistan, he declared, 'mosques and *madrassas*'—'not all' of the latter, but 'a few'—were being 'misused' to 'spread hatred' and 'create divisions'. Neither did it require a non-Muslim critic to point to 'failed' Muslim or Arab regimes. In November 2001, in Egypt's *al-Ahram*, the academic Edward Said condemned Arab governments in general—and the Palestinian Authority in particular—for being 'unable or unwilling to stop either the rise of Islamic extremism or an astonishingly flagrant corruption at the very top'. A 'huge dank cloud of mediocrity and incompetence'—much the same as the 'darkness' of Musharraf—'hangs over everyone' in the Arab world, he added. It gave rise, among other things, to what Said called a 'cult of death'.

Should there be non-Muslims who hold—in what might otherwise be regarded as a 'racist' slur—that Muslims settled in the West have a limited conception of what their new citizenships entail, there were Muslims who thought so too. In the *Washington Post* in April 2002, Mansoor Ijaz, an American-born Pakistani and member of the American Council on Foreign Relations, complained of the (to him) misplaced 'anger' of Muslims in the United States over Justice Department interrogations. According to Ijaz, his fellow-Muslims were demonstrating an 'inability to put citizenship before religious and ethnic allegiances, and US national security interests before dubious claims of civil rights violations'. 'Many of America's Arabs and Muslims', Ijaz further objected, were now debating not only the 'limits of their civic duty' but even its 'merits'.

Muslim responses to their own circumstances, especially in the diaspora, are necessarily complex. They are also partially or wholly concealed from non-Muslims, as the violence of Islamism and its cause in the world advance. Moreover, the device of blaming non-Muslims for whatever afflicts the Islamic world generally crowds out self-criticism, from a justifiable unwillingness to make moral concessions to the non-Muslim. Yet there have been some Muslims who have grasped this nettle also. 'We Muslims cannot keep blaming the West for all our ills', declared Izzat Majeed, a Pakistani writer, in an open letter to *The Nation* in November 2001. 'We have failed as a civil society by not confronting the historical, social and political demons within us.... We have reduced Islam to the organised hypocrisy of state-sponsored *mullah*-ism'.

Moral courage was required of a Muslim to speak in these terms. In November 2001 Nabil Luka Babawi, a professor of criminal law, asserted in the Egyptian paper *al-Ahram* that '[sc. Muslim] terrorists don't know the methods of rational, calm debate'. Instead, they imposed 'darkness'— Musharraf's 'darkness' and Said's 'dank cloud' again—'on the climate of the intellect, because they try to force their backward ideas on public opinion under the veil of religious correctness'. Such sentiment was of the kind which most non-Muslims again wished to hear expressed by Muslims, and which they have continually asserted is not. Babawi even described acts of violence by Muslims against innocent non-Muslims as 'insane'.

Many non-Muslims also wished it said, for example, that 'the Palestinian Arabs invented airplane hijacking'; or that 'Arab Muslims' were the 'masters of terrorism towards their own citizens' as well as 'towards the innocent people of the world', and that in this they had 'the support of some of the clerics'. But it was not necessary to look to Western 'prejudice' for such views. They were the words of a Kuwaiti professor, Ahmad Baghdadi, in Kuwait's *al-Anbaa* in November 2001. He went further, asserting that 'the Arabs and Muslims claim that their religion is a religion of tolerance. But they show no tolerance for those who oppose their opinions. . . . Now the time has come to pay the price'.

It has been generally assumed, too, that the Palestinian cause is dear to every fellow-Arab and fellow-Muslim, as if by fraternal reflex. As was indicated earlier, matters have not been so simple. The rhetoric of Arab and Islamic support for the Palestinians has throughout concealed a variety of judgments, from outright hostility to a support which is more qualified and conditional than that of the Palestinians' Western sympathisers. Muslim governments' declarations of intent to provide financial aid to the Palestinian Authority have rarely been fulfilled to the extent promised, or at all. In particular, many Arab countries showed themselves unwilling to house the Palestinian movement.

The large-scale physical violence carried out in 1970 against Arafat and his forces in the 'Black September' civil war in Jordan has already been noted. In 1982, the expulsion by the Israeli army of Palestinian militia members from Lebanon was supported by many Lebanese. In retaliation for the political support given by Arafat to Saddam Hussein in the Gulf War, hundred of thousands of Palestinians were expelled from Kuwait; many were expelled from Libya also. Syria and several of the militant groups which it sheltered had in common their antipathy towards Arafat, while Hashemite Jordan would not willingly share a common border with a future independent Palestinian state. It was thus made clear by neighbouring governments, in particular those of Egypt and Jordan, that the Israeli threat in 2002 to expel Arafat from the occupied territories was unwelcome. For they were not prepared to provide him with a new base from which to conduct his operations.

Moreover, not even an intransigent common enemy has conciliated—or conciliated for long—internal clan and factional hostilities among the Palestinians themselves, and the power-struggles and running battles to which they have given rise. Arab intellectuals were also to be heard expressing views about Arafat during his lifetime which differed little from those of the most acerbic Israelis. He was a 'hapless, inept leader' in Edward Said's description of him in January 2002, while his Palestinian Authority, with its 'corruption and brutality', had been a 'dismal failure'. The most right-wing of Israelis would have said the same. They would also doubtless have agreed with the judgment in September 2002 of the leading Lebanese journalist, Khairallah Khairallah, that the Palestinians had 'paid dearly' for the 'insistence of a backward group among them on glorifying suicide operations that repel the entire world'.

The spirit of criticism and self-criticism, of condemnation and objection therefore cannot be said to have been absent from internal Islamic debate. To think that it could have been would be aberrant itself. Indeed, it is such debate which has served to demonstrate the nature of the moral confusions and conflicts among Muslims. These conflicts are very various, and refute the 'Islamophobic' notion that Islam is a monolithic or undifferentiated entity whose only internal dynamic is provided by the clash between mindless inertia and equally mindless rage. The historical divisions between and among Sunnis and Shi'as are as deep as those by which Christianity was (and is) riven. The distinction between Wahhabi-inspired Muslims and other Muslims is a profound one. Moreover, to attribute the major responsibility for the upheavals and violences of the current Islamic revival to 'fanatical Wahhabis' is itself simplistic, since Muslims who are not followers of the Saudi Wahhabi sect have also played a turbulent and aggressive role in Islam's advance.

Others, again simplifying, have seen the conflicts within Islam as predominantly battles between 'liberal', 'secular' and 'Westernised' Muslim intellectuals on the one hand, and religious 'fundamentalists' or dynastic despots on the other. This, too, is a reductive distinction even if the recoil (in some Muslim intellectuals) from 'fundamentalism' is profound, and has even induced a desire for reconciliation with the world of 'infidelity' itself. For Islamic 'moderation' has offered some of the most ambiguous responses to the collision between the Islamic and non-Islamic worlds, having a foot in both camps. Moreover, 'secular' or 'Westernised' Muslim intellectuals have made no less use of the devices of argument discussed in an earlier chapter than have their 'non-Westernised' fellow-Muslims.

'I have heard Islamic members of the clergy comparing the Jews to pigs and other disgusting animals', thus exclaimed the ostensibly dissenting Tunisian scholar, Rajaa bin Salamah, at a colloquium held in London in May 2002. 'What kind of Islam are these people spreading?' she asked. The answer to her rhetorical question, as she and other Muslims themselves know, is, for example, in Sura 5:60 of the Koran—among other texts—where it is declared that the Jews have been cursed by God, and 'some of them changed into apes and swine'.

Such 'liberal' or dissenting Muslim interrogation, or self-interrogation, is therefore not always—or even often—what it seems. Bin Salamah's 'challenge' appeared on its surface to imply a disavowal of the comparison made by 'Islamic members of the clergy' between Jews and pigs. Yet such comparison gains its legitimacy from Muslim Holy Writ itself. Other objections which have seemed to signify the taking of a moral distance by Muslims from

Islamist actions have also been less straightforward than they appeared. Villagers in Luxor in November 1997 spat on the bodies of slain Islamist gunmen who had massacred fifty-eight tourists. But reports suggested that what they had in mind were their lost livelihoods as much as ethical reproaches of the killers. Nor has there been any shortage of apparently moral objection to Islamism's acts, but by Muslims and Arabs with blood on their own hands from acts of like kind, or who silently approve of them. For example, the Muslim Brotherhood in Egypt, with its long history of murder, was quick to describe as 'inhumane' the attack on the World Trade Center. Saddam Hussein also had no difficulty in condemning the 'massacre' at Jenin.

However, 'Muslim values' can also be genuinely cited as the ground for objection to an act or behaviour which is held to offend such values. The moral *bona fides* of the complaint in September 2001 by Husain Haqqani, a former high-ranking Pakistani diplomat, that 'celebrations by some Muslims on seeing images of a human tragedy'—the blazing towers of the World Trade Center—were 'totally incompatible with Muslim values' was not to be doubted. Yet the same values have also been invoked in order to deny that Muslims could have committed a particular crime, when the facts were clear that they had. This procedure was still being utilised three weeks after the July 2005 London bombings, as when Mohammad Naseem, the chairman of Birmingham's Central Mosque—one of Britain's largest—felt able to claim that there was 'no proof' that Muslims were involved at all; information to the contrary, he suggested, was the work of 'the CIA'.

These and other forms of avoidance of truth, ambiguity and contradiction were vividly illustrated during the US invasion of Iraq and its aftermath. Relief among many Iraqis at the overthrow of the regime, and applause at the US action, could be combined with shame at Iraqi 'humiliation' at American hands, mental erasure (by many) of the regime's record and increasing anger at the US presence. In Teheran, in April 2003, the Iraqi embassy was stormed and photographs of Saddam Hussein were torn down, but to the accompaniment of shouts of 'Death to America!' from those who besieged the building.

Such 'combined' (or ambivalent) positions were also expressed in the Muslim diaspora. Those who had overthrown Saddam Hussein were 'as much the enemies of Arabs and Muslims as of Saddam', according to Jihad al-Khazin in the London-based *al-Hayat*. 'Islamists have always hated Saddam', declared Azzam Tamimi, director of the Institute of Islamic Political Thought in London, 'but many Muslims are praying for America to be defeated'. Inayat Bunglawala—'media secretary' of the Muslim Council of Britain—asserted in *The Times* in March 2003 that there was 'little hope' that the 'hearts', 'minds' or even the 'loyalty' of British Muslims could be won to the British military presence. On the contrary, British Muslims were 'not going to forget' what 'their Government' had done 'in their name'. Or, in the words of Fuad Nahdi in the *Guardian* in April 2003, British mosques 'up and down the country' were 'for peace, but also for the defeat of the invading coalition'.

A different version of this ambiguity, expressed by some Muslims in Britain, was to 'support the British troops, but not the United States'. In the US itself, according to survey findings published in September 2004, no less than '90 per cent' of newly naturalised Muslim American citizens allegedly declared that if there was a conflict between the US and their country of origin they would be 'inclined' to support the latter. Alternatively, one could opt out—or seem to opt out—of moral choice entirely. Thus, in the United States many Muslims could condemn both the violence of the Saddam regime and the American response to it. 'You don't face wrong with massive use of force', declared Imam Ridha Hajjar of Pomona in California in April 2004. But how, or indeed whether, you 'face' it was left unclear.

Beyond these ambivalences was the capacity to combine objection to Saddam Hussein, and gratification at his departure, with pride at Saddam's 'defiance' of his foes, a defiance which could be held to redound to the credit of 'all Arabs'. In another morally complex set of responses, this time to Saddam Hussein's capture, demands for his immediate trial were coupled with a sense of shame at his failure to resist his captors. 'We had hoped that he would resist to the last and in the process fall as a martyr', said the earlier-cited editor of *al-Quds*, Abdel Bari Atwan, in December 2003. Some responses to the seizing of Saddam by US forces were of a different order. It had been 'ugly and despicable' and an 'insult to all Arabs and Muslims', declared Abdel Aziz Rantisi of Hamas. It was 'bad news', announced Azzam Hneidi, an Islamist member of Jordan's parliament. 'We support any person'—including a mass-killer of his fellow-Muslims—'who stands in the face of American domi-nance', he added.

Rare was the converse: approval, without qualification, of Saddam Hus-sein's fall. 'As a Muslim, I felt it was wonderful that Saddam Hussein was removed. The rest of the Muslim countries were standing there doing nothing', commented Malik Hasan, a prominent Arab-American, in February 2004. Among those who had given up on judgment entirely, at least in public, or who had earlier supported Saddam Hussein but now wished to take cover, was the Palestinian prime minister, Ahmed Qureia. 'We support whatever the Iraqi people want', he said in December 2003.

Other responses by Muslims to acts of violence in which fellow-Muslims were implicated often came shadowed, as we shall see further, by qualifications of a distinctive kind. For example, suicide-bombings against civilians were condemned by Edward Said in January 2002 not merely as 'terrible' but as 'stupid'. That is to say, they were 'counter-productive': a purely utilitarian standpoint. Moreover, community pressures both in the Muslim world and in the diaspora have created understandable hesitations—and even fears—about objecting to acts which might otherwise have been condemned without equiv-ocation. Parents of suicide-bombers combined grief for the deaths of their sons and daughters with professions of pride for their martyrdoms, as has been mentioned, but only rarely had the courage to criticise those who despatched them upon their missions. Or, as Amnesty International delicately put it in July 2002, 'many Palestinians...believe that targeting civilians is morally and/or strategically wrong.... But the critics have in general not been as open or prominent in public as [have been] advocates for armed attacks who support, condone or do not criticise attacks on civilians'.

Such judgments pointed to a familiar mixture, despite the significant volume of forthright judgments by some Muslims on what other Muslims have done. The mixture could be described as non-moral, at least in the con-ventional Western understanding of what an ethical position is. There has also been unembarrassed complicity in and incitement of abhorrent acts; the com-mission of violence against civilian non-combatants, despite such violence being repeatedly asserted to be 'non-Muslim'; reticence, chosen freely or under duress, on the whole subject; and the combining, as by Edward Said, of ethical with 'practical' considerations about the wisdom of taking innocent lives.

Even the standard assertion, as in April 2002 by the Malaysian prime min-ister, Mahathir Mohamad, that 'killing innocent people is not Islamic' could have complicating riders attached to it. Thus, Mahathir declared that 'we must show that we do not resort to acts of terror', despite the fact that such acts are resorted to by Islamists almost daily; and that 'Muslims everywhere must con-demn terrorism, once it is clearly defined'. This implied that a 'definition of terms' could exclude some 'terrorist' acts and include others; 'terror' could be 'redefined' as 'non-terror', and even the worst of wickednesses be made good. There were no such weasel words in the pronouncement of the (Muslim) deputy-foreign minister of Bosnia-Herzegovina in April 2002. 'I don't care about race or religion', he stated in rough but ready fashion; 'if a person kills or harms a civilian he is a terrorist, no matter how noble his struggle may be'. No, counterposed the then Palestinian foreign minister, Farouk Kaddoumi— with Mahathir's type of qualification at the ready—'it is not necessary to con-

demn suicide-bombers, because we have to consider the reasons behind somebody [being] willing to lose his life'.

However, not all inter-Muslim argument has been of this kind. Numbers
of diaspora Muslim women in Britain, for example, have been forthright in
moral condemnation of what they do not like about their treatment. In July
1989, Hannan Siddiqui, speaking on behalf of a 'women's refuge' in Southall,
opposed the notion of separate schools for Muslim children—or for children
of any other denomination—on the grounds that they fostered 'bigotry and
apartheid'. She also straightforwardly described women 'within our communities' as having been 'delivered into' the hands of 'male, conservative and religious forces'.

This was an objection on principle of a kind already referred to, distinctive for being free of ambiguity and convolution. So, too, was the anonymous
Muslim woman's *cri de coeur* in the *Guardian*, also in July 1989, that Islam was
'used as a frequently ruthless weapon of control by men'. In 'the shadows', as
she put it—or in the same 'darkness' and 'dankness' referred to earlier—
'women, and especially the girls, wait in hope of some freedoms that most of
the rest of British citizens take for granted'. Muslim women in Europe, such
as the writer Rana Kabbani, also objected in specific terms to what she called,
in January 1992, 'the heavy veiling that we see across the Muslim world'.
Describing it as 'certainly not Islamic' but a 'dead relic from Byzantium which
the Arabs took on', Kabbani pointed out with similar bluntness that the
Prophet Mohammed had 'urged Muslims to teach their children, boys and
girls alike, to swim and hunt and run'. 'Fundamentalism', bravely declared the
Algerian film-maker, Hafsa Zinai Kouddil, in November 1994—while in
hiding from Islamists and in fear for her life—'is the very negation of women'.

However, such protests remained minoritarian in the Muslim world, and
male pressures did not relax. Nevertheless, an Iranian-American woman,
Shahla Azizi, educated in the West and living in Teheran, openly objected in
April 2003 to veiling, to the need to obtain a husband's 'notarised permission
to travel, to the prohibition on women 'singing in public' and to the denial of
women's competence to be 'a full witness in a court of law'. 'We women [sc. of
Iran] badly need the help of the West to curb the fanatics' fascistic dreams',
she bravely protested. In the spring of 2002, Muslim women marched through
the streets of a number of cities in France to demonstrate against the 'prejudice and violence' which they claimed to encounter in their communities.
They objected in particular to the 'dictation' to them of what was acceptable
and unacceptable in matters of 'behaviour' and appearance, and 'punishments'
which include the stigmatising of women who do not wear Muslim dress, or
who commit other infractions of the Muslim moral code, as 'prostitutes'.

In the controversy over the French government's ban on the wearing by girls of the *hijab* in schools, Muslim community leaders were therefore in a quandary. Some were in favour of retaining the *hijab* on grounds of (male) notions of female decorum, or argued against its ban on the ground that it was 'discriminatory' or 'racist'. Others unwillingly supported compliance with the ban on the grounds that the law had to be obeyed. Others, again, vacillated between one position and another.

This quandary, raised for Muslims living in an adopted non-Muslim society, was that of faith's encounter with secularism, and of the struggle to protect a way of life from the non-Muslim world's often scant regard for it. But a minority of Muslim women once more spoke out determinedly in January 2004 in support of the ban on the veil. It would help all Muslim women—and not only in France, they thought—to counter community pressures to 'cover up'. In particular, it gave Muslim girls in France support in refusing imposition upon them by fathers and brothers.

A more substantial encouragement of such positions came in October 2003, when an Iranian woman lawyer, Shirin Ebadi, was awarded the Nobel Peace Prize in recognition of her work in promoting the rights of women and children in Iran. In March 2004, she declared that the 'patriarchal system' in Islamic countries 'rejects the equality of men and women'; women were 'second-class citizens' in Iran, she repeated in Geneva the following month; and in January 2005 was summoned before a Revolutionary Court to answer for her opinions. She courageously refused to appear, and the matter was dropped. In Turkey, also in April 2004, villagers boycotted an imam who had ordered local women to wear full chadors, and who accused them of indecency for travelling on the same buses as men. In the United States, meanwhile, Muslim women were reported as beginning to challenge their exclusion from mosque worship and communal life; it was said that they were customarily 'sent to pray in mosque basements and hallways', and even in 'parking lots and rented apartments down the street'.

But Muslim women's protests against their condition have remained muted. Nevertheless, in their directness of address and straightforwardness of meaning, their declarations have often stood out from the style of male Muslim refusals of intellectual and ethical challenge. Sometimes the latter refusals are justly confident in their righteousness, sometimes merely evasive. Or, where acts committed by Muslims in Islam's name have been regarded by other Muslims with disapproval, such acts have often been condemned not on the ground that they were wrong as such, but that thay did not serve Muslim interests. Especially in the Muslim diaspora, anxieties have primarily been aroused over the 'bad image' of Islam which Islamist violences create. Or fear, often justified, will be expressed that such 'bad image'—rather than the act itself—will lead to discrimination against Muslims, to career disadvantage, to exclusion from opportunity for education and travel in the United States and so on.

When the previously-cited Tunisian scholar Rajaa bin Salamah urged in May 2002 that Arab intellectuals should 'vigorously condemn terrorist attacks on synagogues in Europe and in other parts of the world', she too urged it not because such attacks were wrong but because they 'blunt the acuteness of the Palestinian problem'. That is, they were again counterproductive. Likewise, Arafat's successor Mahmoud Abbas thought it had been a 'mistake'—not wrong as such—to employ armed violence against Israeli civilians in the Palestinian intifada. Again, Australia's Muslim organisations declared that Islamists, in 'victimising the innocent and the defenceless' in their attacks on the non-Islamic world, were not so much doing wrong as 'hurting the people they claim to represent'. 'They are letting us Muslims down', said a Pakistani police official, referring to al-Qaeda's use of violence. But none of these judgments and opinions ranked as principled criticisms of the acts in question, although such criticisms there have been, as we saw earlier.

Instead, Muslim and Arab opinion more often showed preoccupation with the negative consequences of Islamic violence for Muslims rather than for its impact on others. 'Regrettably', declared King Hussein of Jordan at Casablanca in December 1994, 'the message of Islam has recently assumed another darker dimension, that of fear of Islam, thus tarnishing its image'. After the Madrid bombings of March 2004, almost a decade later, the argument was the same. They were a 'major mistake' since they would 'increase hatred for Islam and Islamists', thought Hussein Amin, a former Egyptian ambassador to Algeria. 'The millions of Spaniards who took to the streets' were a 'latent force of rage which we would do well to take heed of', wrote Abdel Rahman al-Rashed in the Cairo daily *Asharq al-Awsat*.

In June 2004, al-Qaeda attacks on foreigners in Saudi Arabia were criticised by the secretary-general of the Muslim World League, Sheikh Abdullah Mohsin al-Turki, for the 'great damage' they did 'to Islam', not to the victims of the attack. The Egyptian Islamist cleric Sheikh Youssef al-Qaradawi similarly declared in September 2004 that if the kidnappers in Iraq of two French journalists had any 'care for the reputation of Islam'—rather than for the well-being of the captives—the journalists should be freed. The same position, a standard one, was adopted by the Muslim Association of Britain. It expressed its 'disgust' at the kidnap of the two men, but it was the likely consequences for Muslims if they were not released which evidently engaged them more. 'It will disrupt everything that the Muslim community has achieved and further tarnish the image of Islam', the association warned. Likewise, in the aftermath of the London bombings, the Islamic Society of Britain in July 2005 condemned Muslim 'extremists' for 'causing damage to our way of life here'; 'we don't want that to happen', it added.

Such type of response has been a constant. The kidnapping of foreigners in Iraq and the 'killing of workers', pronounced Lebanon's Grand Ayatollah Mohammed Hussein Fadlallah, would 'leave its negative effects on Muslims and the image of Islam in the world'; the decapitations themselves seemed to be a lesser matter. As for the mass hostage-taking at the Beslan school in September 2004, it was again not so much morally wrong in itself to the Egyptian Islamist Ahmed Baghat, writing in *al-Ahram*, but an act of 'stupidity, miscalculation and misunderstanding of the nature of the age'. Once again, it had 'ruined and harmed' Islam's 'image'.

In all these cases, concern focused largely and sometimes entirely upon how a heinous act appeared to others rather than upon the ethics of the act itself. Thus, Taliban rule in Afghanistan appeared to cause more pain to Muslim sensibilities for provoking mockery and recoil in the non-Muslim world than for its cruelties and excesses as such. That is, 'fanatics' gave Islam a 'bad name'. Nor did it appear to be a matter of principle which led Nabil Luka Bibawi to assert in Egypt's *al-Ahram* in November 2001 that 'if world Zionism spent billions of dollars to tarnish the image of Islam'—the 'image' argument yet again—'it will not accomplish what terrorists have done with their actions and words'.

Notable exceptions apart, this type of objection has often represented the limits to which most Islamic criticism of Muslim wrongdoing could reach. It was thus held that the Arabs, or the Islamic world, had 'lost most' as a result of the attacks of September 2001; or that 'only by facing facts' could the Arabs 'begin to cut their losses'; or, as the editor of the Arabic daily *Asharq al-Awsat* put it, 'fanaticism does not pay'. These were the metaphors of the gaming-table, or (at best) of utilitarian calculation. Even the most erudite and 'Westernised' of Muslim commentators could anxiously weigh the negative effects of Islamist violence on the 'position of Muslims' in the non-Muslim world, and give less, or no, attention to the moral significance—as commonly understood—of the violence itself. Others could attribute American revulsion at the decapitations of their hostages in Iraq in 2004 to the 'influence of emotions', as did the president of a Pakistani American association in June 2004.

Such inner debate has often been conducted in what appeared to be an ethical void. Ten days after the attack on the World Trade Center, Ali Alarabi, the Palestinian-American president of the United Arab American League, declared that it had 'united everyone against Arab-Americans' and that 'we've lost a lot of ground. This has set us back 100 years', he added. It was again the Benthamite calculus, measured not in moral terms but in harm to Muslim reputation. From such reflex, deeper confusion has often followed. For example, calculation of profit-and-loss served to muddy the arguments—arguments stemming from legitimate anxieties of faith—over the demand for separate schools in Britain for Muslim children. When in 1991 a militant proponent of such schools declared himself ready, if demands for state-aided Muslim schools were not met, to 'withhold taxes' and 'go to jail'—and called on other Muslims to do the same—other Muslims took the view that such conduct would 'inflict permanent damage on the standing of the Muslim community' in Britain.

At issue here was neither Koranic nor other moral principle but the 'image' question. Such preoccupation could be said to have reflected the natural concerns of the incomer about the risks of an 'anti-Islamic backlash'. Moreover, as the war of the worlds has spread, pressures have mounted on diaspora Muslims—the tenets of 'multiculturalism' notwithstanding—to abandon attitudes or practices, central to their identity, as the price of acceptance. Such pressures have in general had the opposite effect. Equivocation and evasion could be said to have increased. This was equally the case whether the moral challenges which Muslims faced were posed by pressures to 'assimilate', or were the consequence of acts carried out by Islamists against the non-Muslim world. Awkwardly caught between contradictory community instincts to 'keep a low profile' or to go on the cultural and political offensive, to express solidarity with fellow-Muslims or—much more difficult—to join non-Muslims in condemning them, these were dilemmas for which few non-Muslims showed any understanding.

In all this, however, it has remained clear that the question of the 'image' of Muslims in non-Muslim eyes, rather than matters of larger moral and cultural significance, has been the dominant issue for many Muslims. 'The regrettable fact', declared Irfan Husain in the Karachi newspaper *Dawn* in December 2002, 'is that as a result of the current wave of Islamic militancy and terrorism, all [*sic*] Muslims living in the West are currently viewed with deep suspicion and distrust, and will be increasingly discriminated against'. The 'regret' expressed was again for the impact of 'terrorism' on fellow-Muslims in provoking discrimination against them; a sense of moral co-responsibility fot their acts was absent. In a similar response to Chechen violence and the increasing popular hostility shown towards Muslims in Russia, a Moscow imam in January 2003 complained that 'it used to be the Jews. Now they have all gone to Israel. Instead of the Jews, now the politicians incite the masses against the Muslims. We are the new Jews'.

Verdicts on the Muslim condition were often free of self-criticism in such fashion. Indeed, moral criticism was often directed only at non-Muslim reactions to Islamist acts. Nevertheless, severe judgments by Muslims of actions carried out in Islam's name there have been, as we have seen. 'The new tribe, known as *jihadis*, who strut about as the saviours of Muslims have in fact become their scourge', declared Rafiq Zakaria in one such judgment in *The Asian Age* in December 2002. 'They commit the most heinous crimes in the name of Islam', he continued. 'Those Muslims who have taken to this perilous path are doing the greatest harm to both Muslims and Islam, inducing young Muslims to take up arms and to throw bombs in buses, hijack planes, bomb temples.... Their mindless acts', he added, 'have made the lives of Muslims everywhere so unliveable—they are being shunned by non-Muslims and cut off from the rest of the human race'.

Zakaria was also concerned with the 'image' issue, which is to say the unfortunate practical consequences of ill-doing. But unusually it was not his main point. Here, there were none of the moral ambiguities, sly qualifications and other devices, including blame of others than themselves, to which the arguments of many Muslims have resorted. 'After the horrendous bombing in New York and Washington', Zakaria asserted, 'Muslims in America are going through hell. They are harassed by agitated Americans and are made to feel unwanted.... The process of exclusion of Muslims from different walks of life [sc. in the non-Islamic world] is gathering momentum. How long will Muslims ... tolerate the madness of a demented group of Muslims, who are bringing disaster after disaster upon them? How long will Muslims continue to cower in fear of them? ... If they do not act, what future can they and their posterity have?' Zakaria asked.

The questions were rhetorical, and the argument coloured by non-moral considerations. But not for Zakaria was the standard rejoinder of apologists that acts of violence carried out by Muslims in Islam's name were 'non-Islamic'. He gave the lie, too, to those who claimed that Muslims never speak out clearly against wrongful acts when they have been committed by fellow-Muslims. Nevertheless, Muslim self-criticisms could also ring false from excess, relatively infrequent as they have been. When Mahathir Mohamad proclaimed in May 2002 that Muslims had 'only themselves to blame for the poverty, misery and violence afflicting much of the Islamic world', it was a *mea culpa* too far; on the battlefields of the Islamic advance there are many, non-

Muslims and Muslims alike, who do not have clean hands, including those who have provided Islam with the means to wage war upon itself and upon others. Mahathir's form of self-castigation was another element in the confusion which the Arab and Islamic revivals have brought in their wake. It was a confusion in which the issues of 'who we are and where we want to stand in the world'—as the editor of the Pakistani weekly *The Friday Times*, Najam Sethi, put it in September 2001—divided every community of diaspora Muslims.

A wide range of tensions about where Muslims 'want to stand in the world' has come to light in these years of battle. The Rushdie affair was in this respect a paradigm case. The death-sentence against the author, with its open calls to Muslims to murder him, not only gave rise to attacks and killings but to rival 'scholarly' interpretations of Koranic provision. Belligerent threats were combined, typically, with Muslim alarm-over-consequences should such threats actually be carried out. The usual assertions were made by some Muslims that the conduct of other Muslims was 'non-Islamic'. In the confusion, there was characteristically equivocal approval of the principle of the *fatwa* but not of the means prescribed for its execution. Other Muslims kept silent. Some Muslims accepted that the decree against the author was immutable and even of divine provenance, while others, a minority, condemned the *fatwa* outright. It is worth examining some of this in detail, since matters of large import both for the Islamic and non-Islamic worlds were disclosed by the affair.

A marked degree of paranoia, or of paranoid rhetoric, accompanied and followed Khomeini's decree of 14 February 1989, as Rushdie went into hiding, pursued by clerical curses and warnings that he would 'go to hell'. Muslims, Khomeini declared, 'must wake up to the West's plots against us'. In objecting to the *fatwa*, the 'world of arrogance and barbarism' had 'unveiled its true face of chronic enmity against Islam'. The already-cited Cambridge-educated Shabbir Akhtar, echoing Khomeini, even thought there was a 'Western conspiracy' detectable in the 'passions aroused' among non-Muslims by the death-sentence. 'The next time there are gas-chambers in Europe', he declared, 'there is no doubt concerning who'll be inside them'.

The liberal *Guardian*, which made plain its editorial support for Rushdie's freedom of expression, was similarly accused by the British Islamist, Kalim Siddiqui, of being 'engaged in a most invidious witch-hunt against the entire Muslim community'. Yet this was said at a time when Rushdie was himself moving from one safe house to another under police protection. A British convert, Daud Musa (David) Pidcock, the leader of the Islamic Party of Britain, similarly identified the author as 'an agent of the occult establishment' who was being 'well paid and praised for his contribution to this last crusade'. Not surprisingly, there were Jews involved in the plot. Or, as Khomeini put it in February 1990, Rushdie's novel was 'the result of years of effort by American, European and Zionist so-called experts on Islam, gathering in international seminars and conferences, with the aim of finding the best way to insult and undermine Islam's highest values and traditions'.

Inversion (of a type identified earlier among the Twelve Devices) also transformed the hunted author into the huntsman. 'Rushdie', declared Shabbir Akhtar in the *Muslim News* in January 1991—almost two years after the novelist had gone into hiding—'must immediately stop persecuting his brothers. *The Satanic Verses* must be withdrawn'. Even the defence of Rushdie's freedom of expression was transformed by Akhtar into a 'liberal Inquisition'. With Rushdie still under sentence of death more than two and a half years later, and with a large Iranian bounty on his head, President Rafsanjani continued to see in the actions of those who defended the writer a 'Western conspiracy to put pressure on Iran'. Iran was thus more sinned against than sinning, more conspired against than conspiring.

Despite the distortions of perception which these inversions revealed (and required), many Muslims plainly believed that Rushdie's novel was part of a plot against Islam. The verbal violence of the epithets attached to the author and his work was also self-inflaming. He was a 'blasphemous bastard' to Ayatollah Ali Khamenei, and a 'blasphemous dog' to the chief imam of the Jama Masjid, Delhi's main mosque. He had been a 'devil' to Khomeini. To Ali Azhar, the Muslim Action Front's lawyer in the attempt to bring a prosecution for blasphemy against the book in the British High Court, the novel contained 'greater filth than one can find on the bottom of the seven seas'. To the Murabitun European Muslim movement, Rushdie was a 'hooligan'; to the already-mentioned Inayatullah Zaigham (of Gravesend), his existence was 'rat-like'; to the secretary of Bradford's Council for Mosques, Sayed Abdul Quddus, Rushdie was 'a Satan' and his work was 'full of shit'. Ahmed Deedat, a South African Muslim leader, went further, informing the British public that Rushdie 'eats your food, yet shits in the pot from which he eats'. To Shabbir Akhtar, Britain had been 'contaminated' by the 'Rushdie virus'.

Familiar sanguinary images were employed in the polemics. The 'blood of an apostate' was held by several schools of Islamic learning to be a fair target, explained Inayatullah Zaigham. If nothing was done in Britain to meet Muslim objections to the novel, 'blood would be spilled', warned Rehmat Khan, secretary of Derby's Islamic Affairs Action Committee. In May 1989, some 20,000 Muslim demonstrators in Westminster bore banners which included slogans such as 'Kill the Bastard' and 'Rushdie Must Be Chopped Up', the latter beside a drawing of a blade dripping blood. In Holland, in September 1989, a leading book-chain was similarly threatened by an Islamic group that 'blood' would 'flow' if the book was stocked. Even when the author, from his hiding-place, offered charitable help in June 1990 to the victims of an Iranian earthquake, he was accused by Hojatoleslam Sadeq Khalkhali—described as the 'most renowned practitioner of summary justice' in Iran—of 'want[ing] to bargain for his blood'.

Much of the emotion expressed in the public book-burnings, in the tearing apart of effigies of Rushdie—including in Parliament Square in London in May 1989—and in the burnings of British flags, as in Istanbul in May 1993, was merely symbolic. Violent protests, as in India, Iran, Kashmir, Pakistan and Turkey, in which police were attacked or demonstrators killed, were more serious. Bookshops in London were firebombed and death-threats were made against publishers, translators and bookshop-employees—the Khomeini *fatwa* had 'condemned to death' all those involved in the dissemination of Rushdie's novel.

A Japanese translator, Hitoshi Igarashi, was stabbed and killed; an Italian translator, Ettore Capriolo, was stabbed at his Milan flat and survived; a Norwegian publisher, William Nygaard, was shot and seriously wounded. 'We won't let you live', the publisher of the Japanese edition of the book was told by the vice-president of the Pakistan Association in Japan in February 1990. The leader of Belgium's Muslim community, Abdullah Ahdel, who had declined to call for Rushdie's novel to be banned in Belgium, was shot at point-blank range in March 1989 and killed. Even a British television news-reader received death-threats after speaking in defence of Rushdie, and had to be guarded; and when an Iranian student in Britain was detained on charges of setting fire to a London bookshop, the Iranian student association in Teheran threatened reprisals in January 1990 against Britons 'all over the world' if he were not released. His release followed.

Four years after the *fatwa* had been pronounced, Iranian agents in Britain were still trying to track Rushdie down; three of them were expelled in July 1992. When a local radio-station in Bradford made plans to broadcast a phone-in with the author, the president of the Muslim Youth Movement of Great Britain, Mohammed Siddique, threatened the station by letter that, if the programme went ahead, 'it will be difficult to see how Muslims will continue to allow you [sc. the radio station] to operate'. In India, a New Delhi professor, Mushirul Hasan, who in 1992 had called for India's ban on the Rushdie novel to be lifted, was attacked by Muslim students wielding iron-rods and knives. In

Turkey, distributors of a left-wing newspaper, *Aydinlik*, which in May 1993 had begun to publish extracts from the novel, refused to handle the paper after receiving threats from the Turkish Hezbollah movement. Staff at the newspaper were attacked, and copies of the paper were ordered by an Istanbul court to be seized.

Despite Muslim accusations of an international conspiracy, this turmoil—a feature of the 'vortex' described in a previous chapter—was essentially internal to the world of Islam, not least because Rushdie was himself a Muslim. Offended Muslim reaction to the novel also fed upon itself. Demands were made by Iran that Britain denounce Rushdie and his book, and by Ayatollah Khamenei in June 1990 that the author be 'handed over to British Muslims so that God's decree could be implemented against him'. There were also blackmail threats that British hostages, at the time being held in Beirut, would suffer unless Rushdie was 'deported' from Britain. There were still larger warnings of a 'declaration of holy war on the House of Rejection' if the non-Islamic world did not do Islam's bidding in the matter.

The perverse Muslim propensity to self-harm exacted a greater toll on the 'image' of Islam during this episode than any damage which Muslims could inflict upon an individual 'apostate' and 'blasphemer'. In February 1989, Ayatollah Khamenei declared that 'the arrow has been launched towards its target. It is now flying towards its aim'. But this was a sentence—in both senses of the word—taken from Islam's stock of morally self-disabling poses. They were poses struck in a drama which was being conducted on a stage constructed by renascent Islam itself. Nevertheless, they were also designed to strike fear in others, as larger and more terrifying events were to do in the following years. 'Either he stays in hiding', Lebanese Hezbollah's leader Sheikh Hassan Nasrallah shouted to 5,000 demonstrators in a Beirut suburb, in February 1989, 'or he comes out and will be killed'. The following month in Damascus, the leader of the Popular Front for the Liberation of Palestine, Ahmed Jibril, joined in the drama, or act. 'We in the PFLP', he annnounced, 'will confront this new conspiracy and work to execute the legal action against Rushdie'. The author, declared Jibril, would be 'hunted down and killed, in order to defend Islam and its prophet'.

Incitements and promises to kill the author were openly made even in liberal democracies in which Muslims of the diaspora had found their homes. A Bradford Muslim leader, Liaquat Hussain, 'prayed' in June 1989 that Ayatollah Khomeini's 'aspirations' for Rushdie would be 'pursued with undiminished zest'; a senior Muslim scholar from Pakistan, Mulana Ziyaul Qasmi, told a London conference in August 1989 that Muslims in Britain should seek out

Rushdie and take him to an Islamic country in order that he might face justice. 'The decision would be to kill him', said Qasmi laconically. The head of the Iranian judiciary, Muhammad Yazdi, pronounced in February 1990 that Muslims who 'possessed the means' to kill Rushdie, but did not do so, were 'sinners in the eyes of God'.

'It is Islamic law. He must die', asserted Sayed Abdul Quddus, the Bradford Muslim leader, in January 1991. 'The time is ripe for devout Muslims to kill Salman Rushdie', Ayatollah Ahmad Jannati, the senior Iranian cleric, declared in a 'sermon' at Teheran University in July 1992. 'He does not deserve to exist', an adviser to Iranian president Rafsanjani, Javad Larijani, said in February 1994 on the fifth anniversary of the *fatwa*. A Bradford seventeen-year-old, Mohammed Zia Ulhaq, speaking freely to the British press, echoed Iranian judgments: 'He should be killed. There is only one thing, kill'. More concerned with the practical problems but not with the morality of it, a Cardiff Bangladeshi restaurant-manager declared in February 1990 that 'with Rushdie in hiding we can't do anything'. 'We should have kept quiet, and then we could have gone straight to him and done the job', he said.

Nor was there was any shortage of volunteers for 'the job'. 'I would be prepared to kill him', Akbar Khan, supervisor of a Birmingham mosque's day-centre, told the *Guardian* in February 1989. 'Ninety-nine per cent of Muslims would be prepared to kill him', declared Mohammed Ismail Janjua, president of the Dudley mosque. 'I hope he will be killed. I would be prepared to kill him', he openly stated. Even Iran's ambassador to the Vatican announced on 16 February 1989 that he was personally 'willing to carry out the order' to kill the author. Muslims from all walks of life made similar declarations. 'I would give my life to kill him, and my parents feel the same. Everybody wants to kill him before somebody else gets there', Tariq Mahmood of Balsall Heath told the *Independent*. 'If I see him, I shall kill him. There's no need to discuss it with him, just kill him', said a thirty-four-year-old welder, Sultan Mubirak, also from Balsall Heath. 'If he was in this cab, I would kill him', a Bradford taxi-driver told a journalist for the *Observer*; 'if any Muslim gets the chance, he [sc. Rushdie] won't avoid it [sc. getting killed], and he should not', said the Bradford community leader, Sayed Abdul Quddus.

In this 'vortex', a welder and an ambassador, a café manager and a cab-driver, mosque officials and community elders, young and old, men and women, whirled together. All had the death of a 'Satan' in mind. How to kill him, as we have seen, occupied some; where to kill him, others. 'I would welcome the opportunity to kill him myself', declared Mohammed Siddique, president of the Muslim Youth Movement of Great Britain, 'if he was in an

Islamic country'. 'Let us take him to Medina', said a sixteen-year-old Bradford schoolgirl, Safia Sheikh, 'and let us stone him to death'. Others, despite the bravado, were morally less certain—as we shall see—about whether Rushdie should die at all. This doubt took many forms. 'Death, perhaps, is a bit too easy for him', said Iqbal—later Sir Iqbal—Sacranie of the UK Action Committee on Islamic Affairs shortly after the *fatwa* had been issued. 'His mind must be tormented for the rest of his life unless he asks for forgiveness to Almighty Allah', added Sacranie. But Khomeini had ordered Rushdie's life to be taken without delay, and without possibility of such forgiveness as Sacranie was proposing.

On closer examination, the divisions and uncertainties among Muslims about what to do with Rushdie were profound, notwithstanding the absolute terms of the *fatwa* itself. Some Muslims held that Khomeini had been right in theological principle and right in decreeing the sanction of death. Other Muslims held that he was right in principle, but wrong to call for Rushdie to be killed. Yet others havered indecisively over both the principle and the practicality of the thing. In Britain, Muslims were buffeted—in the fashion described earlier—by internal community conflicts between loyalty to faith and the need to observe the domestic law, between inflamed hostility to Rushdie and fear of the consequences for Muslims should he be killed. There were also those who thought—and a minority who said—that the *fatwa* was not only mistaken in theological principle but ethically wrong. But there were few Muslims who defended Rushdie's freedom of speech, while those who approved of the novel itself were fewest of all.

There was thus no homogeneous British Muslim standpoint, even if the rhetoric unleashed on the subject and the media's preference for stark conflict suggested the opposite. Many Muslims around the world, including in Britain, appeared ready to wield the knife themselves, or to applaud those who did. But aggressive as were their responses to the insult to faith, many—perhaps most—diaspora Muslims were uncertain about what should be done.

On the side of absolutism, all was relatively plain. The *fatwa* was held to be not only theologically correct but irrevocable, valid to all eternity. Khomeini had done his duty by Islam, and could have done no other. His was not man's order but God's decree, and must therefore be obeyed. After Khomeini's death, and lest there be any doubt upon the matter, it was promulgated from Iran that 'nothing' could change the *fatwa*, since 'only the person who issued it can change it'. Nor could there be any question of pardon, the Iranian president declared in September 1994, more than five and a half years after the *fatwa* had been pronounced and with Rushdie untouched.

That is, the threat to the author and the Muslim propensity to self-harm were to continue *sine die*.

Denunciation of Rushdie could involve an obsessive gyration about a single spot. To observe it in the case of one British Islamist, Kalim Siddiqui, was also to understand something of the problems which the resurgence of Islam has posed to Muslims in the non-Islamic world. In July 1989, Siddiqui, a former *Guardian* journalist and founder of the self-styled 'Muslim Parliament' in Britain, threateningly but ambiguously declared that 'We [sc. Muslims] cannot live in this country together with *The Satanic Verses* and Salman Rushdie. They will have to go'. Whether this meant that the book had to be pulped and Rushdie killed, or that the latter would merely have to leave the country, was characteristically left unclear. At a meeting in Manchester Town Hall in October 1989, to cries of 'Death to Rushdie!' Siddiqui asked his audience to raise their hands if they thought the author should die. In large majority they did, at Siddiqui's prompting. But in the same month, with a prudential regard for the English law of incitement, Siddiqui declared that the author was 'already serving a well-deserved *life-sentence*'; a different matter, once more, from suffering death at a fellow-Muslim's hands.

By February 1990, worldwide Muslim support for the *fatwa* produced another seeming shift in Siddiqui's position. Rushdie was 'up for the high jump', said Siddiqui. It was an ambiguously militant phrase, capable both of a literal and a metaphorical interpretation. That it was designed to conjure up the image of an execution was clear from the remarks that followed. 'We are a very, very angry people', he proclaimed, 'but Muslims in Britain are not hangmen. We are not here to execute *fatwas* from Teheran'; even the word 'execute' was a *double entendre*. A week later, also in February 1990, at a meeting of '500 Muslim leaders' in central London—and to chants from the audience of 'Salman Rushdie, death to him!'—Siddiqui declared with further ambiguity that 'we want to stay within the law, but we will also see to it that the law does not protect the enemies of Islam'. To cries from the hall for the death of Rushdie, there was menace in Siddiqui's undertaking about what would be 'seen to' in relation to the 'enemies of Islam'. But he was also expressing (for safety's sake) a contradictory desire to obey the British law.

In May 1992, Siddiqui was openly acknowledging this incoherence, in which moral introspection appeared to play no part. Declaring that the issuing of the *fatwa* and its death-sentence were 'absolutely right', he nevertheless urged Muslims to obey British law. That is, he was urging them to disobey the religious obligation of Muslims to kill the author, despite the justice (in his view) of the decree itself. It was put to him by *The Times* that this was 'inconsistent'. 'This is the contradiction of our existence', he nimbly replied. By January 1993 he had once again changed his stance. Now, Siddiqui told British Muslims that 'we should put the [Rushdie] affair behind us, and both sides should forgive and forget as we try to become integrated members of the community'. It was, or at least appeared to be, an entire *volte-face*. It also reflected the dilemmas created in liberal democratic societies for Muslims who are willing but unable, or able but unwilling, to act with the ardour which their more militant fellows expect of them. They are dilemmas, among others, of how to fulfil contradictory obligations to extraterritorial faith and to domestic law, and of how to side-step the demands of pietists without appearing to resile from faith itself.

In the Rushdie case, there were grounds for compassionating with such awkward circumstances but not with the dilemma itself: whether to kill in cold blood a writer in Britain at distant Islamist command. In this dilemma, considerations of right and wrong took second place—when they had any place at all—to a wrestling with the duties of a Muslim in the non-Muslim world. They were the dilemmas of Mia Chand and Abdul Aziz, as set out by a reporter in the *Independent* in February 1989. 'Mr. Chand said Mr. Rushdie should be killed. His friend [Abdul Aziz] contradicted him: "No, not killed, you mean punished". Mr. Chand was insistent. "No, killed. You say what you say, and I say he should be killed"'.

The inner doubts of Mohammed Zaman of Balsall Heath, also reported in the *Independent*, had equally little to do with ethical considerations as conventionally understood. He objected not to the death-sentence against Rushdie but to the blood-price offered for his head. 'I'm cursing him all day in my prayers', said Zaman. 'But I don't approve of the reward for his death, because that is bribery which is against Islam, and somebody might kill him for money and not for the sake of his pride'; another non-moral distinction. At book-burnings, as in Nottingham in February 1989, there were quarrels among Muslims. 'When one of the protesters set fire to the book', reported the *Sunday Telegraph*, 'it was almost immediately extinguished by another'. But differences about means, and fears over consequences, again seemed to have governed such conflicts. When Ayatollah Mahdari Kani, a former Iranian interior minister and prime minister of Iran in 1981, asserted during a meeting at Hammersmith town hall in February 1990 that 'we do not wish to see Islam victorious by executing a man', this was once more an argument about means. As for the justice of the *fatwa*, it was not in question.

At the Organisation of the Islamic Conference meeting in March 1989, it was declared—as if decisively—that Rushdie had 'blasphemed' against Islam.

Yet the delegates again balked at upholding the *fatwa* in terms. Others, such as the British Muslim Alliance, called for an end to death-threats against the author but failed to condemn the *fatwa* itself. With like ambiguity Zaki Badawi, the chairman of the Imams and Mosques Council in Britain, described 'incitement to violence' in February 1989 not as wrong in itself, but as 'contrary to our faith'. Confusingly, he too distanced himself from those who 'express[ed] themselves in extreme ways' against Rushdie and his book—which would include Khomeini himself—but not from the *fatwa* as such.

This kind of fudged position was common. By recourse to it, Khomeini could be held by implication to be right, but 'rash action' at the same time be discountenanced. The Merseyside Muslim Society, urging 'self-restraint', declared that the death-sentence against Rushdie 'could only be carried out in an Islamic state'; a case, this time, of Muslim transferring moral responsibility to Muslim. Another moral evasion took the form of deciding that the matter was of little significance at all. 'I don't think this book will have any effect on Islam', asserted a minister in the Kuwait government, Suleiman Majdi al-Shaheen, in February 1989. 'Too much importance has been attached to the affair of *The Satanic Verses*', similarly declared the imam of a Paris mosque, Tedjini Haddam, in July 1989, diplomatically turning a blind eye to the *fatwa*, to theological argument and to Muslim doubt, while taking an equivocal position himself.

Indeed, in many of those who had initially condemned Rushdie in the most uncompromising terms such equivocation could be found. 'The book'—not Rushdie, now—'must go', announced Shabbir Akhtar in the *Muslim News* in January 1991. 'We have had enough of Rushdie's fustian nonsense', he added. But 'fustian nonsense' was not the same as a 'blasphemy' worthy of death. As to the book-burning which had taken place, Akhtar now insisted that it had not been what it had been made out to be. 'It was not Nazi-style. We merely burnt one book of Rushdie's, not all his previous works', he explained; or, again, 'Hitler's pyromania was more cultivated [*sic*] than ours. We merely burnt one book for excellent reasons'. Whatever else this was, it was a retreat from a maximalist position, even if the dalliance with Rushdie's fate remained as cruel as before. Daud Musa Pidcock, of the Islamic Party of Britain, chose a different moral side-step. The *fatwa*, he declared in March, May and August 1990, could not be carried out on anyone who was mentally ill. Since Rushdie was 'eligible for hospital treatment', he called for the *fatwa* to be 'suspended'. Once more, the *fatwa* was not wrong. Rather, the object of it was 'clinically insane'.

The manoeuvring of leading Muslim intellectuals around the *fatwa* could be of equally low moral quality. 'Many Muslims still believe that no Muslim should talk to you', the Iqbal Visiting Fellow at Cambridge, Akbar Ahmed, told

Rushdie in January 1991, as if a pope were addressing a Galileo. 'I agreed [sc. to talk to you] in a personal capacity', he informed Rushdie—as well as readers of the *Guardian,* which published the exchanges—'because I hoped it would contribute in a small way to creating some harmony.... Everything that is said in *The Satanic Verses* which is held to be hostile or offensive to Muslim sanctities is material that I personally do not agree with. The ... hostile ideas expressed in those passages are ideas I absolutely, as a person and as a writer, reject'. And having triply squared his conscience, he felt safe to ask ('for myself') whether the apostate-in-hiding considered himself to be still a Muslim. 'Yes, certainly', Rushdie replied. That is, a fellow-intellectual, having made his obeisances to anti-intellectualism, was prepared—'for himself'—to talk to the hunted writer, while not demurring at the death-sentence under which his fellow-Muslim stood. Whether or not Ahmed disagreed with the *fatwa* was unclear. It might only be inferred that he disagreed, from his 'daring' to speak to Rushdie in the first place.

Other responses were even more convoluted; to follow them is to enter the same world 'beyond reason' which was entered in a previous chapter. In February 1990, the Iranian president Hashemi Rafsanjani transferred moral responsibility for the uproar caused by the *fatwa* from those who had promulgated it to those who had reacted against it. As mentioned earlier, he declared that there was 'no need' for the 'kind of ruckus' which had greeted 'the imam's sentence'. This 'ruckus', he claimed, had been 'raised' not by Iran but by 'the enemies of Islam'. 'If they [the West] deal with the issue logically', he continued—speaking from within a logical system conducted according to its own rules, as we saw earlier—'the imam's [death] sentence will be regarded as an issue of Islamic expertise, not anything else'.

Given its degree of opacity, the meaning of this statement could not be made out. It could equally have signified a desire to close the matter, or an intention to pursue Rushdie in whatever way 'Islamic experts' might choose. But the fact that it could not be decoded was itself a form of weapon. It is a weapon—that of intellectual convolution, transfer of responsibility, inversion of the truth and moral evasion—which the Muslim world has used to increasing effect as its advance has proceeded. At best Rafsanjani's statement suggested that the *fatwa* was demonstrative only, like the 'demonstration-effects' discussed in a previous chapter, and that it should not be taken literally. Yet at the same time Iranian 'hit-squads' were known to be in search of the author, while the price on his head, already high, was being further raised in Teheran.

In December 1990, even the scholarly Akbar Ahmed was capable of adopting an argument of the type found in the Twelve Devices. He obscurely declared that Rushdie's book 'fed' the 'negative stereotypes of Muslims'; that these stereotypes 'helped create the hatred against Muslims'; and that this hatred 'produced the anger within the Muslim community'. The argument was labyrinthine, but with effort it could be deciphered. It meant that Rushdie himself was to blame not only for having provoked the *fatwa*, but also for the violent reactions of Muslims to his book *and* the hostility towards Muslims which the latter's attacks had aroused in non-Muslims. The 'logic' of this form of argument was that had Rushdie been murdered, it was he who would have been culpable and his assassins excusable, or even blameless. It was also a type of argument which revealed anxiety for what Islam had unleashed against itself.

A similar anxiety was revealed in the complex theological wrangles among divided Muslim scholars as to whether the death-sentence against Rushdie was in accord with Holy Writ. With learned citations and counter-citations of texts, the issue hinged essentially on precisely what crime Rushdie had committed. Was it, for example, 'blasphemy' (that is 'abuse of the Prophet') or was it 'waging war upon God and his messenger', a crime more serious? If the former, then the penalty was or was not death, according to this or that school of Islamic thought. If the latter, death was not merely a fitting but a necessary sanction.

The imam of the London Mosque, Ataul Mujeeb Rashed, took the view—with others—that Islam did not prescribe the death-penalty for 'blasphemy'. Rather, it upheld freedom of belief and disbelief, even if the deity would not forgive the disbeliever. No, declared Daniel Easterman of Durham University—for Western scholars joined in this disputation—the punishment for 'abuse of the Prophet' had 'traditionally been death'. On the contrary, argued Hesham el-Essawy of the Islamic Society for the Promotion of Religious Tolerance, the correct response (also prescribed in Koranic texts) for 'insults' and 'disbelief' was to 'ignore them and be patient, or even return good for evil'.

Other figures in the Islamic diaspora—including in Britain—disagreed, and were free to state their positions, including in the national press. If Rushdie's offence was construed as the crime of *hirab*, or 'waging war' and 'striving to cause disorder' in the Islamic world, then the only penal choice available (regrettably) was 'to be killed or crucified, or to have hands and feet cut off on alternate sides, or to be exiled from the land'—except in the case of those who had repented before they fell into the power of the Muslim authorities.

According to one school of Muslim experts, *hirab* was indeed Rushdie's offence; he had made a 'public declaration of ideological enmity to the House

of Islam', a capital offence. Furthermore, this judgment of Rushdie's actions
was not a fallible human decree, but 'in accordance with what God has sent
down'. A non-Muslim British scholar of Islam, Malcolm Yapp, disagreed. To
him, the 'oddest feature' of the entire proceeding was not that the *fatwa* was
held (by some) to be the word of God, but that Khomeini's pronouncements
were regarded as 'authoritative statements of law'. Moreover, the possibility of
repentance had been overlooked, while 'the opinion of one man' had 'replaced
all the elaborate mechanisms' by which opinions upon the laws of Islam were
normally compared, and 'consensus achieved'.

Disagreement among Muslim scholars was revealed in the description (by
some) of the *fatwa* as 'non-Islamic' and even 'anti-Islamic', the familiar terms.
The Iranian Ayatollah Hossein Ali Montazeri—a dissenting former associate
of Khomeini—even declared that those who had attacked Islam should not be
'dealt with violently', provided that they were not acting with 'deceit'. They
should instead be answered 'book against book, opinion against opinion'.

There was no reconciling these positions. They ranged from readiness to
slay Rushdie without further debate or question, to the recommendation that
he be treated with 'goodness, gentleness and toleration'. Although not made
apparent, in particular to non-Muslims, theological doubt over the principle,
as well as the means, of killing Rushdie was rife in the Muslim world. In addition, fears about the consequences of taking Rushdie's life were combined
with expressions of fierce hatred for him. As earlier indicated, there was also
a minority of Muslims who sympathised, to a greater or lesser degree, with
Rushdie's predicament. In a rare engagement with principle, the Murabitun
Muslim movement described Khomeini's sentence as a 'crime', and declared
that it could not 'condone' it. Individual Muslims in the diaspora also took
their courage in their hands. Ruqayya Aldridge told the *Guardian* that, 'because
of the powers of reasoning' which European Muslim converts—such as she—
had 'acquired through the education process', they did 'not have the same
problems as Asian Muslims'. Unlike the latter, they did not 'blindly accept the
precepts of any ideology from second-hand, often ignorant sources'.

Beyond this, there were yet other Muslim positions. 'Women Against Fundamentalism', a predominantly Muslim group formed in London in March
1989, expressed 'unequivocal support' for Rushdie; Zebunissa Rizwi of Bradford, writing in February 1989 to the *Independent* one week after the *fatwa*,
'denounced unreservedly the revolting book-burning by fanatical Muslims in
Bradford.' 'Speaking up in the current climate', she continued, 'is not easy,
even for secular-minded Muslims. From the moment of birth...the whole
apparatus of culture, tradition and religion is employed to crush heretical

inclinations. For many of us, our lives are characterised by a grotesque schizophrenia: we understand the faith of our families but we cannot accept it.... I am proud to own a copy of *The Satanic Verses* and proud to be an apostate'.

A year later, a 'seventeen-year-old Asian woman', asking 'forgiveness' for her wish to remain anonymous, thanked Rushdie in the *Independent on Sunday.* 'I want to live in your world, and one day I know I will', she wrote. 'There are dissidents out here, but like me they are often too scared to speak. If only we all lived in enough freedom to speak out against this mad vendetta against Rushdie', she exclaimed. As we have seen, most Muslims—especially Muslim men—lacked this kind of moral courage. One who shared it was a professor of philosophy at Columbia, Akeel Bilgrami. 'What does it say about a religion and its constituency', he asked in February 1990, 'that the publication of a book has provoked...a scenario of international-scale violence and terror?' *The Satanic Verses* had taken a 'courageous stand' against 'the forces within Islam which arrest its reform', he asserted. 'That means standing up for Rushdie'.

These were again minoritarian views. But they existed, and might even be expressed in public. Nevertheless, Kalim Siddiqui of the 'Muslim Parliament' had insisted in December 1989, against evidence to the contrary, that there was 'no division' among Muslims; they were of one mind that the *fatwa* be upheld, that the book be withdrawn, and that the death-sentence be implemented. In the *Independent* in February 1989, Iqbal Wahhab similarly declared that Muslims in Britain could 'take solace' that 'whatever else happens' they were 'now stronger and more united than even before'. British Muslims, Wahhab again wrote in December 1989, were voting 'unanimously' and 'overwhelmingly' in their mosques to 'uphold the death-sentence against the author Salman Rushdie'. Tauqir Malik, chairman of the Leeds Muslim committee, concurred with Wahhab, but the earlier-mentioned Hesham el-Essawy—described by Malik as 'isolated'—disagreed.

According to el-Essawy, 'only four mosques', not the 'one thousand' claimed by Wahhab in the *Independent*, had 'joined this action'. Moreover, declared el-Essawy, most British Muslims did not support the *fatwa*. This was an assertion seemingly confirmed by polls in October and December 1989, which put the figure for such support at less than 30 per cent. Other polls, as by the BBC in the following year, found 42 per cent support. Nevertheless, Siddiqui insisted in the summer of 1990 that 'we know that the real figure is 100 per cent'. At a London conference held in July 1990, it was reported by Iqbal Wahhab (once more) that 'five hundred Muslim religious leaders voted unanimously to support the death-sentence imposed by Ayatollah Khomeini on Salman Rushdie'.

In these disputes about the degree of Muslim support for killing Rushdie, one matter was again clear: the ethics of the issue were lost from sight. Or, as Rushdie had telegraphically asserted at the outset, 'What the religious fundamentalists are saying in effect is "God sent the Koran. Full stop. End of discussion"'. But it was not to be so simple. For by December 1990, Rushdie himself had 'come to the point' where he was ready to 'accept the basic tenets of Islam'. In London, in the presence of six Muslim scholars—including two 'moderate' Egyptian imams from a London mosque—he 'affirmed' his belief in 'the oneness of God and the prophecy of the Prophet Mohammed'. His affirmation was 'honest', he declared; he had also been honest with himself, he said. Had he not been, 'it would be impossible for me to continue an intellectual life'. It had not been his intention to 'offend people'. A paperback edition of the novel would not now be published.

Most Muslims rejected his 'conversion' despite the Koranic provision for a sinner's repentance. Every moral confusion, Rushdie's confusion included, was thereafter confounded further. Khomeini's successor as Iran's 'supreme spiritual leader' pronounced the *fatwa* to be 'irrevocable'. The author remained a 'heretic' despite his repentance and 'must be killed', declared Ayatollah Khamenei, who had earlier prevaricated. If his 'return to Islam' was to be regarded as a 'sign of bravery', further declared the hard-line Iranian newspaper, *Jomhuri Eslami*, Rushdie was invited to 'show greater bravery still' and 'prepare himself for death'. The Egyptian minister of Islamic affairs disagreed: Rushdie, having repented and 'become a true Muslim', Islam—as a 'religion of tolerance'—must accept it. The author claimed that his 'affirmation' of faith had received a 'formal blessing' from the spiritual head of the world's Sunni Muslims, Sheikh Gad el-Haq Ali Gad el-Haq; el-Haq denied it. It was also now being asserted, as by the director-general of Leicester's Islamic Foundation, Manazir Ahsan, that Rushdie's crime had 'become all the more grave', since he was both claiming to be a Muslim and allowing his offensive book to remain in circulation.

This, then was a no-win situation for all parties. The issue (or imbroglio) had long transcended the mere matter of interpretation of an Iranian edict, or of an English-language fiction. 'My understanding of Islam', declared Rushdie, 'is that it is a culture of tolerance and compassion, forgiveness and love'. But his 'conversion' had gained him no reprieve. To most Muslims his 'repentance' was not sincere; to many non-Muslims, too, it was a 'conversion' under duress, a means to get a frightened man off death's hook.

But if fear had indeed led Rushdie publicly to embrace Islam, fear was held by Shabbir Akhtar not to be a 'disreputable motive for conversion'.

'Islam', he asserted, 'is not Christianity; and fear, no less than love, is a worthy emotion'. Voices from the Muslim diaspora 'street' demanded that Rushdie be put to the test of his 'conversion'. 'He must show us all', insisted Mehmood Naqshbandi (of Croydon), writing to the *Guardian* in January 1991, 'that he is a better Muslim than the rest of us. If he is willing to live wholly and completely by the Sharia and Sunnah, as all Muslims must and very few do'— therefore, a hypocritically large price for forgiveness—'I promise that I and my friends will defend him with our lives'.

There were many other tensions in this cultural trial of strength within Islam. At London's Central Mosque in March 1991, Sheikh Gamal Manna Solaiman, one of the two 'moderate' imams who had witnessed Rushdie's 'conversion', was not only prevented by worshippers from leading prayers but was forcibly ejected from the mosque. During the three months since Rushdie had 'affirmed' his belief in their presence, neither imam had been allowed to reach the pulpit. The two imams complained to the press. They were being attacked, they said, 'just for meeting Mr. Rushdie and for bearing witness to his embracing of Islam, as indeed it is our duty to do with any conversion'. The 'ugly scuffles' which they described as having taken place in the mosque were (as ever) 'non-Islamic'. But six weeks later they themselves changed position; according to Hesham el-Essawy, they had been put 'under tremendous pressure', including 'by threats of violence'. Apologising to worshippers in May 1991, the two imams now stated that Rushdie's 'conversion to Islam' could not be accepted. His repentance had not been 'real and honest', since he had permitted his book to remain in circulation.

Seven months later, in December 1991, Rushdie himself repented of his repentance. With some portentousness and at further risk to himself, he explained that he had wanted to 'make peace between the warring halves of the world, which were...the warring halves of my soul'. He had sought to make formal peace with Islam 'even at the cost of my pride', but at the time of his 'conversion'—which he was in effect now disowning—he had been 'in a state of some confusion and torment'. Upon this new declaration, he was attacked as 'insincere' by mediators who had brokered his 'return to Islam'. Rushdie in turn accused them of being 'untrustworthy', an undeserved reproach. For its part, Iran repeated that there could be 'no reprieve, whether the apostate repents or not'.

Among most non-Muslims the *fatwa* had from the outset been greeted with dismay and incomprehension. Moreover, it was evident that the lengthening reach of Islam's revival had made a deep incursion into a non-Muslim society's cultural life and traditions of free speech. But division was quickly generated in liberal ranks, too. It was essentially a division between those for whom Western liberal freedoms had moral precedence over Muslim hurt and anger, those for whom they did not, and those who could not make up their minds where they stood. They were positions which in some respects, but in different proportions, coincided with those of Muslims.

To the *Daily Telegraph*—'we should not mince words', it pugnaciously stated—Khomeini's edict was 'barbaric', 'bereft of humanity and reason', and the threats against Rushdie 'demented'. To the French president, François Mitterrand, such threats were 'absolute evil'. For the *Independent*, the burning of books had 'followed the example of the Inquisition and Hitler's National Socialists'. The 'intellectual terrorism' of the *fatwa*, it declared, was not only 'shocking and dangerous' but 'counter-productive' since it could only 'rebound on the Islamic community', the argument of many Muslims also. It was additionally pointed out that protests of the kind mounted against Rushdie by Muslims in Western liberal societies would not have been tolerated from religious minorities in Muslim countries. Muslim conduct, declared a group of British writers of the left in February 1989, could only 'reflect adversely on a faith which has given birth to a great civilisation'. The novelist Anthony Burgess was less circumspect. The *fatwa* was 'the tactics of the gangster. Islam once did intellectual battle, but now it prefers to draw blood', he wrote.

The 'excesses' of Islam were held by much of the British press to be 'abhorrent' and its creed 'bigoted', while the 'Teheran mob' was driven by 'blood-lust'. Islamic 'obscurantism' was 'fanatical'; a 'holy war' was being conducted 'against argument itself'; this was 'terrorism' both intellectual and religious. However, there was little comfort for the author in the calculation, by the *Guardian*'s literary editor, that 'killing Salman Rushdie would give the West its own Mohammed and martyr'. Nor did Rushdie's 'conversion', temporary as it turned out to be, win many plaudits among the secular non-Muslim intelligentsia. It left a 'bad taste in the mouth', since it was also seen as a victory for intolerance of dissent 'on pain of death'. Some of those who had stood by the author declared him to be not 'worth defending' after his 'surrender' to Islam.

But even before his 'conversion'—and its retraction—Rushdie had come under personal attack from non-Muslims for his book. Indeed, by the 1980s Islam had made sufficient cultural and political progress in the diaspora for some non-Muslims to be ready to share the Muslim view of Rushdie's book; a phenomenon of a type which was to become more common, especially on the 'left'. In March 1989, former US president Jimmy Carter used Islam's own vocabulary: *The Satanic Verses* was not only an 'arrow pointed at Muslims' but at 'religion in general'. There had been an 'insult' to the 'sacred belief of our Muslim friends', said Carter. Rushdie had 'vilified the Prophet Mohammed'. The British Conservative peer Viscount Massereene and Ferrard told the House of Lords that the author 'must have made a lot of money out of his scurrilous and blasphemous book'; Baroness Strange thought that Rushdie should 'contribute some personal cash out of that gain to the long-suffering British public'.

The historian Lord Dacre, formerly Hugh Trevor-Roper, even echoed Islamism's incitements. 'I would not shed a tear', he wrote in July 1989, 'if some British Muslims, deploring his manners, should waylay him in a dark street and seek to improve them'. In February 1990, Professor Michael Dummett of Oxford, referring to Rushdie in language akin to that of Muslim objections, held it to be a 'disgusting thing' to 'defile what other men regard as holy'. More abusive still, Dummett asserted that although the *fatwa* was itself an 'abominable act', Rushdie had become 'an honorary white'. He was 'merely an honorary white intellectual, it is true', declared the actually-white intellectual, 'but an honorary white all the same'.

In September 1990 and in similarly vicious *ad hominem* mode, the former Tory cabinet minister, Lord Tebbit, described Rushdie's 'public life' as 'a record of despicable acts of betrayal of his upbringing, religion, adopted home and nationality'. 'He is immensely rich', he continued, 'perhaps the world's richest multiple renegade'. He had used the right of free speech to 'insult, demean and degrade', and was, in short, a 'villain'. It was 'a pity', Tebbit added, that Rushdie had chosen to live in 'our country'. Muslims who had supported the death-sentence against the author could not have wished for more. He had 'betrayed' and 'degraded' Islam and was being damned for it, including by non-Muslims.

On closer examination, there were even some uncertainties among those in Britain accustomed, by cultural reflex, to value freedom of speech almost above life itself. 'Are we committed in the name of freedom of literature to defend this novel against those who think it should never have been published?' asked a London University academic. 'The answer must surely be yes', he told himself, 'but it is a reluctant and deeply troubled yes'. The 'reluctance' and 'troubled' feelings were because of the novel's 'assault on the feelings of Muslims', he explained. Tenderness towards freedom of speech and tenderness towards Muslim sensibilities were here at war, and the result was a near-draw. 'In the name of tolerance we cry for a total autonomy of the arts', a similarly-divided clergyman wrote in August 1989 to the *Independent*, but 'does not authorship have responsibility to social well-being?' he inquired.

The answers to this question varied, at the same time as the costs of Rushdie's protection were being largely borne by the taxpayer, the Muslim taxpayer included. The government of the day appeared to be unequivocal (for a time) in its address to British Muslims; the latter's intolerance of Rushdie would not itself be tolerated. 'Those who wish to make their homes in Britain', the British education secretary Kenneth Baker declared, 'cannot deny to others the very freedoms which drew them to this country in the first place'. Muslim demands that censorship protect their religious feelings, including by an extension to them of the laws of blasphemy hitherto applicable only to Christians, were rejected. The Campaign Against Censorship insisted on Rushdie's behalf that there was even a 'right to offend' others, whomever they might be. 'If you don't have that right', it stated, 'you don't have any literary freedom'.

Indeed, the quality of debate on the difference between Muslim and non-Muslim values reached levels in this period which it was never subsequently to do, as the war of the worlds turned increasingly to guns and bombs. Muslims had 'no right to call for the destruction' of Rushdie's novel, declared the writer Anthony Burgess. 'If they do not like secular society they must fly to the arms of the Ayatollah or some other . . . guardian of strict Islamic morality. . . . They cannot have the privileges of a theocratic state in a society which, as they knew when they entered it, grants total tolerance to all faiths, so long as those faiths do not conflict with that very principle of tolerance', Burgess continued, two days after Rushdie had gone into hiding. 'I am within my rights in inveighing against an aggressiveness which denies to a free society its privilege of allowing its citizens to speak their minds without fear of brutal reprisal', Burgess further asserted.

But the more articulate Muslim spokesmen gave as good as they got. 'Appeals to "matters of principle" and "historically hard-won liberties"' were 'not convincing when placed in the context of double or even triple moral standards', Shabbir Akhtar told the *Guardian* a few days later, when the *fatwa* was a fortnight old. Nor did such Muslim counter-positions lack for non-Muslim support, as we have seen. Indeed, the very 'right to offend' which had been claimed on Rushdie's behalf by opponents of censorship was turned on its head, as argument transcended the particular instance and became more searching. 'A tolerant, open society', declared the Labour MP Gerald Kaufman, 'means tolerance of opinions which may not suit some but which suit those who express them'—by implication including Muslim opinions that Rushdie and his book should be cast into the nether world.

Emboldened by such moral sympathy, Muslims—notably those educated in Britain—cunningly asked why they should 'behave like liberal secularists in order to secure their rights as citizens'. At the time this debate was under-appreciated, as had been earlier arguments about education in a 'plural' society. Yet it was of considerable historical importance in the losing cultural battle with Islam in the non-Muslim world. It raised, even if it could not settle, issues about the nature and limits of the freedoms of the individual in a Western liberal society; about the sacrifices which could, or could not, be expected of all citizens in the name of the 'common interest' and of the need to adapt to a dominant value-system; and as to whether such 'common interest' or 'value system' existed at all in a 'plural' social order.

Hence, the arguments of the literary critics were dwarfed, as was the text's author himself, by larger matters. The critics disputed whether the controversial text was a 'moral parable', an account of a 'hallucination', or a 'good', a 'bad' or even a 'wretched' novel. But on the political front, the issues were large indeed. 'Ethnic minorities' were told peremptorily by government ministers to 'accept the need for greater integration'. A question—presumptuous or urgent, according to judgment—of how 'reasoned enlightenment' might be 'encouraged among British Muslims' was answered by suggestions that this was a task which the established Church should assume on the nation's behalf. There was 'no better and more effective way' of achieving the 'disarming' of a 'potential book-burner', wrote Andrew Brown in the *Independent* in August 1989, than to 'take him to tea at Lambeth Palace and draw him into the endless Anglican conversation'. It was not clear whether he was joking. From the 'left' came a view, expressed by John Torode in October 1989, that if Muslims in Britain were 'given decent housing and better job opportunities', and if 'racist attacks and insults' were ended, Muslim 'youngsters' would 'cease to carry banners reading "Die, Rushdie bastard!"'

Some of these propositions—directed to 'solving' what was perceived as the 'Muslim problem'—were again naive. The playing upon Muslim feelings and interests by some Labour members of parliament who had large minorities of Muslim constituents was a different and unedifying matter. In Leicester East constituency, where there was a Labour majority of less than two thousand, Keith Vaz led three thousand Muslim demonstrators in an anti-Rushdie protest in March 1989, during which the police prevented the burning of an effigy of the author. Himself a Catholic, Vaz not only declared that 'today we celebrate one of the great days in the history of Islam and Great Britain', but attacked his own party, on his Muslim constituents' behalf, as a 'godless party'. With a fellow-British citizen under sentence of death and in hiding, it was a form of opportunism which made its own amoral contribution to the incitements of the hour.

Two months later, on 27 May 1989, when tens of thousands of Muslim demonstrators in Parliament Square burned the Union flag, and tore apart an effigy of Rushdie—to shouts of 'Rushdie die, Rushdie scum!' and 'We want Rushdie, dead dog Rushdie!'—Vaz described the occasion as a 'great celebration of freedom'. In July 1989 he did not trouble to hide what was (for him) at issue. Muslims, he stated, had not only 'begun to wield political muscle' but could 'probably determine the outcome of the election in several cities'. He named six such cities. They included his own.

Gerald Kaufman, who also represented an inner-city parliamentary seat with a significant Muslim presence, was more subtle in his argument. But in March 1989 he stoked the pyre at Rushdie's feet. The British attitude to 'Asians', he stated—while all about him raged Muslim ire—was that they were to be 'championed as long as they conduct themselves appropriately as an impotent minority'. If they had 'the cheek to assert themselves', said Kaufman, 'they had better watch their step'. In May 1989 the deputy-leader of the Labour Party, Roy Hattersley—in whose Birmingham constituency of 80,000 voters no fewer than 35,000 were Muslim—announced his 'vehement opposition' to the banning of books, but at the same time called for the paperback edition of Rushdie's novel not to be published. The Writers' Guild accused Hattersley of 'hypocrisy' and of 'trying to have it both ways'—as well he might have done, given his constituency's composition. 'He wants freedom of expression', the Guild's secretary commented, 'but hopes people will not make use of it'.

Far from being abashed, Hattersley pressed on into the moral labyrinth, following in Kaufman's steps. 'The proposition that Muslims are welcome in Britain if, and only if, they stop behaving like Muslims is a doctrine which is incompatible with the principles which govern and guide a free society', he pronounced in July 1989. For good measure, he added that such a proposition could 'only be described as racist'. The morally and politically testing question of what might be the bounds, in a non-Muslim society, to Muslims 'behaving like Muslims' (whatever that meant) was evaded. Street opinion was less sophisticated, or less devious. Rejecting Hattersley's defence of Muslims who 'behaved like Muslims', it typically declared that 'no one can be allowed to carry on like that in Britain'; which was to say burning books, threatening or volunteering to kill an author, and so forth. Objection to this was 'a necessary defence of our freedoms, and there is nothing racist about it', a letter-writer told the *Independent*.

With 35,000 Muslim voters to concentrate his mind, the deputy-leader of the Labour Party was persistent, but only to add to the incoherence of his position. He declared himself to be personally in favour of the abolition of the crime of blasphemy, but promised Muslims that, if elected to government, the Labour Party would extend blasphemy's scope to cover Islam. He held in disdain accusations of blasphemy in respect of any faith, yet described Rushdie's novel as an 'intentional blasphemy'. 'What most Muslims want', he assured the country, 'they have now got from the Labour Party'. It was a position described by a *Sunday Times* commentator as 'abjectly deferential to a bunch of Islamic clergy firmly planted in the fifteenth century'. 'In liberal Britain', the journalist continued, 'we have a right to tell Muslims that you can believe whatever you like, worship in whatever way you think right, but you may not take away our liberties'. Another voice declared that the vote-bank politicians were 'yellow-bellied and confused'; yet another, that they were 'opportunistic and muddled'.

But such 'opportunism' and 'muddle' were not surprising, since politicians in many Western liberal democracies were having to watch their backs as their Muslim electorates grew. In 2003 and 2004, Muslim spokesmen in Britain, France and the United States issued increasingly open warnings, and on some occasions threats, about their leverage in polls; in US swing states such as Michigan, Florida and Ohio there were sizeable Muslim populations. British Labour MPs and ministers—such as the British foreign secretary, Jack Straw, whose constituency contained many thousands of Muslim voters—faced a 'backlash', they were told, for their support of the US-led invasion of Iraq. 'Straw will have a lot of problems', asserted Ahmed Versi, editor of the *Muslim News*, in September 2003; he had 'upset' his constituents, declared a spokesman for the Muslim Association of Britain in May 2004.

When a Labour candidate went down to defeat in September 2003 in a constituency with a large Muslim presence, Ihtisham Hibatullah, also a spokesman for the Muslim Association of Britain—alleged to have links with the Muslim Brotherhood—described it as a 'warning'. 'We have a very substantial vote-bank', he added bluntly. Likewise, Denis MacShane, a Labour Foreign Office minister who had infelicitously told local Muslims that they had to 'choose between' the 'British way' and 'support for terror', apologised to them in December 2003 for his statement; as MP for Rotherham, with its large Muslim minority, he had no choice. In France, a different but equally threatening kind of warning was issued by a Muslim organisation in February 2004: if candidates for election did not reflect the country's 'ethnic diversity', Muslims would extract themselves from the political process. 'Politicians simply do not resemble the French population', it was rightly said.

By 2005, the confidence of diaspora Muslims had grown in parallel with the dilemmas and confusions of the non-Muslim world. In March 2005 in

Britain, for example—with a general election drawing near—the Labour chancellor of the exchequer, Gordon Brown, praised Islam in terms not heard before. 'It teaches us', he declared, that 'we are all part of one moral universe', while Muslims in Britain were 'our modern heroes' who were 'bringing hope to Britain'. Among the things 'we share in common', the chancellor added, was 'the belief in fair play'.

Seemingly unimpressed even by this testimonial, the Muslim Association of Britain in April 2005 told politicians that 'if you want our votes, work for them'; that Muslim opinion could now be 'decisive' in 'forty constituencies' in which Muslims accounted for from 10 to almost 50 per cent of the electorates; and that their support would depend upon 'where each candidate stands on the most vital issues', which were said to include 'Palestine and Kashmir'. In the event, in May 2005 there were substantial swings against Labour in many constituencies—from 10 to almost 15 per cent in some of them—where there was a high Muslim presence. Muslim objection to British participation in the Iraq war and to 'anti-terror' legislation had weighed more heavily than opportunistic praise of Muslims in Britain as 'heroes' who believed in 'fair play'.

The confused combination of 'respect' for, fear of, contempt for and truckling to the Muslim community was not governed by electoral considerations alone. Even in 1989 it ran deeper, and caught up other than politicians. The local police advised booksellers in Bradford to withdraw Rushdie's novel from sale. Bradford Council told its public libraries not to put the book on their open shelves, and to insert in all copies a warning that the novel 'could be offensive to Muslims'. A gesture welcomed by Muslims, it was denounced by critics as 'peace at any price'. Race relations workers up and down the country exerted their own moral pressures against Rushdie's book. The deputy-chairman of the Commission for Racial Equality declared that Britain could not 'afford' to have a 'large, proud and law-abiding minority withdrawing in a mood of deep sulk'. Others thought there was more than 'deep sulk' to it; the London School of Economics in June 1989 cancelled a meeting in support of the author, fearing 'violent reaction from Muslim extremists'.

Likewise, the Crown Prosecution Service refused in February 1989 and January 1990 to authorise the bringing by the police of any charges of incitement to murder Rushdie. Muslim leaders in Britain who had publicly endorsed, often in blood-curdling terms, the call for his killing went unprosecuted. It was explained that there was 'insufficient direct evidence to bring charges at this time', and that the question of 'whether prosecutions would be in the public interest' had to be 'taken into account'. That is, there was anxiety, openly expressed, that enforcing the law 'would make matters worse'. Deference to such anxiety took other forms still. British Airways refused to carry the author on its flights. In March 1989, after a recall of European diplomats from Teheran for 'consultation', European Community members, including Italy, Greece and Ireland, backed away—with the sword of Damocles suspended over Rushdie's head—from an initial intent to present a common front of disapproval towards the Iranian regime. It was swiftly exploited. The envoys, declared Ayatollah Khomeini, were returning to Teheran 'humiliated, disgraced, and regretful of what they had done'.

This was skilful, the skill of a powerful force in motion. So, too, was the use made by the Muslim and Arab worlds of their knowledge that Western liberal societies were increasingly afraid of the progress of Islamic self-confidence and strength, and even more deeply divided over how to respond to it. These divisions have widened in the last decades. Moreover, the need to 'take a stand' of 'principle' against Islamism's excesses was often outweighed by the greater need for prudence where the West's economic interests were involved, as Muslims again know better than any.

All this was made clear in the ostensibly minor matter of a novelist's right in a free society to invent whatever fiction he chose. Thus, Britain, while seemingly engaged with multiple challenges to individual liberty, to the safety of Rushdie, to public order, to race relations and even to the political fortunes of individual politicians, was also under pressure from trade lobbies which had no interest in such dilemmas. If Muslims in Britain were engaged in a utilitarian calculus, or cost-benefit analysis, of the practical consequences of supporting an Iranian *fatwa* against a British Muslim author, British businessmen and politicians were equally weighing the impact on balance-sheets of moral principle, and of the defence of a single individual's intellectual freedom.

Many clearly considered this freedom to be of little significance in the commercial and diplomatic scale. On the grounds that it would 'harm relations with Iran', Conservative members of parliament criticised the expulsion in July 1992 from Britain of three Iranians who had allegedly been plotting to assassinate Rushdie. Likewise, after the author had been publicly invited to the Foreign Office for discussions of his predicament, complaint was made in parliament that Britain's trade with Iran was being put at risk by such gestures of support. 'I see no reason why we should ruin our relationship with Iran, which can be a very profitable market', declared Sir Edward Heath in March 1993.

However, such 'pragmatism' could not gain much ground on the Iranian regime. It was initially insisted by the Foreign Office that the *fatwa* be lifted before diplomatic relations, severed by Iran in 1989, could be fully restored. This insistence was dropped. Britain's concerns for its practical interests had by August 1990 given Iran part of what it was seeking. But pressure by Iran, using the fate of the British hostages then being held in Lebanon as blackmail, did not diminish. Teheran sought to get Britain publicly to acknowledge that Iran was in the right, that Rushdie had been justly condemned and that the protection of his life was therefore wrong.

Indeed, according to Ayatollah Mohammed Emami Kashani, speaking at Friday prayers in Teheran, this was very close to what Britain did then concede. The British foreign secretary, Douglas Hurd, had not only 'expressed respect for Muslims in defending their beliefs', but had also 'condemned Salman Rushdie'. By doing so, the ayatollah triumphantly declared, Britain had 'come close' to 'meeting Iran's conditions for restoring diplomatic relations'. Britain's precondition for such restoration—the lifting of the *fatwa*—had disappeared; diplomatic relations were resumed; the *fatwa* remained in force. In February 2003, the edict was declared to be 'irrevocable' by Iran's Revolutionary Guards, while the bounty on Rushdie's head was raised to $3 million; and in June 2004, an Iranian 'Committee for the Commemoration of Martyrs of the Global Islamic Campaign'—a title to ponder—claimed that it had 'registered some 10,000 names' of individuals ready to carry out 'martyrdom operations' against 'defined targets', including Rushdie, whose 'attack on Islam' was described as 'much worse than a military assault'. In January 2005, almost sixteen years after it was first promulgated, the *fatwa* was reaffirmed by Teheran.

Whether or not Ayatollah Emami's account in 1990 of the British foreign secretary's position on Rushdie had been truthful, Hurd did not himself demur at the interpretation of his views by the Iranians. It was in any case on record that he had pronounced Islam to be 'one of the world's great religions', and had acknowledged the novel to be 'deeply offensive' to Muslims. But 'subtle' as such manoeuvres by the British might have been thought (by the British) to be, British diplomacy was left standing on its head. Trade interests, the desire to do nothing that would harm Western hostages held under Iran's aegis in the Middle East and the supposed benefits of a 'low-key approach' to profound moral issues had gained the day. The Iranian death-sentence still stood, while open public endorsements of it by Muslims in Britain were continuing.

In consequence, non-Muslim critics of the approach to the Rushdie affair had concluded, by 1990, that 'no one may say anything about Islam which in any way displeases Muslims, irrespective of its foundation in truth'. At the affair's height, it was also instructive to observe how easily the non-Muslim world was knocked off balance by the Muslim challenge, a phenomenon which was to become more common as the Islamic advance continued. Non-Muslims, whether individuals or states, have veered unsteadily between, or tried to combine, contradictory approaches to such challenges. They have included violent military assault on its Muslim and Arab foes, and treading on diplomatic egg-shells in the hope of not offending 'valued' Muslim allies; expressions of 'respect' for Islam, as in 1990, and alternations of deference towards, and disdain for, Muslims and Arabs; and the de facto acceptance, and therefore legitimation, in the diaspora of many Muslim excesses. They were excesses to which liberal societies simultaneously declared themselves to be opposed.

Such ambivalence, alternately resisting and surrendering to pressures in face of the Islamic revival, has sometimes mirrored the ambivalence of the Muslim to the non-Muslim world. More important, it has played a significant part in the growth of Muslim self-confidence, and thus in that revival itself. It also made it difficult to demand of Muslims greater intellectual coherence, or greater attention to moral scruple, than the non-Muslim world itself has demonstrated. For the non-Muslim world has been unable to respond to the political, military and intellectual challenges which face it without using many of the same methods used against it, violent attack included.

Trapped in this labyrinth are those Muslims in the diaspora who are opposed to Islamist violence and mayhem, but who cannot speak out against it as long as Islam itself is, or makes out that it is, under attack. Many of those who have spoken out have not been heard, since the *via media*—in the media—has been less newsworthy than the extreme. Moreover, for a Muslim to disclose to a non-Muslim, or *kafir*, his or her disapproval of the acts of fellow-Muslims has required boldness and even courage; more courage than could be grasped by Western liberals habituated to a culture of free thought and of the right to dissent. Moreover, dilution of their faith and the risk of dissolution of their communities have been felt by many diaspora Muslims to be larger threats to their well-being than hostile reactions by non-Muslims to Islamism's attacks.

In this labyrinth, the equivocal attitude of Muslims towards their adopted societies, and the increasing unwillingness of many younger Muslims to recognise the duties they owe to these societies as citizens, is not a matter for surprise. In 1989, in the argument over Rushdie, this equivocation and unwillingness were already clear. However, most Muslims who wished to kill the author of *The Satanic Verses*, and most non-Muslims who instinctively defended Rushdie's rights, had at least one thing in common: they had not read the book. Many of the older generation of Muslims in Britain could not read it. Most Muslims, whatever their own views, would not break ranks with their fellows. For these and other reasons, the conclusion reached at the time in Britain that 'all Muslims' were 'extremists' or 'fundamentalists' was false, and has remained false. It also discounted the moral courage of those Muslims, albeit a minority, who have been ready throughout the last decades to run the gauntlet of community pressures.

Some have acted alone, and were often unsupported by non-Muslims. In November 2001, Yasser Alvi, for example, allowed his name and address to be published in the *Daily Telegraph* when describing Omar Bakri Mohammed, the leader of al-Muhajiroun, as a 'malevolent clown' whose aim was to create 'hatred and turmoil'. Mohammed Usman of Bradford, although said to have been 'terrorised' for his actions and his house vandalised by Muslim youths, displayed the Union flag in his windows on several British national occasions in 2000 and 2002. With less courage, but distinctive nonetheless, some Muslim organisations determinedly let it be known that they were taking their distance from the 'extremist and sectarian groups' in their midst.

Nevertheless, ambivalence has remained the hallmark of Muslim diaspora responses to moral challenge. For the position of Muslims in non-Muslim societies is a riven one, that of self-division, in which harm to faith is a price of 'belonging' which few Muslims are prepared to pay. Moreover, increasing hostility to Islam in the non-Muslim world has also increased the need of diaspora Muslims to transfer blame to others for the dilemmas they face. In 1989 and 1990, it was as if such habits of moral transference, or evasion, had led Muslims to make Rushdie the focus of responsibility for their own troubles in the diaspora. Moreover, Muslims were made 'anxious' by the very uproar that many in their own communities had created, yet most refused to accept responsibility for it, on the grounds that the 'insult' done them by the book took moral precedence over all other considerations. Hesham el-Essawy, who had urged Rushdie to try to make his peace with Islam and had been his interlocutor with clerical Muslim opinion, told me that Muslims had said in private to him, 'We are confused, we are in terrible trouble, we don't know what to do. Our future is bleak here. Who is going to employ our children? Who is going to respect us? What can we do to show that not all of us are fanatics?'

Such fears of illiberal responses in liberal societies to the very presence of Muslims have grown with the increase in Islamist violence. But so, too, has the pride felt by many Muslims at Islam's assertiveness in the world. Nevertheless, a minority of Muslims has continued to admit to their part in the dilemmas they face. 'We are an intolerant people and rarely brook disssenting voices or differing opinions', declared Irfan Husain in the Karachi newspaper *Dawn* in December 2002. 'Muslim institutions and groups freely use (and abuse) all the freedoms allowed to them in the West', he continued, 'but hate and despise the liberal civilisation that has produced those very liberties. Listen to a Muslim intellectual, *mullah* or politician, and you will hear a litany of complaints and criticisms against Western sins of omission and commission, past and present. Ask him where he wants to send his children to university and, if he is honest, he will reel off the names of the top American universities'. As for Western criticisms of the Islamic world, 'Muslim leaders respond by claiming that their societies have the right to behave as they do because they have "different values". This claim', bravely wrote Husain, 'covers a multitude of sins, ranging from repulsive dictatorships to the subjugation of women and minorities, and brutal punishments'.

This was again not the Muslim silence upon moral questions of which many non-Muslims complained. It treated of matters of right and wrong without transfer of responsibility or other evasion. But its candour about the use, and abuse, by Muslims of the liberties of the non-Muslim world also pointed to the increasing confidence of many Muslims in taking from the non-Muslim world whatever they chose to take—as non-Muslims have for long done with the resources of the Muslim world.

CHAPTER SEVEN
Taking Liberties

Liberties may be taken, or denied, as a result of the absence of democracy or of the rule of law. Liberties may also be taken, in another sense of the phrase, *with* democracy or the rule of law. This can occur, for example, when individuals or groups claim rights and entitlements which are inimical to the general good. It can also occur when democracy's own guardians grant freedoms, or allow licences, to those who harbour hostile intent towards the societies of which they are members. Such complaisance may arise from inertia, from incompetence, from hidden sympathy with such individuals and groups, or from fear lest the latter do worse should their claims be denied. The resulting scope given to the pursuit of ends which are harmful to the democratic and liberal civic order, and which may even have the downfall of such order in mind, is a threat to the liberties of all.

In the relations between diaspora Muslims and the non-Muslim world, the wrongful giving and taking of liberties in this fashion has been a common feature. In their attitudes to their places of settlement and to the norms and values of such places there has been much moral confusion and internal division among Muslims themselves, as earlier noted. But often there has been something morally hard-edged and brass-necked about it; something which goes beyond the right and need to protect the faith which Muslims bring with them into the non-Muslim world.

In this moral 'hard edge', there has been expressed not only pride of identity and belonging. Sometimes, a direct challenge is being made to the (generally disintegrating) value-system of whatever non-Muslim society Muslims have chosen, or have been driven to choose, as their homes. A minority of Muslims, large or small according to judgment, has evinced antipathy towards, and contempt for, the civic orders whose citizen rights it shares, at the same time as it has sought to extend such rights in its own behalf. In addition, this minority has often been ready to applaud the cause of enemies of the non-Muslim world; and in extreme cases, while remaining citizens, even to join the foe.

To expect or to demand citizen rights, protections and entitlements from civic societies for which only ambiguous loyalty is felt is not confined to Muslims. Indeed, the 'taking of liberties' *with* free societies, as well as *from* them, is part of the wider crisis of the liberal civic order. Moreover, in non-Islamic societies, liberties harmful to the public or common good have been given to Muslims—and not only to Muslims—even without the need to seek them.

Amid the flux and internal turmoil of the Western liberal order, there has developed a wide spectrum of relations between non-Muslim and Muslim citizens in the various polities which they now inhabit together. They have included, in some non-Muslims, a deep intolerance towards incomers, an intolerance which has not been confined to responses to Muslims. It is an intolerance which can be manifested in vicious forms. Arousal to 'vigilance' has also prompted, in some, a readiness to take 'pre-emptive action', whether at home or abroad, against perceived threats to the integrity and safety of this or that non-Islamic society. In mid-spectrum, there have been varying degrees of indifference or passivity towards Muslims and other incomers. Such attitudes are not to be confused with tolerance, even if the indifferent and passive often believe their indifference and passivity to be the marks of toleration.

Further along the spectrum of positive responses to incomers, a welcome has been given to 'plurality' in Western liberal democratic societies. Beyond this, there has been sympathy—principally among what remains of the 'left'—for the claims which incomers to these societies make and even for the hostilities which they express. This sympathy for incomers may also be accompanied in some non-Muslims by disdain for, and the placing by them of obstacles in the way of, fellow non-Muslims who seek to defend their own societies' ways of life. At the spectrum's furthest extreme, and among proportionately very few, there has been active engagement by some non-Muslims with their own polity's foes, to the extent of joining them in battle or in other acts of violence.

These are analytical categories only. In the real world, and in the ebb and flow of real event, the same individual has been able to combine—or veer between—several of these responses, whether or not such responses were inconsistent with one another. The striking of mere poses has also suggested adherence to this or that standpoint when it has not actually been the case. Non-Muslim action, inaction and reaction in response to the Muslim presence in the non-Islamic world, or to Islam in general, have also matched and reflected the volatility of the Islamic upheaval itself. But in the matter of the 'taking of liberties' by Muslims in, and from, the non-Islamic world, there have been several constants. Among them has been the making of often inordinate moral and other demands to entitlement in and against non-Islamic societies. Such demands have often not only gone unopposed but have sometimes been promoted by non-Muslims themselves.

In consequence, some Muslims in the United States, in Britain and in other European countries have shown support for Islamism's attacks on the West while expecting that their civic and other entitlements will be satisfied in full. It is an expectation which has generally been justified in the event. 'Taking liberties' here has had its common-or-garden sense. Some Muslim leaders, notwithstanding that many were British citizens, therefore felt able publicly to ask Iran not to lift the *fatwa* on Salman Rushdie, a British citizen also.

In October 1990, an Islamic conference in Bradford of mainly British Muslims also endorsed Iraq's call for a 'holy war against Western forces', British forces included, in the Gulf. Of Saddam Hussein, it was freely declared by local Muslim citizens—even if the declaration was an exaggeration—that 'every Muslim in Birmingham supports him'. A 'savage war' was being waged by Britain and others with the intent of 'destroying an Arab country', declared a National Muslim Conference of two hundred 'British imams' in January 1991, at the time of the Gulf conflict. 'We will never rest', a Muslim speaker told the crowd at a central London rally in February 1991, 'until the forces of the allies are destroyed, until the desert sands are wet with their blood'; the 'blood', doubtless, of fellow-British citizens included. The speaker would not give his name. 'We are all called Abdullah', a representative of the rally told the press.

In a democracy, the 'national interest' may of course be construed to be whatever the individual believes it to be. It could in this instance have dictated belligerency, or non-intervention, or conscientious pacific resistance. But 'national interest' was not the issue in this non-civic debate. Instead, a victory over fellow-citizens was being willed. 'It is not a question of Saddam Hussein, but of the land and resources of the Muslim people', declared Sher Azam, a Bradford Muslim leader. The putative 'national interest' was not a consideration to him, British national as he might be. The French Islamic Association similarly expressed strong support for Saddam Hussein in the 1991 Gulf War, whatever might be the fate of fellow-Frenchmen. A song entitled 'Go on Saddam, Strike Them Down!' was said to be the 'top selling cassette' of 1991 in Muslim areas of Paris.

After a further ten years of the Islamic and Arabic revival—and of the weakening of the 'national idea' in the West itself—it could come as no moral or political surprise that, in the wake of the attack on the World Trade Center, no less than 40 per cent of British Muslims declared (according to a *Sunday Times* poll) that bin Laden 'had reason to mount a war against the United States'. More than one-third of respondents thought that efforts to capture or kill bin Laden were 'unjustified'; 40 per cent even thought that 'Britons'—which is to say fellow-Muslim citizens of Britain—who decided to 'fight with the Taliban' were 'justified' in doing so. The gloss put on this by the chairman of the Council of Imams and Mosques of the United Kingdom was that Muslim support in Britain for the West's foes was a demonstration of the 'natural sympathy which the British show for the underdog'. This was itself an explanation redolent of the Twelve Devices.

The holding of public position, or civic office, by a Muslim in a Western liberal democratic society has also appeared to be no moral barrier to espousing and expressing views which took no account of, or even threatened, the public good. In November 2001, a Muslim city councillor in Glasgow declared that Osama bin Laden's 'grievances' were (again) 'justified', even if his 'actions' were 'wrong'. It was a familiar division of the moral spoils, but one to be found among non-Muslims also. In September 2002, on the anniversary of the attack on the World Trade Center, other Muslims went further. At a conference held at London's Finsbury Park mosque, the attack was described—with a morally infelicitous pun—as a 'towering day in history'.

Not only was the attack 'legitimate', declared a 'British-based Saudi', Muhammad al-Massari, but there was 'still much more to do'. In August 2003, a conference called in London by the radical Muslim group al-Muhajiroun celebrated 9/11 as the 'come-uppance of the USA', and described the hijackers as the 'Magnificent 19' in posters put up in London streets. In November 2004, the above-mentioned al-Massari again told *The Times* that British soldiers—'they are the enemy'—were 'legitimate targets for the Iraqi people. I don't know what universe you are living in', he added. 'Do you think it is okay to kill British troops?' his interviewer asked. 'Indeed it is', he replied. Of two Iraqi-born British Muslims discovered in August 2004 to be fighting for Moqtada al-Sadr's 'Mahdi army' in Najaf in Iraq, the Muslim Council of Britain thought, with related insouciance, that it would be 'bizarre' if they were to be prosecuted for treason. Yet the two British citizens had declared that it was ' good to protect your country'—meaning Iraq, not Britain. After the London attacks of July 2005, there were similar responses. The 'disbanded' al-Muhajiroun's former leader, the Syrian-born Omar Bakri Mohammed—who, after being deported from Saudi Arabia in 1993, was granted 'indefinite leave' to remain in Britain, an entitlement revoked in August 2005 while he was 'on holiday' in Beirut—was said to have described the suicide-bombers as the 'fabulous four'. Widespread 'understanding' of the motives for, if not the methods of, the attacks was expressed by both Muslims and non-Muslims; and the proposal that militant Islamist groups in Britain be banned was swiftly decried by their supporters as 'part of an anti-Islamic agenda'.

Slyer Muslim argument in the diaspora could regard Islamist violence and threat of violence as exaggerated, and object to the taking of protective measures against attack. An increase in police 'stop and search' methods directed at 'Asians' in Britain was described in July 2004 by the Islamic Human Rights Commission as 'appalling'; it was an expression of an 'institutional Islamophobic society', and was 'alienating Muslim youth'. National security measures were the outcome of a 'hullabaloo over the terrorist threat to the UK', asserted a Muslim writer in the *Guardian* in April 2004; the 'bogey of terrorism' needed to be 'banished' from British legislators' minds, similarly argued Faisal Bodi in August 2004, again in the *Guardian*.

Yet also in the *Guardian*, in April 2004, Fuad Nahdi had contradictorily suggested that Britain indeed faced the trouble about which his fellow-Muslims were so dismissive. Unless a 'serious strategy' was adopted to deal with the 'poverty, exclusion and discrimination' experienced by the 'new underclass' of Muslims in Britain, 'I am afraid', Nahdi wrote, 'there is little hope for a safe Britain tomorrow'. Also in April 2004, the Islamist cleric Omar Bakri Mohammed had warned that 'several attacks' were being 'prepared by several groups'. He further described it as his 'dream' to see the 'banner of Islam at 10 Downing Street'. 'This is my country, I like living here', he explained. As to such attacks, Bakri felt able to add that 'we don't make a distinction between civilians and non-civilians, innocents and non-innocents, only between Muslims and non-Muslims. The life of an unbeliever has no value, it has no sanctity'.

Indeed, in August 2004, there were arrests—which were reported to have 'angered' some Muslim leaders—in various parts of Britain in connection with an alleged plan to attack Heathrow airport. Over these and other arrests there was said by the Muslim Council of Britain to be 'growing bitterness in the Muslim community'. The premise of much objection was that it was the authorities who were the malefactors, the arrested innocent, and the whole thing, once more, a mere 'hullabaloo'. 'He's a good boy, he respects his elders', insisted a Muslim community spokesman in Gloucester in November 2003, after the arrest of an individual with explosives in his home; he pleaded guilty at the Old Bailey in February 2005 to conspiring to blow up a transatlantic passenger aircraft, had received training in Pakistan and Afghanistan for the purpose, was studying in Britain to become an imam and was jailed for thirteen years.

When 600 kgs of potentially explosive ammonium nitrate fertilizer had been seized in raids from a number of young Muslims in March 2004, it was likewise suggested that the possession of these materials was for a benign purpose. 'What evidence is there to say that these guys who've been arrested were planning to do anything bad with the fertilizer stuff they had with them?' said the father of one of the detained. They were 'just normal kids', 'Manchester United fans', while 'fish and chips' was their 'favourite food' said another father. According to an uncle, they were 'just regular English guys. They are as British as they come. They don't even have beards'. Instead, it was the police who had acted 'like terrorists' during the arrests. 'It's like the Soviet Union', similarly declared a Muslim in Luton, Mahmud Ahmad, after an arrest in the town in August 2004. Again in July 2005, in Leeds, the uncle of one of the London Underground suicide-bombers asserted that his nephew was 'proud to be British'; he was a 'normal lad' and a 'bowler and batsman', a cricketing friend added. Likewise, a trainee journalist at the *Guardian* who was disclosed to be a member of the Islamist Hizb ut-Tahrir—which campaigns for the restoration of the caliphate under Sharia law and is banned in several countries—described himself in an article on the London bombings (entitled 'We Rock the Boat') as 'a Yorkshire lad, born and bred'. In the same fashion, the Yemeni-American members of an alleged 'sleeper cell' in Lackawanna, New York, charged in September 2002 with association with al-Qaeda and each sentenced to prison terms, were 'all-American regular guys', 'cool dudes' and, according to local opinion, 'fond above all of playing soccer'. The similarities in these descriptions on each side of the Atlantic were impressive.

Indeed, it is instructive to consider the actions which some diaspora Muslims have thought it fitting to take in their countries of birth, adoptive citizenship, permitted long-term stay, temporary (and sometimes illegal) residence, higher education, diplomatic posting or asylum. In Australia, Britain, Canada, France, Germany, Spain, the US and many other nations, arrests have been made—leading to trial, sentence or acquittal, detention without trial, deportation, extradition or release—for aiding or trying to aid 'terrorist groups', as by providing them with equipment, including arms and other weapons both for use at home and far afield. There have been arrests for seeking, collecting, laundering and transferring funds from country to country for 'terrorist' ends, sometimes under the guise of charitable purpose; and arrests for providing false and stolen passports, documents and other means to facilitate the movement of Islamists.

There have been arrests for recruiting 'militants' to 'terrorist groups', for joining 'terrorist groups' and for being members of 'sleeper cells' of 'terrorist groups'; and arrests for training at 'terrorist' camps in the use of weapons and explosives. There have been arrests for instigating, volunteering or preparing to carry out attacks in one's own country or elsewhere, as by acquiring documents on military movements, reconnoitring potential targets and making plans of them; arrests for attempting to acquire or acquiring the means, including weapons and explosives, in order to carry out such attacks; and arrests for carrying them out. There have been arrests for fighting alongside other Islamists in active combat abroad, including against forces of one's own native or adoptive country; and arrests for threatening to kill or killing fellow-citizens, Muslim and non-Muslim, or inciting others to do so.

Although involving only relatively small numbers in each country, all this has followed a consistent pattern: that of promoting Islamism, including its worst excesses, avoiding detection, (often) pleading innocence and (often) attempting to appeal to the rule of law and doctrines of human rights for help against detention or prosecution. In the Muslim diaspora in Europe, individuals—always in small numbers—have been found to be, or have been alleged to be, associated with al-Qaeda, including in the planning of the 9/11 attacks. They have similarly been claimed, or have been proved, to have acted as mentors and guides—generally behind the shelter of a 'clerical' role—to Islamist volunteers; to have recruited jihadists for service, or themselves joined combat, in Afghanistan, Bosnia, Iraq and elsewhere; to have provided recruitment video-tapes and 'sermons' of incitement for distribution abroad; to have raised funds for Islamist organisations and activities by mosque-collections of 'charitable' donations, as well as by cheque and credit-card frauds; and to have attempted to make, to have made or to have used explosive devices.

In August 2003, a Saudi diplomat was even expelled from Britain for trying to bribe a British Muslim police-officer to furnish him with information—from the police national computer—on certain individuals living in the United Kingdom who had 'connections with the Middle East'. In December 2003, an Algerian asylum-seeker was arrested on evidence that he was preparing himself for a suicide-bombing in Britain. Of some of these matters, involving an again proportionately small but nevertheless always significant number of individuals, there was often only the briefest notice before a veil of silence—arousing protest from civil libertarians—was drawn over them.

Some Muslims in the United States—whether citizens, 'permanent residents', illegal immigrants, diplomats or students—have been alleged to be, or found to be, engaged in all these types of activity, and in many states of the Union. Cases against Muslim American citizens, whether by birth or naturalisation, have included document fraud and helping to process bogus applications for Muslims for asylum and work visas; giving false information to immigration officials; concealment of affiliation with Islamist organisations; membership of al-Qaeda 'sleeper' cells; and spying on Iraqi dissidents on behalf of the Saddam regime. Funds and military equipment have been sent to Islamist groups, or attempts made to do so; and there have been conspiracies to attack buildings in the United States and in other countries. 'My loyalty is to the Muslims, not the Americans', said one individual charged with the latter.

In Virginia, in New York, in Michigan, in Oregon, in Florida, in Texas, in Washington State and elsewhere, there has been 'terrorist financing', even involving prominent members of the American Muslim community, including through mosque-donations and again false 'charitable' organisations, among them an 'orphan charity', and variously for the benefit of al-Qaeda, Hamas and Lebanese Hezbollah. In upper New York State, jihadists were recruited for action in Afghanistan; in California, prior to the Iraq War, funds were raised for arms purchases for Saddam Hussein. 'I wanted to serve this nation which is dear to me', declared the Iraqi organiser, a permanent resident in the United States, referring to Iraq.

Other cases against Muslim American citizens or residents originating from Iran, Lebanon, Pakistan, Palestine, Saudi Arabia, Somalia and Yemen, among other countries, have included the jailing of a Pakistani American in Ohio in October 2003 for 'aiding and abetting terrorism' and 'conspiring to bring down Brooklyn Bridge'. In January 2004, a Somali Canadian living in Minnesota was charged in Minneapolis with 'conspiring to provide material support and other resources to al-Qaeda'; in June 2004, in Ohio, the Palestinian-American imam of the Islamic Center of Cleveland, Fawaz Mohammed Damra, was convicted of concealing his links to Islamic Jihad.

A prominent Iranian American was similarly accused in February 2004 of attempting to conceal his alleged channelling of funds (through a Saudi 'charity') to Muslim separatists engaged in the civil war in Chechnya. Of a Somali indicted for plotting to blow up a shopping mall in Columbus, Ohio— home to 30,000 Somalis—his brother declared in June 2004 that 'he loved it here. He never had as much freedom. He said it was good to raise his kids here'. 'He was a good American', his cousin added. In October 2004, a founder of the American Muslim Council was sentenced to a twenty-three-year term of imprisonment for taking part in a plot to assassinate the then crown prince Abdullah of Saudi Arabia; in July 2005, a Yemeni cleric was sentenced in New York to seventy-five years imprisonment for conspiring to support al-Qaeda and Hamas; and also in July 2005, an Algerian 'associated with al-Qaeda' was jailed for twenty-two years for plotting to blow up Los Angeles airport.

Some serious indictments against Muslims were dropped at trial, were reduced to lesser charges or collapsed. They included charges of attempted espionage brought against an interpreter and a Muslim chaplain at Guantanamo. Also retracted were suspicions that an Oregon lawyer, a convert to Islam, had been involved in the Madrid bombings of March 2004. 'He is a regular, run-of-the-mill guy', protested his attorney in May 2004. Convictions against Detroit Muslims in June 2003 of 'conspiring to provide material support for terrorism' were overturned by a federal court because of the failure of the prosecution to disclose key evidence to the defence.

But the pattern of these cases has been of complicity, on the part of a minority in the heart of the non-Muslim world itself, with the aims and actions of Islamist organisations of varying stripe. In Belgium, for example, it involved conspiracy to bomb a Belgian air-base used by NATO, which led to a ten-year sentence in October 2003; provision of false passports and other documents for Islamist itinerants in the world; recruitment (yet again) for jihadist training, trafficking of arms to the Islamist movement in Algeria and so on.

In December 2003, a Palestinian Canadian admitted planning to carry out attacks, on behalf of Hamas, upon Israeli diplomats and other officials visiting Canada and the United States. In France, 'charitable' fronts, among them day-care centres and kindergartens, were closed for their links to Maghrebian Islamist groups. Investigations were launched and charges brought against French Muslim citizens and residents, including mosque officials, for falsification of identity papers, again for recruitment of jihadists, and even for the planning of attacks against Russian interests in France in reprisal for the violences committed by Russian forces in Chechnya—another long filiation of the kind earlier referred to.

In Germany in November 2003, an Egyptian graduate of an Afghan training-camp was jailed for plotting bomb-attacks on Jewish targets in Germany; twenty-two German citizens and residents (some illegally in Germany) of Algerian, Bulgarian, Egyptian, Libyan and Tunisian origin—one of whom had used eight false identities, and some of whom also had French, Belgian and Dutch travel documents—were arrested in five German states in January

2005, accused of recruiting for jihad, providing false documents to jihadists and so on. In Switzerland, there were arrests in January 2004 of resident Muslims, said to be associated with al-Qaeda, for having provided 'logistical support' for attacks on Western residential compounds in Saudi Arabia. Also in January 2004, a group of Turkish Muslims in Switzerland were said to be leading members of the Great Eastern Islamist Raiders' Front, alleged to have been involved in the bombings in Istanbul in November 2003.

As has been shown, the actions of certain diaspora Muslims have not been confined to their places of domicile. Temporarily leaving the non-Islamic world, usually in the expectation of returning to it with rights and entitlements intact, a small minority has journeyed far and wide in order to pursue Islamism's aims. British Muslims have trained at al-Qaeda camps in Afghanistan; been implicated in bombing-campaigns in Jordan; carried out a suicide-bombing in Tel Aviv; been involved in kidnapping foreigners for ransom in India; lured the journalist Daniel Pearl into a deadly trap in Karachi; fought—and were killed, wounded and captured—in Bosnia, and with the Taliban and al-Qaeda; and joined Islamist forces in Iraq.

In the letters pages of *The Times* and *Daily Telegraph*, debate was joined—as in November 2001—upon whether the joining of the ranks of al-Qaeda by Muslims of British citizenship was an act of 'treason'. Yes, argued one side, for it constituted 'adherence to the sovereign's enemies' under ancient statute. No, argued the other, for Britain was not at war with Afghanistan, for example, and al-Qaeda was 'not a state'; while Muslims rejected the very idea that a British Muslim could be charged with treason.

American Muslims, again small in number, trained in Afghanistan, fought with the Taliban, went to Libya to collect funds for Islamists operating from Syria and so forth. French and Spanish Muslims passed to and fro between their countries of adoption and Islamist fronts in the Maghreb and further afield, including in the US and many other countries of Europe. An Indian Muslim was jailed in Bombay for seven years in July 2005 for plotting to hijack passenger aircraft at Heathrow airport and fly them into the House of Commons and Tower Bridge. All these movements and acts have become relative commonplaces. They have not been confined to Muslims by birth, since converts to Islam have also been involved in them.

An Australian Muslim convert received explosives training at an al-Qaeda camp near Kandahar and planned to blow up the Israeli embassy in Canberra, describing it as 'fair game', pleaded guilty and was jailed in June 2004 for nine years; a second Australian convert from Adelaide saw combat in Kosovo and Kashmir, trained at an al-Qaeda camp in 2001 and fought for the Taliban; a third trained in Afghanistan and agreed to be an al-Qaeda 'sleeper' in Australia. British converts to Islam have, among other things, sought to blow up a transatlantic flight with explosives in a shoe, fought with the Taliban and against Indian forces in Kashmir, been tasked with blowing up targets in Britain and been jailed in Egypt for supporting an outlawed Islamist group there.

American converts to Islam, described in the *Washington Post* in September 2002 as a 'particularly dangerous subset of al-Qaeda because they may not draw much scrutiny and can travel easily on US passports', also fought with the Taliban and associated themselves with al-Qaeda. An American Muslim convert killed fellow-soldiers in Kuwait; a former US Marine, also a convert to Islam, established links with violent Islamist separatists in the Philippines; another was charged with helping to train Pakistani Islamists fighting in Kashmir; and a convert tank-crew member of the National Guard's 81st Armour Brigade was said to have attempted to pass military information to undercover agents posing as members of al-Qaeda. He was sentenced to life imprisonment at a court-martial in Seattle in September 2004. A French convert to Islam was jailed in September 2003 in Morocco for plotting to 'foment an uprising', and another, after training at al-Qaeda camps, was convicted in June 2004 of plotting an attack on the US embassy in Paris. A Filipino convert to Islam confessed to having planted explosives on a ferry which caught fire in February 2004 in Manila Bay, killing more than a hundred people; a German convert to Islam, with links to Hezbollah, was sentenced to ten years' imprisonment by an Israeli court in 1999 after carrying out a 'scouting mission' in order to look for suitable supermarkets or cinemas in which to blow himself up.

In most instances in which diaspora Muslims were involved, the rights of citizenship or the protections of residence had not been requited, despite the fact that these rights and protections were sometimes gained after flight to safety from fellow-Muslims in non-democratic Islamic countries. In January 2003, during a protest in Washington against the Iraq War, Mousa Masjid al-Islam, an imam, took the podium to declare that the 'world's problems' would 'never be solved as long as we have these greedy murderers and imperialists like George Bush sitting in the White House'. It was 'revolution time, brothers and sisters', he declared. This has long been a convention of rhetoric, but his assertion that the 'people of the world' were 'waiting for us'—the 'us' including Muslim citizens and residents of the United States—was less so. It implied not merely a sympathy for 'the oppressed', but support for the foes of the nation upon whose rights he was reliant for his own freedom of speech. It was 'taking liberties' once more.

However, his argument was securely grounded in the hostilities of some non-Muslims to their own liberal democratic societies. It did not need an imam to put the view that the United States was a 'terrorist state', or that America was 'the greatest danger to peace on the planet', since Islamist attacks on American 'imperialism' or American 'aggression' were echoed by some non-Muslims themselves. It was a commonality of view which could be said to have given licence to Islamist excesses. The assertion that 'the West' was the 'force of all evil', as the radical British Islamist, Kalim Siddiqui, put it in February 1991, was plausible even to a minority of non-Muslims.

Moreover, non-Muslim support, express or implied, for Islamist or Arab causes did not require training at an al-Qaeda camp or actual participation in combat to make its influence felt. Thus, the non-Muslim US attorney of Sheikh Omar Abdel Rahman, convicted in October 1995 for masterminding the first attack on the World Trade Center in 1993, was herself convicted in February 2005 for, among other things, knowingly transmitting the imprisoned Rahman's violent instructions to his followers in Egypt and elsewhere. Indeed, for non-Muslims to 'see matters the Muslim way' became increasingly widespread as the confidence and strength of Islam in the world grew, and was both an aid to, and evidence of, this advance. The claim, by Senator Jay Rockefeller of West Virginia in July 2004, that Americans had 'fostered' a 'deep hatred in the Muslim world' against themselves—which would 'grow', he threateningly added—was of this type.

As we shall see later, there was also no shortage of non-Muslims ready to argue that 'jihad', for example, did not have a threatening meaning. Euphemisims for violent jihadists were systematically used in the Western press and other media. 'Our editorial policy', explained Reuters managing editor, 'is not to use emotive words' and 'protect editorial integrity'. Hence, although national policies had already decreed that the Third World War was a 'war on terror', 'terrorist' was for many a taboo word, as already mentioned. After the murder of Theo van Gogh in Holland in November 2004, the *New York Times* even used the term 'conservative Muslims' for violent Islamists, and 'conservative Islamic revival' for the Islamist advance.

In a statement by Osama bin Laden vowing to 'bleed America', he was described by the Associated Press in November 2004 as 'calm', 'forceful' and 'shrewd'. 'God help Bush', exclaimed an American commentator in the *Guardian*, also in November 2004, 'if America suffers another terrorist attack'. It was an inversion which played the Islamist game for it. At Yasser Arafat's death in the same month, the UN secretary-general was 'deeply moved'; President Chirac learned 'with emotion' of the death of a 'man of courage'; the

EU praised him for his 'single-minded commitment'; Tony Blair referred to the award to Arafat of the Nobel Peace Prize; and Chancellor Schröder regretted that 'it was not granted to Yasser Arafat to complete his life's work'.

Similarly naive have been the injunctions to parlay with the most violent of Islamist groups. In June 2002, in a letter to *The Times*, a Clifford Hughes even argued that what was required was 'a meeting between al-Qaeda and the United Nations', in order to 'find out what really motivates al-Qaeda' and to ascertain whether there was a 'means whereby some understanding and coop-eration might evolve'. In January 2004, in the *Guardian*, it was likewise asserted that the time had come to 'bite the political bullet'—an unfortunate metaphor—'and open talks with the Taliban'. And when five British Muslims who had been arrested in Afghanistan and detained at Guantanamo were released in March 2004, an article in the *Guardian*, entitled 'The Famous Five with Stories to Tell', listed in admiring detail the 'media deals' which were being offered to them; their release, the newspaper reported, had 'sparked a bidding war among newspapers'. Lurking behind some of this, there could even be detected a Lawrence of Arabia–like romanticisation of Islam.

In domestic matters concerning the Muslim diaspora, other varieties of non-Muslim naivete were potentially helpful to the Islamist cause. For example, they posited the development of a 'British Islam' resting upon the 'state-supported training of Imams', and the 'teaching of Arabic to young Muslims in Britain' under state auspices, as the *Guardian* proposed in April 2004. Public policy in Britain was said to require 'religious sensitisation'; the French state should help finance the construction of mosques, thought its finance minister, Nicolas Sarkozy, in October 2004; the British education system was said in June 2004 to be 'failing Muslim pupils'. In April 2004, Man-chester city council even announced that it wanted to set up and fund a school in Bangladesh for British Muslim pupils who had been taken out of their schools for extended periods during term-time, so that they could 'continue their education'. It was said by supporters of the scheme to be a 'price worth paying to invest in the education of these children'.

There were other 'prices', some idiotic, which were held in the non-Muslim world to be 'worth paying' in order to accommodate Muslim wishes and scruples. In December 2004 alone, these 'prices' included banning Father Christmas from a shopping centre in Birmingham, the concealment of a stained glass portrait of Saint Luke at a hospital chapel in Calgary in Canada, the return to City Hall by local elementary schools in a rural French district of gift chocolates shaped like Christian crosses, the substitution in a school near Milan of the word 'Jesus' with the word 'virtue' in a Christmas hymn and of a Nativity play with 'Little Red Riding Hood' in the Italian city of Treviso, in order not to offend Muslim children. For the same reason, in March 2003, the head-teacher of a nursery school in West Yorkshire allegedly banned books from the classroom which contained stories about pigs.

There have been equally naive attempts, but of larger scope, to accommodate host cultures to minoritarian Muslim interests. This has been despite the fact that few Muslims, especially Islamists, would have countenanced similar respect being shown to the expectations of non-Muslims living in Muslim countries, especially in matters of religion; Saudi Arabia will not even permit non-Muslims to become citizens of the country. Such accommodations included announcements by public officials in a provincial French town of the intention to 'place Islam on an equal footing with Catholicism in all respects' in the town's public life. In the *Observer* in December 2003, it was similarly asserted that 'for too long Islam has been considered a foreign religion. It is no more so than that other great Middle Eastern religion, Christianity', an editorial announced. In Holland, the state provided funding for Islamic clubs run by militant Islamist clerics but withdrew its subsidies to the Salvation Army in June 2005 when the latter refused permanent employment to two Muslims. In Ontario, proposals— from non-Muslims as well as Muslims—to allow the court-system to administer Sharia law in civil disputes between Muslims were rejected in May 2005 by the Quebec legislature. But in Canada pressures for the establishment of Sharia courts to settle family disputes continued.

In December 2003, a Saudi-backed conference held in Texas included an address by an Islamist cleric, Allamah ibn Jibreen, who only two months before had invoked the blessings of the deity on Osama bin Laden. 'May God aid him and bring victory to him and by him', the cleric had declared; while in May 2005, at the behest of an Italian Muslim activist who had earlier objected to the presence of crucifixes on the walls of his children's school, a judge in the city of Bergamo ordered the writer Oriana Fallaci to stand trial for defaming Islam in her book *The Force of Reason.*

Hence, it was not necessary for Muslims, or Muslim converts, to fight in Bosnia, Kosovo, Kashmir or Iraq for Islamism's point to be made, and for Islam's cause to be promoted in the non-Muslim world. More might be achieved by pronouncing—as did a British member of parliament during the Iraq War—that the British and American invaders of Iraq were 'like wolves'. As there were communist 'fellow-travellers' in the past, so now (and again on the 'left'), there were what one might regard as fellow-travellers of Islamism. In the late 1930s, sections of the 'peace movement' were not shy about sharing platforms and even positions with Nazi sympathisers. In Britain, France, Italy and other countries, the 'peace movement', anti-'globalisers' and Church activists similarly did not hesitate, despite their 'progressivism', to work alongside the most militant and reactionary of Islamist organisations and individuals as well as with benignly pacific Muslims.

Such stands also served to revive the fading Western 'left's' near-lost sense of purpose. As a spokesman for the Muslim Association of Britain put it in May 2004, 'the alliance between Muslims and the left in Britain has been a significant phenomenon. Nothing can better illustrate the compatibility of Islam and the West than the diversity of people marching side by side for peace and justice'. In August 2004, anti-war, civil rights and Muslim groups in the US declared that they stood 'shoulder to shoulder' in demanding an 'end to the US government's wars of aggression and disregard of civil rights and liberties'.

These stands were not confined to the 'left'. In March 2003, on the eve of the Iraq War, an anonymous British 'serving officer' declared (to the 'right-wing' *Sunday Telegraph*) that he was 'going to the Gulf with a heavy heart'—as who would not have done?—and that there was 'something McCarthyite about the atmosphere which has spawned this war'. In September 2003, the *Guardian* gave space to a 'serving US soldier' to describe the war in Iraq as the 'ultimate atrocity'. The 'war on terror' itself was termed—again by a commentator in the *Guardian* in July 2003—as 'callous and futile', and a month later as an 'easy-to-assemble tool-kit' and a 'smokescreen'. Yet the 'pan-global' campaigns of the most radical of Islamist groups in Britain, al-Muhajiroun, was described as 'seductive' in the same paper in May 2003. In September 2003, to the *Guardian*'s commentator, Hugo Young, the war against Iraq was 'shameful'. In October 2003, it was declared by another commentator in the same paper as 'one of the most audacious smash-and-grab enterprises in the history of thievery'. It was a proposition to which a minority of Muslims did not even assent themselves.

Criticism of the invasion of Iraq was justified and necessary in the cause of free debate. It also encouraged the further taking of liberties with and from democratic societies. Moreover, the barrage of criticism had its own momentum, once more feeding upon itself. The former UN weapons inspector, Hans Blix, told a Danish newspaper in April 2004—and was eagerly taken up by the Western press agencies—that the 'negative aspects' of the war in Iraq outweighed the benefits of overthrowing the Saddam regime. Fifty former British diplomats declared in the same month that the policies being pursued by Britain and the US in Iraq were 'doomed to failure'. Commentators in Britain and the US asserted that they had been 'hoaxed' by the 'neo-cons' in the Bush administration. The father of a beheaded US hostage declared in May 2004 that his son had 'died for the sins of George Bush and Donald Rumsfeld'.

In the *Guardian* in July 2004, an editorialist, using the language of Islamism, went further. He described the Iraqi interim prime minister as a 'collaborator', the legal proceedings against Saddam Hussein as a 'show trial'—the same view as Saddam's—and the Islamist insurgency in Iraq as a 'classic resistance movement'. In the language of Islamism, another *Guardian* commentator had already proclaimed that 'liberation' would 'only come [to Iraq] when the Americans leave'. Two Italian hostages—released for ransom in September 2004—pronounced that the 'guerrilla war' against the Americans was justified, and that elections held in Iraq while US and other forces were in the country would have 'no legitimacy'. A former British cabinet minister in October 2004 likened insurgents in Iraq to the French Resistance in the Second War, and their fight to that conducted against British colonialism in Ireland.

Honorary Arabism and Islamism could go further. 'Iraq is fighting for all the Arabs', pronounced George Galloway, MP for a Glasgow constituency. 'Where are the Arab armies?' he demanded to know. The wish, or will, to see the United States brought down could thus be shared, and sometimes in almost identical terms, by Muslims and non-Muslims alike. Among 'intellectuals' there was often more open-mindedness about the Islamist or Arab causes than there was about the motives of those who opposed such causes. In October 2003, the archbishop of Canterbury pronounced (of al-Qaeda) that terrorists could have 'serious moral goals'. Moreover, such 'goals' might be 'intelligible or desirable', notwithstanding the 'unspeakably wicked means' used to pursue them.

But there was relatively little readiness to consider that there might have been 'intelligible or desirable' goals involved in going to war against Iraq. To many it was clear, and even a matter which did not merit debate, that there had been no just cause for the Iraq War. It was similarly clear (to some), as in the *Guardian* in October 2003, that the Iranians not only had no nuclear weapons but, in the teeth of growing evidence to the contrary, had 'no plans for one'. Whether true or false, it was a position fully in accord with what Iran was itself asserting, while such case as there might be for the invasion of Iraq was often assumed to be beneath consideration: a double standard.

Many have proceeded from the assumption that the non-Muslim world's actions are almost by definition wrong. This view has been held even without the encouragement given to it by the falsehoods which preceded the Iraq War. That is, there has been a predisposition to accept the notion of Western 'evil' as the *primum mobile* of Islamic angers, and thus to vindicate a large part of the

Islamist case and cause. Hence, the worldwide counterattacks and counter-measures against Islamism and Islamists, and the violence and illiberalism of some of the means used, merely intensified the opposition of many non-Muslims to their own governments' policies and actions. Such opposition, both just and unjust, was further to Islamism's gain.

In some of these countermeasures, the laws of war were observed. In others, the abrogation of such laws, as by the US, was sought to be justified on the grounds that its opponents did not themselves observe them. In many places, anti-Islamists shot first and asked questions afterwards, or covered the bodies over and moved on. In Russia, even the old Stalinist language returned as Islamist 'bandits' in the Caucasus were 'liquidated'. Extra-judicial killings of Islamists were most used in Afghanistan, Algeria, Egypt, by Israel, in pre- and post-Saddam Iraq, Kashmir, Kuwait, Pakistan, the Philippines, Russia, Saudi Arabia, Syria and Yemen; that is, in Muslim and non-Muslim countries alike. 'Clashes', 'crackdowns', 'encounters', 'gun-battles', and 'shootouts' covered a multitude of sins, including the mistaken shooting by police, at point-blank range, of an innocent Brazilian electrician on the London Underground in July 2005.

But in 2004 alone, those disposed of in such fashion included a Taliban senior commander; leaders of the Algerian Salafist Group for Preaching and Combat and of Kashmir's Jamait ul-Mujahideen; the reputed second-in-command of Ansar al-Islam in Iraq; Hamas, Islamic Jihad and al-Aqsa Brigades' leaders in the Palestinian territories and in Syria; the rebel leader of the 'Believing Youth' movement in Yemen; and several senior al-Qaeda figures in Saudi Arabia. They included Khaled Ali Haj, a Yemeni, described as the 'most dangerous' al-Qaeda operative 'in the region', who was shot dead in March 2004; 'al-Qaeda's leader' in the kingdom, Abdulaziz al-Muqrin, killed in June 2004; Abdulkarim al-Mejjati, said to have been the 'mastermind' behind the May 2003 bombings in Casablanca, who was killed in a 'shootout' in April 2005; Younis Mohammed Ibrahim al-Hayari, killed 'during a dawn raid by security forces' in Riyadh in July 2005; and Saleh al-Awfi, thought to have been 'al-Qaeda's successor leader in Saudi Arabia', killed in a 'gun-battle' in Medina in August 2005. In March 2005, similarly, three of the leaders of the Abu Sayyaf group were killed by Filipino police inside a maximum security prison in Manila during the 'suppression of a revolt'.

Between 2003 and 2005 in Afghanistan, Algeria, Chechnya, China, Egypt, India, Indonesia, Israel, Jordan, Kazakhstan, Kyrgyzstan, Lebanon, Malaysia, Morocco, Oman, the Philippines, Russia, Saudi Arabia, Singapore, Syria, Thailand, Tunisia, Turkey, Pakistan, Uzbekistan and Yemen—among other countries—Islamists by the hundreds, in total, were arrested, detained, arraigned, convicted and sentenced to terms of imprisonment or death. 'Dozens of militants' were also reported in March 2004 to have been detained, often under American pressure, in Djibouti, in Ethiopia, in Eritrea, in Kenya— where four men were tried for the November 2002 bombing of a resort hotel and acquitted in June 2005—and in Sudan.

Among those seized were Rachid Ouakali (also known as Abu Tourab), leader of the radical Armed Islamic Group, the GIA, captured in Algeria in November 2003; Mohammed al-Zawahiri, the brother of al-Qaeda's second-in-command, detained in Egypt; four leaders of the Salafia Jihadia group, put on trial in Morocco in August 2003 and sentenced to death, and its 'spiritual leader', Muhammad al-Fizazi, sentenced to thirty years' imprisonment; Jamal Badawi, one of Yemen's leading Islamists, wounded in a 'shoot-out' and captured in Yemen's Abyan province in March 2004; and Riduan Isamuddin, *alias* Hambali, a 'senior operative of al-Qaeda' in south-east Asia, who was captured in Thailand in August 2003 and transferred to US custody. Other leading 'al-Qaeda' and Islamist operatives, sometimes described as 'big catches', were detained in Britain, Dubai, post-Saddam Iraq, Lebanon, Libya, Pakistan and the Philippines. They included Khaled Sheikh Muhammad, the alleged 'mastermind' of the 9/11 attacks; Ramzi bin al-Shibh, one of the 9/11 planners; Ahmed Khalfan Gailani, said to have been implicated in the 1998 bombings of two US embassies in East Africa; Abu Faraj al-Libbi, described as 'third in command of the al-Qaeda terror network', captured in Pakistan's North-West Frontier province in May 2005; and Haroon Rashid Aswat, a 'senior British al-Qaeda operative', arrested in Zambia in July 2005.

Islamist organisations were proscribed; funds were blocked, as by Britain, Switzerland and the US; individuals and groups were put under covert surveillance; and plots, sometimes of large dimension, were said to have been 'foiled' in Britain, France, Germany, Jordan, Indonesia, Kuwait, Lebanon, Pakistan, the Philippines, Russia, Saudi Arabia, Singapore, Spain and Turkey, among other countries. Individuals round the world were seized in 'swoops' and 'raids', held for interrogation, in some cases tortured for evidence, released without trial, brought before judges—both military and civilian—and sentenced to terms of imprisonment, sometimes very long, or to death as in Afghanistan, Jordan, Indonesia, Morocco, Pakistan, the Philippines, Syria and Yemen; seven of these eight Muslim countries.

In most Western liberal democracies, new legal measures, or a toughening of old ones—including by the creation of new offences—were adopted in the name of 'anti-terrorism'. Such acts included the Patriot Act (2001) in the US, and in Britain the Terrorism Act (2000), the Anti-Terrorism, Crime and Security Act (2001) and the Prevention of Terrorism Act (2005). Both the British and American legislation of 2001 made possible internment of foreign nationals without trial.

Thus, in Britain, the powers which were taken included those of holding foreign detainees on grounds of mere 'reasonable' suspicion, a lower standard of proof than required in the normal criminal process, and even of denying access to the information on the basis of which the detentions had been made. Foreign detainees, who were few in total, included 'senior figures' in al-Qaeda and in an Algerian Salafist group, as well as others 'linked to al-Qaeda'—the majority Maghrebians—among whom were individuals who had been convicted *in absentia* for 'terrorist' offences in their own countries. Some at first fell into a limbo of imprisonment, in some cases with their names unknown. It was asserted by defenders of these emergency powers that trials in open court would compromise the means of investigation, the investigators and their informants; the courts were to take a different view.

Moreover, the right given to foreign detainees held in Britain under the 2001 Act to leave the country of their own volition was (in most cases) nugatory. Indeed, most of the foreign nationals found themselves with, in effect, an absolute right to stay in Britain, albeit under detention. This was because the European Convention on Human Rights, to which Britain is a signatory, prohibits deportation to countries—including the United States with its death-penalty, and whether or not such country be a detainee's country of origin—where there is a risk of suffering inhumane or degrading treatment. Suspected 'terrorists' who were wanted in their own countries, and where the fate which awaited them might involve forbidden forms of treatment, therefore had nowhere else to go than the 'high-security' cells in which they found themselves. For the British state was not prepared to release them, until given no choice but to do so under human rights lobby and judicial pressures.

Thus, in December 2004, Britain's Law Lords unanimously declared illegal the detention of foreign nationals without trial. They did so on the grounds that human rights legislation made such detention 'discriminatory'— the diaspora Islamist argument also—and that such response to the threat of 'terrorism' was excessive. For the emergency powers taken by the government singled out foreign nationals for special treatment, and made possible indefinite incarceration without proper judicial process. Although the detainees included individuals who were alleged to have been involved in the planning of attacks in Britain and elsewhere in Europe, and despite the fact that they were believed by the government to pose a serious threat, they were ordered to be released.

The 'real threat to the life of the nation', Lord Hoffman, one of the Law Lords, declared, 'comes not from terrorism but from laws such as these', that is laws which permitted detention without trial. In the view of Lord Steyn in June 2005, the governments both of the United States and Britain had even 'whipped up public fear since September 11 2001' and been 'determined to bend established international law to their will and to undermine its essential structures'. Such judgments as his, and that of Lord Hoffman, were to be severely criticised (by some) after the July 2005 London bombings on the grounds, among others, that they had placed considerations of liberty above those of security, and of human rights above those of the public good.

Among those released was Abu Qatada, a Jordanian-born 'cleric' with alleged connections to Mohammed Atta, the leader of the 9/11 hijackers. He was set free in March 2005 under 'control orders' designed to restrict his activities, but was re-arrested in August 2005 after the London bombings. 'Control orders', which had been introduced by the government in the 'national security interest' and provided for a range of measures from house-arrest to electronic tagging and restrictions on the use of mobile phones and computers, themselves provoked a storm of parliamentary protest. Not only *habeas corpus* but Magna Carta was invoked. In the wake of the London bombings, however, 'the public mood' was declared to be 'different'; 'things' had 'changed'; a 'new balance' needed to be struck.

There followed proposals, plans and decisions to create new criminal offences, and to introduce new 'administrative' measures not requiring legislation. The offences would include 'indirect incitement' of 'terrorism'—as by preaching 'hatred' and 'condoning' or 'glorifying' 'terrorism'—and giving or receiving training in 'terrorist techniques'. New 'administrative' measures would make it easier to deport and 'exclude' those held to be guilty of 'unacceptable behaviours', including the advocacy or justification of violence and the fostering of 'hatred'; would increase the permissible period of pre-charge detention; and would extend existing powers to strip British citizens of their citizenship, whether acquired by birth or naturalisation. It would also be made 'easier' to vet incoming imams, to close mosques and to ban Islamist groups. There was even a threat, 'should legal obstacles arise', to amend the Human Rights Act.

After 9/11, the United States had introduced the Patriot Act. Under it, those designated 'enemy combatants'—that is, neither ordinary criminal defendants nor prisoners of war—could be held indefinitely in secret locations inside and outside the United States, and without access to lawyers. The US held many of its mainly-foreign prisoners in Cuba, intendedly so that they were out of the reach of US constitutional protections of due process and of fundamental rights. As in Britain, the American authorities refused to release the detainees' names. Again it was argued that by disclosing who was in custody, too much would be revealed of the trails which had been followed, the information used, and the identities of suspects who had been left at liberty by design. For the act also provided enhanced powers of covert surveillance, rights of search—including of library and medical records—and phone-taps; and in July 2005, both the House of Representatives and the Senate, unanimously in the latter case, voted to extend 'indefinitely' almost all the main provisions of the Act, but introduced greater judicial oversight of anti-'terrorism' operations and required increased reporting upon them to Congress.

Provision had also been made in the United States in November 2001 for trials before military commissions of captive foreign nationals, under detention in Afghanistan, Cuba and elsewhere, who could be accused of having violated the laws of war. In American estimation, fighters for the Taliban or al-Qaeda, and other members of 'terrorist groups', were not 'lawful combatants' but mercenary irregulars or mere 'killers'. They were therefore denied prisoner of war status on the grounds that they had failed to distinguish themselves from civilian non-combatants, as an army's soldiers (in theory) must. They had 'waged war' as members of fighting organisations which were not armies in the 'accepted' sense. But in their own eyes most saw themselves as foot soldiers in an Army of God, fighting a holy war. There could never have been a wider gulf in perception.

Trials would be held in secret, statements which had been made under duress would be admissible in evidence, and there were to be lower standards of proof (once more) than in ordinary criminal trials. There would be a right of appeal, although not to the US courts. On the one hand, the great majority of the prisoners taken in Afghanistan and Iraq were released. On the other, the Department of Justice went further: even illegal immigrants and asylum-seekers in the US with no known links to 'terrorism' could be detained indefinitely, if it was felt—without hearings of their cases, or right of recourse to release on bond or bail—that to release them might 'endanger national security'.

Taken together, such provisions in Britain and America, both those enacted and those further proposed, could be said to have been a taking of liberties in liberty's name, in order to meet the risk that still greater liberties would be taken by those who had been detained, or were active in their adoptive countries, or who sought entry to them. Civil libertarians fell upon the measures without restraint. Their cries of horror at a 'Kafkaesque nightmare' and a 'new dark age of injustice', or at the 'utter lawlessness' and 'shameless authoritarianism' of these provisions, matched the threats by Islamists of reprisal for the conditions under which detainees were being kept, as at Guantanamo in Cuba, or who had immediate resort to the courts in protest at infringements of their human rights. Others, including those British Islamists who had called on their followers in their adoptive countries to attack fellow-citizens in Afghanistan and Iraq, protested in Britain at the 'betrayal' of Muslims when laws, including against incitement, were sought to be tightened; in July 2005, one British Islamist, Anjem Choudhry, even complained—as if Sharia law were already in force in Britain—that the prime minister had 'broken a covenant in the Koran' by not treating the 'life and wealth of Muslims with sanctity'.

American and British lawyers denounced—again in the words of Britain's Lord Steyn, in November 2003—the creation at Guantanamo of a 'legal black hole' and decried the 'monstrous failure of justice'. Released detainees joined them with complaints of 'torture', 'beatings' and unspecified 'horrific things', and launched legal actions for compensation against the US government. A successful prosecution in Virginia for 'soliciting others to levy war against the United States' was even said by the defendant's lawyers in April 2005 to have been an 'assault on his religious and free speech rights'. Politicians and commentators in the United States spoke of the 'dismantling' of American democracy itself, and in cascades of rhetoric—as in a *New York Times* editorial in November 2003—found not only that a 'mockery' had been made of the American constitution but that 'every American's liberty' had been 'put at risk'; while a leading British trade unionist denounced the 'continuous assaults [sc. of the British law] upon those who seek refuge here as a safe haven'.

In Britain perhaps seven hundred arrests of its citizens had been made by mid-2005, with over one hundred charged but only some twenty convicted. In Spain, during 2004, more than 130 suspected terrorists were arrested. In Russia, some '10,000' individuals were said to have been swept up in September 2004 after the Beslan school seige. In the US in the three years to September 2004, more than three hundred people had been charged with 'terrorism'-related offences. One hundred and eighty had had been convicted, but often only on minor charges, and in a number of cases were acquitted, most often for lack of proof. In some countries, individuals were re-arrested after release from detention, while some ex-Guantanamo detainees released to their home countries were kept in custody, as in Pakistan and France.

Extraditions were also made of wanted 'terrorist' suspects. For example, they were sent from Belgium, Germany and Italy to Spain, from Portugal to

Holland, from Spain to France, from Sweden to Egypt, from Libya to Algeria, from Zambia to Britain, from Malaysia to Indonesia and (allegedly in 'hundreds') from Pakistan to the United States. Suspects and wanted individuals were also handed over by Syria to France and Kuwait, and by Syria and Yemen to Saudi Arabia, and Saudi Arabia to Yemen. France, Germany and the US were among the nations which carried out deportations of Islamists to their home countries, while the Russians deported Muslims back to the Caucasus region from Moscow and other northern cities. The US also carried out covert abductions—or 'renditions', as they were euphemistically called—of 'terror suspects' from foreign countries and had them transported to third countries where they were wanted, including Egypt, Jordan, Morocco and Uzbekistan.

There were other forms of action taken against Islamism and its works in non-Muslim countries, action which could be broadly described as 'cultural'. Between 2001 and 2005 the French interior ministry deported several dozen Muslim clerics, mainly back to the Maghreb; only 10 per cent of France's more than one thousand imams were said in April 2004 to be French citizens, less than half were said to speak French, and 'probably a majority' were said to be illegal immigrants. Those expelled were held to have expressed views which were a threat to 'public order', to 'incite violence', and to offend French conceptions of human rights. These views included pronouncements—as from a Lyons imam with two wives and sixteen children—in favour of polygamy, wife beating and stoning of unfaithful women, as well as approval of the Madrid bombings in March 2004. France's Council of State in December 2004 also ordered the operators of a French satellite to stop carrying transmissions by a Beirut-based Hezbollah television station which, for example, had accused Jews of 'spreading AIDS'.

In May 2004, Germany similarly agreed on new measures to make it easier to deport 'spiritual extremists', while Spain's interior minister announced that he was 'drawing up plans'—which were withdrawn in a chorus of protest—to 'control Islamic radicals', including by 'finding ways' of 'monitoring' the content of preaching in mosques. In September 2004, Germany also banned an 'Arab-Islamic Congress' scheduled to be held in Berlin in order to rally support for 'resistance and intifada'. In November 2004, it cancelled a Pakistani's German citizenship after it was discovered that he had a wife both in Germany and in Pakistan, and also ordered a Turkish Islamist who had been extradited to Turkey—to face charges of treason—to repay a large sum which he had received in social security benefits. Similarly, in December 2004 Germany ordered the deportation to Turkey of a Berlin imam who in a sermon described Germans as 'stinking physically in the eyes of man and morally in the eyes of God', and in February 2005 a Stuttgart imam who had called on worshippers to 'fight or die for Islam', and who had described the United States as a 'Satan', was deported to Egypt. In Holland in January 2003—even before the murder of Theo van Gogh—'political correctness' was declared to be 'in shreds', and even 'multiculturalism' to be 'more a problem than an enrichment'. The '700,000' Muslim immigrants (in a Dutch population of some fifteen million) were told by leading figures across the political spectrum that they were bound, in common with other citizens, to 'assume the obligations of the Dutch humanist tradition'.

Again, in July and August 2005 in the aftermath of the London bombings, France, Italy and Spain each expelled Muslim clerics and preachers, while the French announced that imams who had acquired citizenship would not be protected from deportation. A large number of prayer-halls and mosques in France were also said to have been placed under surveillance. The British planned similar measures, and immediately detained ten 'foreign nationals'. They included, as mentioned earlier, the 'al-Qaeda cleric' and British resident, Abu Qatada, who had been sentenced in absentia to life imprisonment by Jordan in 1998 for involvement in bomb-plots. The government announced that they would be deported for 'reasons of national security'—their human rights defenders and the judiciary allowing—including to countries such as Algeria with unsavoury records of maltreatment of detainees. For its part, Pakistan announced plans in July 2005 to expel an estimated 1,400 foreign students attending the country's Islamic (and Islamist) *madrassas*.

Another type of 'cultural' action had been taken in October 2001 by the mayor of New York, Rudolf Giuliani, when he refused a ten-million-dollar donation to the 'Twin Towers Fund' by Prince al-Waleed bin Talal of Saudi Arabia. As the latter paid over the sum, his simultaneous press-statement criticised American policy in the Middle East and described how 'our Palestinian brethren continue to be slaughtered at the hands of Israelis while the world turns the other cheek'. In response, and handing back the donation, Giuliani accused bin Talal of implicitly attempting to 'rationalise the deadliest attack in history [*sic*]'. There could be 'no justification for savage acts of mass murder', declared Giuliani. Attempts (with cash in hand) to justify them, whether on 'historical, political or religious grounds', were an 'assault on the very principles of civilisation', while 'moral relativism' had 'no place'; there was 'no moral way to sympathise with grossly immoral actions', said the mayor. Harvard University in July 2004 likewise returned a donation from the United Arab Emirates intended to fund a chair in Islamic religious studies, because of the 'anti-Semitic statements' made by individuals connected with the gift.

Similarly, in August 2004 a work visa was denied by the United States—on unspecified 'public safety or national security interests'—to the Swiss Islamist writer Tariq Ramadan, who had been offered a professorship (including in 'peace-building') at the University of Notre Dame. In September 2004 the already-mentioned Fawaz Damra, imam of Ohio's largest mosque, was stripped of his US citizenship for lying about his connections to 'terrorist groups'. In the US this 'cultural' conflict also had other dimensions: in March 2004 publication of a book exploring the links between prominent Saudis and US politicians, including President Bush, was cancelled under legal and other pressures.

Nevertheless, the scale and variety of the 'counter-attacks' in many countries against Islamism did not reduce the sense in diaspora Muslims of entitlement. On the contrary, they tended only to increase it, so that Islamist clerics threatened with deportation felt able to claim a 'right' to continue preaching jihad, while other Islamists sought protection from justice in the rule of law itself. At their side stood civil libertarians who, in Britain for example, described 'anti-terrorist' measures as 'repressive', declared that 'our liberties' were being 'removed', and that an 'authoritarian state was in process of construction'. Moreover, there were sufficient grounds for thinking so, despite the already-mentioned decision by the House of Lords that the imprisonment of foreign nationals without trial was unlawful. For example, the British Court of Appeal had ruled by a majority in August 2004 that evidence obtained through torture carried out by *other* governments—but not evidence obtained in this way by British authorities themselves—could be used in decisions to detain 'terrorist' suspects in Britain. It was known that the CIA, for example, had used 'coercive interrogation methods' against al-Qaeda operatives, including by pushing their heads under water and other forms of duress.

Such judgments, and the introduction—or attempted introduction—in 2004 and 2005 by many Western governments of tougher 'anti-terrorism' measures, were held to be justified by supporters on public policy grounds. However, human rights lawyers and liberal press commentators found such measures themselves 'terrifying' and 'worse than the disease'. They would 'shut down the very democracy that we say we are trying to defend'; would 'alienate' and 'radicalise' Muslims of the diaspora still further; were 'doomed to failure', and so on. Indeed, the argument that Britain, and other countries, by offending or appearing to offend the rule of law themselves, were 'taking liberties' rather than protecting them was now true for many. During 2003 and 2004, US judges struck down as unconstitutional or otherwise unlawful the denial to 'terrorism suspects', American and non-American, of access to lawyers and courts in order to challenge their detentions, expressly and by implication holding that the US administration had exceeded its powers. They also struck down certain of the wide search powers given the FBI under the Patriot Act. A New York federal appeals court in December 2003 ruled that no American citizen could be designated an 'enemy combatant', or be otherwise deprived of his civil rights, without the consent of Congress. The British Law Lords in December 2004 had followed these examples.

In general, the governments of liberal democracies trimmed their sails to such type of decisions as little as possible. They appealed against them when they could, and circumvented them—or sought to circumvent them, as in Britain—when they could not. Moreover, strong arguments continued to be put that human rights law and the Geneva Conventions did 'not apply to terrorists', who were held to be using 'illicit means to conduct armed conflict'. It was therefore thought necessary to meet them on their own ground, and increasingly in their own ways. In addition, Muslims of the diaspora were thought by large numbers of non-Muslims to have a myopic sense of their rights in a liberal order. Thus, a spokesman for the Federation for American Immigration Reform objected in September 2003 that there was 'something almost Orwellian for people violating the laws to demand their rights under the law'. But this 'Orwellian' situation was at the same time being sedulously defended by other non-Muslims, for whom protection of the rights of Muslims in non-Muslim societies had ethical precedence over arguments that such rights were being abused.

Acts of discrimination against Muslim Americans in the United States, for example, were justly condemned. But when Muslims indicated, by their own acts, that their primary loyalties were to their adoptive society's foes, diminishing public sympathy was shown. Therefore, complaints by American Muslims of 'witch-hunts'—as when bogus 'charities' alleged to have channelled 'millions of dollars to terrorists' were raided by federal agents in northern Virginia in October 2003—fell on generally stony ground. Also to fall on deaf ears was the complaint by Abu Qatada, the Jordanian cleric said to have acted as al-Qaeda's point-man in Britain, that he had been a victim of 'prejudice' after his bank-assets were frozen. Similarly, an Algerian—arrested in northern Ireland in November 2003 and accused of receiving training in the making of explosives—protested that he was the victim of 'discrimination'.

'They talk about human rights, they talk about democracy', complained a French Muslim protester in December 2003 against the ban on the *hijab*, 'but where is the liberty here?' Indeed, Muslim appeals in the diaspora to the principles and values of non-Muslim codes of jurisprudence were frequently combined with allegations of the denial of right and 'discrimination'. 'What I don't like', complained Abdul Razak, referring to Muslims arrested in police raids in Leicester in January 2002, 'is that they are considered guilty until proved innocent'. Zacarias Moussaoui, charged in the United States with conspiracy in the attacks of 11 September 2001, similarly declared to a Virginia court in April 2002—during hearings in which he denounced the American justice system—that he was 'innocent until proven guilty'.

Likewise, a former professor at the University of South Florida, Sami al-Arian, who was arrested in February 2003 and indicted for allegedly having been for years a leader of the Palestinian Islamic Jihad—and of having helped to manage its world-wide finances—had also been the American chairman of the National Council to Protect Political Freedom; its Web site advised Arab-Americans to 'know your rights'. Even the earlier-mentioned conviction in April 2005 of a Muslim American for urging fellow-Muslims to 'join the Taliban and fight the United States' was held by a community leader to 'bode ill for the First Amendment'. 'Let Omar Bakri benefit from democracy!' exclaimed the Syrian-born Islamist cleric Omar Bakri Mohammed in April 2004, boasting of his 'sixteen' arrests and releases and at the same time 'dreaming' of Britain's conquest by Islam.

In other ways, too, the laws of a free society were turned to for the protections they offered. For example, Muslim organisations in the United States sought and obtained tax-exempt status as 'charities' under American law, while collecting funds for Islamist groups engaged in violence.

In Britain, Islamists resisting deportation and extradition had recourse to lengthy (and costly) appeals procedures, often supported by the taxpayer. A radical Muslim cleric, accused by the Pakistani authorities of involvement with an Islamic terrorist organisation, took his case to the House of Lords in seeking 'indefinite leave' to remain in Britain and out of the reach of Pakistani justice. Similarly, three alleged associates of Osama bin Laden, one Saudi and two Egyptians, who were wanted for extradition to the United States in connection with the 1998 bombings of US embassies in Kenya and Tanzania, fought a three-year legal battle as far as the House of Lords, at a cost of some £1 million, in order to resist removal from Britain.

In Germany, in September 2004, the Islamist Hizb ut-Tahrir similarly went to the Federal Administrative Court in Leipzig to challenge a banning order against it by the Interior Ministry; the ban had been imposed on the grounds that the group had had contacts with the neo-Nazi German National

Party. In the US, too, the Islamist head of the United Muslim American Association, a non-citizen, objected to his 'unfair treatment' in being excluded from
the country and took his complaint to the Supreme Court, which refused to
hear the case. Other Muslims, sometimes citizens and sometimes not and generally aided by civil libertarians, have brought legal actions and sought damages in their adoptive countries for being finger-printed and searched at borders, for being asked to remove the *hijab* as a condition of employment, and
even for being prevented by deportation from finishing their studies.

Indeed, some diaspora Muslims have demonstrated a sense not only that
they have the same rights as other citizens and residents in non-Muslim societies—as they do—but that a non-Muslim society has special *duties* towards its
Muslim community, as has already been indicated. In November 2001, the
Islamic Society of Britain, in the name of promoting mutual understanding
between Muslims and non-Muslims, sought to have public figures sign a
'pledge' of commitment *to* Muslims, as a token of 'long-term support for
Muslim people'. Some British public figures signed the 'pledge', others did
not. The more acerbic of the latter declared that a 'pledge of tolerance' was
required of Muslims themselves. But this response itself missed the point: a
liberal civil society requires not only mutual tolerance among its members,
but the fulfilment of their obligations to it.

To think otherwise was again a 'taking of liberties'. Moreover, for a non-
Muslim to sign a 'pledge' of support to the members of one religious
minority, and not to the members of another, would itself be a derogation
from a 'plural' society's values. But that Muslims could seek such a 'pledge' at
all was the product of already well-established expectations: that in conditions
of an exploitable political and moral disarray liberties might be taken by those
minded to do so.

In the balance of things, all incomers to Western liberal societies had
good enough prima facie grounds for believing that they were pushing against
a moral open door. This was made clear when, for example, Islamist clerics in
the diaspora felt able to justify, in public, acts committed against the non-
Muslim world, or when entitlements were claimed which could reasonably be
held outlandish in a non-Muslim culture. For there were always sufficient
numbers of non-Muslims to argue that Muslim objectors to, and claimants
against, the societies in which they had settled had a legitimate case, whatever
that case might be.

Indeed, Western human rights activists generally remained staunch in permitting, and even inviting, liberties to be taken in—and from—democratic
civic orders by citizens who were so only in name, or who were not citizens at

all. Such staunchness has not often been deterred. This has been so, even when it was demonstrably productive of consequences harmful to the wider good. Freedom of judgment by some Muslims about the non-Muslim societies which they had joined could therefore be simultaneously confident and amoral. In December 2002, a Muslim organisation in the United States backed by Saudi Arabia—a royal autocracy which has regularly been found to be in gross breach of human rights, and where, as mentioned earlier, no non-Muslim can become a citizen—condemned without a blush an American registration requirement for male non-citizens from a number of (mainly Muslim) countries. It was described as an 'ineffective and inefficient' 'dragnet policy'; exactly the same terms used by American human rights organisations.

Condemnations by Muslims of security measures of this kind have often incongruously combined human rights objections with epithets and threats taken from the vocabulary of Islam. 'If they arrest us', declared Omar Bakri Mohammed in January 2003, referring to investigations by Scotland Yard, 'we will become martyrs'. In October 2001, he described British Muslim citizens who had been reported killed in action in Afghanistan—while fighting for the Taliban—as 'martyrs, beyond doubt'. In such statements, it could seem as if an implied *civic* right were being claimed even to take up arms against a non-Islamic polity in which the Islamist had made his home, and to assail its security in whatever fashion such individual might choose.

To the diaspora Muslims who sought to have it all ways, such combination of anti-civic standpoints has not appeared anomalous. They have again been aided in this by non-Muslims who have assigned a higher priority to individual rights than to civic duties. In moral consequence, arguments and demands advanced against non-Muslim societies by some Muslims have not needed to be defensive or apologetic. Such arguments and demands can be couched not only in the language of democratic rights, but also with a growing sense of righteousness which derives from adherence to Islam itself. The combination of claims-to-rights and claims-to-righteousness is a potent one. It has been capable of driving a liberal society to defensive apologia itself, even as it was being threatened.

From April to August 2004, for example, there were threats by Ahmet Azzuz of the Arab European League against the city of Antwerp—attacks were 'nearly unavoidable', he declared—if the Antwerp Jewish community did not 'distance itself from the state of Israel'; a jihad was threatened by the Ansar al-Qaeda Brigades if Spain did not withdraw its troops from Iraq; Italy was threatened by the Abu Hafs al-Masri Brigades that it would be 'burned' if Berlusconi remained in office; and the Islamic Army in Iraq gave France 'forty-eight hours' to revoke its ban on the *hijab* or face the consequences. But such threats of attack, although they might be harmful to the 'image' of Islam in the non-Muslim world, could also co-exist with an increasing sense of their rights on the parts of Belgian, Spanish, Italian and French Muslims.

There have also been other types of amoral contradiction in the standpoints and actions of some diaspora Muslim organisations and individuals. The purpose of the (Iranian-funded) Muslim Institute in London was to 'keep Muslims free from the corrupt bogland of Western culture and supposed civilisation', declared its director in August 1990. Yet not only was he himself a London University graduate, but his son, far from avoiding this 'bogland' by pursuing his education in a Muslim seat of higher learning, was attending a British university when the statement was made.

Among the militant Arab-American, Malaysian, Pakistani, Palestinian, Qatari, Saudi, Syrian and Yemeni Islamists who were arrested, charged, jailed in, or deported from the United States between 2001 and 2004 for 'assisting terrorism' in various ways were students, graduates, post-graduates and even teachers from US academic institutions. They included Brandeis, Bradley University in Illinois, California State University, the University of California at San Diego, City University of New York, Howard University, the University of Idaho, the University of Maryland, George Mason University in Virginia, the Massachusetts Institute of Technology, the University of Mississippi, the University of South Florida, Southeastern University in the District of Columbia, Syracuse University, New York and Wayne State University in Detroit. In February 2003 a Jordanian graduate student working for a master's degree at a Texan university admitted that he had 'considered becoming a suicide-bomber' if the United States were to invade Iraq. He openly told a Dallas court—which ordered his deportation—that 'I was looking at America as my enemy. If someone had approached me and asked me to do something against the country, I was willing to do it'.

Zacarias Moussaoui, the alleged 'twentieth hijacker' who by misadventure missed participating in the attacks of 11 September 2001, held the United States to be 'a place not fit for Muslims to reside'. Yet after the completion of his flight-training, undertaken with lethal intent, he had planned a long car-tour in order to 'see America'. Exploitation of, and overt or covert admiration for, the technology, or the educational facilities, or the openness of a free Western nation have not been incompatible with disdain for and even with killing designs against it. In 1998, bin Laden and al-Qaeda declared that it was 'the duty' of Muslims everywhere to 'kill Americans'. Yet his family had earlier made an endowment of $1 million to Harvard Law School, from which his brother had graduated.

These no longer constitute moral puzzles. Rather, like the Twelve Devices of argument, they have possessed their own morality and their own logic. As the Islamic and Arab revivals have gained momentum, they have increasingly been the morality and logic of a value-system whose strength lies in part in its readiness to say or do anything which might serve its ends. At the same time, objections to the treatment by liberal democratic societies of their Muslim citizenries—objections which are sufficiently often justified—have generally been indifferent to the issue of whether the latter be sinned against, or themselves sinning. It could also be asserted, as by a Muslim contributor to the *Guardian* in August 2002, that the 'confidence of diaspora Muslims' was being 'eroded' by the 'unscrupulousness' and 'incompetence' of British government agencies. As if there could have been no conceivable grounds for it, the birth of a 'colder', 'harsher' and 'less forgiving' Britain was likewise detected by another Muslim writer in the *Observer* in June 2002.

Innocence of ill-intent, in the manner of the Twelve Devices, can also be pleaded not only without embarrassment but with confidence, once more, in its righteousness. 'Why would they want to arrest me?' a radical Islamic cleric asked sardonically after having called publicly in Britain (on the BBC) for the death of the president of Pakistan for his insufficient Islamist commitment. 'I have done nothing wrong', he added; and in his own eyes he had not. From 2003 onwards, with a similar sense of guiltlessness, spokesmen for Islamic Jihad, Hamas and other 'terror organisations' repeatedly demanded the release by Israel, 'without condition', of all the prisoners the latter held; as the Israelis put it, whether or not they had 'blood on their hands'.

Warnings, subtle and less subtle, to non-Muslims that they should beware of the sense of Muslim grievance have also covered a wide spectrum of threat. Complaints about the intolerance shown to Muslims by the far-right have been increasingly coupled with reminders, as by Faisal Bodi in the *Guardian* in May 2002, to beware of the 'emergence' of a 'large-scale Muslim presence in Europe'. In August 2002, after police had raided its offices, the leader of al-Muhajiroun told a Trafalgar Square rally that the British government was 'sitting on a box of dynamite', and would have 'only themselves to blame'—a familiar argument, as we saw earlier—'if it all blows up in their faces'. It was a metaphor with its own resonance.

It could also be asserted by a Muslim writer, Rana Kabbani, in June 2002 that attacks on Muslims in Europe, particularly Muslims of the 'second and third generation', were attacks on those 'whose continent this is'. The war in Iraq brought an increased spate of warnings, sometimes coupled with similar claims to that of Kabbani, that the Muslim presence in Western liberal societies had created a new world. In April 2003, in the *Guardian*, the British Muslim Fuad Nahdi used the term 'we', and the possessive 'our', when warning (non-Muslims) that diaspora Muslim 'rage' over the US-led invasion of Iraq was likely to prove 'dangerous'. 'We' needed to be 'scared, very scared', he added; the 'end of the war in Iraq' might 'usher in the beginning of our own intifada'. That is, Nahdi was warning of an outbreak in Britain of violence of 'our own', but the identity of the 'we' who needed to be 'very scared' was not wholly clear.

In May 2003, Fuad Nahdi similarly warned in the *Guardian* that without a 'decent settlement for the Palestinians', 'we', once more, 'should brace ourselves for the coming *intifada* in the streets of Birmingham and Detroit'. There was therefore nothing distinctive in, say, the threat by al-Qaeda's Ayman al-Zawahiri in August 2003 that 'Crusader America' would 'pay dearly for any harm done to any of the Muslim prisoners it is holding'. To differing degrees, and whether in hints or in clear terms, they were warnings of retribution against non-Muslims, and they were made with an equal sense of entitlement by the innocent Muslim and the guilty, by the diaspora intellectual and the Islamist al-Qaeda leader.

Claims by Muslims that a non-Muslim society was 'ours' gradually became more common both in Britain and the US. In the United States, spokesmen for a variety of Muslim diaspora organisations, some with covert Islamist links, could also be found on many occasions between 2001 and 2005 praising 'American values of tolerance and democracy', and condemning erosions of civil liberties as if they were such democracy's most loyal adherents. In April 2003 in the *Observer*, the Arab-American writer Edward Said claimed that Americans had been 'cheated' over Iraq and that 'we must have our democracy back'.

In objecting in January 2002 to the conditions under which Muslim detainees, supected of involvement in Islamist terrorist planning, were being kept in a high security prison in London, the Muslim Council of Britain also declared that 'the war on terrorism was meant to be a war on behalf of civilised values'. These values, it asserted, were values 'we [sc. Muslims] hold dear', and such values required to be 'upheld'. In August 2005, when a proposal was made by the British government after the London bombings to ban the 'radical' group Hizb ut-Tahrir, the Muslim Council of Britain again objected. 'By banning this group'—rather than 'prosecuting them in the courts'—'we are undermining our own democratic values', it asserted.

The Muslim Public Affairs Council in the United States similarly condemned President Clinton's attack in August 1998 on Osama bin Laden's bases in Afghanistan as 'un-American'. In December 2002, Sabiha Khan of the

Southern California Chapter of the Saudi-funded Council on American Islamic Relations described the treatment of Muslim detainees in Guantanamo not merely as wrong but as violating 'American ideals of fairness'; in Canada, Mohamed el-Masry, president of the Canadian Islamic Congress, accused those who 'spread hate' as acting 'against Canadian values'.

In March 2002, Abdel Bari Atwan, the editor of the London-based *al-Quds al-Arabi*, also declared that the 'humane foundations of Western civilisation' were 'being questioned by Muslims worldwide'. 'Tolerance, democracy, a fair and independent judiciary, equality before the law and respect for human rights' constituted Atwan's list in *al-Quds* of the betrayed moral principles whose passing he was purporting to lament. America, he asserted in December 2001, had 'turned against all its values'; yet none of these values was truly to be found in an Arab or Muslim country.

Muslim declarations of identification with a non-Muslim society could sometimes sound more like threats than expressions of loyalty to it. Britain was 'our country' and 'our nation', declared Anas Altikriti in the *Guardian* in August 2004. 'We are this nation', similarly asserted Kareem Irfan, chairman of the Council of Islamic Organisations of Greater Chicago, in November 2004. Such claims could also be self-protective. In Britain in December 2003, Muslims in Gloucester were clearly alarmed at the arrest of a suspected Islamist, referred to earlier, who had been found with explosives in his home. He represented no threat to 'our country', they explained. Indeed, some of these usages of 'we' and 'our' expressed pride of belonging—as in 'America is our country. This is where our life is'. 'Harm' had been done to 'our country', similarly declared Inayat Bunglawala of the Muslim Council of Britain in August 2004, expressing apparently sincere dismay over the presence of British troops in Iraq. But other statements of this kind had more in common with the style of the Twelve Devices, being made in bad faith.

Demands made by Muslims of non-Muslim societies that the latter sacrifice their principles in order to satisfy Muslim interests were of a different order of significance. In May 2002, the chairman of the London Muslim Coalition, Kumar Murshid, described a public rally in support of Israel as a 'provocation'. It was a criticism that could not properly be made in a democratic and non-Islamic society. In January 2003, the Dutch member of parliament, Ayaan Hirsi Ali—a lapsed Muslim herself, and later at the centre of the storm over the murder of Theo van Gogh—made disobliging remarks about the Prophet Mohammed. In response, Yassin Hartog, a spokesman for Holland's main Muslim lobby-group 'Islam and Citizenship', pronounced that freedom of speech was 'one thing for an ordinary citizen' but that 'members of parliament should not be allowed to say exactly what they wanted in public'. Demands followed from Dutch Muslims that the parliamentarian be barred from public office.

Similarly, allied action against Saddam Hussein in the 1991 Gulf War was described by two hundred British imams in January 1991 to be 'anti-Muslim', as if not only Muslims but non-Muslims too should have acted in accord with Muslim prescription. In the following years, despite (or because of) the scale of the counter-measures taken against Islamism across the world, such sense of Muslim right and power grew. The non-Muslim world, in contrast, was increasingly disabled by obstructions and divisions in its own ranks, misjudgments of the strengths of those who stood against it and failures of intelligence in both senses of the word. Indeed, it was upon many forms of misunderstanding and error—technical, cultural, intellectual, political, military—that the 'taking of liberties' with and from democratic societies has depended.

Failures of intelligence ranged from the relatively trivial to the disastrous. In the first category it made possible, for example, the unwitting (or witless) choice by the American State Department as its unofficial envoy to Muslim countries during the 1990s—in order to speak on 'religious tolerance and Muslim life in the US'—of a prominent Arab-American who was simultaneously treating with, and providing funds to, Islamist organisations. But this was a matter of minimal significance compared with the failures that preceded and followed the 9/11 attacks.

They revealed uncoordinated effort in America's fifteen intelligence agencies; organisational chaos in the CIA, FBI, Border Patrol and Department of Homeland Security; and rivalries within as well as among them. There were also legal restrictions—based on civil liberties considerations—on the sharing of intelligence between one agency and another. In consequence, there were fatal failures to analyse and respond to the information which they possessed. As a former US attorney-general testified in April 2004 to the commission investigating the attacks, 'The FBI didn't know what it had. The right hand didn't know what the left hand was doing'. The same defects existed at the CIA, whose director George Tenet resigned in June 2004. Even their computer systems were obsolete, and prevented efficient communications within agencies as well as between them.

Perhaps as many as eight of the 9/11 hijackers, in several cases after questioning, were allowed into the country despite carrying doctored or suspicious passports and visas, or possessing only one-way tickets, or both. Without follow-up, several also broke US immigration laws by overstaying their permits, or by failing to study at the colleges which they said they would attend and for which their visas had been issued. In August 2005, it was also alleged (and denied) that in the summer of 2000 a US military intelligence unit had identified Mohammed Atta and three other of the 9/11 hijackers—within two months of their arrival in America—as likely members of an al-Qaeda cell, and that the Pentagon had failed, or been unwilling, to pass the information to the FBI; and there was a similar lack of response to the observations of FBI 'field agents', who in the summer of 2001 had reported that known Islamists were in training at American flight-schools. In late August 2001, one of the group designated to carry out the 9/11 hijackings, Zacarias Moussaoui, was even arrested by the FBI for overstaying his visa limit, and after he had aroused suspicion at a Minnesota flight-school where he had enrolled to learn how to fly a Boeing 747 even though he had had very little previous flight experience. In April 2004, Tenet admitted that US intelligence agencies 'never penetrated the 9/11 plot'.

Yet in 1977, a report by a US government 'Committee to Combat Terrorism' had already identified the hijacking of commercial aircraft, and their potential use in an attack on the United States, as one of the threats against which the civil aviation industry had to increase its guard. In 1995, the CIA not only repeated the warning that civil aviation in the US was at risk, but that Islamists might strike at landmarks in Washington and New York; 'threat reports' specifically mentioned the possibility that an 'explosives-laden aircraft' might be 'flown into a US city'. By 1999 Osama bin Laden had also been described by the CIA as 'interested in targeting US territory' and 'well-prepared to consider hijackings as well as bombings'.

In April 2001, the Federal Aviation Authority in turn warned US airports that hijackers intended to commit suicide in a 'spectacular explosion'. By May 2001, there was information that 'bin Laden supporters' were planning to enter the US through Canada' in order to mount an attack. Five weeks before 9/11, the White House was informed that al-Qaeda members were present in the US and that there were 'patterns of suspicious activity consistent with preparations for hijackings'. Al-Qaeda messages intercepted on 10 September, declaring 'tomorrow is zero hour', were not translated until days later. Some of the hijackers, believed to have been carrying knives, set off alarms as they passed through metal detectors, but were inadequately searched and allowed to proceed.

Moreover, even when it had become clear to the Federal Aviation Authority that several aircraft had been hijacked, 'the American skies were in chaos' as a result of delayed alerts to the US Aerospace Defense Command and failures of communication even at the White House and Pentagon. By the

time the last hijacked aircraft hit the latter, nearly one hour after the first airliner had struck the World Trade Center, scrambled air force fighters were
still one hundred miles away. It was only after the last of the hijacked aircraft
had crashed that the vice-president, on the president's behalf, ordered that
they be shot down.

Three years later, in September 2004, more than 120,000 hours of intercepted recordings had not yet been translated because of the shortage of
qualified linguists at the FBI. Other 'intercepts' had been deleted because of
'limited storage capacities' in the FBI's computer systems. 'It will take another
five years of work to have the kind of clandestine service our country needs',
the FBI director had declared in April 2004. Nor have such things been confined to the US. In Germany, the city of Hamburg served as a base of operations for three of those involved in the attacks of September 2001. 'We must
say we failed to see it', the German interior minister, Otto Schily, declared in
their aftermath; 'we have to re-examine our security system'.

Similarly in Britain, Mohammad Sidique Khan, one of the four 'successful' London suicide-bombers, was said to have been investigated early in
2004 in connection with a plot to build a fertiliser bomb for use in a London
attack, yet allegedly did not have his activities monitored thereafter. Moreover,
Hussain Osman, a suspect in the second 'unsuccessful' attack in July 2005, was
able to leave Britain from London's Waterloo station five days after it. This was
despite the manhunt for him, the wide circulation of his photograph—
including at the station—and the surveillance under which the station had
been placed.

Other forms of bungling led to the presence of a 'highly-placed al-Qaeda
operative' in the US army's Special Forces; he pleaded guilty in 2000 to conspiracy in connection with the 1998 bombings of the US embassies in East
Africa. Because of the rarity of Arabic-language skills among non-Muslim
Americans, inadequate security checks—including in the counter-intelligence
services—were made on civilian personnel hired to serve as interpreters and
as translators of documents. Among those found to be training Islamist
fighters in Bosnia in the 1990s and in Kashmir, as earlier mentioned, were
Muslim converts who had been discharged from US military service. In September 2004, many agents assigned to Arab countries were still reported to be
unable to speak Arabic; in April 2005, US airport security was said by a congressional committee to be still inadequate; and in May 2005 the FBI was
reported to be still hiring intelligence analysts in insufficient numbers.

Letting slip suspects or allowing them to escape; failing to recognise or to
follow up clues; allowing materials for bomb-making, blank passports and

other documents to be stolen; leaking information; failing to choke off funds destined for Islamist uses and taking decisions without the will or means to enforce them have all made their contributions to Islamism's progress. Pakistani political and military authorities for years failed (or refused) to impede the nuclear 'black market' activities of Abdul Qadeer Khan. France, Iraq (under US control), Russia, Spain and other countries between them permitted fertilizer used in bombs, high explosives, artillery shells, mortar rounds and nuclear equipment and materials to disappear. In March 2004, 'several hundred' Soviet-built surface-to-air missiles were reported 'missing' from Ukraine's military arsenal. 'We cannot find them', Ukraine's defence minister announced.

Even police cars and military and police uniforms were stolen by al-Qaeda in Saudi Arabia; during 2004, 'dozens' of 'terror suspects' in the US were said by a congressional investigating committee in March 2005 to have made legal purchases of firearms, despite being on federal 'watch-lists', since US gun-laws protected their 'privacy' when making their applications; in Minnesota a suspected member of a 'sleeper' al-Qaeda cell similarly applied for, and was issued with, a licence to haul hazardous materials. In addition, blank passports stolen from the thirty-four countries which notified the losses to Interpol in February 2004 were said to number 'hundreds of thousands'. In October 2004, Interpol further reported that stolen and forged 'virgin' travel documents and passports together ran to millions in total. Such documents, purloined from consulates, printers and elsewhere, permitted applicants not only to obtain false visas but to establish false identities in moving about the world.

In Britain, it was reported to Parliament in April 2004 that seven thousand official security passes were 'missing', including three thousand from Ministry of Defence premises. In France, '10,000' passports and travel documents were similarly reported in April 2004 to have been stolen. Italy—with its history of general failures of the rule of law—has long led the way in Europe in 'accidental' bungling, and other laxities, when dealing with Islamism and its works. The tally of passports, visa documents and identity-cards reported in February 2004 by Interpol to have been stolen or 'lost' in that country totalled '200,000'. Likewise, in June 2004 it was reported that fake passports were being 'smuggled' from Indonesia into Malaysia; in July 2004, it was said in Johannesburg that 'al-Qaeda militants and other terrorists travelling throughout Europe' were using South African passports sold to them by 'crime syndicates'. In Russia, in September 2004, it was said that the going price for a passport was $500; and in August 2005, an Algerian-born 'Briton' was arrested in Thailand carrying 452 forged documents, including fake Belgian, French, Portuguese and Spanish passports.

But the movement of militants across borders—including across the US border with Mexico—often had no need of documents. It saw Islamists coming into Iraq from Syria, Iran and far beyond, while in 2004 it required some 75,000 Pakistani troops deployed on the Pakistan-Afghan border to stop cross-border attacks. Bribery of Russian guards and security personnel at checkpoints brought Islamists into Chechnya. Bribery also appears to have permitted Chechen women suicide-bombers to avoid security checks and to board two Russian passenger jets, brought down in August 2004. In December 2004, a suicide-bomber wearing Iraqi uniform was able to gain access even to a US military mess-hall at a base in Mosul and kill twenty-two people, while leaks of information and tip-offs were said in May 2005 to be 'undermining' the battle against insurgents.

In 2004, further laxity or connivance reportedly 'lost track of' '400' al-Qaeda-trained fighters in Morocco, and allowed Islamist suspects and prisoners a getaway in Bahrain, Pakistan, the Philippines and Saudi Arabia. In April 2004, it led to the storming of a Gaza prison and the release of detainees accused of bombing a US diplomatic convoy in October 2003, while militants suspected of involvement in a Tel Aviv suicide-bombing in February 2005 'escaped' from a Palestinian jail in Tul Karm two months later. In the Philippines, the Indonesian Fathur Rohman al-Ghozi of Jemaah Islamiyah—who had confessed to involvement in five bombings in Manila in December 2000—was similarly permitted to 'escape' in July 2003 from the command-building of the national police headquarters in the capital; al-Ghozi's three guards were 'investigated' and sacked. In March 2005, militants of the Abu Sayyaf group, awaiting trial on charges of kidnapping and murder—including by a beheading—shot dead with handguns three of their guards within a Manila detention centre. In Afghanistan, in October 2003, more than forty Taliban inmates escaped from a 'high security' prison in Kandahar by digging a thirty-foot tunnel with help from prison officials, five of whom were also found to be missing; in July 2005, four 'senior figures' in al-Qaeda even escaped from US custody at Bagram air-base near Kabul. Similarly, in Yemen, ten Islamist militants involved in the bombing in 2000 of the USS *Cole* 'escaped' from prison in Aden in April 2003. But when the Yemeni authorities, under American pressure, ostensibly changed their policy, the 'escapees' were recaptured in March 2004.

'Leniencies' which often seemed to have more to do with sympathy or fear than with due process let off lightly—or completely—Islamists detained, under trial, or already jailed in Afghanistan, Bahrain, Jordan, Kuwait, Pakistan, the Palestinian territories, Thailand and Yemen. In March 2005, an Indonesian court found the cleric Abu Bakr Bashir guilty of conspiracy in the Bali bombings of 2002, which took the lives of more than two hundred, and jailed him for thirty months, further reduced by four and a half months in August 2005. Iraqi courts, many of them presided over by former Saddam loyalists, handed out sentences of as little as six months to fellow-Sunni insurgents convicted of serious weapons and explosives offences; while in August 2005, two Shi'ite clerics, who had been detained for the earlier-mentioned killing—or 'hacking to death'—of a rival cleric, Abdul Majid al-Khoei, in Najaf in April 2003, were released without trial. But there were many precedents for such leniency in non-Muslim countries themselves. In Italy, after the hijacking of the Italian cruise-ship *Achille Lauro* in 1985, and the forcing down in Sicily by US navy fighters of the aircraft carrying the hijack-leader, Abul Abbas, the Italian authorities freed him within forty-eight hours on grounds of insufficiency of evidence. They filed charges against him only after he had safely left the country—with a diplomatic passport—sentencing him in 1987 to life imprisonment *in absentia* when it was clear that he would not serve the sentence.

In October 2001 in Milan, judicial 'errors' were given as the explanation when suspected members or associates of al-Qaeda, having been granted bail 'because the paperwork was deficient', disappeared. There were acquittals in 2003 and 2004—often against strongly incriminating evidence, including the possession of chemical compounds, TNT, false documents and maps, and in one case a plan of the US embassy in Rome—of Algerian, Egyptian, Moroccan, Pakistani and Tunisian 'terrorist' suspects. In Naples in February 2003, twenty-eight Pakistanis were arrested after police had discovered that they had explosives and a detonator hidden behind a false wall, as well as maps with NATO and American military installations highlighted, together with photographs of *'jihad* martyrs'. They, too, were freed after a judge decided that, notwithstanding the maps, explosives, detonators and the rest, there was 'little evidence' to justify holding them. Within hours they were gone. In January 2005, and again in Milan, five Maghrebians accused of recruiting jihadists to fight in Iraq also had their 'terrorism' charges dropped, on the grounds that theirs were 'guerrilla activities' which did not 'constitute terrorism as such'. They received short sentences for immigration offences.

In Holland, in December 2002, a Rotterdam court acquitted four men accused of planning a suicide-bombing of the US embassy in Paris on the grounds that there had been 'no independent investigation by the [Dutch] police'; the information on which the indictment was based had been gathered by foreign intelligence agencies, and was therefore held to be insufficient. On

the same grounds and again in Holland, twelve men accused of providing
material support, safe haven, and false documents to members of an al-
Qaeda-related organisation, as well as recruiting and indoctrinating young
Muslims in the Netherlands 'for jihad', were acquitted in May 2003 by a Rotterdam court. In Israel, held to be a byword for the severity—and even
brutishness—of its conduct towards 'terrorism', an Islamic Jihad member convicted of 'intending to carry out a terrorist attack' was granted early release
from prison in July 2003; within eight weeks, on the eve of the Jewish New
Year, he was reported to have killed two civilians.

However, these 'leniencies' were themselves matched and even exceeded
by some of the sentences handed down at court-martials, and in other proceedings, against US soldiers found guilty of crimes of violence and abuse
against detainees, and other captives, in Afghanistan and Iraq. The 'primary
torturer' at Abu Ghraib prison in Baghdad, who pleaded in classic fashion that
he was 'just following orders', received a ten-year sentence from a military jury
in Texas in January 2005. But terms of three years and one year were given to
two US soldiers for 'putting out of his misery' a severely wounded Iraqi sixteen-year-old found in a burning truck, who had 'made no hostile gestures'.
Sixty days of hard labour and demotion was a sentence for abusing inmates at
Camp Whitehorse in Iraq. Light sentences of up to one year, reduction in
rank, forfeiture of two weeks' pay, reprimands and bad conduct discharges
were other sentences for mistreatment of prisoners, while four of the top US
commanders at Abu Ghraib were exonerated in April 2005. An army sergeant
who ordered his soldiers to throw two Iraqis—one of whom drowned—into
the Tigris River in Samarra in January 2004 was given a six-month sentence
and a reduction in rank; an Indiana National Guard soldier, charged with the
murder in November 2003 of an Iraqi police officer, received an eighteen-
month sentence in July 2005 for 'negligent homicide' in a plea bargain. British
soldiers accused of abuse of Iraqi detainees blamed superiors, and received
sentences of similar kinds, including five months for stamping on a bound
man, while four Russian soldiers were acquitted in May 2005 of murdering six
Chechen civilians on the plea that they were 'acting under orders'.

They were mere incidents in a larger trial of strength, in which every
form of abuse, falsehood, error, cowardice and misjudgment played their parts
on all sides, as in all wars. Islamists used the weapons of hostage-taking,
ransom demands and extremes of cruelty against their captives; American
troops humiliated prisoners and laughed for the camera over their heaped-up,
naked bodies. Ostensible allies betrayed one another, Arab and Muslim nations
betrayed the Palestinians, and Western and other governments surrendered to

hostage-takers' threats, ensuring that more kidnapping of innocents would follow. Indeed, just as obstacles were attempted to be set in the path of Islamists by (some) Muslim and Arab rulers, so every form of division, internal and external, obstructed and fragmented the efforts of Western powers to stop Islamism's advance.

From Greece to India, hijackers' demands were met (by some nations) from the late 1960s onwards, and the 'tradition' was to be maintained as Islamism, emboldened to take further liberties, moved on. In 2003, Germany paid a ransom of nearly $6 million to free a group of tourists seized in south-eastern Algeria by Salafists 'linked to al-Qaeda'. France, Indonesia, and Somalia pleaded in 2004 for the release of their hostages in Iraq on the self-exculpatory grounds that they had not contributed troops to the war and were opposed to it. Italy, as it always had done, paid ransom. Such payments to kidnappers were commonplace in Iraq, explained Barbara Contini, the Italian interim governor of Dhi Qar province, in April 2004. 'Everyone pays. It's been done for centuries and centuries. There is always a price to pay in these situations', she added. It brought release only for some of Italy's own captives, while the real 'price' was the capture of others.

This was equally a matter of moral indifference, in July 2004, to the Philippines government. After the abduction of one of its nationals and the threat to behead him, it met kidnappers' demands to withdraw its small contingent of troops from Iraq. On the captives' release, the Filipino president, Gloria Macapagal Arroyo, claimed that it was a 'time of triumph'. 'Every life is important', she added, as other nationals' hostages—twenty in the following fortnight—were taken, some of them to be subsequently beheaded.

The political and ethical principles, divisions of opinion, rivalries and duplicities among those confronting—or, in many cases, appearing to confront—Islamism's onward march have been very various. Sometimes justly, they led to the placing by civil libertarians of obstacles in the way of the free prosecution of Islamist crimes and excesses; they also led to wrecking obstructions, again sometimes justified, of Western and usually American policy decisions which were thought by other nations to be misguided or wrong. Competition among the larger Western powers for influence with Arab and Muslim leaders also played a large part in determining differences of judgment and in shaping biases in policy. All these differences, inevitable as they may have been, permitted further licence to be taken by Islamists with an often fractious and disunited non-Muslim world.

Thus, Islamists benefited from the differences in policy and perspective between the continental European powers and the United States. In relation to the Palestinian cause in particular, and the means by which its purposes had been pursued, divisions of attitude were deep. They ranged in Europe from wholehearted sympathy with the Palestinians, almost whatever methods they adopted, to open hostility towards the Palestinian cause among many in the US. In July 2003 the European Union had pugnaciously reaffirmed its intention to keep up dialogue with Yasser Arafat 'as we see fit', on the ground that he had been 'democratically elected as president of the Palestinian Authority'. Other powers, led by the United States, gave him a wide berth to the end.

The European nations also provided substantial financial as well as moral and political support to Arafat's Palestinian Authority. In the decade to 2004, the total of bilateral and multilateral aid which was given to it by the EU and its member-states came to some $5 billion; in January 2004, the foreign minister of the Palestinian Authority described the EU as its 'ally of choice'. These resources were throughout known to have been used to finance Palestinian paramilitary groups, as well as providing a slush-fund for cash handouts to individuals who were in the authority's favour, or to buy off opponents. In 2003, an IMF report asserted that 'senior Palestinian officials' had funnelled some $800 million in funds from donor countries to overseas bank accounts, and had done the same with profits from corrupt business monopolies in the Palestinian Territories. The Palestinian finance minister, Salam Fayyad, himself conceded in January 2003 that there had been a 'breakdown of financial controls'.

Yet in June 2002, the EU's commissioner for external relations was still insisting that there had been no evidence of misuse of EU funds. Only towards the end of 2003 did the EU's fraud investigation agency begin its own enquiry into these misappropriations. This had been due less to lack of evidence than to moral indifference over the uses to which the funds were being put. Such indifference could be said to have made as little contribution to peace as did the acts of the Palestinians and Israelis themselves. The European Union also contributed funds to the social works carried out by the 'political wing' of Hamas, until doubts began to grow in late 2003 about whether the distinction between the 'political' and 'military' wings of the movement could be sustained.

Nevertheless France, in particular, consistently pronounced throughout 2003 that to try to 'sideline Hamas' was 'counter-productive'; and while the Israelis, supported by the United States, continued to regard Hamas as a 'murderous terrorist movement', Hamas claimed in June 2005 that its senior officials were holding meetings with 'European diplomats' 'every ten days to two weeks', its claims to recognition enhanced by its electoral advances from December 2004 in Gaza and the West Bank.

Similarly, in October 2003, while US pressure was building on Syria to retreat from its support of 'terror organisations', the European Union was negotiating an 'association agreement' with Damascus. 'We do not believe in policies of isolation', declared the EU's commissioner for external relations. And from March to December 2003, the European Union's 'anti-racism' monitoring body prevented publication of the results of independent research, carried out on its behalf, which had concluded that Muslims were responsible for much of the increase in attacks on Jews and Jewish institutions in Europe; the researchers claimed that their findings had not 'fitted in' with the EU monitoring body's agenda. As the much greater degree of European opposition to US policy in Iraq from 2003 was to disclose, these were all tokens—some minor and others likely to prove historically decisive—of resistance to the establishment of a common front between Europe and the US in relation to the Islamic world and Middle Eastern issues.

It could be said that the United States had set a precedent in non-cooperation in refusing support to, or approval of, the Franco-British military assault on Egypt at the time of the Nasserite closure of the Suez Canal, in the earlier days of the Arab and Muslim revival. A half-century later in November 2004, France, Germany and Spain—for example—were agreeing to 'work more closely together' in order to build a 'stronger Europe' as a counterbalance to the United States. The wheel had turned full circle. It was manifested in matters small and large. They included, at one level, the prolonged refusal, during 2004, of the European Parliament to agree to joint measures with the US to improve airline safety; at another, resistances of all kinds to cooperation with the US in the most significant matters of military and political action in Afghanistan, Iran, Iraq, Palestine and elsewhere. In Afghanistan, European nations were unwilling to offer either substantial military help to the United States in its pursuit of the Taliban and al-Qaeda, or significant economic aid in Afghanistan's reconstruction after the Taliban's fall.

Other obstacles to US purposes in the world were numerous. Thus, years of rivalry and mistrust, and differing political, cultural and economic circumstances among nations in south-east Asia, impeded cooperation in combating the advances of Islamism in the region. In February 2004, 'some Asian nations'—unnamed—were declared to be 'unable or reluctant to pull their weight' in matters of extraditing suspects to other countries, in sharing information, and even in introducing 'anti-terrorist' legislation. 'Charities' based in Pakistan and Saudi Arabia, with known financial ties to al-Qaeda and its associated organisations, were reportedly shut down by their governments but continued to operate freely. In March 2004, the European Union reported

likewise that member-states had either failed to implement, or had not yet
enacted, EU measures introduced after 9/11. They had not fully cooperated in
the introduction of a Europe-wide search-and-arrest warrant and in sweeping
away time-consuming extradition procedures, nor had they made sufficient
progress in cutting off the flow of 'terror financing' in Europe. In June 2004,
Greece and Italy were singled out for having failed to implement 'almost all'
of the EU's measures; and in July 2005 the German federal constitutional
court, refusing to permit the extradition to Spain of an al-Qaeda suspect with
dual German and Syrian nationality, ruled that the European arrest warrant
was not valid under German law.

Sedulous obstruction also blocked efforts to call Iran effectively to
account for its secret nuclear programmes. There was 'no proof' that Iran was
seeking nuclear weapons, Russia declared in September 2003, when the evidence that this was not so was becoming clearer. Similarly, as evidence grew of
clandestinity and misreporting by Iran—complained of by the International
Atomic Energy Authority—Javier Solana, the European Union commissioner,
asserted in November 2003 that the Iranian government had been 'honest' in
declaring its intentions. In 2003, Britain, Germany and France broke Western
ranks in order to pursue their own diplomatic interests in finding a 'compromise' between the US and Iran. They brokered what they thought was an
agreement for the suspension by the Iranians of uranium enrichment. But
they were continuously out-maneouvred during 2004 and 2005 by Teheran,
while China and Pakistan, in their own geopolitical and other interests, gave
their political support to Iran.

Likewise, the UN Security Council in 2003 and 2004 obstructed, vetoed
or rendered ineffectual policies to confront 'terror' and 'terroristic' capacities,
both real and imagined; it also lacked both the will and the power to enforce
such collective decisions as it did arrive at. In respect of al-Qaeda itself, only
a minority of UN members fulfilled their obligations under UN resolutions
to try to shut off its funding, and to impede and track the movement of its
operatives; most did not even file reports to the UN on what they had done, or
had failed to do. In September 2004, the UN secretary-general also declared
the US-led invasion of Iraq to be 'illegal'; in October 2004 rejected a request
from Iraq's interim leaders to help train judges and prosecutors; in November
2004 refused to commit more than a handful of UN staff members to assist in
the Iraqi elections. Conversely, the Islamist regime in Khartoum was permitted to remain a member of the UN's human rights' commission, despite
the reported 'crimes against humanity' and other violations being committed
by the regime. UN security council members, including Russia and China,
also blocked the imposition of sanctions on Khartoum.

But among the European powers the French did most, and in consistent fashion, to prevent the formation of a common policy with the US in relation to the Arab and Muslim world. It had warned in July 2001 that the authority of Yasser Arafat must not be 'undermined', as the United States joined with Israel in diplomatic and other moves to achieve such end. It opposed US proposals that NATO forces be deployed to help secure the Afghan election in September 2003, and that NATO should take over from the US-led military mission. In its pursuit during 2003 and 2004 of its commercial interests in Iran, it evinced no concern, according to French human rights organisations, at the abuse of human rights in the country, and led the way in trying to broker a 'deal' with Iran as the latter continued its nuclear development programme. In October 2003, President Chirac even blocked collective condemnation by European heads of government of Mahathir Mohamad's assertion, earlier referred to, that Jews 'run the world by proxy', and was publicly thanked by Mahathir for his 'understanding'.

Before the US-led invasion of Iraq, sanctions against Iraq, the disarmament of Iraq and ultimata to Iraq were all resisted or undermined by France and other nations, including Russia. The war against Iraq, the post-war political settlement sought (by the United States) for Iraq and the contribution of soldiery and funds to the 'new Iraq' were likewise resisted or delayed by combinations of European states, by Russia, by China, by the European Union and by the United Nations. Switzerland and Austria refused over-flying rights to United States aircraft. Austria, citing its neutrality, also refused to permit American troops to cross its territory by road or rail should they choose this less-than-obvious route to the Gulf. Similarly, France, Germany and Belgium, acting in breach of Article Four of the NATO treaty which provides for mutual aid between its members, vetoed military measures designed to protect Turkey in the event of war with Iraq. But France—often in conjunction with Russia and China—carried its opposition to the war in Iraq to greater lengths than other nations.

As war neared, it was said to have accepted—with Russia—oil revenues from Saddam Hussein in exchange for exerting pressure on the UN security council to condemn the war. Interrogation in November 2003 of Iraq's former foreign minister, Tariq Aziz, revealed that France and Russia, 'through intermediaries', had assured Saddam Hussein that they would block a US-led war through 'delays and vetoes' at the Security Council. They would also seek to gain 'enough time' for a 'settlement' with the United States, which would be brokered by France and Russia. 'No matter what the circumstances, we will vote "No"', announced President Chirac in March 2003, in advance of the presentation to the Council of a resolution designed by the US and Britain to authorise the use of force against Iraq.

Moreover, even before the Saddam regime had rejected it, France also rejected a 'compromise' proposal under which Iraq would be set tests of compliance with earlier resolutions which had demanded that the latter disarm. Indeed, as France's diplomacy on the eve of the Iraq War strove to thwart American and British plans, a popular English daily paper stridently asked its readers, 'With friends like our Euro-partners, who needs enemies?' and even 'Where the fuck are the French?' And after Saddam Hussein's fall, President Chirac declared that 'Saddam Hussein should have been overthrown without a war', while Arab television stations were reported in April 2003 to be treating President Chirac as a 'hero'. In September 2003, the French even prevented a French charter-airline from ferrying British troop-reinforcements to Basra.

France had further refused to participate—along with Germany and Russia, for example—as peace-keepers in Iraq, whether or not foreign troops were put under UN command, and even in circumstances in which the new Iraqi government had full sovereignty in the country. This was despite acknowledging (with Russia) that a 'secure environment' needed to be created. In May 2004, even against the opposition of the new Iraqi government and in moves which were described by a participant in the discussions as 'harassment by gamesmanship and grief', France (again with German support) wanted an expiry date set for the presence of the US forces in Iraq and a virtual Iraqi veto over the uses of these forces while they remained.

In June 2004, France not only scotched proposals for NATO's direct involvement in securing peace in Iraq, but also opposed a NATO decision to help train the new Iraqi army and refused, with Belgium, Germany and Spain, to send instructors to join the NATO team. Also in June 2004, with the US pressing for a write-off of some 90 per cent of Iraqi debt, France expressed reluctance to forgive more than half of it. 'You can't expect European taxpayers who felt pretty hostile to the military intervention to feel hugely enthusiastic about spending a large amount of money on Iraq', the EU's external affairs commissioner had already declared in October 2003. In September 2004, France even called for representatives of 'those who have chosen the path of armed resistance' to be present at an international conference on Iraq, while in November 2004, President Chirac refused to meet Iraq's interim prime minister on the latter's visit to the EU.

All this was seen differently in December 2003 by Hoshyar Zebari, the new post-Saddam foreign minister of Iraq. Speaking to a closed meeting of the Security Council, he accused the council of having earlier been divided between 'those who wanted to appease Saddam Hussein, and those who wanted to hold him accountable'. The UN, he added, had 'failed to help rescue the Iraqi people from a murderous tyranny that lasted over thirty-five years'. But these divisions in non-Muslim ranks again aided the Islamists' cause, emboldening them to greater violence in Iraq—and helping to justify such violence in their own eyes and to much of the Muslim world—as the major European nations publicly distanced themselves from the US.

Indeed, differences among the non-Muslim powers about how to conduct their relations with a resurgent Islam and with the oil-rich Arab nations have been profound. Moreover, such differences have characterised the non-Muslim world's responses to the Islamic 'reawakening' since the late 1940s. They have divided Europe itself, both between and within nations. Thus, when the Spanish government, which had supported the US-led invasion of Iraq, fell in March 2004—three days after bomb-attacks on Madrid attributed to al-Qaeda or its associates—the incoming 'left-wing' prime minister, Jose Luis Rodriguez Zapatero, promptly described the war as having been a 'disaster' and a 'fiasco'. He was in turn accused of 'appeasement' when he undertook to withdraw Spanish troops from Iraq.

Islamists were quick to seize the advantage. From his prison cell the Indonesian cleric, Abu Bakr Bashir, gave his immediate approval (in a 'secretly filmed' interview with Australian television) to Zapatero's electoral victory, and his political stance. 'My advice to all governments who support America', he declared, 'is to retreat'. In order to maintain Islamist pressure on the Spanish government and people, the Abu Hafs al-Masri Brigades, which had claimed the 'credit' for the Madrid bombings, in turn announced that it would suspend all 'operations' in Spain in return for the fulfilment by the new government of its promise to withdraw Spanish forces from Iraq. This 'deal' opened up further divisions. 'The message to bin Laden', asserted a German politician, 'is that bombing and killing pay off'. But to the European Union president, Romano Prodi, it was US policy in Iraq which had made 'terrorism' 'infinitely worse'. Zapatero was himself asked how 'terrorism' was to be 'combated'? 'Terrorism', he replied, 'is combated by the state of law', a position whose meaning was opaque.

In relation to the US invasion of Iraq, differences among the European nations, and between them and the United States, could not therefore have been deeper. In September 2002, the American ambassador to Germany was even summoned to the foreign ministry in Berlin to answer for the US government's criticisms of German refusal to support military action against Baghdad. And while Europeans accused Americans of 'primitivism', 'unilateralism' and even of being a 'terroristic' danger to world peace, Americans accused Europeans of 'irrelevance' in world affairs and of being 'free-riders on American power', with its nations said to be divided between an 'old' Europe implied to be hostile to US purposes and a 'new' Europe supportive of them.

But the United States was itself inconsistent, and in relation to matters of no less import in the struggle with the Islamic and Arab worlds. It acted obstructively in withholding from both American and foreign courts testimony obtained from its own detainees, often under duress, and in preventing the latter from being cross-examined. Indeed, the intelligence services of the major powers were less than willing to pass on to others what they knew, save in diluted form, and were often more anxious to protect the sources of their information than to share it. The result could be procedural stalemates—as occurred in Germany in 2004—and unsafe acquittals of suspected al-Qaeda operatives. On 'national security' grounds, collaboration and documents were also denied by the US authorities to American courts themselves.

In its own geopolitical and other interests, the US also largely ignored the roles both of Pakistan and Saudi Arabia in some of Islamism's direst acts against the non-Muslim world. In July 2003, it even went to the lengths of striking twenty-eight pages from a US congressional report which gave details of the provision of financial and logistical help to 'terrorist groups' by prominent Saudis in the royal household, diplomatic service and security agencies. On the grounds that the alliance between Pakistan and the US was 'crucial to winning the war on terror', the United States—to India's anger—likewise promoted Pakistan in March 2004 to the status of 'major non-Nato ally'. This made it eligible for priority delivery of advanced military hardware in return, among other things, for its handover into US detention of many of its captives. It was one of many such trade-offs, in the course of which competing geopolitical interests among the leading non-Muslim powers—the US, China, Russia and the major European nations—were continuously in play. Such reconciliations as there were between them, as in June 2005 when EU leaders pledged their support to the 'new Iraq', were more apparent than real.

Open demonstrations of the non-Islamic world's internal conflicts helped provide a grandstand view to Islamists not only of almost every major political and moral debate and disagreement, but even of the West's military intentions and plans. They furnished further opportunities for the advance of the Muslim cause, and helped compensate for the divisions in Muslim and Arab ranks. This advance was aided by accusations from within America itself, and not only from Muslim Americans, that the strategies of the US were the product of hostility to Islam as such. In consequence, Americans were defensively driven to claim that the United States had 'saved' the Kuwaiti people in the Gulf War of 1991 and the Iraqis from Saddam Hussein in 2003, 'saved' Bosnian Muslims by its intervention in the Balkans and 'saved' the Muslims of Kosovo from the Serbs.

Much of this internal debate was strident. Even when conducted in private diplomatic conclave, it became publicly known. In much of the Islamic and Arab worlds, these differences were perceived not as the outcome of divergent choices of policy in liberal democratic societies, but of confused disagreements in face of the challenges which those societies were facing. Such disagreements were long-standing—as earlier mentioned—and repetitious. For example, in January 1991 President Mitterrand, with the then three million Muslims in France at his back and with France's standing in the region in mind, attempted to broker a Middle East conference in order to avert allied military intervention in Kuwait. In this respect little had changed, or could change, in the impediments to concerted Western action. At the same time, the opportunities which such incoherence offered for the further 'taking of liberties' with the West in Islam's name increased.

However, liberal societies were not deterred—nor by their own lights could they be—by the vulnerabilities to which their open disagreements and contentions exposed them. In February 2002, the Spanish foreign minister, with his large domestic Muslim audience, declared himself 'deeply worried' about American policy in the Middle East, while a Swedish foreign minister described the then predisposition of Washington to side-line Yasser Arafat as 'madness'. These disagreements continued to encourage Islamist and Arabist intransigences. In Venice in April 2002, Romano Prodi, the European Union president, not only pronounced Arafat to be 'the only interlocutor for the Israelis' but suggested that the EU should consider economic sanctions against the latter. Once more, it was a declaration made at the very time when the United States was (in effect) giving Israel a free hand in denying Arafat that role.

This type of public display of opposed sympathies often derived from distinct histories in the exertion of colonial and other forms of power over Arab lands. The advance of Arab national movements, for example, owed much to the patronage of the Soviet Union. Non-Muslim nations have also had varied histories in instigating and equipping the Islamist forces themselves. Thus, the 'destabilisation' of the Soviet Union was accelerated by investments in Islamist movements in central Asia by the United States, especially under President Carter. 'Do you regret having supported Islamic fundamentalism, giving arms and advice to future terrorists?' Zbigniew

Brzezinski, Carter's security adviser, was asked by *Le Nouvel Observateur* in January 1998. 'What matters more to world history', Brzezinski asked by way of reply, 'the Taliban, or the collapse of the Soviet empire? Some stirred-up Muslims, or the liberation of Central Europe and the end of the cold war?' 'Some stirred-up Muslims?' responded his questioner with evident incredulity. 'But isn't Islamic fundamentalism a world menace today?' the journalist inquired. 'Nonsense, there is no global Islam', the former national security adviser to President Carter replied.

Such state of denial has been relatively rare. More common has been fear of Islam, a fear which has been openly demonstrated by non-Muslims in many ways. Among the mildest of the tokens of it has been the anxiety on the part of politicians in Western liberal democracies lest a national or local Muslim constituency be offended. Some examples of the political and moral consequences of deferring to it were set out earlier. It was an anxiety which could be expressed directly, as by British politicians over the power of a Muslim 'vote-bank' to rob them of their parliamentary seats. Or it might be expressed in more general terms, as by *La Stampa*'s description of France in April 2002 as not merely the 'leading Muslim country in Europe' but as the 'most forward front in the war being fought for Jerusalem'. Or it could be declared, as in a despatch in May 2002 by a United Press International correspondent, that 'from Paris and London to Berlin and Brussels, European leaders are likely to fear'—the operative word—'outbursts of violence from their huge, recent, Muslim immigrant populations far more than angering tiny Israel'.

This anxiety over the scale of the 'Muslim presence' has again served to boost a sense in diaspora Muslims of power and entitlement, alongside less positive feelings of insecurity and victimisation. But there could also be a frivolous (Anglo-Saxon) disdain for radical Islamism, and for the supposed foolishness of taking it more seriously than it warranted. To Lord Rees-Mogg, writing in *The Times* in October 2001, Osama bin Laden was no more than an 'immature charismatic', a 'playboy revolutionary', 'a poseur', a 'silly but lethal boy'; by April 2003, however, he had grown from 'silly boy' to 'evil man' in Rees-Mogg's judgment. Sir John Keegan, in the *Daily Telegraph* in December 2001, felt able to dismiss the Taliban as 'merely a local eccentric religious movement which had offered al-Qaeda shelter'; Tim Hames, in *The Times* in October 2001, was confident that the United States would have 'achieved the majority of its objectives' in Afghanistan 'before Christmas'.

To Professor Sir Michael Howard in January 2002, the members of al-Qaeda were similar to the 'puritan iconoclasts' who had 'surfaced' in the English civil war. America and Britain, declared another contributor to *The Times* in February 2003, had 'ludicrously overestimated the al-Qaeda menace' and 'boosted' its 'tawdry credit'. To Mary Riddell, in the *Observer* in May 2003, al-Qaeda—'commercially acute and offering an elastic franchise'—was 'the Starbucks of terrorism', no less. In March 2004, as each new Islamist attack conformed with long-established pattern, an editorial in *The Times*, with no greater percipience, described the 'terrorist threat' as 'random'.

To another member of the commentariat in February 2003, again in *The Times*, the 'things' which al-Qaeda had done were 'relatively crude'—the carefully calibrated and skilfully carried-out attacks on the World Trade Center notwithstanding—and their 'technology modest'. That is to say, the technology was too unsophisticated to earn the commentator's admiration. As for the 'shoe-bomber' Richard Reid, he had been no more than 'an imbecile'. If he was 'the cream of al-Qaeda', it was declared, then 'things' were 'less dire than we feared'. 'Bin Laden is turbulence, but it passes', Peter Preston likewise assured *Guardian* readers in February 2004, while 'too much mindless jaw about jihad' was 'tosh'. And even after the July 2005 London bombings, a longstanding *Times* commentator, Matthew Parris, thought suicide-bombing to be 'just another craze', even a 'grizzly sort of terrorist chic'; 'the war' was 'not against evil but against silliness'; and the bombers were 'not evildoers' but 'credulous muppets'.

In a similarly infantile perception, the *Guardian* represented the British prime minister, Tony Blair, as 'British Robin to the American Batman'. America had 'gone ape' in the two years following the 9/11 attacks, thought a commentator in the *Guardian* in January 2004. Similarly, reference by President Bush in his State of the Union address in January 2004 to 'terrorist attacks' on 'Bali, Casablanca, Riyadh, Mombasa, Jerusalem, Istanbul and Baghdad' were met in the *Guardian* with the comment 'Well, better not go on holiday there'. To Hugo Young, in the *Guardian* in July 2000, Iran and Iraq were no more than 'gnats'; while Tim Hames, in *The Times* in April 2003, enquired—with foolish parallels adduced—whether Saddam Hussein was 'the new Elvis Presley'. In minimising what stood before it, it was a disposition which signalled a vulnerability to being taken for a ride, as in the 1930s.

Other forms of misjudgment were based on wishful thinking, or were errors which derived from the media commentariat's self-importance. Expressing surprise at the extent of American determination to make Islamism answer for its attacks, a *Guardian* columnist in December 2001 declared, 'I've been coming to the United States for many years, and thought I knew it. Yet it turns out I did not know it'. The fault, however, was implied to be that of the Americans rather than of the observer. 'Until 9/11 and the

Afghan war, perhaps America did not fully know itself', he suggested by way of explanation.

At the same time, the mass media snatched eagerly at every communiqué and video threatening dire consequences for the non-Islamic world, and showed indecent enthusiasm for carnage. Many in the public turned away in disgust from this passing 'show', while callow media interpreters themselves often had a free run in 'taking liberties' with the truth. In such soil cynicism flourished, despite the seriousness of the issues. A senior British government adviser, a mere one hour after a second passenger-jet had struck the World Trade Center, thus felt able to send a message to other officials that it was 'now a very good day to get out anything we want to bury'. That is, a convenient opportunity had been offered in which to release news unflattering to the government. On a 'dull day', so it was calculated, such news would have had greater negative impact.

Such disjunction from reality was clear in the diary-notes made by the editor of *The Times*, Peter Stothard, at the time of the attack on the World Trade Center, and published in December 2001. 'It seems wrong to write in these notes', he told himself on 12 September 2001, 'let alone to say out loud, how wonderful is a pictorial story about skyscrapers, about architectural creations so perfectly designed for a broadsheet page.... When airlines hit office blocks, the space is the thing'. On 15 September, 'the more often the images were repeated on TV, the harder the act of empathy became'; on 9 December, 'it meant something for only a very short time'; and on 10 December, he recorded, 'the books on Islam and political history are back on the office shelves, piled in a sort of order but with no pattern or theme, just like the events described within their covers'.

To admit such lack of engagement was at least candid. Together with other types of intellectual and moral failure to respond adequately to the impulses which have been coursing through the Islamic world, 'these notes' did not match the historic moment. Stridency of judgment served the truth even less. 'Time seems to have run out on this alliance'—the alliance between the United States and Britain—declared John Lloyd in the *New Statesman* in July 2002. 'The realities of Bush's policies now clash with the realities of Blair's', he pronounced, beneath a headline which read 'America, with Relish, Spits on Britain'. This was false, the product of an overwrought desire to shock.

Indeed, imperatives set by the need for sensation have brought further dangers. Files discovered in late 2001, in an al-Qaeda computer in Afghanistan, revealed that attempts to develop chemical and biological weapons had commenced 'when the enemy drew our attention to them by repeatedly expressing concern that they can be produced simply'. The American media has not only explained to all and sundry the vulnerabilities to attack of nuclear power-plants, but also given their locations, pointed out in detail how they might be sabotaged and graphically described what the effects of such sabotage would be.

Another form of naivete has been expressed in the American desire to be loved by its rivals and even, it sometimes seems, by its foes. Thus, shortly after the attacks on the United States, Newt Gingrich, the former speaker of the American House of Representatives, declared that it was 'unmistakable that some people really hate us. They understand what America is and what we stand for', he protested, 'and still they want to kill us'. That what they 'understood' might have been the ground for their animus appeared to be beyond his perception. A study-panel set up by the US government, and which included a leading Arab-American among its members, likewise announced in October 2003 that 'hostility toward America' had reached 'shocking levels'. There had been a 'catastrophic loss of America's reputation abroad', declared a typically self-lacerating commentator in the *Herald Tribune* the following day, putting salt on the wound with seeming satisfaction; adding, again falsely, that 'people outside the US don't think terrorism is an Evil force'.

In related fashion, the *New York Times* in September 2003 went far out of its way [to Jakarta] in order to ask Indonesian Muslims why America was 'unloved in the Islamic world'. The paper duly reported that it would 'take time' for the United States to 'build trust again' among Muslims, rather than the other way about. In a half-page spread, readers of the *New York Times* were also told by Indonesian students that America needed to be 'more sensitive'. In other words, the United States had to distinguish between Muslim right and American wrong; the Islamist case once more. Also sufficiently close, paradoxically, to Islamist excoriations, were the views expressed in September 2001 by the Baptist minister Jerry Falwell. According to Falwell, God had 'lifted the curtain of protection' which had shielded the United States, in anger at 'those who have tried to secularise America'. 'You helped this happen', he declared of 'pagans', 'abortionists', 'feminists', 'gays', 'lesbians' and others. America, declared Falwell, had 'probably' got what it deserved.

Other assertions, corresponding as little with reality as Falwell's, have informed us that 'in a battle between religion and technology', and 'between theocracy and democracy', the West was 'bound to win', as a *Times* columnist confidently put it in November 2001. According to the *New York Times* in September 2002, it similarly did not appear to be 'right' to argue that 'September 11 was the beginning of World War Three'. This, at least, was correct; such war had been in progress for decades, with its fronts spreading across the globe.

Western naivete has also taken the form of an over-demonstrative benignity to Islam, especially unpersuasive at times of exacerbations of tension and armed conflict. When the American president invited fifty-two Muslim diplomats to a traditional lamb-and-rice dinner at the White House in November 2001—in order to wish them a 'blessed Ramadan' while simultaneously bombing Afghanistan—this was naivete indeed. So, too, was the invitation, five months earlier, to a 'briefing' in the White House executive office-building of 160 members of the American Muslim Council, a prominent member of which had been under investigation for at least six years by the FBI for links to terrorism, and for which he was subsequently indicted. 'I sat on the front row', he declared.

A related British foolishness permitted a commentator in *The Times* in November 2001 to assert that the Koran was 'broadly ecumenical'. The future British foreign secretary, Jack Straw—with a large proportion of his parliamentary constituency Muslim, as was earlier mentioned—likewise declared in London's Regent's Park mosque in July 1989 that 'allegations about how Islamic society treated women' should be 'dealt with head-on'. Islam, Straw proclaimed, accorded women 'at least as important a position' as 'societies in the Judaic and Christian tradition'. This attempt to refute alleged misconceptions about Islamic teaching was both deluded and presumptuous. 'We do not need the likes of Jack Straw to tell us what the Koran teaches us … we know', was one Muslim woman's rejoinder. The similar assertion by the editor of the *Wall Street Journal*, Paul Steiger, that the murder of Daniel Pearl in February 2002 in Karachi had made a 'mockery' of 'everything' which his kidnappers 'claimed to believe in' was also not a realistic judgment.

Such expressions of seeming 'goodwill', necessary as may be in some circumstances, have again made for greater vulnerability at the hands of those who were ill-intentioned. Moreover, it was often hard to draw a line between benevolence and crassness. When Thomas Friedman in the *New York Times* in August 2002 expressed the wish that, along with passages from the Old and New Testaments, his school-age daughter 'had also been assigned the Koran' for study, it was a just suggestion. But to add that he could not 'conceive' of 'any Christian who would not deepen his own faith by reading the Koran' was unpersuasive in its excess. And what of the *Guardian* editorial in June 2002 entitled 'Our Muslim Future', with its subtitle 'Britain and Islam Can Make It Together'?

Whether benign or naive, each such statement expressed a position which was capable of being seen by Muslims as weakness not strength, as foolishness not wisdom. That which represented, to some, the virtue of 'tolerance' or 'understanding' was often no more than playing the sitting duck for Islamism's further progress. In this tragi-comedy, there have been many elements combined. They have included greater tenderness towards the malefactor's rights than to the public good, wilful obstructiveness in the attempts to find a common policy towards Islamist harm-doers, and misguided fear of the possible worse consequences of taking action than of doing little or nothing.

Evidence of Islamist incitement and recruitment, given to the authorities by Muslims themselves in Britain, was reported to have been 'virtually ignored' by the police until after the attacks on the United States. According to Charles Shoebridge, a former British intelligence officer—whose account was published in the *Guardian* in December 2001—such evidence was held to concern 'areas of cultural sensitivity' which were 'best left alone'. It was likewise revealed in December 2002 that two FBI agents, Rupert Wright and John Vincent, had been ordered by a superior in the 1990s to 'let sleeping dogs lie' and to cease their investigations of a pro-Islamist group in Chicago, later discovered to have been involved in the funding of the al-Qaeda attacks in 1998 on the US embassies in Kenya and Tanzania.

Letting 'sleeping dogs lie' was undoubtedly the motive, at least in part, for the refusals during the Rushdie conflict to prosecute Muslims in Britain for incitement to kill, as earlier discussed. More than a decade later, complaint was still being made—as in *The Times* in February 2002—that a 'certificate of immunity' appeared to have been 'unofficially issued to Muslims, and to Muslims alone, who publicly call for people to be murdered'. By February 2003 an exception had been made in the case of the already-mentioned Abdullah el-Faisal, a British Muslim cleric sentenced to nine years' imprisonment for 'soliciting murder' and 'inciting racial hatred'. But the general point was a just one.

In such abstentions, unwillingnesses and failures, as in some of the bunglings, flippancies and naivetes noted earlier, there has often been something more than mere incompetence, inadvertency or misjudgment at work. Terms such as 'cultural sensitivity' give a clue to what this 'something more' might have been: a desire—which manifested itself in local administrative decisions as well as in the Security Council of the United Nations—to be *thought well of* for the breadth of one's sympathies and understanding. This has arguably not been a moral stance at all, but the absence of it; not a token of engagement with actuality, but of retreat from it.

Depending on circumstances, the balance of moral opinion in the Western liberal democracies has also shifted, and shifted again, on the relative merits of this or that policy towards the Muslim world. Immediately after the

September 2001 attacks on the United States President Chirac declared that France would be 'in the front line in the combat against international terrorist networks, shoulder to shoulder with America, its ally forever'. 'We are all Americans' was then the common cry, but in general it did not last. The attempt to promote French prestige in the wider Arab world—as well as the opinion held of President Chirac by millions of Muslims in France—weighed more heavily on French policy than sympathy with the United States, once the dust of 9/11 had settled. 'We are all Americans' disappeared from the lexicons of political pretence, and the United States was left by the French to shoulder its own burdens in Iraq.

Indeed, there were many issues on which the US found itself as embattled in its relations with its allies as with its foes. Objectors to 'American unilateralism' were charged by the US with preferring to do nothing. In the case of Iraq, the US accused its opponents of permitting Saddam Hussein to 'take liberties' with the United Nations, while the UN was accused of prevarication and weakness. It was a weakness reminiscent (for some) of the causes of failure of the League of Nations in the 1930s. As the Islamic *ummah* looked on, ends were willed—or pretended to be willed—but not means; and angry Americans declared Europe to be militarily and economically weak, inward-looking, and 'lacking in seriousness' in its positions.

The equally anomic times of the 1930s brought profound political differences between the Western powers, and varying degrees of fear of, and complicity with, the cause of the dictators. Now, the progress of militant Islam and large increases in the size of the Muslim diaspora in the West have made for new forms of *raison d'état*, especially in Europe. In this rapidly changing world-order, resentment—shared by Muslims and many non-Muslims—has grown at the use and abuse of American power, as well as the belief that those who have carried the fight to Islam have lacked prudential foresight. There has also been sympathy (on the 'left') for the awakening from its torpor of the ex-colonial underdogs of Islam and Arabism, whom some would pat encouragingly on their heads as they rise. Thus, even 'rogue states' and 'terrorism' are capable of being perceived in ways which have often been incomprehensible to policy-makers in the United States.

It has faced moral objection, passive resistance and active impediment at almost every step it has taken. In January 2003, the Labour parliamentarian George Galloway shouted in the House of Commons for a 'stop' to attempts to protect Britain from what the prime minister, referring to Iraq, described as 'a threat to our country'. In the same month a *Guardian* commentator described the recalcitrant French president as 'speak[ing] for England'. Also in January

2003, Galloway accused Labour ministers, again *à propos* Saddam's Iraq, of 'mobilising mendacity on a military scale not seen since Dr. Goebbels denounced Czech and Polish aggression'. In February 2003, a German commentator, Josef Joffe, the editor of *Die Zeit*, argued that those who took such stands ended up 'on the side of Saddam, in an intellectually corrupt position'.

These divisions, themselves generated by militant Arabism's and radical Islam's pressures on the non-Muslim world, were naturally fastened upon by America's Arab and Muslim foes. 'The scepticism [sc. about reports of Iraq's possession of 'weapons of mass destruction'] which we read of in America and other countries', declared General Amir al-Saadi, one of Saddam Hussein's principal advisers, in February 2003, 'is very heartening'. The ambassadors of Syria and of the Saddam regime, addressing the Security Council in March 2003, praised the Catholic Church, and the French, German, Russian and Chinese governments, as well as demonstrators in many countries, for their opposition to war. Shortly before air-attacks were launched on the city, a Baghdad newspaper, *Babel*, celebrated the 'humiliating international isolation' of the United States and Britain; Abdul-Razzaq al-Saadi, one of Baghdad's leading imams, proclaimed from the pulpit that 'the entire world, Muslims and non-Muslims, curses the aggressive intentions of the American administration'.

Whenever the 1930s parallels were pressed, charges of 'appeasement' were heard. But for others in the West, the United States was the principal malefactor. Indeed, for some 'on the left', it was the 'current American elite'—described by John Pilger in the *Daily Mirror* in January 2003 as the true 'Third Reich of our times'—which was being 'appeased' by the British. In consequence, there was often more concern shown for the 'victims' of US policy than for those who had come under Islamist or despotic Arabist attack. Many objectors to the imminent Iraq War focussed not on 'the danger it threatens to one's own side but, paradoxically, [the danger] that it threatens against the other', as Sir John Keegan wrote in January 2003. 'The people I'm concerned about', declared a Labour MP on the eve of the attack on Iraq, 'are the Iraqi citizens who are going to get killed'. 'Dictators' had been appeased in the 1930s, argued Keegan; now those being appeased included the 'Arab street', 'liberal opinion at home', and 'legalists in the United Nations and other international organisations'.

Some non-Muslims seemed to lose their senses entirely. The United States was not comparable with 'the Third Reich', and Jerry Falwell's abortionists and gays did not 'help' the attacks of 11 September 2001 to 'happen'. Other notions could be even more surreal. The German modernist composer Karl-Heinz Stockhausen not only praised the attack on the World Trade

Center for the 'imagination of the act' and the 'precision of its execution', but called it 'the greatest work of art for the whole cosmos'. An editor of the journal *Index on Censorship* similarly described the killing of Theo van Gogh in November 2004 as a 'marvellous piece of theatre'. 'What are 20,000 dead in New York?' the Italian Nobel laureate Dario Fo asked after 9/11, exaggerating the total of casualties in order to posture more strikingly at a safe distance from the ruins. 'This violence', he declared, 'is the legitimate daughter of the culture of violence, hunger, and inhumane exploitation'.

Very different moralities were made manifest after the attack on the World Trade Center. New York firemen and police sacrificed their lives without need of being summoned to their civic duties; American Roman Catholic bishops declared that the United States had a 'grave obligation' to 'defend the common good'; a curmudgeonly individual testified to the *New York Times* that, despite 'not being of a benevolent nature', she had 'in one blink become a citizen of the *polis*'. Some Americans talked of a 'wound' that would heal, others of a wound that would not. Patriotic citizens spontaneously paraded and sang on New England village-greens. Yet within only a year, a Yale professor, Stephen Carter, could be heard declaring that 'our brief moment of unity' had 'become but a frail memory, fading fast', and 'perhaps was after all a chimera'.

Against this cultural self-doubt was ranged the rhetoric of 'resoluteness', of certitude of direction in the teeth of the suicidal hijacker or the fulminating cleric. In August 2002, the 'peace lobbies' were accused by Richard Perle, head of the Pentagon's defence policy board, of 'feckless moralising', while a clenched toughness became the order of the day among American war-planners. 'Why are we in such doubt', asked one, 'and worried more about what the Muslim world thinks of us rather than we of them? Why have we not seen one American offer a "Who cares?" or a "Too bad"?' Treating with those 'compromised by terror' was declared to be 'out of the question'. 'No concessions' could, or would, be made to 'terrorism'. It would be neither 'winked at', nor 'contained', but destroyed.

In high places and low, especially in the Anglo-American world, the time of 'taking liberties' with America and the West was pronounced to be at an end. 'This nation and our friends', proclaimed George W. Bush in January 2003 in his State of the Union address, 'are all that stand between a world at peace and a world of chaos and constant alarm. Once again, we are called to defend the safety of our people and the hopes of all mankind'. 'Old' Europe's equivocations and the United Nations' attempts to slough off its responsibilities were scoffed at, while before his fall Saddam Hussein was colourfully accused of 'stiffing the world'. There was much talk of 'coming clean', of clocks ticking, of time being 'short' or 'running out' and of 'games' being over. 'If we need to act', Bush declared in March 2003, 'we will act. When it comes to our security, we don't need the UN's permission to do so', he added. 'Let no one be in any doubt, the rules of the game are changing', similarly asserted the British prime minister in August 2005, shortly after the London bombings.

There were those for whom this was too tough by half; there were others for whom it appeared not to be tough enough. The *Daily Telegraph* had proclaimed in August 2001 that 'irresistible force' was the 'only answer' to suicide-bombers; a former US Navy chief petty officer expressed the view in the *New York Times* in September 2001 that Osama bin Laden should be 'buried with a pig-skin'. Members of the crowd at a pro-Israeli rally in Washington in April 2002 called for Israel's prime minister, Ariel Sharon, to be 'tougher'. Even a pastor of the First Church of Christ in Highland, Indiana, thought in September 2001 that the Americans should 'just make glass out of Afghanistan'. Another voice of middle America declared that 'nothing would be cruel enough' for bin Laden.

'I'd skin him alive and pour salt on him' was the word from a customer at the Pink House restaurant and bar in Ogden, Illinois, three days after the World Trade Center attack. As for Afghanistan, 'the whole country' should be 'levelled'. From the Pentagon on the same day came the opinion of the deputy-secretary of defence, Paul Wolfowitz—later retracted—that states which 'sponsor terrorism' should be 'ended'. A year later, a retired bank-clerk in Tampa, Florida, thought it was necessary not only to 'clean up all of Afghanistan' but also 'all of Iraq'. 'We need to get our troops out there and clean up the mess. This is what the government should do—mop it up', she said.

In the event, precisely this was attempted and failed. There was no 'clean-up' of the 'mess', because no such 'clean-up' was possible whether in Afghanistan, Iran, Iraq, Palestine, Somalia or Sudan. Nor could there be a 'clean-up' of the related 'mess' in the Muslim diaspora itself. Instead, after the fall and capture of Saddam Hussein, there was still greater moral and political confusion about the tasks America had assumed. For all its fire-power—or because of its fire-power—it appeared only to have increased the number of its foes, including among the politicians and publics of its allies. But why this should be so, and what to do about it—the sources of the moral confusion— were more awkward matters for Americans to grasp. Some, including a former director of military history at the United States air force academy, believed that 'the war' would escalate. Radical Islamists would 'not go easily into the night', he wrote in an e-mail circulated in the United States after the September 2001 attacks. 'They do not fear us', he declared, concluding that 'in spite of our overwhelming conventional strength as the world's only super-power, we are the underdog in this fight'.

This was a rare perception. More common were fears about 'Trojan horses', 'fifth-columns' and 'sleeper-cells' at work in the heartlands of the United States and other countries. 'I notice you and it worries me', John Maniscalco, a pilot with American Airlines—whose aircraft were hijacked in September 2001—declared in July 2002. He was referring to 'Arab Muslims in America'. 'I need your help', he continued. 'As a rational American, trying to protect my country and my family in an irrational and unsafe world, I must know how to tell the difference between you and the Arab/Muslim terrorist. ...Do you pray in your many daily prayers that Allah will bless this nation, that He will protect and prosper it? Or do you pray that Allah will destroy it in one of your 'jihads'?...Do you love America? If this is your commitment, then I need you to start letting me know about it....It is up to you to show me where you stand'. The anxieties which he expressed were more crudely for-mulated by a gunshop-owner in Amarillo, Texas. 'I'll be honest with you', he told a reporter. 'I see somebody that's Arabic, Pakistani or Indian. I'm looking at him, like "What the hell do you have under your coat?" Everybody is scaring me to death right now'.

There was more harshness in the view expressed in August 2002 by the British Indian writer Farrukh Dhondy. 'Fellow-Brits'—that is, British Mus-lims—who had gone to Afghanistan in order to fight with the Taliban 'went out to destroy this civilisation and now cry to return to it', he declared. They were 'clearly not terrorists' but 'traitors to our society' who 'should be tried for treason'. Such trial was 'necessary for the future of Britain', wrote Dhondy, if the 'venom' of such 'traitors' was not to be 'spread' in the 'land of their birth and citizenship'. Rihal Ahmed, a British Muslim from the English midlands who had been captured by US forces in Afghanistan, was reported to have gone into hiding in fear of his life on returning to Britain from Guantanamo. 'Racial trouble', it was said, was expected if he reappeared in his home-town. The situation of diaspora Muslims was thus deeply contradictory: one of increasing strength vis à vis the non-Muslim world as Islam advanced, but often worsening at the day-to-day level in ways which Muslims feared.

Yet this predicament was balanced by human rights and civil libertarian criticisms of most measures—legal, political or military—which had been adopted in the 'war against terror'. There were 'no circumstances' that could justify the death-penalty in a trial of Saddam Hussein, according both to an official spokesman for the European Union and to Kofi Annan in December

2003. The war in Iraq, declared Human Rights Watch in January 2004, was not justified as 'an intervention in defence of human rights, even though it ended a brutal regime'. True, it said, Saddam Hussein had an 'atrocious human rights record'. But there had been 'no imminent or ongoing slaughter', and in its absence the assault on the regime was wrong. Intervention, the organisation added, 'should not be used belatedly to address atrocities that were ignored in the past'.

When the World Trade Center fell, human rights experts were quickly on the scene while the citizens of New York and elsewhere struggled with their civic duties and tasks. In a full-page advertisement in the *New York Times* on 24 September 2001, Amnesty International described the attacks as a 'massive violation of human rights'. They were not. They were a violation of a nation's security and of the security of its citizen-body. 'We must unite to fight terrorism', the advertisement read, 'but we should also unite to protect the human rights of all'. That was to say—and it was swiftly said—Amnesty International expected the rights of both malefactors and victims to be respected and protected. But a clear moral distinction was not made between the perpetrators and the objects of terrorist attack, 'abhorrent' or 'outrageous' as civil libertarians might in passing have held such attacks to be.

'Now we really need rights'—as if we had not already got them—the 'academic director of the Human Rights Act Research Project' at the University of London declared in the *Guardian* in October 2001. 'As we stand on the brink of war in the name of democracy', she wrote, 'we should ask ourselves what kind of democracy we wish to defend'. As others cleared the rubble of ruined buildings, treated the harmed, buried the dead and comforted the living, this question was not required to be asked, and least of all asked of those who were doing such works of duty. 'No one denies the awesome responsibility on the Government to protect us', the siren voices nevertheless cried, 'but it is when fear is stalking the land that bills of rights'—rather than determination of purpose to defend the civic order—'are needed most'. That is, such rights were not merely needed, as indeed they are, but 'needed most'.

Furthermore, in December 2002, after the British government had published a dossier on the Saddam regime's human rights abuses, the secretary-general of Amnesty International held it to be 'nothing but a cold and calculated manipulation of the work of human rights activists'. On the one hand, the concept of human rights implied an equal regard for all involved in the 9/11 attacks, perpetrators and victims alike. On the other, a sense of outrage at breaches of human rights by the Iraqi dictator could be diluted by greater disapproval of those who sought to draw attention to, or to correct, them.

Likewise, the United Nations High Commissioner for Human Rights, Mary Robinson, addressing a meeting of the Organisation of the Islamic Conference in Geneva in September 2002, condemned the United States for having 'eroded civil liberties at home and human rights standards around the world', while asserting that 'no one can deny the acceptance of the universality of human rights by Islamic states'. Yet articles 24 and 25 of the 'Cairo Declaration on Human Rights in Islam', adopted in 1991 by the Organisation of the Islamic Conference, make the Universal Declaration of Human Rights 'subject to the Islamic Sharia': the latter is described as the 'only source of reference' for the Islamic position on the subject. Hence, in 1992 the International Federation for Human Rights and the International Commission of Jurists condemned the 'Cairo Declaration'. It was said by them to 'threaten the inter-cultural consensus upon which international human rights instruments are based', to 'introduce an intolerable discrimination against both non-Muslims and women', and to 'reveal a deliberately restricted character in regard to certain fundamental rights and freedoms'. Notwithstanding this, the UN High Commissioner for Human Rights had not only pronounced the contrary, but had done so before a gathering of the representatives of the world's Muslim nations.

In the name of Western Enlightenment ideals—and of the United Nations—a public invitation was again being extended to the illiberal, and worse, to consider themselves to be enlightened too. It was also an invitation to take whatever further liberties they wished with the non-Muslim world. Indeed, as Islamism advanced, most human rights activists remained more exercised by the 'taking of liberties' from Muslims than the 'taking of liberties' by them; even after the London suicide-bombings of July 2005, British human rights advocates objected to the creation of new criminal offences of 'glorifying' or 'endorsing' 'terrorism', and of giving or receiving 'terrorist' training. Moreover, while countries represented on the United Nations Commission for Human Rights could elect Libya—with what was described as an 'appalling' human rights record—as its head in January 2003, international lawyers, the UN Security Council and European nations adjudged many American actions to be 'illegal' and even 'international crimes'.

Plain foolishness could also stand in for policy. 'If you are serious about terrorism', declared Tony Benn, the veteran of the Labour left, in October 2001, 'the first thing you do is ban the arms trade'. A knowing impossibility, it therefore amounted to a counsel to do nothing. Other music to Arabist and Islamist ears was provided by the sounds of Western breast-beating and self-incrimination. 'Britain to Blame for Many World Problems, Says Straw', ran a headline in *The Times* in November 2002. 'There's a lot wrong with imperialism', the foreign secretary told the *New Statesman*, and 'a lot of the problems I have to deal with now are a consequence of our colonial past'. True as might be, his confessional criticisms of Britain's historical role in the Middle East, in Afghanistan, in India, in Pakistan and in Africa could only be taken by Islamists as further moral justification for whatever they might choose to do.

This instinct in some for self-flagellation could be taken to inordinate lengths. After a twenty-one-year record of unblemished service, a British prison-officer at Blundeston Prison in Suffolk was dismissed in May 2002 for 'misconduct'. It was said that he had made 'insulting' and 'insensitive' remarks about Osama bin Laden which 'could have been' heard—although there was no evidence that they had been heard—by three Muslims visiting an inmate. A tribunal which reversed the decision in January 2004 revealed that the prison governor had ordered his staff to 'say nothing about terrorist attacks because of the high number of Muslims in the prison'. Even reference to a 'British way' in matters of conduct was described in November 2003 by the Commission for Racial Equality not merely as 'offensive' but as liable to 'drive young people [sc. Muslims] into the hands of extremists'.

'Culturally sensitive' *mea culpas* of this kind invited the taking of the moral initiative by those to whom such deferences were paid. They took their (minor) place among the encouragements provided to Islamism by the non-Muslim world's moral conflicts. Competing interests and policy divisions, the taste for media sensation, and human rights scruples between them strengthened Islamism's hand. In this 'vortex', the violator of the law could be transmuted into an innocent victim of the law, and treasonable acts could be made to seem permissible acts of moral choice. Often, moral and legal focus was entirely lost under the pressure of claims by some Muslims to ethical autonomy in their adoptive countries, and by the exploitation both by Muslims and non-Muslims of the precedence given in democratic societies to civil liberty over public safety.

In such circumstances, the tolerances, moral inertias and hidden sympathies of the corrupted liberal could themselves become liberticidal, and the distinction between the giving and taking of liberties dissolve.

CHAPTER EIGHT

Thinking within Limits

There have been many moral evasions and intellectual side-steps by which inconvenient and unwelcome truths about the Arabic and Islamic revivals are sought to be kept at a distance in the non-Muslim world. These evasions and side-steps often require as much self-deception as the Twelve Devices of argument discussed earlier. They are also as stereotyped and easily recognisable as the latter.

In the non-Muslim case they can be used to provide a rationale for passivity of response, or non-response, to the ethical, cultural and political challenges which the Muslim revival poses to the non-Muslim world. Some non-Muslims have used exaggeration and outright falsehood to justify their hostile and violent responses to this revival. Others have preferred to wish it away by denying or minimising it; others again have explained (or justified) Islamist anger and violence by attributing responsibility for it to the non-Muslim world. Some of these devices overlap with, or are the mirror-images of, those adopted by Muslims who feel themselves under pressure to answer for what is said or done in Islam's name. Others again are *sui generis*. But all have expressed in their own ways the preferences of many in the non-Muslim world for not knowing, or not accepting, what is afoot.

These responses, as we have already seen, can be presented in moral guise, or as issues of 'sensitivity' to diversity of belief and culture. They can be based upon 'pragmatic' considerations. Some have derived from 'liberal' good-will, others from hard-headed *realpolitik*; others have sought to compensate for the rough or racist will-to-harm Muslims who have settled in the non-Muslim world. Other responses again can be understood as products of a psychologically complex proneness to self-blame and even, sometimes, as expressions of Western self-hatred.

I set out here Nine Arguments which have been commonly used to keep at bay 'unwelcome and inconvenient truths' about the Islamic revival and its advance. As with the Twelve Devices of Muslim argument they are presented here in schematic form for analytical purposes. In practice, these types of argument are not mutually exclusive. They can be employed in combination, as well as singly. Each is also flexible enough to be put to use in almost any set of circumstances, or can be swapped for another as changing occasion is thought to warrant.

TYPE A: *'Your-"facts"-are-mere-suppositions-or-are-suspect'.*

Regular resort has been had to this argument. It has much in common with the devices of Muslim argument, examined in an earlier chapter, by means of which assertions against Islam and Islamism are claimed to be false. The Type A argument has been employed by non-Muslims in order, for example, to oppose an 'activist' or 'interventionist' stance towards the Muslim world. In this type of argument, it will be held—sometimes justly—that what is alleged against Islamists, Islam or the Arab world is untrue or cannot be proven. It is an argument which, again conveniently to Islamism's advance, frequently coincides with the latter's own positions.

Thus, in October 2001, not long after the attack on the World Trade Center and the Pentagon, a commentator in the *Guardian* declared that the evidence of the involvement of bin Laden in the attack consisted 'largely' of 'supposition and conjecture'. Similarly, a *Guardian* editorial asserted—of a video of bin Laden, released in December 2001, which showed him in company with associates celebrating the attacks—that it was 'impossible' not 'to think that something about it [sc. the video]' was 'a put-up-job', and that 'it should not be taken wholly at face-value'. The following day it pressed the Type A device further, citing 'special effects' experts in order to suggest that the tape would have been 'relatively easy to make'.

As we saw earlier, Muslims also doubted whether fellow-Muslims could have carried out the 9/11 attack, pointing their fingers elsewhere. Indeed, the suggestion that 'the CIA or Mossad' 'must have known about September 11 in advance'—but had 'failed to stop it' for their own sinister purposes—was widespread in the Arab and Muslim worlds, as the *New York Times* reported in

January 2002. Hence, when the American writer Gore Vidal called for an 'investigation into 9/11' and declared that 'we still don't know by whom we were struck that infamous Tuesday', his argument—that this was a Type A 'suspect' act—was congruent, by implication, with that of many Muslims themselves. He was also suggesting that mere supposition ruled; and that the attack might have been carried out by other hands than those of the Islamists who claimed and celebrated it.

In such Type A questioning of the given facts, responsibility has often been transferred from unknown foes to the non-Muslim world itself, the converse of the strategy seen in the Twelve Devices of Muslim argument. The attribution of falsehood to American government pronouncements has been for many, especially on the 'left', a reflex response. Indeed, it was so even before the imbroglio over supposed 'weapons of mass destruction' in Iraq gave support to users of the Type A device. Moreover, when this device has been employed at full stretch, almost anything—exactly as in the Twelve Devices of Muslim argument—could be asserted, but now by non-Muslims, as to the culpability of the non-Muslim world. Here it once more coincided, in style and often in content also, with Islamist apologia.

Thus, just as the Indonesian cleric Abu Bakr Bashir was 'certain' that the Bali bombing was 'engineered by foreign intelligence', so too the British Labour MP, Michael Meacher, was certain in September 2003 that the 9/11 attacks were an 'extremely convenient pretext' to put a 'blueprint for US world domination' 'into action'. The Type A proposition has therefore been as flexible an instrument in non-Muslim hands as the Twelve Devices are in Muslim argument. Like the latter, the former is available to sustain a variety of interchangeable positions. But the device has chiefly served in polemics with those who have been seen as hyperactive in their responses to the Islamic challenge. Those who use the Type A device have therefore held the non-Muslim world to be itself at fault in whatever befalls it; have argued that belligerent responses to the Muslim world rest upon exaggerating or inventing the dangers it poses; and have accused belligerents of failing to understand the reasons for such assaults, of having foreknowledge of them or even of having carried them out themselves.

In debates from 2002 to 2005 about whether Saddam Hussein did or did not possess 'weapons of mass-destruction', the Type A argument came into its own. Continuous denials by Iraq of such possession, and categorical claims by the US, Britain and other 'coalition' countries to the contrary, were crisscrossed by assertions and counter-assertions, inferences, innuendoes, qualifications, retractions and further falsifications. The Type A argument was deployed by partisans of every view. Type A doubt—which divided the West—was in particular mobilised to great effect against American and British claims of the imminence of the threat posed by Saddam Hussein.

It is essential that the truth be known, but in the labyrinth of the struggles between the Muslim and non-Muslim worlds such truth has often been difficult to ascertain. Propaganda and counter-propaganda, exaggeration, deception, fear, the promptings of special pleading, wishful thinking, and misinformation governed and clouded judgment about Iraq's 'weapons of mass-destruction'. The Type A argument not only came into its own, but appeared to be vindicated, as apparently certain knowledge—of 'uranium purchases', chemical weapons, mobile laboratories, bio-organisms kept in scientists' homes, surface-to-air missiles, ballistic weapons of prohibited ranges, and so on—became subject to Type A dismissal as imaginary or overstated. Other assertions that such weapons had been hidden or 'sent abroad' were in turn rejected.

By serving, or seeking, to diminish the sense in non-Muslims of the dangers to others of the Saddam regime, the Type A argument fulfilled its primary and most common purpose for those who deployed it. It was that of using the 'supposition-and-conjecture' device not merely to discredit 'over-reaction' but to suggest that discretion, and even inaction, in the non-Muslim world was the better part of valour. Moreover, its implications often were exactly those which Islamist action and argument sought to achieve: the sense that to grasp the Arab and Muslim nettles was a risky undertaking, and at worst a crime.

Another form of argument in which the Type A device was implicit lay in the suggestion that, whatever general threat the non-Islamic world might face from Islamism, it was a threat which was 'amorphous', as the dean of the Stanford Law School chose to put it in September 2002. Likewise, threats could be held to be not evident, or not 'immediate'—as in the Iraqi case—according to choice. Even when it was conceded there was a threat of some kind, it was often held to be one which had been given falsely definite shape and dimension by overstatement and distortion, in order to furnish pretexts for the Western conquest of the Muslim and Arab worlds—an argument which reappears in the Type C device.

TYPE B: *'You-have-the-facts-completely-wrong-and-your-judgments-are-therefore-wholly-false'*.

This is the 'strong' variant of the Type A device, and has generally been employed to suggest that supposed 'facts' should not have been attended to at all. As we saw with the Twelve Devices, it is also among the commonest forms of argument presented by Muslims to the non-Muslim world, and has similarly been adopted by non-Muslims in seeking to refute the arguments of fellow non-Muslims. The Type B device has been of particular service in debate with those who are held to be unduly bellicose about, or insufficiently understanding of, the Muslim (and even the Islamist) case or cause.

The assertion that 'the-facts-are-quite-different' is everywhere a gambit of debate upon almost any subject under the sun; refusal of an opponent's premises is a commonplace of disputation, whoever the disputants are. But in polemics among non-Muslims about the sources of Muslim anger, fundamental disagreements about facts make the finding of common ground hard, or even impossible, to find.

Events are denied to have occurred and seeming facts are elided by all parties, according to their choice (again) of what may be unwelcome or inconvenient to have generally known and discussed. Whether Islam is or is not a 'religion of peace', whether the 'war on terrorism' is or is not a war against Islam, whether the existence and conduct of Israel is or is not the cause-of-causes of the conflict between the Muslim and non-Muslim worlds and whether this or that Muslim nation is or is not a danger to others, are objects not simply of contending political judgment. They are also differences over how historical events should be interpreted, and even over whether disputed events took place at all.

As was shown earlier, such differences among non-Muslims could be taken to the length of attributing the events of 9/11 to the Americans themselves. Using the 'strong' Type B variant of the Type A device, the French writer Thierry Meyssan argued in his book *L'Effroyable Imposture* ('The Horrifying Fraud' or 'The Appalling Lie'), published in the spring of 2002, that the Pentagon was not hit by an aircraft but by a guided air-to-ground missile which had been fired on the orders of 'extreme right-wingers' in the American government and military itself. Similarly, the two aircraft which struck the World Trade Center were said to be pilotless and empty 'drones' 'programmed' to crash into the building, and were not manned by Islamist associates of Osama bin Laden. The further suggestion made by Meyssan in his Type B argument was that the events of 9/11 were foreknown, were supported, were instigated or were organised by the United States to provide grounds for its invasion of Iraq, and in order to promote its plans to conquer the world by a combination of trickery and force of arms.

Inconvenient or unwelcome truth was in this way again kept at a dis-

tance—here by a non-Muslim—through an again near-paranoid application
of the Type B device. It was a conspiracy theory which converged with the
type of argument adopted by Muslims, often from anxiety lest they, or their
'image', be harmed by the acts of fellow-Muslims. 'This was an American
action, 100 per cent', Muhammad Kamel Khamis, an Egyptian neighbour of
the family of Mohammed Atta, the leader of the attacks, insisted to the *New
York Times* in September 2002. 'It's not easy even for a pigeon to fly in America
without permission. How could an Egyptian do this?' Khamis asked.

Type A or B arguments have thus been used equally by both Muslims and
non-Muslims. They have most often been employed to enable the user to take
a distance from events, in the first case to avoid a sense of moral implication
in such events, and in the second case to avoid a sense of obligation to call
attacks on the non-Muslim world by their right names. They have had in
common a denial of the veracity (and the honesty) of assertions by non-Muslims who have been critical of Muslim and Arab actions. Such commonality
of position could extend, for example, to the claim—adopted by a number of
non-Muslim 'experts', politicians included—that a fellow non-Muslim had
'no-understanding-of-the-true-nature-of-Islam'. Here, disputation has frequently turned upon the supposed 'misperception' of the 'true meaning' of
jihad. It is a 'misperception' which a minority of non-Muslims will seek to
correct in the same terms as those adopted by Muslims.

In May 2002, in his 'commencement address' to fellow-Harvard students,
Zayed Yasin, a Muslim American born in Chicago, denied that the word had a
belligerent sense. In a speech which was at first entitled 'American Jihad'—
until protest forced him to change it to 'Of Faith and Citizenship'—Yasin
declared that jihad was not to be equated with 'holy war'. Rather, it essentially
meant 'a struggle to do the right thing'. Far from being a term of bellicose
intent in requital of harms done to Islam, it signified, said Yasin, 'a struggle for
the refinement of self', 'a struggle for the perfection of one's own inner
morality'.

A half-truth, this revised version of the meaning of jihad was endorsed
by some non-Muslims on the Harvard faculty. 'Jihad' was not a word of summons to war-for-faith. Instead, according to members of the Harvard pro-
fessoriat, 'true jihad' signified a 'struggle without arms', and even an effort to
'do good in society'. The Right Reverend Michael Nazir-Ali, Anglican
bishop of Rochester, similarly explained in May 2002 that 'the root verb
jahada', from which jihad is derived, meant only 'to make an effort'. There
were circumstances, explained the bishop, in which it might be used as a
term to 'justify armed conflict when Islam is in danger'. But its core meaning

was morally worthy. To think otherwise was to invite a Type B reproach: 'You-have-no-understanding-of-the-true-nature-of-Islam'. To this subject of jihad I will return.

The 'lay' variant of this Type B device was the common argument that 'You-have-no-real-understanding-of-the-Arab-and-Islamic-world-or-of-its-culture'. This was a device adopted by non-Muslim 'experts', once more, as well as by Muslim interlocutors. It served to refute—sometimes justifiably—the drawing of negative inferences and conclusions from known facts or patterns of events. But led by this form of the Type B argument, the way was also opened to evasions and inversions of truth of a kind similar to those found in the Twelve Devices.

With the Type B assertion as a premise, leading 'left'- and 'right'-wing political figures in the non-Muslim world could for example deny that anti-civic Muslim conduct in the diaspora, or a related lack of democracy in the Islamic world, were what they seemed. Those who were sufficiently 'sensitive' to cultural difference, or sufficiently informed about the history of colonialism, would recognise that Muslim separatism in the diaspora was merely an aspect of the rich diversity of a plural and tolerant society. Similarly, a nepotistic Arab monarchy or Muslim military tyranny could be re-presented as defending a nation's interests from Western subjugation.

Hence, when non-Muslims understood the real import of Arab and Islamic political actions, they would also recognise, for example, that Israel was similar to South Africa at its apartheid 'worst', as the editor of the *Guardian* expressed it in May 2001; or that Palestinian militants were engaged in a 'vicious anti-colonial war', in the already-cited words of Robert Fisk of the *Independent* in May 2002. Such *aperçus* were again not distinct from those of Islamism itself. They rested upon a corollary of the Type B argument, also shared with most Muslims: that the critic of Islam's ethics or of Islamism's actions, being saddled with the wrong facts and with misperceptions based upon them, must necessarily reach erroneous moral and political conclusions on the subject.

The motives for arguing this have often been complex. They have included the reductive need of some liberal and 'left' non-Muslims to simplify the issues before them, in order that they could be fitted within a pre-existing schema of interpretation. In many Muslims there was a parallel need to dismiss Western responses to Islamism's excesses as vitiated by ignorance, or as wholly unfounded. However, some non-Muslims who held other non-Muslims to be under-informed, or wrong, in their assertions about Islam could adopt Type A and B arguments for worthier reasons; indeed, in the cause of rationality itself.

Here, objection by non-Muslims to the alleged insensibility of Western interpretations of the internal affairs of the Muslim world could be presented as a 'thoughtful' corrective to broad-brush generalisations. Nevertheless, the line between sweet reason and 'liberal' apologia—even for Islamism's most abhorrent actions—has often been a fine one. This line was trodden, and crossed, in such arguments as that 'Islamists in general neither rule out violent means nor, as stereotypes suggest, joyfully embrace them', as a *Guardian* commentator declared in November 1997. However, he continued, 'once they have taken up such means, they are as subject as other extremist groups everywhere to the corruption of violence'.

This could be seen as a valid attempt to compensate for immoderate judgments about the methods to which the more violent Islamists resort. But, once more, by the device of implicitly suggesting that Islam and Islamism had been misunderstood by the unsubtle, it was both a tempering of unwelcome truth and a near-exculpation of Islamist violence. It offered the proposition that those who practised violence in Islam's name became subject to inner pressures difficult or impossible to resist. A more blatant use of this device was the 'explanation' in July 2001, also by a *Guardian* commentator, that, like the word *jihad*, the Arabic word *hamas*—that of the eponymous Palestinian 'terror-group'—had been misinterpreted.

Citing the 'great Islamic activist Hamza Yusuf Hanson', George Monbiot told *Guardian* readers that *hamas* meant 'enthusiastic but intelligent anger'. Moreover, such meaning was not only 'radical' but 'comprehensible'. The word *hamas*, Monbiot declared, 'explains itself'; and, by inference, the violent acts carried out by Hamas were also 'self-explanatory' as acts of anger, but presumably of 'enthusiastic' and 'intelligent' anger. Once more, this was clearly intended as a Type B 'corrective'—grounded (by a non-Muslim) upon the authority of a 'great Islamic activist'—to the supposedly crass misjudgments of the under-informed. But it was also an implicit apologia for violence.

Going further down this Type B path, 'suicide hijackers' were not 'cowards' or 'deranged', as some averred. Such popular responses' to them in America, after the attacks of '9/11', showed a 'lack of perception', declared Jonathan Clark in *The Times* in November 2001. Instead, they were 'intelligent, courageous religious zealots'. In the *London Review of Books* in March 2002, the Cambridge classics don, Mary Beard—similarly correcting others' 'lack of perception'—saw 'extraordinary acts of bravery' in terrorism. In bin Laden's version in September 2003 of the same argument, 'he who wants to learn... courage in support of religion should follow in the footsteps of Said al-Ghamdi, Mohamed Atta, Khaled al-Mihdar, Ziad al-Jarrah and their brethren', the hijackers of 9/11.

In the *Observer* in June 2002, the thwarted plan of a young Saudi, Zuher al-Tbaiti, to blow up a British or American warship in the Strait of Gibraltar was likewise presented as a 'daring operation'. In March 2002, David Hirst in the *Guardian* described Yasser Arafat as 'the world's most exalted political prisoner' and the 'supreme, heroic embodiment of his people's will'. In December 2001, in the *Melbourne Age*, the Australian commentator Michael Leunig called for a national prayer for Osama bin Laden on Christmas Day. 'It's a family day and Osama's our relative', he declared. Bin Laden was even described in the *New York Times* in September 2001 as having 'gentle eyes'; while Saddam Hussein, in the view of the former US attorney-general Ramsey Clark— expressed in January 2005 after the latter had offered to defend him at trial— had been 'demonised' by his captors, and was in fact 'reserved, thoughtful and dignified'.

Like the 'explanations' of the true meanings of *jihad* and *hamas*, these were moral judgments. They had in common that they were arrived at by non-Arabs and non-Muslims. Together, they rested upon the premise that contrary moral judgments arrived at by other non-Muslims upon these matters were wrong: wrong in fact, or wrong in interpretation of word and event, or both. Sometimes intended genuinely to provide an intellectual or ethical counter-balance to excess or falsehood, Type A and B arguments often served instead to keep truth at a distance.

TYPE C: *'Even-if-you-are-right-about-the-facts-you-should-keep-your-sense-of-proportion-in-judging-them'.*

This device is a milder, or fall-back, version of the Type A and B devices. It could be described as the 'keep-your-cool' position in relation to the Arab and Islamic revivals and advance. The Type C position has been much espoused, implicitly or explicitly, by those who see greater virtue—often rightly—in *sang-froid* than in fear or anger, whatever their provoking cause. But it has also been adopted by those unwilling to make moral or other distinctions between one value-system and another, between friend and foe, or between action and reaction. (This position is even more manifest in the Type E argument, to which I will come.)

It might be said that the 'keep-your-cool' position was conventionally British. Indeed, it conformed with a familiar model of British demeanour. 'Look', the novelist Margaret Drabble told me in January 1991 at the time of the Gulf War, 'we are all a mass of reason, superstition and self-interest mixed together. They [sc. Muslims] are not as irrational as we think they are, and we are not as rational as we think ourselves to be'. This was an intellectually well-calibrated expression of the Type C argument.

As in the fine line trodden between 'sweet reason' and 'liberal apologia' in some versions of the Type B position, so here the line between dispassion—or 'standing back' from the immediacies of event—and unconcern was easily crossed. 'Keeping cool' might involve such degree of disengagement from the sordidly real as to become something quite other, a *sang-froid* which was truly cold-blooded. Thus, when it was mooted in February 1995 that Ramzi Ahmed Yousef—accused of involvement in the first bombing of the World Trade Center in 1993, and in 'a string of other terrorist plots'—had studied engineering at a British university, it was said in the *Guardian* to 'raise the intriguing possibility that a British university supplied the skills he has allegedly employed to wreak mayhem around the world'. To suggest that it was 'intriguing' was, from one point of view, to keep a Type C 'sense of proportion'. From another, it was an adjective of moral indifference, or worse.

'Keeping cool' was therefore not always what it seemed. When a number of British Muslims went to Afghanistan in order to fight alongside the Taliban, Ken Livingstone, London's mayor, urged in November 2001 that they not be prosecuted on their return to Britain. 'We've got to accept', he declared—although the source of this moral imperative was unclear—'that these people went off because of a deep sense of injustice about what's happening in Israel and the West Bank'. Livingstone's call to the police to 'be lenient' was, again at one level, a 'keeping cool' in the face of cries of 'treason'. At another, it could be regarded as a mixture of apologia and moral indifference in the name of 'keeping a sense of proportion'.

A detached calm in the face of ill-doing could be counted stoical when harm was being threatened against, or done to, oneself. But it remained indifference when the harm was being committed against others. This was so, even if the phlegmatic believed that such calm or proportion was dictated by a higher code of morality than that which agitated those who did *not* 'keep their cool'. Such phlegm was also not confined to the British. 'The attacks on the Pentagon and the World Trade Center', declared Lewis Lapham, the editor of *Harper's Magazine*, in December 2001, 'provide an impressive occasion for timely remarks on our [sc. US] foreign and domestic policy, as well as an opportunity to ask what we mean by the phrases "public service", "common good" and "civic interest"'. The adjective 'impressive', like the adjective 'intriguing', was an adjective of moral disengagement. It again expressed that distancing—or alienation—from brute truth earlier noted in respect of the Type A devices, but here in service of Olympian reflection upon ostensibly larger matters.

In some instances, 'keeping cool'—as when a former British cabinet minister argued in September 2002 that Saddam Hussein was 'no threat'—represented a genuine effort to be judicious. But when the deaths of almost three thousand innocent citizens at the hands of suicide-hijackers could be held to provide no more than an 'impressive occasion' for debate, the business of keeping one's head, or keeping a sense of proportion, ceased to be a virtue. For under the Type C rubric, unpleasant verities could even be cancelled outright. In more complex and divided fashion, the impulse to 'keep cool' could enter into conflict with itself, as when a *Guardian* commentator in December 2001 described 'these times' as both 'threatening' and 'overheated'.

Type C insistence upon calm and proportion could not only be a mark of sound judgment. For it could conceal as great a hostility to the objects of Islamist attacks—Israelis, for example—as for those who carried out such attacks. As in the resort to Type A and B devices, the Type C argument could also serve to evade or cancel unwelcome facts, as well as glibly to minimise the significance of whatever the 'overheated' had exaggerated. It could also be used to counsel 'restraint' when a repressed odium—as for the United States in much of the non-Muslim world—furnished the actual impulse for the advice.

Domestic anti-terrorist measures, such as those taken in the United States and Britain, were very widely regarded as Type C 'over-reactions'. Moreover, Type A, B and C devices could be in play together, with facts argued to be mere suppositions or plain wrong and with judgments held to be awry. The conduct of open hostilities against Islamism, or emergency security measures, or (especially) an invasion of Saddam's Iraq, then became 'disproportionate responses', the responses of misguided hotheads. Knowing better, the cool retained their poise and balance, kept alarms—and unpleasant truths—at a distance and rejected charges that the Type C device was an alibi for complacency and inertia, or concealed a sympathy for the foe.

TYPE D: *'If-you-respond-too-forcefully-to-Islamist-plans-and-outrages-you-will-undermine-your-own-society's-and-even-the-whole-world's-freedoms'.*

This device of argument has been widely deployed in Western liberal democracies during the Arab and Muslim advance. In form, it is not dissimilar to that used by Muslims who fear that their interests will be harmed by Islamist actions, as earlier discussed. For the Type D device expresses anxiety lest an 'own goal' be scored by excess. Its argument is also essentially utilitarian and seeks, like its Muslim variant, to curb responses which are believed to be self-harming. In the non-Islamic world, the Type D or 'own goal' argument is generally linked to, and overlaps with, the proportionality argument of Type C. That is, those who 'keep cool' are less likely to score 'own goals'.

As with the three types of argument already identified, the Type D device has been used to justify not reacting decisively, or at all, to moral challenge or physical threat. It is a device which has proved potent, has appeared in a variety of forms in ethical and political debate, and has been advanced with differing degrees of urgency and intensity of expression. In its commonplace form, it could be asserted, for example, that responses to 'terrorism' 'amplify the threat to liberty', as a *Guardian* commentator put it in September 2002. This was clearly the 'own goal' thesis. But such position often did no more than exhibit that 'pale cast of thought' by which 'resolution' is 'sicklied o'er', in Hamlet's words, or is stopped in its tracks by paralysis of the will. For the Type D device, whether in its strong or weak variants, emphasises—often to the already-hesitant—that there are risks in decision, in this case risks to liberty by liberty's defence.

In its stronger versions, the Type D argument could be used to assert that almost any measure of guardedness was not simply an illiberal imposition upon the free society but a step towards a 'police state'. To act upon disquiet for public safety was to be in the grip of 'panic', or of a 'rage' for 'anti-terrorism measures'. Equally extravagant misuse of language—generally in the cause of Type C moderation—could transform the citizen's awareness that the liberal order requires to be defended into a base or 'cowardly acquiescence' with 'sinister', 'brutal', 'shameless', 'ruthless' and 'draconian' assaults upon civil rights. These epithets were all employed, whether in the British or American press, to decry 'anti-terrorism' measures.

Taking the Type D device to its limits, the 'terror threat' was said to have been 'used' by those 'hungry for power' in order to 'attack civil rights', according to the *Guardian* in December 2001. Those who did so were conducting a 'war on America', as the same paper had it in April 2004. In the same spirit, it was 'difficult to think of anyone who has inflicted more harm on Americans than their current president', declared a *Guardian* contributor in May 2004; the US had been 'turned into a byword for man's inhumanity to man', he added. The 'hard question', asserted Timothy Garton Ash in the same place in October 2002, was 'whether the conduct of the "war against terrorism" in this atmosphere of menace might not end up being as much a threat to our own freedoms as terrorism itself'.

This 'question' was a 'hard' one only if the premise upon which the strong variant of the Type D argument rests was accepted: that the open society was equally at risk from its ardent, or too ardent, defenders as from its ardent foes. It was also characteristically implied that the *via media*—whether that of 'keeping cool', or avoiding an 'own goal'—was a sager path to take than any other. At the same time, advocates of such moral equilibrium, whether they adopted the Type C or Type D positions, generally overstated their case, themselves employing a panic-stricken vocabulary when condemning the panic of others.

In February 2002 a Yale professor of law, Bruce Ackerman, perceived, or claimed to perceive, the lineaments of 'repression' in America's national security measures; by July 2002, such 'repression' was described by an Australian journalist, John Pilger, as 'stark'. To a Columbia Law School professor, the measures in question amounted to a 'new martial law'. Under it—according to Anne McIlroy in the *Guardian* in October 2002—'a whisper of suspicion may be enough to destroy a man's life'. Susan Sontag went still further in May 2004: the US military had created a 'new, international carceral [*sic*] empire' which went 'beyond Soviet Russia's Gulag system'. To such extreme conclusions could those who adopted the Type D device of argument, whether implicitly or explicitly, be led; in the name of a rational concern-for-consequences, and in order to guard us from others' zeal and authoritarian excess.

TYPE E: '*Even-if-the-facts-about-Islamism-are-as-they-are-asserted-to-be-the-conduct-of-the-non-Islamic-world-is-as-bad-or-worse*'.

This device of argument again had a broad range of uses, especially on the 'left'. It could serve not only as the premise for Western self-laceration, but also as the ground upon which the refusal to meet Muslim challenges to the non-Islamic world could be made to stand. It also took the form of a simple moral equation. 'Two radicalisms—al-Qaeda's and Washington's—are at work, and in 2003 they will continue to feed on one another', the American commentator William Pfaff predicted in December 2002. Employing the same type of 'equivalence' argument, it could be said that 'by fighting bin Laden, we sink to his level and he wins', in the words of the editor of the 'right-wing' *Spectator* in October 2001. Not dissimilarly, the Italian 'far-left' party, Rifondazione Comunista, claimed in May 2004 that 'Bush and bin Laden' were 'two links in the same chain, two aspects of the same crisis of civilisation'. That is, each 'side' was either in danger of becoming, or was, 'as-bad-as-the-other'.

A stronger version of the Type E device was at work in much of the language used in criticisms, by non-Muslims themselves, of the non-Muslim world's attitudes, policies and acts. As their criticisms ascended the Type E scale from simple arguments of moral equivalence, they increasingly implied that matters were ethically and politically *worse* on the non-Muslim 'side' of the fence than they were on the other. Even the less hostile could call the American military action in Afghanistan an 'embarrassment' and 'morally tainted', as the future archbishop of Canterbury, Rowan Williams, put it. Or the US intervention in Afghanistan could be more severely described as nothing but a 'reprisal', in the words of the *Observer* in September 2002. Harsher versions of the Type E case, such as that advanced in December 2001 by Tiziano Terzani in the Italian *Corriere della Sera,* held that it was 'now the turn of the Taliban to be made victims of Americans seeking to avenge their dead [of 9/11]'. Similarly, in February 2003, *Le Figaro* argued that America was seeking to act against Iraq out of a 'spirit of vengeance', a phrase more commonly reserved to Israel and Jews, as we saw in a previous chapter. In January 2002, even the distinguished British historian, Professor Sir Michael Howard, could describe the 'American people' as driven by a 'visceral demand for vengeance'.

Such Type E criticisms could converge in form, and even in vocabulary and content, with those made of the non-Muslim world by radical Islam itself, as was previously noted. Malignities could be attributed to American purpose, by non-Muslims, which were not morally distinguishable from accusations made by sworn enemies of the United States.

Thus, Zacarias Moussaoui, on trial in Virginia for conspiring in the attacks of 9/11, described the American government from the dock as an 'evil force'. But this was no greater a condemnation than were the commonplaces to be found in the Western press. Indeed, it was milder than many. To a *Guardian* commentator in October 2002, President Bush was using 'fear and the threat of violence to promote his policy', and was a 'reckless warmonger' to an editorialist in the *Atlanta Journal* in September 2002. In March 2003, to the former deputy-leader of the Labour Party, Roy Hattersley, the actions of the US defence secretary, Donald Rumsfeld, were those of 'crude brutality'; a judgment not greatly different in degree from that arrived at in May 2004 by Ameer ul-Azeem, spokesman for the hard-line Bangladesh group Jamaat-e-Islami, that the United States had 'reached the extremes of wickedness in Iraq'. Similarly, to a *Guardian* commentator in March 2003, Rumsfeld was 'responsible for a series of crimes sufficient, were he ever to be tried, to put him away for the rest of his life'. To an American columnist in the *Guardian* in May 2004, US deputy secretary of defence Paul Wolfowitz was a 'neo-conservative Robespierre'.

To the Labour MP George Galloway, the British government was com-

posed of 'liars, forgers, war criminals and murderers'. There had been resort
to 'crude American gun-law' in Iraq, and there was a 'strong war crimes case'
against US and British leaders, agreed Richard Overy, author of *Interrogations:
Inside the Mind of the Nazi Elite*. To a *Guardian* commentator in April 2003, the
'enterprise' in Iraq had been 'crudely colonial'. Indeed, Saddam's tyranny had
been 'replaced by a tyranny of the occupation forces', who had 'unleashed'
'Vietnam-style "search-and-destroy" raids on Iraqi people's homes', a contributor to the same paper asserted in June 2003. But as early as November 2001,
within a few weeks of the 9/11 attacks, a *Guardian* columnist had described
the United States as a 'raging colossus', its 'ruthlessness' a potentially 'greater
threat than the Islamist fanaticism that provoked it'.

Here, the common Type E implication that 'each-is-as-bad-as-the-other'
was no more than a hair's breadth from the proposition that 'we' are 'worse'
than 'them'. It was an argument which not merely tended towards Arabism's
and Islamism's own moral terrain, but could even come to rest upon it; as when
an editorialist in the *Guardian* in April 2003 lauded the 'bravery of many
[Iraqi] fighters, who have confronted tanks with AK-47 rifles and died in their
thousands'. Only the word 'martyr' was missing from this encomium.

However, the Type E argument could also remain poised between the
milder and the more extreme versions, moving back and forth across a moral
no-man's land between the 'as-bad-as' and the 'worse'. Iraq might be an autocracy, but there was 'creeping totalitarianism' in Britain, too, according to a
leading British trade unionist in September 2002. Under these conditions, the
'rights of citizens' were being 'incrementally taken away'. If this or that
Muslim regime was 'repressive', then so too was the United States. It had
'loosed war and repression on the world', in the view of some seventy prominent American intellectuals and artists published in June 2002; a larger indictment than the same individuals would have levelled against America's foes,
thus signifying that America was 'worse'.

Such Type E arguments, if accepted, also dictated that the conduct of the
non-Islamic world, and especially of the United States, should be morally disowned or be actively opposed. Conversely, those who did not disown or
oppose such conduct were held to be wanting in morality, while those who
were in favour of it were clearly beyond the moral pale. They might even be
out of their senses, as was suggested by the term 'rabidly pro-American' used
by the *Guardian* of the Australian prime minister, John Howard, in February
2003. However, the Type E argument carried those who pushed it to its limits
into their own moral limbo. In this limbo, hard-line Type E condemnations of
the policies of the non-Muslim world as 'brutal', 'draconian', 'vengeful', 'evil',

'shameless' and the rest, lost real meaning. If the 'American regime' was termed 'abhorrent', as in the *Guardian* in September 2002, the truly abhorrent could no longer be effectively described; if economic sanctions against Iraq were held to be not merely unfair or harsh in their effects but 'barbaric', as in the *Observer* in July 2002, then barbarism could not be distinguished from them.

Moreover, the Type E device of moral argument, the further it was pressed, set many of those who employed it upon a trajectory which disabled their own judgments. For example, it could be argued that the 'transatlantic alliance' might be 'strategically important' for Britain, but was 'hardly a moral necessity'. The thesis of the 'abhorrent regime' was implicit in this, but it was a mild statement of its kind. When resort to the Type E device was ratcheted up, as it often was, the Anglo-American alliance could become not that of 'poodle' to 'master' but 'profoundly dangerous' for 'the British people', as *Guardian* commentators held it to be in September 2002 and February 2003. Even at this (relatively anodyne) point in the West's debate with itself, the militant Islamist could happily, and gratefully, agree with its terms. But criticisms of Western 'brutality', 'barbarism', 'repression', 'shamelessness', 'vengefulness', 'wickedness' and the rest drove the non-Muslim caravan much further onto Islamism's sands.

Beyond lay further excesses in Type E argument which were more complex. In them non-Muslims could be found applying to their own societies, even to the letter, criticisms which were made of the polities and cultures of the Islamic world itself. The forms of this perverse will to self-condemnation were detectable even in the most rational analyses and observations, and could again be placed on an ascending scale. A mild version of this procedure was represented by 'I have no problem with nation-building in Afghanistan, but what I'm really interested in is nation-building in America', in the words of Thomas Friedman in the *New York Times* in January 2002. That is, America's proclaimed task in the Hindu Kush had been taken over into an American criticism of the United States.

Further along this path of transposition, the American notion of the need for 'regime change' in Iraq could be turned upon America itself, and by non-Americans and Americans alike. 'The problem with America is its government. What they, and we, need is regime change', declared Martin Kettle in the *Guardian* in September 2002, among many who made this transposition; 'what we need, now', likewise proclaimed the Democratic presidential challenger, Senator John Kerry, in September 2003, 'is not just a regime change in Iraq but a regime change in the United States'. In October 2002 and January 2003, respectively, the American writer Gore Vidal and the British writer John le Carré both called the American government 'the Bush junta'. In similar transferences, the American 'junta' or 'regime' was said to be composed of 'conspirators', or of 'warlords'. It was even asserted by the left Labour MP George Galloway, in August 2002, that George W. Bush had become president in a 'distinctly Tikriti-style-fix'. The very name of Saddam Hussein's clan-town had been taken over into a metaphor by which to criticise failures in the American electoral system.

When the Type E device was being used at full stretch, such transpositions could make America into the true 'rogue state'. Bernard Cassen, one of the leaders of the European 'anti-globalisation' movement, described it as such in September 2002. It was a procedure followed, and invited to be followed, by spokesmen for those states against which American hostilities had been directed. 'The outlaw here is America, not Iraq', declared the latter's deputy prime minister, Tariq Aziz, in February 2003; it was the American president, not Saddam Hussein, who was the true 'despot' and 'dictator', according to Saddam Hussein's foreign minister, Naji Sabri, in March 2003.

Similarly, just as Islamism was accused of acts of 'terrorism', so some non-Muslims, employing the 'bad-as-each-other' Type E thesis, held that America was itself a 'terrorist regime', committing the same kind of 'terrorist acts' as those whom it condemned. From many examples, Bishop Thomas Gumbleton of Detroit declared in September 2002 that for the United States to strike first at Iraq would be an 'act of terrorism'; the American scholar Noam Chomsky shared the view that the United States administration was a 'terrorist regime', a view which he described as being held by 'much of the world'.

Going further, the notion that 'each-is-as-bad-as-or-worse-than-the-other' could lead to the suggestion, put forward in the *Guardian* in November 2002, that arrest-warrants be issued by the International Criminal Court against 'the CIA operatives' who had recently 'blown away six al-Qaeda "terrorists"' in Yemen; the quotation marks around the word 'terrorists' also signified that the term was less than just.

Under the rules of equivalence and transposition in which the Type E device deals, even the critique of the religious 'fundamentalism' of Islam could be turned (by non-Muslims) upon the West. In January 1991, at the time of the Gulf War, the Oxford philosopher Bernard Williams told me that it was 'difficult to be enthusiastic about Western fundamentalism also'. A decade later, the 'fundamentalism' of the 'economic prescriptions of the IMF, the World Bank and the World Trade Organisation', as well as the 'fundamentalism' of the 'ideology of business', were held to have 'called forth' an answering 'fundamentalism' in the Islamic world, according to the writer Jeremy Seabrook in December 2001. A senior research fellow at London's Institute for Defence Studies agreed, asserting in August 2002 that 'American fundamentalism' and the 'fundamentalist policies' of the White House equally required to be 'contained'. The 'poison of religious certainty'—here Christian, there Islamic—was described in *The Times* in July 2002 as 'seeping into the mainstream democratic politics' of the United States. It was upon such symmetries that the Type E device rested.

Those who transposed the terms of criticism of Islamism (and Islam) into criticisms of the West would hold, sometimes plausibly, that there were objective grounds for doing so. Nevertheless, the lengths to which this procedure could be taken were also unwittingly revealing. Thus, Saladin-like metaphors could be used of Western responses to the Islamist challenge, as when America was described—in the *Guardian* in September 2002—as taking its 'sword' from it 'scabbard'. Or if Islamism was engaged in a holy war, then so too was the non-Islamic world. A 'Western jihad' had been launched against Iraq, I was told by Seabrook during the Gulf War.

Type E arguments, in order to make their case, necessarily sought to establish moral parallels between Islamic and Western—especially American—excesses. Some of these parallels have been just. Others have been forced, to the point of falsehood. But in the latter case, the issue of truth often appeared secondary to the satisfaction to be gained from turning an argument round upon the Western and non-Muslim self. In order to achieve such satisfaction, the truth might even be turned entirely on its head by the intellectual or political cross-dresser. Thus, the Labour MP George Galloway, referring to the bombing of Afghanistan, declared before thousands of protesters in London on 18 November 2001 that Britain was 'standing shoulder to shoulder with the world's biggest terrorist state; the United States of America'. On the same day in Quetta, before other tens of thousands, a Pakistani Islamist leader, Hafiz Hussain Ahmed, also called America 'the biggest terrorist state'. But although the terms were the same, the ardours they expressed were distinct. In the first case, it was that of a vicarious or second-hand identification with America's foes; in the second that of a first-hand, and therefore psychologically more authentic, identification by an Islamist with Islamism's cause.

Type E declarations by non-Muslims have their own resonance for those who make them, and a force independent of their falsehood or truth. In part, their *éclat* derives from their 'daring', in which the very act of ravaging the non-Muslim world seems to furnish its own pleasures. To have argued, as did

George Monbiot in the *Guardian* in August 2002, that the United States not only 'presents a danger to the rest of the world' but 'is becoming our [sc. Britain's] foremost enemy' was, at one level, no more than riskless attitudinising. At another level, like many of the devices of Muslim argument earlier examined, it possessed its own logic, the logic of the Type E device.

TYPE F: *'Even-if-you-have-the-facts-entirely-or-partially-right-about-political-Islam-and-its-actions-you-must-first-look-to-the-underlying-causes-of-such-actions'.*

This argument rests upon the belief that Islamism is an effect before it is a cause, and that much of the responsibility for what has been done in Islam's name lies elsewhere than in the Muslim world itself. It has again been an especially popular proposition on the 'left', although not confined to it. Like certain other devices of non-Muslim argument, it has often coincided with and echoed Islamism's self-justifications. In common with the latter, it has also transferred responsibility for Islamism's acts to others.

The Type F argument could be expressed in simple and direct terms, as well as in oblique and complex form. When expressed directly, the language of the Type F device has commonly been that of the muscular 'tackling' of the 'causes' of Muslim hostility towards the non-Muslim world. These 'causes' are generally described as 'core' causes, 'global' causes, 'prime' causes, 'root' causes or 'underlying' causes, the last adjective being the most frequently employed.

It could thus be claimed, in an *Independent* editorial in October 2002, that 'the real issue [posed by terrorism] is how to deal with the underlying causes'. Standard Type F propositions—for example, in a *Guardian* editorial in November 2003—held that 'Al Qaida's business' was 'rebellion', but that it was the West which, 'by its actions and inactions', had 'too frequently given these rebels a cause'; or, in another *Guardian* editorial in December 2003 after the Iraqi leader's capture, that 'Saddam Hussein was a horror of our age. But the guilt for his deeds is not entirely his alone'.

Impressive, too, has been the range of voices which has spoken to the argument that the 'root' or 'underlying' causes of 'terrorism' needed to be 'addressed', 'tackled', or 'removed'. In 2004, it included the British cabinet secretary Sir Andrew Turnbull, various spokesmen for the Council on American Islamic Relations, President Musharraf of Pakistan, Prince Talal bin Abdul Aziz of Saudi Arabia, and the former director of the Institute for Strategic Studies in Beijing.

Even the former head of one of Britain's intelligence services, Stella

Rimington, employed the device: the 'underlying causes' of terrorism would have to be addressed, she declared, if the 'war' against it were to be won. Or the Type F argument could be put in interrogative form. 'Who is tackling the global causes of suicide bombing?' asked a *Guardian* commentator in November 2003. The view implicit in many such assertions and questions was that the non-Islamic world was to blame for whatever blows were struck against it; they could be variously attributed to the 'disadvantage' and 'exclusion' of Muslim citizens in the diaspora, US partiality in the Palestinian issue, 'abusive American detention methods', 'unemployment and poverty' in the Muslim world and so on. Yet the argument was not more plausible than would have been an assertion in the 1930s that the 'underlying causes' of German Nazism or Italian fascism had to be 'addressed'—or 'tackled'—before any action against them could be held to be morally justified. Moreover, the arguments were often contradictory. Some wanted the US to desist from whatever it was doing and vacate the field, while others wanted it to assume responsibilities for helping Muslim and Arab states out of the circumstances in which 'terrorism' was 'bred'.

Those who urged the moral and intellectual priority of the 'underlying causes' of Islamist hostility towards the non-Muslim world could often be accused of also wanting to exonerate, to a greater or lesser degree, those guilty of violence. This was sometimes done by directly exempting the actors themselves from blame, as in the extremer forms of the 'desperado' case made for Palestinian and other suicide-bombers; an argument to which I will come. It could also be done by attributing culpability to a wide range of current or antecedent events or, on a larger scale, to the legacies of the former colonial powers. 'Is it possible', thus asked the Canadian philosopher Ted Honderich, 'that the September 11 attacks had nothing at all to do with...Malawi, Mozambique, Zambia or Sierra Leone?'

Impatience with those who had resort to the Type F device could lead to accusations that those who used it were guilty of 'appeasement', as has been mentioned. This charge was in turn refuted, sometimes with justice, by those so accused. As the European Union commissioner Chris Patten protested in October 2002, 'discussion of the causes of [sc. Muslim] alienation and hatred' could not be taken per se to be 'evidence of appeasement'. Nevertheless, in the years before the outbreak of the Second World War, similar Type F 'discussion-of-causes'—in this case the 'causes' of Nazism—was common among the 'appeasers' of the day, as well as among those who felt some sympathy for Nazism itself. Moreover, recourse to the Type F argument has seldom been the outcome of dispassionate or scholarly inquiry for truth's sake. Instead, it has typically proceeded from premise to foregone conclusion without breaking its stride.

Those who have sought to identify the 'underlying causes' of Muslim hostility to the non-Muslim world have had differing opinions as to the nature of the West's crimes. A severe version of the Type F argument, as we saw earlier, was articulated in September 2001 by Italian Nobel laureate Dario Fo. It was 'the culture of violence, hunger and inhumane exploitation' which had led to the attacks on America. Indeed, 'exploitation' by 'global capitalism' has been one of the 'underlying causes' of 'terrorism' favoured by the 'left'. But in Dario Fo's argument that the attacks were 'legitimate', he indicated that the Type F device could be employed not merely to 'explain' but also to justify the actions of which it treated.

This procedure could be taken even further, as by Honderich. Given the nature of the antecedent—or 'underlying'—causes which impelled their acts, Palestinians, for example, not only had a 'moral right to their terrorism', but were 'right to engage in it', the philosopher declared in Toronto in September 2002. Indeed, it was 'permissible if not obligatory' for them to do so, he added, while those who 'killed themselves in the cause of their people' had 'sanctified themselves'. This was for a non-Muslim to press the Type F argument to its furthest limit; and at this limit it became, once again, identical with the Islamist case.

Even in more modest forms, the Type F device has rarely been used for the genuine purpose of grounding events in their necessary historical context, properly examined, but in order to sustain a simple 'backlash' thesis. As in the severer forms of the Type F argument, Western fault is thus made the prime mover in the Arab upsurge and Islamist violence. The frequent use by non-Muslims of the Type F device has also invited Muslims to adopt it without restraint, including in the civil libertarian terms favoured by many non-Muslims after the 9/11 attacks. It was 'American policy' with its 'denial of the principles of justice, human rights, democracy and self-determination' which 'help[ed] terrorists to exist', declared Jihad al-Khazzen in September 2001 in the Arabic daily *al-Hayat*.

This form of Muslim moral evasion squared well with the use of the Type F argument by those non-Muslims for whom Western foreign policy, past and present, ranked high among the 'core', 'global', 'prime', 'real', 'root', or 'underlying' causes of Islamist and Arab violence. Hence, just as Muslim apologists blamed the United States for al-Qaeda's attacks, the American director of the Center for Muslim-Christian Understanding, John Esposito, held American foreign policy to have been responsible for them. But as early as

October 1984, George Schultz, the then US secretary of state, had asserted that to explain 'terrorism' by finding fault with American foreign policy was to invite 'moral confusion'. Nevertheless, the policy and conduct of the United States cannot be so easily sidelined from discussion of the causes for Islamist violence against it. However, to attribute 'blame' for Islamism to the United States was again to understate the degree to which the Muslim advance is governed by its own internal dynamic and by dictates of belief which the non-Muslim world cannot alter.

But the Type F argument as to 'underlying causes' possesses a powerful appeal. It provides a quick and easy means of short-circuiting debate about the questions which it promises to answer. It equally serves Muslims who seek to transfer responsibility for their actions to others, and non-Muslims for whom self-criticism (and hostility to the US) have their own attractions. With the aid of the Type F device, Islamist actions have in consequence often been permitted to pass either with diminished reproach—on the grounds that they were overshadowed by their causes, whatever such causes might be—or to pass without reproach at all, on the grounds of the moral innocence of the actors. Worse, the Type F argument has often implied that the violent effects of these causes can now be expected to be unbounded and even unending. That is, the scale of prior historic wrong-doing is held (by some) to be of such great magnitude or long-standing that it cannot be redeemed, in particular when new crimes are being committed by the non-Muslim world which can also be laid at the latter's door.

The Type F device can therefore provide Islamism with grounds for a permanent evasion of responsibility, or a moral *carte blanche*. For one of the commoner implications of the Type F device is that those who are to blame for the actions of Islamists are also disentitled from reacting to whatever is done to them in return. 'Playing the world's policeman' was therefore 'not the answer to the catastrophe in New York', a *Times* columnist argued in September 2001, since 'playing the world's policeman' was 'what led to it'. That is, the United States was not only to blame for the attack upon it but was disqualified from taking up the cudgels on its own behalf. Out of this closed circle of argument there is no escape.

Moreover, even when adopted by non-Muslims for the moral purpose of attempting to arrive at a just settlement of accounts with the past, the Type F argument is open to exploitation. Thus, where 'understanding' has been expressed for the 'underlying' causes of this or that challenge to the non-Islamic world, unreason could seize gratefully upon it as moral justification for the morally worst of acts. 'Anger breeds terrorism', argued a non-Muslim about suicide-attacks in Israel, using the Type F argument in abbreviated form; al-Qaeda 'draws on a pool of grievances', declared another non-Muslim in the same Type F vein; a Muslim apologist, following in the van, could similarly pronounce that it was not Saddam Hussein who was the 'real criminal' but 'Western governments' who had 'made him what he is'.

Seeking to understand the motives for an act carried out against the non-Muslim world has not always signified a desire to transfer responsibility from the actor to others. Nor has it necessarily implied sympathy for such act. But in standard apologias for Islamist excesses, and whether the apologist was Muslim or non-Muslim, the Type F device in practice almost always achieved such ends. For inquiry into 'root' causes generally served to transform the Islamist into a victim who had neither moral nor practical alternative but to respond to such 'root' causes, including with great violence. Indeed, these 'causes' could provide *rights* to act so in the eyes both of a Canadian philosopher and a bin Laden.

The syllogisms to which use of the Type F device led have varied in quality and range. If the 'underlying cause' of Palestinian 'terror-attacks' on Israel was held to be the absence of a viable Palestinian state, the creation of a viable Palestinian state was therefore simplistically inferred to be 'the way' to stop such attacks. At a lower level, it was posited by the *Sydney Morning Herald* that the victims of the Bali bombing, and others accustomed to holiday in Bali, had not sufficiently 'respected and nurtured the place'. They had failed to 'give enough back to the people who belong there, whose home it is'. This procedure of 'explanation' of causes, and moral exemption from responsibility for their effects, could be even more telegraphic. 'American policy nourishes anti-Americanism' was Type F reasoning at its simplest. In most cases of a rational search for explanatory causes some truth was necessarily found. But almost always it was at the cost of providing moral alibis for the worst of acts.

In some instances of the use of the Type F device, something like relish could again be detected among non-Muslims for the more disastrous effects-of-the-underlying-causes. 'The bigger they come', declared Matthew Parris in *The Times*, referring to the United States and the September 2001 attacks, 'the harder they fall'. Here, the transfer of responsibility, characteristic of Type F arguments, was implied rather than stated, and pain as well as pleasure could be derived from the metaphor of the 'hard fall' of a colossus. There was less obliqueness in the sentiments of the *Guardian* commentator who, using the Type F device, asserted in August 2004 that 'in every action Bush has swelled the ranks of those who cheered in the streets' at the 'fall of the twin towers'.

The writer John Berger, in responding to 9/11, combined the Type E argument—'each-is-as-bad-as-the-other'—with the Type F alibi for the malefactor. The Type E device dictated to him that 'the number killed in the attack on the Twin Towers' was merely equal to 'the number of innocent civilians killed collaterally in Afghanistan by the US bombardments'. The Type F device—according to which effects are the just consequence of their causes—was at work in his claim that, while watching the attack on the World Trade Center on television, Berger had been 'instantly reminded of August 6, 1945'. He made the nature of the parallel plain. The destruction of Hiroshima, he wrote, had been a 'blinding demonstration' of 'a remote and ignorant ruthlessness' on the part of the United States; the attack, or counter-attack, on the World Trade Center was a fitting response to a continuing 'ignorant ruthlessness' in American policy, or so he implied.

The Type F thesis could be more crudely formulated. 'However tactfully you dress it up, the United States had it coming', a contributor to the *London Review of Books* put it, *à propos* 9/11. A young Muslim from Luton thought the same of the suicide-bombings in London in July 2005. 'I think they had it coming with the war in Iraq', he told the *Guardian.* To Susan Sontag, the 9/11 attacks were a 'monstrous dose of reality'; once more the 'dose of reality' was implied to be the effect of precedent causes. It was the 'had-it-coming' thesis, otherwise stated. This Type F argument was present in all propositions that those who struck at the West were merely 'striking back'. That is, their violence was not an initiative for which they were ethically accountable, but an 'inevitable' response for which they could not ultimately be blamed.

'Al-Qaeda Strikes Back' was the title of a major BBC documentary in October 2002. A *Guardian* commentator likewise declared in November 2001 that 9/11 had taught that 'the empire can strike back'. The same Type F argument as to precedent-cause-and-just-effect could be more obliquely expressed through metaphor, as by Noam Chomsky in September 2002. In 'addressing the roots of hatred' for the United States, he warned that 'if we insist on creating more swamps, there will be more mosquitoes'. Moral responsibility for the 'swamp' which had bred the 'mosquitoes'—a reductive and disparaging characterisation of the many impulses which have contributed to the Arab and Islamic revivals—was again transferred, without qualification, to the non-Islamic world.

Such resort to the Type F argument, whether by Muslims or non-Muslims, again did scant justice to the morally autonomous and self-propelling nature of the Islamist (and Islamic) challenge to the West. To attribute the world-wide mobilisation of Islamic thought-and-action to a mere effect of impoverishment, or of exploitation, or of imperialism was to diminish Islam itself. To perceive this 'reawakening' as a response to American foreign policy, or to Israeli settlement activity, or to even lesser causes was to demean it further. Indeed, it was a paradox of the Type F device that, in the search for the 'underlying causes' by which Islamist violences and excesses might be explained, the West came to blame itself for actions which many Muslims were proud to have committed.

TYPE G: *'The-United-States-is-the-root-of-evil-in-the-world'.*

This proposition is one of the forms in which the Type F device of argument as to 'underlying causes' is presented. It has bulked so large that it merits consideration in its own right. It is similar to the lesser but related thesis, examined in an earlier chapter, that Israel and 'Jews' are ultimately responsible for the ills of the Middle East, or even the ills of the entire world. The Type G device—the 'Argument Against America'—is again of great potency, utility and reach. For many, it possesses sufficient truth to gratify the need for a large object upon which political dissatisfactions of many kinds may be focused. In addition, it seems to have served as object of the 'primitive' or 'anthropological' desire for a scapegoat, as well as furnishing an explanation for the undermining of whatever it is that individuals, or even entire nations, may hold dear. It is not surprising, therefore, that the 'Argument Against America' has come to bestride so much of the world; even some Americans adopt it, on occasion in terms which barely differ from those used by Islamists themselves.

The Type G device has deep roots; political and cultural criticism of America is a hoary phenomenon as well as a volatile substance. As earlier mentioned, on the day after the 11 September attacks, *Le Monde* proclaimed in an editorial that 'We are all Americans'. Twelve months later, its author declared that there was 'a wave in the world' which now led him to believe that 'we have all become anti-American'. Or, as Salman Rushdie put it in February 2002, 'anti-Americanism is presently taking the world by storm'. By May 2003, the novelist Margaret Drabble could openly admit in the *Daily Telegraph* that her 'anti-Americanism' had 'become almost uncontrollable. It has possessed me like a disease. It rises up in my throat like acid reflux....I now loathe the United States'. This Type G argument could be adopted by Americans themselves. 'As an American, all I can say is, Thank God for French knee-jerk anti-Americanism', a letter-writer declared to the *Herald Tribune* in October 2002. 'Without France's steadfast opposition to all things Yankee, the world would be in a far worse state than it already is', he asserted. In addition, the very term 'anti-Americanism' could be dismissed by a *Guardian* columnist in October 2001 as an 'inane slur', a 'thought-killing smear' and a 'McCarthyite label'.

Others confined their criticisms to American foreign policy, or even more narrowly to particular individuals, the American president for example. In whatever form, the Type G 'root-of-all-evil' argument against America generally held a central and versatile place as a premise of analysis among Muslims and non-Muslims alike. The defects of American policy could serve equally to 'explain' event, to attribute responsibility for such event, and even to uphold entire structures of perception. Recourse to the Type G device has also been the simplest means of foreclosing debate, as well as of discharging on America what would otherwise be an anxiety without focus, or an anger without object.

It is a device which can be summoned up at once, and without effort, in order to make the United States—like the Soviet Union before it—the cause-of-causes of the world's ills. To *al-Quds al-Arabi*, in March 2002, 'the world' itself felt 'hatred for America'. Even to a *Times* commentator in July 2002, the America of George W. Bush—an America of 'self-righteous Christian fundamentalists', 'military machismo', 'anti-abortion zealots', 'gas-guzzling pickup trucks' and so on—was 'feared, distrusted and increasingly disliked in the rest of the world'. Indeed, the Type G argument was of broad, almost cosmic, sweep. Moreover, those who adopted it, whether Muslim or non-Muslim, often appeared to do so with that 'uncontrollable' sense of distaste to which Margaret Drabble had confessed.

Upon the figure constructed of the United States, as upon the effigies which were burned in demonstrations, much spleen was vented. It could be declared, apparently with a sense of gratification—or of relief at the act of discharge of spleen itself—that America was 'becoming a global hate-figure', as a *Guardian* columnist put it in March 2002. Or hostility to America was presented as a dormant or latent force so powerful that only a single spark was required to set it ablaze. Thus, a Saudi political analyst declared in September 2002 that, if the 9/11 attacks on the United States had been marked in Saudi Arabia with an official first anniversary commemoration, a 'country-wide loathing' for American policy would have been 'inflamed'.

For Muslims and some non-Muslims together, the Type G device made the United States, not those who assailed it, the real 'problem'. It established a moral bond between Islamists who would see the United States brought down and the severer Western critics of American actions. The America which was a 'global hate-figure' in the view of a commentator in a liberal Western newspaper in March 2002, and the America described to a Western reporter by a Palestinian in a refugee-camp in October 2001 as 'the biggest evil around', were the same. Opinions might differ about how this object of the 'root-of-evil' argument should have its wings clipped or its neck wrung. But the view that America required to be resisted, humbled or brought down was shared in large degree by all those for whom the Type G 'root-of-evil' proposition was true.

The Type G argument could be found in many different versions and cover a wide range of objections. 'We no longer reckon ourselves lucky that this superpower is at the helm', wrote a commentator in the *New Statesman* in July 2002; 'it's cool to be un-American', declared a twenty-one-year-old student at the Berlin Free University in September 2002. Divisions within the UN Security Council, the European Union, NATO and the British House of Commons over the invasion of Iraq in 2003 evinced dislike not only of American leadership and American policy, but of the supposed 'nature' of America as such. It was a dislike which appeared to loom larger in many minds than did recoil from Saddam Hussein's tyrannical regime itself.

Indeed, the Type G thesis was continuously deployed against the United States by all and sundry. It was directed at 'hawkish' American counsellors to the president, at American policy in the Middle East, at American 'war-mongering', at American oil-interests or at all of them—and others—together. They were, again, the 'real problem'. It was a problem which for some seemed to dwarf the problems posed by the (unnameable) Islamic advance itself. Counter-views that it was 'easy to be anti-American', or invocations of the American role in liberating Europe during the Second World War, made little ground against those for whom the Type G argument was tantamount to an article of faith. Indeed, there were those in the West who did not hide their desire to see the United States and most of its works defeated. In May 2003, the mayor of London, Ken Livingstone, 'looked forward' to the US administration 'being overthrown' 'as much' as he had 'looked forward to Saddam Hussein being overthrown'—although how the latter was to have been achieved without American intervention he did not make clear.

Others wanted more harm done than this. If Iraq was to 'regain its independence', declared an editorialist in the *Guardian* in April 2004, 'the Iraqi resistance will have to sharply raise the costs of occupation'. 'Mutiny' was described as an 'entirely rational and principled response' and the 'only way out' in Iraq by a *Guardian* columnist in May 2004. Guy Rundle, in the *Sydney Morning Herald* in April 2003, similarly regretted that the United States had not met more 'serious resistance' in Iraq. 'That', he declared, 'will have to wait for another time. In Syria. Or Iran. Or Cuba. Or China'. By November 2003 the veteran Hampstead Trotskyist, Tariq Ali, was able to praise the 'anti-colonial' Iraqi resistance; the 'Iraqi maquis' he called it, comparing it with 'the

Algerian maquis almost half a century ago', as others had compared it with the French Resistance in the Second World War. Approvingly citing (Iraqi) descriptions of local supporters of the American forces as 'jackals' and 'quislings', Ali identified what was happening in Iraq as the 'classic first stage of guerrilla warfare against an occupying army'.

Similarly, the Italian anarchist, Tonio Negri, who had approved of the 9/11 attacks, described the Americans as the 'Talibans of the dollar'. Even the word 'homeland', used by the American government in reference to its domestic measures of self-protection, was put in sardonic quotation marks by a commentator in the *Observer* in March 2003. 'The only true heroes', asserted Nicholas de Genova, a Columbia University professor in April 2003, were 'those who find ways that help defeat the US military', further declaring that 'we have to believe in the victory of the Iraqi people and the defeat of the US war machine'. French journalists, too, according to Alain Hertoghe—fired from his newspaper *La Croix* at the end of 2003 for his accusations against the French press—were 'dreaming of an American defeat'. Islamist and (some) Western judgments were again in agreement.

Such death-wish attached itself with greatest ardour to President Bush. Here, the Type G device again knew no bounds. A chorus of voices in Britain, among them those of politicians, journalists and psychologists, described him as a 'bully', 'extreme', 'fanatical', a 'poisonous political pygmy', 'politically alien', a 'Texan psychopath', a 'reckless brigand', a 'combination of ignorance, piety and swagger', a 'complete and utter menace to the future security of the world', and even as the 'greatest threat to life on the planet'. He was also the 'most corrupt president since Harding in the twenties', according to the mayor of London; his 'anger rules the world', diagnosed the psychologist Oliver James; he was 'weak' and a 'moral coward', asserted the former US vice-president Al Gore; to a former senior adviser to President Clinton, his 'public persona' was 'inherently fragile'. The defeat of President Bush, said the financier George Soros in November 2003, was not only the 'central focus' of Soros's life, but a 'matter of life and death'.

Nevertheless, it was Bush himself who was declared to be 'obsessed', whether with the 'war on terrorism' or with Iraq, while his policies on the Middle East were held to be 'ignorant', 'absurdly unreal', 'puerile', 'ludicrous', 'vacuous' and 'fantastic'. In the *Guardian* in June 2002, it was implied that he was 'off his head'; in the same place in August 2002, 'a gale of laughter' was being aroused in 'the British people' at the 'idea of their fate being in the hands of George Bush'. In March 2003, again in a *Guardian* editorial, he was being 'played' 'like an open-mouthed trout on a line' by Ariel Sharon. In

December 2001, a *Times* commentator similarly suggested that President Bush, a man without 'real stature', lacked both 'the intelligence' and 'the leadership ability' to 'overcome' the 'fanaticism' of those around him.

He was 'one of the most unqualified people ever to have run for the highest office [in the United States] let alone to have attained it', according to Christopher Hitchens in the *Guardian* in January 2002; his 'dumbness' was 'scripted'—whatever that might mean—and his 'ignorance' was 'wilful', or intentional, according to other *Guardian* pundits. Moreover, he had had a 'reputation for 20 years' as an 'obnoxious drunk', as Hitchens put it. The Indonesian Muslim leader, Din Syamsuddin, agreed: the president was a 'drunken horse'. To the Labour MP Alan Simpson, in October 2002, Bush's 'needs to satisfy his thirst for power and oil' were again those of a 'drunk', and it was the British prime minister's duty 'not to pass the bottle'.

In the view of the Labour MP Gerald Kaufman, expressed in August 2002, he was 'the most intellectually backward American president of my lifetime'; to a leader of the European anti-globalisation movement, the already-cited Bernard Cassen, he was 'an imbecile, it's clear'; to the *Observer*, he was 'tone deaf to the rest of the world'. To Nelson Mandela, in February 2003, it was evident that President Bush 'cannot think straight'; to the writer Martin Amis in March 2003, Bush was not only 'intellectually null' but 'more psychologically primitive' than Saddam Hussein. To the *Observer* in October 2004, he was 'palpably unstable', with a 'creepy, inane grin on his face' and 'manifestly unfit to be President'. To the Democratic presidential contender, Wesley Clark, in February 2004, Bush did not 'have a clue about where this country should be going'; to the Iraqi foreign minister, Naji Sabri, speaking on the eve of the Iraq War, he was an 'ignorant, idiot man'; to a North Korean spokesman in August 2004, he was similarly 'an idiot, an ignoramus'; to New York's state Democratic chairman, Herman Farrell, in September 2004, the president was 'simple'; and in July 2005 he was likened by Senator Hillary Clinton to a half-witted character in a comic magazine.

Yet to others he possessed a 'warrior mind', if he had a mind at all. In March 2003, a German defence minister, Walter Kolbow, described him as a 'dictator' and in August 2004 the North Koreans called him a 'tyrant'. A further chorus of British voices also spoke of him as 'semi-articulate', 'impotently inarticulate', 'verbally inadequate', 'stumblingly inept with the language', a 'bumbling embarrassment' with a 'missing brain' and 'with all the eloquence of a yokel'. So self-persuaded was the British commentariat by its portrait of President Bush—drawn for the purposes of advancing the 'root-of-evil' thesis—that the *Guardian*'s deputy editor, Jonathan Freedland, was driven to express 'surprise' on discovering, during the November 2002 mid-term US elections, that Bush 'on the campaign trail' was not a 'linguistically-challenged dunce'. In particular, it was a 'surprise' to 'see him speak fluently and without so much as a glance at any notes'. 'It will break liberal hearts to admit it', Freedland revealingly added, 'but he's good'.

In the balance of things, however, this was no more than a passing aside. For the Type G device required that stereotypes be continually reinforced. Hence, for those whom the device served, more comfort was provided by 'Texan cowboy' epithets than by complications of description which could not be squared with the purposes of the device itself.

'Bleak philistinism' was thus discovered—as in the *Observer* in September 2002—at Bush's Texas ranch, described as his 'spiritual home'. In the *New York Times*, in the same month, the president's opinions were described as 'cowboy bromides'; to a British trade union leader, also in the same month, Bush's were 'cowboy tactics'; to Richard Gephardt, the American Democratic politician, he had a 'cowboy kind of belief' that issues were 'black and white'; to Albert Scardino, an American executive editor of the *Guardian*, he would have been 'inept' even as 'a cowboy'. The BBC's political editor, Andrew Marr, suggested in February 2003 that 'smiting Babylon and razing Nineveh again', which was to say attacking Iraq, might 'actually sound attractive to a biblical Texan'. In December 2001, the head of the British defence staff, Admiral Sir Michael Boyce, himself had oblique recourse to the 'cowboy' allusion when he mocked the idea of an American 'high-tech twenty-first-century posse in the new Wild West'.

Some of the hostilities expressed were evidently visceral. Margaret Drabble could 'hardly bear to see the faces of Bush and Rumsfeld'. 'Just seeing Bush's face or hearing his voice', and the 'way he walks and talks', aroused a similar 'physical reaction' in the American writer Jonathan Chait; Bush's 'upper lip' was described as 'faintly simian' in the *Guardian*. When the president visited London in November 2003, he was described by a protest-leader as the 'most unwelcome guest this country has ever received'.

Bush was depicted as a 'Hitler' on protest-banners; he was in pursuit of a 'totalistic [*sic*] ideology' in the judgment of Al Gore in August 2003; a month earlier, he was the 'Genghis Khan of the century' according to the hook-handed London cleric, Abu Hamza. He was a 'killer' according to the *Socialist Worker* in November 2003, and also a 'killer' on placards in Ireland in June 2004 during his presidential visit; he was the 'World's No. 1 Terrorist' said Islamists and Western demonstrators together. A 'huge crowd'—its numbers inflated by media excitement—cheered in Trafalgar Square when an image of Bush was brought down in imitation of the felling of Saddam Hussein's statue in Baghdad. Arundhati Roy, the Indian writer, similarly expressed the hope in January 2004 that Bush would 'share Saddam Hussein's fate' and be tried for 'crimes against humanity'. Bin Laden would have agreed.

Those who had resort to the Type G 'root-of-evil' argument often claimed that it was not America or Americans, but an odious American administration to which they objected. Yet distinctions between America-as-a-nation, American comportment in general in the world, American foreign policy, American leaders and ordinary American citizens were frequently blurred. Verbal assaults upon the United States in Type G arguments denoted 'America'-as-such to be aggressive, arrogant, barbarian, brash, brutal, its capitalism feral, flaunting its powers, high-handed, hypocritical, ruthless, savage, supremacist and vengeful. These epithets were used by Muslims and non-Muslims alike, including by an Islamist condemned to death in August 2003 for the Bali bombings, by an American financier, a distinguished British historian, Muslim clerics, and a raft of British media commentators. Even US aid to victims of the December 2004 earthquake and tidal-wave in south-east Asia was described in the Muslim world as 'exploiting the suffering of the people' in order to 'improve America's image'.

Amid the plethora of such condemnations, the United States was held guilty of military and colonial 'adventurism', of 'vast carelessness', of 'exceptionalism', of 'foolishness', of 'hubris', of 'imperialism', of 'infantilism', of 'terrorism', of 'triumphalism', of 'heedless' and even 'grotesque' 'unilateralism' and so on. In February 2002, America's view of the world was described by Chris Patten, the European Union's external relations commissioner, as 'absolute and simplistic', and to suffer from 'unilateralist overdrive': a form of political hemiplegia, or one-sided paralysis of its political vision. 'Gulliver can't go it alone', Patten added. Once more, many of the diagnoses of American ills were agreed by Muslims and non-Muslims. According to Prince Turki bin Faisal of Saudi Arabia in September 2002, the United States was not only 'unilateralist' and 'interventionist', but a 'xenophobic' power.

More crudely, the Bush administration could be described as, say, 'grisly' by the *Observer* in September 2002, or as 'the most unappetising I have ever known', by the Labour MP Gerald Kaufman in February 2003. It was even composed of 'power-crazed global bullies', according to a *Guardian* commentator in March 2003; while a professor emeritus of political science at Boston University, Howard Zinn, in August 2005 described the US president as 'surrounded by thugs in suits who care nothing about human life abroad or here'. These were stronger terms even than those used by bin Laden, who in April

2004 merely referred to 'the gang in the White House'. That it was America which 'wants war and means war', as it was put by a *Guardian* columnist in September 2002, again accorded fully with the standard Type G characterisation of American predispositions-as-such. Or, as Arundhati Roy expressed it in the same month, 'the US...has been at war with one country or another every year for the last 50 years'.

The 'America' of the Type G device was typically 'rapacious' for 'oil, money and power', and with its 'boundless appetite for domination' was bent on the 'tyrannical control of other nations'. According to a Bradford University professor of peace studies in February 2002, its 'war on terrorism' was no more than a 'euphemism for extending US control in the world', the argument of Islamists also. In the words of a British commentator in the same month, its exercise of 'imperial power' was 'overweening'; America was no less than a 'global behemoth'.

This 'behemoth'—a term also applied to Israel, as we saw earlier—was the 'terrorist king' to the Indonesian vice-president, Hamzah Haz, in September 2003; a 'danger to the world' and 'in the hands of a group of extremists' in the view of George Soros in November 2003; a 'hegemon', a 'hyperpower on the march', an 'idiotocracy', a 'monster out of control', 'in danger of turning into a military state' and the 'greatest threat to national sovereignty in Britain' in the opinion of a *Guardian* columnist in July 2003. Indeed, it was 'no longer just a nation' but 'a religion', he argued, and no longer needed to 'call upon God' because 'it was God'.

More serious (or less fatuous) were Type G comparisons made between the politics of the Bush administration and those of Nazism; comparisons also made, again as we saw earlier, in the case of Israel. Sometimes this Type G slur was indirect, as when the attacks on America in September 2001 were described by Bernard Cassen, the French 'anti-globalist', as 'having provided a shocking pretext to advance American interests *über alles*'. Of the same kind was the assertion in March 2003 of the veteran British Labour MP, Tony Benn, that a '*blitzkrieg*' was about to be launched on Iraq.

More direct were the declarations, as in September 2002 by Germany's justice minister, Herta Daeubler-Gmelin, that President Bush's methods of putting pressure on Iraq were similar to those employed by Hitler; that the 'attempts' of the US to 'rebuild all the world' were 'fraught with the same dangers as the Nazis taking over the world' in the judgment of a Russian commentator, Dmitri Ostalsky, in September 2003; that America 'more and more resembles Nazi Germany in its ambitions', in the view of the playwright Harold Pinter in November 2003; and that the US was an 'unbridled country that presents a global threat similar to Germany in the 1930s', according to Richard Gott, again in the *Guardian*, in April 2005. In November 2003 President Bush's 'You're either with us or against us' had 'conjure[d] up' for George Soros 'memories of Nazi slogans'. Even a US federal judge, Guido Calabresi, in June 2004 compared President Bush's election in 2000 with the rise to power of Mussolini and Hitler, while a *Guardian* writer in May 2004 likened the US army to the Wehrmacht. The head of Turkey's parliamentary human rights group took the analogy further, declaring in November 2004 that the 'genocide' in Iraq was on a scale 'never seen in the time of the Pharaohs nor of Hitler'.

In an alternate version of what was essentially the same thesis, but without resort to the word 'Nazi' or reference to the Hitler regime, America's conduct spoke to a 'new sense of Caucasian superiority' and a 'new desire to subjugate those of other colours and cultures', according to the journalist Martin Jacques in May 2002. The intentions and actions ascribed to the US when the Type G device was in use could thus be extravagant indeed. Paul Bremer, the American civil administrator in Iraq—or 'occupation chief'—was even claimed by a commentator in the *Guardian* in April 2004 to be 'deliberately' 'provoking a war' in Iraq, in order to 'create the chaos it [sc. the United States] needs'.

Attribution to the US of outlandish misdeeds, the worse the better, was a necessary feature of the Type G device. In November 2002 Osama bin Laden claimed that AIDS was a 'satanic American invention', while the historian Eric Hobsbawm declared in January 2003 that the American administration had 'wrecked NATO', 'deliberately sabotaged the European Union', and even 'aimed' to 'ruin' the 'prosperous democratic social welfare states' of the West. Similarly, in September 2002, the *Observer* discovered a 'frightening propensity' in the United States to 'crush free-thinking', while in May 2003 a journalist on the same paper asserted that 'the role of the social' in America had been 'banished', no less. There were therefore no bounds, once more, to the kinds of proposition which the Type G device engendered when President Bush came to be re-elected in November 2004. The US was being 'taken to a dark, puritanical tyranny'; the Republicans had become a 'quasi-clerical party'; America, by electing Bush, had shown itself to be a 'gun-happy land of religious maniacs' and so forth.

However, the Type G argument was again flexible enough to offer an entirely different view of the United States, according to choice. It could then become a nation held to be guilty of childish 'tantrums' and to possess a 'pitiful worldview'—in the words of the *Guardian*'s Hugo Young in July

2002—as when it rejected the jurisdiction of the International Criminal Court. But the device was equally available to make of 'America' a ruthless, world-dominating and predatory force. If you preferred, it could also be a witless, cow-punching and obese 'behemoth', or be suffering from a combination of 'chronic attention deficit disorder' and 'curious obsessions' according to a British academic writing in the *New York Times* in October 2002. Alternatively, it was 'rotting at its core', as another *Guardian* commentator put it in March 2003; or, perhaps, it could be all these together.

Whatever the particular 'Argument Against America', the Type G device has generally been employed reductively, often at the same time as complaint was being made of American simple-mindedness in its worldview. Likewise, those who used the device could be rhetorically violent even as they complained of American aggression, and were as high-handed in their mode of address as the American traits to which they were objecting. Users of the Type G device also tended to abuse of language, the better to gain notice in public debate. Hence, Pentagon officials could be described as acting with 'improper *ferocity*' in pursuing their ends, while 'America' was accused by Nelson Mandela in February 2003 of committing '*unspeakable atrocities* in the world'. In the *Observer* in February 2002, the United States was declared to be in '*pathological* condition', and to be 'an organism grown so large it is *sick*'.

In Type G argument, the terms of mental illness could be used not merely of its president but of America-as-a-whole. Its 'post 9/11' mood was described as that of 'national paranoia'; at the World Economic Forum in New York in February 2002, an 'incoherent paranoid mood' was detected by a *Times* columnist. 'American politicians, businessmen and media commentators' were 'on the brink of a collective nervous breakdown', he declared, while the 'wider American public' seemed to be in the grip of 'manic-depression'.

With 'paranoia', 'arrogance' and other such mental and moral disorders afflicting the United States, those who adopted the Type G argument could readily find a president 'whipping up war hysteria'—in *The Times* in February 2002—or a nation, according to John le Carré in January 2003, in 'one of its worst periods of historical madness'. To Günter Grass, in May 2003, the Iraq War was nothing but 'organised madness'. 'America' was thus being diagnosed to be in thrall to a darkness of mind as great as when seventeenth-century Puritans fought the devil. Or, as Matthew Parris explained in January 2002 in *The Times*, 'America has simple gods and likes to keep her satan simple too.... In Salem it was once witches. In Senator Joe McCarthy's heyday it was Commies. Now it is al-Qaeda', he asserted. This use of the Type G device therefore implied that the United States was striking out at phantoms.

The symptoms of America's political pathology identified by those who employed the Type G device varied in degree but not in kind. For the premises of the 'Argument Against America' have been constant: that the United States, whether in its character as a nation, or in its policy, or in the nature of its administration, is 'the problem'. The corollary of this is that violence and odium of word or deed directed against America are not simply responses to this 'problem'; they contain the makings of a 'solution' to it.

In the transposition of moral attention from acts carried out against America to acts carried out by it, the combined force of the Type F 'underlying causes' device and the Type G 'root-of- all-evil' thesis served Muslims and non-Muslims equally well, some Americans included. Skilful use of the logic of the Type G argument increasingly dictated that America was morally disentitled to perceive its foes as themselves 'evil'; while the Type E device dictated that, if the latter were 'evil', they were only as 'evil' as, or less 'evil' than, was the United States itself. Between them, these arguments further helped to disable the non-Muslim world's responses to the challenges it was facing.

TYPE H: *'Many-acts-by-Muslims-are-those-of-desperate-individuals-who-lack-other-means-to-express-their-despairs'.*

This device presented the perpetrator of violence, especially random and suicidal violence, as the morally helpless object of circumstances. It was a proposition frequently linked to the Type F thesis as to 'underlying causes'. In its mildest variant, the Type H argument invested ill-doing with less moral significance than it would (or should) otherwise have had. A middling position—reflecting the Type E notion that 'each-is-as-bad-as-the-other'—gave moral parity to desperate perpetrator and often innocent target.

The Type H argument was often used as the ground for expressions of sympathy or admiration for the perpetrator's courage. In an ultimate moral inversion, the device could also be employed to make the victim of a Type H 'desperate' act responsible for his or her own wounds or death. When the Type F 'underlying-causes' and the Type H 'desperado' thesis were combined, perpetrators could acquire absolution not only in the eyes of Muslims—where they were seen as 'martyrs'—but also in the eyes of non-Muslims to whom the argument appealed.

In a characteristic use of the Type H device, Yasser Arafat could therefore be perceived as 'the temporising victim, not the master of events', as Peter Preston described him in the *Guardian* in December 2001. The implication of many such assertions, whether offered in Muslim self-legitimation or in non-

Muslim 'liberal' apologia, has been that 'terroristic' acts are not truly 'terroristic' if they are carried out by those who are 'desperate'. A rider to this is that even the most reprehensible of acts become less reprehensible when they are 'correctly' understood. This moral, or amoral, argument is again a commonplace. At different times it has been put forward by Christians and Muslims, by Nazis and Jews, and by many others besides.

A difficulty with the argument when used of Islamist violences is that only a very small minority of those whom the Type H device would identify as 'desperate' have struck out at others with 'terrorising' effect. Nevertheless, the Type H thesis was found persuasive by many non-Muslims in respect of certain types of Islamist act. When two Palestinian suicide-bombers destroyed themselves and passers-by in a Jerusalem Street in December 2001, 'you may heap any combination of adjectives on them you like', declared Peter Preston once more, 'but leave "cowardly" out of the equation'. 'Desperation', he explained, 'carries its own lexicon'.

This was so, but it has been a 'lexicon' in which the Type H device has been inscribed on its first page. According to it, 'desperation' could transform an act of carnage into an act of courage. Those working with the Type H device generally acknowledged the tragic nature of an act of public self-destruction which had as its end 'taking others with it', whoever these others might turn out to be. The act could even be declared, with a nod to its *terribilità*, to be wrong. But those who used the Type H argument frequently implied that such wrong at the same time had its rights. It might even be held, on the last page of this 'lexicon', to *be* right.

Once more, Muslim and (some) non-Muslim arguments have coincided. In particular, Israeli sins of omission and commission have generally been held—including by some Israelis—to be Type H exemplars of that-which-causes-despair. The user of the Type H argument, whether Muslim or non-Muslim, will also commonly hold that the consequences of causing such despair in others can not only be anticipated and explained but even justified; at worst celebrated. Conversely, there are others who reject the Type H justification-by-desperation thesis. They include Muslims who are not only pre-occupied with the 'image' of Islam but those who are ready to accept Muslim responsibility for Muslim acts. But, Muslim objection to the Type H thesis can also be amorally cold-eyed, as in Edward Said's assertion that 'in the end desperation only produces poor results'.

The device has been applied both to the particular instances of an Islamist attack and to the general circumstances of the Muslim, and especially of the Arab, condition. 'A balance of the Arab world shows a meagre present and bleaker future', thus wrote Marwan Bishara in the *Herald Tribune* in February 2002, pointing to a generalised Arab 'despair'. The Indian Muslim writer, M. J. Akbar, went further, declaring that in an 'age of despair', 'the need for a hero' who 'can inspire pan-Islamic victories' was 'acute' among Muslims. That is, Muslims were by implication 'desperate': the premise, potentially, for a Type H argument again without moral or geographical limits.

'Hopelessness' was also a common condition of those to whom the Type H device was applied. Such 'hopelessness' could be termed 'absolute', as Karen Armstrong, the religious historian—in an interview with *al-Ahram* in July 2002—described the circumstances of Palestinian suicide-bombers to be. Indeed, they were so 'hopeless' that a British Liberal Democrat member of parliament (and physician) could declare in January 2004 that in such circumstances she would herself 'consider' becoming a suicide-bomber.

That the 'despairing' and 'hopeless' should have advocates in their behalf is, from one point of view, a saving grace; that 'despair' and 'hopelessness' should be addressed and redeemed is a demand of justice. But the Type H device has generally not been employed in this way or to this end. Instead, it has more often served as apologia—once again—than as a genuine explanation of motive. In moral consequence, violent acts carried out against innocent non-combatants, taken unawares, have been vindicated in the perpetrators' own eyes not only by the dictates of faith but also by non-Muslim apologetics for such violence. In consequence, violence has acquired a measure of ethical legitimacy as a means both of armed warfare and mere protest.

'Despair' and 'hopelessness' are outcomes of multiple and complex causes. These causes have included not only inflictions of wounds upon Muslims by others, but inflictions of harm by Muslims upon themselves. But the Type H device, like other such devices of argument, is reductive of complexity. 'Despair', whatever its etiology, has for some been sufficient in itself to explain or justify desperate acts, however cruel and violent such acts were.

This reductiveness has been matched by the falsehoods of those who have argued a contrary case: that there is 'no evidence whatever that the suicide-bombers ... act out of poverty, hopelessness and despair', as Edward Alexander asserted in the *American Spectator* in June 2003. Yet in the previous month, in attacks in Casablanca by fourteen suicide-bombers—who were reported to have come from the 'sprawling slum' of Sidi Moumin—most were young, indigent, unemployed and unmarried, and with one exception poorly-educated. However, many suicide-bombers, including most of those who helped plan or took part in the 9/11 attacks, have been quite other than the impoverished desperadoes who figure in standard uses of the Type H device.

Choosing from a number of instances, Omar Khan Sharif, one of the two British Muslims who carried out a suicide-attack in Tel Aviv in April 2003, came of a prosperous family, was privately-educated, was married and had been at university; Hiba Azzam Darajme, a nineteen-year-old girl who blew herself up in the northern Israeli town of Afula in May 2003, was a student of English literature at al-Quds University; and Abdel Madi Shabneh, an eighteen-year-old who carried out a similar attack on a Jerusalem bus in June 2003, killing himself and seven others, was a high-school student who had been planning to study electronics and who was said to have 'never previously spent a night away from home'. Likewise, co-ordinated suicide-bombings in a crowded Jerusalem café and outside a Tel Aviv army-base in September 2003 were carried out by two university students, while bombings in India by Islamists in December 2002, and in January, March and August 2003, were said to have involved computer professionals, an engineer and a doctor. In particular, such attacks have almost everywhere been commanded and organised by the better educated rather than by the less, and by the relatively prosperous rather than by the most deprived and 'despairing'; Mohammed Atta, the principal 9/11 pilot, had a German university degree, and Shaikh Khalid Mohammed, the alleged 'master-mind' of the 9/11 attack, studied engineering in North Carolina.

The Type H 'desperation-and-hopelessness' argument posits that the acts which it seeks to explain, and even justify, are acts of unappeasable last resort. However, for their organisers such acts are strategic choices, made in the belief that an enemy can ultimately be brought to its knees by their use. In addition, as a *Times* commentator argued in June 2002, Islamist *kamikaze* actions have not been the 'noble stands of outnumbered warriors like the Spartans at Thermopylae', but 'the calculated acts of men and women whose ideology celebrates death in a fashion which almost defies Western comprehension'. That is, many of Islamism's 'despairing' attacks have been carried out in the firm belief not only that they were a means to defeat the foe-on-earth but in order to obtain a sure reward in heaven.

Islamists have themselves categorically denied—as did Islamic Jihad—that 'depressed peple' were chosen as suicide-bombers. Nevertheless, non-Muslims who employed the Type H device continued to find a rationale in 'desperation' and 'hopelessness' even for the worst of acts, and to earn silent Islamist gratitude for it. Indeed, the logic of the Type H argument is that the more 'desperate' or heinous the acts, the more entitled to 'understanding' became the perpetrators. Worse, the Type H device depends upon fittingly violent acts of 'hopelessness' and 'desperation' for its case to be made, as those who organise such acts and send the suicides upon their tragic errands know. For there can be no 'age of despair', in M. J. Akbar's phrase, without desperadoes.

Use of the Type H device has had a larger moral and political significance than this. Not only has it been employed to 'explain' culpable acts but to present 'desperation' as a form of *force majeure*, and to make a norm of 'desperate' acts of 'resentment', 'frustration'and 'rage'. Those who have retained their hopes, or who have not responded violently to their circumstances, have been made to appear tolerant or passive exceptions to the rule upon which the Type H generalisation rests.

The Type H device has also had morally innocent ends. It has been employed by many non-Muslims in the expression of compassion for those, especially the young, who have committed extreme acts of self-immolation. Nevertheless, in many cases there has been a small moral distance between compassion and 'understanding', and between 'understanding' of a cause and sympathy for it, as has already been indicated. The Type H argument has been found serviceable in each of these cases, morally distinct as they are. More important, the 'desperation-and-hopelessness' thesis, when allied with the 'underlying-causes' and 'root-of-evil' arguments, has often been intended to lead to a single and again simplistic conclusion: that the recruiting-sergeant for Islamist 'terrorism' is not Islamism itself but the misdeeds of the non-Muslim world.

Such conclusion, like the Type H 'desperado' thesis itself, misperceives the nature of the Arab and Islamic resurgence. For over the last decades, despite internal division and blood-letting, Islam and Islamism have drawn their strengths from their own energies and resources, and not from 'hopelessness' and abjection.

TYPE I: *'To-take-determined-action-against-militant-Arabism-or-Islamism-will-have-dire-consequences'*.

This device of argument has frequently been deployed in conjunction with, and as a conclusion drawn from, the Type F, G and H propositions. Use of it has increased during the acuter phases of conflict between the Muslim and non-Muslim worlds. Some of the forms in which it has appeared have been more oblique than others. Thus, it could be suggested that the taking of measures, particularly aggressive measures, against this or that perceived threat from the Arab or Islamic world was to overlook the 'real issue' (Type F), and that by doing so the consequences would be even more serious. The 'real issue', as we have seen, was most frequently the culpability of America, of Israel or of the non-Muslim world as a whole for creating circumstances to which Islamism was merely a reaction. In addition, the Type I device again served as a means of transferring attention from the nature and significance of Islamist acts, to the risks of taking determined counter-measures against them.

Like some of the other devices which have been examined, the argument was of great flexibility. At any given moment an action or reaction on the part of the non-Muslim could be denoted to be the wrong one. Once more, it was a position which could be shared with Muslims and Islamists themselves. Using the Type I device, a war against Iraq was declared by a contributor to the *New York Times* in October 2002—and by the Democratic presidential candidate, John Kerry—to be 'the wrong war at the wrong time'. Something else would typically be held to be the 'real issue', in this case the pursuit of al-Qaeda. When 'something else' was required to displace the matter-in-hand—whatever such matter might be—it was often one of the standard Type F 'underlying causes', in particular the Palestinian-Israeli dispute, which was said to demand prior attention. Other alternative issues could include the interests of 'peace and stability' in this or that region, the avoidance of offence to Muslim sensibilities, the need for 'better intelligence', the need for more development aid, or the need for 'democracy' in the Muslim world and so on.

All these were significant issues in their own right. All were also serviceable to the 'wrong target' thesis, in which 'taking-your-eye-off-the-ball' was held to invite greater trouble than already existed, whatever such trouble might be. From time to time, this form of argument could be found in inter-Muslim discourse also. Thus, in October 2002, the Algerian president declared himself opposed to a war against Saddam Hussein on the grounds that it would 'draw the focus from the Palestinian cause'.

Warnings about the consequences—preferably dire or catastrophic—of taking this or that action, again whatever such action might be, have again been commonplaces in all cultures, and in any crisis. As the writer John Wain described the situation in the late 1930s, a 'vociferous pacifist movement... hammered home its message: "Leave Hitler alone. Let him have what he wants, or we might end up having to fight him"'. Use of the 'dire consequences' device in the conflict with Islamism has once more been versatile. It could be employed for the purposes of astute procrastination and in skilful diplomatic manoeuvre. It could recommend itself equally to those with long-sighted strategic purpose, to those with a morally inert preference for inaction and to those with—once more—a hidden sympathy for a foe. Resort to the Type I argument could also be prompted by inability to do anything about a given problem, by genuine and well-grounded fear of taking action and by self-interest.

In some of the other devices I have examined in this chapter, the Type I thesis is implicit. For example, the Type C 'principle' of keeping a 'sense of proportion' and even of 'letting sleeping dogs lie'—lest they stir and bite— dictates caution or 'cultural sensitivity' in face of Islamist challenge, lest worse befall. The Type F 'underlying causes' thesis, in expressing a predisposition to see effects as essentially a 'backlash' against such causes, holds out the (naive) promise that in the absence of such 'causes' the dire effects will not occur. All these arguments rest upon a similar premise: that to assail, even upon justifiable grounds, the perpetrator of a violent or other hostile act against the non-Muslim world is likely to lead to consequences worse still.

In addition, the 'underlying causes' of actual or feared effects are often of such large scope or of such generalised nature—say, 'American imperialism', 'global capitalism', 'racism', 'Zionism' or 'hostility to Islam'—as to appear, or to be, irredeemable whether in the short term or at all. The Type I argument then enters a political and moral cul-de-sac. It warns against the fateful consequences of a course of action which is held to be misjudged and wrong, while generally calling for prior attention to be given to 'underlying causes' which are almost always beyond immediate (or any) solution. The Type I argument is thus often a proposal—in effect—to do little or nothing. Moreover, the argument that 'if-they-hit-you-don't-hit-them-back-or-they-will-hit-you-again' again offers *carte blanche* to the Islamist cause.

However, the Type I argument as to 'dire consequences' has on many occasions been salutary. This has been the case when warning was given of the risks of taking actions against the Muslim and Arab worlds which were practically misguided, morally indefensible, or illegal. In the case of the intervention in Iraq in 2003, such warnings offset bland assertions that right was being done, that 'victory' was at hand and so forth. But these warnings were often given in standard 'catastrophist' form, and again with a barely-disguised relish for the worst that could be anticipated. Those who used the Type I argument declared, for example, that a 'nightmare' was beginning and that the 'spirit of war' had been 'unlocked', as if it had not already been 'unlocked' in the long decades of the Islamic revival.

'President Bush and his government', declared Günter Grass in April 2003, were bringing 'sure disaster to their own country'. A retired British diplomat, Sir Martin Berthoud, told *The Times* that 'what we are doing out there' was having a 'horrendous impact' on Britain's 'international standing'; an *Observer* commentator even claimed that, 'when we get to the other side of this war', the entire 'world order' would have to be 'put back together again'. By implication, the 'world order' was in the process of being destroyed not by the upheavals generated by the advance of Islam, nor by Islamism's spreading assaults, but by the actions which the American 'hyperpower' was taking against them.

Appeal to the Type I 'dire-consequences-of-action' argument has derived much of its impact from the fact that the argument itself arouses fear. Indeed, its force has rested in large part on the ease with which it could be translated into populist terms. Moreover, the case that 'things-will-only-be-made-worse' by this or that action, or counter-action, is not only simple to put but can be made to appear sophisticated with little intellectual effort. Arguments that a misjudged Western response to challenge would consolidate Islamism's existing grip on parts of the Muslim world, or would set back the 'transition to democracy' in autocratic Islamic states, were therefore often heard when the Type I device was in use. The 'dire consequences' argument has also been media-friendly, since it held out the prospect of spectacular televisual disasters. Even in its milder variants, it offered the promise of Muslim 'reprisals' and 'revenge attacks'.

The Type I could also be used to suggest that the consequences-of-action would be the opposite of what the West intended. Hence, the bombing of Afghanistan would 'probably freeze the Taliban in their hold on power as long as it lasts, as is usual with bombed regimes', predicted a *Times* commentator in October 2001. The American intervention in Iraq, likewise declared the Duke of Devonshire in the *Daily Telegraph* in March 2003—immediately after the invasion had begun—had 'strengthened the hold of the [Saddam] regime over its people'. A similar form of argument has long been employed by radical Muslims; in April 1992 the Sudanese Islamist leader, Hassan Turabi, warned that 'if America tries to stand in our way, it will only increase the momentum', the 'momentum' being that of the Islamist (and Islamic) cause. 'Every time a martyr falls, Hamas is strengthened', likewise proclaimed Ismail Haniya, a senior Hamas official, in April 2004.

Thus, both non-Muslims and Muslims could together assert that the more direct the action taken against Islamism or tyrannical Arab regimes, the greater in strength they would grow. This view was expressed not only by Islamist leaders but by many in the 'Arab street'. 'They [sc. the Israelis] don't seem to understand that the more deaths they cause us', an inhabitant of Ramallah told the *Guardian* in August 2001, 'the stronger we get'. It was even argued that to pursue Islamism's most violent figures endangered the pursuer more than the pursued. 'If the state machinery goes after what it calls extremists', the former head of Pakistan's security services, General Hamid Gul, warned in April 1995, 'then the reaction could be very nasty'.

There has therefore been little to choose among the predictions made by those, whether Muslim or non-Muslim, who have adopted the Type I device. 'Any American victories in Afghanistan', declared a *New York Times* editorial in September 2001, four days after the attacks on the World Trade Center and in advance of America's counter-assault, 'would quickly turn into a catastrophic defeat, if the war there turned Pakistan...into an Islamic fundamentalist state'. Likewise, warned Indonesian Islamists three days later, any attack by the United States on a Muslim country would cause a violent response. It was a proposition with which the *New York Times* agreed. Such attack would 'strengthen the hand of Islamic radicals in Indonesia'. The Type I argument was not only being used both by radical Muslims and by East Coast liberal opinion-formers, but at the same time and in the same fashion.

Moreover, whether the West's purposes were held to be justified or mis-guided, the Type I device dictated that they could equally exact a dreadful toll of one kind and another. There was 'likely to be an arduous house by house, street by street, fight in Baghdad', thought a correspondent in the *Guardian* as American troops began their action. 'To kill Saddam', prophesied a *Times* columnist, the Americans would have to 'fight their way to his bunker across the bombed streets of a sullen city'; it would be like Stalingrad, thought the *Guardian*, 'millions of women and children would be killed', predicted Baroness Shirley Williams.

Or if the actual consequences did not entirely live up to expectations, it could be made to seem as if they had. In April 2004, a 'revolt within the mil-itary against Bush' was asserted in the *Guardian* to be 'brewing'; by May 2004, under the headline 'America's Military Coup', a commentator in the same paper announced that 'the US officer corps' had 'turned on the government'. As for the consequences of the French ban on the wearing of the *hijab* in schools, they could be 'quite literally catastrophic', warned Madeleine Bunting in the *Guardian* in December 2003. To Jon Henley, in the same paper in Jan-uary 2004, the prospect was equally bad, or worse. The ban 'looks increasingly like turning into a debacle of gargantuan proportions', he wrote.

In some cases of the usage of the Type I argument, whether by Muslims or non-Muslims, the prognosis as to the likely 'dire consequences' of this or that action was judicious, or pointed to evident truth. In others, it was falsified by events. When Islamists employed the device in their own cause, it served to 'terrorise' others; when non-Muslims used it they terrorised themselves. The argument could be put by the prudent and reflective as well as by those who were simply hostile to the United States; it could be the expression, at some remove, of a pacifist ethic, or of Western self-hatred. It could be the product of a need to fill out a newspaper-column and to wring the withers of a tele vision audience, or to put a citizenry on its guard against mistakes of judgment by the non-Muslim world.

The Type I argument has also served as a great—and perilous—unifier of understandings. It has passed back and forth across the boundaries between Muslim and non-Muslim perceptions, between 'left' and 'right', and between those with experience of military combat and mere armchair strategists. Thus, Sir Michael Boyce, chief of the British defence staff, warned in December 2001 of the dangers in American policy of 'radicalising the opinion of the Islamic world'. He too was using the Type I device, just as the Western press has done from the need to create alarm, or as Islamists do by way of threat. In particular, the argument held out the prospect of some form of catastrophic result for which those who had taken the action would have only themselves to blame. Once more, this was precisely what the Islamist would wish the non-Muslim to think.

As I have indicated, the consequences which have been predicted should this or that policy be pursued, or this or that action be taken, have been of varied direness. At the lower end of the scale, Western support for, or tactical alliances with, undemocratic Muslim and Arab states have been said—both by Muslims and non-Muslims—to put their imagined democratisation at risk. In October 2002, it was argued by one of Iran's vice-presidents, Massoumeh Ebtekar, that 'external pressures' to speed up the country's (putative) reform process would have the effect only of strengthening the hands of anti-reformists. Somewhat more severe was the commonplace Type I prediction, whether from Muslims or non-Muslims, that Western actions could 'create instability', whether in a particular nation or region, or even in the 'entire world'. The range of those subscribing to this 'instability' proposition was wide. They included Muslim and non-Muslim politicians, members of the liberal Western commentariat, retired diplomats and many others. And when instability already existed in a particular region, as in the Middle East, a Type I variant would have it that such instability would be 'increased'.

The Type I argument could often be said to imply that any action, save succumbing to Islamist pressures, would be ill-advised. Moreover, the great strength of the device has been that its prognoses have necessarily proved right in many instances, since, independently of what non-Muslims may or may not do, Islam and Islamism are on the advance. Hence, users of the Type I argument could safely offer the prospect, or promise, of 'more trouble', preferably severe. In *The Times* in October 2001, the bombing of Afghanistan was thus held to be 'likely to increase anti-Western hysteria in the Middle East', while the *Guardian* thought in July 2004 that the 'killing fields'—itself a catastrophist cliché—of the Iraq War 'could eventually stretch from Afghanistan to Palestine'. And as the anticipation of the 'dire consequences' of action, especially that taken by the United States, became more fearful, the sentiments of Islamists and the judgments of some Western pundits increasingly converged. 'The more America brandishes its military power, the more it will be met with antagonism, revulsion and misunderstanding' was the prediction of a *Times* commentator in February 2002; 'revulsion' is a word of shared recoil.

Most Type I prognoses were repetitious and revolved around the same sets of premises and conclusions. Thus, President Chirac in September 2002 saw the 'alienation of the Islamic world' as the likely consequence of a war against Iraq. A large-scale prospect, it was nevertheless merely one of the commoner forms of middle-intensity forebodings as to the risk of 'precipitate action' against the Saddam regime. Another commonplace mid-range form of Type I assertion had it that war with Iraq was 'not just a substitute for the war against terrorism' but would 'impede' it, as the *New York Times* argued in October 2002 in chorus with a thousand other voices.

More common still was the kind of prognosis offered in February 2003 by a former British ambassador to Syria and Saudi Arabia, Patrick Wright, that action against Iraq would 'contribute to the terrorist threat'. Similar was the argument when put, also in February 2003, in cruder populist terms: the West, declared a *Times* columnist, would experience 'vengeance in return' for an assault on Iraq. Indeed, Type I arguments continuously blamed US actions for the 'growing support' of Islamism, for the 'expansion' of 'terrorism' and for 'creating the conditions'—as if there were no others—in which al-Qaeda could 'thrive'. These were again truisms bound to be vindicated by events. For 'terrorism' has its own trajectory, that of the Islamist advance.

The standard feature of all such prophecies, as I have noted, was the implication that another course than the one chosen should have been chosen instead, and that the price of having made the wrong choice was that worse now beckoned. Sometimes this 'worse' was made menacingly imprecise, as in the suggestion by the writer Martin Amis in March 2003 that a 'kaleidoscope of terrible eventualities' would follow an attack upon Iraq. Indeed, the nouns and adjectives of escalating Type I prediction themselves followed a predictable path, especially when the 'worst-case scenarios' were rehearsed.

According to the German foreign minister, Joschka Fischer, 'mass' casualties, 'mass' opposition and the 'endless suffering of countless people' were promised in March 2003 to be in the offing if a war with Iraq took place. To the British journalist Max Hastings, also in March 2003, 'years of global crisis' lay ahead if America did not mend its ways—as if such years of 'global crisis' did not lie ahead in any event, and whether the Iraq War was misguided or not. It was 'possible', thought Nicholas Kristof in the *New York Times* in February 2003, that 'invading Iraq will trigger precisely the scenario we fear'—the much-repeated Type I 'own-goal' thesis—and that it would lead 'thousands of young Arabs to join al-Qaeda'. It would 'make attacks like the bomb in Bali more likely', declared the *Independent* in October 2002; it would give rise to 'one hundred years of terrorism', declared one of Italy's left leaders, Massimo d'Alema, in January 2003; it would 'fuel an upsurge in terrorist attacks world-wide', declared the Malaysian prime minister, Mahathir Mohamad, in February 2003—as if Islam's and Islamism's progress in the world did not presage all this independently of whether or not America 'brandished its military power'.

Those who resorted to the Type I 'dire consequences' device generally had another characteristic in common. They were unable to allow that a 'tough response' to Islamism or Arabism's excesses might at least serve as some deterrent to them, or that open divisions and almost palpable fears in the non-Muslim world invited attack. 'Next time a large bomb goes off in a Western city, how far did this policy'—that of going to war in Iraq—'contribute to it?' the former Tory government minister, Kenneth Clarke, rhetorically demanded to know in the House of Commons in February 2003. 'Next time an Arab or Muslim regime is toppled by a regime far more extreme, how did this policy contribute to it?' he asked further.

The swelling ranks of al-Qaeda, one hundred years of terrorism, the toppling of regimes and much else besides were offered by Muslims and non-Muslims, and by 'right' and 'left', as Type I consequences of Western errors of judgment. In the view of the already-mentioned serving British army officer, writing under cover of anonymity in the *Sunday Telegraph* on the eve of the Iraq War, there was even the 'worrying prospect' of 'public opinion turning against the Armed Forces'. In February 2003, the writer Norman Mailer added his own 'dire prospect' to the heap: that America was 'going to become a mega-banana republic, where the army will have more and more importance in Americans' lives', and that its democracy might 'give way'. This was even more hectic than some Muslim uses of the Type I thesis; it clearly took a non-Muslim to predict the transformation of America into a 'mega-banana republic'. In comparison with it, 'one missile on Baghdad and things are going to go crazy, especially in the universities' was the relatively modest prospect offered by the Egyptian journalist Amira Howeidi in March 2003.

Metaphors of 'explosions' of terrorism, or of 'whirlwinds' which would 'affect us for generations to come', according to a Labour MP speaking in the House of Commons, merged easily with those favoured by Muslim rhetoric, including its metaphors of consuming flame. The 'whole region' would be 'set ablaze' if Iraq were attacked, declared Yassin Ramadan, one of Iraq's vice-presidents in February 2003. The Egyptian president similarly warned that war with Iraq would light a 'gigantic fire'. According to Amr Moussa, the sec-retary-general of the Arab League, it would yet again 'open the gates of hell'.

Type I arguments as to the 'dire consequences' of taking action against actual or intending Muslim or Arab assailants permitted both Muslim and non-Muslim to predict anything whatever, including generalised calamities of largest scale. The other devices examined in this chapter between them made a principle out of scepticism as to facts, questioned others' moral judgments, counselled a sense of proportion, addressed the risks to liberal societies of over-reaction and turned criticism round upon the non-Muslim world. But the specialty of those who employed the Type I device was to discount the possi-bility that the actions to which they objected, and against whose consequences they warned, might have been the least bad choice among the limited options which faced the non-Muslim world. It was a device which also relied greatly upon illusion and, yet again, wishful thinking. Moreover, those who resorted to it were usually confident in their predictions of catastrophe, but rarely offered genuine or realistic alternatives to the policies or acts of which they disap-proved. Use of the device often involved little more than nay-saying, even when dressed in the guise of decision.

For those who employed the Type I argument, it was not the 'dire conse-quences' of the *acts* carried out by a United States or by an Israel, but the dire nature of the *actors*, which was generally the real issue.

****

I have described all these devices as forms of 'thinking within limits'. Yet, as I have shown, each might be pushed to its own extremes, even to the 'gates of hell'. For the most part, they were arguments which were directed to con-straining or deterring action and reaction by non-Muslims in the face of chal-lenge. At best, each might be defended as conducing to prudential foresight, or to the inhibiting of excess as a response to excess. But when one device was heaped upon another, and complex combinations of open animus and concealed sympathy informed them, they could cease to be rational antidotes to the perceived risks of unreason, and become merely perverse. Moreover, unlike those devices of Muslim argument which sought to divest Muslims of moral responsibility for their own acts and transfer it to non-Muslims, many of the devices examined in this chapter showed a predisposition in non-Muslims to assume moral responsibility themselves for attacks which Islamists had made upon them. The devices often suggested, too, that inaction by non-Muslims in the face of such attacks was the best course to pursue.

This perversity could take a profounder form. Where Muslim actions were often suicidal, both metaphorically and in fact, their Western correlates sometimes seemed to be those of a death-wish, as has been noted. Such death-wish has been displayed in media-driven enthusiasm for disaster, the larger the better; in excoriating self-criticisms of the history of the West; in expressions of the belief that the West, and especially the United States, 'had it coming'; and in other forms besides.

They could go so far as to signal the hope, and not merely the expectation, that America would take a beating at Islam's hands, a beating it was held to deserve. It was a hope not greatly distinct from that entertained by America's declared foes. Thus, a *Guardian* commentator in July 2000 not only described as 'world-destabilising' America's 'missile-knockout system', but declared that 'tomorrow's test may fail. Let's hope it does'. Such ballistic system might indeed be both costly and unfeasible. But to express the 'hope' that it would fail was of a different order of criticism. It was criticism which willed, as Islamism also wills, that America's purposes be dashed. 'We should cross our fingers', similarly urged George Monbiot in the *Guardian* in August 2002, 'and hope that a combination of economic mismanagement, gangster capitalism and excessive military spending will reduce America's power to the extent that it ceases to use the rest of the world as a doormat'.

Such 'hopes' have presented themselves as protective of the general good. But it was clear that they were also impelled by hostility, and by the desire to see the United States brought down, whether as a military or economic force, or both. The ills it wreaks were often held to outweigh any good it might purport to do, as Islamism also holds. Moreover, many Western fatalists not only perceived further disasters ahead—without understanding the nature or scope of the Muslim advance—but appeared to gain gratification from the prospect. 'What happened in Bali could not only happen in many other places', declared a contributor to the *New York Times* in October 2002, but 'surely will'. It was again as if there was some satisfaction to be gained from the assurance.

Even when such certitude was less, the likelihood of America's collapse could still be looked to confidently enough. It was a 'mighty empire' which, 'when the time comes', could 'implode from within', the Indian writer Arundhati Roy speculated in September 2002. 'It looks as though structural cracks have already appeared', she declared. 'As the war against terror casts its net wider', she added, 'America's corporate heart' was 'haemorrhaging'. It was a violent image. But just as the cry of 'Death to America!' is heard in the Muslim world, it is common enough, too, in some non-Muslim hearts and heads.

CHAPTER NINE

The Force of Faith

No faith can be summed up in a phrase. Christianity is no more describable, in essence or in practice, as a 'religion of love', or Judaism as as a 'religion of justice', than is Islam as a 'religion of peace'. Islam, now in an ascendant phase and strong in its sense of righteousness and truth, is at the very least a faith both of peace and war. Moroever, it is not open to Christians or Jews to dispraise it for its militancies, when the Old Testament sagas, the annals of Christianity and the history of 'civilised' twentieth-century Europe are together steeped in gore. Indeed, Christianity has a long and bloody record of taking the sword to Muslims and Jews alike, and used the epithet 'infidels' to describe Muslims exactly as do Muslims of Christians and Jews. Furthermore, the most solemn ethical principles of Hebraism are betrayed daily in the politics of the state of Israel, and in the conduct of some—even many—of its citizens towards the Palestinians.

The speed and force of Islam's current advance also cannot justly be the subject of non-Muslim handwringing. Christians, Jews and others would do better to look to the shoring-up of their own ethical domains, weakened as most of them are by the conduct of their own adherents. For an intense trial of faith is now in progress—and under arms—in many parts of the world. In it Islam's powers, which are the powers of its believers, have thus far proved more than a match for opponents. It is also clear that 'Islamophobia', 'Judeophobia', obsessive anti-Americanism and other related fixations are intellectually one-dimensional and threadbare responses to the contradictions of the real world, in particular of a world at war.

387

Nevertheless, these narrow responses can be expected when firm faiths—whether the faith be in God, in gods, in no-God, or in the destiny of peoples and nations—are in conflict. In such circumstances, believers, opponents, apostates and sceptics inevitably take up their respective battle positions. In the babel of present struggles between Muslim and 'infidel', Arab and Jew, American and anti-American, 'New World' and 'Old Europe', almost every partisan position is simplistic. Muslims are not all thirsty for 'Crusader' blood; Christians are divided among themselves about the just response to the Muslim and Arab worlds; Americans are not all 'gun-happy cowboys'; Jews are not all bent upon world conquest and many are not even 'Zionists' and so on.

It is similarly clear that if Islam were truly a religion of compassion, mercy, patience, balance and peace, many of the acts which have been recorded in this work—whether carried out by Muslims or against them—would not have taken place. Moreover, if Islam was the embodiment of the above-mentioned virtues, no writer or scholar, whether Muslim or non-Muslim, would have felt inhibited in commenting on its history, its protagonists, its texts or its ethics, as can be done in respect (or disrespect) of other faiths.

Yet no such restraint has been observable in the judgments passed by Islam on the faiths of others. As the Indonesian cleric Abu Bakr Bashir put it, 'human beings without Islam are like cattle in the eyes of Allah'; to the Syrian cleric Sheikh Mahmoud al-Ghassi, in a 'sermon' in October 2003, 'atheist dogs'—including Christians and Jews—were waging war against Islam in the Middle East. Even a lesson for six-year-olds in Saudi schools reads 'All religions other than Islam are false'. The Koran thus dismisses Christianity's central, or iconic, event. 'They slew him not', reads Sura 4, 'and they crucified him not, but they had only his likeness'. Moreover, 'no sure knowledge had they about him', the Koran asserts, 'but followed only an opinion, and they did not really slay him', it repeats. Several Suras also deny that God had, or could have had, a son. Indeed, Islam arrogates to itself licence not merely to criticise the faiths of others but to condemn their 'infidel' adherents to theological perdition as a matter of divinely-ordained duty.

Although the Koran is a work of many dimensions and injunctions, pacific and less so, statements on the 'infidel', as in Sura 9, are clear. 'Fight', it declares—or, in other translations 'make war upon'—'such of those to whom the scriptures [sc. the Old and New Testaments] have been given as do not believe in Allah...and who do not acknowledge the religion of Truth [sc. Islam], until they pay tribute and are humbled'; that is, the 'unbeliever' must bow to Islam or pay the price, both literally and metaphorically. Similarly, in

Sura 4, God is described as having 'cursed' the Jews for their unbelief. In Sura 5, Muslims are even enjoined 'not [to] take Jews and Christians as friends', a proposition found in school text-books in many parts of the Muslim world; and in Sura 2, for example, is found the imprecation that 'the curse of Allah be upon the infidels'.

Hence, when an al-Qaeda spokesman, Mohammed al-Ablaj, declared in November 2003—after a suicide-bomb-attack on a residential compound in Riyadh—that it was 'forbidden' for Muslims to 'work with and mix with Americans', it was an injunction which rested upon Holy Writ at least as securely as did contrary protestations that such declaration was 'anti-Islamic'. The same was true when in June 2004 al-Qaeda called on 'all Muslims' to 'separate themselves' from 'American and Western crusaders and all non-believers in the Arabian peninsula'. Osama bin Laden's many invocations to Muslims to 'fight the Crusaders and Jews', and other similar declarations such as that 'the battle is between good and evil, God's soldiers and those of Satan', or that 'it is the duty of every Muslim to threaten US and British interests anywhere'—in the words of the Iranian cleric Ayatollah Ahmad Jannati in Teheran in June 2004—were as much in accord with faith's prescriptions as their opposites were claimed to be by the equally devout.

However, the common ground between them was expressed by Saleh al-Wohaibi, the US-educated secretary-general of the World Assembly of Muslim Youth, in April 2004. When he declared that 'to say that the Jews and Christians are infidels is part of our religious dogma', he was correct, but modestly so. For the Koran in its severest texts—there are others less severe—frequently attributes 'evil-doing', 'wretchedness', 'baseness' and much else besides to most unbelievers. It also holds them to be cursed in God's eyes, offers Jews and Christians—*ahle kitab*, the 'People of the Book'—the prospect of protection only in return for submission to Muslim rule and offers those of other faiths even less. There is, however, an alternative: if disbelievers 'convert and observe prayer, and pay the obligatory alms, then let them go their way, for God is Gracious, Merciful', declares the ninth Sura of the Koran. That is, the 'infidel' will again be let off the hook—whether literally or metaphorically—but only by bending the knee to Islam, as mediaeval Jews were forced to do if they wished to escape the Christian fire. That such an ethic remains active in the thought of some Muslims is clear. 'If Bush wants peace and security', declared an Israeli Arab leader, Ra'ed Salah, four days after the attack on the World Trade Center, 'the only solution is for him to convert to Islam'.

Nevertheless, while Muslims are put on their guard against both 'infidel' Jews and Christians, respect is also expressed for Christ's (and Moses') prophetic mission. That is, Muslims can deny Christ's divinity and crucifixion while accepting his apostleship, and have incorporated such acceptance into the Muslim belief-system. But this is to do no more than make a transfer of part of the Christian story into Islam on Muslim terms, as did Christianity itself with some of the basic tenets of Hebraism, while many elements of Hebraism are to be found in Islam. Both Judaism and Christianity are held to have been superseded by Islam, the final revealed religion on earth, a claim which by definition reduces the 'unbelieving' followers of other religions to inferior moral and social status. Muslim expressions of regard for, and genetic affinity with, the Hebrew patriarchs and the prophets, including Christ, thus co-exist with many expressions of rejection of Jews and Christians alike. Yet this rejection is also an expression of Islam's pride of belief, and no more deserving of criticism than Hebraism's rejection of the un-'chosen' non-Jew, or Christianity's claim to have 'abrogated' and 'transcended' the belief-system of the Jews, while incorporating a large part of it in its own teachings.

Moreover, Islam's claim that the only authentic existence is a Muslim existence is essentially the same claim made by Jew or Christian as to his or her own faith and belonging. The Muslim notion that the pre-Islamic past at best contained forerunners of Islamic truth, together with polytheistic and pagan deformities of mind, is not greatly distinct from the beliefs of Jews and Christians about their prehistories also. And just as Jews destroyed or appro- priated Canaanite temples, and Christians destroyed or appropriated syna- gogues and mosques, the physical destruction and vandalising, under Islamist rule, of pre-Islamic Buddhist and other artefacts in Afghanistan, for example, cannot justly be singled out for exceptional condemnation.

None of this is without logic and a powerful logic at that, like it or not. It is a logic which is incompatible with the acceptance by Muslims of 'infidelity', or with the possibility of any long-term assurance to 'infidels' in a Muslim land that they will be secure, unless it be on the basis of paying deference to true faith. It is also a logic of closure to the non-Islamic past, of combative- ness (at worst) and wariness (at best) in the face of 'disbelief', and of certitude in the promise of a Muslim future. With equal logic—Islam being a coherent belief \ system—it requires the prevention, under sanction of punishment for apostasy or blasphemy, of moral criticism of the historical protagonists of Islam. It similarly refuses sceptical exegesis of its texts and articles of faith, and provides for the custodianship of its truth-claims by an increasingly ener- getic clerisy both in the Muslim world and in the diaspora. It also rejects that which is 'not-Islam' as 'alien' to it; indeed, as an otherness which must, at the last, be humbled if Islam is to come into its foreordained dominion.

Even without the provocations offered to Islam by the non-Islamic world, all this furnishes the preconditions for a sense of embattlement in Islam's relations with other belief-systems. It sets Islam at odds with ethical and political practices which diverge from those fostered by Muslim culture and tradition; in Saudi Arabia revised school-texts introduced in November 2003 warned that even those supporting Western methods of government deserved 'excommunication from Allah's mercy'.

Moreover, the meaning of the word 'Islam' is not 'peace'—even if Muslims (and some non-Muslims) are given to asserting it—but 'submission' to God's will and Holy Writ, a wholly different idea. To reduce Islam to a mere 'religion of peace' also denies its militant sense of righteousness. 'No interpretation ever said so', correctly declared Mohammed al-Rameh, a member of Saudi Arabia's Supreme Institution for the Judiciary in October 2001, 'and God said to fight all the infidels'. Indeed, it is as a fighting faith, comparable with that of the 'Church Militant' in times past, that the principal force of Islam lies. It is this force, made more redoubtable as non-Muslim value-systems falter and fail, which has been aroused in the current period of its revival and advance. The emphasis upon 'justice' in Islamic moral injunction, and the manifold virtues found in the Muslim conduct of life, are those of a righteousness which knows its moral way, and will not brook interference with it.

Injunctions to act towards the world of man and Nature with 'compassion' and 'mercy', in the name of a God who is continuously attributed with these virtues, are also present throughout the Koran. Even divine promises to harm the infidel—as in Sura 22, where 'garments of fire', 'boiling fluid' and 'hooked rods of iron' await 'those who disbelieve'—are uttered in the name of the same divine virtues. But under a threat to faith, whether from apostate fellow-Muslims or hostile non-Muslims, meekness of conduct would be a betrayal of religious duty. Just as the deity has prepared 'manacles, iron-collars and a raging fire' for 'disbelievers', as Sura 76 proclaims, so 'disbelievers' should 'find harshness' in 'those who believe', as Sura 9 instructs. Yet just as such duty is demanded of the faithful so, too, is charity. 'Woe to those who pray ... who make a show of devotion, but refuse help to the needy', as Sura 14 expresses it.

There is no doubt that many Koranic passages enjoin intolerance towards, and rejection of, the 'infidel', in particular those who have caused Muslims harm. But such passages must be set alongside the words addressed to 'unbelievers' in Sura 109, for example. 'To you be your religion, to me mine', it declares. They are words which suggest, at least on the surface, quietude in the face of 'disbelief' [in Islam]. 'Do not thrust away those who cry to their Lord morning and evening', further enjoins Sura 6, 'it is not for you to judge their motives, nor for them to judge you. If you thrust them away, you will be doing wrong'; and again, 'do not revile those who call on other gods, lest they, in their ignorance, revile your God'.

However, the (predominating) sense of Muslim Holy Writ remains that of an ethical and intellectual recoil from non-Muslim modes of life, and at its severest perceives recalcitrant 'infidels' to be 'fuel for the fire', as Sura 3 has it. At the last day, the error of 'unbelievers' in not having acknowledged the true faith will be painfully revealed to them in 'grievous torment'. But Christianity offers unrepentant non-believers no greatly different fate, despite its 'gospels' of love and forgiveness. The Hebraic Bible and the New Testament contain great wisdom, but little good was vouchsafed to the enemies of ancient Israel in the first, or to the hardened sinner at the Day of Judgment in the second.

The verses of Sura 2 also temper the rigour of Islam's rejection of the 'faithless' by forbidding the irruption of Muslims into the latter's sacred places. 'Think over, O people! Who commits a greater wrong than the one who hinders prayers and tries in his zeal to ruin the places of worship of others?' it demands to know. There are no bombings and desecrations of synagogues, nor arson-attacks on Christian churches, allowed for here. It is not even fitting, the Sura adds, that Muslims should enter the temples of others unless they have 'the fear of Allah'; without such fear, they themselves will face 'nothing but disgrace', and be 'tormented in the world to come'.

Yet the great majority of Koranic references to the non-Muslim 'unbeliever' are those of disdain and dire forewarning, even if there are gradations of both. The greatest scorn is reserved for 'infidels' who are polytheists. Thus, Sura 9 commands the faithful—'when the sacred months [of Shawal, Dul Qaadah, Dul Hajja and Muharram] are past'—to kill 'those who join other gods with God', 'wherever you find them'. 'Seize them, besiege them and lie in wait for them with every stratagem but, if they convert, let them go their way', it instructs. Indeed, in the Muslim schema those who follow other faiths than Islam are by definition misguided and wrong. Their faiths are not simply 'not-Islam', but a blind and even 'rebellious' refusal of Islam's obvious truth, as Christians held the rejection of Christ's divinity by Jews to be. But such absolutism is a badge of faith itself, again like it or not; and Islam again cannot be singled out for condemnation, least of all by Christians and Jews, on this ground.

As the price of their refusal of Islam, non-Muslims must take their places in a hierarchy of Muslim rejection. For 'infidelity', although the common characteristic of all who have not seen Islam's light, is also a matter of degree:

the Jews and Christians being of the second class, while Hindus, Buddhists, Sikhs, Animists and others are of the third class and effectively beyond the moral pale. But then Jews, too, look down on the non-Jew as a *goy*, and Christians generally see those who reject Christ as having forfeited the possibility of 'salvation', or posthumous redemption. Indeed, Christian theology and iconography consign the 'deicide' Jew and the Prophet Mohammed to the nether world together, and equally offensively to Jew and Muslim.

The violence of emotion displayed in epithets about, and warnings to, 'unbelievers' is of considerable intensity in certain of the Koran's Suras, but not more so than in the Christian Book of Revelation, in many of the writings of the Church Fathers, or in the language of the Old Testament prophets. Despite frequent Muslim denials that it is so, the morally bleakest of threats are made against Christians, Jews and other 'infidels'. 'When you encounter Unbelievers [in combat], then strike their necks', Sura 47 enjoins; 'I will cast terror into the hearts of those who have disbelieved, so strike them over the necks, and smite their fingers and toes', declares Sura 8. Yet women and children were put to the sword with moral abandon and God's approval in the Old Testament, while the Crusaders and Christian hunters of 'heresy' struck down uncounted numbers of innocents to the glory of God. Now it is Islam which successfully brandishes the old Jewish and Christian weapons of faith, and marches on.

It claims, as Jews and Christians once did, both the high moral ground and possession of the final truth. Even the rhetorical declarations of a member of the Mahdi army in Najaf in May 2004 that 'for me, bullets smell like flowers and I dance and sing as I kill Americans', and of an al-Qaeda militant in Saudi Arabia in the same month that 'blood and more blood' would 'heal souls', echo the sentiments of past warriors doing God's work. When Yasser Arafat on the 56th Anniversary of the creation of Israel called on the Palestinians, also in May 2004, to 'find what strength you have to terrorise your enemy and the enemy of God', he was quoting Sura 8 of the Koran. But he was also speaking in the same accents as those of his predecessors of other faiths who led their troops to battle against Caananite idolaters, heretical Albigensians, or 'cut-throat Moors'.

Hence objections, for example in a State Department report in December 2003, that 'freedom of religion does not exist' in Saudi Arabia and that non-Muslim worshippers risked 'arrest, imprisonment, lashing and deportation' were naive. Naive, too, was the observation in the same report that in Iran 'Bahai's, Jews and Christians' suffered varying degrees of 'officially sanctioned discrimination' including 'intimidation, harassment and imprisonment'.

Expressions of 'disillusion' in Britain, also in December 2003, that the Saudi Arabian interior ministry—which had 'seemed to be moving towards moderation'—should have banned the import of 'crucifixes and models of Buddha' were misguided; it was bound to be so, since faith had decreed it.

Muslims who find al-Qaeda threats against the West to be 'embarrassing', or even 'non-Islamic', are being as falsely ingenuous as are non-Muslims who reel in seeming incomprehension from such threats. When bin Laden was described by Abu Bakr Bashir as a 'Muslim hero and member of Allah's army, not a terrorist', or when Abdel-Samie Mahmoud Ibrahim Moussa, the Egyptian imam of Rome's main mosque, cried out in June 2003, 'Allah, let us destroy the enemies of Islam! Allah, help us crush the enemies of Islam! Allah, ensure the victory of the nation of Islam!' these were not moral aberrations. They were felt by each speaker to be consistent with the duties of the believer and the destiny of 'unbelief'.

There have been significant numbers of clerics and Muslim spokesmen, as earlier mentioned, who have denied that this is the authentic voice of Islam, and who have publicly taken their distance from it. Lay Muslims have declared that they 'detested' being 'associated with terrorism', since Islam was, as ever, a 'religion of peace'. The kidnappings of foreigners and slaying of hostages in Iraq were regularly condemned across the Muslim world, despite assertions to the contrary by 'Islamophobes' and others. In June 2004, 'killing a soul without justification' was declared 'one of the gravest sins under Islam', and even 'as bad as polytheism', by the Saudi cleric Sheikh Saleh bin Abdullah al-Humeid, speaking at the Grand Mosque in Mecca. In the same month, a Syrian government official called the decapitation in Iraq of an American hostage a 'shameful crime, alien to Arab and Muslim morals'. In January 2005, also at the Grand Mosque in Mecca, its state-appointed preacher Sheikh Abdulrahman al-Sudeis, one of the leading voices of Islam, denounced 'terror attacks' as 'putrid' and condemned 'delinquent and void interpretations of Islam based on ignorance'. Faith, he proclaimed, 'does not mean killing Muslims and non-Muslims who live among us, it does not mean shedding blood, terrorising, or sending body-parts flying'.

Nevertheless, despite al-Sudeis's pleas to Muslims to espouse 'moderation', he himself had earlier described Jews as the 'scum of the human race', the 'rats of the world' and so forth. Moreover, it remains the case that fear, siege, ambush, fetters, fire, hell, a 'helpless journey's end' and suchlike are promised in Islam to 'the worst of created beings'—the 'disbeliever'—as well as to other rebels against the faith, both Muslim and non-Muslim. 'Infidels' who attack Muslims and Muslim lands must be fought, while most of the pains which Muslims are enjoined to inflict upon aggressors, or which will be their inevitable fate at God's hand, are physical, and physical in detail. They include the above-mentioned smiting of necks, exposure in chains to hell-fire, filth to eat, the pouring of boiling water upon the head, and the like. Where Muslims are held to have made war on their own faith—as was discussed earlier in relation to the Rushdie case—they face dire punishments, again physical, or, as a more lenient alternative, expulsion from the land but with an 'awful doom in the hereafter'. But it is again the same kind of 'doom' as awaits the unrepentant Christian sinner.

Distinct, however, in Islam is the aspiration to reduce the 'infidel' to subjection and subordination *in this world*, as a vindication of the truth of Islam and in its name. Such absolutism makes conversion to Islam necessary (in theory) if the infidel's 'natural' fate, that of subordination to Muslim rule, is to be avoided. It is matched by the punishment—the death penalty—allotted under strict *S*haria law to those who seek to convert Muslims from Islam to another faith. Both speak equally to that sense, reflected in Sura 8 of the Koran, that the 'worst beasts in the sight of God are the thankless who will not believe', the 'cattle' to whom Abu Bakr Bashir referred.

Yet, once more, this sense that the non-Muslim is beneath the rank of the truly human is not much distinct from atavistic Jewish taboos of related kind. The true moral difference in Islam is that believers are enjoined in many sacred Muslim texts to gird their loins and fight the obdurates, described in Sura 2 as 'the perverse', who 'will not believe'. Some Muslims hold that such calls-to-arms are figurative only. But in their 'popular' sense these injunctions are plain, leaving scant space for their interpretation as metaphors or theatrical postures only, rhetorical as their language may be. Furthermore, it could be said that a 'reawakened' Islam's truest expression—and its greatest strength—lies in the revived ardour with which instruction to the faithful is being attempted to be followed. And since other faiths look to, or hope for, ardour in their faithful, it must be expected of Islam also.

'Think not the infidels shall escape Us!' Sura 8 warns. 'Make ready then against them what force you can, and strong squadrons'—not squadrons of mind alone—'whereby you may strike terror into the enemies of God and your enemies', the very text invoked by Yasser Arafat in May 2004. When the 'radical' Iraqi Shi'ite cleric, Moqtada al-Sadr, similarly urged his followers to 'terrorise your enemies', in this instance the coalition-forces in Iraq, his was again the language of faith. It was a terrorisation not only enjoined in faith's cause but sanctioned by it. 'I will cast a dread into the hearts of the infidels', Sura 8 has the deity promise. When bin Laden's closest associate, Ayman al-

Zawahiri, warned the American president in February 2004 to 'fortify your targets' and 'tighten your defences' 'because the fighting Islamic community has decided to send you one squadron after the other', this was again an echo of the language of the eighth Sura, and in accord with its dictates.

Despite the objections of other Muslim sages, the Indonesian Bashir was equally orthodox—and more than a mere 'terrorist'—in asserting from his prison-cell in March 2004 that 'we have to oppose America physically, such as to bomb and do other things. Every effort to attack America is good because it is according to religion'. Nevertheless, the eighth Sura also instructs that if 'they [sc. the 'infidels'] incline to peace, then you incline to it also'; almost exactly as Arafat himself declared in May 2004, referring to the Israelis. 'If they want peace', he declared, 'let's have peace', which was orthodoxy once more. But if they do not, the same text declares, 'strike off their heads, and strike off their every finger-tip, because they have opposed Allah and his apostle'; or, again, 'fight against them till strife be at an end'. 'If only you could see what occurs when the angels cause the infidels to die!' the Sura exclaims; 'they smite their faces and their backs, and declare "Taste the torture of the burning"'.

These quatrains may be held to be literary devices, and again no more violent than many passages in the Hebrew Bible or in the more vivid prophecies of the Book of Revelation. They also derive from the tribulations of Islam in its first days, when its existence was threatened, as many Muslims believe their faith to be threatened now. Indeed, cited today, these verses have ceased to be, if they ever were, the poetics of heroic saga. They are the active battle-cries of a living faith, a summons to take up arms in its defence and in emulation of the martyrs who slew Islam's foes, and who were slain in turn. Again, suicide is forbidden in a brief aside in Sura 4. But standing above such prohibition is the much greater moral weight of the repeated calls to carry the fight to the faithless enemy, by any means, 'until strife be at an end'. Moreover, those who 'turn aside' from such struggle are warned in Sura 8 that they will incur the deity's 'wrath', while those who 'fight for the cause of Allah...he will bring into Paradise', as Sura 47 promises.

The ethics of these injunctions are clear. The 'infidel', especially the irreconcilably hostile 'infidel' who threatens and assaults Islam's honour and the Muslim's faith, deserves what he gets; 'I was motivated by the law that commands me to cut off the head of anyone who insults Allah and his prophet', declared the killer of Theo van Gogh at his trial in Amsterdam in July 2005. Indeed, it is morally incumbent upon the faithful to teach 'infidelity' the lessons which it is held to merit. To 'congratulate martyrs' who lose their lives in such works of faith, or to pray that 'we are all granted that same fate', are again commonplaces, but devout commonplaces, of Friday pulpit-sermons throughout the Muslim world. This is notwithstanding the dissenting strain in Islam which takes a distance from such invocations, or fears for the 'image' of Islam if they are acted upon. Moreover, it is not open to Christians, whose own martyrs earned sainthood by shedding blood or dying for faith, to look on Islam's concept of martyrdom with scorn.

The crowds at the funeral of an Israeli-assassinated Palestinian leader who demanded 'more martyrs!' and 'more sacrifice!' might seem to the 'infidel' to speak to a morally reprehensible code of values. So, too, might the Yasser Arafat who told a crowd of supporters in April 2004 that 'all of us are martyrs-in-waiting', to which the crowd responded with 'We will sacrifice our blood and souls for you!'; or the Hamas spokesman, commenting on the death of a young mother in a suicide-bombing in January 2004, who declared that 'martyrdom' was a 'higher quality than motherhood'. But, on the contrary, all such cries, statements and acts could be held to be in accord with an ethic which knows itself to be divinely-sanctioned, and possesses its own covenant, norms and prescriptions—as do Hebraism and Christianity—for what is considered to be, and to express, the faithful life.

It was therefore just, in its own terms, that Imam Samudra should have told a court in Bali in August 2003, on being sentenced to death for the bombings there in October 2002, not only that he felt no remorse, but—more to the Islamic point—that he had been 'waging war against injustice'. It is an impulse which non-Muslims dismiss at their peril. Non-Muslims might shake their heads in bewilderment that members of a Pakistani Islamic coalition, Mutahida Majlis-e-Amal, should have demonstrated in February 2004 in support of the Pakistani nuclear scientist Abdul Qadeer Khan, 'father of Pakistan's bomb' after he had been accused of spreading nuclear weapons technology to anti-Western nations. But militant faith—not 'fundamentalism'—issues its own commands to the faithful, of which the 'faithless' are (rightly) regarded as knowing nothing.

Moreover, to 'march on and fight for the cause of God' is as much a Muslim duty as it was once held to be a duty of the Christian. It is therefore not more wrong that a mosque in Baghdad should go by the name of Um al-Qura ['Mother-of-all-Battles'] than that returned Crusaders should lie in hallowed ground in many English churches. Similarly, when the mayor of Istanbul, Recep Tayyip Erdogan—who was later to become prime minister of Turkey—declaimed in public in 1997 that the mosque's minarets 'are our bayonets, their domes our helmets, and the believers our soldiers', his was the same kind of inspiration as activated those who celebrated an *auto da fé* during the Inquisition. Indeed, Erdogan's was a poetic rendering of orthodoxy for which it was arguably unjust that he should have received a ten-month jail sentence for 'inciting religious hatred'.

It is unsurprising that, during the current Islamic advance, mosques and mosque compounds in several countries, and especially in Iraq—including in its holy cities of Karbala and Najaf—should have been found to have weapons and ammunition stored in them, or should have been used both for shelter and as vantage-points for attack. Once more, the Christian West is not entitled to its incredulity. In the Second World War, even a monastery and a bishop's residence in Italy were used to hold prisoners awaiting deportation to German death-camps. Moreover, just as Western armies are attended in battle by chaplains and padres, so in Iraq, in combat with 'infidel' forces, clerics with their own militias perceive themselves to be armed for God's work.

The 'infidel's' fatal destiny in Islam's moral structure can therefore no more be wished away than can the 'deicide' Jew's role in the equally manichean system of the Christian faith. As 'the Jew' is to the Christian, so the 'infidel' is to the Muslim. Without them, there would in each case be no darkness to serve as foil to the light of faith. Many of Islam's holy texts, like Christianity's, also breathe the spirit of the highest moral endeavour. 'Whosoever saves a life', declares Sura 5 for example, 'it is as if he had saved the whole of mankind'; the fact that the verse is followed by a warning against those who 'make war against God' cannot detract from the humanity of the words themselves. But in Islam's and Arabism's current advances, it is not this ethic which has been in command of their growing forces, to the distress of Muslims who hold Islamism's grosser acts to be sinful. As pointed out in an earlier chapter, such Muslims disown those who can declare, as did the jailed London cleric Abdullah el-Faisal, that it is 'wonderful' to 'kill an infidel'. 'You crawl on his back', he told an audience of young followers, 'and while you are pushing him into the hellfire, you are going into paradise'. To other preachers of Islam, including those who speak from Mecca, such counsels are 'delinquent and void'.

In order to compensate for the reductiveness which associates Islam only with insatiable belligerence, Muslims and non-Muslims seek to draw distinctions between Islamism's acts and 'that compassion and tolerance which the Koran teaches', as *The Times* put it in August 2001, five weeks before the attack on the World Trade Center. But, once more, well-intentioned accounts by non-Muslims of what Islam 'is' generally underestimate its strengths. They also ignore Islam's claims to the moral superiority of its teachings. 'You are the best community raised up for mankind—you enjoin what is right, forbid what is wrong, and believe in Allah', the Koran declares.

Yet non-Muslims have continued to give false assurances to one another as to the 'essential nature' of Islam. Less than four weeks after the 9/11 attack, the *Daily Telegraph* pronounced that Islam was an 'essentially peaceful faith', and that 'this quarrel' was 'not with any religion, nor yet a clash of civilisations, but a war for civilisation against barbarism'. In *The Times,* also within a month of 9/11, Islam was a 'religion of compassion' and to President Bush— speaking to this issue many times as the counter-attack on Afghanistan proceeded—it was a faith 'committed to morality', a faith of 'learning', a faith of 'love'. The theme was a constant on both 'right' and 'left'. To the *Guardian* in August 2003, Islam's 'message' was one of 'peace'; to President Bush, in September 2003, Islam's 'teachings' were 'peaceful'; in October 2003 to Condoleeza Rice, the US administration's then national security adviser, Islam was a 'peaceful religion'. To President Bush again, also in October 2003, Islam had even become a 'religion of liberty and tolerance', which 'terrorists' who claimed it as their inspiration were 'defiling'.

There was a clearly concerted US diplomatic effort to argue such case, in the throes of troubles with the Muslim world following the invasion of Iraq. The statements rested not only upon genuine conviction (in some) that they were true but upon anxiety lest Muslims conclude that the 'war on terror' was a war upon them alone. The 'cultural sensitivity' discussed earlier, as well as the need of the non-Muslim world for Muslim allies, also played their parts. Islam could thus be represented—or re-presented—by the non-Muslim Western politician not merely as an 'essentially peaceful faith' but as a 'religion *of* peace' as such. On this basis, and for many Muslims also, Islamist violences became aberrations committed by those who had distorted its profoundest values. As early as June 2000, it was also reported that the British prime minister, out of a 'particular interest' in the 'links between Christianity, Judaism and Islam', had read the Koran 'three times'. By December 2001, his view that the acts committed by al-Qaeda were not compatible with Islam's teachings had been repeated on several public occasions; and in January 2002, in the southern Indian city of Bangalore, he declared that the 'true voice of Islam itself' would confront the 'fanatics' who distorted Muslim principles, principles which were 'caring and decent'.

To the anger of evangelical Christians who declared him to be 'not a theologian' and to be 'simply mistaken', President Bush in turn expressed the belief in November 2003 that Christians and Muslims 'worship the same God'; and in December 2003, the British foreign secretary similarly described the 'values of our faiths and cultures' as 'shared'. A decade earlier, in October 1993 at the Sheldonian Theatre in Oxford on the occasion of his visit to the Oxford Centre for Islamic Studies, Prince Charles had even presumed to speak for the Prophet, in declaring that the latter had 'himself always disliked and feared extremism'.

Muslims, especially those anxious for Islam's 'image', often spoke to the same themes. The Malaysian prime minister, Mahathir Mohamad, described Islam in February 2002 as a religion of 'peace and moderation'. If it did not 'appear' to be so 'today', he added, it was 'not due to the teachings of Islam' but to 'interpretations made by those who are apparently learned in Islam in order to suit their patrons or their own vested interests'. At the same time, siren voices off-stage in the non-Muslim world held, for instance, that 'the more you examine Islam, the more militaristic it seems'; or declared that it was 'neither a religion of tolerance nor peace'; or demanded to know 'who are US politicians to talk about Islam?'

They were countered by diaspora Muslim leaders who were quick to hear in hostile comment the language of 'civilisational conflict', or, worse, of that 'war against Islam' which praise of Islam by non-Muslims was designed to offset. Western leaders continued to insist upon their 'respect for the faith of Islam, even as we fight those whose actions defile that faith', in the words of the American president in September 2002. It was repeatedly asserted by non-Muslims that Islamists had 'hijacked' a tolerant and peace-loving faith, while diaspora Muslims in particular insisted that to sow terror and mayhem among innocent civilians was 'non-Islamic'; those who wished 'evil on the world' could not properly 'call themselves Muslims', they declared.

Many Muslims and some non-Muslims therefore agreed—or pretended to agree—that Islamists were 'corrupting, misinterpreting and misrepresenting the word of God to generate support for their political mission', and that they stood 'condemned out of their own mouths for committing the most hideous crimes in the name of God'. In March 2002, commenting on the contents of training-manuals found in the ruins of Taliban and al-Qaeda camps in Afghanistan, a *New York Times* editorialist even wondered how it was possible for al-Qaeda trainees to have gone 'from the peaceful message of the Koran to the warlike practicality of these notebooks'. It was 'one of the tragedies of our times', the leading article asserted.

A scholarly Muslim version of this, presented for the attention of non-Muslims, was that 'balance' and 'compassion' were the 'central features of Islam' but were now 'under threat', in the words of Akbar Ahmed. Indeed, Islam's more majestic aspects and ethical strengths were steadily lost from view amid violences generated by the Islamic advance itself. A measure of this was that it had still been possible in December 1996 for a diaspora Muslim intellectual to declare in the *Guardian* that what he found 'attractive about Islam' was that it 'appeals to man to use his intellect'. Islam, he asserted, was the 'middle path' and rejected 'extremism of any sort'. In the years that followed, the case for Islam's appeal to the 'intellect' was rarely heard.

Nevertheless, whenever tensions between the Muslim and non-Muslim worlds increased, the greater the stress that was placed by Western diplomacy upon Islam's 'essential' virtues. For example, the 'tradition of mercy and forgiveness enshrined in Muslim beliefs and practice' was emphasised by the British foreign secretary in February 1989, during the uproar over the Rushdie affair. This emphasis became even more common in the aftermath of the 9/11 attacks on the United States. 'Islam', declared a *Times* commentator in October 2001, 'is no more a threat to world peace than Christianity, Buddhism or communism have been in the past'.

But praise by non-Muslims for the virtues of Islam has been continuously contradicted by the acts of Muslims themselves. Such praise has clearly been taken by most Muslims to be insincere, and with good reason. Indeed, many Muslims have blamed their belligerencies upon what they see as the increasing offences and outrages committed against them by non-Muslims, praise Islam as the latter might. 'Muslims were always peaceful', asserted the Bradford Muslim leader Sayed Abdul Quddus, who in February 1989 had himself helped consign Salman Rushdie's novel to the flames in public, calling him a 'Satan'. 'Islam means peace', he declared inaccurately, 'but if someone criticises and throws dirt on religion there will be retaliation'. Muslim *vox pop* repeated the assertion in February 1990, as the trouble over Rushdie continued. 'Islam means peace', a Cardiff Bangladeshi assured a journalist, 'but the Koran says that if anyone says anything about the Prophet, you can do what you want'. According to such view, 'compassion', 'peace', 'mercy' and 'toleration' were conditional only, whatever the efforts to present them as defining characteristics of Islam's value-system.

Here the purposes of the attribution to Islam, by Muslims and (some) non-Muslims, of 'peace', 'tolerance' and so on as its cardinal virtues converged. From mutual fear, they sought to provide each other with earnests of benign intention as acts of reciprocal hostility increased. 'Islam is a title of peace', pronounced another Bradford Muslim elder, Sher Azam, at the height of the angers and incitements over Rushdie; Islam 'preaches peace among all mankind' proclaimed a third. But other Muslims could be less politic, or more honest. 'We Muslims all pray for peace', I was told in March 1991 by the leader of the 'Muslim Parliament' in Britain, Kalim Siddiqui, 'then we pick up our weapons and go forth to battle'.

Itself a reductive view, denial of its truth by well-meaning non-Muslims has been at the cost of failing to address the awakened sense in Muslims that they face increasing threat at 'infidel' hands. A wider and more informed perspective has dictated a different view. 'The relations between Muslims and people of other civilisations—Catholic, Protestant, Orthodox, Hindu, Chinese, Buddhist, Jewish—have been generally antagonistic', wrote Samuel Huntington in 1998. 'Most of these relations have been violent in the past, many have been violent in the 1990s', he continued. 'Wherever one looks along the perimeter of Islam, Muslims have problems living peacefully with their neighbours. . . . Muslims make up about one-fifth of the world's population but in the 1990s they have been far more involved in intergroup violence than the people of any other civilisation. The evidence is overwhelming'.

His thesis of a 'clash of civilisations' was widely rejected as 'Islamophobic', over-schematic and even apocalyptic. But the evidences he cited also made impossible the opposed simplification which denoted Islam a 'religion of peace'. Words such as 'enemy', 'battle', 'war', 'victory' and 'chastisement' are constantly repeated in Islam's holy writings. Many of its ordinances invite, instruct or incite those of true faith to destroy the 'works of infidelity', and to gain victory over the 'unrighteous' and the 'ringleaders of infidelity'. Hence, it was as an expression of faith that Zacarias Moussaoui, the alleged 'twentieth hijacker' of September 2001, intended to 'work in any way possible to make the lives of non-believers more difficult', as a fellow-Muslim testified in the judicial proceedings against him.

Yet, once more, Islam cannot be singled out for special condemnation for this; the distinction between true faith and false which underlies such aspiration is an organising principle dictated by the religious spirit itself. 'Be not like the infidels' is a *leit-motif* of the Koran. But, as argued earlier, the distinction between Muslims and 'infidels' is not morally distinct from that between Jews and 'Gentiles', or between those with and those without faith in Christ. They, too, are allotted their separate places in a macrocosm whose terrains are forever divided; in the case of Islam, between the 'House of Islam' and the 'House of War'.

By the light or darkness of all such conceptions, the faithful and the faithless, those who belong and those who do not, 'true brethren' and others, stand apart. In Islam's case, according to a rule set by its predecessors of other faiths, the natural state of their relations is one of division until a final peace is achieved in the victory of true belief. It is the same kind of peace as Hebraism and Christianity offer after the coming of the Messiah. All such schemata reject, to a greater or lesser degree, that sense of the common condition and fate of mankind upon which a true 'humanism' alone can rest. Or, as the archbishop of Sarajevo complained in October 2002, humanitarian aid sent to Bosnia from Arab countries during the civil war was permitted to be distributed only to Muslims; the same charges were made against Muslim charities after the *tsunami*, or tidal wave, struck south-east Asia in December 2004.

In general, however, this binary system of perception, upon which most faiths rest, cannot and does not exclude the ordinary civilities, hospitalities, exchanges and understandings between the *Homo sapiens* in the faithful, and the *Homo sapiens* in the faithless. Nevertheless, such distinctions as that between the Jew and the *goy*—or between the sacred and the unclean in every anthropological structure of taboo—do much to obstruct the sense of the common lot of mankind. In the Islamic case, the binary distinction between the Muslim and the 'infidel' or *kafir* has furnished justifications since early mediaeval times for differences of treatment and status in Islamic polities between Muslims and non-Muslims. Even in the 'golden age' of Muslim Ummayid rule over Andalusia, Christians and Jews who occupied high official positions remained subject to special taxes according to Koranic provision and were marked out by dress-codes, precisely as Christians in their domains marked out the Muslim and the Jew.

Hence, when Osama bin Laden declared in November 2001 that the world had been 'divided into two camps', 'one under the banner of the Cross' and the other 'under the banner of Islam', he spoke to this schema in orthodox Islamic fashion. It is a schema which lumps Jews and Christians together on one side—even if they may not wish it—and Muslims on the other. After the bombing of the UN headquarters in Baghdad in August 2003, the 'Armed Vanguards of the Second Muhammad Army' claimed 'proudly' that they had 'not hesitate[d] for one moment to shed Crusader blood'. But more typically, in September 2003, Ayman al-Zawahiri—bin Laden's al-Qaeda associate—not only 'saluted' their 'brothers' in Iraq for their 'sacrifices and valour in fighting the Crusaders' but also called on Muslims to 'fight the Christian-Zionist crusade aimed at eradicating Islam and Muslims'.

Likewise, in October 2003—among many such pronouncements—bin Laden exhorted Muslims to 'attack Christians and Jews who occupy Muslim lands'; in January 2004, occupation of Iraq was a 'link in the Zionist-Crusader chain of evil'. At one level, such statements were hyperbole. At another, they were calls-to-arms rooted in Islam's sacred texts and driven by impulses beyond the reach of the non-Muslim's weapons. They were also derived from a worldview falsely described as that of 'fanaticism'or 'fundamentalism', and one which is untouchable by arguments that 'true Islam' is 'betrayed' or 'besmirched' by an al-Qaeda movement. On the contrary, al-Qaeda and its associated organisations and fractions can easily be shown—when wishful thinking ceases—to be doing what many of Islam's teachings demand of true faith and the faithful.

Indeed, Muslim history is a lengthy tale of martyrdoms in battle, suicidal sacrifices, declarations of jihad against the 'infidel' myrmidons who have continually crossed Islam's path, and martial deeds of conquest. The establishment of Arab control over the Iberian peninsula in the eighth century took only seven years to achieve but seven hundred years to bring to an end. It is a history which Muslims are as entitled (or disentitled) to celebrate as the Jews and Christians celebrate their own; and Muslims in future generations will doubtless celebrate in the same way many of the deeds committed in its present renaissance.

If this were not so, and if Islam were truly a 'religion of peace', numerous *fatwas* would have been issued by Muslim clerics against those who commit or organise violence in Islam's name; as earlier mentioned, the Islamic Commission of Spain was the first significant body to do so in respect of bin Laden and al-Qaeda, but not until March 2005—the first anniversary of the Madrid bombings—and with an eye to the interests of some one million Muslims in the country. Instead, during the last decades, declarations of jihad have been made which are the very stuff of Islam's binary perception of the world. Marxists, too, saw our world as riven, but by classes, not faiths. They also were engaged in convulsive 'struggle', an end to which could only be brought by the 'universal victory of the proletariat', as Islam looks to the ultimate victory of faith through 'struggle' over the 'unbeliever'. Indeed, Islam, far from being a 'religion of peace', is a faith *of* struggle, has faith *in* struggle and, when the defence and advance of faith demands, formally declares jihads against the objects of its struggle and striving.

The 'theology' of the call to jihad is, however, a contested one. As was indicated earlier, some Muslims (and non-Muslims) give the word the anodyne sense of a mere striving 'in the path of God'. For others, it is a summons to arms or a declaration of war. Or 'two currents' may be stated to exist in Muslim thought: one which makes of jihad a solemn obligation to 'take to the field' against an encroaching foe, and the other which counsels caution, patience and even silence until a Messianic saviour reappears. Or, again, it is argued by some Muslim schools of thought that jihad has two senses: one, the 'greater' sense, that of spiritual effort, praying and fasting included, and the other, the 'lesser' sense, that of defensive military combat against threats to Islam's safety and well-being. But the concept of jihad espoused by the Wahhabi sect of Islam, despite the Koranic injunction in Sura 2 not to 'begin hostilities' against a foe, rests upon a sense of continuous duty—a sense shared by Christians in their heyday—to fight for faith by all available means. Such duty may include that of attacking the hostile 'infidel' before his presumptive intent to 'destroy' Islam can mature, a doctrine not dissimilar to that of the contested policy of 'pre-emption' adopted by the United States in the Iraq War.

The assurance of Islamists as to the rightness of what they do could not be so absolute if they were not convinced that there was 'theological' justification for it. Such assurance has survived denunciations by some of Islam's leading figures, who have pointed to Koranic prohibitions of many of the acts which Islamists have committed. For example, in March 2004, after suicide-bombings which claimed innocent lives were carried out in Karbala in Iraq against fellow-Muslims—denoted as the 'stooges' of 'American Crusaders'—an al-Qaeda statement declared that it did 'not kill innocent people except in carrying out justice'. That is, even innocents, contrary to injunctions in Holy Writ itself, might expect to be sacrificed to a higher cause. In September 2003 Ayman al-Zawahiri, with equal confidence that he was fulfilling Islam's commands, asserted that what the West called 'terrorism' *was* the Muslim's jihad.

Jihad has been held by anti-Muslims to be an 'ugly concept'. But it is again no 'uglier' or less logical—according to the logic of the binary system earlier discussed—than Marxist concepts of 'class' and 'class struggle'. In each thought-system, the complexities of the world are reduced to a simple schema. Moral privilege is accorded to a select entity, in Marxism the 'proletarian', in Islam the Muslim; and this entity is seen as pitted ineluctably against its 'dialectical' foe. In Marxism's case, this was the 'bourgeois', in Islam's it is the 'infidel'. Moreover, without the labour of the 'proletarian', according to the Marxist schema, the 'bourgeois' would have been nothing; and, as has already been argued, without the 'infidel' and the machinations against Islam of 'unbelief', Islam would have no fit foe against which to defend true faith.

As Islam's advance has continued, declarations of jihad have been increasingly made or threatened by clerical and lay defenders of Muslim interests. These declarations have been many and various; even a Saudi newspaper, *al-Bayan*, called on the Islamic world in July 1995 to wage a jihad against the Bosnian Serbs. With the supporting signatures of 'six hundred' clerics, the Taliban's escaped leader, Mullah Mohammed Omar, renewed a call in March 2003 for a jihad both against US troops and Afghans working with them. Also

in March 2003, Mohammed Sayed Tantawi, Grand Sheikh of al-Azhar—who
in February 1991 had declared the overthrow of Saddam Hussein to be a 'religious duty'—now called on Muslims to wage a jihad in support of the Iraqi
people against the invading 'infidels'. In May 2005, Afghan Muslim clerics
threatened a jihad against the United States if, within three days, it failed to
'hand over to an Islamic country for punishment' the military interrogators at
Guantanamo who were reported to have desecrated the Koran. But in July
2005 President Musharraf urged his fellow-Pakistanis to 'wage a jihad against
extremism' itself, the 'extremism' which other jihadists were seeking to
promote.

Rival Muslim clerical authorities similarly differed over whether, when,
by whom, and against whom a jihad should be declared. In March 2003, the
Russian Supreme Mufti Talgat Tadzhuddin, in response to the invasion of
Iraq, called for a jihad against the United States. The Chief Mufti of Russia,
Ravil Gainutdin, disagreed. 'We must be realists', he pronounced. 'Jihad
against the US has already been declared by Saddam Hussein. This is enough'.
Both in 1991 and 2003 Saddam, although a secular nationalist who had been
responsible for the imprisonment and execution of leading Iraqi Shi'a
clerics—and was named an 'infidel' by other Muslims—several times called
for a jihad to be waged against the invaders of his country. Even from hiding,
in July 2003, Saddam called for a jihad to 'resist the occupation'. And while the
imam of Amman's al-Kurdi mosque was describing the Iraq War as 'a fight
between the apostate America and the apostate Saddam Hussein', the latter
was himself denouncing as 'infidels' the armies at Baghdad's gates.

In general, however, both the meaning of jihad and its preferred targets
have been constant. Thus, in April 2003 one of the Taliban's leading commanders, Mullah Dadullah, not only declared a jihad against American forces
present in Afghanistan but also vowed to drive 'all Jews and infidels' out of the
country. 'Oh God, strike the oppressor, Oh God, make the infidels and aggressors drown', likewise proclaimed Sheikh Abdul-Razzaq al-Saadi, imam of
Baghdad's 'Mother-of-all-Battles' mosque. 'It is the duty of Muslims today,
Iraqis and others', he added, 'to threaten American interests wherever they are,
to set them on fire and to sink their ships. This is jihad in the name of God'.

It has also been in the logic of a fighting faith that Islamist movements
have had clerics as their 'advisers' and in many instances as their 'spiritual
leaders'. In the case of Hamas, it was Sheikh Ahmed Yassin until he was assassinated by the Israelis; in the case of Lebanese Hezbollah, Sheikh Hassan
Nasrallah; in the case of Jemaah Islamiyah, Abu Bakr Bashir; in the case of
Ansar al-Islam, Mullah Mustapha Krekar; in the case of the Taliban, Mullah

Mohammed Omar; in the case of the Tawhid and Jihad group in Iraq, Sheikh Abu Anas al-Shami, killed in a US airstrike in September 2004; and so on. Yet Israelis, too, have their rabbinical 'spiritual advisers' who, as we have seen, counsel intransigence and worse towards the Palestinians. Indeed, some Christian evangelical preachers, especially in the United States, have also dealt out fire and brimstone to America's foes. Thus, when three leading American Christian evangelists, Jerry Falwell, Franklin Graham and Pat Robertson, separately made criticisms of Islam, including by crudely calling it an 'evil religion', the Iranian ayatollah Mohsen Mujtahid Shabestari promptly condemned them to death. 'In our opinion, to kill these three is necessary', he declared.

As has already been noted, murder has not been a stranger even in the holiest of Muslim shrines. In April 2003, the Iraqi Shi'ite cleric Abdul Majid al-Khoei was 'hacked to death'—in the familiar media phrase—within the Grand Imam Ali mosque in Najaf, built over the tomb of the Prophet's son-in-law, the fourth caliph of Islam, himself murdered in 661. In August 2003, also in Najaf, the cleric Sheikh Mohammed Baqer al-Hakim, leader of the Shi'ite Supreme Council of Islamic Revolution, was assassinated by fellow-Muslims; he had returned to Iraq from exile four months earlier at the head of a many thousands' strong militia, the Badr Brigades, trained and armed by Iran's Revolutionary Guard. But Christians, with their long history of internecine and sectarian conflict, again cannot cast the first stone. Popes, too, have been murdered, and in 1170 an archbishop of Canterbury, Thomas Becket, was slain before his cathedral's high altar.

In the world of Islam, as was also common in the Christian past, lay figures and pulpit preachers share an often inflamed vocabulary of faith, whose rhetoric was examined in an earlier chapter. 'Anyone who has dust on his feet from the field of battle', proclaimed the prayer-leader of Baghdad's Abdel Qadr al-Gaylani mosque, Abu Bakr Sammerai, in March 2003, 'will never enter hell on judgment day'. Whatever deeds, or misdeeds, the holy warrior might have committed in faith's name, he was (by inference) secure. Conversely, there was 'not a tyrant or hypocrite whom God has not slashed with his sword', declared Abdul-Razzaq al-Saadi, a Baghdad imam, equally violently, as the Iraq War neared. Iraqis around the world should 'threaten American interests and set them ablaze', he urged. The description of the suicide pilots of September 2001 as a 'convoy of Muslims granted success by God', and at whose success 'the infidels cried out', was that of bin Laden. It was faith's language, a language spoken inside and outside the mosque.

It was in this spirit, too, that the Taliban leader, Mullah Mohammed

Omar, called in November 2001—in God's name—for nothing less than the 'destruction of America'. It was a 'huge task' which was 'beyond the will and comprehension of human beings', he declared to the BBC, and not a 'matter of weapons' but of the 'extinction of America with God's help'. By means of it 'America'—not America's government alone—would 'fall to the ground'. 'May God destroy America!' prayed Ibrahim al-Munah, of Mosul's al-Zia al-Iraki mosque, in April 2003. Nor was this rhetoric of threat and harm idle or random, often being rooted in the language of the Koran itself. For example, the 'vengeance' taken against 'unbelievers' includes, in Sura 7, 'night-raids while they slumbered in their cities'; in Sura 22, more to the point, the 'laying low in ruin' of the 'infidels' 'lofty towers'.

Thus, in May 2003, al-Qaeda's second-in-command, Ayman al-Zawahiri, declared to the Muslim world that 'the only thing that will benefit you is car-rying arms and spiting your enemies, the Americans and the Jews.... The cru-saders and the Jews understand only the language of murder and bloodshed, and are only convinced by coffins, destroyed interests, burning towers'—an echo of Sura 22—'and a shattered economy'. Hamas similarly threatened in September 2003 to strike the 'houses and towers of Israel', while bin Laden recalled in October 2004 how he had decided to 'destroy towers in America'. Such allusions to 'towers', their provenance recognisable, were resonant, and the 9/11 destruction of the 'Twin Towers' a fulfilment, religious, political and even 'poetic'.

Such fire-in-the-belly is not pacific. Moreover, when faith is insulted or put under 'infidel' siege, 'meekness' and the turning of the other cheek are seen in Islam not as virtues but as cowardice and backsliding. Indeed, among Islam's strengths is the fact that, as it advances, its injunctions retain a greater capacity to instruct the actions of the faithful than do the threats and promises of the Old Testament, or the homilies and parables of the New.

However, some clerics and dissenting Muslim spokesmen have risked the ire of the more militant with open counsels of caution. After Iraq had been invaded by American troops, Grand Ayatollah Sistani of Najaf issued a *fatwa* in April 2003 advising Iraqis not to hinder the 'coalition' forces. In contrast the Grand Mufti of Syria, Sheikh Ahmad Kiftaro, speaking on behalf of the 'Arab nation', had called a month before for 'all Muslims' to use 'all possible means' against the 'warriors'—'American, British and Zionist'—who had entered Iraq. Kiftaro specified that these means should include 'martyrdom operations'. Whether the Saddam regime had been just or unjust, or whether Saddam was himself an 'apostate', were for Kiftaro no longer of significance, when set against the obligation of the faithful to repel the 'unbeliever' from an 'Arab land'.

Nevertheless, non-Muslims make errors of judgment when they set up a permanent dichotomy between the 'moderate' and the 'extremist', as has already been indicated. They hear 'fanaticism' in violent diatribes; they are predisposed to hear 'reason' in carefully modulated Muslim positions. But the generalised hostility felt towards the non-Muslim world's policies and actions makes the distinction an increasingly false one. Relatively few Muslims might go as far as the earlier-mentioned Sheikh Abdullah el-Faisal, the London Muslim cleric jailed in March 2003 for incitement to murder, who pronounced in a 'promotional video' that it was 'the duty' of young British Muslims to 'wage war' against and to 'kill unbelievers', specifying 'Hindus, Jews and Americans'. But in his own defence he declared that he had 'preached only what he had learned from the Koran'. Furthermore, it was a sense of the justice of his preaching which provoked incredulity and anger among his Muslim supporters at the court's sentencing of him to a prison term.

In February 2003, Abu Hamza al-Masri, subsequently detained under Britain's 'anti-terrorist' laws, described the lost *Columbia* space-shuttle crew—composed of American Christians, an Indian-born Hindu and an Israeli Jew—as a 'trinity of evil against Islam', and asserted that Muslims saw their deaths as a 'punishment from God'. The Muslim Council of Great Britain quickly expressed its 'disgust' at his words on behalf of the 'vast majority of Muslims' in Britain. Yet his views were also an echo of the sentiments of the 'Arab street'. In Egypt, for example—as the *New York Times* reported—passers-by in Cairo described the deaths of the astronauts as 'divine retribution against America', including for its war preparations against Iraq. 'God cannot forgive unfairness', they said; and that an Israeli was among the dead was openly declared to be 'good news'. Similarly, an 'Islamic scholar' and native US citizen, Ali al-Timimi, sentenced to life imprisonment by a court in Virginia in July 2005 for exhorting his followers to join the Taliban and fight American troops, had described the *Columbia* shuttle disaster as a 'good omen that Western supremacy, especially that of America, is coming to an end, God willing'.

These judgments, whether pronounced in a mosque sermon, presented in an 'instructional' video, addressed to followers or given *en passant* in the streets of a crowded Muslim city, were again not aberrant. They flowed from a powerful sense of right. The imam of the Grand Mosque of Mecca, Islam's holiest shrine, could thus call on all Muslims in June 2002 to unite against a world-wide conspiracy of 'Hindus, Christians, Jews and secularists' which was threatening Islam's 'sublime truths'. 'Worshippers of the Cross', 'idol-worshipping Hindus' and the secular West's 'poisonous culture and rotten ideas' were ranged together against true faith. Praying to God to 'humble the infidels and destroy the enemies of religion', he called upon the deity to 'support our brother *mujahideen* in Palestine, Kashmir and Chechnya', and in particular to bring down the 'usurper Zionists' and 'aggressor Jews'.

Such worldview may be held to be irrational by others, some Muslims included, whose notions of the good and the true differ. But it is rooted in Islam's historical memory, its sacred texts, its renewed strength of belief, its distaste for the infidel's world, and its recent sense of wrong. These can no more be changed than can the articles of faith of the Christian or Jew. Even the humblest Muslim who bends in submission to the tasks which such worldview enjoins can be found to speak and to act in accord with its commands. Thus, the alleged 'twentieth hijacker', Zacarias Moussaoui, describing himself in April 2002 at a court-hearing in Virginia as a 'slave of God', depicted his trial as one between faith and a conspiracy of 'pagans, Jews, Christians and hypocrites', or false Muslims. They were the same foes who had been denounced in June 2002 from the highest shrine of Islam in Mecca.

'From the Shi'a mosque in Poona [in India] where I grew up', wrote Farrukh Dhondy in the autumn of 2001, 'there emerged every Moharrum night, the end of Ramzaan, a procession of chanting Muslims in black shirts, cutting themselves with chains and little daggers strung together, in frenzied and bloody penance through the night'. It was, said Dhondy, a 'demonstration of a belief beyond the threshold of pain. They believed that theirs was the only creed, that their book was dictated by God, that Hindus were idolaters and the worshippers of trees and monkeys, that Zoroastrians were fire-worshipping infidels and that Christians were an ancient military enemy. Their faith seemed to me even at the time to exclude what it had not invented'.

Since the beginnings of Islam, many harms have been attempted against, and done to, Muslims by those of other faiths. But from its outset Islam has also perceived 'non-Islam', in all its forms, to be an actual or potential foe. Hence, that Islam should have had 'bloody borders', as Samuel Huntington wrote in 1993, has arguably been in the necessary order of things; so too, that during the decades of the current Islamic advance, there should have been violence between 'Muslims and orthodox Serbs in the Balkans, Jews in Israel, Hindus in India, Buddhists in Burma and Catholics in the Philippines', as Huntington summarised it. Islam, if truly mindful of its sacred prescriptions, is bound to be unable to brook offence by 'infidels'. In consequence, members of many faiths and ethnicities, in one part of the world and another, have suffered at Muslim hands, as Muslims have suffered at the hands of others in the last decades.

Even before the Khomeinite revolution in 1979, adherents of the Baha'i faith, to take one example, were sentenced to death in Iran as 'heretics', as they had been in Morocco in the 1950s. In 1990, Amnesty International again expressed deep concern about the condition of Iranian Baha'is, whose lives were reported to have been spared only on condition of conversion to Islam. In Algeria, Islamists have shown deep hostility to the Berbers, the largest ethnic minority in Algeria, killing many during the course of its long civil war, while Islamists have killed Sikhs as well as Hindus in Kashmir, and Nepali Hindu hostages (by the dozen) in Iraq. The suffering of Buddhists in Muslim-ruled parts of India was centuries-long and severe, slain *en masse* by invaders in the twelfth century, and driven north to Tibet and Nepal and south to Sri Lanka during the Islamic conquest of the subcontinent. The destruction in March 2001 by the Taliban of the four giant statues of Buddha at Bamiyan in Afghanistan—statues which had survived even Genghiz Khan—was thus no more than an incident in Islam's historic combat with the 'idolatry' of Buddhism; as were attacks in 2004 and 2005 in southern Thailand on Buddhist clerics and temples, officials and ordinary citizens by a resurgent Muslim separatist movement which included decapitations among its methods.

But among the many targets of Muslim recoil from polytheists, Hinduism—not always a tolerant faith itself—has earned Islam's particular contempt for its theogony and totems, and the eclectic embrace of its beliefs. The culture of the Hindus, perceived by Islam as the very antithesis of true faith, could be said to have sustained the longest and most continuous of all Muslim sieges. The very name 'Hindu Kush' given to the mountain range of Afghanistan—across which Muslim invaders passed into the plains of India—literally means 'kills the Hindu', or 'Hindu slaughter'. With long historic memories, many members of the Hindu community of Kabul fled the Afghan capital in April 1992 at the Taliban takeover; those who remained were ordered by edict in May 2001 not only to wear distinctive yellow badges or yellow clothing but to 'stop living in proximity to Muslims'.

'The decision is in line with Islam', the head of the Taliban's 'religious police', Mohammed Wahli, declared at the time. 'Religious minorities living in an Islamic state must be identified', he added. The edict was subsequently withdrawn, and replaced by the issuing of special identity-cards to Afghan Hindus. But a long Islamic shadow had crossed the polytheistic Hindus' path; as it did also in the slaughters of Hindus carried out by the Pakistani army in 1971 in East Bengal, when the homes of Hindus were painted with a yellow 'H'. Indeed, the creation of Muslim Pakistan and Bangladesh brought about a mass-exodus of Hindus from both. In the first, it reduced the pre-independence proportion of Hindus from about one-quarter to less than 2 per cent, and in the second to less than 10 per cent. Moreover, violence against Hindus in Bangladesh—and against other religious minorities, including Buddhists—has continued to be reported.

The Muslim conquest of the Indian subcontinent was a matter of successive waves of invasion, beginning in the seventh and eighth centuries under raiders such as those commanded by the Arab Muhammad bin Kasim, and followed, for example, by Mahmud of Gazni's eleventh-century pillages and killings and by Muhammad Ghauri's late-twelfth-century conquests in northwestern India and the plains of the Ganges. Marked by frequent mass-slaughters of Hindus, by their forcible conversion, and by the destruction of Hindu places of worship, Islam assaulted that multi-headed and many-armed theism which it perceives as the idolatrous sin of sins. 'Oh Prophet', prayed Timur Beg, or 'Tamerlane'—who sacked Delhi in 1398, slaying '50,000' Hindu captives before the battle, and 'about 100,000' after it—'make war upon the infidels and treat them severely, and let the army of Islam gain from the plunder of the Hindus' wealth!' Similarly, the Mughal emperor Akbar is said to have ordered the massacre of 'about 30,000' Hindu prisoners in 1568, after the battle of Chitod.

The emperor Jehangir, who ruled India from 1605 to 1622, spared the Hindus the wholesale killings meted out to them by his predecessors, but warned them—in the manner, once more, of the Old Testament prophets or the Puritan iconoclasts of the Reformation—that as 'adorers of images snared in the web of their own inventions' they would not 'escape the retribution prepared for them'. Aurangzeb, crowned emperor of India in 1659 with the title of 'al-Amgir' or 'world conqueror', sought to convert all Hindus to Islam by means of pressures ranging from discrimination to extremes of physical violence. He declared it a 'sin for a Muslim even to look at a temple' of the Hindus; a court-historian described his reign as that of a 'destroyer of false gods', whose 'idols' were 'taken from the infidels' temples' and 'pressed under foot by the true believers'.

There has been an imposing historic continuity and universality in Muslim disposition towards the 'unbeliever'. It has been tempered at different periods, and for differing durations, by amiable cohabitation, mutual respect, intellectual collaboration and other forms of relatively peaceful relation. But even if there have been varying degrees of hostility demonstrated towards 'infidelity' by Muslims, and at times no marked hostility at all, 'infidelity' has remained 'infidelity'. Moreover, the passive acceptance of 'unbelief', particularly should the latter become or be seen as a danger to true faith, is a betrayal of Islam itself. Indeed, the long history of aggressions against Muslims and their lands has merely served to confirm the threat to Islam which 'unbelief' represents *per se*. Non-Muslim bewilderment at the violence of word and deed of Islamist 'terror groups', or at the intractability of the conflict between Muslims and Jews in the Middle East, is therefore misplaced.

When the 'twentieth hijacker', Zacarias Moussaoui, told a Virginia court in April 2002 that he prayed to God for 'the destruction of the United States of America' and the 'Jewish people and state', as well as for the victory of 'Muslims fighting in Chechnya, India and elsewhere', he was speaking to that sense of the eternal 'infidel' whose overthrow has been decreed by God. And when he added that he mistrusted his court-appointed lawyers for having 'no understanding of terrorism, Muslims and the *mujahideen*', he was expressing both a sense of election—unknown and unknowable to the non-believer— and of having right upon his side.

This sense of election and right has remained constant, even if it has not been acted upon in periods of Islamic quiescence. However, in such periods, the long record of offences, conquests and defeats suffered at the hands of the 'infidel' has been preserved in the historic memory of Muslims. This collective memory is the common property of Islam. Moreover, its store has of necessity been increasing. For the Muslim revival has itself provoked the 'infidel' to ever more hostile and violent responses to it. For each infliction upon Islam of further outrage—in Afghanistan, in Iraq, in Palestine, in the Muslim diaspora—a further reckoning must be made. In this dance, often a dance of death, the Muslim and the 'infidel' become partners. By committing acts perceived to be disrespectful of Islam, it has been the Hindu in one place, the Jew in another and the Christian in a third who has fulfilled the role of bringing the Muslim to a deeper sense of faith.

Indeed, for an 'infidel' to show temerity towards Islam has always been to court danger. In the case of Christian proselytising, it has led to the killing of missionaries by Islamists, as in southern Lebanon in November 2002 and in Yemen the following month; for a non-Muslim to proselytise among Muslims, and for a Muslim to convert from true faith to false, are punishable by death under a strict interpretation of Sharia law. During the period of Taliban rule, foreign-aid workers were even prohibited from visiting the homes of Afghans, let alone attempting to convert them, while the offices of Christian relief agencies were sealed in August and September 2001 and evangelical Christian charity-workers arrested. Accused of 'promoting Christianity', they were freed during an American air-attack on Afghanistan.

In Pakistan, Christians have played their familiar parts in Muslim

demonology, even though Christians, perhaps half of them Catholic, constitute not more than 3 per cent of the Pakistani population. Many belong to the
poorest and least influential stratum of Pakistani society, yet they have often
enough been targeted for harassment and attack. But for the Muslim pietist
their fewness and powerlessness cannot render their 'infidelity' less. Charges
of blasphemy have been levelled at Pakistani Christians, using laws passed in
1985 which also made blasphemy a capital offence. The alleged inscribing by
Christians of graffiti on mosque-walls and the alleged defacement by Christians of copies of the Koran—acts attributed to 'unbelievers' in a number of
countries during the Islamic revival—have brought death-sentences,
including in 1995 against a fourteen-year-old boy. The judgment was quashed
after international outcry. In that case, the two Christian defendants, the
second of whom was an adult aged forty, were claimed by their counsel to be
illiterate. They were nevertheless accused of having 'thrown papers into a village mosque with blasphemous remarks written upon them'. A third Christian
accused in the case was killed by unidentified gunmen in April 1994 before the
matter could come to trial.

An appeal against the death-sentences was launched, while pietists ominously pronounced the defence-lawyer a 'heretic', calling on fellow-Muslims
to kill her; she left Pakistan. The appeal, heard within a fortnight of the original verdict as news of the judgment gained publicity abroad, was brought on
the grounds that the evidence against the accused had been 'concocted'. The
appellate judges—who had themselves received death-threats—conducted
the hearing under heavy police-guard, with crowds outside the court-building
shouting for the executions of the accused. Nevertheless, the judges courageously acquitted the two Christians. In February 1997, after the spread of
similar rumours that Christians had torn pages from the Koran, written blasphemies upon them and 'thrown them into a mosque', some 20,000 Muslim
rioters drove Christians from their homes in Pakistan's Punjab region, looted
and set their property on fire and wrecked more than a dozen churches.

In October 2001, with Islam's energies further whetted by the 'success' of
the 9/11 attacks on the United States, sixteen Pakistani Christians were
gunned down by radical Islamists during a church service in Bahawalpur in
southern Pakistan. As the gunmen opened fire, they were reported to have
shouted 'Pakistan and Afghanistan, graveyard of Christians!' and 'This is just
a beginning'. The Christians had been slain in revenge for Muslim deaths in
Afghanistan. But beyond the murders lay a broader horizon, since those who
had been killed belonged to a larger genus: 'we have killed the non-believers',
a spokesman for the Islamist group Lashkar-e-Jhangvi declared. In January

2002, Daniel Pearl, kidnapped in Karachi, was a rare catch as an American Jew. But in August 2002, it was again the turn in Pakistan of the Christian 'unbeliever', in a massacre carried out at a Christian hospital and school.

In September 2002, in a further attack, gunmen entered the premises of a Christian charity in Karachi—the Institute of Peace and Justice—separated Christians from Muslim nurses, and shot seven of the former in the head. In December 2002, on Christmas Day, members of Pakistan's Jaish-e-Mohammed, or 'Army of Mohammad', set off a blast in a Protestant church in Chianwala, near Daska in central Pakistan, killing three young Christian girls at worship and injuring others. In a mosque sermon three days prior to the attack, a local Muslim cleric, Mohammed Afzal, had allegedly declared it to be the 'duty of every good Muslim to kill Christians'. 'You should not even have food until you have seen their dead bodies', he was reported to have said.

It was an instruction of a type at which other Muslims have raised their hands in dismay, holding it to be 'non-Islamic'. Yet in April 2003, according to the bishop of Faisalabad, an eighteen-year-old Pakistani Catholic, Javed Anjum, was seized by students of a *madrassa*—or Islamic seminary—in the town of Toba Tek Singh, 300 kilometres south of Islamabad, imprisoned and severely beaten in an effort to get him to recite the *kalma*, or Muslim credo, and to abjure his faith. He refused and died of his injuries in Faisalabad in May 2003. Similarly, in Bangladesh in September 2004 and May 2005 respectively, a council member of the Bangladesh Baptist Fellowship and a Baptist lay pastor were beheaded by Islamists. However, at issue in such cases was not the catch-all charge of 'barbarism' which the 'civilised' level at Muslim fervours. For Christianity itself is historically no stranger to such mutant forms of the proof of faith. Moreover, the respect paid by Muslims to their Holy Book and its teachings is not more egregious than that shown by the members of other faiths to the icons of their belief; the ghosts of the innocent burnt at the stake for 'desecrating the Host' mock such notion.

Islamist severities will also not abate as long as its faith is felt to be under threat from whatever source, including from the mere presence of 'infidels' or 'apostates'. In Iran, said to be home to some 300,000 Christians, Pastor Hussein Soodman was charged with apostasy and hanged in 1989; its most prominent Christian cleric, Bishop Haik Hovespian-Mehr, was kidnapped, tortured and murdered in January 1994; in June 1994, Pastor Tateos Michaelian of St. John Presbyterian Church in Teheran was shot and killed; Pastor Mehdi Dibaj, a Muslim-born evangelical Protestant who had been imprisoned for nine years on a charge of 'apostasy', was freed but only to be stabbed to death in July 1994. In September 1994, Pastor Mohammed Yusefi was found hanging from a tree.

'Western observers' characteristically blamed the murders on Muslim 'fanatics'—an erroneous term—acting under the patronage of the Iranian government. The Iranians, for their part, blamed the Iraqis. However, by April 2003 and with the United States army established in neighbouring Iraq, Iran's foreign minister, Kamal Kharrazi, expressed his 'pride' that 'Christians, Jews, Armenians, Zoroastrians and Muslims' were 'living peacefully together in the Islamic Republic'. Iran's religious minorities were represented in its parliament, and Iranian law recognised the marriage, divorce and burial customs of those belonging to faiths other than Islam. But a nuclear-arming state ruled by an Islamist clerisy could not be a permanent haven for any 'infidel', least of all in conditions of internal and external political tension.

Thus, during 2004, there were 'harassments' of church-going Teheran Christians, and arrests of Christians in northern Iran in May and June. In September 2004, police raided the annual meeting of the General Council of the Assemblies of God, an evangelical Protestant movement. More than eighty Iranian Christians, including pastors, were detained before all but one—a convert from Islam—were released. A former Iranian army colonel and convert to Christianity, he was sentenced to three years' imprisonment for not having declared his conversion: non-Muslims are forbidden to serve as military officers in the Islamic Republic.

In parts of Indonesia, especially on its islands, Muslim groups—similarly defending true faith against false—have taken up arms against local Christians, who form about 10 per cent of Indonesia's population; the Laskar Jihad movement, for instance, has been described as 'specialising in fighting Christians in the Maluku [Malacca] islands'. Christian churches, schools and Christian-owned houses and stores have been looted and torched. Of many examples of such actions taken against 'unbelievers' in Indonesia—including against the Chinese—twenty-five churches were razed in Java in October 1996. These events took place after a sentence deemed by Muslims to be too lenient was handed down against a Christian accused, once more, of blasphemy against the Koran. In the ensuing depredations, 'No to Jesus!' and, for good measure, 'No to Jews!' were inscribed on local walls.

Despite the wishful thinking of non-Muslims (and some Muslims), the logic of such words and deeds was again a coherent one, objectionable as this logic might be according to other standards of reason and right. In April 2000, five thousand Muslims in Indonesia's capital Jakarta called for a jihad against all Christians living in the Malaccas. The call was heeded in part. On the mainly Christian island of Halmahera, for example, a church and some three hundred houses owned by Christians were firebombed by Islamic fighters. In

June 2000, over one hundred Christians were killed there, and an 'unknown number' of women and children were kidnapped.

Similar actions against Christians, sometimes as a consequence of missionary activity among Muslims, continued to occur elsewhere in the Malaccas. By late 2002, it was reported that on the island of Sulawesi nearly two thousand Christians had died, with many more thousands left homeless. In the Malaccas as a whole, the death-toll from religious violence—in which many Muslims also lost their lives—was said to have reached nine thousand. In April 2004, Muslim gangs, provoked by a march by a Christian separatist movement, again attacked Christian homes, setting fire to a Protestant church and the campus buildings of a Christian-run university in the provincial capital of the Malaccas, Ambon, during several days of armed clashes between Muslims and Christians. 'This is a holy war', a Muslim street-fighter was reported as saying; adding, correctly, 'we are obliged to defend our faith'. There were other clashes and attacks of similar kind. In one of them, in July 2004, a Protestant minister was shot dead in church in eastern Indonesia while delivering a sermon.

Violent attacks on Christians by Islamists in the Philippines, where the great majority of the population is Catholic, have also been in accord with pattern. For example, in December 1993, grenades were thrown into the cathedral in Davao on the island of Muslim-dominated Mindanao; in June 1994, fifteen Christians were separated from Muslims at a road checkpoint by members of the Islamist Abu Sayyaf group, and gunned down. There were subsequently many similar incidents in areas of Muslim insurrection in the Philippines, in which foreign Christian 'infidels' were taken hostage—of whom some were killed, including by beheading—and in which Christian places of worship were attacked. In January 2005, a suicide-bombing of a popular Catholic festival in a suburb of Manila was said to have been foiled and sixteen Islamists arrested.

Across Africa from west to east, Islam's battles of faith with Catholic, Anglican and evangelical Christians, including Pentecostals, have also intensified. They have provoked riot and other violence from the Ivory Coast and Liberia—where churches and mosques were set on fire and there were reciprocal killings in October 2004—to the Sudan. Here, where there has been a long history of Christian-Muslim (and inter-Muslim) hostility, decades of civil war in southern Sudan, referred to earlier, cut a murderous swathe through the African Christian population. Formally declared to be a jihad—although other matters than religious difference, including control over natural resources, have been involved—it brought years of slaughter in Christian communities as well as forcible conversions to Islam.

In Nigeria, a nation of some 130 million—or about one-fifth of Africa's population—tensions between Muslims and Christians during the last four decades have often ended in bloodshed. The secessionist Biafran civil war of 1967, earlier referrred to, could be traced—at least in part—to the hostility felt by Muslim Hausa-speakers for Christian Ibo immigrants in Muslim-dominated northern Nigeria. On this interpretation, and although other factors were again involved, the victims of Muslim-Christian conflicts since the 1960s in Nigeria have numbered more than one million. Continuing communal religious riots, objections to job discrimination against Christians, land disputes between Muslims and Christians and Nigerian Christian resistance from January 2000 to Sharia law in the Muslim north have regularly led to bouts of reciprocal killing. They have occurred in and around the Muslim-dominated city of Kaduna, for example, as well as in the central city of largely Christian Jos. There has also been the familiar targeting of Christian pastors and worshippers, and the razing of churches by arson.

Among numerous instances of unrest during 2001 in Nigeria's Plateau state, there were at least one thousand killings in Muslim-Christian clashes. Further fighting between Muslim Fulani herders and Christian farmers in the same state in 2004 left many hundreds of dead, on both sides. In February 2004, Muslims attacked the mainly Christian town of Yelwa in central Nigeria and were reported to have pursued local Christians to a church, which was set on fire and some fifty, including the pastor, were killed. In April 2004, there was an attempted coup by northern Muslim officers in the Nigerian army against the Christian-led central government in Lagos. Again in Yelwa, and also in the city of Kano, riot and massacres in May 2004 carried out by rival gangs—or 'militias'—armed with guns, swords and clubs, led to many hundreds of deaths. Churches and mosques were set ablaze, and some twenty thousand Christians were reported to have been driven from their homes. There were great cruelties on both sides; 'the pagans', declared a Muslim eye-witness, 'have killed our people'.

Some of these conflicts in Nigeria had to do with battle between Muslims and Christians for resources, in which hostilities of faith played only a part. Others were the consequence of the introduction of Sharia law into twelve Muslim-dominated northern states. In Zamfara state, it brought into existence Islamic courts with the power to order beheadings, amputations and lashings, in the last case including for drinking alcohol in public. Similar restrictions introduced in 2004 required that businesses close five times a day for Muslim prayers. Opposition from Christians to the Islamic penal system brought tension, violence and counter-violence, with militant mosque-sermons arousing the faithful against local 'unbelievers'. Christians attacked Muslims and Muslim property in reprisal, and were again attacked in turn; gun-battles, in which both Muslims and Christians died, broke out over seemingly minor offences to religious sensibility and scruple.

In Jos, at a time of Friday prayer—and on the day before the attack on the World Trade Center—a Christian woman's attempt to cross the street in front of a mosque was ill-fated. Infringing a taboo which was similarly punished in Muslim lands in the Middle Ages, it led to Muslim rampage and killing. In November 2002, with empty-headed frivolity or intention to insult—depending on point of view—a Nigerian newspaper columnist implied that the Prophet would have been happy to marry one of the contestants in the 'Miss World' competition, then being held in Nigeria. In three days of riots in Kaduna and other cities, several hundred Christians and Muslims died—the majority Christian—thousands were forced to flee their homes, curfews were imposed, and twenty-two churches and eight mosques were destroyed.

In Nigeria, as elsewhere, Christians have been the principal targets of Islam's increasing militancy and raised self-awareness. It has been manifested in a readiness, among other things, to attack the 'infidel' for demonstrating even minor insensitivities to true faith, let alone for committing the greater offences of which the non-Muslim world stands accused. In some instances, the anger and violence which have ensued have been swiftly suppressed or soon exhausted; in others, they have been the occasion for a wider-scale call to jihad.

In contrast with such violences, the tensions referred to in earlier chapters between Muslims and non-Muslims in Europe, although growing, remained relatively minor. Threats, assaults, desecrations and a gradual diminution of toleration—together with rare outbreaks of local riot, as in Britain in the summer of 2001—still stood at the outer limit of events. However, there were serious Muslim-Christian clashes during disturbances in Kosovo in March 2004, after the death in suspicious circumstances of a Muslim child. In reprisal Albanians of the majority Muslim community set fire to some fifteen Serbian Orthodox churches—some of great historic significance—and mosques were burned down by Serbians in reprisal. There had been, among other things, a quick arousal of hostility in Muslims to a sense of threat at 'infidel' hands.

It was a response which became increasingly common, including where Muslims were in the majority and not under attack by 'unbelievers'. Thus, at the height of the Algerian civil war, Christian cemeteries were desecrated and Christian priests—as well as workers for a Christian religious foundation—

were murdered. The Islamist GIA declared that these murders had been carried out as part of a 'campaign of annihilation and physical liquidation of
Christian crusaders', even though such 'crusaders' were not party to Algeria's
internal conflict.

In Egypt, similarly, the Islamist upsurge from the beginning of the 1990s
brought increasing discrimination against and attacks on Coptic Orthodox
Christians in particular, of whom there are said to be seven million or more in
a population of over seventy million. Assaults on Christians, allegedly encouraged in certain instances from the mosque pulpit and which met with little
police response, included the sacking and burning of churches, such as that of
the Free Methodists in Cairo in October 1991; the killing of Copts and the
destruction of their shops and homes, particularly in the rural areas of upper
Egypt; and resort to punishments for the refusal by Copts to pay the *jizya*, the
traditional tax which finds sanction in the Koran itself. In December 1992,
physical violence—including having the right arm and both legs broken—was
reported by David Hirst in the *Guardian* as being inflicted on Copts for acts of
'disobedience'. Similarly, in February 2000, on the eve of a papal visit, some
twenty Coptic Christians who had been attending mass were killed by
'Muslim mobs' at al-Kosheh, again in upper Egypt.

Samir Hafez, one of the victims of this attack, was said to have been
'hacked to death'—again in the stock vocabulary of the media—when he
refused to renounce his Christian faith. 'They found tattoos of the Virgin
Mary and Saint George on his arms and beat him', his mother, Samihia Hafez,
told Sam Kiley of *The Times*. 'They said they would stop if he said he was a
Muslim, but he said he would rather be murdered, so they smashed his head
in and cut off his arms'. A lurid example of the 'bad press' discussed in a previous chapter, the demands made of the victim, and the consequences of his
recalcitrance, were clearly understood by the perpetrators as a translation into
act of the demands of faith. In July 2003, Christians were again reported to be
facing 'increasing discrimination' and to be 'leaving the country in considerable numbers'; while in December 2004 further wrecking of Coptic property
in upper Egypt, together with allegations of forced conversion to Islam, led to
public protests in Cairo.

Under Saddam Hussein's Ba'athist regime, Christians—who include
Assyrians, Mandaeans and members of the Eastern-rite Catholic Chaldean
church, numbering perhaps 800,000 in total or some 3 per cent of the Iraqi
population—were mostly spared the brutalities suffered by Shi'ite Muslims, as
was the small population of Jews. There were also generally cordial relations
between Christians and Shi'ites, whose preoccupations lay elsewhere. Never-

theless, as has already been observed, violently anti-Christian diatribes began to flow from Baghdad's pulpits on the eve of the Iraq War, as the Ba'athist regime grew increasingly threatened. They led the Chaldean bishop of Baghdad, Shlemon Wardouni, to lodge a formal protest in March 2003 against denunciations 'from the minaret' of the approaching 'Crusaders'; he feared the taking of reprisals against his community if there were a Western invasion. Wardouni's forebodings were justified. With the country quickly occupied by an army of foreign 'infidels', Islamists began to assert themselves in familiar fashion against Iraq's 'unbelievers'.

There were early reports in May 2003 of Iraqi Christians being murdered for selling alcohol; and, in November 2003, of clashes—involving deaths—between Muslims and Christians in areas of the fiercest Sunni resistance to the invasion forces. In Ramadi, west of Baghdad, local Assyrian Christians spoke of their 'suffering', of being 'terrified' and of being 'blamed for the war'. Iraqi Islamists were described as 'putting pressure' on Christians 'as never before', while Bishop Wardouni expressed his fears to the Vatican in October 2003 about the future in Iraq of the Christian community as a whole. Indeed, immediately upon the fall of Baghdad, some Iraqi Christians, alarmed at the prospects in an Islamic republic under Shi'a control, were already leaving the country.

During 2004, attacks on Iraqi Christians in their churches increased, with death-threats, abductions and ransom demands; more than one hundred Christians had been killed by the autumn. For example, in August 2004 six Chaldean and Assyrian churches in Baghdad and Mosul were bombed in a coordinated attack. In October 2004, at the start of Ramadan, four Baghdad churches suffered similar coordinated firebombings, and other churches were attacked in Baghdad and Mosul in November and December 2004, while 'most' Assyrian Christians were said to have been prevented from voting in the Iraqi elections of January 2005. Throughout this period, 'record numbers'—running to tens of thousands—of Iraqi Christians were said to have left for Lebanon, Jordan and Syria, as well as European countries and the United States.

But the Christian population of Lebanon—some 60 per cent of the total in the early 1950s—had itself been reduced by flight and massacre during years of civil war; and the small Christian community in Jordan had dwindled also. In Syria, a degree of tolerance historically characterised relations between Muslims and Christians. But the Syrian army showed little mercy when it took over Christian eastern Beirut and other Christian areas in 1990. Thousands of Christians were killed, and there was an exodus of hundreds of thousands more. Fellow-Christians in Lebanon also led the way during the following years in protesting at the presence of Syrian troops in the country until the latter's departure in April 2005; as they left, there were numerous reprisal bombing-attacks on Christian neighbourhoods in and near Beirut.

Moreover, during a period of intensifying Islamist diatribe against the 'Zionist-Crusader' foe, and with Israel on their borders, all Christian communities in the Middle East faced increasing insecurities as Islamism advanced in the region. A tortuously complex situation also included attempts by Syria to gain the Vatican's sympathy for its hostile stance towards Israel, a matter to which I will return; and in a further intricacy, both Catholics and Muslims in Lebanon objected, as in other countries, to the proselytising activities of evangelical Christian missionaries in the country, one of whom was shot by a Muslim gunman in September 2002.

In Saudi Arabia, Christian or Jewish observance, and visible symbols of 'unbelief' such as the Cross or Star of David, are disallowed. Even during the 1991 Gulf War, when hundreds of thousands of coalition troops were based in Saudi Arabia—including in order to defend it from possible Iraqi attack—army padres were instructed to 'show discretion regarding their clothes'; that is, not to appear in public in clerical dress. The Christian Mass and Jewish rites were required to be celebrated inside desert tents after the Saudi authorities had banned open-air, 'infidel' ceremonial. It was therefore consistent with such recoil that in 1992, on Christmas Day, the Saudi authorities should have sentenced to death two Filipinos for 'preaching Christianity', a capital crime.

The Filipino president, Fidel Ramos, was forced to plead for clemency for them. However, the securing of such 'compassion and mercy' for the two Christians commanded its own price. In being driven to petition for mercy in their case, the Filipino president, like other non-Muslims who have had to approach the Saudi throne with cap in hand, had no choice but to accept the presumption of the two Filipinos' 'guilt'. But the logic of Muslim recoil from 'infidelity' itself dictates the refusal to tolerate proselytising in the holiest land of Islam; for non-Muslims to have expected that their objections to Muslim 'intolerance' would be persuasive was again naive. Under milder Muslim circumstances too, as in the Gulf state of Qatar, neither Christian nor Jew may show signs of his or her faith in public, nor hold religious services lest 'offence' be given to Muslim sensibilities, although in Bahrain observance of Christmas is permitted.

Nevertheless, the freedom of worship which Western liberal democracies provide to Muslims and others goes unreciprocated in most Muslim countries. Indeed, in December 2004, the Saudi defence minister, Prince Sultan, declared that churches would 'never' be allowed to be built in the kingdom, while forty Pakistanis were detained in Riyadh in April 2005 after 'performing Christian religious rites' in a private apartment, and—since a Muslim was present—were also accused of 'spread[ing] the poison of their beliefs to others'. Yet, at the same time, Muslims resist restraints put upon the observance of their faith in Christian lands, and have even objected to 'infidelity's customs and practices in 'infidelity's own countries. In April 2003, Muslim employees at the Pentagon protested at the conducting there of its traditional Good Friday service by an evangelical preacher, Franklin Graham, on the grounds that he had earlier criticised Islam in strong terms. A Saudi prohibition on carol-singing on the one hand, and Muslim objections in a Catholic country to the presence of a crucifix in a hospital-ward or a school on the other, are relatively trivial. But they were a combination which could arouse anger in non-Muslims. They again spoke to the intransigences of a faith which rejects 'unbelief', if in a fashion of which reason knows nothing.

Under the aegis of the Palestinian Authority, too, Christians of all denominations have suffered. In the 1960s, there were forty churches in Gaza alone. Three decades later, with only two churches remaining, the community was described as 'facing extinction'. There had earlier been some 60,000 Arab Christians in Gaza. But with Christian women required by local Islamists to cover themselves in Muslim fashion, and under the duress of the Arab-Israeli conflict, the Gaza community's numbers had fallen to no more than a few hundred. 'All of us', declared a Palestinian Christian woman in November 2003, 'are afraid of the ultimate insult, being called a *sharmouta*', or prostitute. 'No father wants his daughter labelled like this', she added. The population of Bethlehem, which had been 80 percent Christian during the 1960s, was only one-third Christian four decades later, while Nazareth's Christian population was reported in July 2003 to have been reduced to a small 'hounded minority'.

During the 1990s, with the Palestinian Authority exercising control over church property and church affairs in the West Bank, Gaza and east Jerusalem, there were also reports of the vandalisation of Christian cemeteries and robberies of churches, as well as of the 'harassment' of Christian pastors, young Arab Christian men and 'apostate' Muslim converts to the Christian faith. These charges were dismissed by Authority spokesman as 'minor incidents', or even as the reports of 'Christian fanatics'. It was clearly the case that the continuing exodus of Palestinian Christians was also attributable to the increasing damage to the Palestinian economy caused by the Palestinian-Israeli conflict, which brought its own inducements to Arab Christians to leave in search of opportunity elsewhere. Nevertheless, the hostility of Muslim militants, together with pressures by the Palestinian Authority on the leaders of shrinking Arab Christian communities in the Palestinian territories to make clear their allegiance to the Palestinian cause, were said to have driven many Arab Christians away.

Some of the factors at work in the relations between Muslims and non-Muslims in Palestine were familiar, others unique. They included the presence, amid an overwhelmingly Muslim population which was host to many Islamist groups, of Arab 'apostates' who were simultaneously Arabs, Palestinians and 'unbelievers'. Moreover, close at hand and exerting an unacceptable domination over local Muslims, was a Jewish state which was a principal object of calls to jihad and which stood at the heart of a supposedly universal 'Judeo-Christian' axis. Further complexity included divisions among Palestinians, divisions which added to their weakness before a more powerful foe. In Israel also, there were incidents of hostility between Muslims and Christians, as in February 2005 when members of the Muslim Druze sect—Israeli citizens—attacked Christian families and their property in the northern town of Mughar; the Israeli police did not intervene.

In such setting, as elsewhere in the world, Christian interests, and especially the diplomacy of the Catholic Church, have faced difficult challenges as Islam's confidence has grown. Furthermore, although Muslims are divided and engaged in battle with themselves as well as with the 'unbeliever', the Christian world is not less so. Thus, traditional or conservative Catholicism generally perceives Protestantism—and therefore Protestant America—as little better than the embodiment of an individualist and materialist spirit which is responsible for most of the vices of the age in the non-Muslim world. Deep-rooted 'Judeophobic' sentiments among many Catholics are shared by many Muslims, but have been at odds with the support shown by sections of the Christian evangelical movement for Israel and the Jews.

Thus, there are 'Christian Zionists' in the American evangelical movement who believe—contrary to the mainstream of the Catholic Christian tradition—that the Jews have a 'divine right' to claim most or all of the Holy Land as their own; and that Israel is 'not the problem but the solution', as the majority-leader in the US House of Representatives, Tom DeLay, put it in July 2003. The perceptions of most Catholic Christians are remote from these. As the Vatican's *Osservatore Romano* expressed it in May 1948, 'Modern Israel is not the true heir of biblical Israel, but a secular state.... Therefore, the Holy Land and its sacred sites belong to Christianity, the true Israel'; the actual state of Israel, as mentioned earlier, was not recognised by the Vatican until late 1993. This taking of a distance by Catholicism from Israel, and its long history of hostility to the Jews, has prima facie made possible an accommodation between Rome and Islam on the 'Jewish question', one based upon an antipathy which they share. However, the hostility shown equally to 'Crusaders' and 'Zionists' by Islamists has served to confound repeated Vatican attempts to find such accommodation, not least when Catholics and Catholic places of worship have been subjected to Islamist violence and attack.

For their parts, Muslim leaders have long made efforts to gain Christian and especially Catholic diplomatic support for Islamist and Arab policy towards Israel. In 1950, for example, Azzam Pasha, the secretary of the Arab League, proposed to the Vatican a Christian-Muslim alliance against 'the Jews and communism'. More than a half-century later in December 2004 the Lebanese Shi'ite cleric, Sheikh Sayed Hussein Fadlallah, called on the Vatican to join Muslims in opposing the 'war on terrorism' on the grounds that it was harming the interests of both Christians and Muslims. In particular, and despite the ill-treatment of Christians at Muslim hands, including in Palestine itself, Muslim appeal to Christian sentiment in respect of the Holy Land has been both well chosen and necessary to the Palestinian cause.

Yasser Arafat frequently called Palestine by the Church's own term, the '*Terra Santa*'. In September 1983, he even described Christ as the 'first Palestinian *fedayin* who carried his sword along the path on which the Palestinians today carry their Cross'. Depictions of Jesus nailed to the Star of David have been used in al-Fatah posters. Likewise, the wall or 'security fence' erected by the Israelis was condemned by the Palestinian leader in February 2004 on the ground that it 'prevent[ed] Christians from going to the city of Jesus, God bless Him'. Indeed, the 'Christian card' has been attempted to be played in the Muslim and Arab worlds as well as in the diaspora, even while Christians continued to be assailed as latter-day 'Crusaders'. In July 2003, Saddam Hussein appealed to members of the Chaldean Catholic church to join the struggle in Iraq against the supposed 'American-Zionist' enemy; while in March 2004, from many such examples, the imam of the Italian city of Gallarate, Mohamed Mafoudi—who was shortly afterwards deported from Italy for his alleged contacts with Islamist 'terror-groups'—expressed the wish of Muslims to 'embark upon a journey with Christians in constructing a world of brotherhood and peace'.

There were many elements in this *pas de deux*, among them the belief expressed by the Vatican in July 1990 that Islam and Christianity were on a 'dangerous collision course' which it would take 'great prudence to avoid'. There were also Church anger at the treatment of Christians, fear of Islam's advance, the desire for a pacific compromise between the two great religious powers of the world and rival claims upon the Holy Land. The outcome of these often irreconcilable sentiments has been confusion in the Catholic Church's address to Islam.

On the one hand it has sought, generally with uncertain voice, to meet Muslim opinion in matters small and large. Such efforts have had a wide range: from, say, a contested proposal in May 2004 to remove from the cathedral of Santiago de Compostela a statue of Saint James, Spain's patron saint—which has heads of decapitated 'Moors' at its feet—to condemnations of the invasion of Iraq in 2003. On the other hand, the Jesuit journal *La Civiltà Cattolica*, published with Vatican approval, described Islam in October 2003 as having had a 'warlike face' throughout its history. Two months later, however, Arab sensibilities were directly addressed by Cardinal Roger Etchegaray when he expressed his 'sadness' at seeing images of the 'humiliating' capture of Saddam Hussein. It was a position from which the Pope let it be known— through a 'senior Vatican official'—that he dissented. Days later again, Cardinal Jean-Louis Touran, the Vatican's former foreign minister, strongly objected to the treatment of Christians in 'too many Muslim countries', denounced the 'extreme case' of Saudi Arabia where freedom of religion was 'violated absolutely', and declared that Christians and Muslims faced an 'enormous task' in establishing relations of 'mutual tolerance'.

In May 2004, the head of the Vatican's Pontifical Council for Inter-Religious Dialogue, Archbishop Michael Fitzgerald, in similarly tough tones refused the request of Muslims to resume prayer in the cathedral of Cordoba—a mosque during Arab rule over Spain—telling them to 'accept history' and not to 'take revenge' on the Catholic Church. In January 2004, on another religious front, the Pope assured Israel's chief rabbis of his commitment to improve Catholic-Jewish relations; yet in March 2004, after the Israeli assassination of Sheikh Ahmed Yassin, the Hamas leader, the bells of the remaining churches in Gaza rang out in sympathy with the Palestinians.

The Christian churches differed among themselves, too, about the nature of the challenge which a resurgent Islam posed. In some cases—despite the death-rate in Muslim-Christian conflict—there was doubt about whether it posed a challenge at all. In August 2003, the archbishop of Canterbury, Rowan Williams, even felt able to support the creation of educational *madrassas* in Britain, regarded by others, Muslims included, as seminaries of Islamism. The churches differed, too, in the degree of their fear that militant responses to the advance of Islam might only offer further provocations to it; a fear which was least manifest among evangelicals, despite the killing of their missionaries in a number of Muslim countries. These divisions could be said to have been the church counterparts of divisions among the Western powers, whose strategic interests in accommodating themselves to Islam's strengths were in conflict with the desire to stop it in its tracks. This complex response to the Islamic world—both fearing and courting it at the same time—has been a particular mark of the policy of the Church of Rome.

Adding to this complexity, was Islamism's coupling together of Christianity and Judaism as 'infidel' allies allegedly engaged in a joint war against the Muslim world. Such thesis was anathema to the many Christians who disapproved of Israel and 'the Jews' as strongly as, or more strongly than, they disapproved of Islam. Islamists could be said to have made Jews and Christians one in their fates, but it was not an identity which all Christians could accept. In part, this was because the predisposition of many Christians, clerics and lay alike, was to 'make peace' with Islam and the Arab world. Christian peace-groups, such as Pax Christi in Britain, took the position that military action against Saddam Hussein was both 'illegal' and 'immoral'; that is, wrong as a matter both of law and faith. Other Christians, drawing on the writings of Aquinas, for example, held that the decision to invade Iraq did not meet Aquinas's criteria that there be both just cause and just intent in war.

Other issues, even older than those raised by Aquinas, loomed amid the hostilities between Muslim, Christian and Jew. In April 2002, a nine-foot-square mural on display outside St. John's Church in the centre of Edinburgh, which—like the Palestinian Fatah posters—depicted a crucified Jesus lying dead between Roman and Israeli soldiers, was removed after protests. In the same month, Hilarion Capucci, the former Syrian Orthodox archbishop in Jerusalem, took a prominent part in a demonstration which was held in Rome's Piazza del Popolo to show solidarity with the Palestinians in their struggle against Israel; the Syrian Orthodox Church acknowledges the authority of the pope, and Capucci was at the time being lodged in the Vatican itself. During his oration the archbishop—in clerical dress, but with an Arab *keffiyah* about his neck and standing alongside Nemer Hammad, a representative of the Palestinian Authority in Italy—described suicide-bombers, in Islamist terms, as 'martyrs who go to their deaths as to a party'.

In this form of Christian response to the Palestinians' plight, the sub-text or implication—made explicit in Edinburgh—was that Palestinians were victims of 'the eternal Jew'. Such victimhood being reminiscent of that of Christ and at the same hands, it was incumbent upon Christians to act for the Palestinians' protection. Hence, 'dialogue' was conducted between some Christians and Muslims, and common positions were discovered, both on the politics of the Middle East and on matters of personal moral conduct. At the same time, conventicles of Christian evangelists pledged themselves to the defence of 'Zion' on Israel's behalf, notwithstanding that Islamism continued to do battle with its 'Crusader' foes. Unremitting, too, was the contest between Christianity—Catholic, Anglican and evangelical—and Islam to win converts to their respective faiths, a contest particularly intense in parts of the 'developing' world.

Violence between Muslims and Christians in the last decades has claimed many lives, even while the faiths have striven against one another for souls. Indeed, competition for adherents was often a factor in the conflicts which set Muslims and Christians against one another, from the southern Philippines to northern Nigeria. Moreover, the waning of Christian influence in the life and thought of much of the West has coincided with the growing strength and confidence of the Muslim diaspora in nominally Christian nations. And as during the struggles of the mediaeval Church to contain an earlier mobilisation of Islam's might, problems have been raised for a now unarmed Rome which are beyond the reach of diplomacy alone.

Nevertheless in 1991, for instance, the Roman Church and Muslim leaders signed an 'agreement', void in its outcome, not to try to convert each other's followers in Africa and Asia. Again, in February 1992, when launching a 'Decade of Islamic Revivalism' in Britain, the president of its Imams and Mosques Council, Zaki Badawi, called for a 'no-poaching agreement' among the main religions in the United Kingdom in order to 'protect our [sc. Muslim] community from predators'; that is, from Christian evangelists in search of potential 'apostates' from Islam. Despite it, a Christian evangelical campaign—which had been given the uncompromising title of 'Spearhead'—defiantly announced that there would be 'no no-go areas' for evangelism in Britain, its Muslim communities included.

However, it is the Catholic Church which, of all the non-Muslim faiths, has been most sorely tested during Islam's long march from strength to strength. The former has tried to steer a path—often on behalf of all Christians, whatever their denominations—between the need for self-defence, the pacification of religious passions, and the pursuit of its own cause. Consistency of response to Islam's advance has therefore been impossible. During a visit in February 1993 to Sudan, Pope John Paul II roundly criticised Khartoum's Islamist regime for its assaults on the Christian minority in the south. But by March 1994, as the dilemma posed to the Church by manifestations of Islam's fighting spirit grew sharper in many parts of the world, the Pope's address to the Muslim world became more placatory. It was now 'urgent', he declared, for the Catholic Church to 'strengthen its dialogue with other religions in Africa, especially Islam'.

In May 1998 a committee was set up, in line with Vatican diplomacy, to 'promote dialogue between Christians and Muslims'. Composed of the Pontifical Council for Inter-Religious Dialogue on one side, and al-Azhar's Permanent Committee for Dialogue with the Monotheistic Religions on the other, it expressed an aspiration to find common moral ground between Christians and Muslims. As Islamism struck directly at the United States, the Pope in Kazakhstan in September 2001 pleaded that Christians and Muslims 'work together for peace', declaring—impotently—that 'religion must never be used as a reason for conflict'. Muslims and Christians, his spokesman added, 'can live together, work together, and pray together'; similarly in August 2005 the new pope, Benedict XVI, urged Muslims to join Christians in trying to combat 'the spread of terrorism' in the world.

But although 'common ground', including on social and moral issues, might be found by some Christians and some Muslims, the 'true faith' of Islam could not be reconciled, by definition, with 'unbelief'. This was so even if Christianity and Islam held themselves to be—with Judaism—united in their 'monotheism'. Indeed, there was no greater prospect of a theological reconciliation between Islam and Christianity than there was between Islam and the Jews, Christianity's co-'infidels'; that is to say, no prospect at all. Only in the matter of Israel, and the bloodletting between Muslims and Jews, could Islam and (in particular) the Catholic Church be seen to be intermittently in close accord. 'Zion' it might be to Christian evangelicals, but Israel was little better than the embodiment of the anti-Christ for many Catholics, and an equivalent source of harm in the eyes of most Muslims.

Here, the linking hyphen between 'Judeo' and 'Christian', kept in place in Islamist diatribe, was for many Christians dissolved. With the image of the refugee-camps of the Palestinians before them, Muslims and Christians, despite their divisions, could be found looking with equally baleful eyes upon Jerusalem's Jewish custodians. In February 2000, for example, the Vatican and the Palestinian Authority jointly declared that 'unilateral actions' by Israel on the future of Jerusalem were 'morally and legally unacceptable', and that there should be an 'internationally agreed statute' for the city. In March 2000, the Pope on a visit to the region chose Bethlehem not merely to speak of Palestinian suffering, but to link this suffering—as did the Palestinians—with that of Christ. 'How often has the cry of innocents been heard in these streets?' the Pope asked. By such analogy, the gulf between the Islamic and Christian worlds, traversed by few other bridges, was attempted to be crossed.

In the course of wider Catholic efforts at 'bridge-building'—amid the explosions of suicidal Islamist mayhem, and a fortnight after the attack on the

World Trade Center—the Pope on his aforementioned visit to Kazakhstan had diplomatically 'reaffirmed' the 'Catholic church's respect for Islam'. Only days before, Osama bin Laden had declared a jihad against 'Crusaders', and thousands had been slain in its cause. But this, the Pope pronounced, was 'not the act of authentic Islam', an Islam which 'prays' and is 'concerned for those in need'—yet another one-sentence declaration by a non-Muslim of what Islam 'is'.

The motives for caution were put with candour in January 2003 by Cardinal Angelo Sodano, a Vatican secretary of state, as Islamist violence continued. 'Is it worth the trouble to provoke a billion Muslims?' he asked. Whether or not to go to war with Iraq, he added, was a matter of *convenienza*, meaning 'suitability', 'fitness' or 'profit'; utilitarian considerations all. Both in the short and long terms, Sodano argued, the principal issue for the Church remained that of finding what he called a 'realistic' way to 'live in harmony with the Islamic world', rather than advancing against it along the path once taken by the mediaeval popes.

In February 2003, Cardinal Roger Etchegaray was dispatched to Baghdad in an effort to persuade Saddam Hussein to comply with UN resolutions, and to avert war. The Vatican also hosted visits from the foreign ministers of the two Western governments most opposed to conflict, Germany's Joschka Fischer and France's Dominique de Villepin, as well as from Iraq's Catholic foreign minister Tariq Aziz, the UN secretary-general Kofi Annan, and the British prime minister Tony Blair. The joint Pontifical Council and the al-Azhar Committee, referred to earlier, also met in Cairo in February 2003. In a statement it emphasized the 'role of religions for peace', declared it to be the latter's 'responsibility' to 'confront terrorism', proposed further meetings to 'facilitate common reflection on the teaching of a religion that is not one's own'—a theologically limited objective—and thanked the Pope for his efforts at mediation.

The Pope's own anxieties, disclosed on several occasions during March 2003, were more revealing. He feared that a war with Iraq would 'harm relations between Muslims and Christians'; a few days later he expressed the hope that it would not 'set Muslims and Christians against one another'. By Cardinal Sodano's test of *convenienza*, an invasion of Iraq by the Anglo-American alliance was being held to be imprudent, and (on balance) contrary to Church interest. But since *convenienza* was an insufficient moral criterion, it was announced by the Vatican, on the Pope's behalf, that an Anglo-American attack on Iraq would also be a wrong. The grounds—which plainly did not exclude *convenienza*—were that 'peaceful means' for resolving the conflict had 'not yet been exhausted'. Those who went to war, the statement continued, would therefore be assuming a 'grave responsibility before God, their conscience and history'.

After the war had been launched, President Chirac of France, who had done the most within the European Union and through the Security Council to deny the legitimacy of the allied action, therefore felt able to turn publicly to the Vatican for moral support of his position. In the name of the 'most fundamental human values, starting with respect for one another and tolerance'— but ignoring the Saddam regime's human rights' record—Chirac, in a personal letter to the Pope, called for 'the Holy See and France' to 'work together so that law, justice and dialogue between peoples prevail'. On 'all these subjects' France and the Vatican held 'very similar views', the French president declared, implying thereby that the Vatican shared the political position which France had adopted.

Instead, the Roman Church found itself in a moral labyrinth as tortuous as any examined in earlier chapters. For the most part, its responses continued to be confused. In August 2004, the Vatican's leading theologian Cardinal Joseph Ratzinger—who succeeded Pope John Paul II on the latter's death in April 2005—objected to the possible admission of Turkey to the European Union on the grounds that its membership would 'dilute the culture of a Christian continent'. In September and October 2004, using the historic language of Rome's hostility to Islam, John Paul II himself denounced Islamist 'terrorism' and the taking of hostages as 'barbarity'. But in November 2004, at Arafat's death, the Vatican described the Palestinian leader as the 'illustrious deceased', calling on God in the Church's name to grant 'eternal rest to his soul'. And in April 2005, the new Pope expressed his 'appreciation' for the 'growth of dialogue' which had taken place between Muslims and Christians.

In this labyrinth were incoherently combined traditional Church stances towards Islam, Vatican pragmatism or *convenienza*, concern for the fate of millions of Christians embattled in Muslim countries, ethical objection to 'terrorism' and war, antipathy towards Israel and sympathy for the Palestinian cause. All of these bore upon the strategic problem of how the Church was to manage its relations with world-Islam as it advanced. Moreover, with an inner fire which much of Catholicism no longer possessed, Islam was challenging Christendom to a contest of faiths for which most Christians—with the exception of militant evangelicals—had no stomach; many continued to be in denial that such challenge existed at all. Yet the fact that the focus of the bitterest conflict between Islam and the non-Muslim world was in Christianity's, and Arafat's, '*Terra Santa*' made Christians as much protagonists in this conflict as Muslims and Jews.

To add to the complexity, there were divisions in the ranks of all faiths, Christians, Muslims and Jews. There were Israelis who sympathised with the Palestinians more than with the policies of Israel, Muslims who—apart from being citizens of Israel—were weary of strife and opposed to suicide-bombing, and Christians who were better disposed to 'Zion' than to Rome. Moreover, the complex dance of the faiths about one another was not confined to the theatre of the Levant. For example, in February 1990 the British Muslim Action Front argued in the High Court in London that Islam and Christianity were 'so intertwined' that the 'blasphemy' of Salman Rushdie's *The Satanic Verses* was equally offensive to both, since 'all the apostles and all the prophets described in the Old Testament and the Koran are the same'. In February 1993, the speaker of the Iranian parliament, Ali Akbar Nateq-Nouri, likewise called on Christians to join Muslims in 'hunting down and killing' Rushdie, on the grounds that he had insulted Christianity also.

These latter arguments fell on stony ground. Nevertheless, there were many such invitations, implicit or explicit, for the tactical or temporary setting aside of differences between Muslims and Christians in order to combat common foes, generally the United States and Israel. A typical appeal was once more that of Saddam Hussein, who on Christmas Day 2000 had called on Christians and Muslims to 'rise up against Israel and the Zionist conspiracy'. After an audience at the Vatican in February 2003, before the outbreak of the Iraq War, a more convoluted version of the same message was given by the Saddam regime's Chaldean Catholic foreign minister, Tariq Aziz. 'Muslims and Christians', described by Aziz as 'people who believe in God', were 'trying to fight against this aggression [sc. threatening Iraq] and to mobilise the forces of God against the forces of evil'. He was implying that whatever their other differences, Muslims and Christians—and in particular Catholics—had a common duty to resist an 'evil' which, by further implication, was being promoted by those without belief in God. Muslims and Christians shared such belief; others—in this context, Jews—did not.

The assertion that Jews were 'enemies of God' (and of 'humanity') was explicitly made in communiqués issued by the al-Aqsa Martyrs' Brigade and the People's Front for the Liberation of Palestine, for example, when claiming responsibility for an attack at a crowded railway-station outside Tel Aviv in April 2003. During a visit to Damascus by the Pope in May 2001 and in his presence, the Syrian president, Bashar al-Assad, was more specific, reviling 'those who try to kill the principles of all religions with the same mentality with which they betrayed Jesus Christ'. It was an observation which recalled Saddam Hussein's condemnation, a decade earlier, of the first President Bush for 'betraying the teachings of Christ in the same way that Judas betrayed Jesus'.

In the course of the same papal visit, Syria's minister of religious affairs, Muhammad Ziyadah—in an address delivered at the Ummayad mosque in Damascus in the presence of the silent Pontiff—again implicitly invited the Roman Catholic Church to make common cause with Muslims. 'We must be fully aware of what the enemies of God'—that is, the Jews—'and malicious Zionism conspire to commit against Christianity and Islam', Ziyadah asserted. Seated beside the Pope as Ziyadah spoke was the Grand Mufti of Syria, Sheikh Ahmad Kiftaro, who two years later in March 2003 was to call for 'all possible means' to be used by 'all Muslims' against the coalition-forces in Iraq, as was earlier mentioned. Questioned as to whether the Pope would make any formal reply to the Syrian president's comments, the papal spokesman, Joaquin Navarro-Valls, declared 'The Pope will absolutely not intervene'. As for the observation that Jews seek to 'kill the principles of all religions', this was Assad's 'opinion', said Navarro-Valls. 'I wouldn't call it strong, I would call it clear', he added.

The papal reserve and his spokesman's judgment were comprehensible enough. In the conflict in the Holy Land, the Roman Church's interests in establishing what Cardinal Sodano had called a 'realistic' 'harmony with the Islamic world' invited the keeping of a judicious silence where *convenienza* dictated. Jews complained about the references to them, in the presence of a pope, as 'enemies of God'. But such complaints could not have been expected to command sympathy from most Christians—as Muslim politicians in the Middle East know—when Christian faith is itself grounded in belief in the historic 'culpability' of the Jews. At the same time, when the Roman Church's support was being sought in the Middle East, Muslim and Arab diplomacy could set aside the fact that Christians equally with Jews are 'unbelievers', and 'Crusaders' to boot.

Nevertheless, Islam's judgment against the 'infidel' Christian faith is a judgment against which there is no appeal. Islam, therefore, cannot make the kinds of concession to Christian scruple which many Christians are ready to allow Islam, as an earlier chapter demonstrated. Nor need it make such concessions, being strong in its sense of the finality of its faith and the superiority of its values. Thus, despite Vatican efforts to establish a working 'harmony' with Islam for *convenienza*'s sake, it is Muslims who have remained more adept in the attempted instrumentalisation of each by the other.

It was again in the Holy Land that this was most clearly seen. When Yasser Arafat sought to defy an Israeli ban on his travelling from his ruined headquarters in Ramallah to Bethlehem in December 2001 for the purpose of attending Christmas Mass, he protested—with a sharp eye to Christian public opinion—that no one had the right to 'prevent us from fulfilling our duty to God'. This was a well-struck ecumenical pose; the Church's manoeuvres in quest of Islam's favour have been both less shrewd and less brazen. The Palestinian information minister, Yassir Abed Rabbo, gilded the Christian lily further: the Israeli government, he declared, wanted 'blood and tears instead of Christmas carols'. These were the same carols which in Saudi Arabia Christians were forbidden to sing.

Nevertheless, many Christians have been able to establish a bond of common interest with Muslims which is grounded in shared objections to Israel's command over the Holy Land, to Jewish rule over Jerusalem and even to the Jews themselves. Such common cause was demonstrated after some one hundred armed Palestinian militants chose Bethlehem's Church of the Nativity as a place of sanctuary in April 2000. The consequent siege of the church by the Israeli defence forces permitted Christians and Muslims to share a sense of wrong. Fatah-Tanzim and Hamas fighters, many of them with records of involvement in attacks upon civilians and bearing Kalashnikovs within the church, knew that a forcible entry by Jews into the fourth-century Christian shrine would have a disastrous impact. It would 'send a fatal image around the world', wrote an Italian journalist, fortuitously trapped inside the church. With the Palestinians firing from the roof of the adjacent convent and being fired at—Muslim against Jew and Jew against Muslim, in a Christian place—it was a 'trump card', he added.

This 'trump card' had been well played, as immediate statements from Rome showed. The Vatican's *Osservatore Romano* accused Israel, not the gunmen at the altar, of 'desecrating' the 'birthplace of Jesus'; it was Bethlehem's 'painful Calvary', declared the Pope, again hinting at a link between the sufferings of Christ and of the Palestinians at the hands of Jews. With the Israeli army encircling the church, the Arab media and Palestinian leaders—seizing the opportunity of this theological round-dance—joined their voices to those of the Christian world. Israelis, stated Yasser Arafat, were 'attacking churches and mosques', 'ruining' the first and 'burning' the second. The governor of Bethlehem, Muhammad al-Madani, asserted that the Israeli army was 'killing Palestinians inside the church'.

'Occupation of Bethlehem by Israel' was thus exacting a high moral price, a price higher than that paid by the armed fighters who had seized the Church of the Nativity in the first place. Sacrileges committed inside the church by the gunmen were attributed to the *force majeure* of the siege itself. The Holy Land seemed to be 'approaching apocalypse', *The Times* had declared. But the

Palestinian gunmen knew better what they were about. As their leading figures emerged from the church to face a 'deportation' brokered by the Vatican, one of them, Ibrahim Abayat—the Bethlehem commander of the al-Aqsa Martyrs' Brigade, wanted for a series of bombing and shooting attacks on civilians—announced that they were accepting exile to Rome 'for the sake of the church'.

The choice by Muslim fighters of a Christian shrine as a sanctuary from the aggressor-Jew—attracting the intercession of a Church seeking 'harmony' with the Muslim world—had been a deft move in a battle of arms and wits. It was also a mere episode in a long-term and universal struggle being waged by Islam with the 'unbeliever', whether Christian, Jew, Hindu or other. This struggle is not that of a 'religion of peace', but of a faith of deep devotion, of periods of passivity—not the same as peace—and of militant or warrior duties which require to be discharged in God's name. It is a struggle which Allah will not permit true faith to lose, and which 'unbelief' does not know how to win.

CHAPTER TEN

Against Illusion

T he Islamic advance and the upheavals it has provoked have been met in the non-Muslim world by a combination of lack of historical knowledge, naivete, misnaming of the foe as mere 'terrorists' or 'fanatics', divisions of interest—and therefore of policy—and violence. The naivetes included the belief that whenever 'freedom takes hold, terror will retreat', in President Bush's words in September 2003; or, at his second inaugural address in January 2005, that 'the best hope for peace' was the 'expansion of freedom in all the world'.

With this naivete was associated the notion that the 'democratisation' of Arab and Muslim regimes would promote such ideal. It was linked, for instance, to the proposition that an election in Iraq based on universal suffrage would offer an 'example to all in the Muslim world who desire freedom', as a US official put it in September 2003. Yet America has been constrained by its geopolitical interests to keep in place numbers of dictatorships and other unsavoury regimes. Moreover, in March 2004, a twenty-two-nation Arab League summit held in Tunisia was unable to make a collective commitment to 'democratic reforms' because of the refusal of some countries—unnamed, but including Saudi Arabia and Syria—even to include such words as 'democracy', 'parliament' and 'civil society' in a joint declaration. Dissenters at the summit insisted that 'Arab and Islamic values' should take precedence over all others.

Apart from seeing such initiatives as Western-inspired intrusions into the

Muslim world, the dissenters were—in their own terms—right. For there can
be no truck in authentic Islamic and Arab cultures with popular sovereignty,
independent parliaments, secular justice, an unimpeded plurality of competing parties, and the moral autonomy of the individual. The non-Muslim
world also cannot reasonably expect the will of a majority to prevail in often
artificial nations, some carved out on the map in geometrical lines by the colonial powers, and which are composed of rival ethnicities and traditional
authority systems.

In addition, Muslim and Arab emirs, sultans, sheikhs, kings and 'republican' autocrats—the latter of whom also aspire, in general, to quasi-regal,
dynastic rule—have usually been unable to brook true opposition. This was
particularly the case where they came to power by coups. Furthermore,
Islamic norms of rule predispose most in the Muslim world to expect only
limited forms of participation in the political process, even when something
akin to a democratic election is held. Political prisoners are held in almost
all Arab and Muslim countries. Not only military or factional paramilitary
dictatorships but also royal and civilian 'republican' regimes have
obstructed, or attempted to crush, whatever latent democratic aspirations
there might be in their countries. Or, where something like free elections
with a relatively unrestricted suffrage have taken place, they not infrequently brought further advances to, and even victories for, Islamist parties.
Alternatively, by rigging and other forms of manipulation, elections served
to entrench the authority of existing monarchs, tribal leaders, warlords and
so on. It also proved possible for a robed clerisy in Iran to rule with absolute
powers over a notional parliamentary system, by arrogating to itself the
right to disqualify candidates for election—including to the presidency—
and to veto parliament's legislation.

In the lesser Gulf states and Saudi Arabia, as in many Arab and Muslim
countries, political rights were in the grant of rulers to concede, to delay, to
restrict or to withhold entirely. Even where a 'democratic' extension of suffrage was conceded (by men) to women in Kuwait in April and May 2005, it
was made subject to an ambiguous condition—sufficiently vague to permit the
future curtailment of the right itself—that 'females abide by Islamic law'.
Moreover, elections themselves were often confined to consultative bodies, in
the authentic Islamic tradition, with power retained in the hands of ruling
families and clans, royal and other; in Saudi Arabia, the monarch chooses all
150 members of the consultative council. There might also be elections to
merely municipal bodies without real powers, as in Saudi Arabia in February
and April 2005; or to part-elected and part-appointed institutions without sov-

ereign authority. Dynastic succession itself could be by 'election', as in the United Arab Emirates.

Human and political rights, such as the rights of free expression and assembly and to form political parties, either did not exist in the Gulf sheikhdoms and Saudi Arabia—there were none allowed in Saudi Arabia—or existed only in shadow forms. Even token rights were routinely abused and objectors to the existing political dispensation, ranging from liberal intellectuals to Islamists, might be rounded up, as in Bahrain in October 2004, and in Saudi Arabia in October 2003 and March 2004. Also in Saudi Arabia, which does not even have a constitution and where, as mentioned earlier, non-Muslims cannot become citizens—for such is the lack of reciprocity between what Saudis expect of the non-Muslim world and what they are prepared to grant—fifteen peaceful anti-monarchical demonstrators, including two women, were sentenced in January 2005 to be lashed for their protests. Similarly, three 'democracy activists' who had called for genuine elections in Saudi Arabia, reform of the judiciary and a limitation upon the powers of the ruling family received jail terms of from six to nine years in May 2005. The arguments of the Saudi authorities against such protests and campaigns were both telling and again authentic: reforms had to be 'gradual' and not disturb the 'unity of the homeland'. Protesters, accused of 'creating political instability and sowing dissent', were described in March 2004 by the Saudi defence minister, Prince Sultan, as 'rebels against their fathers'.

In the pyramidal theocracy of Iran, political protesters have been routinely arrested in large numbers, as in 1999 and in June 2003, journalists have been jailed and dozens of liberal publications closed down. Not surprisingly, the ostensibly democratic parliamentary 'elections' of February 2004, as well as the presidential 'elections' of June 2005, saw the disqualification—by the clerics and Islamic jurists on the ruling (and unelected) Guardian Council— of 'moderate', 'liberal' and 'reformist' candidates by the thousand, together with the rigging of figures of turnout and results; the Council also has the power to reject the outcome of an election. At the same time, voting in Iranian elections has been described by the authorities as a 'religious duty' and boycotts of the polls pronounced to be 'religiously forbidden' and 'treason'.

In February 2004, the more than two thousand 'disqualified' parliamentary candidates included eighty existing parliamentarians. More than one-third of the Iranian parliament resigned in protest, and as in the presidential elections of June 2005 there was a high degree of abstentionism in the 'polls'. Two-thirds of the electorate in Teheran failed to vote in February 2004. Nevertheless, the turnout was described by Iranian state television as 'massive'—it was also called 'remarkable' by the government-supporting newspaper *Jomhuri Eslami*—while Iran's Supreme Leader called the event a 'national and Islamic epic in the true sense'. In March 2004, even attempts made by the then Iranian president, Mohammad Khatami, to reduce the powers of the Guardian Council were rejected—by the Guardian Council—as 'unconstitutional' and 'against Islam'.

In June 2005, after all but six of more than one thousand candidates—including all the women aspirants—had been 'disqualified' and with regime vigilantes present at polling-stations, the 'election' brought to office Teheran's 'hardline' mayor, Mahmoud Ahmadinejad. A former member of Iran's Revolutionary Guards, he was attributed with declaring, in reference to the 1979 ousting of the Shah by the followers of Ayatollah Khomeini, that 'we did not have a revolution in order to have democracy'. He was right. During his 'election campaign' he further declared that 'the wave of the Islamic revolution' would 'soon reach the entire world', and after his 'election victory' that 'the world must now bow down and respect the will of the Iranian nation'. 'The Iranian nation cannot be intimidated', he added as he took the oath of office; his new government, announced in August 2005, was composed of men—there were no women—who were mainly former military commanders or who had close links with Iran's security services.

In Iraq, 'democracy' was attempted to be introduced by the United States, but in effect at the point of a gun. It was accompanied, therefore, by continuous violence; obstacles were set in the path of America's political 'reconstruction' of Iraq by some of the European powers; and doubts and divisions grew in the US over whether it could, or should, maintain its military presence in the country. Above all, the process of 'democratisation' was beset by internal Iraqi forces whose divergent ends, and mutual hatreds, were not compatible with such process.

Indeed, the elements of the US plan to establish 'sovereign self-rule' in Iraq (under US suzerainty) were changed several times in an attempt to accommodate rival Iraqi interests. Eventually, this plan involved the serial setting-up of a 'governing council'—whose chairman, rotated monthly among the sectarian and sub-national groups represented on it, was killed by a suicide-bomber in May 2004—the creation of an 'interim national assembly' and the holding of a national election in January 2005. The election was conducted under a state of emergency, with parts of the country in armed insurrection. Most of the 20 per cent minority Sunni population, long accustomed to rule in Iraq and opposed to a poll which could not deliver victory to its interests, failed to vote and therefore gained only a handful of seats in the 'interim national assembly'. Conversely, most of the majority Shi'as had looked forward to, and gained, the advantages which a majoritarian-ruled national system would bring them.

At the same time, the (non-Arab, but mainly Muslim) Kurds, turning out in force in the north of the country where they were numerically dominant, had their long-standing claims to regional autonomy strengthened by the 'democratic' process itself. For its part, much of the Christian population, as earlier mentioned, was prevented by intimidation, including by Kurds, from voting; while in the oil-rich south, where a fiefdom of Iran and an Islamic sub-state had been in process of creation from the time of the US invasion, Islamic parties were easy 'electoral' victors, with secular democratic parties gaining only some 2 per cent of the vote. Others, especially militant Sunnis and Sad-damite loyalists backing the insurgency, were entirely opposed to the attempted reconstruction of the Iraqi polity to US prescription; while others again, with violent foreign Islamists also at large, denounced 'democracy' itself as alien to Islam.

Described euphemistically as having produced a 'fractured mandate', the January 2005 election was nevertheless seen by the US as part of a step-by-step process of new 'institution-building' by the occupying forces. Thereafter, it took almost three months of wrangling before the new 'interim government' was formed in April 2005, with a Kurdish president, a devout Shi'ite prime minister and a Sunni speaker of the assembly making a sectarian division of the political spoils. It was in this setting, with the insurgency continuing to rage and after further wrangling between Shi'as, Sunnis and Kurds over the balance of its composition, that a seventy-one member committee—one of whose Sunni representatives was gunned down in Baghdad in July 2005, and a Sunni adviser to the committee also assassinated—drew up a draft constitution for the 'new Iraq'.

It did not meet the American illusion that it might serve as a model for the wider 'democratisation of the Middle East'. Instead, so many and so divergent were the interests involved that the proposed constitution envisaged a state which was to be simultaneously not only 'republican, parliamentary, democratic, and federal' but also Islamic, and in which laws were expected to accord both with Islamic and democratic 'standards'. Moreover, amid the ruins of the tyrannical Ba'athist regime, this 'new' state-form was being attempted to be created in face of continuing violence, the influence of the Shi'ite clerisy, tribal and clan affiliations, Kurdish insistence upon regional autonomy, Sunni refusal to accept the political consequences of its minoritarian status and bitter Islamist hostility towards the 'infidel occupiers of Arab lands' and those seen as doing their bidding. A functioning democracy based on the free exercise of independent choice, and the subordination of religious and other loyalties to a secular, liberal-minded and non-denominational general, or national, will could not rest upon such unfavourable ground. Illusion believed, and seemingly needed to believe, that it could. The further notion that the 'democratic example' of Iraq would 'strike a blow at the heart of global terrorism'—as the British prime minister put it in January 2005—was even more naive.

Even Tunisia's 'moderate' regime with its self-proclaimed 'secularism' and 'democracy'—and policies of 'economic liberalisation'—was one of the most oppressive in the Arab world. In October 2004 its president, Zine el-Abidine ben Ali, gained a fourth term under its 'democratic' system with a '94.49' per cent popular mandate, compared with (a more successful) '99.4' per cent in 1999. Meanwhile, in 2002, Morocco's slowly incremental democratic reforms brought advances, not to American hopes of the universal spread of 'freedom', but to the fortunes of the Islamist Justice and Development party. Indeed, since 1987, the electoral process in many Muslim countries— including in Algeria, Bangladesh, Egypt, Kashmir, Kuwait, Lebanon, Pakistan and Turkey as well as in the Palestinian territories—has produced more Islamist gains then losses.

Thus Algeria, as earlier mentioned, was governed by the single party National Liberation Front, with army support and in effect under military rule, after having cancelled an Islamist victory at the polls. Its president, Abdelaziz Bouteflika, thereafter ruled by vote-rigging in a country where basic political rights were severely curtailed and human rights abused. Libya, which silenced internal opposition to President Ghaddafi by resort to repressive measures—and which, according to Amnesty International, tortured and executed political prisoners—sought in 2004 to combine such continuing form of rule with a seeming 'turn' to the West and the abandonment of its weapons programmes.

Syria, a 'secular' society under Ba'athist rule, changed its constitution to permit President Bashar al-Assad to succeed his father. Despite some 'lightening' of the 'political atmosphere rather than its institutions'—there were intermittent amnesties for political prisoners—it was a one-party nepotistic police-state, self-described as 'open-minded and tolerant', yet ruled under a state of emergency since December 1962. With some cultural but few political freedoms, its jails in 2005 contained hundreds—or, by other accounts, thousands—of political prisoners. Some of them had been held for two decades, and included both dissenting liberal intellectuals and Islamists. Its minority Kurdish population, of whom some 150,000 to 300,000 had been denied Syrian citizenship, was forbidden to form political parties or to publish newspapers in Kurdish. Moreover, pro-democracy activists have in familiar style been convicted of 'trying illegally to change the constitution', while in May 2005 the head of a Syrian human rights organisation was arrested only two months after President Assad had promised an Orwellian 'great leap in reform', a promise repeated by the ruling party in June 2005.

In Jordan, there was another Muslim variation upon the same undemocratic themes. With an ostensible parliamentary system, its monarch could nevertheless veto legislation, dismiss parliament itself, rule by decree and postpone 'elections', as was done in 2001. By manipulating the 'electoral' system, 'party' politicians (or tribal followers allied to the ruling Hashemite dynasty) were guaranteed domination in parliament, as in Kuwait in the case of the ruling royal al-Sabah clan, and in Egypt under President Mubarak's control. Advocates of a genuine democracy in Jordan were barred from participation in the political process, while to accuse officials of corruption could result in a conviction—in the style of Saudi Arabia or Syria—for 'insulting the dignity of the state'. Concessions to 'democratisation' in Jordan also took the form of the creation, announced in January 2005, of elective 'councils', again without effective powers, to 'oversee development' in the country.

In pro-American and US-backed Kuwait—where no political parties but only 'movements' were allowed—limited elections in July 2003 increased the strength of Islamists opposed to both political and economic liberalisation and in favour of the introduction of Sharia law, while liberal parties were almost extinguished. After the election (to the all-male parliament) the emir—who under the Kuwaiti constitution is unaccountable and above rebuke—appointed his brother as 'prime minister'. But in April and May 2005, as earlier mentioned, cosmetic or token changes brought about under US pressure led for the first time to the appointment of two women—one of them a member of the royal family—to its 'municipal council'; while in June 2005, against opposition by male lawmakers on the grounds that it was 'unconstitutional', a woman was appointed to Kuwait's cabinet. Her first speech in government was shouted down.

Across the Arab and Muslim worlds, many consistencies could be made out, even in European Muslim or proto-Muslim nations such as Albania, Bosnia or Kosovo. They made fallacious the proposition, or hope, that such countries were looking to the Jeffersonian and Westminster models of democracy as guides and inspirations, or could be brought by example to do so. Even in the miniature Muslim autocracy of the Maldives in the Indian Ocean,

opposition parties were disallowed and its president, Maumoon Abdul
Gayoom, 'won' his sixth successive five-year term in a 'referendum' in 2003. In
Muslim Brunei on the north coast of Borneo, which had been ruled by decree
under a state of emergency since 1962—a similar time to those in force in
Syria and Egypt—its sultan, Hassan Bolkiah, was both its ruler and its 'prime
minister'. He suspended the Legislative Council, all of whose members were
in any case appointed, in 1984; but reconvened it in September 2004, signing
into force a 'new constitution' that would allow for a partly-elected parliament
while leaving his own absolute powers unaltered. 'These changes', he warned
(in familiar style), 'have not been created to bring about chaos and trouble'.

Indeed, where in Muslim states there was the semblance of a 'democratic'
process, it was often hedged round with undemocratic limitations, either
restricting the franchise or the rights of assembly, organisation and criticism,
or all of them together. Where there were polls, malpractice often accompanied them. Such systems also rewarded loyalty to an existing ruler or regime;
or if the 'wrong' result was delivered, as in Algeria, the incumbent regime was
predisposed not to give way to it, or suspended the electoral process entirely.
Whatever the result, it rarely, if ever, gave sovereign authority to an elected or
partially elected legislature over the existing powers in the land. Often, too,
the polity—or what passed for such—was riven by sectarianisms which transcended any notion of general public obligation.

Moreover, superficially 'democratic' systems could be combined with various forms of autocratic absolutism which provoked Islamists to demand their
overthrow, as did Osama bin Laden in respect of the 'corrupt and oppressive'
Saudi regime in December 2004.

Authoritarian non-Muslim societies also demonstrate some of these features. But no other culture in modern times has shown Islam's and Arabism's
impressive adherence to their own deeply-rooted political traditions: above
all, those of resisting—by whatever means—genuine accountability to popular will, including in states with parliaments and other appurtenances of
modern rule, and even where a more plural political system might have
existed in the past.

Thus even in Lebanon—a Muslim-and-Christian nation, but from the
time of the 1975–1990 civil war until April 2005 reduced to a satrap of
Syria—President Emile Laboud in October 2004 had the country's constitution amended by parliament, with its pro-Syrian Muslim majority, in order to
maintain himself in power at Syria's behest for a further three years. He
formed a government composed entirely of pro-Syrian politicians, which by
February 2005 had resigned under the pressure of popular demands, led by

the Maronite Christian minority, for a restoration of the country's independence after a wave of revulsion had greeted the assassination of the anti-
Syrian former prime minister of Lebanon, Rafik Hariri. Damascus and its
clients in Beirut, bolstered by the 25,000-strong private militia of the Shi'ite
Lebanese Hezbollah movement—which is backed by both Syria and Iran—at
first sought to resist concessions of any substance. The Syrian army and intelligence services made new dispositions of its forces within the country, but by
the end of April 2005 Syria's troops—although allegedly not all its intelligence operatives—had left Lebanon after nearly thirty years of occupation.

Yet even after the Lebanese elections of May and June 2005—in which
anti-Syrian and pro-Syrian candidates, including those of Hezbollah, won in
their respective fiefdoms, but with an overall anti-Syrian victory—the old
complex political dispensation in essence remained in place. It was based upon
the sectarian and confessional, not democratic, considerations which had
determined the division of power after the 1975–1990 civil war, with the presidency of Lebanon 'reserved' to a Maronite Christian, the prime ministership
to a Sunni Muslim, the presidency of the chamber of deputies to a Shi'a and
religious sects allocated parliamentary seats according to their size. In 2005,
this division of spoils was again made. Moreover, Syria continued to exercise
influence in the country through the armed Hezbollah movement—which for
the first time entered the Lebanese government—through the Syrian intelligence services and through Palestinian organisations active in Lebanon's
twelve refugee camps, together with the help of Syria's allies in the Lebanese
political and police apparatuses.

In Egypt, ruled under emergency laws since 1967, President Mubarak
announced in January 2005, after twenty-three years in office, that in the (again
characteristic) interest of 'stability', and rejecting direct elections to his office,
he intended to seek a fifth six-year term. As in the past, this would be secured
through nomination by the ruling party—the 'National Democratic Party'—
and approval of the nomination by a 'parliament' in which his party had more
than 85 per cent of the seats. A month later, under US pressure—and after the
arrest (on a trumped-up charge of 'forgery') of Ayman Nour, the head of a
reformist movement challenging the Egyptian leader's continuous rule—
Mubarak appeared to change direction, asking Egypt's 'parliament' to alter the
constitution in order to 'permit' direct multi-party elections to the presidency.
Described by opponents as merely 'formal changes' and 'deception', the cunningly amended rules in effect gave a veto to the ruling party over who could
run against the incumbent. In September 2005, Mubarak was duly 're-elected'
with '88.6' percent of the vote. The poll was conducted under continuing
emergency rule, with outside observers denied access to monitor the election.

Here, too, there were thousands of political detainees, dissidents were attacked and arrested for taking part in 'unlicensed demonstrations' or 'endangering public peace', while the Muslim Brotherhood was outlawed and other Islamist parties were banned. Repressive police actions and the use of torture were combined, as in Syria, with intermittent releases of political prisoners, the abolition of only minor emergency regulations, and the again characteristic use of the vocabulary of 'reform', but not its substance. Thus, Mubarak had declared in March 2004 that 'nobody imagines that we can press a button and freedoms will arrive. If we completely open the door'—at which the Islamist wolf stands—'there will be chaos'; the opposite assertion to the American proposition that when 'freedom takes hold, terror will retreat'.

In Pakistan—ruled by the military for more than half of its years since becoming an independent state in 1947—political developments in 2002 and 2004 were also in accord with pattern. In October 2002, relatively free elections delivered the crucial border regions of Baluchistan and North-West Frontier Province not to democrats but to outright control by Islamists committed to uphold 'Islamic standards'. The introduction of Sharia law was approved in May 2003; and, among other things, the playing of music and singing in public were banned, and music-tapes were burned in a bonfire in Peshawar.

Differently, but also in accord with pattern, President Musharraf, who took power in Pakistan by coup in October 1999, won a five-year term as president in April 2002 in a rigged referendum in which he was the only candidate. In September 2004 he reneged on his promise, made in December 2003, to give up his command of the army and to return to civilian status. Instead, he decided to keep both his offices, with both houses of a pliant parliament—dominated by pro-military parties—approving a bill to permit it. The bill ran counter to the constitution; Musharraf himself signed it into law. In addition, it was announced in May 2005 that Musharraf would stand for 'election' in 2007 to a second five-year presidential term.

In the Palestinian Authority's system of rule, the possibility of forming viable political and other institutions was continuously undermined by Israeli action. Yet many of the Authority's undemocratic and anti-democratic features were again according to the underlying pattern. Nepotism, corruption, the absence of rule of law in its 'courts', the maintenance under Yasser Arafat of multiple security forces, or private armies, and his overriding of demands from within the Palestinian Authority for accountability and 'reform' were all familiar. So, too, was the appointment by Arafat of 'prime ministers' beholden to him. Yet all these features could coexist with a notionally 'democratic' electoral process, planted in ground not only ravaged by the Israeli occupation but by factional Palestinian loyalties. These latter could not be transcended by 'party politics' on the liberal democratic model, nor could such be expected.

After Arafat's death, leadership elections in December 2004 produced a successor chairman, Mahmoud Abbas, who, as one of Arafat's 'prime ministers', had earlier tried and failed to exert his authority over this morass. He attempted to do so again, and in effect declared the second Palestinian intifada at an end. But Arab-Israeli violence continued, if on a reduced scale. In February 2005, the Palestinian 'parliament'—which had last submitted to election in 1996—objected to the 'cabinet' presented to it for approval and forced changes in its composition; a modest token of progress. At the same time, lawless inter-factional Palestinian feuding and score-settling also continued. There was violence within the Palestinian 'security forces', which Abbas attempted to reorganise, including by opening their ranks to fighters from the militant groups and armed gangs; gunmen from his own Fatah faction even fired at his Ramallah compound in March 2005.

More significant, and now part of a familiar pattern in the Muslim world, was the outcome of local Palestinian elections in January and May 2005. Although the faltering Fatah movement held on, the elections led to advances in the occupied West Bank and Gaza for the growingly popular armed Islamists of Hamas. Their campaigns, notionally democratic but directed to the ultimate creation of an Islamist Palestinian state, were described by observers as 'well-organised political operations'.

The consequences of this progress by Hamas—one of whose spokesmen declared in April 2005 that 'we will not remove our finger from the trigger'—included the postponement by Abbas in June 2005 of the 'parliamentary elections' scheduled for the following month. In July 2005 he also invited Hamas and Islamic Jihad to join a new Palestinian 'national unity government'. Both refused, since the 'democratic process' was itself delivering victory to Palestinian Islamists on their own terms, while the 'disengagement' of Israel and withdrawal of its settlements from Gaza was hailed by Hamas militants as a victory for their 'armed struggle'; more, it marked the 'beginning of the end for Israel', according to Khaled Mashal, the Hamas political leader.

As in Iraq, so in presidential elections in Afghanistan in October 2004, the 'democratic process' was brought to the country after its (partial) conquest by US and other external forces. Also as in Iraq, voting was conducted in conditions of sectarian, clan, 'ethnic' and armed sub-national conflict, with a large protective US and NATO military presence. In Afghanistan, the rules of liberal democracy and of 'free and fair elections' were hoped to be grafted onto a society the writ of whose government in its capital did not extend far. It was also beholden to local power-brokers and to warlords with their own militias. Like the government itself, voters were therefore not free political agents and were not exercising—and again could not have been expected to exercise—their 'choices' in the unfettered 'privacy' of a truly democratic election. Again as in Iraq, and in many other parts of the Muslim world, they had extra-civic loyalties, in this case Pashtun, Tajik, Uzbek and other; some 80 per cent of the votes in October 2004 were thought to have been cast according to 'ethnic' identity.

Nevertheless, it continued to be ingenuously believed that the norms of Western democracy and the traditions and dictates of Islam could be reconciled. Thus, an 'Islamic Republic of Afghanistan'—like the neighbouring 'Islamic Republic of Pakistan'—was sought to be created under a constitution, agreed in January 2004, which formally protected human and civil rights. It also notionally established an independent judiciary and other separation of powers—in a country where the rule of law barely existed—and all in a form which was hoped to be consonant with Islamic prescription.

The nature of this dilemma was made apparent in October 2003 by a leader of one of Afghanistan's fledgling Islamic parties. 'Afghanistan is a Muslim country that wants freedom and peace', he declared, 'but never such a freedom or peace at the expense of Islam'. As in Iraq in January 2005, so in Afghanistan in October 2004, Islamist threats from a reviving Taliban movement did not deter millions of voters. But the outcome of the Afghan constituent assembly and of the process of 'democratisation' had again been according to pattern. It resulted in the acquiring by the (weak) president, Hamid Karzai, of near-dictatorial powers in the interests of creating order, the establishment of a parliament with limited authority, and concessions to regional strongmen demanding local autonomy; one of Afghanistan's leading warlords, Abdul Rashid Dostum, was even chosen by the president as his military chief of staff.

In essence, a non-democratic regime had been created by ostensibly democratic methods under a foreign aegis, and with little or no control vested in a nominally sovereign Afghan government over the 30,000 NATO and US troops in the country. Moreover, as the security situation deteriorated, parliamentary elections planned for June 2004 had to be repeatedly postponed on what were called 'technical' grounds. 'We don't want America, we don't want Karzai, we want Islam', demonstrators in Jalalabad shouted in May 2005, during protests over the desecration at Guantanamo of copies of the Koran.

In other Muslim countries there were some democratic forms, but they generally coexisted, as in Bangladesh, with growing oppression of minorities and infractions of civil rights, intensifying struggles (both open and denied) with an Islamism on the rise, political violence, and justifications of strong rule. Indeed, such rule was usually required—in a vicious circle of cause and effect—to repress the consequences of the very methods which strong rulers employed. In many Arab and Muslim countries the army therefore had to uphold the political system, whatever the form taken by its state institutions. In Pakistan, the role of the military, with its ranks divided between pro- and anti-Islamists, increased indifferently whether democratic practices were being observed in the country or not; whereas in Turkey, in a succession of coups, the army had sought to defend the nation's 'secular' tradition.

But the general tendency in most Arab and Muslim countries, again whatever the form of rule, was for the advance of Islamist movements. Where there were democratic, or quasi-democratic, processes they on balance served the Islamist interest; where there was repression, long-term Islamist prospects were also improved. Moreover, many Arab and Muslim regimes provided good ground for Islamist condemnation of them. In Indonesia—with its entrenched corruption, dictatorial political legacy and long-standing Islamist separatist insurrection—support for the minority Islamist Justice and Prosperity party increased significantly in elections in April 2004. 'For us', said its leader, 'politics is one of the ways to spread true Islam'.

In all these Muslim countries and many others, there was therefore no correlation between 'democracy', the march of 'freedom' and the retreat of Islamism. Malaysia, where ostensibly democratic elections took place in May 2004—under its new leader, the Islamic scholar Abdullah Ahmad Badawi— might be cited as a counter-example. There, victory was gained by 'moderate' Muslim parties over an Islamist party seeking to make Malaysia an Islamic state. But the outlines of an ominously familiar pattern were clear in Malaysia also. It included the steady Islamisation of a previously open multi-ethnic state, in which 40 per cent of the population was non-Muslim, diminishing toleration of opposition and respect for political rights, together with the erosion of judicial independence and the rule of law. Moreover, democratic forms yet again coexisted with the concentration of power in corrupt hands. The results of the polls in May 2004 could therefore be said to have been irrelevant to the deeper processes under way in the society as a whole. They were those of the gradual advance of Muslim expectations that Islam's ethical and social norms would be adhered to; expectations which in turn could only be held in check by authoritarian rule, and by the manipulation of the electoral system itself.

In other Muslim countries such as Somalia—where an agreement was made in January 2004 to form the country's first national government since the overthrow of a dictatorship in 1991 and the state's collapse—there were not even democratic forms at all. Indeed, there was no central rule but uncontrollable internal warfare. Yet here, too, the anti-democratic pattern was repeated in 'democracy's name. A 'government' was thus sought to be formed in October 2004 from the members of a 'parliament' chosen by traditional clan and sect leaders in pursuit of their own interests, as was in effect the case, despite a popular suffrage, in Afghanistan and Iraq also. However, so severe was the chaos created in Somalia by factional combat that such rule as there was had to be exercised from neighbouring Kenya by the Somali transitional federal 'government', a government opposed by Somali Islamists. In June 2005, 'president', 'prime minister' and 'cabinet' returned to Somalia in an attempt to rule a country in which, after nearly fifteen years of anarchy, the capital city and many provincial towns remained unsafe, and in which the warlords whose private militias continued to control them had been transmuted into 'lawmakers'. Indeed, so divided was the new Somali 'federal administration' that its two principal factions established their headquarters in different Somali cities.

Where Islamism had gained power, as in war-torn Sudan—the size of the continental United States—or in the northern states of federal Nigeria, the attempted imposition on non-Muslims of Sharia law also brought great strife. In Sudan, however, attempts to settle the more than twenty-year civil war between the Arabised Muslim north and 'rebels' in the ethnically-African Christian, Muslim and Animist south led in January 2005 to a 'peace deal' between them. It saw a new and precarious power-sharing settlement, whose price for the Islamist regime in Khartoum included the promise of 'democratic' elections within three years and the installation in July 2005 of the southern Christian leader, John Garang, as a vice-president. But only three weeks later, Garang was killed when his helicopter crashed near the Uganda-Sudan border.

The 'settlement' itself had been a rare outcome, produced by a seeming 'victory' over Islamism but at the cost of millions of lives. Commoner was Islamism's steady advance in conditions of strife. And the greater the strife, the greater the need for 'strong rulers' or military rule; and the greater the need for such rule the less the tolerance of opposition, and the more illusory the notion of a future of 'freedom' through a rolling process of 'democratisation' in Muslim and Arab lands. This was not least because, as we have seen, 'democratic' and 'parliamentary' forms proved compatible in Muslim states—where such forms existed—with absolutist, dynastic, military or clerical rule of every kind.

The unique Muslim exception to this was held to be Turkey, the relict of the Ottoman Empire. But here too, as earlier mentioned, its powerful army had for decades dictated terms to its civilian politicians through a National Security Council. In this case it was to defend Turkey's official 'secularism' from its foes, a 'secularism' established with the abolition of the caliphate in 1924 by Kemal Atatürk, Turkey's founder. Indeed, despite the formal reduction in August 2002 of the army's role in Turkey's affairs, as recently as 1997 it had procured the ousting of an Islamist government from office. Turkey had also been locked for decades in internal struggle with a separatist Kurdish movement, and had had recourse to harsh laws and practices against political dissenters. In addition, as a consequence of the wider Islamist advance, it saw a gradual increase in Muslim self-awareness and confidence among its population while at the same time it sought entry to the European Union. Moreover, its Justice and Development party, although tailoring its policies in government to the democratic and other requirements of 'Europe', had deep Islamic roots.

The Turkish government was therefore constrained to try to reconcile Muslim 'values, traditions and identity' with liberal democratic expectations of it on the part of the European Union's powers. Thus, familiar tensions existed in 'secular' Turkey as elsewhere in the Muslim world. They were manifested in 2005 in Turkish government proposals, rejected by the Turkish judiciary, which would have promoted an Islamic rather than a secular agenda. Furthermore, some of Turkey's more far-thinking Islamists themselves expressed 'pro-European' sympathies, on the ground that the protection of civil liberties under European human rights' provisions would give them greater freedom to promote the Islamist cause in Turkey.

Here, the nature of the American 'democratic illusion' was again made clear. Rights and liberties, especially those of a free electoral system, gave as much scope to Islamism as to other forces openly to pursue its ends. In some instances, as we have seen, this has led to the suppression of its parties, or to the rigging of election procedures and results in order to prevent such parties gaining ground. But if the American illusion could not survive examination of the nature of Muslim and Arab cultures and of Islamism's strengths, the *realpolitik* demanded of oil-rich and oil-dependent states alike was even less compatible with the ideal of a democratic world-order. In particular, the needs of the mainly non-Muslim and oil-hungry powers, led by the United States, imposed their own demands on the forms of government which could be permitted to the oil-rich Muslim states.

From the province of Aceh in Indonesian Sumatra to Algeria, from the states of the Arabian Gulf to the states of west Africa's Gulf of Guinea, there were natural resources upon which the well-being and material progress of much of the globe depended, or which required to be further exploited. In the Caspian states and the Caucasus, in Iran and Iraq, in Nigeria and Sudan, in Saudi Arabia and elsewhere, many varieties of instability, authoritarian rule, corruption and internal conflict therefore prevailed, and true democracy and liberty were necessarily at a premium.

The rich non-Muslim world accounts for four-fifths of the global consumption of oil. The United States alone spends some $100 million a day on the import of crude oil in order to fuel its levels of production and consumption, while gasoline demand alone amounts to some 10 million barrels a day. For its needs it takes one-quarter of the world's oil supplies, but itself possesses only some 3 per cent of the world's oil reserves, perhaps 60 per cent of which are in the Muslim states of the Gulf. It was thus not surprising that 'freedom' and 'peace' were rarely found in 'developing' nations which supplied the resources upon which the Great Powers depended—powers now joined by India and China as their economic strengths (and needs) grew greater.

The expectation that there could be 'genuine democracy' in Iraq, say, was unreal. For it was estimated to possess the world's second-largest crude oil reserves, perhaps one-tenth of the world's total or even more, and also some 100 trillion cubic feet of natural gas—and this at a time when, for example, Britain's gas and oil reserves were dwindling towards exhaustion. This 'balance of forces', unfavourable to the non-Muslim powers, spans the world, like other transnational phenomona associated with the Islamist advance. For example, China, short of natural resources, shared nuclear technology with Iran in exchange for oil. Japan for its part strengthened its alliance with the United States—to the length of sending 'non-combat' troops to Iraq—in order to help ensure the flow of oil to it, under American protection, from the Middle East.

The fates of the Muslim oil-possessing nations intimately affect almost every aspect of the non-Muslim world's economic life-expectancy and lifestyle. This was not merely reflected in the years of combat on foreign fields—oil and natural gas fields chief among them—but was expressed, almost by the minute, on the stock-exchanges of the world. Oil prices rose in 2004 with each major act of sabotage of Iraq's oil production system; fell immediately in June 2004 'on a wave of optimism' that the conflict in Iraq would 'ease'; rose in August 2004 with the 'knock-on effects' on retail prices of threats by the Iraqi Shi'ite cleric Moqtada al-Sadr to halt oil production in Basra, threats which were said to have 'rattled oil markets'. They rose to 'record highs' in September 2004 in the wake of similar 'rebel' threats against Nigerian oil facilities; and likewise rose immediately in December 2004 after al-Qaeda had attacked the Saudi interior ministry in Riyadh, triggering what stock-exchange reports called a 'jittery bump-up in prices'. Similarly, the death of Saudi Arabia's King Fahd in August 2005, nervousness over the possibility of sanctions being imposed upon Iran and refinery breakdowns in the US each had the effect of raising oil prices on the world market.

However, falls in prices in periods of relative peace also reduced the revenues of already-unstable regimes, as in Saudi Arabia. Yet, on balance, such states had a larger long-term interest in suppressing internal unrest than in maximising their oil profits, and were aided in this political choice by the needy Great Powers themselves, led by the United States, which benefit from cheap oil. In such circumstances, once more, there could be no reconciliation between 'freedom' and the 'retreat of terror'. For unfreedom, or a 'crackdown' on dissent and disorder, was seen by both sellers and purchasers as a prerequisite for the uninterrupted flow of oil and natural gas.

At the same time, the correlation between Western-supported authoritarian rule in oil-rich states and the Islamist advance has been unmistakable. The appeal of the Islamist cause in Muslim states—whether or not they possessed oil—which were held to be the corrupt clients of the 'infidel' world necessarily increased also. Clear, too, was the correlation between making modest, or fake, moves towards 'democratisation' and the growing impatience of the liberal minority in a Muslim or Arab country with such token measures. Moreover, for immobile regimes to take cosmetic measures in the hope of abating internal opposition, while drawing a halt to them before matters 'got out of control', was to walk a political tight-rope. Oppression was thus an easier and simpler option, as well as being in greater accord with traditions of rule in many oil-rich states. Nor was such repression objectionable to Western powers—despite their 'democratising' rhetoric—for the (short-term) benefits it brought, provided that repressive regimes did not threaten the non-Muslim world itself, as had seemed to be the case in Iraq. Thus, when President Abedelaziz Bouteflika of Algeria, with its great oil and gas reserves, announced in April 2004 that he needed another five-year term of oppressive rule in order to bring 'total stability' to the country, there were no audible protests from purchaser-nations.

In Iraq, intervention led to repeated attacks by Islamists and former Ba'athists against the country's oil wells, pipelines, and other oil facilities in north and south. These attacks damaged the Iraqi people's patrimony, but were carried out in order to inflict greater damage—if possible—on oil-dependent non-Muslim nations. Oil politics played a large part, too, in Kurdish demands for political autonomy in northern Iraq, since it would bring with it control of the Kirkuk oilfields; the Kurds also demanded an increased share in the national oil revenues, a familiar source of internal conflict in oil-rich states. Libya's 'turn' to the West in 2004 was also not all it seemed. It was driven less by a 'change of heart' than by Libya's desire—reciprocated by the United States, subordinating the 'democratic illusion' to its own interest—for billions of dollars of new investment in its economically crucial but declining oil sector, its main source of foreign earnings. And in return for the dropping of US sanctions against Libya, the position of US and other Western oil corporations in the country was, at least temporarily, secured. The absence in Libya of political liberties, and the abuse of elementary human rights, were not involved in this equation.

This was even more the case with Saudi Arabia. Access to its immense resources of oil at the best available prices—kept down (insofar as they could be) in the Western interest—was exchanged for US and Western support of an autocratic and dynastic regime, which was itself dependent on the sale of oil for 70 to 80 per cent of its revenues. Or, as the Saudi ambassador to the US, Prince Bandar bin Sultan, correctly expressed it in April 2004, 'oil prices and Saudi Arabia and American politics are intertwined'. And as al-Qaeda's attacks in the kingdom increased, the more-freedom-less-'terror' proposition was again overshadowed by the shared interest of the regime and of its principal supporter that the 'crack-down' approach should succeed.

In Saudi Arabia matters were also too complex, politically and culturally, for the American 'democratic illusion' to have much relevance. The regime and the country stood at the very fulcrum of the struggle between the Muslim and non-Muslim worlds. Saudi institutions and resources were the principal support of the Islamist cause in dozens of countries. Yet it was also the oil nation on which the non-Muslim world was most dependent. In sum, it was the very heart of Islam, yet its regime was reliant upon the protection of the 'Great Satan' itself. Indeed, al-Qaeda had right on its side—by its own lights— when it objected to such a regime. Thus in October 2004 Osama bin Laden called on Islamists to 'be active and prevent them [sc. 'America', 'the enemy'] from getting hold of our oil and concentrate your operations on it, in particular in Iraq and the Gulf'. 'The main driving reason behind the enemy's hegemony over our countries is to steal our oil', he added.

In August 2003, the last US military unit officially left the kingdom. It was a tactical withdrawal required by the Saudi regime as a concession to Islamism's demands for the removal of 'infidels' from sacred soil. But—in continuing protection of the regime—the US necessarily kept its forces near at hand elsewhere in the Gulf and, whether temporarily or permanently, in Iraq. Yet al-Qaeda attacks in Saudi Arabia, equally inevitably, did not abate.

Other oil-rich Gulf states shared many of the characteristics of Saudi Arabia. In the case of Dubai, it included professions of support for the non-Muslim powers, the provision of military facilities to the United States on its territory, and service as a crucial hub for the movements of Islamists and their funds. As with Saudi Arabia, the oil-dependent Western powers—again in their own interests—helped to sustain the other Gulf regimes, autocratic and feudal as they might be. The reasons were not far to seek; Qatar, for example, in which Shell, Total and Exxon Mobil were all heavily invested, has the world's third-largest reserves of natural gas.

Kept afloat on a sea of oil, like the royal absolutism of Saudi Arabia, was the clerical absolutism of Iran. In consequence, it had extensive commercial relations with oil-dependent non-Muslim nations, particularly in Europe. They were relations which enabled Teheran to proceed with its nuclear pro-gramme in a political and economic trade-off, in which both sides of this again anti-democratic equation had an interest. Indeed, Iran—OPEC's second-largest oil producer—and Syria made clear in 2004 their awareness of the Great Powers' vulnerability to pressures in which the latter's oil needs were involved. For example, Iran called on the US to lift economic sanctions, imposed on it in 1995, which prevented US companies investing or trading in its oil; Syria similarly warned the US in March 2004 not to impose sanctions upon it if American corporations active in the Syrian oil industry were to retain their contracts.

This form of interest tied America's hands in many countries. It therefore made hollow its public commitment to the principle of ending 'tyranny' in the world, and strengthened the case of Islamism in its conflicts both with the US and with the Arab and Muslim oil regimes upon which the non-Muslim world depended. Oil also accelerated the American search in 2004 for suitable bases and deep-water ports in the west African Gulf of Guinea, whose oil-rich (and therefore coup-ridden and authoritarian) regimes already supplied the US with some 15 per cent of its oil; the region had the potential to provide one-quarter in the coming decade.

The most powerful of the African states, Nigeria—the world's eighth-largest oil exporter and the fifth biggest source of US oil imports, but with some two-thirds of its 140 million people said to live on 'less than a dollar a day'—had a history of years of military misrule, abuse of human rights and the squandering of its resources, together with a Sharia-ruled Muslim north,

as we saw in a previous chapter. Between 2003 and 2005 it not only saw uprisings by poverty-stricken local populations, denied benefit from the nation's oil
riches, but the sabotage of oil installations in the Niger delta—the source of
nearly all the nation's output of some 2.3 million barrels per day. The 'democratic' process in the oil-rich south again followed close to the near-universal
pattern: that of postponed or rigged elections, rule by corrupt local power-
brokers, and the absence in the oil-region of elementary political rights.

The 'democratic illusion' was even more obviously so in the dictatorial
west African oil-states of Equatorial Guinea—said to have 'massive' oil
resources and where there was a failed coup in March 2004—and the Islamic
Republic of Mauritania. With its offshore oil reserves due to be 'exploited' for
the first time in 2006, a military coup overthrew the pro-American Mauritanian government in August 2005, and led to the immediate release of some
of the Islamists held in the fallen regime's jails. On the other side of the continent, more than two decades of civil war in southern Sudan from 1983—
most of Sudan's oil is in the south—had cost the lives of some two million
people, as earlier mentioned. The war had had much to do with the refusal of
the Arab Islamist government in Khartoum to countenance the southern
demand for a 50-50 share of oil revenues of some $3 billion a year—against
an offer of 5 per cent—and the north's fear of the south's secession. With
Chevron a major player in the Sudanese oil industry, the US also had its own
interests in the brokering of peace efforts in Sudan's internal conflicts. They
were efforts in which the 'democratic illusion' was again set aside in favour of
the politics of oil, and the potential of access to Sudan's still untapped
reserves.

Indeed, the US sought to maintain its presence, as it must, wherever there
was oil. It therefore made increasing efforts in 2004 and 2005 to keep a
watchful eye on the Malacca Straits between Malaysia and Singapore, in part
on behalf of its client Gulf state oil-producers; through these straits some ten
million barrrels of crude oil from the Gulf were estimated to pass each day.
In Indonesia Aceh's province, one of the nation's poorest regions but rich in
natural gas—and bitterly contested by government and Islamist forces—it was
equally logical that the military-backed regime in Jakarta had for almost three
decades fought to prevent the province falling to a Muslim separatist movement; a 'peace treaty' signed in August 2005 left thousands of Indonesian
troops and police still in the province.

On Palawan island in the Philippines, the Malampaya gas field with its 2.5
trillion cubic feet of gas contains the country's largest foreign investment project, led by a consortium of Western oil corporations including Shell and

Chevron. It was therefore again logical that Philippine and US troops should have conducted joint military exercises there in February 2004, which involved jointly fending off a mock-attack on the project by imaginary Islamist forces.

Together with huge reserves of natural gas, there were also estimated to be from 100 to 250 billion barrels of crude oil in the Caspian Sea and in the Central Asian nations which border Afghanistan, Iran and Russia; there were perhaps 130 billion barrels in Azerbaijan and Kazakhstan alone. The presence of these resources produced the familiar pattern of phenomena. Autocratic regimes presided over the local riches to their own benefit, and would not give way easily, or at all, to 'democratic' pressures. Competition between the Great Powers—in particular the United States, Russia and increasingly China—also intensified for the favour of these regimes, whatever their nature and whether they were oil-rich or not, in order to establish military bases in them, as in politically turbulent Kyrgyzstan and Uzbekistan. It was a competition both to guarantee access to the region's resources and to deny such access to rivals, as well as to provide staging-posts within easy striking distance of the battles with the Islamist advance in Central Asia and its neighbouring nations.

In Muslim Azerbaijan, corrupt familial rule by President Geidar Aliyev from the 1970s also involved the amendment of the constitution—as in Syria—in order that Aliyev's son, Ilham, might be appointed 'prime minister' in August 2003; he thereafter succeeded his father as president in October 2003. It again corresponded to the oil regime pattern. With its strategic geopolitical position on the Caspian, its immense oil reserves, the presence of Western oil corporations and its key oil pipeline—inaugurated in May 2005 to avoid Russian territory and Iran, reduce dependency on Middle Eastern oil, and pass through Georgia to Turkey and on to the US market—abuses of human rights and the absence of democratic institutions in Azerbaijan were to be expected. For such abuses were again perceived by the country's rulers and by oil-dependent Western nations as the necessary price to be paid for the security of the large corporate investments made in Azerbaijan's energy resources. Equally necessary, US military advisers helped train its army and 'special forces', while US military aid to the country as a 'strategic US ally' was increased in 2004; in June 2005, thousands of protesters took to the streets demanding 'freedom' and denouncing the 'robber government'. It was therefore again ground in which Islamism could prosper.

In Muslim-majority Kazakhstan, the family members of President Nursultan Nazarbaev, who by 2005 had ruled for sixteen years, controlled the oil economy—with its large off-shore oil-reserves at Kashagan, for example, still to be explored—supervised the state-owned news media and ran their own political party. In September 2004, with a gradually burgeoning Islamist movement, the country also held falsified 'elections' to its largely powerless 'parliament', again according to pattern. Also according to pattern, the United States further developed its military ties and other relations with Kazakhstan in 2003 and 2004; and a deal between the autocracy and a consortium of Western oil firms, including Chevron Texaco and Exxon Mobil, was signed in February 2004. Natural gas-rich and majority-Muslim Turkmenistan—the starting-point of a projected $3 billion pipeline through Afghanistan and Pakistan to the Western market—had similarly been ruled with an iron hand, and by decree, since 1985 by President Saparmurat Niyazov who has tolerated no dissent in the country. Despite this—or because of it—he, too, gained the support in 2004 of the United States for his regime's aims to 'bring stability to the region'.

This was now accepted code for the need in oil-rich areas of the world—and again whether individual nations in the midst of such regions were themselves oil-rich or not—to face down political challenges, but often at the cost of provoking them further. Even in oil-poor Muslim-majority Kyrgyzstan—on China's border, home to both Russian and US bases and also an Islamist refuge—regional contention for resources and the consequent absence of genuine political freedoms provoked upheaval in the country. In March 2005, the once 'liberal' but increasingly repressive family regime of Askar Akayev was swept away in a wave of popular protest. It saw the storming of government buildings, mass looting and the freeing of political prisoners from Kyrgyz jails, followed by a 'landslide electoral victory' in July 2005 by Akayev's successor, Kurmanbek Bakiyev. However, after these events, it was being said that 'little or nothing' had changed.

Similarly, in May 2005, strategically well-placed Uzbekistan's authoritarian and corrupt 'secular' regime, led since late Soviet times by Islam Karimov, put down a bloody uprising during which some two thousand political prisoners, many of them Islamists, were said to have been freed. Earlier closely supported by the United States—but with occasional protest at the practices of its regime—Uzbekistan had signed a 'partnership agreement' with Washington in 2002, permitting it a military base in Karshi-Khanabad, ninety miles from the Afghan border. The US had also helped fund Uzbek security forces despite acknowledging their use of torture against the regime's detainees.

At the same time, Uzbekistan's Islamist movement was said to be Wahhabi-influenced, to be 'linked to al-Qaeda' and to be aided by outside Islamist groups such as the already-mentioned Hizb ut-Tahrir or 'Party of Liberation'. The Uzbek movement not only fought alongside the Taliban and continued to be active in nearby Afghanistan, but mounted attacks on the US and Israeli embassies in the Uzbek capital, Tashkent, in July 2004. Kazakh Islamists who were said to have been involved in these attacks were put on trial in the southern Kazakh city of Taraz in March 2005. Uzbek Islamists also carried out bombings in January 2005 in Dushanbe, the capital of neighbouring Tajikistan, whose previously-mentioned civil war between Islamists and the 'secular' government's forces from 1992 to 1997 had claimed tens of thousands lives. Tajikistan was yet another autocracy in which 'elections' were rigged and little dissent tolerated.

More important, China's industrial advance and oil needs—it became a net oil importer in 1993, and was the world's second-largest oil consumer after the United States—also made it an increasingly significant player in the oil-politics of the area, not least because of the long-standing pressures upon it of a violent Muslim separatist movement in its own oil-rich western province of Xinjiang. In November 2004, it concluded a 30-year oil and gas deal with Iran, and openly backed the embattled Karimov in Uzbekistan during his repression of the uprising of May 2005. There was much at stake in these intensifying struggles for Great Power influence over an unstable region; and in the ebb and flow of it, the US was ordered by Uzbekistan in July 2005 to close its base at Karshi-Khanbad.

The combination of a dependent but armed US presence in Central Asia, oppressive local regimes and rivalrous American, Chinese and Russian support for such regimes again provided the ground both for political turmoil and for the Islamist advance—the very advance against which these regimes were pitted in the first place. Even the need of the US to protect the safety of the earlier-mentioned pipeline bringing natural gas from Azerbaijan to the Caspian, and across Georgia from the Caucasus to the Black Sea, could be said to have played its part in the 'velvet revolution' which ousted Eduard Shevardnadze from the Georgian presidency in November 2003. He was replaced by the pro-American Mikhail Saakashvili. At the same time, US military assistance was provided to train and equip Georgia's border guards. With its military base at Krtsanisi, the US was not surprisingly described by the new Georgian leadership in November 2003 as having 'done a lot for our country', while US involvements in the region deepened. But this was again an American strategic necessity, given Georgia's proximity to the Middle East, Turkey and Russia.

Moreover, the US, now better placed in Georgia than under its previous regime, had its own interests (and hand) in the ultimatum given to Russia in March 2005 by the Georgian government to remove its two military bases from the country; in May 2005, the Russians agreed to a 'phased withdrawal' of its forces by 2008. An equal object of contention, the oil port of Batumi in the breakaway Georgian province of Adzharia on the Turkish border—from where up to 200,000 barrels a day of crude oil and petroleum products from Kazakhstan and Turkmenistan are shipped—was likewise secured in May 2004 after a successful trial of strength between Georgian troops, some trained by US forces, and Adzharia's rebel leader.

Oil and the siphoning-off of oil revenues by Muslim-dominated Chechnya's first rebel president, Dzhokhar Dudayev, was also a major factor in the Russian army's invasion in December 1994 of the province, across which pipelines pass from the Caspian. In subsequent years of brutal war in Chechnya, which had itself formerly been an oil-producer, Chechen separatists—who, as we saw, had declared a jihad against Moscow—were gradually joined by Islamists from far afield, including Wahhabi-inspired Saudis and former fighters with the Taliban in Afghanistan. In the war, tens of thousands of civilians and soldiers died. According to pattern once more, sham 'democratic' elections, held under martial law, delivered '80 per cent' turnouts and 'victories' in the province for Russian placemen, including a former Muslim cleric. There were gross human rights' violations, assassinations and 'disappearances', with the conflict also affecting the neighbouring provinces of Ingushetia, Muslim-majority Dagestan and North Ossetia. The war ravaged the entire area, keeping some 100,000 Russian troops pinned down in Chechnya alone. But a Russian defeat would have left Islamists astride a principal oil route from Central Asia to the Black Sea.

The politics of oil were inevitably a greater determinant of the strategies of an oil-dependent United States than of an oil-rich Russia. But defenders of US foreign policy found many other grounds for supporting these strategies. Chief among them were the increasing scale and reach of support—financial and logistical, covert or poorly-concealed—for 'terror groups'. It was support, as has been mentioned, which was provided not only by the enemies of the US but by some of its notional allies in the Muslim and Arab worlds. The latter ran with the hare and hunted with the hounds, and included Saudi Arabia, Pakistan, Yemen, Jordan and several Gulf states. They co-operated in their own interests with US efforts, but also provided sustenance and encouragement in numerous ways to Islamism and Islamist groups. This support was provided through state bodies and officials, by para-state agencies such as 'charities', or by powerful individuals acting in a 'private' capacity. Blame might be attributed to 'rogue elements', as in Pakistan, but their activities were often known and connived at.

There were more direct forms of support for 'terror'. Saudis and Yemenis, Algerians, Moroccans and Tunisians, together with the citizens or nationals of many other Arab and Muslim countries from Mauritania in west Africa to Malaysia in south-east Asia, and from Syria to Somalia, constituted the cadres and activists of Islamism from one end of the world to the other. Some of these countries' authorities, again knowingly, gave them free passage to and fro. Other fighters passed 'unofficially' across their borders—as in the case of al-Qaeda operatives moving in and out of Iran—or acted in clandestinity where local Muslim and Arab regimes were themselves hostile to the Islamist threat.

Arab banks based in the Gulf states, in Jordan, in Saudi Arabia and Syria, for example, also provided conduits through their international branches for 'terror financing'. Syria's authorities, in particular the Syrian intelligence services, aided the passage of Islamists across its porous borders while simultaneously making the claim (as in May 2005) that it had detained 'many hundreds' of foreign *mujahideen* trying to enter Iraq. Among many others, fighters from Lebanon, home to Iranian-financed Hezbollah, were enabled to reach Iraq through Syria and to return. Likewise, Egyptian authorities at various times and places controlled, turned a blind eye to, or helped prevent tunnelling activities and the smuggling of weapons and fighters into Gaza for Hamas and for the Palestinian Authority. Simultaneously, the Egyptian state sought to play the role of peace-broker in the Palestinian-Israeli conflict, as well as collaborating with the US against 'terror'—which was a threat to itself—in return for Washington's large financial subventions.

The intricacies of Syria's positions were similar, their net effect much the same. It provided a home and logistical support to Islamist organisations at war with Israel, while 'cooperating' with the US in providing information on al-Qaeda. That is, it gave tokens of support, sometimes of substance, to the United States, and ostensibly sought better relations with it. But it coupled this with actions beneficial to Islamism's assaults on the non-Muslim world, despite the longer-term threat of Islamism to its own regime. Many of these actions were therefore incoherent. Syria had little or nothing to gain from the collapse of post-Saddam Iraq into chaos, yet, as stated, it facilitated the movement of Islamists, including Syrian nationals, together with their *matériel* and funds, into Iraq. It provided haven to members of the fallen Saddam regime and their funds, was alleged have taken in some of the regime's weapons, and in February 2005 the Syrian intelligence services were even accused (by a Syrian officer captured in Iraq) of having helped to train and equip Iraqi insurgents, its decapitators included. But also in February 2005, Damascus handed over to Baghdad thirty wanted former Ba'ath Party officials—including Saddam Hussein's half-brother—who had taken refuge in (fellow-Ba'athist) Syria.

In the Gulf, the United Arab Emirates—which had been one of only three governments, along with Pakistan and Saudi Arabia, to have recognised the Afghan Taliban regime—pursued policies of similar complexity. They demonstrated an openness to 'modernisation' and to increasing commercial relations with the non-Muslim world, but without 'democratisation'. It had close trading and other links with Iran; and tolerated the passage of Islamists en route to and from the planning and carrying out of attacks. Thirteen of the nineteen hijackers of 9/11 were said to have flown from Dubai to the US. Dubai was also a transit-point in the movement of funds and weapons to Islamists, and even in the smuggling of nuclear equipment.

Qatar similarly combined acceptance of US military bases in the sheikhdom, and the making of deals with Western oil giants, with service as a hub for Islamism's funds and personnel. In addition, payments were made to al-Qaeda from 2003—the agreement was renewed in March 2005—of millions of dollars in order to buy off attacks against Qatar. 'We are not the only ones doing it', a Qatari official in Doha laconically told *The Times* in May 2005. Qatar provided sanctuary to numerous Islamists, including the Chechen leader, Zelimkhan Yandarbiyev, until he was assassinated in Qatar in February 2004. It was also hospitable to the leader of Algeria's Islamic Salvation Front as well as to leaders of Hamas, for whom it provided a secure refuge. 'Thank God I have freedom of movement', declared the latter's Khaled Mashal, after moving back and forth between Syria and Qatar in May 2003, for example. At the same time, Qatar claimed in February 2004 to be 'at the forefront of the fight against terrorism'.

Such type of 'combined' policy offered more support than opposition to Islamism, provided that the latter's energies were primarily directed against the non-Muslim world, and not against the local regime or its allies. This was most evident in the policies of Saudi Arabia. But such policies did not prevent assaults both upon 'infidels' in the country and upon the kingdom's institutions by al-Qaeda, which was said to have 'infiltrated' the Saudi security services, national guard and other agencies. Nevertheless, these attacks did not end the kingdom's 'twin-track' approach to the advance of Islamism in the world.

For the 'infidel' was inevitably more alien to Saudi culture and tradition than was the Islamist, whatever the methods the latter might use. As the home of Islam's holiest places, Saudi Arabia's stances were not capable of being abandoned, or even tempered to any significant degree by US pressures, despite the former's need of the latter for its own protection. In the face of such complexity, US diplomacy was inevitably leaden-footed. During the last decades, it had faced a Saudi regime which in its own interests—but ultimately to the risk of the regime itself—had permitted 'infidels' to set up military bases in the kingdom. In the interests both of itself and the US, it had cooperated with the US in the tracking down of members of al-Qaeda and its associated groups. But since the mid-1970s, according to some estimates based on Saudi official publications, it had channelled over $70 billion in 'charitable' funds to Wahhabi institutions across the world, from Bonn in Germany to Bosnia and Bangladesh, and from Michigan to Mogadishu in Somalia. Its funds reached Afghanistan and Pakistan, and even war-torn Aceh in Indonesia. Half of the budget of Hamas was said to have come from Saudi Arabia, and similar support was given to the Palestinian intifadas and Palestinian suicide-bombers. Despite strenuous denials, Saudi individuals linked to its intelligence service also appeared to have aided the 9/11 hijackers, of whom fifteen—as already mentioned—were Saudis. Indeed, Saudi nationals were prominent among Islamism's fighters; more than one in six of the detainees in Guantanamo were Saudis.

Yemeni nationals and those with familial roots in the country also played a large role in Islamism's progress. They included Osama bin Laden himself, Abu Bakr Bashir, Ramzi bin al-Shibh—a 9/11 plotter—and Islamists active in the US. Yemen was also the site of the bombing of the USS *Cole* in October 2000. But it too pursued a many-sided policy. For many years it tolerated the activities of Islamists until it was itself threatened—or seemingly threatened—by them. Yemen gave some assistance to the US in the 'hunt for al-Qaeda'; but also turned a blind eye to, or was unable to control, the movement of explosives and even SAM missiles in and out of the country. At the same time, it both imprisoned and killed Islamist 'rebels' in the country, while allowing others to escape, including from its jails, as noted in an earlier chapter.

There was no power on earth which could have hoped permanently to master such wiles and stratagems, whether practised in Pakistan or Syria, or by Palestinians, Qataris or Saudis. However, it could be said to have been Shi'ite Iran—a foe of Sunni Saudi Arabia—which led the way in the outmanoeuvring of the non-Muslim world, whether in the matter of the advance of its nuclear programme or in its support for Islamism's attacks. Pursuing familiar obfuscatory policies, it claimed in June 2003 to have 'several' leading al-Qaeda members 'in captivity', under 'house arrest' or 'waiting to stand trial'. Refusing to disclose their identity, Iran was instead accused of 'protecting' them. Yet in October 2003, the Iranian president also declared that Iran would 'never support them [sc. 'terrorists']', and that they would have 'no place in our country'; it 'might' even be ready to extradite them to 'friendly'—which was to say non-'infidel'—countries. In July 2004, Iran further claimed to have arrested and repatriated 'hundreds' of suspected al-Qaeda members, and to have 'dismantled' al-Qaeda cells in Iran. Nevertheless, it was asserted by the Arabic daily newspaper *Asharq al-Awsat* in December 2004 that Iran was 'sheltering' 'several hundred' al-Qaeda members at Revolutionary Guard facilities in the country.

Not in doubt was Iran's implication, as paymaster and organiser, in attacks carried out by a variety of Islamist organisations in many countries, from Argentina in July 1994 to suicide-bombings in Israel during the following decade. Both the Saudis and the Americans also accused Iran of being behind attacks in Saudi Arabia in 2003 and 2004. And like other Muslim nations it permitted the passage of Islamists to and fro across its borders, allegedly including nine of the 9/11 hijackers—acknowledged as a 'possibility' by Iran itself in July 2004—as well as to and from training-camps in neighbouring Afghanistan. On the admission in December 2003 of one of the participants, Iran was also involved in the suicide-attacks by Islamists in Istanbul in November 2003, as well as in Iraq after the US invasion of the country.

Yet all this too was unsurprising. The struggles of faith against the 'infidel' world have almost everywhere called upon Muslim and Arab nations, governments, organisations, groups and individuals to demonstrate where their deepest loyalties lie. Bosnian 'charities' diverted resources to violent Islamist use; Turkey served as a staging-post for Islamist operatives in movement, while Turks of Chechen origin channelled funds to their brethren fighting the Russians in the Caucasus. Jemaah Islamiyah throughout south-east Asia similarly depended upon funds and recruits drawn from a dozen countries in the region and beyond, including (so it was said in July 2004) from Afghanistan and Pakistan.

The ramifications of support for the Islamist cause have been very wide. Funds were raised for al-Qaeda in the west African state of Liberia through diamond-trading; one of the leading figures in al-Qaeda, Abu Hafs, was a Mauritanian; the failed Muslim state of Somalia served as a base for al-Qaeda attacks in Kenya. Similarly, Sudan provided refuge to bin Laden in the 1990s, offices of Hamas and Islamic Jihad were set up in Khartoum, Sudanese 'charitable' funds were reported to have reached as far as Missouri, and there were Sudanese fighters in Iraq.

Of the ostensible allies of the US, it was Pakistan whose role in relation to Islamism was again among the most ambiguous. It was described as 'staunch' and 'courageous' in its 'pursuit of al-Qaeda leaders'. But there continued to be Islamist camps on its soil, including near its capital Islamabad. There, Islamists from countries as diverse as China and Turkey were said to have received training, while 'charities' funding Islamist action continued their distributions of resources largely undisturbed. At the same time, the Pakistani army harried the forces of the Taliban operating on its borders with Afghanistan, yet significant numbers of its intelligence operatives, officer corps and police—who between them constituted a parallel state apparatus— remained more sympathetic to the Islamist movement in the region than to its opponents; in 2005, Pakistan was being increasingly blamed for failing to stop insurgents crossing into south and south-east Afghanistan and even for 'encouraging them on their way'.

Against such ambivalences there was no effective weapon. Nor could a single power, whether the United States or any other, hope to master the multiplicity of forces—of faith, funds, weapons and helping hands—increasingly ranged against the non-Muslim world. Moreover, in the latter's own backyards were often to be found Islamist bases, some serving as temporary way-stations and refuges, and others as more permanent sources of assistance to a near-worldwide cause.

In many European countries, inciters to jihad and recruiters of jihadists, procurers of false or stolen documents and furnishers of funds and arms found scope for their activities. With links to Islamist movements from Afghanistan to Algeria and Malaysia to Morocco, there were cells of activists in Belgium, France, Germany—also the focus in Europe of the Muslim Brotherhood— Italy, the Netherlands, Spain, Sweden, Switzerland and the United Kingdom, among other European nations. There was also continual movement of such activists in and out of these countries and across their borders.

In Belgium, nationals of Egypt, Jordan and Morocco and Palestinians were among those apprehended, as in June 2004. In France, Maghrebian Islamists were active and often well-ensconced in diaspora life. In Germany, nationals from the Maghreb, Egypt, Iraq, Jordan, the Palestinian territories, Bulgaria and Turkey were among Islamists arrested between 2003 and 2005 during raids in Augsburg, Bonn, Frankfurt, Hamburg, Ulm and other cities. In the Netherlands, detainees came from the Maghreb, Syria, Turkey and elsewhere.

With its 7,600 kilometres of largely unpoliced coastline, already referred to, Italy was an easy point of entry to Europe and served as a principal focus of Islamist organisation and movement, sometimes aided both by the mafia and by the far-'left'. Maghrebians, Egyptians, Palestinians and others were arrested (and often released) in raids in Cremona, Florence, Genoa, Milan, Naples, Perugia, Prato, Siena, Turin and other cities. In Spain, Moroccans and Moroccan-born Spaniards, and other Maghrebians, were among the Islamists under surveillance or arrested. In Switzerland, Yemenis were detained in August 2004 for alleged involvement in the attack on the USS *Cole* in October 2000 and in attacks in Riyadh in May 2003. In the United Kingdom, many members of Islamist organisations—including groups active as far afield as Uzbekistan, Pakistan and the United States—found refuge, sources of recruitment, funds and the means of acquiring false documents, while those detained (and released) included suspects from Algeria, Egypt, Jordan, Libya and Syria. The 'twentieth hijacker', Zacarias Moussaoui, had earlier lived in London for nine years; other foreign Islamists wanted by third countries were found to be living, or at some time to have lived, in Britain. Indeed, not only other European countries such as France but even Muslim nations, such as Pakistan and Saudi Arabia, complained—however hypocritically—at the numbers of Islamists, many wanted in the complainants' countries, who had found 'shelter' or 'operated with impunity' in Britain.

The reach of the connections of individuals picked up in non-Muslim states was often bewildering. It outdid the reach of those who would stop them, even without taking into account the laxities, obstructions and failures of co-operation detailed in an earlier chapter. Examples of this 'reach' were many. Thus, a Caribbean-born French citizen with links to the Kashmiri Islamist group Lashkar e-Taiba ('Army of the Pure') was arrested in Australia in October 2003. In Gemany, in November 2003, an Algerian was arrested in Hamburg on an Italian warrant for organising the recruitment of fighters for Iraq. In the Netherlands, the assassin of Theo van Gogh in November 2004 was a Dutch-Moroccan who belonged to a militant network with links in Belgium, Portugal and Spain; the Syrian 'spiritual' leader of the network had himself earlier sought 'asylum' in Germany. Several of the same group had been trained in Pakistani camps. It was a chain of connections involving at least eight countries. Similarly, in March 2005, an Algerian-born French Islamist jailed for ten years for plotting to blow up the US embassy in Paris had lived in Britain, Germany and Pakistan, had trained at al-Qaeda camps in Afghanistan, was arrested in Dubai and had contacts in Belgium, the Netherlands and Spain—a ten-country link. Again, the attackers in the 'successful' and in the failed London bombings included British-born Pakistanis from Yorkshire, an Anglo-Jamaican Muslim convert, an Ethiopian who had assumed a Somali identity in order to obtain refuge and subsequently citizenship in

Britain, and who had previously lived in Italy, and a naturalised 'Briton' from Eritrea who was said to have spent time in Saudi Arabia.

In Poland, an arrested Algerian suspect was carrying a British passport. In August 2003, Kurdish forces in Iraq arrested a Tunisian carrying an Italian passport who was attempting to cross the border from Iran. In March 2004, Islamist fighters captured by Pakistani paramilitary police on the Afghan border included Uzbeks, 'Arabs', Chechens and ethnic Uighurs from Muslim western China's Xinjiang province. In Spain, also in March 2004, a Moroccan-born Frenchman arrested in connection with the Madrid bombings was said to have previously been in Britain, Iran and Turkey. Again, one of the accomplices of the Turkish Islamists who blew up a synagogue in Istanbul in November 2003 had links with Iran, had received military and explosives training in Pakistan and had fought in Bosnia and Chechnya.

Likewise in Egypt, in September 2003, twenty-three arrested Islamists allegedly planning to enter Iraq included individuals from Bangladesh, Indonesia, Malaysia and Turkey, as well as Egypt, while in May 2004 an asylum-seeker from Yemen who had settled in the British city of Sheffield died in the suicide-bombing of a US military checkpoint in Iraq. Almost every significant blow struck by members of Islamist networks has disclosed similar transnational, and even transcontinental, connections. Abdulaziz al-Muqrin, al-Qaeda's leader in Saudi Arabia—shot dead in an 'encounter' in Riyadh in June 2004—trained in Afghanistan, had fought in Algeria and in the 1992–1995 war in Bosnia and had been a member of a group which had attempted to assassinate President Mubarak of Egypt in Ethiopia in 1995, a six-country link.

There were equally far-reaching transfers of armaments of many kinds to Arab and Muslim nations and Islamist groups. Some were carried out by state and para-state bodies, others by arms' traders and often through a 'black market' in weapons. These transfers involved everything from small arms and night-vision goggles to missile technology and the means, often 'dual use', for the production of chemical weapons and nuclear devices. These transfers were conducted by China, North Korea, Pakistan and Russia among other nations, while 'black market' trading involved both Muslims and non-Muslims, and included nationals or citizens of countries from Kyrgyzstan to Sri Lanka and Switzerland to Armenia. Western powers, including the United States, and Western corporations acting with or without the knowledge of their governments were also co-responsible for building up the military capacities of the foes of the non-Muslim world. It was a global trade which could involve exchanges of know-how and hardware as well as onward transfers to third countries of acquired knowledge, materials and weapons, as in the 'triangular trade' between China, Pakistan and Libya.

China was a major player in these transactions. It transferred nuclear and missile technology to Pakistan—which in turn received nuclear warhead designs from China—and made the same technology available to Iran, sometimes as a *quid pro quo* for earlier-mentioned oil deals. China also assisted in domestic Iranian uranium-extraction processes. In addition, it provided Silk-worm missiles to the Saddam regime and gave assistance to Saudi Arabia in missile production, a deal itself said to have been brokered by Pakistan. Iran in turn helped Libya with its missile programme and sold arms to Syria.

North Korea, for its part, aided Iran's ballistic missile and nuclear programme—the latter begun under the rule of the Shah with US encouragement and help; Iran's first nuclear engineers were trained at MIT. North Korea was also said to have provided Syria, Libya, Egypt and Pakistan with missiles and missile designs, in Pakistan's case in exchange for the latter's centrifuge technology. It was alleged, too, to have supplied Libya with uranium hexafluoride, said to be of Pakistani origin; and Yemen with missiles and related equipment. In January and March 2004, it was reported that North Korea, as well as Pakistan, had agreed to share missile technology with Nigeria.

Pakistan exceeded even North Korea in its proliferation activities. In alleged 'black market' deals in the 1980s and 1990s, often made with the aid of middle-men and conducted by Abdul Qadeer Khan, the Pakistani nuclear scientist, nuclear know-how, technology and materials were transferred to Iran, North Korea, and Libya among other countries, as well as to private corporations. According to Iran, Saudi Arabia—which had itself helped to finance the Pakistani nuclear programme—was, in turn, also a beneficiary of these transfers.

Many contested the 'black market' nature of Pakistan's actions. Equipment and materials were said to have been transported, at least in part, in government cargo planes, as well as with the knowledge—according to Khan himself—of leading members of the Pakistani military and its para-state apparatus. In what appeared to be a charade, Khan made a detailed 'confession' of his activities in February 2004, seeking 'mercy', and was duly 'pardoned' by President Musharraf. The transfers by Pakistan to Iran between 1988 and 1991 were also alleged to have been authorised at the time by Pakistan's pro-Islamist chief of army staff, General Mirza Islam Beg. Although he denied that this was so, Beg declared his belief in January 2004 that an alliance between Pakistan, Iran and Afghanistan was destined to become the 'core of the Muslim world'.

In this cat's cradle of relationships, the United States could not therefore expect more of Pakistan than an ambivalent response to the former's geopolitical needs and military problems. This was not least since the United States—together with Pakistan—had itself backed the Taliban in the Afghan war with Russia. Indeed, Pakistan could be said to have done as much as might reasonably have been asked of an 'Islamic Republic' in a period of growing conflict between the Muslim and 'infidel' non-Muslim worlds.

Russia's military and technological aid to Arab and Muslim nations raised other kinds of issues, above all those of its long-term geopolitical rivalry with the United States. It played a decisive role in Iran's nuclear progress, as we saw, providing it with its nuclear reactor at Bushehr and undertaking to furnish it with enriched uranium. It also assisted in Saddam Hussein's failed missile programme and in Syria's arms and missile acquisitions. Other non-Muslim powers were equally involved in equipping the Arab and Muslim world with its military arsenals and other strengths. Until December 2003, the US, Japan, South Korea and the European Union were themselves engaged in building a nuclear plant in North Korea. The US also furnished military help to Saddam Hussein in the 1980–88 Iran-Iraq War, and provided missile-systems to Egypt and Saudi Arabia. Moreover, while relations between Iran and the US were deteriorating in 2003, US firms—through a British front company—were reportedly supplying vital military components to Teheran.

In Europe also, combinations of state and private interest made possible the continuous transfer of lethal weapons to many parts of the Muslim and Arab world. In 2003, the British government even licensed the export of 'toxic chemical precursors' to Syria. France helped Iraq build its nuclear reactor at Osirak, bombed by Israel in 1981, and in exchange for oil provided Saddam Hussein with missiles and Mirage fighters in the Iran-Iraq War; Germany was also involved prior to the 1991 Gulf War in assisting Iraq's missile and chemical weapons programme.

This interplay of interests and hostilities within and between the Muslim and non-Muslim worlds was yet another labyrinth. In the midst of it the nuclear genie was let out of the bottle, never to be returned. Questions as to whether Saddam Hussein's Iraq had 'weapons of mass destruction' in 2003, if so at what state of readiness and where—if they existed—they had gone, formed only a small part of this labyrinth. Across the Middle East there were lethal weapons—including missiles, nerve agents and other chemical and biological arms—being sought, in process of acquisition, and in successful or unsuccessful attempts at their manufacture. In Egypt, in the Gulf sheikhdoms, in Iran, in Israel, in Saudi Arabia, in Syria and in Yemen weapons were held in store, technologies were being exchanged and weapons' scientists were at work, often in clouds of threat, counter-threat and denials of the truth.

From the 1980s, Iran's covert advance to nuclear power status gradually accelerated. It was aided by possession of its own uranium mines, by technical assistance from many countries, and by its skills of manoeuvre in holding off effective inspection. It alternately agreed and refused to suspend, but not to cease, uranium enrichment. Buying time, it outwitted European diplomatic efforts to strike a 'compromise' with it; and claimed to be engaged in nuclear energy development for peaceful domestic purposes only, while producing and testing missiles of increasingly long range, using solid-fuel technology, which were capable of carrying nuclear warheads. Yet Iran asserted in June 2003—in the manner of the Twelve Devices—that it 'had no intention of ever building atomic weapons', pledged 'full transparency' in October 2003, accused its critics of 'deceit' in March 2004, and in June 2004 declared—with sufficient justice but ominous prospect—that it did 'not take orders from for-eigners'. In November 2004, it added not only that there was 'no place for weapons of mass destruction in Iran's defence doctrine' but that a Muslim nation 'could not use nuclear weapons'.

Between April and June 2005, Iran's manoeuvres continued. It repeated that its activities were 'transparent', but reports suggested that it was smug-gling nuclear weapons material into Iran, and even negotiating with North Korea to build a network of underground bunkers in order to conceal its nuclear weapons work. It agreed to a 'temporary suspension' of nuclear activ-ities, some of which had no non-military purpose, while carrying on with such activities; and reiterated that it was not seeking nuclear weapons while also declaring that the 'national will' demanded that uranium enrichment con-tinue. It was also asserted by former president Rafsanjani that not to do so would be a 'stain of shame on our history'. And despite offers of a 'non-aggression pact'—among other political and economic inducements—if Iran were to stop its uranium enrichment, enrichment was 'resumed' in August 2005, while the US made clear that the 'use of force' against Iran, although a 'last option', was an 'option on the table'.

Israel, clandestinely aided by Britain in the 1950s and with perhaps as many as two hundred nuclear devices in its arsenal, was even more successful than Iran in becoming a significant nuclear power, while refusing to acknowl-edge that it was so. It also avoided scrutiny by the International Atomic Energy Authority, with the exception of a single research reactor. Moreover, Israel would have had the same right as Iran, if the former had acknowledged the truth about its nuclear weapons, to refuse to abandon the means of annihilating others without those others doing so too. Hence, calls to Israel to abandon its strategies (and stratagems) fell upon deaf ears, as did those to Iran. Indeed, Iran and Israel each became increasingly threatening to the other. The latter considered the former an 'existential threat' to its survival, while Iran warned in December 2003 that the 'Zionist territory'—described by Teheran as a 'universal threat'—would be 'swept away' should it attack Iran.

This was merely one more potential theatre in a war whose conflicts engaged dozens of states across the world. They were conflicts which brought 'infidels' face-to-face with believers in Muslim lands, as well as in non-Muslim societies where Muslims of the diaspora had settled; and, as we saw in the opening chapter, divided Muslim nations internally as well as setting Muslim nations at loggerheads with one another. Indeed, most of the conflicts referred to in this work remained unresolved. Civil wars continued, were ended by fragile pacts and were resumed. Islamist insurrections might temporarily abate, but the tide of them was not turned back. Muslim and Arab nations, and especially the oil-rich, tended to become more authoritarian not less under the pressure of internal disturbances often generated by Islamism's increasing appeal. Sectarian divisions within the Muslim world were not set aside—often they became more bitter—in the presence of 'infidel' invaders. Divisions among the dependent non-Muslim powers also deepened as the challenges, short-term and long-term, to their security and to their economies grew larger, or appeared to do so; while the Muslim presence in the diaspora was increasingly seen by some as a threat to national cultures and to domestic social peace.

In their broader context, it could therefore be argued that no particular conflict—whether in the Middle East, in the Caucasus, in the Horn of Africa, in Afghanistan, in south-east Asia or elsewhere—was more significant than any other. This was so even if media attention, or exploitation of single conflicts for partisan ends, made this or that contention, insurgency or war the supposed cause of causes. Such emphasis also led to the illusion that, once a particular conflict had been resolved, a general peace would return to a region, or even transform the relations between the Muslim and non-Muslim worlds.

The Palestinian issue was correctly described in October 2004 by an Arab commentator as 'sensitive' for 'all Muslims'. However, it was also clear that Islamism's advance both within Muslim nations and against the non-Muslim world was being made independently of the fate of the Palestinian cause. Although it could be held that the US had made strategic errors in its incursion into Iraq, non-intervention would similarly have had no impact upon the wars in Kashmir, Sudan or Chechnya, upon the insurrection in Thailand, upon the strife between Muslims and Christians from the Philippines to Nigeria, upon Islamism's assaults in India, north-western China and Central Asia, or upon the struggles of the rulers of the Gulf kingdoms and sheikhdoms to keep their thrones.

Moreover, the fact that Afghans, Algerians, Chechens, Egyptians, Jordanians, Kuwaitis, members of Lebanese Hezbollah, Libyans, Palestinians—with Jordanian passports—Saudis, Sudanese, Syrians, Tunisians and Yemenis, as well as Muslims from several European countries, were among those found (in relatively small numbers) fighting in Iraq from 2003 spoke less to any misjudgment by the US than to the scope of the Islamist movement. The rivalries of the existing Great Powers, and the rise to pre-eminence of new forces in the world, also dwarfed the specific toils in which the US might find itself in any part of the world at any given time. Indeed, the gloating—by Muslims and some non-Muslims alike—which accompanied every American discomfiture pointed to the scale of the challenge faced by the United States. 'The Americans, whether they want it or not, whether they accept it or not, are defeated in Iraq', Iran's supreme leader, Ayatollah Ali Khamenei, declared in June 2004. It was a sentiment which many in Europe, including among its leading politicians, hoped privately was true.

Yet even a US 'defeat' in Iraq would have been no more than an incidental event in the wider interplay of forces set loose in the world by Great Power rivalry, natural-resource dependency, the revival of Islam, the spread of nuclear weapons technology and the exacerbation of differences—ethical, political, cultural, religious—between the Muslim and non-Muslim worlds. As early as February 1989, Iran's Ayatollah Khomeini had called upon the Soviet Union, as its regime tottered, for closer ties between the two countries in order to 'confront the devilish acts of the West'. Caught up in the centre of these 'devilish acts' in the following years, the US was both the strongest and the most vulnerable of the Western powers. In seeking to keep up with the Islamic advance, whose scale few had anticipated, it became increasingly overstretched, not least as a result of the refusal of many of its notional allies to support its policies and worldview. From 2003, its active duty combat brigades, its National Guard and its reserve forces were being drawn upon to their limits.

The consequences of this included extended tours of duty for its soldiery, the speeded-up 'rotation' of forces from one theatre to another and the increased use of the National Guard and of reserves—and even of retired and discharged soldiers—for active service, many of whom required retraining; some 40 per cent of the forces in Iraq in 2005 were members of the

National Guard and the Reserve. Difficulties of recruitment, including among black Americans whose representation in the US army was declining, added to the strain; as did efforts to maintain levels of re-enlistment to an all-volunteer army which was too small for the demands upon it, and which had to shoulder duties criticised by many both at home and abroad.

As a result of conflicts in and with the Muslim and Arab worlds, there was a US military presence—simultaneously or successively—in many parts of the globe. In Afghanistan in 2005, for example, there were seventeen thousand US personnel were at twenty-six different locations, some of them remote military outposts. They were about 140,000-strong in Iraq. They were also in Bosnia, in Kuwait—in a strength of 30,000—in the Central Asian states of Uzbekistan and Kyrgyzstan, and at Camp Lemonnier in Djibouti in the Horn of Africa. There, a small US 'task-force' sought to 'cover' Islamist movements in seven countries with a combined area two-thirds the size of the United States. US forces were not only located in the Pakistani tribal areas but helped train Pakistani army units in airborne assault tactics; trained 'police units' from the Caucasus to Indonesia; engaged in combat exercises in the Philippines and Kenya; and, in May 2005, the US renewed for a further ten years a military cooperation pact with Malaysia.

US forces also collaborated with the Algerian army in tracking down Islamists belonging to the Salafist movement, used training areas in Tunisia, were offered similar facilities in Morocco and helped 'hunt down Saudi Arabian terrorists in the mountains of Sudan'. Further small numbers of 'special forces' aided the 'equipping and training' of armies in Mali and in Mauritania, where Algerian Islamists attacked a military post in June 2005, and in Chad and Niger, on whose border over forty Islamists were killed in clashes in March 2004. In order to try to 'counter' the movement of fighters across the thousands of miles of the Sahara, a new US military programme—announced in May 2005—planned for increasing cooperation with the armies of nine African nations, now to include Senegal and oil-rich Nigeria. The US also 'looked at sites' for potential bases, and sought other facilities, in Cameroon, Gabon and Mozambique, as well as on the west African islands of Sao Tome and Principe, and elsewhere in the Gulf of Guinea. The US was said to be covertly present in other Muslim states besides, or in non-Muslim states bordering upon them.

The costs of such activities and engagements by the US, to say nothing of its total defence spending—including on the continuous modernisation of its armaments and other military equipment—rose inexorably from 2003 to 2005; it was said to have accounted for almost half the world's total military expenditure in 2004. Such spending helped heap up the US deficit (and national debt) to very high levels, described by the chairman of the Federal Reserve in April 2005 as 'on an unsustainable path'; over $1 billion was needed each week in Iraq alone, and $1 billion a month in Afghanistan. Large sums were spent in support of Israel, Egypt and the Palestinian Authority, hundreds of millions were allocated to the building of a new embassy in Baghdad, and almost $800 million to 'combating the drug trade in Afghanistan'. Substantial resources of all kinds were required both for 'homeland defence' and in order to counter the movements of funds, arms and individuals through an increasingly widespread network of Islamist cells and support organisations.

The US was therefore driven to reduce its forces in the heart of western Europe where over 100,000 were stationed—it left Hungary, for example, in June 2004—as well as to reduce its force levels in Japan and South Korea, and to plan for the closure and 'consolidation' of bases in the United States itself. For America now needed to be strategically better placed, including in the central and eastern Mediterranean, in or near the Black Sea as in Bulgaria and Romania, in the Caucasus, in Central Asia and in West Africa. Increased protection of oil supplies, interdictions of the movements of Islamists, new training locations for US forces and an enhanced capacity to assist 'allied' Muslim states which were facing internal insurgencies and rebellions were among the new determinants of these relocations.

Yet the advance of Islam was not of a kind that could always be met by logistics, armament, security measures, 'containment' and counter-attack. For it was estimated that in the course of the twentieth century the number of Muslims in the world had shown the largest increase of any religious group. They had risen from some 12 per cent of the global population in 1900 to 20 per cent—or some 1.3 billion—by the century's end. This rate of growth was itself accelerating, and it was estimated that Muslims would number some 2.3 billion by 2025.

Statistical projections of the future sizes of Muslim populations, especially in non-Muslim countries, have been affected by subjective—or racist—alarms. Statistics also lie, and demographic projection is both an inexact science and fruitful ground for the incitement of fear and hatred. Although birth-rates had dropped in some Muslim countries, such as Egypt, it could nevertheless be said that half of the world's significant population growth was taking place in only six countries, three of which—Pakistan, Indonesia and Bangladesh—were overwhelmingly Muslim, and two of which, India and Nigeria, had large Muslim populations. The sixth, China, the world's most populous country—but with only some 20 million Muslims—was thought likely to be overtaken in numbers during the twenty-first century by India. In contrast, the 'developed' world was expected to show little growth in populations and in many cases a decline, with the exception of high immigrant countries such as the United States.

Many countries where Islamism was advancing, or could be expected to advance, were also the same countries where population growth was projected to be the most rapid. By 2050 Nigeria's population could triple to over 300 million. The population of Bangladesh, a mere 44 million in 1951 but 111 million only four decades later, could more than double again by 2050 to some 280 million. Yemen's population could rise by over 250 per cent, that of the Palestinian territories by over 200 per cent, that of Afghanistan and of Kuwait by a little under 200 per cent. The proportion of Muslims in most non-Muslim majority countries had also risen and on present trends must rise further, in some cases steeply. For example, in India the Muslim population rose from 35 million in 1951 to some 140 million in 2003, with a reported 30 per cent increase between 1991 and 2001 alone.

Approximately half the population of the African continent is estimated to be Muslim: over 90 per cent in the Maghreb; between 80 and 90 per cent in the west African states of Gambia, Mali, Mauritania, Niger and Senegal; perhaps 50 per cent in Nigeria; perhaps 25 per cent in East Africa. These proportions have been increasing from high birth-rates and in some countries, such as Rwanda and Sierra Leone, from quickening rates of conversion also; the number of Muslims in Rwanda was said to have doubled in ten years to some 'one million', or to about 15 per cent of the population. Even in South Africa the Muslim population had shown significant growth, from perhaps 12,000 in 1991 to estimates of '2 million' in 2003.

Realism, not racism, made all such figures important, approximate as most were and with many hypothetical projections among them. But, without them, no true assessment could begin to be made of the moral and political significance of the great weight of belief, of numbers and of an aroused sense of identity and entitlement which confronted the non-Muslim world. Although instrumentalised by 'Islamophobes', such statistics and estimates required to be faced above all by those who naively believed in the power of 'democracy' to defeat demography, or in the power of the gun to defeat the 'force of faith'. Moreover, as indicated, similar changes in totals and proportions of Muslims (but on a smaller scale) appeared also to have taken place in the non-Muslim societies of Europe, as a result of immigration and of natural increase as local birth-rates fell. Again, estimates of the numbers varied widely, especially in countries whose censuses excluded such categorisation. Muslim organisations themselves often exaggerated the figures for their own political ends, while the numbers of illegal Muslim (and other) immigrants in Europe could not be assessed.

But since the late 1980s the Muslim population in western Europe might have more than doubled to over 20 million; other estimates made it about 15 million. In many European countries, Islam was also clearly established as the second-largest, and everywhere growing, religion. In Italy, where there were '43,000' Muslims in 1970, there were variously said to be '600,000', '800,000' or even 'one million' in 2004. There were roughly the same estimates of the total of the Muslim population in the smaller Netherlands—where Muslims were said in 2003 to 'outnumber Calvinists'—and in Spain, where there were said to be 'one million' in 2005. There were '3.5 million' Muslims in Germany, and 'over 2000' mosques; and '3.7 million', '5 million' or even '7 million' Muslims in France, with 'one-third' of all Muslims said to be under the age of eighteen, nearly twice the proportion of young people as in the general population. Indeed, some demographers estimated that a 'quarter' of the French population under twenty-five was Muslim. Even in Switzerland there were said to be some '500,000' Muslims, and '150,000' in Denmark. There were also said to be '30,000 to 50,000' converts to Islam in France—others made out the figures to be higher—and in total many tens of thousands of Muslim converts in Spain and in other European countries.

In Britain, where Islam was again the second-largest and fastest-growing faith—with more Muslims said to be attending mosques than Anglicans attending churches—there were said to have been '1.54 million' in 2001, and '1.8 million', 'nearly 2 million' or even '2.5 million' in 2004, more than half estimated to be under thirty-five, and with the 'great majority' said to have been born in Britain. In Athens, Berlin and London, in Milan and Barcelona, in Rotterdam and Leicester, there were tens and even hundreds of thousands of Muslims; in Hamburg alone, a centre of Islamist activity, '120,000'. In the US, there were '1.88 million', '2.6 million', '3 million', '5 million', or even—according to American Muslim sources—'7 million'. In Australia, there were said to be '285,000'; in Canada, whose Muslim population was expanding rapidly, '600,000'. But in all these countries the proportions of Muslims in the population remained small: less than 1 per cent in Australia, some '3 per cent' in Britain, '5 or 6 per cent' in Holland and Sweden, '8 per cent' in France and perhaps '14 per cent' in the Russian Federation, where estimates of the Muslim population ranged widely between '14 million' and double that number.

However, more important than such head-counting, which could be put to morally base uses, was its context. It was one in which Islam and Muslims constituted a growing physical, political and ethical force, proportionately increasingly young, and with religious observance maintained to a more ardent degree than was generally the case with the other great faiths. This was despite report of a significant number of apostates in Muslim communities in the non-Muslim world. Moreover, most Muslims possessed a strong sense of belonging to a world-wide commonality of tradition and belief. Of this tradition Islamism was an authentic expression, despite some Muslim disclaimers that this was so.

Above all, the Muslim presence in the non-Muslim world, especially in the West, was a presence in societies with diminishing knowledge of their own pasts, let alone the pasts of other cultures. They were societies increasingly governed by the atrophied ethics of 'the market' and by a belief in the self-realisation of the individual as the highest of values. They were also societies over-dependent on a 'culture' of consumption, and upon the resources of Muslim lands—among others—which sustained it. Their citizens' aspirations for, and sense of, the future had in many cases similarly shrunk to dimensions compared with which Islam's moral and religious goals were grandiose, however unacceptable they might be to most non-Muslims.

In addition, many—perhaps most—non-Muslim members of Western civil societies prized the possession of personal rights more than they did the virtues of either faith or reason. Defenders of such rights often showed themselves ready to go to almost any moral or legal lengths in the protection and promotion of them, even making rights out of mere wants or desires. They were therefore ethically disqualified from demanding of Muslim immigrants, for example, a greater degree of citizen consciousness than they themselves possessed. Furthermore, they were prone to offer 'integration' to Muslims who did not wish it, or who wished it only upon their own terms.

The non-Muslim world's secular value-systems as well as its religious institutions had also waned in authority while Islam's reach in the world, and Islamism's violences in its name, had increased. Catholicism's internal moral disorders, for instance, reduced even wealthy American dioceses to bankruptcy in lawsuits brought against them for the crimes and delinquencies of God's ostensible servants, and led to the resignations not only of American bishops, but of bishops from Austria to Argentina and from Canada to Poland. For many, these disorders—found on a lesser scale in Anglicanism also—compromised Christianity itself, even if Christian evangelism, especially in Africa and Latin America, grew stronger in the contest of faiths, or new wars of religion.

Many seminaries, monasteries, convents and churches closed in western Europe and North America—despite the religious vitality of Hispanic

Catholic immigrants to the United States—while the number of mosques grew; in Britain, for example, mosques sometimes took over vacated church buildings. Some three thousand Catholic schools also closed in the US in the four decades from the 1960s, while the Church of England lost half its membership in thirty years. In many countries outside the 'developing' world, callings to the Catholic priesthood fell, in some cases—as in Britain and Ireland—precipitously, while imams entered Europe in increasing numbers to attend to, and in a minority of cases to incite, their faithful. Only one priest was ordained in Dublin in 2002, and eight in Ireland, and only a mere eighteen in the whole of England and Wales in 2004. In 1965 one in thirty Catholic parishes in the US had no resident priest; by 2002, it was one in six.

Together with their priests, Christian worshippers of most denominations had also aged, while young Muslim males in the diaspora continued to crowd their mosques. The average age of Anglican churchgoers in England and Wales was said in November 2001 to be over seventy; the average age of priests and monks in Ireland in 2004 was sixty-three; and the average age of Jesuit priests world-wide was fifty-seven in 2002. These clergy were not being replaced in any numbers by younger men. In April 2002, the Church of Scotland itself predicted that it would 'become extinct within 50 years' at its current rate of decline, and fewer than 3 per cent of Londoners were said in 2004 to be regular churchgoers. Even in Spain, where half a century ago '98 per cent' declared themselves to be practising Catholics, only 18 per cent did so in 2004. 'Europe is no longer Christian', the general-secretary of the United Reform Church in Britain asserted in June 2003. 'I would be hard pushed to say we were a Christian country', similarly declared the archbishop of York in December 2004; in a British poll published in March 2005, less than half of the respondents knew why Christians celebrate Easter.

Although internally diverse and divided, the Arab and Muslim states and peoples represented a sharp contrast to this. They possessed an ultimately unified and advancing sense of identity and purpose, while the 'post-Christian' 'West', a disparate and indeterminate category, now lacked such sense of supranational identity and ethos. Beliefs in the intrinsic merits of 'Judeo-Christian' morality, or of Western paliamentarism, or of technological rationality, could no longer compose an ideal of equivalent force, since each of these elements was increasingly subject to, and corrupted by, the demands of 'the market', among other pressures.

The Muslim sense that there was a single, boundariless and transcendent 'Muslim nation'—'the Muslim nation of more than one billion people', as the secretary-general of the Arab League, Amr Mousa, put it in September

2001—made most of the ends to which non-Muslims aspired seem paltry or arrogant, or both, especially in pious Muslim eyes. It permitted a Bradford Muslim leader to declare in August 1990 that, although British Muslims had joined the British armed forces, they remained 'part of a wider, international Muslim nation'. Or as Hassan al-Banna, the founder in the 1920s of the Muslim Brotherhood, expressed it, 'Islam is a country and a citizenship together'.

Inter-Arab and inter-Muslim bloodletting contradicted the universalist ideals which could be said to bind the 'Arab nation' and the wider Muslim world community, or *ummah*. Muslims have killed uncountably more fellow-Muslims than have non-Muslims during the present Islamic advance. 'Pan-Arabism' was also more ideal than real. Nevertheless, the understanding that there is a 'land of Islam', a land which has been extended into the non-Muslim world through the Muslim diaspora, has become increasingly potent. Indeed, Muslim supranationalism, the sense of which is disseminated with growing ease through the Internet and a (willingly) instrumentalised Western media—it has been called an 'electronic jihad'—is more significant than Islam's internal conflicts.

The Muslim nation-state of course exists, including in the most repressive forms. But there is no concept of the political state as such in the Koran, whose teachings are universalist in their scope. Pietists as well as many 'ordinary' Muslims hold that an 'Islamic nation' is a religious before it is a political entity, and as such part of an Islamic world community whose interests transcend those of a mere state; Yemen is described by its own jurists as 'totally subject' to Islam. Even teaching materials for Muslim children in the diaspora, such as those issued by the Islamia Schools Trust in London, have made this clear, and in their own terms justly so. 'The injunctions and commands of Allah take priority over all other laws, even though social pressures and attempts at indoctrination by the state's institutions take place', it is declared.

Hence, the Muslim and (even more) the non-Muslim state, and citizenship of them, are contradictory and temporary phenomena when judged by the aspirations of the Islamist who seeks 'Islamist rule on earth', and who carries Holy Writ in one hand and a weapon in the other. All geographical boundaries—and moral limits when occasion demands—can be crossed when the common fate of Muslims is felt to be at stake. Chechnya, asserted Ghafoor Ahmed, leader of Bangladesh's Jamaat-e-Islami party in January 1995, 'will prove to be another Afghanistan for Russia': four countries of the world were girdled more swiftly than by Shakespeare's Ariel in one instant of Muslim thought. In an era of other 'globalisms', this is globalism indeed. It is a globalism not merely of faith but of all-embracing perception. For Muslims not only see the Islamic world as ultimately a unity; they see the 'infidel' world as a unity also, its differences and divisions notwithstanding. Within the permanent binary structure of this perception, discussed earlier, the 'non-Islamic' is the antithesis of Islam's essence, identity and purpose. When a Yemeni Islamist group, the Abyan Islamic Army, mistakenly attacked a French tanker instead of a United States navy frigate in October 2002, it declared that it 'made no difference' since 'the unbelievers' nation' was 'one'.

Yet the US is also being driven by necessities which cannot be withstood. 'We are relentless, we are strong, we refuse to yield, we will bring these killers to justice', proclaimed President Bush in March 2004. Such necessities, whose nature is plain, and of which oil-dependency is merely one, bring America into collision with other interests, belief-systems and powers, old and new, the principal of them now being Islam. The US is caught up in matters which it aggravates by its involvement in them—although not on the scale of the 'dire consequences' thesis discussed in a previous chapter—but from which it cannot extract itself without incurring even greater danger.

The US has also intervened in settings of great complexity whose circumstances eluded external control. Moreover, even when Islamists suffered local defeats, they were generally perceived by them as temporary setbacks only. For in Muslim hearts the certitude remains that the more Islam is attacked the stronger it grows. Moreover, the conditions under which Islamism has advanced have been those in which the non-Muslim world's efforts to 'rein in' such advance by force, diplomacy or covert means have been least effective. Sometimes this was because the US was driven to uphold regimes unsupported by their own people; or because existing local conflicts were too intricate to be settled, or even to be fully understood, by outsiders; or because the counter-influence of other Great Powers, or newly ascendant forces in a region, obstructed American purpose. In the last circumstances, other nations, whether acting singly or together—as in the case of members of the European Union—have refused to allow the US unchallenged dominion.

In addition, the strength of the 'Muslim presence' in most Western nations must increase and cannot be diminished. It is no longer to Islam's scholarly traditions nor to its cultural achievements that the Muslim impact on the world is owed. Instead, Islam's advance has been quickened by the developed world's increasing need for migrant labour and for the material resources of others, coupled with Islam's internally-generated conviction of its moral supremacy over a dependent West's system of values.

Against this the West, and in particular the US, has pitted both firepower and the belief that there is a widespread desire in Islamic lands for their 'democratic deficit' to be made good by the general adoption of Western liberal democratic norms. However, this belief is largely a projection onto the Islamic world of 'the West's', and especially of America's, desires for such outcome. The 'democratic illusion' rests upon two related beliefs. The first is that Western concepts of democratic citizenship can be successfully planted in cultural ground deeply sown and tilled for centuries by Islam. The second belief is that such concepts can not only subordinate to their command Islamic laws and customs morally and politically incompatible with those of liberal democracy, but bring their clerical guardians to docile heel at a time of Islam's world-wide renewal.

Both beliefs are naive. The Iraqi Shi'ite leader Ayatollah Mohammed Baqer al-Hakim, assassinated in August 2003, declared that even were 'democracy' to come to Iraq, it would not be a 'western-style democracy' but a 'democracy' which prohibited 'behaviour acceptable in the West but forbidden in Islam'. This was not the kind of democracy which the 'democratic illusion' had in mind. According to Abu Musab al-Zarqawi in January 2005, to displace the 'rule of God' with the 'rule of the people' was 'infidelity itself'. Indeed, it is an article of true faith that the purposes of 'unbelievers', whatever the latter may say or do, cannot ultimately be Islam's purposes. Thus, the US-devised reconstruction of the Iraqi polity was held to be 'blasphemous' by bin Laden in December 2004.

Even when not measured by such harsh criteria, the 'democratic illusion' is a slender reed when set against the counter-processes of Islamisation, or re-Islamisation, which are in progress in much of the Arab and Muslim world. They permit attacked groups of Islamists to re-form, and autonomous or only loosely-linked new groups to replace those which are broken up by anti-'terrorist' measures. They also make unnecessary a centralised organisation to take command of Islamist actions. Indeed, the failure of the Soviet imperium and the ultimate moral unacceptability to most Muslims of western liberalism's values, together with the persistence of corrupt and self-serving regimes across much of the Muslim world, have left political Islam, or Islamism, without serious long-term rivals on its own ground.

Islamism's advance has also posed doctrinal and political problems to the western 'left', problems which can barely be resolved at all. For example, in the eyes of some 'progressives', opposition even to violent Islamist revivalism raises the presumption that the opponent is 'Islamophobic' or 'racist'. Yet for a 'leftist' to support the Islamist cause—a cause which is itself hostile to most 'left' or 'progressive' presuppositions—is to draw uncomfortably close to the

'Islamo-fascist camp'. The latter term is no idle one. The principle of submission to authority; the reduction of all 'out-groups' to inferior status; disbelief in the virtues of free thought; contempt for democracy; the corporatist dissolution of distinctions between the public and the private realms; the perception of all cultures save that of Islam as morally decadent; the subordination of women to men and to the home; and the readiness to use extremes of personal cruelty and violence, together with the odium expressed for Jews and homosexuals, were among the main constituents of the fascist creed.

Indeed, fascist models of rule were consciously adopted by the founders of the Arab nationalist Ba'athist (or 'Renaissance') movement, which succeeded in establishing regimes in Syria and Iraq. Chechen Muslim irregulars fought alongside the invading Nazis in the Second World War, while in the 1930s and 1940s leading Arab clerics and nationalists—the predecessors, and in some cases the inspiration, of today's Islamists—made no secret of their ardent support for Nazism's cause. 'Holocaust-denial' has also been a commonplace theme, as noted earlier, of radical Islamist diatribe against Israel's existence. Moreover, the adoption by Islamists of an anti-imperialist, or anti-colonialist, stance again evokes echoes of the fascist past. As the commentator Thomas von der Osten-Sacken put it in October 2002, 'The Germans in 1939 said they were fighting against universal capitalism and for self-determination in the colonial world. They used anti-colonialist language. The same words and phrases as are being used now were being used in the 1940s, when the Germans were supporting the revolts of India and the Arabs against the British. Today, Germany is again being praised in the Middle East for taking the same side that it took fifty years ago', he declared, referring to Germany's opposition to the Iraq war, and 'France, too, is again in the same position'.

A minority of Muslims themselves see a 'new fascism' in Islamism and in some of the dictates of Sharia law. Many Muslims have suffered grievously from the denial of their human rights under absolutist Muslim and Arab regimes; 'actually existing Islam has failed to create a free society anywhere', as Salman Rushdie put it in December 1991. But for much of what remained of the Western 'left'—with its own 'socialist project' in ruins—the appeal of a politics of anti-colonialism, anti-racism and (especially) anti-Americanism weighed more heavily in the ethical scales than did the defects of Muslim and Arab societies. Indeed, veteran leftists and neo-fascists alike, including the Austrian Jörg Haider and Russia's Vladimir Zhirinovsky, paid court in Baghdad to Saddam Hussein, expressing their 'solidarity' with and 'esteem' for him; Zhirinovsky even invited the Iraqi dictator in 1995 to 'join a new coalition against the West'.

It was the 'left' which had the larger dilemma. For it had no viable cause greatly distinct from that of Islamism in expressing its hostility to the policies of the United States. Yet peace-marches in 'solidarity' with those suffering from the latter's 'imperialist aggression' and 'oppression', or 'anti-globalisation' demonstrations, brought 'progressives' shoulder-to-shoulder with Islamists whose belief-system was, at its heart, remote from their own.

In September 2002, in protests in London against the approaching Iraq War, the Socialist Workers' Party, Islamists, anarchists, 'anti-globalisers', peace activists, the Campaign for Nuclear Disarmament, pro-Palestinian sympa- thisers, Jewish leftists and thousands of British Muslims—some of whom, a decade earlier, had been calling for Salman Rushdie's head—marched together. Slogans declaring 'No to War!' 'No to Capitalism!' 'No to Global Imperialism!' were borne through the streets along with Palestinian banners, the Union Jack and the hammer-and-sickle; Muslims and non-Muslims alike wore *keffiyahs*. A minority took this a step further, even to the point of ill- concealed sympathy with violent Islamist actions; and while the suicide- bomber attained the martyr's heaven, the Western 'anti-imperialist', afflicted by another form of suicidal impulse, looked forward to America's defeat. Indeed, in March 2003, a surviving member of Italy's Red Brigades called for the 'left' to 'show solidarity' with Islamists in their 'struggle' against an 'Israeli- Anglo-American plot'.

Such 'identification' on the 'left' with Islamism is as presumptuous as the notion of 'democratising' the Arab and Muslim worlds. Short of conversion, non-Muslims cannot make Islamism their own; the non-Muslim, however 'progressive', remains an 'unbeliever'. However, the left's anti-Americanism has given further political space to Islamists to pursue their ends against a divided non-Muslim world. Now, neither Islamism nor repressive Muslim and Arab regimes face serious ethical opposition from Western 'leftists' who, before the defeat of socialism, could otherwise have been expected to object strongly to them on doctrinal grounds. The 'left' has also been aware that Islam and Islamism have had a gradually increasing appeal to part of the con- stituency which it has itself now lost: the socially, culturally and economically marginalised, for whom Islam, like socialism before it, has come to be seen as the 'faith of the oppressed'. It is an evolution which can (for some) make a hero even of a bin Laden.

The Islamic advance has also had a mixed reception on the 'right'. In Britain, anti-Americanism, even if less marked on the 'right' than on the 'left', spans the political spectrum. Moreover, the 'old right' has been philo-Arab since British colonial times, and this tradition has remained influential—and divisive—in the British diplomatic service. Some leading Tories were opposed to the 'poodle' role they attributed to the British Labour government in following the US into the 2003 Iraq War; the tradition of resentment in the upper ranks of the British armed forces at US military pre-eminence continued also. Confused British conservatives who were hostile to Israel—and often to Jews as such—nevertheless admired the ruthless methods of the Israeli defence forces.

There was confusion, too, on the 'far-right'. Despite its anti-Muslim and anti-immigrant stance in domestic politics, the British National Party, like sections of the 'far right' in the United States, was opposed to the overthrow of the Baghdad regime. It shared the belief with many on the 'left' that it was carried out in the Jewish interest and at Jewish prompting. In February 2005, on the sixtieth anniversary of allied raids on Dresden, neo-Nazis marched through the city behind slogans denouncing 'allied bomb terror' against 'Hiroshima, Nagasaki, Dresden and today Baghdad'. Hostility to the 'Jewish cabals' allegedly determining American and even British foreign policy thus brought Islamism, the American and European far-right and significant parts of the Western 'left' into a degree of political accord. Islamist condemnations of 'imperialists' and 'Crusaders', of 'theft' of 'Muslim oil' and of 'Zionist racism' have a resonance for many on the 'left'; Islamism's (and Islam's) recoil from the moral defects of Western liberal societies is a recoil shared by much of the 'right'.

'The West calls for freedom and liberty', preached Sheikh Mohammed al-Tabatabi to tens of thousands of worshippers at the Qadhimaya mosque in northern Baghdad in May 2003. 'But Islam is not calling for this. Islam rejects such liberty. True liberty is obedience to God and to be liberated from desires', he declared. Yet the illusion has persisted that Western 'Enlightenment' principles can make progress on Islam's terrain. It is again presumptuous in old colonial fashion. For it pretends to a knowledge of what would be best for the objects of its attentions. It fails to grasp that Islam and Muslims possess their own divinely-sanctioned sense of a just cause, a true order and the good life, regressive as some of its forms might appear according to a different logic and a different ethic. It is not universal suffrage but universal knowledge of Islam, and not the sovereignty of the people but the sovereignty of God, to which pious Muslims aspire. There might be differences among the faithful about the means to attain such ends, but not about the ends themselves.

Moreover, where 'secularisation' has occurred in the Muslim and Arab world, resistance to it has generally redoubled. Similarly, where war against Muslim interest has been offered by the 'unbeliever', it can now be expected that every effort will be made to pay him back in kind. In their own terms, Islam's ideals are fully the equal of the universal 'liberation' aspired to in the 'American dream'. It is a dream which Islam—and especially Islamism— clearly rejects, even if some Muslims aspire to be Americans themselves. But the West, and especially the United States, persists in transposing to the Islamic world its own preferences for 'free thought', for the separation of God's realm from Caesar's, for the 'free market' and so on.

Yet the principles which Arab and Muslim regimes are being expected to espouse have themselves brought Western liberal societies to a condition of increasing dysfunction. In true faith's eyes, these principles are the route to social disaggregation and moral chaos, the twin ills which Islam has diagnosed as afflicting the American way of life. Moreover, Islam's moral strength—or blindness, according to point of view—resides in its refusal of the flexibilities, compromises and 'relativist' virtues and vices of most non-Muslim ethical systems, religious and lay. 'I cannot accept that there are liberals and fundamentalists within Islam', the president of Bradford's Council for Mosques declared in July 1989 during the Rushdie affair. 'For me, you are either Islamic and hold to your beliefs; or you do not hold to them and you are not Islamic'.

Such type of view is likely to become an increasingly formidable challenge to the non-Muslim world. For Islamic (and Islamist) ethical judgments upon the 'vices' of the West can only grow in confidence as such 'vices' become more blatant and self-harming. As objection to the disorders of non-Muslim societies also come to be shared across the political spectrum—and not only by dangerous radicals of the 'far-right'—it is Islam's critique which is more likely to be vindicated than defence of the corrupted liberal *status quo* by human rights lobbyists, moral relativists and free-marketeers. Although bin Laden had by his own acts lost the entitlement to take the ethical high ground, in his 'Letter to the American People' in November 2002 he described 'acts of immorality' as 'pillars of personal freedom' in the American value-system. This was a gross overstatement. But if the contrast between American ideals and the actuality of its internal social and moral condition continues to deepen, the belief of Muslims that only Islam can provide a curative to such ills is likely to increase also. The Muslim on his way to the mosque might be seen, by many non-Muslims, as living in darkness. But armed by his faith, whether literally or metaphorically, he himself sees most non-Muslims as lost souls, morally unfit to pass judgment upon him.

The Muslim world suffers from lack of productive activity, intellectual as well as economic, from high levels of unemployment and from political repression. But Western liberal democracies suffer from the inability of perhaps the majority of their citizens to grasp that individual self-realisation, in 'freedom's' name but at the continuous expense of others, has finite possibilities of fulfilment. That which the West has increasingly forgotten, and which entire generations have never known, Islam to its honour remembers: that individual wants, desires and rights cannot be elevated over those bonds of reciprocity and obligation upon which any social or moral order must rest.

The trial of strength between the values of Islam and the 'philosophy' of 'democracy', 'human rights' and 'free markets' is dialectically connected. Each is a foil to the other. To declare 'terrorism' rather than Islamism to be the true foe of the non-Muslim world, and especially of 'the West' and its ways, is therefore an error of judgment. It is not less so for having been dictated by fear of the truth or by tactical prudence. Moreover, American policy-makers are currently no real match for the hundreds of millions of faithful with a broader historical perspective and a longer attention-span than their own—or than that of the Western mass media.

Islam is also of necessity expansionist. If it were not, the universal 'House of Islam' could not be built. As Zaki Badawi, the 'moderate' head of the Muslim College in London, expressed it in 1981, 'A proselytising religion cannot stand still. It can either expand or contract. Islam endeavours to expand in Britain'. 'Islam isn't in America to be equal to any other faith but to become dominant', similarly declared the chairman of the board of the Council on American Islamic Relations, Omar Ahmed, in July 1998. 'Think of this as the beginning', said Abu Musab al-Zarqawi during the siege of Fallujah in Iraq in November 2004; the 'spirit of resistance [to America]' would persist into 'future generations', promised al-Qaeda's Ayman al-Zawahiri in June 2004. 'Islam is advancing according to a steady plan. America will be destroyed, but we must be patient', stated the Saudi scholar Nasser bin Suleiman al-Omar, also in June 2004. 'We will control the land of the Vatican, we will control Rome and introduce Islam in it', declared Sheikh Muhammad bin Abd al-Rahman al-Arifi, the imam of the mosque of the King Fahd Defence Academy in Saudi Arabia in the summer of 2004.

Coexistence is a necessary ideal. But Islamism is on its guard against 'infidel' attempts to deflect its energies by negotiation, bribery, co-optation, 'containment', 'democratisation' and 'modernisation'. In his address in February 1989 to the students of Iranian religious seminaries, Ayatollah Khomeini asserted that the 'committed clergy' had 'never' been in a 'state of conciliation' and 'never will be'. Not even all Islamists share this rigorous view. But it is clear that as long as faith's ardours continue to burn, the non-Muslim world, and especially the United States, will continue to be tested not only diplomatically and militarily but ethically also.

It is not the case that a 'war of civilisations'—described as such by some Islamists themselves—is a 'war we cannot win', as a commentator in the *New York Times* asserted in October 2001. Nevertheless, Islam is considered by the faithful to be invincible, and the West's 'materialism' to be doomed to systemic and moral failure. Indeed, it is the United States, seen by Islamists as 'insecure', which faces the largest difficulties in its contest with what it has chosen to misname as 'terror'. For its military and economic strengths invite continuous challenge. It is a challenge which has been reflected in the hostility shown to it even by its erstwhile allies in Europe. As long as its overwhelming military capacity subsists, the US will also be inevitably suspected of being bent upon world-conquest.

The scale and riches of its corporate interests, combined with its thin ethic of individual self-fulfilment as the primary good, also make it susceptible to large-scale economic, social and moral crises. A globalised economy and a putatively global 'democracy', dominated by a single mega-force, is inherently unstable. The greater its size the greater that mega-force's dependency upon the material resources, the purchasing-power and the political goodwill of others. Thus, when al-Qaeda's Ayman al-Zawahiri told the leaders of the US and Britain in a video released in August 2005 that 'there will be no salvation until you withdraw from our land, stop stealing our oil and other resources, and end support for infidel [Arab] rulers', they were demands which would always be impossible to meet. The challenge to the rich non-Muslim world which Islam and Islamism represent is also merely one challenge among others. When over a billion people in the world are estimated to live on less than a dollar a day—or, according to another estimate, nearly three billion on less than two dollars—any economic megalith, whether it was the United States or another, would be facing a mounting moral challenge; particularly a megalith governed by the ambitions of corporate monopolies which are too large for their own good or for the good of others.

It is also clear that Islam will not ultimately defer to the 'infidel'—indeed it is obligated by Holy Writ not to do so—nor Islamists shrink away to defeat under a hail of fire. In his account in April 2003 in the *Washington Post* of the resumption, after Saddam Hussein's fall, of the tradition of Shi'ite pilgrimage to Karbala in Iraq, Anthony Shadid wrote of 'tens of thousands marching under green, black and red banners, beating their chests as they surged into a shrine of gold-leafed domes and minarets.... Shi'ites cut their heads with the flat edge of swords, blood pouring down their faces. In a spectacle not seen in three decades, others swung heavy chains, which caught the glint of a blazing sun before crashing down on their backs. "The people are stronger than tyrants", one of their banners read'.

The Losing Battle with Islam

But naive incomprehension of the nature of Islam's varied strengths remains. 'I love the stories about people saying: "Isn't it wonderful to be able to express our religion, the Shi'a religion on a pilgrimage?"' commented the president of the United States. Yet, for all that, he was described by a Hamas leader in March 2004 as the 'enemy of God'. 'We are rolling back the terrorist threat to civilisation, not on the fringes of its influence, but at the heart of its power', Bush further declared in September 2003.

Such judgments spoke to a significant failure of understanding. 'Faith is as faith does', wrote the Cambridge-educated British Muslim, Shabbir Akhtar, in February 1989. 'Against the militant calumnies of evil, the Koran is bound to have the last word'. Yet if this was also an illusion, it was no greater than the non-Muslim world's illusions both about Islam and itself.

Index

Abayat, Ibrahim, 435

Abbas, Abul, 311

Abbas, Mahmoud, 51, 202, 214
  attempted assassination of, 55
  on intifada, 242, 447

Abd al-Jabbar, Falih', 27, 28

Abdel-Wahhab, Mohammad ibn, 49

Abdullah, Ali, 189–90

Abdullah, Ouled, 78

Abdullah, Radwan, 152

Abdullah bin Abdulaziz (former crown
  prince), 55, 189, 281

Abdullatif, Fadi, 211–12

Abercrombie, William, 223

Ablaj, Mohammed al-, 389

Abrams, Elliott, 222

absence of historical sense, 30, 35, 36

absolutism, 251, 392, 395, 444, 455

Abu Bakr, Yasin, 20

Abu Dhabi, 22

Abu Ghraib, 70, 230, 312

Abu Hafs al-Masri Brigades, 159, 208,
  301, 319

Abu Hanifa mosque (Baghdad), 189

Abu Rudeineh, Nabil, 187

Abu Saâda, Hafez, 82

Abu Sayyaf ('Father of the Sword')
  Islamist group, 62, 161, 289, 310,
  417

Abu Zaid, Nasr Hamid, 131

Abyan Islamic Army, 480

academia and Islam, 34

Achille Lauro (ship), 311

Ackerman, Bruce, 349

Action Committee on Islamic Affairs
  (Britain), 251

'Action for Peace' (Italy), 203

Adult Literacy and Basic Skills Unit, 115

Afghanistan, 15, 37, 71, 99, 162, 331, 390,
  411, 468
  Afghan warlords' treatment of cap-
    tives, 60
  anti-Americanism, 81, 448
  assassination of vice-president, 54
  attacks on foreigners, 56, 57
  bombings in, 67
  civil war, 25
  clan rivalries, 49

defence of Islamic taboos, 127, 129
displacement of population, 16, 17
elections in, 82, 447–48, 450
funding of violence in, 463, 464
hostage-taking in, 59, 60
inter-Muslim hostilities, 54, 63–64, 67,
    69
Islamists' transnational use of, 466, 467
Northern Alliance, 49, 52–53, 54
and oil, 457
pipelines, 458
represented in fighting against US in
    Iraq, 472
statistics on, 475
support of Iraq in Gulf War, 25
as training ground for Islamists, 26, 30,
    36–37, 148, 168, 278, 282–83, 400,
    464, 466, 467
treatment of women, 80, 82, 85
US attack on bin Laden's bases, 304
use of Twelve Devices of Muslim
    argument, 145
US financial support of, 474
US presence in Afghanistan, 473–74
See also Soviet Union/Afghan war
    (1979–1989); Taliban; Taliban,
    US led coalition against
Africa, Islam's relations with other reli-
    gions in, 417–19
Afzal. See Munir, Afzal
Afzal, Mohammed, 415
Agence France Presse, 99
Agha, Dol, 70–71
Aghajari, Hashem, 133
Ahdel, Abdullah, 248
Ahl al-Bait, 204
ahle kitab, 389
Ahmad, Mahmud, 278
Ahmadinejad, Mahmoud, 440
Ahmed, Abou Abed, 134–35
Ahmed, Abu Abdallah, 82
Ahmed, Akbar, 107, 117, 150, 254–55,
    400

Ahmed, Ghafoor, 479
Ahmed, Hafiz Hussain, 354
Ahmed, Iftikhar, 117
Ahmed, Mahieddine, 78
Ahmed, Omar, 486
Ahmed, Rashid, 147
Ahmed, Rihal, 332
Ahsan, Manazir, 259
AIDS, 295, 369
aircraft, attacks on
    Air France airliners
        bombing in 1989, 58, 59
        hijacking in 1994, 33, 41
    Pan Am Flight 103 over Lockerbie, 20,
        30, 58, 65
    Russian airliners, 310
    See also 9/11 attacks
Ajami, Fouad, 133
Ajloun massacre, 51
Akaileh, Abdullah, 83
Akayev, Askar, 458
Akbar (emperor), 412
Akbar, M. J., 373, 375
Akhtar, Shabbir, 32, 42, 120–21, 246, 247,
    254, 259–60, 263, 488
Akhund, Mullah Dadullah, 161
al-Ahram (Egyptian newspaper), 205, 212,
    213, 215, 229, 233, 234, 243, 373
al-Akhbar (Egyptian newspaper), 205,
    214–15
Alamoudi, Abdurrahman, 211
al-Anbaa (Kuwaiti newspaper), 235
al-Aqsa Martyrs' Brigade, 160, 289, 432,
    435
al-Aqsa mosque (Jerusalem), 8, 64, 151
Alarabi, Ali, 244
al-Arabiya (TV), 226
al-Azhar University (Cairo), 87, 96, 228,
    406
Albania, 13, 17, 26, 30, 51, 419, 443
al-Bayan (Saudi Arabian newspaper), 405
Aldridge, Ruqayya, 257
Alexander, Edward, 373

al-Fatah, 425
  See also Fatah movement
al-Furdus Square (Baghdad), 210
al-Gama'a al-Islamiyah, 62, 220
Algeria, 19, 191, 289, 364
  advanced weapons assistance from
    China, 24
  Algerian Islamists active in Europe,
    311, 465, 466
  Algerian Islamists in Britain, 39, 40,
    279, 298, 309, 466
  association with al-Qaeda, 281, 313
  attacks on foreigners, 36, 59, 61, 232
  ban sought on teaching, 134–35
  bombings in, 42, 69, 232
  civil war, 21, 25, 36, 37, 50, 70, 72, 77,
    125, 419, 420
    assassination of Boudiaf, 54, 55, 56
    death tolls, 15
    mass murders in, 77–79
    media coverage of, 70
    support from other Muslim coun-
      tries, 22, 23, 24
  defence of Islamic taboos, 134, 135
  displacement of population, 17
  electoral process, 442, 444
  extradition of terrorists, 295, 296
  and GIA, 33, 59, 290, 419
  hijackings, 33, 41, 58, 232
  independence from France, war over
    (1954–1962), 19, 125
  inter-Muslim hostilities, 13, 21–22, 36,
    50, 65, 67, 69–70, 74, 77–79, 135,
    138, 151, 201, 210, 232
  and Islamic Salvation Front, 20, 462
  Islamists' transnational use of, 21,
    309–10, 467
  kidnappings and hostage-taking in, 59,
    313
  nuclear programme, 23
  oil, 451, 453
  represented in fighting against US in
    Iraq, 472
  support for terror, 461
  terrorist attacks not based on Pales-
    tinian issue, 191
  training and recruitment for Islamist at-
    tacks, 37, 166, 281–82, 298, 461, 466
  treatment of Christians, 419–20
  treatment of women, 82, 84–85, 132,
    240
  unemployment of youth, 166
  use of torture, 74
  US military presence in, 473
Algerian Islamist movement, 33, 39, 40. *See
    also* Armed Islamic Group, Salafist
    Group for Preaching and Combat
Algosaibi, Ghazi, 162
al-Gumhouriya (Egyptian newspaper), 189
al-Hayat (London newspaper), 237, 357
al-Hayat al-Jadida (Palestinian news-
    paper), 214
Ali, Ayaan Hirsi, 85, 305
Ali, Tariq, 363–64
Alibhai-Brown, Yasmin, 223
al-Imane mosque (Lille), 148
Aliyev, Geidar, 457
Aliyev, Ilham, 457
al-Jazeera, 62, 166
al-Jumhuriyah (Iraqi newspaper), 157
al-Kindi University (Baghdad), 84
al-Kurdi mosque (Amman), 406
Allam, Magdi, 225
Allawi, Iyad, 54, 160
Allende, Salvador, 53
al-Madina mosque (London), 231
al-Maqreze Centre for Historical
    Studies (London), 143
al-Muhajiroun ('the Emigrants'), 168,
    208, 212, 271, 276, 277, 287, 303
al-Qadisiyah (Iraqi newspaper), 157
al-Qaeda ('the base'), 44, 60, 143, 158,
    242, 285, 315, 322, 323, 349, 359,
    381, 382, 394, 404, 405
  in Afghanistan, 148, 168, 282–83, 324,
    400, 466

agents for, 49, 58, 106, 143, 189, 278, 279, 389, 393, 464, 467
and Ayman al-Zawahiri, 96, 157, 160, 290, 304, 403, 408, 486, 487
and Bali bombing, 84, 208, 382
in Bosnia, 282
and Britain, 282, 288, 298, 360, 399
in Europe, 311, 312, 313, 316, 319, 320
formation of, 20, 30, 56
funding of, 201, 280, 315, 316, 327, 462, 464
International Islamic Front for Jihad Against Jews and Crusaders, 30
in Iran, 461, 464
in Iraq, 82, 136, 282
in Kenya, 327, 464
in Libya, 232
linked to other Islamist groups, 59, 68, 153–54, 159, 160, 189, 313
and Madrid bombings, 319
in Morocco, 310
and Osama bin Laden, 30, 43, 101, 226, 227, 302, 454
in Pakistan, 465
in Saudi Arabia, 189, 230, 242, 282, 309, 453, 454, 455, 462, 463, 467
in Somalia, 21
in Syria, 461
in Tanzania, 327
in Tunisia, 29
and United States, 278, 280, 281, 283, 284, 297, 307, 308, 309, 349, 357, 363, 370, 376, 463
use of Islam for justification, 389, 399, 403–404
use of past grievances for justifying violence, 359
in Uzbekistan, 458
'Al-Qaeda Strikes Back' (BBC documentary), 360
al-Quds (Palestinian newspaper), 155
al-Quds al-Arabi (London newspaper), 152, 238, 305, 362

al-Quds University (Palestinian territories), 374
al-Riyadh (Saudi newspaper), 52, 212
al-Shahid mosque (Khartoum), 189
Alter, Robert, 204
al-Thawra (Iraqi newspaper), 155
Altikriti, Anas, 305
Alvi, Yasser, 271
al-Waleed (prince), 296
al-Zia al-Iraki mosque (Mosul), 408
ambiguity, 147, 155, 274, 465
of Muslims on use of violence, 226–33, 236–40, 245
ambivalence of Muslims towards non-Muslim world, 99, 226, 228, 237, 269–72, 465
American Airlines, 332
American Arab Anti-Discrimination Committee, 91, 228
American Conservative, 221
American Council on Foreign Relations, 234
American Muslim Council, 198, 211, 281, 326
American Presbyterian Church, 179
American Spectator, 373
Amis, Martin, 365, 381
Amnesty International, 74–75, 124, 177, 194, 195, 239, 333, 411, 442
amputations as punishment, 71, 72, 93, 418
Amrozi. *See* bin Nurhasyim, Amrozi
Amsterdam Council of Churches, 104
Anjum, Javed, 415
Ankara University, 96
Annan, Kofi, 125, 191, 332, 430
Ansar al-Islam (Iraq), 189, 289, 406
Ansar al-Jihad (Iraq), 160
Ansar al-Qaeda Brigades (Iraq), 301
Ansari, Abd al-Hamid al-, 226
anti-Americanism, 29, 31–32, 33, 35, 81, 359, 361–71, 384, 387–88, 448, 482, 483

anti-Islamic backlash, 243–45
anti-Muslim feelings, 17, 62, 70, 97,
    101–108, 112, 115, 116–17, 123–25,
    126
anti-Semitism, 14, 118, 205, 207, 212,
    215–18, 296
Anti-Terrorism, Crime and Security
    Act, Britain (2001), 291
anti-terrorism efforts. *See* 'War on
    Terror'
Apogevmatini (Greek newspaper), 206
Appalling Lie, The. See L'Effroyable Imposture
    (Meyssan)
'appeasement', 356
Arab European League (Belgium), 108,
    301
Arab-Islamic Congress, 295
Arab-Israeli conflict, 123–25
    Arab-Israeli war of 1948–1949, 18,
        182–84
    displacement of Palestinians, 16,
        183–84
    Arab-Israeli war of 1967 (Six-Day
        War), 14, 18, 29, 184, 185
    Arab-Israeli war of 1973, 18, 29, 186
    See also Israeli-Palestinian conflict
Arab League, 175, 209, 383, 425, 437, 478
    statistics on, 174
    use of Twelve Devices of Muslim
        arguments, 138, 139, 144
Arab nationalism, 11, 12, 13, 17, 27, 47,
    50, 123, 133, 141, 142, 145, 191, 321
Arab News (Saudi online newspaper), 229
Arafat, Yasser, 141, 178, 223, 434
    calling Palestine '*Terra Santa*', 425, 431
    and corruption, 165, 235, 446
    death of, 192, 209, 284, 431, 447
    and European countries, 314, 317, 321
    and Jordan, 23, 235
    on martyrdom, 156, 397
    Nobel Peace Prize, 201, 285
    ordering killings, 56
    on Osama bin Laden, 192

and Saudi Arabia, 141
on terrorism
    condeming, 138, 150
    justifying, 163
    urging, 144, 393, 395
    treatment by Israelis, 185, 206, 222,
        235, 345
    use of Twelve Devices of Muslim
        argument, 138–39, 141, 144–45,
        149, 150, 151, 371
    West Bank headquarters, 29, 156,
        433–34
Araud, Gérard, 215–18
Argentina, 464, 477
    bombings in, 22, 68, 69, 202, 211
'argument against America', 361–71
Arian, Sami al-, 299
Arifi, Muhammad bin Abd al-Rahman
    al-, 486
armaments used by Islamists, 467–71
Armed Islamic Group, 33, 59, 290, 419
Armed Vanguards of the Second
    Muhammad Army, 403
Armenia, 416, 467
    civil war with Azerbaijan, 16, 20
Armstrong, Karen, 373
Army of Ansar al-Sunna, 52
Arnold, Matthew, 109, 112
arson attacks, 34, 62, 67, 105, 135, 195,
    216, 392, 418
Ash, Timothy Garton, 348
Asharq al-Awsat (pan-Arab newspaper),
    231–32, 242, 243, 464
Ashura, festival of, 63
Asian Age, The, 244
Asmat, Haji Mohammed, 128
Assad, Bashar al-, 205, 208, 432, 442
Assad, Hafez, 19, 24, 50, 433, 443
    attempted assassination of, 55
    use of Twelve Devices of Muslim
        argument, 142
Assal, Riah Abu el-, 187
assassinations, targeted, 53–56

Associated Press, The, 10, 61, 63, 81, 148, 284

Aswat, Harron Rashid, 290

asylum seekers, 16, 90–91, 93, 107, 279, 293, 467

Atatürk, Kemal, 451

Atlanta Journal, 350

Atta, Mohammed, 40, 83–84, 151, 292, 307, 342, 344, 374

Atwan, Abdel Bari, 152, 238, 305

Aurangzeb (emperor), 412

Ausaf (Pakistani newspaper), 214

Australia, 242, 278, 345, 351
  anti-Jewish attacks, 215–16
  anti-Muslim attacks, 62, 104
  Australian hostage in Iraq, 226
  converts to Islam involved in violence, 168, 282–83
  embassies bombed, 69
  and Jemaah al-Islamiyah, 25
  Muslim statistics, 476
  support of Gulf War, 25
  terror cells in, 466
  troops in Iraq War, 158, 226
  warned to withdraw from Iraq, 158–59

Austria, 16, 61, 67, 101, 209, 317, 477

Avvenire (Italian newspaper), 190

Awadh, Abubakr, 211

Awali, Ghalib, 54

Awfi, Saleh al-, 289

Aydinlik (Turkish newspaper), 249

Ayodhya mosque, 68, 90

Azam, Sher, 154, 275, 401

Azeem, Ameer ul-, 350

Azerbaijan, 16, 20, 457, 459
  and oil, 457

Azhar, Ali, 247

Aziz, Abdul, 253

Aziz, Shaukat, 55

Aziz, Tariq, 208, 223, 317, 353, 430, 432

Azizi, Shahla, 240

Azmeh, Aziz al-, 99, *233*

Azzuz, Ahmet, 301

Ba'ath party, 12, 482
  in Iraq, 11, 12, 19, 27, 54, 76, 161, 210, 420–21, 441, 462, 482
  in Syria, 11, 19, 27, 206, 442–43, 462, 482
    massacres, 16, 50
    use of Twelve Devices of Muslim argument, 138
    treatment of Christians, 420–21

Babawi, Nabil Luka, 234

Babel (Iraqi newspaper), 329

Babri Masjid mosque (Ayodhya), 23

'backlash' thesis, 357, 377

Badawi, Abdullah Ahmad, 449

Badawi, Jamal, 290

Badawi, Zaki, 117–18, 231, 254, 428, 486

bad press for Islam, 47–87

Badr Brigades, 407

Baghat, Ahmed, 243

Baghdadi, Ahmad, 235

Baha'i faith, 411

Bahrain, 30, 310, 422, 439

Baker, Abdul Haqq, 168, 231

Baker, Kenneth, 263

Bakhtiar, Shapur, 55

Bakiyev, Kurmanbek, 458

Balfour, Arthur, 181

Bali bombing, 68, 84, 150, 166, 323, 359, 382
  and Abu Bakr Bashir, 311, 339
  Amrozi guilty of, 208, 232
  attributed by Islamists to Israel, 189, 221
  Samudra guilty of, 397

Balkans, 15, 25, 40, 321, 410
  See also Bosnia; Kosovo; Serbia

Balukta Party, 21

Bandar bin Sultan (prince), 138, 454

Bangladesh, 15, 81, 135, 449
  assassination of president, 54
  bombings in, 66, 69
  elections in, 442
  inter-Muslim violence, 63, 66

Islamists' transnational use of, 467
Muslim statistics, 474, 475
Pakistan-Bangladesh war (1971), death
    tolls, 15
punishments, 73, 74
response to Gulf War, 25
treatment of other religions, 411, 412,
    415
treatment of women, 73, 74, 82, 85
Bangladesh Baptist Fellowship, 415
'Banglatown,' 92
Banna, Hassan al-, 479
Baraka, Amir, 214
Bashir, Abu Bakr, 60, 388, 395–96, 463
    argues that charges fabricated by US
        and Israel, 190, 221, 339
    found guilty of Bali bombing, 150, 319
        reduction of sentence, 311
    leader of Jemaah Islamiyah, 141,
        153–54, 189, 406
    praise of bin Laden, 44, 394
Bashir, Omar Hassan Ahmed al-, 20,
    189–90
Baz, Osama el-, 215
BBC. *See* British Broadcasting Corporation
Beard, Mary, 344
Becket, Thomas, 407
Beg, Mirza Islam, 468
beheadings, 71–72, 77, 106, 154, 229,
    243, 426
    in Algeria, 78
    in Bangladesh, 415
    of Daniel Pearl, 79, 212
    in Iraq, 51, 61, 90, 139, 143, 228, 243,
        287, 394, 462
    in Kashmir, 60, 75
    in Nigeria, 418
    in Palestine, 75
    in Philippines, 310, 313, 417
    in Saudi Arabia, 71, 72, 73
    in Thailand, 411
Belgium, 294, 301, 465, 466
    anti-Jewish attacks, 216

anti-Muslim feelings, 62, 102, 104, 105
    using educational segregation, 117
attempted bombing in, 281
Islamists' transnational use of, 466
Muslim demands for special treatment
    after immigration, 108
opposition to Iraq War, 317–18
'Believing Youth' movement, 289
Beloufi, Ahmed, 39
ben Ali, Zine el-Abidine, 20, 39, 442
Bencheikh, Soheib, 223
Benedict XVI (pope), 429, 431
Benn, Tony, 334, 368
Berbers, 411
Berg, Nick, 228
Berger, John, 42, 120, 359–60
Berlin Free University, 363
Berlusconi, Silvio, 106, 160, 301
Berthoud, Martin, 376
Beslan school hostage-taking, 59, 60,
    229, 243, 294
    blamed on Israel, 189–90
Biafra civil war, 15, 418
    See also Nigeria, Northern
Bibawi, Nabil Luka, 243
Bible, 392, 396
Biden, Joseph, 200
Biffi, Giacomo (Cardinal), 101, 103
Bilgrami, Akeel, 258
bin Baz, Sheikh Abdel-Aziz, 163
bin Kasim, Muhammad, 412
bin Laden, Osama, 39, 148, 159–60, 204,
    210, 335, 344, 403, 444, 463
    agenda of, 107–108
    attempts to liken to Bush, 349
    call for jihad or killing of Americans
        and Jews, 211, 212, 302, 307, 389,
        403, 408, 430, 454
    calling al-Qaeda 'good terror', 43
    comment on AIDS, 369
    on death, 162
    diaspora Muslims' comments on, 276
    efforts to hunt him down, 101, 276, 304

endowment of Harvard Law School,
    302
fatwa against, 226, 404
founding of International Islamic
    Front for Jihad Against Jews and
    Crusaders, 30
on Iraq reconstruction, 481
on Jews, 189, 211
as a leader, 22
'Letter to the American People', 207,
    221, 485
Muslim condemnations of, 43, 230
Muslims' support of, 101, 148, 230,
    276, 286, 307
non-Muslim views on, 179, 284, 319,
    322, 323, 331, 344, 345, 349, 483
and 9/11, 75, 153, 162, 227, 307, 338,
    341, 408
and Palestine, 32, 192, 193, 210
praised by Bashir, 44, 394
praise of Fisk's reporting, 76
in Sudan, 464
theology of, 28–29, 407
use of Islam for justification, 389, 403
bin Nurhasyim, Amrozi, 208, 232
bin Salamah, Rajaa, 236–40, 241
Bishara, Marwan, 373
black-market arms trading, 467–71
Black Muslim coup in Trinidad, 61
Black Sea ferry, capture of, 59
'Black September', 235
Blair, Tony, 43, 285, 323, 324, 430
    blamed for London bombings (2005),
        151
blasphemy, 233
    in Islam, 131–33, 164, 390, 414, 416
    protecting Islam in Britain, 115, 263,
        266
    Rushdie seen as blasphemous, 121,
        122, 247, 254, 256, 432
Blix, Hans, 287
Blondet, Maurizio, 190
blood

used as metaphor by Christians, 159
used as metaphor by Muslims, 157–60
use of word by media to sensation-
    alize, 60, 61, 63
Bloomberg, Michael, 102
Blüm, Norbert, 197
Blundeston Prison, 335
Board of Deputies (Britain), 116
Bodi, Faisal, 166, 207, 303
Boeing 747, 307
Bolkiah, Hassan, 444
Bombay Stock exchange, bombing of, 69
bombings, 65–71, 158, 166, 229, 403
    in Afghanistan, 67
    in Algeria, 42, 69, 232
    in Argentina, 22, 68, 69, 202, 211
    in Austria, 67
    in Britain, 69, 75
    of USS Cole, 310, 463, 466
    Cruise-missile attacks by US, 30
    in Egypt, 61, 62, 67, 68, 137, 237
    in Germany, 68
    in Greece, 68
    in India, 23, 65, 68, 69
    in Indonesia, 67, 68, 69
        Bali bombing, 68, 84, 150, 166, 189,
            208, 221, 232, 311, 323, 339,
            359, 397
    in Iran, 69
    in Iraq, 64, 67, 68, 129, 189
    in Israel, 39, 57, 62–63, 65, 66, 67, 68,
        69, 139, 152, 197, 198, 211, 372,
        374
    by Israel, 469
    in Italy, 67
    in Jordan, 68
    in Kashmir, 67, 68, 69
    in Kenya, 30, 68, 69, 149, 152, 211,
        223, 299, 327
    in Lebanon, 19, 68, 69
    letter-bombs, 56
    in Morocco, 67, 68, 75, 289
    in Pakistan, 67, 68, 69

Pan Am Flight 103, 20
in Philippines, 67, 68
in Russia, 65, 66, 67, 68, 69, 310
in Saudi Arabia, 30, 67, 230–31
in Spain (Madrid train-bombings), 65,
    158, 190, 229, 242, 319, 467
in Tanzania, 30, 69, 299, 327
in Thailand, 67, 68
in Turkey, 67, 68, 208
by United States, 19–20, 30, 54
in United States, 67
in Yemen, 68
See also 9/11 attacks, suicide-bombings
Bonino, Emma, 81
Bosnia, 12, 15, 27, 239, 321, 403, 443, 464
    citizens attacked in Algeria, 61
    civil war, 15, 21, 22
    displacement of Muslims, 16, 17
    Islamists' transnational use of, 467
    Muslims fighting in, 26, 37, 279, 282,
        286, 308, 321, 405, 467
    near-genocide of Muslims, 13, 26, 70,
        89, 150–51, 193, 194
    US military presence in, 473
Bouckaert, Peter, 195
Boudiaf, Mohammed, 54, 55
Boughedou, Saida, 85
Boughedou, Zoulika, 85
Bouteflika, Abdelaziz, 205, 442, 453
Boyce, Michael, 366, 380
Boykin, William, 108
Bradford, Bishop of, 120
Bradford University, 368
Bradley University, 302
Bradshaw, Ben, 194
Brahimi, Lakhdar, 192
Brandeis University, 302
Bremer, Paul, 157, 369
Britain
    advanced weapons assistance to Pak-
        istan, 24
    anti-Muslim actions, 17, 62, 101, 104,
        106, 107, 116
    controversies over wearing the *hijab*,
        95, 104, 105
    desecration of Muslim graves, 64
    assault on Egypt (1956), 17, 19, 29, 315
    assistance to Israeli nuclear pro-
        gramme, 470
    attacks on its embassies, 68, 69
    blamed for London bombings (2005),
        151
    bombings in, 69, 75
        London Underground bombings
            (2005), 15, 31, 65, 101, 143,
            155, 226, 230, 237, 243, 278,
            289, 292, 308, 360
    Britons accused by Saudis of bomb-
        ings, 73
    citizens attacked in Egypt, 61
    converts to Islam drawn to activism,
        168–69
    decline of Anglicanism and Catholi-
        cism, 478
    foiled attacks, 290
    honour killings in, 86
    Islamists in, 39, 327, 465, 466
        transnational use of, 466, 467
    laws on, and treatment of, terrorists,
        291–92, 293–94
        arrests of terrorists, 290, 294
        extradition of terrorists, 295
    Muslim demands for special treatment
        in education, 109–15, 116–18
    Muslim statistics, 476
    plans for expulsion of Muslim clerics,
        296
    providing weapons to Muslim world,
        469
    support of Gulf War, 25
    support of Iraq against Iran, 24
    treatment of Muslim immigrants,
        91–93, 97–101
    unemployment of Muslims, 116, 167–68
    use of falsehood, 135–36
British Airways, 267–68

British Broadcasting Corporation, 33, 62, 75, 93, 145, 154, 187, 217–18, 258, 303, 360, 366, 408
British Court of Appeal, 297
British Department of Education, 108, 110
British Foreign Office, 183, 191, 194, 199
British High Commissioner for Palestine, 182
British High Court, 116, 247
British Home Affairs Committee (House of Commons), 115
British Home Office, 39, 114
British House of Commons, 115, 203, 328, 363, 382
British House of Lords, 299
British Law Lords, 291–92, 298
British Ministry of Defence, 309
British Museum, 279
British Muslim Alliance, 254
British Parliament, 309
British Scotland Yard, 301
Brixton mosque, 168, 231
Brown, Andrew, 264
Brown, Gordon, 267
Brunei, 128, 444
Brunei Legislative Council, 444
Brzezinski, Zbigniew, 43, 188, 321–22
Buchanan, Patrick, 218, 221
Buddhists, 390, 393, 402, 410, 411, 412
Bukhari, Syed Ahmed, 199, 228
Bulgaria, 281, 465, 474
Bunglawala, Inayat, 227, 237, 305
Bunting, Madeleine, 379
Burgess, Anthony, 263
Burns, William, 79
buses
    bus bombings, 39, 57, 61, 67, 75, 139, 374
    hijackings, 58, 78
Bush, George W., 42, 284, 389
    after 9/11, 144, 399
    attempts to liken to bin Laden, 349

and Blair, 324
blamed for London bombings (2005), 151
condemnation of, 283, 350, 353, 359, 362, 364–69, 377, 433
on democratisation of Muslim regimes, 437
his attack on terror, 43, 480, 488
on invasion of Iraq, 135–36, 287–88, 331
linked to Saudis, 297
State of the Union address, 323, 330–31
support of Israel, 219, 221–22, 224
Bushehr nuclear reactor, 24, 469
Butler, Richard, 223

'Cairo Declaration on Human Rights in Islam', 334
Cairo Museum, 61
Calabresi, Guido, 369
California State University, 302
Cambio 16 (Spanish newspaper), 205
Cambridge University, 107, 150, 180, 344
Cameroon, 473
Campaign Against Censorship, 263
'Campaign Against Islam' (Britain), 102
Campaign for Nuclear Disarmament, 483
Camp David 'peace accord,' 18, 178
Camp Whitehorse (Iraq), 312
Canaan, land of, 178, 181, 390
Canada
    anti-Muslim sentiments, 108
    Canadian accused by Saudis of bombings, 73
    diaspora Muslims aiding terrorism, 37, 278, 280, 281, 307
    Muslim statistics, 476
    settlement of diaspora Muslims, 285
    Sharia law, 286
Canadian Islamic Congress, 305
caning. *See* floggings as punishment

Canterbury, archbishop of, 56, 61, 107, 227, 288, 350, 407, 426
Capone, Al, 54
Capriolo, Ettore, 248
Capucci, Hilarion, 427
car-bombs, 64, 67, 69, 189, 232
Carey, George, 227
Carter, Jimmy, 261–62, 321
Carter, Stephen, 330
Cassen, Bernard, 353, 365, 368
Castro, Fidel, 53
Catholic Church, 329, 410, 414, 422, 424–26, 428–31, 433–35
    decline of, 477–78
    See also Vatican
celebrations after violence, 57, 143, 149, 237
cemeteries, desecration of, 64–65, 216, 419, 423
Center for Muslim-Christian Understanding, 357
Central Mosque (Birmingham), 237
Central Mosque (London), 211, 260
centrifuge technology, 468
Chad, 16, 473
Chait, Jonathan, 366
Chaldean Catholic church, 420, 421, 425, 432
Chalgam, Mohamed Abderrhmane, 232
Chand, Mia, 253
Chanel fashions, 128
charities, 140, 146, 403
    charity as defined by Muslims, 132, 391
    Christian charities, 413, 415
    false charitable organizations, 279, 280, 281, 298, 299, 460, 463, 464, 465
    with financial ties to al-Qaeda, 201, 280, 315
Charles (prince), 400
Chechnya, 17, 410, 413, 471
    assassination of Yandarbiyev, 462

beheadings, 59
bombings, 58, 65, 67, 69, 310
Chechens in Second World War, 482
Chechen use of violence, 76, 244
clan allegiance in, 49
Islamists in, 26, 37
    arrests of, 289
    influx of, 310, 479
    transnational use of, 467
kidnappings and hostage-taking in, 12, 59, 60, 221
oil, 460
represented in fighting against US in Iraq, 472
Russia's use of force to deny independence, 13, 21, 29, 60, 70, 193, 281, 312, 460
separatist movement, 15, 16, 21, 29, 30, 193, 280, 460
    support from other countries, 23, 24
use of Twelve Devices of Muslim argument, 145
'chemical Ali'. *See* Majid, Ali Hassan al-
chemical weapons
    used by Iraq, 50
    used by Syria, 50
Chevron Texaco (oil company), 456, 457, 458
Chile, 53
China, 17, 24, 44, 320, 467–68
    aid to Iran, 24, 316, 452, 468
    as a Great Power, 452
    Islamists in, 465
        arrests of, 289
        transnational use of, 467
    and Israel, 174, 186
    and Khartoum, 316
    Muslim statistics, 474–75
    not supporting Iraq War, 317
    nuclear programme, aiding other countries, 24, 452, 468
    and oil, 452, 457, 458, 459
    praise from Amir al-Saadi, 329

Xinjiang, 13, 15, 16, 20, 25, 26, 90, 459,
    467
Chirac, Jacques, 96, 208, 284, 317–18,
    328, 381, 431
Chitod, battle of, 412
Chomsky, Noam, 353, 360
Choudhry, Anjem, 294
Christ, role in Islam, 389–90
Christian Democratic Party (Germany),
    103, 197
Christian Falange (Lebanon), 125
Christians, 178–79, 402–403, 410
    Christian Ibos, 418
    Christianity as a 'religion of love', 387
    Christian Zionists, 215
    evangelical Christians, 171, 178–79,
        215, 362, 399, 407, 424, 428
    Islam's treatment of, 387–435
    Lebanese Christians, 184
    Maronite Christians, 445
    Nigerian Christians, 418–19
    See also Catholic Church, infidels and
        Muslims, Vatican
'Christmas Letter' (Saddam Hussein), 12,
    432
Churchill, Winston, 22
Church of England, 109, 113, 179
Church of Scotland, 478
Church of the Nativity (Bethlehem), 14,
    434
Chrysostom, John, 223
CIA. See US Central Intelligence Agency
City Journal (New York City), 107
City University of New York, 302
civil liberties, 280, 293, 297, 300, 306,
    333, 335, 357, 451
    of Muslim Americans, 116, 313
    potential danger of eroding, 304, 334,
        347–49
Clark, Jonathan, 344
Clark, Ramsey, 345
Clark, Wesley, 365
Clarke, Kenneth, 382

'clash of civilisations', 27, 190, 399, 402
Clash of Civilisations, The (Huntington),
    172
clerics as advisers to Islamic movements,
    406–407
Clinton, Bill, 304, 364
Clinton, Hillary, 365
Clio (goddess of history), 44–45
Clochemerles, 109
clothing, Muslim, 80–81
    See also hijab
CNN (TV), 199
Cold War, 17, 42
USS Cole, 310, 463, 466
collaborators, 14, 51, 61, 75, 76, 80, 151,
    288
Columbia (space shuttle), 409
Columbia University, 364
Columbia University Law School, 349
Commission for Racial Equality, 112,
    267, 335
Committee for Bangladeshis' Rights, 92,
    109
Committee for the Commemoration of
    Martyrs of the Global Islamic
    Campaign, 269
Congo, 53
Conservative Party (Britain), 268. See also
    Tory Party
Contini, Barbara, 313
convenienza, 430–31, 433
Copts, 420
Cormack, Patrick, 203
Corriere della Sera (Italian newspaper),
    225, 350
Council for Mosques (Bradford), 32, 141,
    154, 247, 485
Council of Islamic Organisations of
    Greater Chicago, 305
Council of State (France), 295
Council on American Islamic Relations,
    198, 305, 355, 486
'Covenant' of Hamas, 212

'Covenant' of the Palestinian Authority, 209

covert abductions of terror suspects. *See* 'renditions'

Croatia, 21, 61

Crown Prosecution Services, 267

Cruise-missile attacks by US, 30, 54

Crusaders, 96, 108, 160, 161, 164, 388, 389, 393, 397, 420, 421, 425, 430, 433, 484

'Crusader America', 304, 405

'Crusaders and Zionists', 49, 175, 403, 408, 422, 428

Cuba, 53

cultural sensitivity, 327, 335, 377, 399

Cunningham, Alan, 182

Cyprus, 19

Dacca, 19

Dacre, Lord, 262

Dadullah, Mullah, 406

Daeubler-Gmelin, Herta, 368

Daily Mirror (British newspaper), 329

Daily Star (British newspaper), 150

Daily Telegraph (British newspaper), 44, 53, 76, 83, 94, 217, 223, 261, 271, 282, 322, 331, 361, 377, 399

d'Alema, Massimo, 382

Dalyell, Tam, 190, 218

Damra, Imam Fawaz Mohammed, 209, 280, 297

Daniel, Isioma, 131

Darajme, Hiba Azzam, 374

Darfur, 15, 21, 161

Darwish, Abdullah Nimr, 158

Dawn (Pakistani newspaper), 243–44, 271

death-squad killings, 50

death-threats, 57, 82, 103, 110, 133, 134, 248, 254, 414, 421

death tolls, 15–17

Decalogue, 202

decapitations. *See* beheadings

deception

used by Muslims, 135, 136–37, 146–56

Twelve Devices of Muslim argument, 137–46, 148, 149, 155, 164, 197, 215, 228, 247, 256, 276, 303, 305, 337, 339, 341, 470

used by non-Muslims, 135–36, 137, 146–47, 150

Nine Arguments to avoid truth about Islamic advance, 338–83

Decourtray, Albert Florent Augustin (Cardinal), 120

Deedat, Ahmed, 247

Defence Policy Board (Pentagon), 218

De Genova, Nicholas, 364

DeLay Tom, 219, 424

democracy, 39, 146, 207, 273, 275, 376, 378, 442, 452, 475, 486, 487

as alien to Islam, 441, 482

choices to be made, 333

illusion of, 451, 481

Western democracy, 45, 99, 304, 305, 448, 481

See also civil liberties; human rights

democratisation of Muslim regimes, attempts at, 437–88

Denmark, 56, 103

anti-Muslim sentiments, 102

prejudices about, 107

and wearing of *hijab*, 95, 105

Muslim statistics, 476

Dermouche, Aissa, 105

Der Spiegel (German newspaper), 206

desecration of sacred places or objects, 62, 64–65, 216, 419, 423

Koran, 81, 406, 414, 416, 448

'desperado' argument, 370–75

destruction of religious artefacts, 390

detention of foreign nationals without a trial, 291–93

devices of Muslim argument. *See* Twelve Devices of Muslim argument

Devonshire, Duke of, 377

Dhalla, Musadiq, 116
Dhondy, Farrukh, 107, 133, 332, 410
Diahnine, Nabila, 85
diaspora, Jewish, 175
diaspora Muslims, 86, 89–125, 166, 175,
        230, 234, 237, 246, 266, 328, 331,
        471
    ambivalence of, 269–72
    demands for special treatment after
        immigration, 98, 275, 285–86
        related to education, 109–15,
            116–18
    expecting rights from country while
        supporting enemies of, 275–88,
        298–305
    fears of, 332
    growth in strength, 428
    sense of power over non-Muslims,
        322
    on treatment of women, 240–42
    use of Twelve Devices of Muslim
        argument, 142, 148
    view of Islam, 400, 401
    See also settlement of Muslims in
        Western countries; education
Dibaj, Medhi, 415
Diem, Ngo Dinh, 53
Die Zeit (German newspaper), 329
di Giovanni, Janine, 193
'dire consequences' as an argument,
        375–83, 480
Disney World and controversy over
        wearing the hijab, 95
Dome of the Rock, 210
Dominican Republic, 53
Dostum, Abdul Rashid, 448
Drabble, Margaret, 345, 361, 362, 366
Druze Muslims, 424
Dubai, 147, 462
    arrests of terrorists, 290, 466
    Islamists' transnational use of, 466
    and oil, 455
Dudayev, Dzhokhar, 460

Dudley mosque, 250
Duisenberg, Greta, 206
Dumas, Roland, 36
Dummett, Michael, 121–22, 262
Durham University, 256

East Africa, Muslim statistics, 475
Easterman, Daniel, 256
East Jerusalem, 64–65, 160, 423
East Turkestan, 25
Ebadi, Shirin, 241
Ebtekar, Massoumeh, 380
Economist, 222
education
    attempt to ban, 134–35
    Islamic schooling demands by immi-
        grants to West, 97–99, 116–18,
        244, 285
    Islamist objection to Jews in British
        educational system, 213
    Muslim demands for special treatment
        after immigration, 108–15
    treatment of women in Muslim coun-
        tries, 82
Egypt, 13, 43, 51, 87, 168, 220, 342, 461
    advanced weapons assistance, 468, 469
    anti-Americanism, 81
    assassinations, 29, 54, 57, 162
    attempt to overthrow Mubarak, 23
    asylum for Nazis, 182
    bombings in, 62, 67, 68
        Luxor, 61, 138, 237
    condemnation of terrorism, 229, 231,
        233, 234, 242, 243
    controversies over wearing the hijab, 96
    displacement of population, 17
    Egyptian embassy in Pakistan
        bombed, 69
    and Gaza, 22, 183, 192, 461
    government of, 442–43, 444, 445
    inter-Muslim hostilities, 53, 56, 64, 72,
        74, 151, 201
    and Iraq War, 383, 472

Islamists in, 19, 23, 25, 26, 37, 40, 50, 58, 61, 73, 135, 162, 213, 281, 283, 284, 289–90
   arrests and trials of, 29
   extraditions and deportations, 295, 296, 299
   extra-judicial killings, 72, 201, 289
   support by Iran, 22
   support of Iraq, 26, 472
   transnational use of, 465–67, 472
and Israel, 18, 37, 179, 183, 187, 191, 205, 212, 235, 461
   attacks on, 29, 182, 183, 184, 186
   formal recognition of, 203
and Nasser, 11, 18–19
Suez War (1956), 11, 17, 19, 29, 315
treatment of Christians, 420
and United States, 474
use of Twelve Devices of Muslim argument, 143, 144
views on *Columbia* disaster, 409
Eid al-Adha, 63
El Al aircraft, hijacking of, 19
Eliot, T. S., 222
El Watan (Algerian newspaper), 78
embassy bombings
   attacks foiled, 69, 466
   attacks on embassies in Uzbekistan, 459
   Australian embassy in Indonesia, 69
   British embassy in Greece, 68
   Dutch embassy in Iraq, 69
   French embassy in Algeria, 36
   Israeli embassy in Argentina, 68
   Jordanian embassy in Iraq, 69
   Philippine embassy in Indonesia, 68
   US embassies in Kenya and Tanzania, 30, 69, 299, 327
   US embassy in Lebanon, 69
Empson, William, 155
'enemy combatants', 292–93, 298
Erakat, Saeb, 144, 180
Erbakan, Nocmettin, 212–13

Erdogan, Recep Tayyip, 199, 397–98
Eritrea, Islamists' transnational use of, 467
Ershad, Hossain Mohammad, 19
   brought down because of Gulf War, 25
Esposito, John, 199, 357
Essawy, Hesham el-, 105, 256, 258, 260
Etchegaray, Roger, 426, 430
Ethiopia, 16, 55, 290, 466, 467
EU. *See* European Union
'Eurabia', 93
European Central Bank, 206
European Convention on Human Rights, 291
European Court of Human Rights, 97
European Monitoring Centre on Racism and Xenophobia, 104
European Union, 38, 77, 356
   admission of Turkey, 431, 451
   anti-racism, 315
   anti-terrorism efforts, 314–15
   'association agreement' with Syria, 315
   condemnation of US, 367, 369
   on Saddam Hussein trial, 320
   and Iraq
      not supporting Iraq War, 317, 318, 319, 363, 431
      pledge of support for 'new Iraq', 320
   on Jenin incursion by Israel, 194
   languages spoken, 108
   on nuclear programmes, 316, 469
   support for Hamas, 314
   support for Palestine, 201, 284–85, 314, 321
Evening Standard (British newspaper), 205, 222
exceptionalism as applied to Israel, 200–201
Exeter University, 99, 233
extradition
   of Jews, 172

of Islamists, 278, 294–95, 299, 316
extra-judicial killings, 72, 131, 201, 289
extremism, 230
Exxon Mobil (oil company), 455, 458

Fadlallah, Ayatollah Mohammed Hussein, 243
Fadlallah, Sheikh Sayed Hussein, 425
Fahd (king), 453
Fahd, Sheikh Nasser al-, 230
Faisal (king), 19
Faisal, Abdullah el-, 213, 214, 327, 398, 409
Fallaci, Oriana, 108, 286
Falwell, Jerry, 325, 329, 407
Farrakhan, Louis, 20, 169, 217
Farrell, Herman, 365
fascism, 36, 103, 172, 240, 482
  anti-fascism, 29
  as basis of Ba'ath party, 11
  neo-fascism, 62, 482
  'underlying causes', 356
fashion, Western, 80–81, 129
Fatah movement, 56, 194, 209, 425, 447
  al-Fatah, 427
Fatah-Tanzim, 434
Father Christmas, 285
fatwas, 404
  against Barbie dolls, 83
  condeming London suicide-bombings, 226
  condeming US in Iraq, 408
  against Isioma Daniel, 131
  against Osama bin Laden, 226
  against Salman Rushdie, 20, 28, 30, 32, 37, 119, 120, 122, 131, 142, 154, 225, 246–65, 267–70, 271, 275
  against Taslim Nasrin, 85
Fayyad, Salam, 314
FBI. See US Federal Bureau of Investigation
fear of Muslim immigrants, 89–125
Federation for American Immigration Reform, 298

Federation of Muslim Organizations (Britain), 227
Feith, Douglas, 222
fellow-travellers of Islamism. See non-Muslims, support of Islamism
'fifth column', 107, 332
Finsbury Park mosque, 276
First Amendment freedom in US, 299
First Church of Christ (Highland, Indiana), 331
'First European War', 110–11
First World War, 22
  beginning of, 18
  demand for renaming of, 110–11
Fischer, Joschka, 381–82, 430
Fisk, Robert, 75–76, 80, 192, 197, 204, 218, 343
Fitzgerald, Michael, 426
Fizazi, Muhammad al-, 290
Flint, Julie, 56
floggings as punishment, 72, 73–74, 85
Fo, Dario, 330, 357
Foot, Paul, 217
Force of Reason, The (Fallaci), 286
Ford, Henry, 190
Forest, William. See Faisal, Abdullah el-
Fortuyn, Pim, 102–103
Fouda, Farag, 135
Fox News (TV), 118
France, 38, 40, 127, 128, 148, 214, 229, 266, 285, 286, 295
  and Algeria, 19, 36, 125, 204, 232
  anti-Muslim actions, 101–102, 104, 105, 240, 241
  controversies over wearing the hijab, 95, 96, 97, 105, 209, 241, 298–99, 301–302, 379
  desecrations of sacred places, 62, 64
  elections in, 216, 266
  Franco-British military assault, 17, 19, 315
  and Gulf War, 25, 321
  indications of Muslim poverty, 167, 168

Muslims in prison, 166–67
unemployment of Muslims, 116, 166
and Iran, 261, 316
and Iraq War, 313, 317, 318, 329, 430, 431, 482
Islamists in, 62, 65, 281, 282, 465, 466, 480
arrests and trials of, 278, 283, 290
attacks on French aircraft, 33, 41, 58, 59
extraditions and deportations, 294–95, 296
as rear base for fundamentalism, 39, 40
transnational use of, 466, 467
and Israel, 204, 215, 216, 218, 221, 223, 314, 322
Muslim demands for special treatment after immigration, 98, 108, 285–86
Muslim statistics, 92
nuclear programme, aiding other countries, 24, 469
security laxity, 309, 310
and United States, 221, 328, 361
Free Democrat Party (Germany), 197
Freedland, Jonathan, 365–66
free markets, 485, 486
Free Methodists, 420
French Islamic Association, 275–76
French Red Cross, 223
Freud, Sigmund, 224
Friday Times (Pakistani newspaper), 246
Friedman, Thomas, 326, 352
Frossard, André, 121
fundamentalism, 11, 12, 39, 236, 240, 321–22, 397, 404
'neo-Islamism', 27
secular fundamentalism, 93
in Western nations, 353–54
funding of terrorism, 280, 281, 298, 299, 460, 463, 464

Gabon, 473
Gaddafi, Muammar al-, 19, 209
Gailani, Ahmed Khalfan, 290
Gainutdin, Ravil, 406
Galilee, 186
Galloway, George, 198, 211, 288, 328–29, 350–51, 353, 354
Gambia, Muslim statistics, 475
Gandhi, Indira, 56
Ganje'i, Ayatollah Jalal, 233
Garang, John, 450
Gayoom, Maumoon Abdul, 444
Gaza, 64, 183, 461
celebrations after violence, 57, 148, 149
and Christians, 14, 423, 426
condemnation of Israeli occupation, 206
under Egyptian control, 22, 192
elections in, 314, 447
hatred of Israel, 158, 161, 202, 210, 214
indications of Muslim poverty, 167
Israel withdrawal, 176, 447
shooting of collaborators, 51
storming of Gaza prison, 310
Gecgel, Imam, 189
Gemayel, Bashir, 55, 184
General Council of the Assemblies of God, 416
Geneva Conventions, 180, 202, 298
Genghis Khan, 366, 411
genocide, 13, 125, 205–206, 369
Gentilli, Marc, 223
George Mason University, 302
Georgetown University, 199
Georgia, 459–60
Gephardt, Richard, 366
German Federal Administrative Court, 299
German Interior Ministry, 299
German National Party, 299–300
Germany, 36, 40, 299, 315, 329, 463

advanced weapons assistance to other
    countries, 24, 469
anti-Muslim attacks, 101, 103, 104
banning of Arab-Islamic Congress,
    295
banning of Hizb ut-Tahrir, 211–12,
    299
bombings in, 68
controversies over wearing the *hijab*,
    95
and George W. Bush, 365, 368
German tourists attacked, 62, 213
and Iran, 316
and Iraq War, 317, 319, 329, 381–82,
    430, 782
Islamists in, 61, 308, 374, 465, 466
    arrests and trials of, 278, 281, 283,
        320
    attacks foiled, 290
    extraditions and deportations, 294,
        295, 316
and Israel, 197, 206
Muslim demands for special treatment
    after immigration, 108
Muslim immigration to, 16, 465, 466
Muslim statistics, 476
paying ransoms, 62, 213
Second World War, 59, 188, 217, 356,
    398, 482
and United States, 319, 368–69
'Gerontion' (Eliot), 222
Ghaddafi, Muammar Abu Minyar al-,
    442
Ghamdi, Said al-, 344
Ghassi, Mahmoud al, 388
Ghauri, Muhammad, 412
Ghazali, el- (Sufi), 134
Ghazali, Muhammed, 72
Ghozi, Rohman al-, 310
GIA, The. *See* Armed Islamic Group
Gingrich, Newt, 325
Giuliani, Rudolf, 296
'global capitalism', 357, 377

global nature of Muslim faith, 479–80
Goebbels, Joseph, 329
Golan Heights, 18, 184
'Golden Age' of Islamic learning, 130
Golden Mean, 202
Goldstein, Baruch, 90
Gomaa, Abdulwahab Hussein, 231
Gorbachev, Mikhail Sergeyevich, 23
Gore, Al, 364, 366
Gott, Richard, 369
Graham, Billy, 120
Graham, Franklin, 407, 423
Grand Imam Ali mosque (Najaf), 407
Grand Mosque (Mecca), 394, 409
Grass, Günter, 370, 376
Great Eastern Islamist Raiders' Front, 282
Great Mosque of Rome, 231
'Great Satan', 44, 454
Greece, 68, 268, 313, 316
Greek Eastern Islamic Raiders', 67
Green, Andrew, 192
Guantanamo Bay, 60, 70, 81, 230, 281,
    285, 294, 305, 332, 463
    desecration of Koran, 406, 448
Guardian (British newspaper), 36, 37, 40,
    41, 69, 71, 72, 75, 92, 105, 157, 166,
    177, 180, 182, 186, 188, 192, 195–96,
    198, 199, 204, 205, 207, 216, 217,
    218, 221–22, 223, 224, 238, 240, 246,
    250, 252, 255, 257, 260, 261, 263,
    277, 278, 284, 285, 287, 288, 303,
    305, 323, 326, 327, 328, 333, 338,
    343, 344, 345, 346, 347, 348, 349,
    350, 351, 352, 353, 354, 355, 356,
    359, 360, 361, 362, 363, 364, 365,
    366, 367, 368, 369, 370, 371, 378,
    379, 381, 384, 399, 420
Guardian Council (Iran), 233, 439, 440
Guinea, 455, 456
Gul, Hamid, 379
Gulf of Guinea, 455
Gulf War (1991), 12, 14, 25, 31, 157,
    202, 354, 422

damage to Kuwait, 52
deaths in, 15, 40
'turkey shoot' of Iraqi army, 13
Iraqi delusions about, 155–56, 157
seen as 'anti-Muslim', 43, 306
support of Iraq during or after
by Arafat, 23
from Belarus, 24
by British imams, 306
by French Islamic Association, 275–76
by Hussein (king), 43
from Iran, 141
from Jordan, 141
from Palestine, 235
from Romania, 24
from Sudan, 23
from Ukraine, 24
US defence of, 321
Gulf War, second. *See* Iraq War (2003)
Gumbleton, Thomas, 353

Ha'aretz (Israeli newspaper), 123, 176
Haddam, Tedjini, 254
Haeri, Kadhim Husseini, 190
Hafez, Samihia, 420
Hafez, Samir, 420
Hafs, Abu, 464
Haider, Jö, 482
Hain, Peter, 199
Haj, Khaled Ali, 289
Hajjar, Imam Ridha, 238
Hakim, Mohammed Baqer al-, 55, 189,
407, 481
Halabja, 20
Halmahera, 416–17
Hamas, 192, 210, 289, 378, 406, 488
arms and funding for, 22, 23, 26, 30,
280, 281, 314, 463, 464
assassination of leaders, 54, 64, 139,
158, 231
revenge for, 160
association of Hamas with terrorism,
197, 199

and Chechnya, 26, 462
and Christians, 434
condemnation of some attacks, 138,
229
'Covenant' of, 212
and Egypt, 461
and elections, 447
inspired by Khomeinism, 20
and Iran, 22, 30
and Israel, 161, 202, 209, 210, 303, 408
in London, 39, 40
meaning of word, 344, 345
and Saudi Arabia, 463
and Sudan, 464
suicide-bombings, 39, 66, 139, 158,
161, 397
and Syria, 23
and United States, 238
Hames, Tim, 322, 323
Hamid, Alaa, 131
Hammad, Nemer, 427
Hammadi, Saddoun, 156
Hamza, Sheikh Abu, 213, 366
hangings as punishment, 13, 72, 73, 80,
415
See also lynchings
Haniya, Ismail, 378
Hanson, Hamza Yusuf, 344
Haq, Sheik Gad el-Haq Ali Gad el-, 259
Haqqani, Husain, 237
Haque, Muhammed, 110
Harding, Warren G., 364
Hariri, Rafik, 55, 445
Harper's Magazine, 33
Hartog, Yassin, 305–306
Harvard University, 296, 302, 342
Hasan, Mushirul, 248
Hashemite dynasty in Jordan, 235, 443
Hassain, Samira Ali el-, 214
Hassani, Hafiz Sadiqulla, 74
Hastings, Max, 382
hate crimes, 104, 229
Hatefi, Rahman, 71

Hattersley, Roy, 265–66, 350
Hayari, Younis Mohammed Ibrahim al-,
    289
Haz, Hamzah, 368
Hazrat-I-Abubakr Sadiq mosque (New
    York), 230
headscarf. *See hijab*
Heath, Edward, 268
Heathrow Airport, 277, 282
Hebraism, 178, 387, 390, 397, 402–403
    See also Judaism
'hell' as metaphor used by Muslims, 160
Henley, Jon, 379
Herald Tribune (newspaper). *See Interna-
    tional Herald Tribune* (US news-
    paper)
Hertoghe, Alain, 364
Herzl, Theodor, 181, 209
Hezbollah ('Party of God'), 79, 197, 211,
    295, 406
    benefited from false charities, 280
    condemnation of decapitation, 228
    condemnation of Israel, 202
    condemnation of kidnappings, 229
    formation of, 18, 22
    represented in fighting against US in
        Iraq, 472
    and Rushdie, 249
    senior members assassinated, 54, 161
    support by diaspora Muslims, 283
    support by Lebanon, 23
    support from Iran, 461
    Syrian influence, 445
Hibatullah, Ihtisham, 266
hijab, 94–97, 104, 105, 241, 298, 300, 302,
    379
hijackings, 15, 16, 23, 29, 48, 207, 234,
    245
    Air France airliners, 33, 41, 59
    attempt at Heathrow, 282
    bus in Algeria, 78
    El Al aircraft (1968), 19
    of Italian cruise ship *Achille Lauro*, 311

    meeting hijackers demands, 313
    9/11 hijackings, 58, 76, 137, 307–308,
        332
    Russian airliner, 58
    suicide hijackers not cowards, 344
Hilali, Sheikh Taj al-Din al-, 226, 228
Hindus, 63, 93, 410, 411–12
    Hindu massacre of Muslims, 70, 90
    Islam's treatment of, 387–435
    massacre by Muslims, 125
    as targets of Muslims, 19, 23, 68, 75, 125
hirab, 256–57
Hiroshima, 54, 198, 359–60, 484
Hirst, David, 105, 169, 180, 345, 420
Hitchens, Christopher, 365
Hitler, Adolf, 18, 31, 181, 188, 205, 206,
    213, 215, 261, 366, 368, 376
Hizb ut-Tahrir ('Party of Liberation'),
    95, 211–12, 213, 220, 223, 278, 299,
    304, 459
Hneidi, Azzam, 238
Hobsbawm, Eric, 369
Hoffman, Lord, 292
Holland. *See* Netherlands
Holley, David, 195
Holocaust, 181
    denial of by some Muslims, 123, 215,
        482
    'inflated' figure of Jewish deaths, 214
Holocaust Remembrance Day, 214–15
Honderich, Ted, 356, 357
Honeyford, Ray, 111–13
honour killings, 86
*Horrifying Fraud, The . See L'Effroyable
    Imposture* (Meyssan)
Hostage-taking, 23, 26, 29, 48, 52, 56,
    58–61, 312–13, 431
    by Chechens, 12, 59, 60, 190, 221, 229
    by Iranians, 19, 61, 69, 269
    by Iraqis, 59–60, 79, 139, 226, 228, 243,
        287–88, 313, 394, 411
    by Jamaat al-Muslimeen in Trinidad,
        20, 61

in Lebanon, 249, 269
by Pakistanis, 61
in Philippines, 417
See also kidnappings
Houellebecq, Michel, 118
Hovespian-Mehr, Haik, 415
Howard, John, 351
Howard, Michael, 322, 350
Howard University, 302
Howeidi, Amira, 383
Hoyer, Steny, 219
Huggler, Justin, 195
Hughes, Clifford, 285
Hull University, 120
human rights, 94, 96, 109, 114, 164, 165,
    297–99, 300–301, 316, 332–35, 486
  in Algeria, 442
  in Azerbaijan, 457
  'Cairo Declaration on Human Rights
    in Islam', 334
  in Chechnya, 460
  European Convention on Human
    Rights, 291
  European Court of Human Rights, 97
  in France, 295, 317
  Human Rights Act, 292
  Human Rights Act Research Project,
    333
  Human Rights Commission of Pak-
    istan, 86
  Human Rights Watch, 195, 333
  and Saddam Hussein, 333
  International Court of Justice, 176
  International Federation for Human
    Rights, 334
  in Iraq, 333, 431
  Islamic Human Rights Commission,
    195, 199, 277
  in Libya, 442
  in Nigeria, 455
  in Pakistan, 86
  in Sudan, 165
  in Syria, 443
  in Turkey, 451
  UN High Commission on Human
    Rights, 334
  Universal Declaration of Human
    Rights, 72, 334
  in US, 104, 333
Human Rights Act Research Project, 333
Human Rights Commission of Pakistan,
    86
Human Rights Watch, 195, 333
Humeid, Sheikh Saleh bin Abdullah al-,
    394
Hundred Years' War, 18
Hungary, US reduction of forces in, 474
Huntington, Samuel, 172, 402, 410
Hurd, Douglas, 269
Husain, Irfan, 243–44, 271
Hussain, Liaquat, 249
Hussein (king), 40, 43, 242
Hussein, Qusay, 157
Hussein, Saddam, 15, 136, 146, 147, 197,
    198, 208, 223, 359, 363
  asking Kuwait for help against US, 145
  attempt to assassinate Qassem, 54
  benefited from false charities, 280
  blaming Jews, 221
  and Catholic Church, 430
  'Christmas Letter', 12, 432
  coming to power, 19
  compared with Goebbels, 329
  cruelty to captives under Hussein
    regime, 60
  death of Muhammad Sadiq al-Sadr,
    55
  dictatorial regime of, 31
  and Gulf War, 25
  human rights abuses, 333
  invasion of Kuwait, 21
  invoking Allah's aid, 12
  on Jenin, 237
  as a leader, 22
  mixed Muslim reactions to, 238
  and neo-fascist support, 482

non-Muslim support of, 288
overthrow of, 228, 406
perceived as no-threat, 347
poison gas attacks on Kurds, 20, 142,
    151, 161
reference to Kuwaitis, 50
refusal to recognize Israel as a state,
    202
statue of, 210
as target of assassination, 56
treatment of Christians, 420–21, 425
trial of, 332, 345
use of Twelve Devices of Muslim
    argument, 142, 145
and weapons of mass destruction, 329,
    339–40
on Zionism, 191
Hussein, Uday, 157
Husseini, Faisal al-, 210
Husseini, Haj Amin al-, 181
Husseini, Ishaq, 133

Ibrahim, Saad Eddin, 231
Igarashi, Hitoshi, 248
Ijaz, Mansoor, 234
Il Manifesto (Italian newspaper), 197
Il Messaggero (Italian newspaper), 193
'image' issue for Muslims
    anti-Islamic backlash, 243–45
    anti-Muslim sentiments and preju-
        dices, 17, 62, 70, 97, 101–108, 112,
        115, 116–17, 123–25, 126
Imam Ali mosque (Najaf), 55, 407
Imam Kadhum mosque (Baghdad), 209
Imams and Mosques Council (Britain),
    254, 276, 428
IMF. *See* International Money Fund
    (IMF)
Independent (British newspaper), 71, 75,
    108, 118, 154, 192, 195, 197, 204,
    205, 218, 223, 225, 250, 253, 257,
    258, 261, 262, 264, 265, 343, 355,
    382

Independent on Sunday (British news-
    paper), 258
Index on Censorship, 330
India, 472
    advanced weapons assistance from
        Israel, 24
    arrests of terrorists, 289
    attacks on Muslim properties in, 62
    bombings in, 23, 65, 67, 68, 69
    gaining economic strength, 452
    Hindu-Muslim 'communalism', 17
    Hindus killing Muslims, 125
    India-Pakistan war, 29
    Muslim attacks on Hindus, 63, 125
    Muslim statistics, 474–75
    relations with Israel, 174
    riots, 82
    use of Twelve Devices of Muslim
        argument, 145
Indian Airlines, 58
Indiana National Guard, 312
Indo-Arab Islamic Association, 195
Indonesia
    arrests of terrorists, 289, 290
    Australian embassy bombed, 69
    bombings in, 67, 68, 69
        Bali bombing, 68, 84, 150, 166, 189,
            208, 221, 232, 311, 323, 339,
            359, 397
    corruption, 449
    extradition of terrorists, 295
    foiled attacks, 290
    hostage-taking in, 59
    Indonesian hostages taken in Iraq War, 60
    inter-Muslim hostilities, 53
    Islamists' transnational use of, 467
    mujahideen role in, 26
    Muslim separatism, 16, 19
    Muslim statistics, 474
    and oil, 456
    riots, 82
    terrorist attacks not based on Pales-
        tinian issue, 191

treatment of Christians, 416–17
use of Twelve Devices of Muslim
argument, 141, 145, 165
Indonesian Ulamas Council, 232
infidels and Muslims, 387–435
See also Jews; names of religions
Ingrams, Richard, 223
Inhofe, James, 179
Inner London Education Authority, 117
innocence, professions of, 141–43
Inquisition, 203
Institute for Strategic Studies (Beijing),
355
Institute for Strategic Studies (London),
18
Institute of Islamic Political Thought
(London), 237
Institute of Peace and Justice (Karachi),
415
insurgency of Muslims. *See* resurgence
of Muslims
inter-Muslim hostilities, 48–52, 54–55,
63–64, 68, 479
in Algeria, 78, 232
mixed Muslim reactions to, 239
use of torture, 74–75
International Atomic Energy Authority,
316, 470–71
International Commission of Jurists, 334
International Court of Justice, 176
International Criminal Court, 353, 370
International Federation for Human
Rights, 334
International Guerrillas (film), 220
International Herald Tribune (US news-
paper), 70–71, 208, 325, 361, 373
International Islamic Front for Jihad
Against Jews and Crusaders, 30
International Jew, The (Ford), 190
International Money Fund (IMF), 314,
353
International Red Cross, 207
Interpol, 308

*Interrogations: Inside the Mind of the Nazi
Elite* (Overy), 351
intifadas
first, 18, 20, 39
death of collaborators with Israel,
51
second, 18, 54, 178, 447
threat of intifadas outside Palestine,
304
Iqbal, Mufti, 37
IRA. *See* Irish Republican Army
Iran, 160, 380
acquisition of lethal weaponry, 469
advanced weapons assistance
from China, 24, 468
from North Korea, 24, 468
from Pakistan, 23, 468
providing to others, 468
blamed by Saddam Hussein for poison
gas attacks, 151
Bushehr nuclear reactor, 24
defence of Islamic taboos, 129, 134,
135
displacement of population, 17
elections in, 233, 439
funding of Muslim Institute
(London), 302
hangings as punishment, 72
hostage-taking in, 59
inter-Muslim hostility, 13
Iran-Iraq War, 23
Islamists' transnational use of, 467
nuclear programme, 21, 22, 24,
141–42, 288, 463, 470
assistance from France, 469
assistance from Pakistan, 23
assistance from Russia, 469
and oil, 457
passenger aircraft shot down by US,
13
providing arms to Palestine, 199
Rafsanjani call for violence by Palestinians, 40

refusal to recognize Israel as a state,
    179–80
revolution (1989), 11
as source of *mujahideen*, 26
support for terror, 463–64
supporting insurgencies, 22, 24
    Hamas, 30
support of Iraq after Gulf War, 141
support of Iraq during Iraq War
    (2003), 26
as a theocracy, 439–40
as threat to world peace, 188
treatment of other religions, 416
treatment of women, 85
unemployment of youth, 167
US embassy bombed, 69
use of torture, 74
use of Twelve Devices of Muslim
    argument, 140–42, 148
against Western fashions, 80
Iraq, 21
    advanced weapons assistance
        from China, 24, 468
        from Germany, 24
        from North Korea, 24
        from Russia, 469
    arrests of terrorists, 290
    attacks on foreigners, 61
    attacks on oil wells, 453
    Australian embassy bombed, 69
    Ba'ath party in power, 19
    bombings in, 64, 67, 68, 69, 129, 189
        mosque bombings attributed to
            Israel, 189
    capture of passenger aircraft, 58
    civil war, 25
    compared with Afghanistan, 447–48
    cruelty to captives, 60
    deaths caused by Saddam Hussein, 15
    decapitations, 90
    defence of Islamic taboos, 135
    democracy as goal, 440–42, 451, 481
    displacement of population, 16, 17

Dutch embassy bombed, 69
elections in, 441
and Gulf War, 13
hostage-taking in, 59
insurgency support from Iran, 22
inter-Muslim violence, 63
Iraq-Iran War
    support by Britain during, 24
    support by US during, 23, 24, 469
Islamists from active in Europe, 465
Islamists' transnational use of, 467
Jordanian embassy bombed, 69
kidnappings and ransoms, 59–60
nuclear program, 18, 198
and oil, 453–54
Slovak embassy bombed, 69
support during and after Gulf War
    Afghanistan, 25
    from Arafat, 24
    from Belarus, 24
    Egypt, 25
    Jordan, 25
    Malaysia, 25
    Pakistan, 25
    from Romania, 24
    South Africa, 25
    from Sudan, 23
    Syria, 25
    from Ukraine, 24
support during and after Iraq War
    (2003)
    from Egyptian Islamist movement,
        26
    from Iran, 26
    from Jordan, 26
    from Saudi Arabia, 26
    from Syria, 26
    from Yemen, 26
supporting insurgencies, 23
terrorist attacks not based on Pales-
    tinian issue, 191
treatment of Christians, 420–21
treatment of women, 84

Turkish embassy bombed, 69
use of chemical weapons, 50, 51
use of Jerusalem as backdrop in some
    art, 210
use of torture, 74
use of Twelve Devices of Muslim
    argument, 139, 145
US financial support of, 474
war against Israel (1948), 182
Iraqi National Assembly, 51, 156, 440–41
Iraqi National Museum, 142
Iraqi Radio, 155
Iraq War (2003), 14, 31, 38, 66–67, 142,
    157, 312, 351
    collaboration with occupying force,
        51–52
    delusions about, 156
    and 'dire consequences' argument, 376
    impact on US, 471–74
    Islamists coming to aid of Iraq, 472
    Muslim responses to, 237–38, 304
    non-Muslim responses to, 286–89,
        317–20, 329, 430–31
    potential of causing more terrorism,
        381–82
    support to Iraq before, 23
Ireland, decline of Catholicism, 478
Irgun gang, 54
Irish Republican Army, 19, 23
Isamuddin, Riduan, 150, 290
Islam
    belief system, 388–89, 391–93, 395–96,
        398–99, 401, 402, 405, 408
    forbidding killing of non-combatant
        civilians, 227, 239
    incompatibility with popular sover-
        eignty, 437–88
    as a religion of peace, 387, 400, 402
    as a religion of submission, 391
    religion of tolerance, 235
Islam, Ansar al-, 289
Islam, Mousa Masjid al-, 283
'Islam and Citizenship' (Holland), 305

Islam-as-politics. *See* Islamism
Islambouli, Khalid, 57
Islamia Schools Trust (London), 479
Islamic Affairs Action Committee
    (Britain), 247
Islamic Army (Iraq), 301–302
Islamic Center of Cleveland (Ohio),
    209, 280
Islamic Commission of Spain, 226, 404
Islamic Council of Catalonia, 148
Islamic Foundation (Leicester), 259
Islamic Human Rights Commission, 195,
    199, 277
Islamic Iran Participation Front, 199
Islamic Jihad, 197, 280, 289, 299, 303,
    312, 447
    Israeli embassy bombing in Argentina,
        68
    in Sudan, 464
    and suicide-bombers, 374
    supported by Lebanon, 23
    and Syria, 142
Islamic Party of Britain, 246–47, 254
Islamic Republic of Afghanistan. *See*
    Afghanistan
Islamic Republic of Pakistan. *See*
    Pakistan
Islamic Research Council (Egypt), 87
Islamic Resistance Movement. *See* Hamas
Islamic Salvation Front (Algeria), 20, 462
Islamic schools. *See madrassas*
Islamic Society of Britain, 243, 300
Islamic Society of North America, 155
Islamic Society for the Promotion of
    Religious Tolerance (Britain), 256
Islamic taboos, enforcement of, 127–37
Islamic Women's Olympics, 83
Islamism, 355–61
    defined, 10, 40
    non-Muslim support of, 284–88
    transposing criticism from to West,
        349–55
    See also Islamists; Muslims

Islamist Justice and Development Party
(Morocco), 442
Islamist Justice and Prosperity Party
(Indonesia), 141
Islamists, 331–32
hatred of US but desire for its benefits, 14
links between, 465–67
taking liberties with non-Muslims,
273–335
as victims of past violence, 359
See also Islamism; Muslims; under
individual country names
'Islamofascism', 482
'Islamophobia', 13, 35, 77, 85, 118, 213,
277, 394, 402, 475
closet 'Islamophobes', 120
racist 'Islamophobes', 41, 230, 481
Islam's dress code, 80–81, 85
Israel, 171–224
acquisition of lethal weaponry, 469
advanced weapons assistance
from Britain, 470–71
to India, 24
to Turkey, 24
from US, 24, 174
aid from US, 174
anti-Muslim sentiments, 123–24
arrests of terrorists, 289
assassination of Yassin, 54, 64
attack on Arafat's headquarters, 29
bombing of its embassies, 68, 69
bombings in, 39, 57, 62–63, 65, 66, 67,
68, 69, 152, 197, 198, 211, 372,
374
branded as a terrorist country, 197–99
brutal treatment of Arabs, 182–83,
184, 203
compared with South Africa's
apartheid, 343
considering all Jews within its
purview, 172
creation of, 18, 123, 172, 182

and exceptionalism, 200–201
first Palestinian uprising (intifada), 18
incursion in Jenin, 193–97
invasion of Lebanon, 18, 30
and Islamophobia, 13
Israel-as-'source-of-the-problem',
187–88
lack of recognition as a state, 179–80,
199, 200–201, 202–203, 207
looting in Ramallah, 197
nuclear programme, 174
assistance from Britain, 470–71
perceived as the 'anti-Christ of
nations', 175
as 'root-of-all-evil' to Muslims, 32
second Palestinian uprising (intifada),
18
shooting down Libyan airliner, 58
statistics on, 177
targeted assassinations, 53–54
as threat to world peace, 188
treatment of Palestinians, 206
ultranationalist Israelis, 206
use of torture, 75
US financial support of, 474
vandalisation of Muslim properties in,
62
willingness to respond to violence,
164
withdrawal from Gaza, 176
world opinion on, 171–224
See also Arab-Israeli conflict; Israeli-
Palestinian conflict
Israeli-Palestinian conflict, 173, 187
hope for resolution, 209
importance to all Muslims, 471
three preconditions for peace in, 38
See also Arab-Israeli conflict
Israeli Justice Minister, 206
Italian cruise-liner, seizure of, 58, 311
Italian Interior Minister, 39
Italian Union of Muslims, 108–109
Italy, 106, 160, 201, 202, 309, 382, 398, 427

'Action for Peace', 203
anti-Muslim feelings, 101, 108
bombings in, 67
comments after 9/11 attacks, 350, 364
and controversy over wearing the *hijab*, 95
and European Union, 316
extraditions and deportations, 294, 296
Islamists' transnational use of, 465, 466, 467
and Israel, 191, 201, 204, 207
Italian fascism, 11, 356
Italian hostages taken in Iraq War, 60, 288, 313
Muslim demands for special treatment after immigration, 108–109, 286, 302
Muslim statistics, 476
peace movement in, 201, 203, 286–87
Red Brigades, 483
Rifondazione Comunista, 203, 349
and Rushdie controversy, 131, 248
terror cells in, 465
threats by Islamists, 159, 160, 301
Ivory Coast, 30, 417

Jabar, Mahmoud, 84
Jaish-e-Mohammed ('Army of Mohammed'), 161, 415
Jakarta, 67
Jamaat al-Muslimeen (Trinidad), 20
Jamaat-e-Islami (Bangladesh), 131, 350, 479
Jamait ul-Mujahideen (Bangladesh), 66, 289
Jamaleddin, Sayyid Iyad, 233
Jama Masjid mosque (Delhi), 199, 228
James, Oliver, 364
Janjua, Mohammed Ismail, 250
Jannati, Ayatollah Ahmed, 55, 56, 158, 250
Japan, 120, 162, 452, 474
    assistance to North Korea's nuclear programme, 469

citizens attacked in Egypt, 61
need for oil, 452
and Rushdie controversy, 128, 131, 248
Jarrah, Ziad al-, 344
Java, 62, 416–17
Jefferson, Thomas, 163
Jehangir (emperor), 412
Jehovah's Witness meetings, 86
Jemaah Islamiyah ('Islamic Community'), 25, 310, 464
    and Abu Bakr Bashir, 141, 153, 189, 221, 406
    in Indonesia, 141, 150, 153–54
    in London, 40
    use of Twelve Devices of Muslim argument, 141
Jenin, 51, 57, 76, 201, 206, 223, 237
    Israeli incursion into, 193–97
Jenkins, Philip, 220
Jenkins, Simon, 185
Jerusalem, 156, 178–79, 184, 192, 210, 219, 224, 322, 429, 434
    bombings in, 57, 67, 139, 372, 374
    Dome of the Rock, 210
    East Jerusalem, 64–65, 149, 160, 423
    historical references to, 160, 178
    inter-Muslim hostilities, 64
    Jerusalem Temple, 178, 179
    'Judaisation' of Jerusalem, 223
Jerusalem Post, 76
Jerusalem Temple, 178, 179
Jesus. *See* Christ, role in Islam
Jews
    as aliens in Israel, 180–81
    as 'enemies of God', 432–35
    hatred of Jews, 208–16, 220–21, 222–24. *See also* anti-Semitism
    Islam's treatment of, 387–435
    and Israel, 171–224
    Jews seen as cause of World War II, 188
    statistics on in US, 219–20

worldwide statistics on Jews, 173–74
See also infidels and Muslims; Judaism
Jibril, Ahmed, 249
jihad
    alternate meanings for, 342–43
    calls for, 406, 430
    theology of, 404–405
jihad, training for, 37. *See also mujahideen*
Jihad al-Khazin, 237
Jihad group (Iraq), 407
jilbab, 95
Joffe, Josef, 329
John Paul II (pope), 428, 430–31, 432,
    433, 434
Johns Hopkins University, 133
Johnson, Boris, 217
Johnson, Daniel, 217
Jomhuri Islami (Iranian newspaper), 259, 440
Jordan
    and Arafat, 185
    Arafat's attempt to overthrow, 23
    arrests of terrorists, 289, 290, 310
    bombings in, 68
    celebrations after violence, 149
    civil war, 235
    desecration of Jewish synagogues in
        East Jerusalem, 64
    embassy bombed in Iraq, 69
    extradition of terrorists, 295
    foiled attacks, 290
    formal recognition of Israel, 179, 203
    and Hashemite dynasty, 443
    hostilities among Muslims, 13
    Hussein (king), 40
    Islamists from active in Europe, 465, 466
    and Israel, 18
    massacre of Palestinians (1970, 1971),
        51, 185
    no help for Palestine, 192
    Palestinian guerrillas in, 23, 29
    relations with Palestine, 235
    represented in fighting against US in
        Iraq, 472

    as source of *mujahideen*, 26
    support for terror, 461
    supporting insurgencies, 23
    support of Iraq after Gulf War, 141
    support of Iraq during Iraq War
        (2003), 26
    support of Iraq in Gulf War, 25
    treatment of women, 83
    use of Twelve Devices of Muslim
        argument, 139, 141, 144
    war against Israel, 184
Jordan Times, 139, 203
Jos (Nigeria), 418–19
Judaism
    as a 'religion of justice', 387
    See also infidels and Muslims; Jews
Justice and Development party (Turkey),
    451
'justification-by-desperation' argument,
    370–75

Kabbani, Rana, 240, 303
Kaddoumi, Farouk, 151, 163, 239–40
kafir, 50, 270, 403
    and Muslims, 387–435
Kamhawi, Labib, 152
kamikazes, 161, 374
    See also suicide-bombings
Kani, Ayatollah Mahdari, 253
Kaplan, Metin, 142
Karadzic, Radovan, 89
Karimov, Islam, 458–59
Karine A (ship), 196
Karlin, Miriam, 224
Karnak Temple, 61
Karouri, Abd al-Jalil, 189
Karroubi, Mahdi, 233
Karzai, Hamid, 54, 71, 191, 448
Kashani, Ayatollah Mohammed Emami,
    269
Kashmir, 12, 13, 21, 37, 145, 286, 289,
    471
    attempted assassinations in, 85

bombings in, 67, 68, 69
defence of Islamic taboos, 85, 129
displacement of population, 17
elections in, 442
inter-Muslim violence, 63
Islamists, training of, 37, 282, 283, 308
Islamist secession movement, 15, 20,
  21, 24, 29
  cruelty to captives, 60
  death tolls, 16
  support from Pakistan, 24
  and Rushdie controversy, 248
  treatment of Hindus, 62, 75, 411
  treatment of women, 85
  use of Twelve Devices of Muslim
    arguments, 145
Kaufman, Gerald, 203, 204, 224, 263,
  265, 365, 367
Kazakhstan, 289, 429, 430
  and oil, 457–58, 460
Keane, Fergal, 217
Keegan, John, 53, 58, 123, 322, 329
Kennedy, John F., 53, 56
Kennedy, Robert, 29, 56
Kenya, 21, 290, 473
  bombings in, 68
  bombing of Israeli-owned hotel, 68,
    149, 152, 211, 223
  bombing of US embassy, 30, 69,
    299, 327
  and Somalia, 450, 464
Kerry, John, 219, 352, 376
Kettle, Martin, 352
Khadimiya mosque (Baghdad), 63
Khairallah, Khairallah, 235
Khalid al-Faisal (prince), 153, 187
Khalidi, Hussein, 182
Khalil, Izz el-Deen al-Sheikh, 54
Khalkhali, Hojatoleslam Sadeq, 248
Khamenei, Ayatollah Ali, 129, 142, 143,
  150–51, 472
  and Israel, 202, 207, 209, 210
  on Rushdie, 247, 249, 259

use of Twelve Devices of Muslim
  argument, 142, 143, 147, 151
Khamis, Muhammad Kamel, 342
Khan, Abdul Qadeer, 21, 309, 397, 468
Khan, Akbar, 250
Khan, Mohammad Sidique, 308
Khan, Rehmat, 247
Khan, Sabiha, 304–305
Khan, Yahya, 19
Kharrazi, Kamal, 199, 416
Khartoum, 15, 19, 27, 189, 316, 450
  kidnappings in, 56
  and oil, 456
  support for terror, 464
  treatment of Christians, 428
  See also Sudan
Khatami, Mohammad, 145, 160, 180,
  218, 233, 440
Khazzen, Jihad al-, 357
Khoei, Hojataleslam Abdul Majid al-, 55,
  311, 407
Khomeini, Ayatollah Ruhollah, 42, 71,
  159, 233, 440, 472, 486
  coming to power, 19
  and Rushdie, 20, 220, 246–48, 251,
    254, 258, 268
  use of Twelve Devices of Muslim
    argument, 138
Khomeinism, 12, 20
kidnappings, 20, 37, 57, 58–61, 229,
  242–43, 282, 310, 313
  See also hostage-taking
Kiftaro, Sheikh Ahmad, 408, 433
Kiley, Sam, 420
King Fahd Defence Academy mosque
  (Riyadh), 486
Kirkuk, 68
  importance of to Kurds, 454
Klarsfeld, Arno, 216
Kolbow, Walter, 365
Koran, 134, 157, 210, 294, 326, 409, 420,
  479, 488
  desecration of, 81, 406, 414, 416, 448

perceived insults to, 57, 128
precepts of, 136–37, 398, 400–402, 405
quotes from, 388–89, 391–93, 395–96,
     398–99, 408
and Rushdie, 259
satirised in literature, 118, 119, 120,
     432
Kosovo, 12, 21, 193, 286, 321, 419, 443
clan allegiance in, 49
displacement of population, 16, 17
killing of Muslim Albanians, 13, 51
mujahideen role in, 26, 282
support from Iran, 22
Kouddil, Hafsa Zinai, 240
Krekar, Mullah Mustapha, 406
Kristof, Nicholas, 382
Kurdistan, 25, 63
Kurds in Iran, 55
Kurds in Iraq, 189, 441, 467
displacement of, 17
inter-Muslim violence, 63, 82
massacre at Anfal, 20
and oil, 454
poison gas attacks by Saddam Hussein,
     20, 51, 142, 147, 151, 161
Kurds in Syria, 443
Kurds in Turkey, 50, 451
displacement of, 17
Kuwait, 254, 283, 289, 321
al-Sabah family in control, 443
defence of Islamic taboos, 129
government of, 442, 443
and Iran, 22
and Iraq, 12, 21, 25, 50, 145, 147
Islamists in, 290, 295, 310
     represented in fighting against US
         in Iraq, 472
Muslim statistics, 475
and Palestinians, 235
treatment of women, 81, 83, 438, 443
US presence in, 473
See also Gulf War (1991)
Kuwait University, 228

Kyrgyzstan, 67, 289, 467
and oil, 458
US military presence in, 473

Laboud, Emile, 444
Labour Party (Britain), 198, 203, 204,
     211, 218, 224, 263, 264, 265–67, 334,
     339, 350, 353, 365, 368, 383
La Civiltà Cattolica (Jesuit journal), 426
La Croix (French newspaper), 364
Lagerfeld, Karl, 128
Lahore, 25, 63, 74, 84, 164
Lapham, Lewis, 33, 346
Lapid, Yosef, 206
La Razon (Spanish newspaper), 205
La Repubblica (Italian newspaper), 191
Larijani, Javad, 250
Lasfar, Amar, 148
Lashkar-e-Jhangvi (Pakistan), 414
Lashkar-e-Taiba ('Army of the Pure'),
     466
Laskar Jihad (Indonesia), 416
La Stampa (Italian newspaper), 194, 322
La Vanguardia (Spanish newspaper), 205
Laws on, and treatment of, terrorists
     in Britain, 291–92, 293–94
     European Union, 316
     in United States, 290, 292–94
League of Nations, 328
Lebanon
anti-Syrian vote, 445
and Arafat, 185
arrests of terrorists, 289, 290
assassination of Gemayel, 184
bombings in, 19, 68, 69
celebrations after 9/11, 150
Christians in, 184, 421–22
civil war (1975–1990)
     death tolls, 15
     displacement of population, 16
death of Gemayel, 55
death of Hariri, 55
displacement of population, 17

elections in, 442
expulsion of Palestinian militia by
    Israel, 235
foiled attacks, 290
funding of Muslim insurgent groups,
    23
and Hezbollah, 23
hostage-taking in, 59
invaded by Israel, 18, 30, 125, 184, 186
refusal to recognize Israel as a state,
    202
represented in fighting against US in
    Iraq, 472
as a satrap of Syria, 444–45
support of Arafat, 23
Syrian troops in, 138, 186
war against Israel, 182
le Carré, John, 353, 370
Leeds Muslim committee, 258
L'Effroyable Imposture (Meyssan), 341
Le Figaro (French newspaper), 121, 350
'left' positions and errors, 481–83
Leicester, and fundamentalist terrorists,
    40
Le Monde (French newspaper), 216, 361
Le Nouvel Observateur (French news-
    paper), 322
le Pen, Jean-Marie, 216
letter-bombs, 56
'Letter to the American People' (bin
    Laden), 207, 221, 485
Lewis, Bernard, 27, 29
Libbi, Abu Faraj al-, 290
Liberal Democrat Party (Britain), 373
Liberia
    support for terror, 464
    treatment of Christians, 417
Liberté (Algerian newspaper), 78
Libya
    airliner shot down, 58
    anti-Americanism, 19, 82
    disavowal of violence, 140, 229, 232
    economic statistics, 167, 174

and human rights, 334, 442, 454
Islamists in
    active in Europe, 281, 466
    arrests of, 281, 290
    extraditions of, 295
    fighting in support of Iraq, 472
and Israel, 183, 191
nuclear programme, 147, 208, 468
and oil, 454
and Palestinians, 235
unemployment of youth, 167
use of Twelve Devices of Muslim
        argument, 140
weapons assistance
    to Northern Ireland, 19, 23
    from other countries, 23, 147, 468
Likud Party (Israel), 190, 222
Lincoln, Abraham, 56
Livingstone, Ken, 363
Llewellyn Tim, 187
Lloyd, John, 324
Locke, John, 94
Lockerbie (Scotland), 20, 30, 58, 65
London
    bombings in, 69
    and fundamentalist terrorists, 40
    London Underground bombings
        (2005), 15, 31, 65, 101, 155, 278,
        292, 308
        disavowed by Muslims, 143, 237
        justification for, 360
        Muslim responses to, 226, 230, 243
        shooting of innocent Brazilian, 289
London Mosque, 229, 256
London Review of Books, 344, 360
London School of Economics, 37, 267
London University, 211, 262
Los Angeles (California), bombings in,
    67
Lumumba, Patrice Emergy, 53
Luther, Martin, 223
Luxor, bombing at, 61, 138, 237
Luzzatto, Amos, 207

lynchings, 14, 51, 76, 77
  See also hangings as punishment

Macapagal Arroyo, Gloria, 313
Macedonia, 17, 26, 30, 69, 70
MacShane, Denis, 266
Madani, Muhammad al-, 434
Madhi, Sheikh Ibrahim, 213
madrassas, 38, 233, 296, 415, 426
Madrid train-bombings, 65, 158, 190,
    229, 242, 281, 295, 319, 404, 467
Mafoudi, Gallarate Mohamed, 425
Maghreb, 295
  clerics deported to, 295
  Islamists in, 281, 282, 291, 311
    active in Europe, 465, 466
  Muslim statistics, 475
  unemployment of youth, 166
'Magnificent 19', 276
Mahdi army (Iraq), 276, 393
  See also Sadr, Moqtada al-
Maher, Ahmed, 64
Mahfouz, Naguib, 135
Mahmood, Tariq, 250
Mahmud of Gazni, 412
Mailer, Norman, 382
Majeed, Izzat, 234
Majid, Ali Hassan al-, 161
Malaccas, 416–17
Malacca Straits, 456
Malaysia, 19
  anti-Americanism, 82
  elections in, 449
  Islamisation of, 449
  Islamists in, 309, 382, 461, 465
    arrests of, 289, 302
    extradition of terrorists, 295
    transnational use of, 467
  and Jemaah al-Islamiyah, 25
  and Jews, 190, 206
  Prime Minister, 190, 206, 239, 382,
    400
  support of Iraq in Gulf War, 25

support of Muslims in Bosnia, 26
unemployment of youth, 167
US military presence in, 473
Maldives, 443–44
Mali, 473, 475
Malik, Abdul, 86
Malik, Tauqir, 258
Maluku Islands, 416–17
Mandela, Nelson, 365, 370
Maniscalco, John, 332
maquis, 364–65
market bombings, 68
Marking, Henry, 191
Maronite Christians, 445
Marr, Andrew, 366
martyrs and martyrdom (Muslim), 39,
    40, 41, 156–60, 161–62, 238, 301,
    396–97, 408
  image of blood, 159
  martyrdom of Saint Sebastian, 75, 80
  Martyrs' Memorial (Oxford), 17
  mujahideen as, 26
  and Rushdie controversy, 261, 269
  use of Twelve Devices of Muslim
    argument, 140
  See also suicide-bombings
Marxism, 38, 404, 405
Mashal, Khaled, 161, 192, 447, 462
Masri, Abu Hamza al-, 409
Masry, Mohamed el-, 305
Massachusetts Institute of Technology,
    302, 468
Massari, Muhammad al-, 276
Massereene and Ferrard, Viscount, 262
Massoud, Ahmed Shah, 21, 54
mass unsettlement of Muslims. *See* dias-
    pora Muslims
Mauritania, 179, 461, 464, 473
  Muslim statistics, 475
  and oil, 456
McCarthy, Joe, 370
McIlroy, Anne, 349
Meacher, Michael, 339

media coverage, 47–87, 100–101, 107,
193–97, 203–206, 214–15, 216–17,
322–24, 420
Mein Kampf (Hitler), 119
Melbourne Age (Australian newspaper), 345
Meldgaard, Anne-Marie, 103–104
Merkel, Angela, 103
Merseyside Muslim Society, 254
Messery, Ali el-, 229
Meyssan, Thierry, 341
Michaelian, Tateos, 415
migration of Muslims, mass. *See* diaspora Muslims
Mihdar, Khaled al-, 344
Mill, John Stuart, 94, 163
Mitterrand, François Maurice, 24, 321
Moghal, Manzoor, 227
Mohamad, Mahathir, 190, 206, 216, 239,
245–46, 317, 382, 400
blaming Jews for violence, 229
Mohammad, Shaikh, 154
Mohammed, Khalid Shaikh, 58, 374
Mohammed, Omar Bakri, 271, 277, 299,
301
Möllemann, Jürgen, 197
Monbiot, George, 205, 344, 355, 384
Montazeri, Ayatollah Hossein Ali, 257
moral arguments, 347–55, 356
Morocco, 411, 442
bombings in, 67, 68, 75, 289
and democratic reforms, 442
denouncing terrorism, 230
inter-Muslim hostilities, 53, 74, 105
Islamists in, 53, 62, 105, 283, 310, 311, 461
arrests of, 289, 290
death of van Gogh, 57, 466
in Europe, 465, 466, 467
'renditions', 295
transnational use of, 467
and Polisario Front guerillas, 19, 176
support of Gulf War, 25
unemployment of youth, 166
US military presence in, 473

Moro Liberation Front, 68
Moscow, 21, 244–45, 295, 460
bombings in, 65, 66, 67
hostage-taking, 12, 15, 59, 60, 221
Moses, role in Islam, 389–90
mosques used for weapon storage, 398
Mossad (Israel), 53, 54, 214, 223, 338
Motassedeq, Mounir el-, 208
Mother-of-All-Battles mosque
(Baghdad), 190, 397, 406
Moumin, Sidi, 373
Mousa, Amr, 478–79
Moussa, Abdel-Samie Mahmoud
Ibrahim, 208, 394
Moussa, Amr, 383
Moussaoui, Zacarias, 212, 299, 302, 307,
350, 402, 410, 413, 466
Mozambique, 473
MTV, 129
Muasher, Marwan, 227
Mubarak, Hosni, 40, 73, 187, 203, 215,
228, 443, 445–46
attempted assassination of, 55, 467
Mubirak, Sultan, 250
Mugabe, Robert Gabriel, 23
Muhammad, Khaled Sheikh, 290
mujahideen, 26, 36, 43, 66, 410, 461
Mukhtaseb, Zuheir al-, 75
Mulki, Hani, 139
multiculturalism, 101–103, 110–11, 117,
118, 244, 296
See also pluralism
Munah, Ibrahim al-, 408
Munich Olympics, 15, 59
Munir, Afzal, 100
Muqrin, Abulaziz al-, 467
Murabitun European Muslim movement, 247, 257
murder in holy places, 407
Murshid, Kumar, 305
Musharraf, Pervez, 30, 233–34, 355, 406,
446, 468
attempted assassination of, 55

use of Twelve Devices of Muslim
  argument, 147
Muslim Action Front (Britain), 247, 432
Muslim Aid (Britain), 227
Muslim Association of Britain, 155, 242,
  266, 267, 287
Muslim Brotherhood, 465, 479
  in Egypt, 54, 209, 237
  in London, 40, 266
  in Syria, 18, 446
  use of assassinations, 54
Muslim College (London), 117–18, 231, 486
Muslim Council of Britain, 142, 227,
  232, 237, 276, 277, 304, 305, 409
Muslim Educational Trust (Britain), 108
Muslim Institute (London), 302
Muslim World League (Saudi Arabia),
  242
Muslim migration. *See* diaspora Muslims
Muslim News (British newspaper), 116,
  247, 254, 266
'Muslim Parliament' (Britain), 22, 110,
  252, 258
Muslim Public Affairs Council (US),
  198, 304
Muslims
  demands for special treatment after
    immigration, 93–102
  global nature of Islam, 479–80
  and infidels, 387–435
  Muslims-as-terrorists, 31
  Muslims-as-victims, 31
  Muslim stereotypes, 87
  Muslim treatment of fellow-Muslims.
    See inter-Muslim hostilities
  population statistics, 474–77
  preference for autocracies, 437–88
  viewed as primitive, 93, 105–106
  See also Islamism; Islamists
Muslim Youth Movement of Great
  Britain, 248, 250
Mussolini, Benito, 31
Mutahida Majlis-e-Amal (Pakistan), 397

Nagasaki, 54
Nahdi, Fuad, 157, 238, 277, 304
Naipaul, V. S., 108
Najdi, Abdel Rahman al-, 189
Naqshbandi, Mehmood, 260
Naseem, Mohammad, 237
Nasrallah, Sheikh Hassan, 161, 202, 211,
  249, 406
Nasrin, Taslima, 85, 131
Nasser, Gamal Abdul, 11, 17, 18, 19, 181,
  315
Nasserism, 27
Nateq-Nouri, Akbar, 432
Nation, The (US magazine), 234
National Alliance (US), 187–88
National Association of Head Teachers
  (Britain), 110
National Cathedral (Washington, DC),
  155
National Council to Protect Political
  Freedom (US), 299
National Democratic Party (Egypt),
  445–46
National Federation of Muslims
  (France), 232
National Islamic Front (Sudan), 27
National Islamic Prison Foundation
  (US), 169
National Liberation Front (Algeria), 442
National Muslim Conference (Britain),
  275
National Party (Britain), 102, 484
'Nation of Islam' (US), 20, 169, 217, 394
NATO. *See* North Atlantic Treaty Orga-
  nization
Navarro-Valls, Joaquin, 223, 433
Nazarbaev, Nursultan, 457
Nazir-Ali, Michael, 342–43
Nazism, 79, 181–82, 221, 261, 368–69
  as basis of Ba'ath party, 11
  and Chechen Muslims, 482
  linked to Israel, 205, 206, 207
  propaganda about Jews, 106–107

'underlying causes', 356
used by ultranationalist Israelis, 206
using Jewish holidays for rounding-up
    Jews, 62
Negri, Tonio, 364
neo-conservatives and Islam, 35, 221
neo-fascism, 62, 482
'neo-Islamism', 27
neo-Nazism, 103, 182, 187, 191, 207, 212,
    213, 216, 299, 484
    National Alliance (US), 187–88
Nepal, 63, 411
Nesin, Aziz, 135
Netherlands
    anti-Muslim feelings, 102, 103
    abuse of women wearing *hijab*, 105
    embassy bombed in Iraq, 69
    extradition of terrorists, 295
    Islamists' transnational use of, 466
    monitoring of sermons of Muslim
        clerics, 97
    Muslim attacks on Christian churches,
        62
    Muslim statistics, 476
    pro-Muslim sentiments, 104
    terror cells in, 465, 466
    vandalisation of and assaults on
        Muslim properties in, 62
Neumann, Michael, 205
New Century Hall (Manchester), 42
New Statesman (British magazine), 324,
    335, 363
Newsweek (US magazine), 28, 81
New Testament, 392
New York Review of Books, 134
New York State University, 302
New York Times, 29, 32, 58, 60, 67, 76,
    137–38, 149, 190, 198, 199, 284, 294,
    325, 326, 330, 331, 338–39, 342, 352,
    366, 370, 376, 379, 381, 382, 384,
    400, 409, 487
Next Christendom, The (Jenkins), 220
Nigeria, 75, 191

advanced weapons assistance, 468
defence of Islamic taboos, 131
displacement of population , 17
fear of polio vaccine programme, 150
Muslim-Christian violence, 30, 62,
    418, 419, 428
Muslim statistics, 474, 475
Northern Nigeria, 15, 131, 428, 450
and oil, 453, 455–56, 473
riots, 419
treatment of women, 74
US military cooperation with, 473
Nine Arguments to avoid truth about
    Islamic advance, 337–83
9/11 attacks
    failure of US intelligence efforts,
        306–308
    lack of belief in bin Laden's guilt,
        338
    reactions to, 328, 331–32
    theory that Pentagon hit by guided
        missile, 341
    theory that World Trade Center hit
        by drones, 341
    See also US Pentagon; World Trade
        Center
Nixon, Richard, 221
Niyazov, Saparmurat, 458
Nobel Peace Prize, 201, 241, 285
non-Muslims
    allowing liberties to Islamists, 273–335
    attempts to placate Muslims, 335
    inability to understand Islamic world,
        343
    Nine Arguments to avoid truth about
        Islamism, 337-383
    perception of Islamism as ineffectual,
        322–23
    support of Islamism, 284–88, 316–23
    transposing criticism of Islamism to
        apply to West, 349–55
North Atlantic Treaty Organization,
    281, 311, 317, 318, 363, 369, 447–48

Northern Alliance (Afghanistan), 52–53,
    54, 70–71
North Korea, 188, 365
    advanced weapons assistance, 147, 467
        from Pakistan, 23, 468
        providing to others, 24, 468
    nuclear programme
        assistance from others, 469
        assistance to Iran, 470
Nottingham Islamic Centre, 128
Nour, Ayman, 445
nuclear devices. *See* weapons of mass
    destruction
Nygaard, William, 248

Observer (British newspaper), 216, 217,
    222, 223, 250, 286, 303, 304, 323,
    345, 350, 352, 364, 365, 366, 367,
    369, 370, 376–77
oil, 21, 52, 154, 164, 317, 484, 487
    America's need for, 220, 363, 365, 368
    oil-rich countries, 174, 319, 441,
        451–60, 471, 473
    'oil weapon', 11, 29
Okaz (Egyptian newspaper), 229
Old Testament, 393
Oman, arrests of terrorists, 289
Omar, Mullah Mohammed, 150, 405,
    406–408
Omar, Nasser bin Suleiman al-, 486
OPEC. *See* Organization of the Petro-
    leum Exporting Countries
O'Reilly, Bill, 118–19
Organisation of the Islamic Conference,
    175, 253–54, 334
    use of Twelve Devices of Muslim
        argument, 144
Organization of the Petroleum
    Exporting Countries, 11, 455
Orr, Deborah, 218
Orthodox Church, 402, 410, 419, 427
Orthodox Jews, 57, 172, 224
Orwell, George, 9

Orwell Prize, 223
Osirak nuclear reactor (Iraq), 18, 198,
    469
Oslo accords, 18, 39
Osservatore Romano, 424, 434
Ostalsky, Dmitri, 368
Osten-Sacken, Thomas von der, 482
Other Side, The (Abbas), 214
Ottoman Empire, 14, 111, 165, 181, 185,
    451
Ouakali, Rachid, 290
Overy, Richard, 351
*Oxford Encyclopaedia of the Modern Islamic
    World* (Esposito, editor), 199
Oxford University, 121–22, 205

Pakistan, 84, 164
    advanced weapons assistance, 147
        from Britain, 24
        from China, 468
        from North Korea, 24, 468
        providing to others, 23, 467, 468
    ambiguous relation with Taliban, 465
    arrests of terrorists, 289, 290, 310
    assistance to terrorists, 320
    attacks on foreigners, 61, 62
    attempted assassination of Musharraf,
        55
    bloodless coup (1999), 30
    bombings in, 67, 68, 69
    British embassy bombed, 69
    and Catholic Church, 414
    concern about becoming an Islamic
        fundamentalist state, 379
    creation of, 18
    defence of Islamic taboos, 135
    displacement of population, 16, 17
    Egyptian embassy bombed, 69
    elections in, 442
    expulsion of foreign students, 296
    extradition of terrorists, 295
    foiled attacks, 290
    hostage-taking in, 59

hostilities among Muslims, 13
India-Pakistan war, 29
inter-Muslim violence, 53, 63
Islamists from active in Europe, 466
Islamists' transnational use of, 466
'Jewish conspiracy' against, 220
Muslim attacks on Christian churches, 62
Muslim statistics, 474
nuclear programme, 21, 30, 147, 309, 397
Pakistan-Bangladesh war (1971), death tolls, 15
recognition of Taliban, 462, 469
riots, 82
ruled by military, 446
as source of *mujahideen*, 26, 36
support for terror, 463, 464–65
supporting insurgencies, 23
support of Gulf War, 25
support of Iraq in Gulf War, 25
unemployment of youth, 167
US embassy bombed, 69
use of stoning as punishment, 74
use of torture, 74
use of Twelve Devices of Muslim argument, 140, 144, 145
US military presence in, 473
Pakistan Association (Japan), 248
Palestine, 16, 21
Arab-Israeli war of 1948–1949 and displacement of Palestinians, 16
arrests of terrorists, 311
as British colony, 181
British embassy bombing in Greece, 68
called '*Terra Santa*', 425, 431
celebrations after 9/11, 148–49
and citizenship in Israel, 176
considered under foreign subjugation, 180
covert support for, 201
displacement of population, 17, 123
establishment of Israel, 18, 172, 182

first Palestinian uprising (intifada), 18, 20, 39
death of collaborators with Israel, 51
hostage-taking in, 59
Iranian call for Palestinian hijackings, 140–41
Islamists from active in Europe, 465, 466
in Jordan, 29
lynchings in, 76
media coverage of deaths, 70
Muslim statistics, 475
partitioning of, 18, 172, 182, 183, 184
aftermath of, 182–86
represented in fighting against US in Iraq, 472
'right of return' to Israel, 219
riots, 82
second Palestinian uprising (intifada), 18, 54, 178
deaths of collaborators with Israel, 75
seizure of aircraft, 58
status of Muslim support for, 235
support for terror, 463
unemployment of youth, 167
US accused of causing deaths there, 150–51
use of torture, 74
use of Twelve Devices of Muslim argument, 141, 144–45
Palestine Liberation Organization, 18
call for rebellion against House of Saud, 141
formation of, 29
insurgency support
from Iraq, 23
from Jordan, 23
recognition as a political entity, 180
Palestinian Authority, 193, 202–203, 209, 210, 461
accused of torture, 147

appeal for joint struggle with Israel against Iran, 144–45
and corruption, 165, 235, 314
corruption, 446–47
relations with Catholic Church, 429
television channel, 213
treatment of Christians, 423–24
use of Twelve Devices of Muslim argument, 138, 144–45, 151
US financial support of, 474
weapons from Iran, 196, 199
Palestinian Islamic Jihad, 299
Palestinian Liberation Front, 58
Palestinian National Liberation Movement. *See* Fatah movement
Pan American Airlines, 58
Pan Am Flight 103, 20
See also Lockerbie (Scotland)
'pan-Arabism', 144, 181, 231, 479
Papon, Maurice, 125
Parekh, Bhiku, 120
Parris, Matthew, 323, 359, 370
partitioning of Palestine, 18, 172, 182, 183, 184
aftermath of, 182–86
See also Arab-Israeli conflict; Israel; Palestine
Pasha, Azzam, 425
Pasha, Nuqrashi, 54
Pasha, Syed Aziz, 227–28
Pasqua, Charles, 36, 40
passports and travel documents
missing, 309–10
misuse of by Islamists, 465–67
Patriot Act, US (2001), 290–91, 292–93, 298
Patten, Chris, 194, 356, 367
Paulin, Tom, 205, 207, 213
Pax Christi, 427
Pearl, Daniel, 37, 58, 79, 212, 282, 326, 415
Pentagon. *See* US Pentagon
'People of the Book', 389
People's Front for the Liberation of Palestine, 19, 432

People's Party (Denmark), 102
Peres, Shimon, 39, 201, 222
Perle, Richard, 218, 222, 330
Permanent Committee for Dialogue with the Monotheistic Religions (al-Azhar), 429, 430
Petmezci, Osman, 213
Pfaff, William, 349
PFLP. *See* Popular Front for the Liberation of Palestine
Philippine Airlines, 58
Philippines, 25, 81–82, 161
bombings in, 68
Islamists in
arrests of, 289, 290
prisoner escapes, 310
violence of, 59, 61, 62, 67–68, 82, 152, 283
oil in, 456
removal of troops from Iraq War, 313
southern Philippines insurgency, 15, 16, 19, 26, 67, 68, 283, 428
treatment of Catholics, 410, 417, 472
treatment of women, 74
use of Twelve Devices of Muslim argument, 145
US presence in, 457, 473
Philistines, 178, 200
Pidcock, Daud Musa (David), 246, 254
Pierce, William L., 187
Pilger, John, 184, 217, 329, 349
Pink House restaurant (Ogden, IL), 331
Pinter, Harold, 368
pipelines, 66, 453, 457, 458, 459, 460
Pius X, refusal to recognize Israel as a state, 180
Plateforme (Houellebecq), 118
'pledge of tolerance', 300
PLO. *See* Palestine Liberation Organization
pluralism, 90, 94, 97, 109, 118, 121, 264, 274, 300, 343, 444
See also multiculturalism; secularism

Polisario guerrillas, 19, 176
Poland, 18, 467, 477
polio vaccine programme, fear of, 150
'political correctness', 35
political prisoners. *See* prisoners
politics of oil, 451–61
Pontifical Council for Inter-Religious
    Dialogue, 426, 429, 430
Popular Front for the Liberation of
    Palestine, 249
population statistics
    for Jews, 173–74, 219–20
    for Muslims, 474–77
Portugal, 294, 466
poverty levels in Middle East, 16, 106,
    167, 175, 226, 245, 277, 356, 373,
    456
Predator drones, 54
Presley, Elvis, 323
Preston, Peter, 223, 323, 371–72
Prevention of Terrorism Act, Britain
    (2005), 291
Principe (island), 473
prisoners, 132, 303, 398, 412
    escapes of, 310
    Iraqis as, 60, 70, 148, 189, 293
    light sentences for those mistreating
        Iraqis, 312
    number of Muslim youth, 166–67,
        169
    political prisoners, 438, 442, 446
        Arafat as a political prisoner, 345
    prisoner exchanges, 165
    prisoner of war classification, 292, 293
    treatment of Muslims, 60, 70, 105,
        132, 189, 229, 304
Prodi, Romano, 319, 321
profiling, 90
propaganda, 340
    used against Muslims, 107
'Propagation of Virtue and Prevention
    of Vice' (Afghanistan, Pakistan),
    80–81, 129

Protestantism, 424
'Protocols of the Elders of Zion', 212,
    213
punishments in Muslim culture, 70–74
Punjab University, 84

Qadhimaya mosque (Baghdad), 484
Qadir, Abdul, 54
Qadr al-Gaylani mosque (Baghdad), 407
Qadri, Hassan, 86
Qaradawi, Sheik Youssef al-, 242
Qaraqirah, Sheikh Husam, 227
Qasmi, Mulana Ziyaul, 249–50
Qassem, Abdal Karim, 54
Qatada, Abu, 106, 296, 298
Qatar, 226, 422, 463
    Islamists in, 301, 462
    and oil, 455
    relations with Israel, 177
    support of Gulf War, 25
Quddus, Sayed Abdul, 247, 250, 401
Qureia, Ahmed, 238

Rabbo, Yassir Abed, 434
Rabin, Yitzhak, 56
'racism', 376
Rafsanjani, Hashemi, 40, 209, 247, 250,
    255, 470
    use of Twelve Devices of Muslim
        argument, 140–41, 142
Rahman, Sheikh Mujib al-, 54
Rahman, Sheikh Omar Abdel, 55,
    149–50, 284
railway bombings, 65, 432
    See also London Underground bomb-
        ings, Madrid train-bombings
Ramadan, Tariq, 229, 297
Ramadan, Yassin, 383
Ramadani, Sami, 157
Ramallah, 180
    and Arafat, 156, 185, 434–35
    violence in, 76, 197
Rameh, Mohammed al-, 391

Ramos, Fidel, 422
Rana, Imam Waheed, 155
ransoms, 52, 56, 58, 59–60, 61, 282, 288, 312–13, 421
Rantisi, Abdel Aziz, 54, 158, 160, 210, 238
rape, proving of, 85
Rashed, Abdel Rahman al-, 226, 242
Rashed, Ataul Mujeeb, 229, 256
Rashid, Ali, 202–203
Ratzinger, Joseph. *See* Benedict XVI (pope)
Rawalpindi mosque, 63
Razak, Abdul, 299
'reawakening' of Islam. *See* resurgence of Islam
recruitment of terrorists in Western countries, 279–80
Red Brigades (Italy), 483
Rees-Mogg, William, 204, 322
Reeves, Paul, 195
Regent's Park Mosque (London), 12
Reid, Richard, 168, 231, 323
'renditions', 295
restaurant bombings, 67
Reuters, 10, 68, 81, 127, 284
Revelation, Book of, 393, 396
revivalism, 13
Revolutionary Guards (Iran), 269, 407, 440, 464
Reza Pahlavi, Mohammed (Shah), 440, 468
Riddell, Mary, 323
Rifondazione Comunista, 203, 349
'right of return' to Israel, 219
'Rights for Whites', 103
Rimington, Stella, 355–56
Riyadh, bombings in, 67
Robertson, Pat, 179, 407
Robinson, Arthur, 20
Robinson, Mary, 334
Rockefeller, Jay, 284
Roed-Larsen, Terje, 195
Roman Catholic Church. *See* Catholic Church

Romania, 474
Rome, bombings in, 67
Roy, Arundhati, 367, 368, 385
Royal Embassy of Saudi Arabia (Washington, DC), 137–38
Royal Institute of International Affairs (London), 36
Rumsfeld, Donald, 29, 288, 350, 366
Runcie, Robert, 107
Rundle, Guy, 363
Runnymede Trust, 169
Rushdie, Salman, 36, 42, 44, 56, 115, 119–22, 131, 132, 154, 220, 225, 246–65, 267–70, 271, 401, 432, 482, 483, 485
    on anti-Americanism, 361
    fatwa against, 20, 28, 30, 32, 37, 142, 275
    restating loyalty to Islam, 141, 259
    repenting of repentance, 260
Russia
    arrests of terrorists, 289
    bombings in, 65, 66, 67, 68, 69
        Russian airliner, 310
    and Chechen revolution, 29
    deaths of Muslim Chechens, 70
    extradition of terrorists, 295
    foiled attacks, 290
    hostage-taking in, 59, 60, 229
        blamed on Israel, 189–90
    and Islamophobia, 13
    need for oil, 457
    and oil, 457
    opposition to Iraq War, 317–18
    providing nuclear assistance, 24, 467, 469
    providing Syria with nerve gas, 24
    relations with Israel, 174
    separatism, 15. *See also* Chechnya
    supporting insurgencies, 24
    undermining 'War on Terror', 317
    withdrawal of troops from Georgia, 460
    See also Soviet Union

Russian airliner, hijacking of, 58
Rwanda, 125, 475

Saadi, Abdul-Razzaq al-, 329, 406, 407
Saadi, Amir al-, 329
Saakashvili, Mikhail, 459
Sabena (airline), 58
Sabri, Naji, 156, 353, 365
Sacranie, Iqbal, 227, 251
Sadat, Anwar al-, 29, 54, 57
Saddique, Mohammed, 231
Sadr, Moqtada al-, 158, 167, 228–29, 276, 395, 452
    See also Mahdi army
Sadr, Muhammad Sadiq al-, 55
Sadr City, 167
Safavi, Sayed, 230
Sahar, Abdullah, 228
Sahhaf, Mohammed Said, 156
Said, Edward, 185, 222, 233–34, 235, 239, 304, 372
St. John Church (Edinburgh), 427
St. John Presbyterian Church (Teheran), 415
St. Peter's Square (Rome), 15
Saladin, 22, 160
Salafia Jihadia (Morocco), 290
Salafist Group for Preaching and Combat (Algeria), 59, 289, 291, 313, 473
Salah, Ramadan, 158
'Salvation Movement' (Iraq), 49
Sammerai, Abu Bakr, 407
Samudra, Imam, 397
San Francisco Chronicle, 214
Santiago de Compostela cathedral, 426
Sao Tome (island), 473
Sarkozy, Nicolas, 285
Sarwar, Ghulam, 108
Satanic Verses, The (Rushdie), 32, 115, 119–22, 135, 141, 246–65, 270, 432
Saud, Abdullah bin Abdulaziz al- (former crown prince), 55, 189, 281

Saud, al-Waleed bin Talal al- (prince), 296
Saud, Bandar bin Sultan bin Abdul Aziz al- (prince), 138, 454
Saud, Fahd bin Abdul Aziz al- (king), 453
Saud, Faisal bin Abdelaziz al- (king), 19
Saud, Khalid al-Faisal al- (prince), 153, 187
Saud, Saud bin Faisal bin Abdul Aziz al- (prince), 153
Saud, Sultan bin Abdul Aziz al- (prince), 422–23, 439
Saud, Talal bin Abdul Aziz al- (prince), 355
Saud, Turki bin Faisal ibn Abdul Aziz al- (prince), 367
Saudi Arabia, 164
    accused by bin Laden of corruption, 444
    acquisition of lethal weaponry, 469
    advanced weapons assistance
        from China, 468
        from Pakistan, 468
    arrests of terrorists, 289
    assassination of Faisal, 19
    assistance to terrorists, 320
    attacks on by Islamists, 462, 464
    attacks on foreigners, 61, 62, 242
    beheadings as punishment, 71–72
    bombings against Americans (1995, 1996), 30
    bombings in, 67, 230–31
    conflict between Sunnis and Shi'as, 49–50
    defence of Islamic taboos, 128, 129, 134, 135
    diaspora Muslims planning attacks on, 282
    elections in, 438–39
    extradition of terrorists, 295
    foiled attacks, 290
    funding of Council on American Islamic Relations, 305

funds for martyrs' families, 161
hostage-taking in, 59
inter-Muslim violence, 53, 63, 201
Islamists' transnational use of, 467
on Jenin incursion by Israel, 195
and oil, 453, 454
recognition of Taliban, 462
represented in fighting against US in
    Iraq, 472
response to 9/11, 137, 149, 153
response to democratisation of
    Muslim regimes, 437
status of youth, 167
support for terror, 461, 462–63
supporting insurgencies, 24
  Muslims in Bosnia, 26
  support of Taliban, 30
support of Iraq during Iraq War
    (2003), 26
treatment of Christians and Jews,
    422–23
treatment of prisoners, 73
treatment of women, 81, 83
use of Twelve Devices of Muslim
    argument, 137–38, 140, 142,
    143–44, 149
US military leaving, 454–55
Scardino, Albert, 366
Schiffer, Claudia, 128
Schily, Otto, 308
Schoenbohm, Joerg, 103
School of Oriental and African Studies
    (University of London), 37
schools. See education
Schröder, Gerhard Fritz Kurt, 285
Schultz, George, 41, 358
Scotland and Pan Am Flight 103. See
    Lockerbie (Scotland)
Scotland Yard, 86
Seabrook, Jeremy, 354
Sebastian (Saint), 75, 80
Second Coming of Jesus, 179
Second World War, 11, 18, 22, 53, 214, 398

America's role in liberating Europe,
    363
Chechen Muslims assist Nazis, 482
Japanese suicide missions, 161–62
Jews seen as cause of, 188
killing of diplomats, 56
use of hostage-taking, 59
use of Twelve Devices of Muslim
    argument, 356–57, 363–64
secularism, 11, 42, 121, 135, 233, 236,
    241, 406, 441, 442, 477, 484
  in Iraq, 12, 406, 441–42
  in Israel, 424
  secular fundamentalism, 96
  secular rationalism, 23
  secular West, 135, 236, 409
  in Tajikistan, 477
  in Tunisia, 442
  in Turkey, 449, 451
  in US, 325
  in Uzbekistan, 458
security barrier for Israel, 176
security from terrorism, problems of,
    306–12
Sedki, Atef, 162
Senegal
  Muslim statistics, 475
  US military cooperation with, 473
'sense of proportion' as an argument,
    345–47, 376
sensitivity to diversity, 337
Serbia, 17, 405, 410
  Albanian collaborators, 51
  death tolls, 21
  killing of Muslims, 26, 70, 89, 321
  Serbian Orthodox churches, 419
Sethi, Najam, 246 settlement of Mus-
    lims in Western countries, 98, 275,
    285–86, 427
settlement of Muslims in Western coun-
    tries, 98, 275, 285–86, 427. See also
    diaspora Muslims; education
Sha'ath, Nabil, 193

Shabestari, Mohsen Mujtahid, 407
Shabneh, Abdel Madi, 374
Shadid, Anthony, 487
Shadjareh, Massoud, 195, 198–99
Shaheen, Suleiman Majdi al-, 254
Shah of Iran, 440, 468
Shaikh, Mohammed Younus, 132–33
Shaker, Nabil, 189
Shami, Sheikh Abu Anas al-, 407
Shapira, Avraham (rabbi), 176
Sharia law, 72, 104, 226, 260, 278, 395,
    482
  demands for imposition of
    in Britain, 294
    in Canada, 286
    in Egypt, 72
    in Kuwait, 443
    in Pakistan, 61
  escaping from, 17
  imposition of
    in Afghanistan, 71, 413
    in Nigeria, 30, 74, 75, 418, 450, 455
    in Pakistan, 446
    in Sudan, 19
  Universal Declaration of Human
      Rights, desire to subject it to, 334
  and women, 85
Sharif, Omar Khan, 374
Sharm el-Sheikh hotel, 68
'sharmouta', 423
Sharodi, Hafiz Hussain Ahmed, 214
Sharon, Ariel, 53, 161, 190, 203–206,
    221–24, 331, 364
Sheffield University, 39
Sheikh, Ahmed Omar Saeed, 37
Sheikh, Safia, 251
Sheikh, Sheikh Abdulaziz al-, 84
Sheldonian Theatre (Oxford), 400
Shell (oil company), 455, 456–57
Sherzad, Mohammed, 230
Shevardnadze, Eduard, 459
Shi'a Muslims, 81, 488
  in Azerbaijan, 20

  in Bahrain, 30
  divisions between Sunnis and Shi'as,
      48–49, 236
  in India, 410
  in Iran, 49, 209, 463
  in Iraq, 25, 50, 51, 55, 63, 64, 143, 158,
      189, 228, 229, 238, 271, 395, 406,
      407, 420, 421, 441, 452, 481, 487
  in Pakistan, 63
  in Saudi Arabia, 49–50
  Supreme Council of Islamic Revolu-
      tion (Iraq), 407
Shibh, Ramzi bin al-, 290, 463
Shinkafi, Mamuda Aliyu, 131
Shkirat, Khader, 205
'shock-and-awe' air-attack on Baghdad,
    54
'shoe-bomber'. See Reid, Richard
Shoebridge, Charles, 327
Shomari, Thaer Ibrahim, 190
Short, Clare, 192
Siad Barre, Mohamed, 16, 19
Siba'i, Hani al-, 143
Siddique, Mohammed, 248, 250–51
Siddiqui, Ghayasuddin, 151
Siddiqui, Hannan, 240
Siddiqui, Kalim, 246, 252–53, 258, 284,
    402
Sidiqui, Muzammil, 155
Sierra Leone, Muslim statistics, 475
Sikhs, 411
Silkworm missiles, 468
Simpson, Alan, 365
Sinai, 184, 186
Singapore, 25, 69, 174, 289, 290, 456
Singhvi, L. M., 37
Sirhan, Sirhan, 29, 56
Sistani, Ayatollah Ali al-, 55, 229, 233, 408
'Six Day War'. See Arab-Israeli conflict
'sleeper cells', 278, 279, 280, 283, 309,
    332
Slovakia, embassy bombed in Iraq, 69
Social Democratic Party (Denmark), 103

Socialist Worker (British newspaper), 366
Socialist Workers' Party (Britain), 483
Sodano, Angelo, 430, 433
Solaiman, Shaikh Gamal Manna, 260
Solana, Javier, 316
Somalia, 15, 331
  anti-Americanism, 82
  civil war, 21, 23, 25, 26
  clan allegiance in, 49
  displacement of population, 16, 17
  Islamists in, 59, 313, 461, 464
    arrests of, 280
    source of funding, 463
    transnational use of, 466
  use of Twelve Devices of Muslim
    argument, 145
Sommaruga, Cornelio, 207
Sontag, Susan, 349, 360
Soodman, Hussein, 415
Soros, George, 364, 368, 369
South Africa, 25, 27, 247, 309, 343
  Muslim statistics, 475
Southeastern University (Washington,
  DC), 302
South Korea, 469, 474
South Vietnam, 53
'sovereign self-rule' as US goal for Iraq,
  440–42
Soviet Union, 17, 20, 24, 278, 321, 472
  See also Russia; Soviet-Afghan war
    (1979–1989)
Soviet-Afghan war (1979–1989), 19, 20
  death tolls, 16
  defeat of Soviet Union, 21, 26, 30
  US support of insurgency, 25
  See also Afghanistan; Taliban
Spain, 295
  bombings in Madrid, 65, 158, 190, 229,
    242, 319, 467
  converts to Muslim drawn to activism,
    168
  decline of Catholicism, 478
  expulsion of Muslim clerics, 296

extradition of terrorists, 294, 295
foiled attacks, 290
Islamic Spain, 14
Islamists' transnational use of, 466, 467
Muslim statistics, 476
Muslim youth in prisons, 167–68
opposition to Iraq War, 318
terror cells in, 465, 466
threats by Islamists, 301
withdrawal of troops from Iraq, 319
Spectator (British magazine), 204, 217, 349
Spitalfields (London), 92
Sri Lanka, 53, 72, 161, 411, 467
Stanford University School of Law,
  339–40
Starbucks, 128
Steiger, Paul, 326
Stern gang, 54
Steyn, Johan van Zyl (Lord), 292, 294
Stockhausen, Karl-Heinz, 329–30
Stoiber, Edmund, 103
stoning as punishment, 72, 74, 295
Stothard, Peter, 324
Strange, Baroness (Jean Cherry Drum-
  mond), 262
Straw, Jack, 266, 326, 335
'submission', 110, 389, 391, 410, 482
Sudan, 21, 471
  attempted assassination of Mubarak,
    55
  civil wars, 15, 19, 20, 25, 52
  displacement of population, 16, 17
  human rights record, 165
  independence of, 19
  insurgency support from Iran, 22
  Islamist Sudanese regime, 28
  Islamist takeover of (1983), 23
  Muslim attacks on Christian churches,
    62
  National Islamic Front, 27
  and oil, 456
  power sharing settlement of civil war,
    450

represented in fighting against US in Iraq, 472
support for terror, 464
supporting insurgencies, 23
terrorist attacks not based on Palestinian issue, 191
treatment of Christians, 417
use of Twelve Devices of Muslim argument, 140, 145, 148
US military presence in, 473
Sudeis, Sheikh Abdulrahman al-, 394–95
Suez Canal, 11, 29, 186, 315
Sufi tradition and Sufis, 134, 230
suicide, place in Islam, 158, 396, 427
suicide-bombings, 57, 65, 150, 161–63, 185, 239, 344, 372, 374, 397, 427
after 9/11, 53
in Algiers (1995), 42
in Israel, 39, 197, 198, 211, 464
London Underground bombings (2005), 15, 31, 65, 101, 143, 155, 226, 230, 237, 243, 278, 289, 292, 308, 360
in Pakistan, 63
perception of heroism, 158
Russian airliner, 310
seen as a 'craze', 323
using Christian/Jewish holidays, 62–63
See also bombings; martyrs and martyrdom (Muslim); 9/11 attacks
suicides by women, 85
Sultan (prince), 422–23, 439
Sunday Telegraph (British newspaper), 36, 253, 382
Sunday Times (British newspaper), 101, 192, 266, 276, 287
Sunnah, 134
Sunni Council (Britain), 226
Sunni Muslims, 236, 259
in Britain, 226
divisions between Sunnis and Shi'as, 48–49

in Iraq, 49, 51, 55, 63–64, 189, 229, 311, 421, 440–41, 445
in Pakistan, 49, 63
in Saudi Arabia, 49–50, 463
Supreme Council of Islamic Revolution (Iraq), 407
Supreme Council of Kenya Muslims, 211
Supreme Institution for the Judiciary (Saudi Arabia), 391
Sura. See Koran
suspicion of Muslim immigrants, 89–125
Suzuki, Hisaaki, 128
Sweden, 295, 465
anti-Muslim sentiments, 102, 104, 107
abuse of women wearing hijab, 105
Muslim statistics, 476
Swissair, 58
Switzerland, 61, 282, 290, 297, 467
Muslim statistics, 476
opposition to Iraq War, 317–18
terror cells in, 465, 466
'sword' as metaphor used by Muslims, 160–61
Syamsuddin, Din, 365
Sydney Morning Herald (Australian newspaper), 359, 363
Syracuse University, 302
Syria, 446
acquisition of lethal weaponry, 469
advanced weapons assistance
from China, 24
from Iran, 468
from North Korea, 24, 468
from Russia, 469
and Arafat, 185
arrests of terrorists, 289, 290
asylum for Nazis, 182
attack on Israel (1973), 29
attempted assassination of Assad, 55
Ba'ath party in power, 19
constitutional change, 442–43

controlling Lebanon, 444–45
extradition of terrorists, 295
inter-Muslim hostilities, 13, 201
invasion of Israel, 63
Islamists from active in Europe, 465, 466
massacres by Ba'athists, death tolls, 16
and oil, 455
refusal to recognize Israel as a state,
    202
represented in fighting against US in
    Iraq, 472
response to democratisation of
    Muslim regimes, 437
seizure of airliner, 58
status of youth, 167
support for terror, 461–62, 463
support of Gulf War, 25
support of Iran during Iran-Iraq War,
    23
support of Iraq during Iraq War
    (2003), 26
support of Iraq in Gulf War, 25
treatment of Christians, 421–22
troops in Lebanon, 138
use of torture, 74
use of Twelve Devices of Muslim
    argument, 138, 139–40, 142, 144,
    147
war against Israel, 182, 184, 186

Tabatabi, Mohammed al, 484
taboos, Islamic (enforcement of). *See*
    Islamic taboos, enforcement of
Tadzhuddin, Mufti Talgat, 406
Tajikistan, 459
    civil war, 15, 22
    civil war (1992–1997), 21
        death tolls, 16
    Islamists in, 20, 26, 37
Talal bin Abdul Aziz (prince), 355
Taliban, 14, 21, 54, 80–81, 161, 289, 293,
    301, 332, 406, 413, 448
    ambiguous relation with Pakistan, 465

assistance in Chechnya, 460
British Muslims joining, 346
defence of Islamic taboos, 129
as 'enemy combatants', 293
and Hindus, 411
meaning of, 38
Muslim condemnation of, 230, 243
non-Muslim support of, 285
and Northern Alliance, 53
prison escape, 310
recognition of, 462, 469
as seen by British journalist, 28
supported by Saudi Arabia, 30
support from Uzbekistan, 458–59
treatment of prisoners, 70–71
treatment of women, 80–81, 82, 84
violence in defence of Islam, 127
Taliban, US led coalition against, 14, 40,
    315, 322, 350, 359–60, 378, 399,
    447–48
    Britain's role in coalition, 335, 354
    British Muslims fighting with Taliban,
        301, 332, 346
    Islamist reactions to, 152, 159, 161,
        279, 280, 406, 413, 414
    potential further danger of, 379, 381
    treatment of after fall, 289–90, 310
Tamerlane, 412
Tamils and Tamil Tigers, 53, 161
Tamimi, Azzam, 237
Tantawi, Mohammed Sayed, 96, 228,
    229, 230, 406
Tanzania, 21
    bombing of US embassy, 30, 69, 327
    defence of Islamic taboos, 127
taqiyya. *See* deception, used by Muslims
Tawhid Islamic Group (Iraq), 407
Tbaiti, Zuher al-, 345
Tebbit, Norman Beresford (Lord), 262
Teheran Declaration (1997), 198
Teheran Times (Iranian newspaper), 139,
    143
Teheran University, 72, 250

Tenet, George, 306, 307
Terrorism Act, Britain (2000), 291
Terzani, Tiziano, 350
Thailand, 19, 21, 471
    arrests of terrorists, 289, 290, 309, 311
    bombings in, 67, 68
    southern Thailand separatists, 16, 19,
        30, 67, 68, 411
Thaiti, Zuher al-, 345
Thani, Hamad bin Khalifa al-, 177
Thatcher, Margaret, 38, 225, 227
theocracy, 439–40
Theodorakis, Mikis, 188, 189, 216
Third World War, 15–29, 35, 42, 48, 284
    and 9/11 attacks, 325
Time (magazine), 179
Times, The (London), 33, 34, 39, 40, 44, 71,
        74, 76, 81, 92, 107, 114, 117, 169, 180,
        181, 185, 191, 192, 193, 194, 202, 203,
        204, 218, 223, 224, 225, 237, 252, 276,
        282, 285, 322, 323, 324, 325, 326, 327,
        335, 344, 354, 358, 359, 362, 365, 370,
        374, 376, 377, 379, 381, 398, 399, 401,
        420, 434, 462
Timimi, Ali al-, 409
Timur Beg, 412
Tomb of the Patriarchs, 90
Torode, John, 264
torture of fellow-Muslims. *See* inter-
    Muslim hostilities
Tory Party (Britain), 203, 484
Total (oil company), 455
Tourab, Abu. *See* Ouakali, Rachid
Touran, Jean-Louis, 426
Toynbee, Arnold, 28, 172
training camps for *jihad*, 26, 30, 36–37,
        148, 168, 278, 282–83, 400, 464, 466,
        467
    See also mujahideen
transnational nature of Islamism,
    465–67
Trevor-Roper, Hugh (Lord Dacre), 262
Trinidad, attempted coup, 20, 61

Tripoli, bombed by US, 19
Trujillo Molina, Rafael Leonidas, 53
Tunisia, 13, 29, 185, 236, 242, 473
    Arab League summit in, 437
    and bin Ali, 20, 39
    controversies over wearing the *hijab*,
        96
    government of, 442
    insurgency
        attempts to overthrow government,
            164
        support from Sudan, 23
    Islamists in, 164, 311, 461, 473
        arrests of, 289
        attacks of, 53, 62, 281
        fighting in support of Iraq, 472
        in London, 39
        transnational use of, 467
    supporting Iraq, 25
Turabi, Hassan, 28, 98, 148, 378
Turkey
    advanced weapons assistance from
        Israel, 24
    arrests of terrorists, 289
    attacks on by Islamists, 464
    bombings, 67, 68, 208
    British embassy bombed, 69
    and controversy over wearing the
        hijab, 96
    defence of Islamic taboos, 127, 135
    desecration of British graves, 64
    displacement of Kurds, 17
    elections in, 442
    embassy bombed in Iraq, 69
    foiled attacks, 290
    government of, 451
    inter-Muslim hostilities, 53
    invasion of Cyprus, 19
    Islamists from active in Europe, 465
    Islamists' transnational use of, 467
    military coup, 449
    Muslim attacks on Jewish synagogues,
        62

relations with Israel, 174
as source of *mujahideen*, 26
treatment of women, 83, 85
unemployment of youth, 167
Turki, Sheikh Abdullah Mohsin al-, 242
Turki bin Faisal (prince), 367
Turkish National Security Council, 451
Turkish Revenge Brigade, 67
Turkish Welfare Party, 83, 212–13
Turkmenistan, 22
and oil, 458, 460
Turnbull, Andrew, 355
Turner, Ted, 199
Twelve Devices of Muslim argument,
137–46, 148, 149, 155, 164, 197, 215,
228, 247, 256, 276, 303, 305, 337,
339, 341, 470

Uganda, bombings in, 66
Ukraine, loss of Russian missiles, 309
ulema, 229
Ulhaq, Mohammed Zia, 250
Ulla, Saber Abu el-, 213
Um al-Qura Mosque (Baghdad). *See*
Mother-of-All-Battles mosque
ummah, 328, 479
Umm al-Qura University (Mecca), 43
Ummayad mosque (Damascus), 433
unbelievers. *See kafir*
'underlying causes' as an argument, 355–
61, 376
unemployment among Muslims, 116
of Muslim youth, 166–68, 169
Union of Muslim Organizations
(Britain), 228
United Arab American League, 244
United Arab Emirates, 71, 147, 296, 439, 462
defence of Islamic taboos, 131
recognition of Taliban, 462
support of Muslims in Bosnia, 26
treatment of women, 83
use of canings as punishment, 73–74
United Kingdom. *See* Britain

United Muslim American Association, 300
United Nations, 125, 136, 145, 147, 191,
193, 200, 201, 208, 223, 284, 287,
328, 330–31
Arafat's speech to, 210
bombing of Iraqi headquarters, 403
on displacement by civil wars, 16
embargo of Iraq, 23, 141
establishment of Israel, 18, 182
General Assembly, 205
Israel as member, 180
opposition to Iraq War, 317
resolution on Iraq, 430
resolution on Israel, 202
Security Council, 202, 316, 317–18,
327, 334, 363, 431
supervision of Afghan elections, 447
United Nations High Commission for
Human Rights, 334
election of Libya as head of, 334
United Nations Middle East envoy, 195
United Nations Relief and Works
Agency for Palestine Refugees in
the Near East, 180, 183, 201
United Nations World Conference on
Racism, 205, 213
United Press International, 195, 196, 322
United States
accused by Saddam Hussein of
looting during Iraq War, 142
accused of eroding civil liberties, 334
advanced weapons assistance
to Egypt, 469
to Iraq, 469
to Saudi, 469
aggression against Muslims, 17
aid to Israel, 174
anti-Muslim sentiments, 102
mistreatment of Muslim prisoners,
105
reprisals against Muslims after
9/11, 104
use of propaganda about, 108

as 'root of evil' in the world, 361–71
assistance to Iraq against Iran, 22
assistance to North Korea's nuclear
    program, 469
blamed for London bombings (2005),
    151
bombings by, 19–20, 30, 54. *See also*
    Gulf War (1991); Iraq War
    (2003); Taliban, US led coalition
    against
bombings in, 67. *See also* 9/11 attacks
cases against Muslim Americans,
    280–81
compared with Iraq, 351
and controversy over wearing the
    hijab, 95
converts to Islam drawn to activism,
    168
covert abductions of terror suspects,
    295
decline of Catholicism, 477
defence spending, 473–74
desire to be liked by other nations, 325
diaspora Muslims planning attacks on,
    280–81, 283
embassy bombings
    attempts foiled, 466
    in Kenya and Tanzania, 30, 69, 299,
        327
    in Lebanon, 69
extradition of terrorists, 295, 302
and fundamentalist terrorists, 39
government agencies. *See* US and spe-
    cific agency name
handling of Islamism, 480
ignoring Pakistan and Saudi assistance
    to terrorists, 320
impact of Iraq War on, 471–74
intifada called travesty by some, 178
invasion of Iraq. *See also* Iraq War
    (2003)
    European response to, 317–20
Islamists from active in Europe, 466

and Israeli-Palestinian conflict, 38
laws against, and treatment of, terror-
    ists, 290, 292–94
need for oil, 457, 460
no right to respond to 9/11 attacks,
    165
registration requirement for Muslim
    men condemned, 301
relations with Israel, 174
relations with Kazakhstan, 458
seen as a terrorist state, 354
shooting down Iranian air liner, 13
stronger Europe to balance US power,
    315
and Suez War (1956), 19
supervision of Afghan elections, 447
supporting authoritarian regimes
    because of oil, 451–61
support of Gulf War, 25
support of Iraq against Iran, 24
terrorists' access to guns, 308
treatment of Muslim prisoners, 70
use and abuse of power, 328
US embassies bombed, 30, 69, 299, 327
US Jews and 'Jewish lobby', 219–21
use of deception, 135–36
vandalisation of Muslim properties in,
    62
viewed as a rogue state, 353
Universal Declaration of Human Rights,
    72, 334
University of California–Berkeley, 204
University of California–San Diego, 302
University of Idaho, 302
University of London, 99, 333
University of Maryland, 302
University of Mississippi, 302
University of North Carolina, 118–19
University of Notre Dame, 297
University of South Florida, 299, 302
UNRWA. *See* United Nations Relief and
    Works Agency for Palestine
    Refugees in the Near East

US
  Aerospace Defense Command, 307
  Border Patrol, 306
  Central Intelligence Agency, 214, 297,
    306, 307, 338, 353
  Committee to Combat Terrorism, 307
  Congress, 219
  Department of Corrections, 95
  Department of Homeland Security,
    306
  Federal Aviation Authority, 307
  Federal Bureau of Investigation, 298,
    306, 307, 308, 326, 327
  Federal Reserve, 474
  House of Representatives, 219, 325
  Justice Department, 105, 221, 234, 293
  Marines, 283
    barracks in Beirut attacked, 19
  National Guard, 472–73
    81st Armour Brigade, 283
  Pentagon, 218, 307, 370
    attack on 9/11, 338, 341, 346
  Senate, 219
  Special Forces, 308
  State Department, 200, 306, 393
    terrorist countries list, 27
  Supreme Court, 300
  See also United States
Usman, Mohammed, 271
Uzbekistan, 49
  and China, 457, 459
  government of, 448, 458
  inter-Muslim hostilities, 74
  Islamists in, 59, 74, 458–59
    arrests of, 289
    'renditions', 295
    support of Taliban, 459
    transnational use of, 466, 467
  and oil, 458–59
  and United States, 457, 458, 459, 473

van Gogh, Theo, 57, 85, 102, 103, 159,
  166, 189, 284, 296, 305, 330, 396, 466

Vatican, 180, 422, 424–26, 429–31,
  434–35
  See also Catholic Church
Vaz, Keith, 264–65
Védrine, Hubert, 204
Versailles Treaty, 188
Versi, Ahmed, 266
victimhood of Muslims. See Muslims
Vidal, Gore, 338–39, 353
Villepin, Dominique de, 221, 430
Vincent, John, 327
violence
  in defence of Islam, 127–37, 164
    celebrations after, 149, 237
    covert support for, 140
    justification for, 89–90, 152–53,
      370–75
  Muslim reactions to terrorist acts,
    226–33, 236–40, 242–43
  'underlying causes', 355–61
  See also inter-Muslim hostilities; spe-
    cific types of violence
Vlaams Blok (Belgium), 102
'Voice of the Republic of Iran', 148
Voltaire, François Marie Arouet de, 94
Vulliamy, Ed, 222

waging war. See hirab
Wahhab, Iqbal, 258
Wahhabi Muslims, 49, 50, 236, 405, 458,
  460, 463
Wahid, Abdurrahman, 165
Wahli, Mohammed, 411
Wain, John, 376
Waleed, al- (prince), 296
Wall Street Journal (US newspaper), 326
war crimes cases, 351
Wardouni, Shlemon, 421
'War on Terror', 12–13, 17, 290, 399
  anti-terrorism efforts, 347
  arrests of terrorists, 289–90
  causing erosion of civil liberties, 304,
    334, 347–49

covert abductions of terror suspects,
295
extradition of terrorists, 294–95
French undermining of, 317
impact of Western naivete on, 323–27
lack of meaning, 42–43
laws against, and treatment of, terrorists, 290, 292–94, 297–98
in European Union, 316
laxity on handling terror threats and
terrorists, 311–14
Muslim reactions to terrorist acts,
226–33, 236–40, 242–43
non-Muslim support of, 284
response to attacks cause further
attacks, 152–53
Russian undermining of, 317
seen as way for US to control world, 368
support for, 461–71
threats by Islamists of more attacks,
302–304
Western response to, 28–35
Warsaw Ghetto, 206
Washington Post, 162, 194, 234, 283, 487
Wayne State University, 302
weapons of mass destruction, 329,
339–40, 467–71
West Bank, 75, 176, 183, 184, 192, 206,
423, 447
and Arafat, 185
attack on Arafat's headquarters, 29
Israeli settlements, 180
treatment of Christians, 14
unemployment of youth, 167
Western response to Islamic revival,
28–35
West Java, 62
Wheatcroft, Geoffrey, 204
Wilders, Geert, 103
Williams, Bernard, 353
Williams, Rowan, 350, 426
Williams, Shirley (Baroness), 379
Wilson, A. N., 205, 222

Wohaibi, Saleh al-, 389
Wolfowitz, Paul, 222, 331, 350
women, treatment in Islamic societies,
57, 80–86, 240–42, 326, 438
controversy over wearing the *hijab*,
94–97
treatment described in *Independent*, 108
'Women Against Fundamentalism'
(Britain), 257
Women in Islam (Mustafa), 81
Woollacott, Martin, 222
World Assembly of Muslim Youth, 389
World Bank, 353
World Church of the Creator (US), 212
World Economic Forum, 370
World Health Organisation, 150
World Trade Center, 22
first attack in 1993, 30, 55, 149–50,
284, 346
second attack (9/11 2001), 26, 53, 66,
346
bin Laden's response, 162
blamed on Israel or US, 44, 151,
153, 188, 214, 338, 339
celebrations by Muslims, 148–49,
237
failure of US intelligence efforts,
306–308
and human rights, 333
justification for, 359–60
killing of Muslims and non-Muslims, 65
lack of belief in bin Laden's guilt,
338
media coverage of, 69–70, 75, 324
Muslim responses to, 50, 137–38,
142, 149, 153, 226, 227–28, 237,
244, 276
planners of, 40, 212, 290
praise of, 329–30
Saudi nationals' involvement, 143
theory that planes were drones, 341
US response to, 330

World Trade Organisation, 353
World War I. *See* First World War
World War II. *See* Second World War
World War III. *See* Third World War
Wright, Patrick, 381
Wright, Rupert, 327
Writers' Guild, 265
'wrong target' as an argument, 376

Xinjiang, 13, 90
  displacement of Muslims, 16
  Islamist separatism, 15, 20, 25, 26
  Islamists' transnational use of, 467
  and oil, 459
  See also China

Yandarbiyev, Zelimkhan, 462
Yapp, Malcolm, 257
Yasin, Zayed, 342
Yassin, Ahmed, 209, 406
  assassination of, 54, 64, 158, 161, 231,
      426
    revenge for, 160, 208, 232–33
  purpose of Hamas, 210
  revenge for, 160
  use of Twelve Devices of Muslim
      argument, 138–39
Yawer, Ghazi al-, 161
Yazdi, Muhammad, 250
Yemen, 26, 49, 72, 152, 176, 191, 413,
    460, 479
  advanced weapons assistance from
      others, 468, 469–70
  ambassador kidnapped in Algeria, 59,
      63
  anti-Americanism, 82
  'Believing Youth' movement, 289
  bombings in, 68
    bombing of USS *Cole*, 310, 463, 466
  and Christians, 413
  inter-Muslim hostilities, 53, 63
  Islamists in, 290, 461, 463
    arrests and trials of, 289, 290, 311

  arrests of in US, 278, 280, 281
  attacks by, 61, 62, 68
  extraditions and deportations, 295,
      302
  extra-judicial killings, 289
  killing of supposed terrorists by
      US, 353, 467
  Muslim statistics, 475
Young, Hugo, 221–22, 287, 323, 369–70
Yousef, Ovadia (rabbi), 176
Yousef, Ramzi Ahmed, 346
Youssouf, Mohammed, 109
youth, Muslim
  in prisons, 167–68
  and unemployment, 166–68, 169
Yusefi, Mohammed, 415

Zahar, Mahmoud al-, 210
Zahid, Anas, 231–32
Zah'ran, Sheikh, 166
Zaigham, Inayatullah, 120, 247
Zakaria, Fareed, 28
Zakaria, Rafiq, 244
Zaman, Mohammed, 253
Zambia, 290, 295, 356
Zapatero, Jose Luis Rodriguez, 319
Zarqawi, Abu Musab al-, 49, 143, 160,
    161, 481, 486
Zawahiri, Ayman al-, 160, 405
  and controversy over wearing the
      hijab, 96
  encouraging Iraqis to violence against
      US, 157, 158, 403, 486
  threats to US, 304, 395–96, 403, 408,
      486, 487
Zawahiri, Mohammed al-, 290
Zebari, Hoshyar, 318–19
Ze'evi, Rehavam, 151
Zeroual, Liamine, 232
Zhirinovsky, Vladimir, 482
Zia ul-Haq, Mohammad, 19
Zimbabwe, 23
Zinn, Howard, 367

Zion, 171, 200
Zionism, 13, 153, 191, 200, 214, 217, 220,
    243, 247, 388, 408, 410, 433
  in America, 143, 219, 220, 221, 222,
    247, 425
  blamed for Muslim violence, 189, 190
  Christian Zionists, 215, 424, 428, 429,
    432
  'Crusaders and Zionists', 49, 175, 403,
    422, 425
  European Zionists, 180

'extreme Zionism', 217
  founder of, 209
  in Israel, 172, 190, 202, 208–209, 210,
    211, 218, 471
  'Protocols of the Elders of Zion', 212,
    213
  as racism, 204, 205, 484
  use of Twelve Devices of Muslim
    argument, 143
Ziyadah, Muhammad, 433
Zoroastrians, 410, 416